The Criminal Justice System

Second Edition

The Criminal Justice System

Volume 2:
Law Enforcement
Courts

Edited by
Michael K. Hooper, Ph.D
Sonoma State University
Department of Criminology and Criminal Justice Studies

Ruth E. Masters, Ed.D
California State University, Fresno
Department of Criminology

SALEM PRESS
A Division of EBSCO Information Services, Inc.
Ipswich, Massachusetts

GREY HOUSE PUBLISHING

Copyright © 2017 by Salem Press, A Division of EBSCO Information Services, Inc., and Grey House Publishing, Inc.

All rights reserved. No part of this work may be used or reproduced in any manner whatsoever or transmitted in any form or by any means, electronic or mechanical, including photocopy, recording, or any information storage and retrieval system, without written permission from the copyright owner. For information contact Grey House Publishing/Salem Press, 4919 Route 22, PO Box 56, Amenia, NY 12501.

∞ *The paper used in these volumes conforms to the American National Standard for Permanence of Paper for Printed Library Materials, Z39.48 1992 (R2009).*

Publisher's Cataloging-In-Publication Data
(Prepared by the Donahue Group, Inc.)

Names: Hooper, Michael (Michael K.), editor. | Masters, Ruth, editor.
Title: The criminal justice system / edited by Michael K. Hooper, Ph.D, Sonoma State University, Department of Criminology and Criminal Justice Studies [and] Ruth E. Masters, Ed.D, California State University, Fresno, Department of Criminology.
Other Titles: Criminal justice. 2017.
Description: Second edition. | Ipswich, Massachusetts : Salem Press, a division of EBSCO Information Services, Inc. ; Amenia, NY : Grey House Publishing, [2017] | Originally published as: Criminal justice / edited by Phyllis B. Gerstenfeld. ©2006. | Includes bibliographical references and indexes. | Contents: Volume 1. Crime, criminal law — Volume 2. Law enforcement, courts — Volume 3. Corrections, special issues.
Identifiers: ISBN 978-1-68217-310-7 (set) | ISBN 978-1-68217-312-1 (v. 1) | ISBN 978-1-68217-313-8 (v. 2) | ISBN 978-1-68217-314-5 (v. 3)
Subjects: LCSH: Criminal justice, Administration of—United States—Encyclopedias. | Criminal procedure—United States—Encyclopedias. | Crime—United States—Encyclopedias. | Criminal law—United States—Encyclopedias. | LCGFT: Reference works.
Classification: LCC KF9217 .C75 2017 | DDC 345.73/05—dc23

Contents

Complete List of Contents....................ix

Law Enforcement
Alcohol, Tobacco, Firearms and Explosives,
    U.S. Bureau of 419
Black Lives Matter Movement/
    Blue Lives Matter Movement 421
Body-worn cameras........................422
Booking..................................424
Border patrols 425
Boston police strike.......................427
Broken windows theory....................427
Campus police............................429
Civilian review boards.....................431
Cold cases 432
Community-oriented policing...............434
Crime analysis............................436
Crime scene investigation..................438
Dallas and Baton Rouge police officer
    attacks (2016) 439
DARE programs 440
Deadly force 441
Discretion 443
Drug Enforcement Administration, U.S. (DEA) ...444
Drugs and law enforcement 445
Evidence-based policing 448
Federal Bureau of Investigation, U.S............450
Frankpledge and watch system..............454
Graham v. Connor (1989) 455
High-speed chases........................457
Highway patrols 459
Homeland Security, U.S. Department of 459
Intelligence-led policing...................462
Internal affairs...........................463
Internal Revenue Service, U.S................465
Interpol 466
Justice Department, U.S....................467
King beating case 472
Knapp Commission.......................474
Kyllo v. United States 475
Law enforcement.........................475
Law Enforcement Assistance Administration 479
Marshals Service, U.S......................480
MOVE bombing..........................481
National Guard...........................482
Neighborhood watch programs..............484
Noble cause corruption....................485

Peace Officer Standards and Training 487
Police....................................488
Police academies 491
Police brutality 493
Police chiefs..............................498
Police civil liability 498
Police corruption.........................500
Police detectives 504
Police dogs...............................506
Police ethics..............................507
Police lineups............................509
Police militarization.......................510
Police powers............................511
Police psychologists.......................514
Police subculture.........................514
Posse comitatus 516
Predictive policing........................517
Preventive patrol.........................518
Private police and guards 519
Problem-oriented policing 521
Procedural justice 522
Racial profiling and criminal justice...........523
Reasonable force.........................526
Resisting arrest 527
Secret Service, U.S........................527
Sheriffs..................................529
Slave patrols 530
Special weapons and tactics teams (SWAT) 531
Stakeouts................................533
State police 534
Sting operations 536
Strategic policing.........................537
Tennessee v. Garner 538
Treasury Department, U.S...................539
Use of force 541
Vehicle checkpoints 542
Warrior versus guardian mentality 544
Wickersham Commission 545
Women in law enforcement and corrections 546

Courts
Acquittal.................................553
Amnesty.................................553
Appellate process 554
Argersinger v. Hamlin.......................556
Arraignment 557
Attorney ethics 557

v

Attorney General, U.S.	559
Attorneys general, state	561
Australia's "Reintegrative Shaming" approach	562
Bail system	564
Bailiffs	567
Barker v. Wingo	568
Batson v. Kentucky	569
Bench warrants	570
Bifurcated trials	570
Bill of particulars	571
Blended sentences	571
Brady v. United States	572
Capital punishment	573
Case law	578
Cease-and-desist orders	579
Certiorari	579
Chain of custody	580
Change of venue	581
Citations	581
Civil commitment	582
Clemency	584
Clerks of the court	584
Coker v. Georgia	585
Competency to stand trial	585
Concurrent sentences	587
Contempt of court	587
Convictions	588
Corporal punishment	589
Counsel, right to	591
Court reporters	592
Court types	593
Criminal prosecution	595
Cross-examination	598
Cruel and unusual punishment	599
Death qualification	603
Defendant self-representation	604
Defendants	606
Defense attorneys	607
Deportation	608
Depositions	610
Deterrence	611
Discovery	612
Dismissals	613
District attorneys	614
Diversion	616
Drug courts	617
Effective counsel	619
Execution, forms of	622
Execution of judgment	624
Expert witnesses	625
Eyewitness testimony	626
False convictions	629
Faretta v. California	631
Fines	632
Ford v. Wainwright	633
Furman v. Georgia	634
Gag orders	635
Gideon v. Wainwright	635
Grand juries	636
Gregg v. Georgia	638
Habeas corpus	639
Harmelin v. Michigan	641
Harmless error	642
Hearings	642
Hung juries	643
Immunity from prosecution	644
Impeachment of judges	645
In forma pauperis	645
Indeterminate sentencing	646
Indictment	647
Inquests	648
Jessica's Law/Jessica Lunsford Act (2005)	648
Judges	650
Judicial review	652
Judicial system, U.S.	652
Jurisdiction of courts	655
Jury nullification	657
Jury sequestration	658
Jury system	659
Just deserts	663
Mandamus	664
Mandatory sentencing	664
Massiah v. United States	666
McCleskey v. Kemp	667
Minnick v. Mississippi	668
Miscarriage of justice	669
Night courts	670
Nolle prosequi	670
Nolo contendere	670
Objections	671
Obstruction of justice	671
Opinions	672
Palko v. Connecticut	672
Pardons	673
People v. George Zimmerman (2013)	675
Plea bargaining	676
Pleas	677
Powell v. Alabama	678
Precedent	679
Preliminary hearings	680

Presentence investigations 681
Prosecutorial abuse 681
Public defenders 683
Public prosecutors 686
Punishment 688
Restitution 692
Restorative justice 693
Restraining orders 695
Reversible error 695
Robinson v. California 696
Rummel v. Estelle 697
Santobello v. New York 698
Scottsboro cases 699
Self-incrimination, privilege against 701
Sentencing 703
Sentencing guidelines, U.S. 705
Solem v. Helm 706
Speedy trial right 707
Standards of proof 707
Stanford v. Kentucky 708

Stare decisis 709
Subpoena power 710
Summonses 711
Supreme Court, U.S., and criminal rights 711
Suspended sentences 714
Testimony 715
Three-strikes laws 716
Tison v. Arizona 717
Traffic courts 718
Traffic fines 719
Trial publicity 720
Trials 721
United States Sentencing Commission 725
Verdicts 726
Voir dire 727
Witherspoon v. Illinois 727
Witness protection programs 728
Witnesses 730
World Court 733

Complete List of Contents

Volume I

Publisher's Note ix
Contributors xi
Complete List of Contents xvii
Introduction xxv

Crime

Abortion 3
Adultery 5
Alcohol use and abuse 6
Animal abuse 9
Anti-Racketeering Act of 1934 12
Arson 12
Assault and battery 15
Attempt to commit a crime 18
Autopsies 19
Bigamy and polygamy 20
Blackmail and extortion 21
Breach of the peace 24
Bribery 25
Bullying 27
Burglary 29
Carjacking 31
Child abduction by parents 32
Child abuse and molestation 33
Commercialized vice 38
Comprehensive Addiction and Recovery
    Act of 2016 (CARA) 41
Comprehensive Drug Abuse Prevention
    and Control Act 42
Comstock law 43
Conspiracy 44
Constitution, U.S. 46
Consumer fraud 49
Corporate scandals 51
Counterfeiting 55
Crime 59
Crime index 64
Crimes of passion 64
Criminal justice in U.S. history 65
Criminal justice system 70
Criminals 75
Criminology 78
Date rape 83
Designer and date rape drugs 84

Disorderly conduct 85
Domestic violence and criminal justice 86
Drive-by shootings 91
Drug legalization 92
Drug testing 95
Drunk driving 97
Embezzlement 100
Environmental crimes 103
Female offenders 104
Feminist criminology 106
Forensic psychology 107
Forgery 109
Fraud 110
Gambling 113
Graffiti 116
Hate crime 117
Hit-and-run accidents 120
Hobbs Act 121
Hoover, J. Edgar 121
Human trafficking 122
Illegal aliens and criminal justice 124
Inchoate crimes 126
Indecent exposure 127
Insider trading 128
Insurance fraud 129
Jaycee Lee Dugard case (2009) 131
Jaywalking 133
Justice 134
Kidnapping 136
Ku Klux Klan 139
Loitering 140
Lynching 141
Mafia 143
Mann Act 143
Manslaughter 144
Mass and serial murders 145
Mental illness and crime 150
Missing persons 152
Money laundering 154
Mothers Against Drunk Driving 155
Motor vehicle theft 156
Murder and homicide 160
National Commission on the Causes
    and Prevention of Violence 166

National Narcotics Act............................167
National Stolen Property Act...................168
Omnibus Crime Control and Safe Streets
    Act of 1968..................................168
Opium Exclusion Act..............................169
Organized crime......................................170
Organized Crime Control Act..................173
Pandering..174
Peacemaking criminology.......................174
Perjury...176
Pickpocketing..177
Political corruption.................................177
Pornography and obscenity.....................181
Principals (criminal)................................185
Prohibition..186
Psychopathy..187
Public-order offenses..............................189
R.A.V. v. City of St. Paul..........................190
Racketeer Influenced and Corrupt
    Organizations Act..........................191
Rape and sex offenses..............................193
Reckless endangerment...........................199
Recreational and medical marijuana movements...200
Regulatory crime.....................................201
Right to bear arms...................................202
Robbery...204
Schools of criminology...........................208
Seditious libel..210
Sexual harassment and criminal justice..........211
Sherman Antitrust Act............................213
Shoplifting...214
Skyjacking..217
Sobriety testing.......................................219
Sports and crime.....................................221
Stalking..225
Suicide and euthanasia............................226
Suspects...229
Tax evasion..230
Telephone fraud......................................233
Television news.......................................235
Texas v. Johnson.......................................237
Theft..238
Treason..241
Treasury Department, U.S.......................244
Trespass...246
Unabomber..249
Uniform Crime Reports..........................251
Vandalism..252
Vigilantism..254
Violent Criminal Apprehension Program..........256

Virginia v. Black......................................257
Voting fraud..258
War crimes..259
White-collar crime..................................261
Wisconsin v. Mitchell...............................266

Criminal Law
Accomplices and accessories...................271
Aggravating circumstances.....................271
Amicus curiae briefs................................272
Annotated codes.....................................273
Antitrust law...273
Arizona v. Fulminante............................277
Arrest...278
Arrest warrants.......................................282
Asset forfeiture.......................................283
Atwater v. City of Lago Vista...................285
Automobile searches...............................285
Bill of Rights, U.S....................................287
Bivens v. Six Unknown Named Agents..........290
Brown v. Mississippi................................291
Burden of proof......................................292
California v. Greenwood..........................293
Chimel v. California................................294
Circumstantial evidence.........................295
Citizen's arrests.......................................296
Color of law..297
Common law..299
Comprehensive Crime Control Act...............300
Confessions...301
Consent searches....................................303
Criminal intent.......................................304
Criminal law...305
Criminal liability....................................309
Criminal procedure................................310
Cultural defense.....................................314
Decriminalization...................................314
Defenses to crime...................................315
Diminished capacity...............................319
Diplomatic immunity.............................319
Double jeopardy.....................................320
Due process of law..................................321
Duress..324
Entrapment...325
Equal protection under the law..............326
Escobedo v. Illinois..................................327
Ex post facto laws....................................328
Exclusionary rule....................................329
Excuses and justifications.......................331
Extradition..331

Federal Crimes Act 334
Felon disfranchisement 334
Felonies 335
Gun laws 336
Harris v. United States 340
Hearsay 340
Hurtado v. California 341
Ignorance of the law 342
Illinois v. Gates 343
Illinois v. Krull 343
Illinois v. McArthur 344
Illinois v. Wardlow 345
Incorporation doctrine 346
Information (written accusation) 347
Insanity defense 347
International law 350
Jim Crow laws 354
Knowles v. Iowa 357
Lesser-included offenses 358
Lindbergh law 358
Magna Carta 359
Mala in se and *mala prohibita* 359
Malice 361
Manhattan Bail Project 361
Mapp v. Ohio 362
Martial law 363
Maryland v. Buie 363
Maryland v. Craig 364
Massachusetts v. Sheppard 365
Mens rea 366
Military justice 367
Miranda rights 369
Miranda v. Arizona 372
Misdemeanors 372
Mitigating circumstances 374
Model Penal Code 374
Moral turpitude 375
Motives 375

Multiple jurisdiction offenses 376
New Jersey v. T.L.O. 377
No-knock warrants 378
Payne v. Tennessee 378
Plain view doctrine 379
Presumption of innocence 380
Preventive detention 381
Privileged communications 382
Probable cause 383
Proximate cause 385
Punitive damages 386
Reasonable doubt 387
Reasonable suspicion 387
Rules of evidence 388
Search and seizure 391
Search warrants 393
Self-defense 395
Sex offender registries 396
Sexually Violent Predator Acts 398
Statutes 400
Statutes of limitations 401
Stop and frisk 401
Strict liability offenses 403
Terry v. Ohio 404
Traffic law 404
United States Code 407
United States Statutes at Large 407
United States v. Alvarez-Machain 408
United States v. Leon 409
United States v. Lopez 409
Vagrancy laws 410
Vicarious liability 411
Violent Crime Control and Law
   Enforcement Act 412
Weeks v. United States 413
Whren v. United States 414
Wilson v. Arkansas 415

Volume II

Law Enforcement

Alcohol, Tobacco, Firearms and Explosives,
   U.S. Bureau of 419
Black Lives Matter Movement/
   Blue Lives Matter Movement 421
Body-worn cameras 422
Booking 424

Border patrols 425
Boston police strike 427
Broken windows theory 427
Campus police 429
Civilian review boards 431
Cold cases 432
Community-oriented policing 434

Crime analysis 436
Crime scene investigation................438
Dallas and Baton Rouge police officer
    attacks (2016) 439
DARE programs 440
Deadly force 441
Discretion 443
Drug Enforcement Administration, U.S. (DEA) ...444
Drugs and law enforcement 445
Evidence-based policing 448
Federal Bureau of Investigation, U.S. 450
Frankpledge and watch system 454
Graham v. Connor (1989) 455
High-speed chases.....................457
Highway patrols 459
Homeland Security, U.S. Department of 459
Intelligence-led policing 462
Internal affairs 463
Internal Revenue Service, U.S. 465
Interpol 466
Justice Department, U.S. 467
King beating case 472
Knapp Commission 474
Kyllo v. United States 475
Law enforcement.......................475
Law Enforcement Assistance Administration 479
Marshals Service, U.S. 480
MOVE bombing 481
National Guard 482
Neighborhood watch programs 484
Noble cause corruption 485
Peace Officer Standards and Training 487
Police 488
Police academies 491
Police brutality 493
Police chiefs 498
Police civil liability 498
Police corruption 500
Police detectives 504
Police dogs 506
Police ethics 507
Police lineups 509
Police militarization 510
Police powers 511
Police psychologists 514
Police subculture 514
Posse comitatus 516
Predictive policing 517
Preventive patrol 518
Private police and guards 519

Problem-oriented policing 521
Procedural justice 522
Racial profiling and criminal justice ...523
Reasonable force 526
Resisting arrest 527
Secret Service, U.S. 527
Sheriffs 529
Slave patrols 530
Special weapons and tactics teams (SWAT) 531
Stakeouts 533
State police 534
Sting operations 536
Strategic policing 537
Tennessee v. Garner 538
Treasury Department, U.S. 539
Use of force 541
Vehicle checkpoints 542
Warrior versus guardian mentality 544
Wickersham Commission 545
Women in law enforcement and corrections 546

Courts
Acquittal 553
Amnesty 553
Appellate process 554
Argersinger v. Hamlin 556
Arraignment 557
Attorney ethics 557
Attorney General, U.S. 559
Attorneys general, state 561
Australia's "Reintegrative Shaming" approach 562
Bail system 564
Bailiffs 567
Barker v. Wingo 568
Batson v. Kentucky 569
Bench warrants 570
Bifurcated trials 570
Bill of particulars 571
Blended sentences 571
Brady v. United States 572
Capital punishment 573
Case law 578
Cease-and-desist orders 579
Certiorari 579
Chain of custody 580
Change of venue 581
Citations 581
Civil commitment 582
Clemency 584
Clerks of the court 584

Entry	Page
Coker v. Georgia	585
Competency to stand trial	585
Concurrent sentences	587
Contempt of court	587
Convictions	588
Corporal punishment	589
Counsel, right to	591
Court reporters	592
Court types	593
Criminal prosecution	595
Cross-examination	598
Cruel and unusual punishment	599
Death qualification	603
Defendant self-representation	604
Defendants	606
Defense attorneys	607
Deportation	608
Depositions	610
Deterrence	611
Discovery	612
Dismissals	613
District attorneys	614
Diversion	616
Drug courts	617
Effective counsel	619
Execution, forms of	622
Execution of judgment	624
Expert witnesses	625
Eyewitness testimony	626
False convictions	629
Faretta v. California	631
Fines	632
Ford v. Wainwright	633
Furman v. Georgia	634
Gag orders	635
Gideon v. Wainwright	635
Grand juries	636
Gregg v. Georgia	638
Habeas corpus	639
Harmelin v. Michigan	641
Harmless error	642
Hearings	642
Hung juries	643
Immunity from prosecution	644
Impeachment of judges	645
In forma pauperis	645
Indeterminate sentencing	646
Indictment	647
Inquests	648
Jessica's Law/Jessica Lunsford Act (2005)	648
Judges	650
Judicial review	652
Judicial system, U.S.	652
Jurisdiction of courts	655
Jury nullification	657
Jury sequestration	658
Jury system	659
Just deserts	663
Mandamus	664
Mandatory sentencing	664
Massiah v. United States	666
McCleskey v. Kemp	667
Minnick v. Mississippi	668
Miscarriage of justice	669
Night courts	670
Nolle prosequi	670
Nolo contendere	670
Objections	671
Obstruction of justice	671
Opinions	672
Palko v. Connecticut	672
Pardons	673
People v. George Zimmerman (2013)	675
Plea bargaining	676
Pleas	677
Powell v. Alabama	678
Precedent	679
Preliminary hearings	680
Presentence investigations	681
Prosecutorial abuse	681
Public defenders	683
Public prosecutors	686
Punishment	688
Restitution	692
Restorative justice	693
Restraining orders	695
Reversible error	695
Robinson v. California	696
Rummel v. Estelle	697
Santobello v. New York	698
Scottsboro cases	699
Self-incrimination, privilege against	701
Sentencing	703
Sentencing guidelines, U.S.	705
Solem v. Helm	706
Speedy trial right	707
Standards of proof	707
Stanford v. Kentucky	708
Stare decisis	709
Subpoena power	710

Summonses 711
Supreme Court, U.S., and criminal rights. 711
Suspended sentences. 714
Testimony 715
Three-strikes laws 716
Tison v. Arizona 717
Traffic courts 718
Traffic fines 719
Trial publicity 720
Trials 721
United States Sentencing Commission 725
Verdicts 726
Voir dire 727
Witherspoon v. Illinois 727
Witness protection programs 728
Witnesses. 730
World Court 733

Volume III

Corrections

Addiction 737
AIDS 740
Ashker v. Brown (2015) 741
Auburn system 743
Battered child and battered wife syndromes 744
Boot camps 746
Chain gangs. 748
Community-based corrections 749
Community service 750
Conjugal visitation in prison. 751
Crime victimization: primary and secondary 752
"Dark figure of crime" 754
Elderly prisoners 755
Forestry camps. 756
Good time 757
Halfway houses 758
History of incarceration 759
Homeless women and victimization 761
House arrest 763
Incapacitation 764
LGBTQ prisoners 765
Medical model of offender treatment. 766
National Crime Victimization Survey 767
National Organization for Victim Assistance. 768
"Not-in-my-backyard" attitudes 769
Opioid treatment breakthroughs 770
Palmer raids. 773
Parole. 773
Parole boards. 777
Parole Commission, U.S. 779
Parole officers 780
Pennsylvania system of corrections. 781
Prison and jail systems 783
Prison escapes 787
Prison guards. 789
Prison health care 790
Prison industries 792
Prison inmate subculture 793
Prison overcrowding 794
Prison/prisoner classification systems 797
Prison Rape Elimination Act (PREA) of 2003. 798
Prison violence 800
Prisoner rights 802
Prisons, Federal Bureau of. 804
Privatization of institutional and community
 corrections, including faith-based programs 805
Probation, adult. 806
Probation, juvenile 809
Realignment (PSR) policy 811
Recidivism. 813
Rehabilitation 815
Scandinavia's prison experience 818
Security threat groups (STGs)/prison gangs. 819
Smith Act 819
Solitary confinement. 820
Supermax prisons 822
Victim and Witness Protection Act 824
Victim assistance programs. 824
Victim impact statements 825
Victim-offender mediation 827
Victim recovery stages. 827
Victimization theories 829
Victimless crimes 832
Victimology 833
Victims of Crime Act 834
Victims of Trafficking Act of 2015 835
Victims services. 836
Walnut Street Jail 838
Work camps. 838
Work-release programs 840
Youth authorities. 841

Special Issues

Adam Walsh Child Protection and
    Safety Act (2006) 845
Antiterrorism and Effective Death Penalty Act. . . . 846
Bloodstains 848
Boston Marathon Bombing (2013). 848
Bounty hunters 850
Bureau of Justice Statistics 851
Civil disobedience. 851
Clear and present danger test. 855
Computer crime 855
Computer forensics. 859
Computer information systems. 861
Contributing to delinquency of minors 863
Coroners 864
Crime labs 866
Criminal history record information. 867
Criminal justice education 868
Criminal records 869
Cybercrime investigation 871
DNA testing 875
Document analysis 878
Electronic surveillance 879
Espionage. 881
Fingerprint identification 884
Forensic accounting 886
Forensics 887
Freedom of assembly and association 890
Fusion Centers 891
Gault, In re. 893
Geographic information systems. 894
Identity theft. 895
Juvenile courts. 899
Juvenile delinquency. 900
Juvenile Justice and Delinquency Prevention
    Act 904
Juvenile Justice and Delinquency Prevention,
    Office of 905
Juvenile justice system 905
Juvenile waivers to adult courts 908
Katz v. United States. 909
Latent evidence. 910
Lone wolf. 911
Medical examiners 913
National Crime Information Center. 914
National Institute of Justice 915
Nonviolent resistance. 915
Olmstead v. United States. 917
Parens patriae. 918
Paris terrorist attacks (2015) 918
Patriot Act. 920
Pedophilia 921
People v. Nidal Hasan (2013). 923
Polygraph testing. 924
Pornography, child. 926
Post-traumatic stress disorder 929
President's Commission on Law Enforcement
    and Administration of Justice 931
Print media 931
Privacy rights. 934
Psychological profiling. 936
Religious sects and cults 938
Roper v. Simmons (2005) 941
San Bernardino terrorist attack (2015) 942
Schall v. Martin 944
School violence. 944
September 11, 2001, attacks. 946
Sex discrimination. 948
Shoe prints and tire-tracks 952
Social media 952
Status offenses. 954
Surveillance cameras. 954
Technology's transformative effect. 956
Terrorism 957
Toxicology 963
Trace evidence 964
Uniform Juvenile Court Act. 965
USA FREEDOM Act (2015) 966
Victims of Child Abuse Act Reauthorization
    Act (2013) 968
Wiretaps and criminal justice 970
Youth gangs 971

Bibliography of Basic Works on Criminal Justice . . . 977
Glossary. 963
Crime Rates and Definitions 1003
Crime Trends. 1007
Supreme Court Rulings on Criminal Justice 1009
Famous American Trials 1019
Time Line 1031

Topics by Subject Category. 1047
Index to Court Cases 1065
Index to Laws and Acts 1069

Personages Index. 1075
Subject Index 1079

Law Enforcement

Alcohol, Tobacco, Firearms and Explosives, U.S. Bureau of

Identification: Federal agency that enforces federal laws involving firearms, moonshine liquor, untaxed cigarettes, and explosives

Date: Established as the Alcohol Prohibition Unit in 1919

Significance: Originally created to enforce the federal prohibition on alcohol, the Bureau of Alcohol, Tobacco, Firearms and Explosives (ATF) has undergone many changes during its history and is now the main federal agency responsible for the enforcement of gun-control laws. It has many other responsibilities, but its involvement in the enforcement of gun laws has made it one of the most controversial federal law-enforcement agencies.

The Bureau of Alcohol, Tobacco, Firearms and Explosives began in 1919 as the Alcohol Prohibition Unit in the Bureau of Internal Revenue (which later became the Internal Revenue Service). It was soon moved to the Department of Justice and was renamed the Bureau of Prohibition. Under that name, it enforced federal laws against the consumption or manufacture of alcohol. After Prohibition was repealed in 1933, the bureau was returned to the Treasury Department's Bureau of Internal Revenue. At first called the Alcohol Tax Unit, it was renamed the Alcohol and Tobacco Tax Division (ATTD).

Federal laws required that alcohol producers and tobacco sellers pay special excise taxes. Some citizens, particularly in the South, produced "moonshine" liquor without paying the necessary taxes and sold their homemade liquor in states or localities where alcohol was illegal. Through the 1960s the ATTD's main law-enforcement responsibility was pursuit of illegal liquor stills, especially in southeastern states. The ATTD also regulated the lawful commerce of alcohol, acting as the administrative agency to enforce alcohol production and sales by legitimate companies, pursuant to the federal Alcohol Administration Act of 1935.

The US Constitution does not explicitly grant the federal government any law-enforcement powers except in a few discrete areas, such as piracy and counterfeiting. That is why it was necessary to add the Eighteenth Amendment to the Constitution in 1919 to empower the federal government to enforce prohibition. In 1934, when Congress wanted to impose federal controls on the possession of machine guns, it used its taxing power. The National Firearms Act that Congress passed that same year required that owners of machine guns—and certain other firearms—pay a federal tax and register their guns with the federal government. The latter requirement was ostensibly enacted for tax purposes but was actually a method by which the federal government gave itself control over firearms ownership. The ATTD was given responsibility for enforcing this new tax law.

Expanding Jurisdiction

As national crime rates rose during the 1960s Congress passed new federal crime laws. The US Supreme Court's increasingly expansive interpretations of Congress's power to regulate interstate commerce provided the basis for new laws enacted on the theory that local crime affects interstate commerce. In 1968, Congress passed the Gun Control Act, which provided detailed regulations for the retail sale of firearms and prohibited large classes of people from buying guns. The following year, the ATTD was renamed the Alcohol, Tobacco and Firearms Division (ATFD) and given responsibility for enforcing the gun control policies under the new act.

In 1970 Congress passed the Explosives Control Act. The ATFD and the Federal Bureau of Investigation (FBI) shared responsibility for enforcing this law's criminal law provisions, but the ATFD took sole responsibility for regulating the lawful production and sale of explosives. Two years later, the ATFD was removed from the Internal

Official seal of the BATFE. (Public domain, via Wikimedia Commons)

Revenue Service. Renamed the Bureau of Alcohol, Tobacco and Firearms (ATF), it became an autonomous law-enforcement agency within the Treasury Department, along with that department's Secret Service and Bureau of Customs.

Gun Enforcement Controversy

The ATF's enforcement of the new gun laws was controversial from the start. Many gun owners—as well as groups such as the National Rifle Association, Gun Owners of America, and Second Amendment Foundation—contended that ATF tactics were unconstitutional and illegitimate. They claimed that the agency often seized guns and refused to return them, even when there was no legal basis for doing so. Critics of the agency also charged that ATF agents entrapped many innocent people into committing technical violations of federal laws and that the agency frequently abused its search and seizure powers.

The ATF denied the charges, but a unanimous 1982 report of the US Senate Subcommittee on the Constitution provided a scathing denunciation of ATF tactics. In 1986 Congress passed the Firearms Owners' Protection Act (FOPA) by large margins in both the House and the Senate. This new law significantly revised the Gun Control Act of 1968, provided more precise definitions of what was covered by federal law, reduced some technical violations of gun laws to misdemeanors, and set limits on the ATF's search and seizure powers.

Expanding Operations

In 1975, the ATF began to take on arson cases under the theory that the accelerants used by arsonists constituted explosives. Later, the federal explosives law was amended to encompass arson, thus making ATF's jurisdiction over arson more legally secure.

During the late 1980s and early 1990s, as the federal war on drugs became a major national issue, the ATF created "Special Response Teams" to conduct violent and high-profile raids into homes that ATF alleged were occupied by drug dealers in possession of illegal firearms. During that period, the bureau began styling itself as "ATF," rather than "BATF," to mimic the three-letter acronyms of the Federal Bureau of Investigation (FBI) and Drug Enforcement Agency (DEA).

The bureau's image was significantly tarnished by a congressional investigation of the case of Randy Weaver. Weaver and his family were white separatists who lived in Ruby Ridge, Idaho. In 1989, an informant working for an ATF agent entrapped Randy Weaver into selling him two shotguns (a legal act) and then sawing off their barrels to shorten them (an illegal act). The case eventually led to an FBI siege of Weaver's cabin in 1992 and the fatal shooting of Weaver's wife in what became known as the Ruby Ridge shoot-out. Weaver himself was tried and acquitted for the original firearms sale charge in 1993. Another controversy followed soon after. In early 1993 an ATF raid on the compound of the Branch Davidian religious cult outside Waco, Texas, went disastrously wrong. Four ATF agents and several civilians were killed, and the ATF's decision-making about the so-called Waco siege was widely criticized.

The Waco and Weaver cases (which were both seen as motivations for the Oklahoma City bombing in 1995), allegations of racial and sex discrimination within the ATF, and other serious management problems, appeared to put the bureau's existence in jeopardy, especially when committees in both houses of Congress held hearings to investigate the bureau in 1995. However, the bureau survived, and afterward avoided major negative publicity. The bureau continues to be criticized by gun-rights groups for its unduly severe enforcement of federal gun laws, while simultaneously receiving criticism from anti-gun groups for excessive timidity in its enforcement of the same laws.

Reorganization

As part of a federal law-enforcement reorganization following the September 11, 2001, terrorist attacks on the United States, the ATF was renamed the Bureau of Alcohol, Tobacco, Firearms, and Explosives and was transferred from the Treasury Department to the Justice Department—where, ironically, its Prohibition ancestor had been transferred decades before. Despite its name change, the bureau retained "ATF" as its official acronym.

In 2004 Congress enacted legislation that restricted the release—except for law-enforcement purposes—of ATF records identifying lawful gun buyers. The new law also restricted the release of the "trace" records used by the ATF to track the sale and ownership of individual firearms. Requests for such information are usually made by local law-enforcement agencies that find guns that may have been used in crimes or guns that have been stolen. Supporters of the new federal legislation argued that law-abiding gun owners, as well as nonowners who may be mentioned in trace reports—such as witnesses to crimes—should have their privacy rights protected. Critics responded that the law interfered with the ability of the public to learn important information about gun ownership and gun-law enforcement.

David B. Kopel

Further Reading

Bureau of Alcohol, Tobacco, Firearms and Explosives. ATF, US Dept. of Justice, 2016. Web. 25 May. 2016.

Hardy, David. *The B.A.T.F.'s War on Civil Liberties*. Bellevue, Wash.: Second Amendment Foundation, 1979. Print.

Holmes, Bill. *Entrapment: The BATF in Action*. El Dorado, Ark.: Desert Publications, 1998. Print.

Moore, James A. *Very Special Agents: The Inside Story of America's Most Controversial Law Enforcement Agency-the Bureau of Alcohol, Tobacco, and Firearms*. Champaign: University of Illinois Press, 2001. Print.

United States Government. *Twenty-first Century Guide to the U.S. Bureau of Alcohol, Tobacco, and Firearms*. Washington, D.C.: Progressive Management, 2002. Compact disc.

Vizzard, William J. *In the Cross Fire: A Political History of the Bureau of Alcohol, Tobacco and Firearms*. Boulder, Colo.: Lynne Rienner, 1997. Print.

See also Arson; Attorney General, U.S.; Entrapment; Gun laws; Justice Department, U.S.; Organized crime; Regulatory crime; Right to bear arms.

Black Lives Matter Movement/ Blue Lives Matter Movement

Definition: Black Lives Matter movement, an attempt to revive the Black Nationalist movement and focus attention on the mistreatment of African Americans

Criminal justice issues: Crime prevention; criminology; arrest and arraignment

Significance: The Black Lives Matter movement seeks to proclaim the dignity of Black people and to make Americans aware of the systematic oppression faced daily by them.

The Black Lives Matter movement is a chapter-based national organization. The killing of Trayvon Martin by George Zimmerman in 2012 and his subsequent acquittal was the spark that led to the organization. Subsequently, Martin faced a posthumous trial in his own death. Further killings of AfricanAmericans, many of whom were unarmed, by police led to the Black Lives Matter movement, an attempt to revive the Black Nationalist movement and focus attention on the mistreatment of AfricanAmericans. Their purpose and manifesto is comprehensive.

According to http://blacklivesmatter.com/about, "Black Lives Matter affirms the lives of Black queer and trans folks, disabled folks, black-undocumented folks, folks with records, women and all Black lives along the gender spectrum. It centers those that have been marginalized within Black liberation movements. It is a tactic to (re)build the Black liberation movement."

The Blue Lives Matter is a reaction to the Black Lives Matter movement. Police officers see the movement as an attack on law enforcement and its practices. The movement began with the killing of police officers in 2014. Additionally, the organization seeks to combat the position of the Black Lives Matter group that police are targeting AfricanAmericans and singling them out for punishment and even killings.

There are those who seek to support both groups and point out that all lives matter. No one should be targeted; police should enforce laws equitably and in turn not be the target of any group at all.

Major Ideas

The Black Lives Matter movement seeks to proclaim the dignity of Black people and to make Americans aware of the systematic oppression faced daily by them. The issue is not simply unfair enforcement of laws but overall oppression and denial of Black humanity. Their manifesto makes clear that this oppression affects every part of Black lives and every class and gender within Black society. The inequality is pervasive and part of everyday experiences.

The Blue Lives Matter movement holds that many, some say all, shootings involving police are justified because of the danger of their jobs. The movement seems to deny any prejudice or discrimination against African Americans and points to the killing of police officers in their view all of whom were targeted. They also explain the shootings of unarmed as well as armed AfricanAmericans as justified.

There is a gap between those who promote civil rights and the tough-on-crime advocates in America. Proponents generally believe that one must advocate for one side or the other. There are those, however, who believe that the two sides can be brought together in holding the American ideal of justice for all and the promotion of human dignity as a right guaranteed to all Americans regardless of race, creed, or color.

Conclusion

The differences between the two organizations may seem insurmountable at times. Most Americans would agree that justice should be equitable and that police should exercise reasonable restraint. Moreover, most Americans would agree that there is a history of grave injustice against AfricanAmericans. These injustices need to be addressed honestly and confronted deliberately. Similarly, no police officer should feel or be targeted while doing her or his job. There is also widespread agreement that training in how to deal with the public is much needed. Efforts are being made to aid community relationships. Less heat and more light is required to help solve these essential problems.

Frank A. Salamone

Further Reading

Black Lives Matter. http://blacklivesmatter.com/about/.
Edwards, Sue Bradford. Black Lives Matter. ABDO.
Gates, Louis Henry, and Kevin M. Burke. *And Still I Rise: Black America Since MLK*. New York: Harper Collins, 2015.
Martinelli, Ron. *The Truth Behind the Black Lives Matter Movement and the War on Police*. Temecula, Calif.: Martinelli & Associates, 2016.
Massey Jr., Joseph Lee. *The Erosion of the Thin Blue Line: Memoirs of My Life as a Washington, D.C. Police Officer*. Raleigh, N.C.: Lulu Publishing Services 2016.

See also Police subculture; Police militarization; Police powers; Police ethics; Police corruption; Police brutality; Police civil liability; Police; Gun laws; Disorderly conduct; Deadly force; Community-oriented policing; Civil disobedience; Color of law.

Body-worn cameras

Definition: Video-recording cameras that are mounted somewhere on a police officer's body, used for recording what happens during police-citizen encounters. These can include cameras that are mounted on an officer's head, lapel, or torso.

Criminal justice issues: Civil rights and liberties; constitutional protections; government misconduct; law enforcement organization; media; police powers; political issues; professional standards

Significance: After several highly publicized police shootings of unarmed black men, there has been growing public and political support for the mass diffusion of body-worn cameras. What appeals to the public is their potential to provide more objective accounts of what happened during police-citizen encounters, however, body-worn cameras can also be beneficial and problematic to the police.

Body-worn cameras (BWCs) are a relatively new technology and have been available internationally for the last decade. In the United States, BWCs first received significant media attention in 2013 when a federal district judge ordered New York City police officers to wear cameras in response to lawsuits over racial bias in stop-and-frisk practices. But it was not until the summer of 2014 with the police shooting of Michael Brown, an unarmed black teenager, in Ferguson, Missouri, that this technology suddenly became part of a national conversation about police reform.

While the research base on BWCs is still small, with increased public and political support for their mass adoption, efforts aimed at understanding this technology have increased exponentially. Such studies have found that the police are largely receptive to BWCs and that the cameras can have positive impacts on several policing outcomes such as reductions in citizen complaints, decreased use-of-force incidents, shorter complaint investigation times, stronger evidence, and less volatile citizen encounters. However, some challenges may also accompany the implementation of BWCs. These include police perceptions of having less discretion and credibility, and the logistical and financial burdens that accompany their adoption and use.

Benefits

Proponents of body-worn cameras claim that they can benefit the police and society in a multitude of ways that include increased police accountability, stronger evidence, improved training practices, and better public relations. However, existing research is yet to verify all of these claims. What we do know is that BWCs do have some positive impacts on certain police outcomes.

First, the adoption of these cameras has been associated with reductions in the number of civilian complaints filed against police officers. These findings have been consistent across a number of jurisdictions within the United States. However, it is still uncertain whether reductions in complaints are due to increased police accountability, because citizens are more likely to withdraw frivolous complaints when faced with the footage, related to factors concerning the complaint process, or a combination of these.

Second, police have reported that BWC footage can help them reduce the amount of time they spend investigating citizen complaints. In some jurisdictions where complaint investigations may last weeks, they can be reduced to a matter of days. While the footage has been beneficial to internal affairs investigators, patrol officers who are often the subject of such investigations also claim that the shorter investigation times have reduced significantly the total amount of stress they relate to open investigations against them.

Despite some mixed findings, the adoption of BWCs has also been correlated with downturns in police use-of-force. Studies that support this notion suggest that this applies to both excessive and appropriate amounts of force. In some situations, officers choose to use their knowledge of case law instead of force to persuade citizens to comply with their commands (even when they could legally use force).

Body-worn camera footage can serve as a stronger source of evidence that helps secure convictions and reduces time spent in court. Officers report that BWC footage can be helpful during all types of cases, but is especially helpful in cases that involve domestic violence, driving under the influence (DUI), or other complex cases. Footage is useful for these cases not only because they document victim injuries or offender behavior, but the footage can be used to help create very detailed and accurate police reports that withstand scrutiny from supervisors, the courts, or others.

While most research on the impacts of BWCs on citizen behavior has involved measuring police perceptions of citizen behavior, these studies have shown that citizen behavior can be affected in two ways. Some citizens can become less angry and belligerent when they find out that they are being recorded since they might fear their actions could be viewed by others. Additionally, some members of the public might feel more reassured or at ease that their rights are being protected when an officer's behavior is captured by BWCs and be more willing to comply.

Challenges

While body-worn cameras offer many potential benefits to police and the public, there are also some inherent challenges associated with their use that must be acknowledged. For instance, low-ranking officers can be very apprehensive about the adoption of BWCs as they fear that the footage would be used as a mechanism to constantly monitor them and get them in trouble for minor violations of departmental policy (e.g., cursing). Additionally, some officers might feel like BWCs limit their discretion concerning minor, ticketable, offenses. These perceptions can lead to more legalistic behavior like increased citation activity as officers fear they might be scrutinized by their superiors. Moreover, some police officers report that members of the courtroom work group occasionally question the veracity of their incident reports when there is no accompanying BWC footage. These attitudes can underlie the misuse, abuse, or abandonment of BWCs at police organizations. However, despite these anxieties, these feelings eventually seem to give way to a willingness to embrace BWCs as officers see that BWCs offer certain practical benefits to their daily work.

While police agencies who are in the market for body-worn cameras have a broad range of products and models to choose from, there seems to be a lot of diversity in the capabilities, features, and cost of these devices. The cheapest option may not always be the best choice. Cameras can differ on many technical features that include their placement, storage options, battery life, aspect ratio, video and audio quality, nighttime recording ability, and radio integration. One of the most important product features is whether the devices are head-mounted (on an officer's sunglasses or a special-made headband) or chest-mounted (attached to an officer's chest or lapel).

Chest-mounted cameras are more affordable but can compromise the capture of relevant information since it may only record data that the officer's body faces. In addition, the view of the camera can be obscured by an officer holding a citation book or notepad or firearm. Head-mounted BWCs align more closely with the direction an officer is looking, may provide a better field of view, and tend to be more stable when officers are in a foot pursuit or fighting a suspect, however, they are almost four times as expensive as their chest-mounted counterparts. Finding a product that adequately meets the needs of a department at the right price point might be a significant challenge.

In addition to the cost of the actual camera devices, video data storage and maintenance can serve as the most notable financial and logistical problem for police agencies. Large amounts of video and audio data need to be regularly downloaded, backed up, and protected, and these data also need to be readily accessible to relevant parties. There are two ways that police organizations can decide to store their body-worn camera footage: on-premises or via third-party services. While storing data on-premises can help ensure their security, departments that house their own data might be forced to allocate additional staff and resources to accommodate the maintenance and access to the footage. Departments that choose to use third-party options (cloud-based data storage services), would not have to allocate additional resources to house the data internally and could have easy access to footage on a secure server, but might have to pay expensive subscription fees.

Whether third-party options or self-storage, many factors could dictate the storage costs. Larger departments with more officers will likely deal with far more footage than smaller agencies. Organizations with mandatory recording policies will also have more storage needs than agencies with discretionary policies. How long departments choose to house data will also impact how much data accrues. Whether departments opt to make footage available to the public, and to what extent, can also have serious financial and logistical implications. This is particularly the case when departments spend additional resources on redacting personal information of the subjects in the footage.

Marthinus C. Koen

Further Reading

Ariel, Barak, Farrar, William, and Sutherland, Alex. "The Effect of Police Body-Worn Cameras on Use of Force and Citizens' Complaints against the Police: A Randomized Controlled Trial." *Journal of Quantitative Criminology*, 31, no. 3 (2015): 509-35. Examination of the impacts of body-worn cameras on use of force and citizen complaints.

Katz, Charles, Kurtenbach, Mike, Choate, David, and White, Michael. *Phoenix, Arizona, Smart Policing Initiative: Evaluating the Impact of Police Officer Body-Worn Cameras*. Washington, D.C.: U.S. Department of Justice, Bureau of Justice Assistance, 2015. Evaluation of the implementation of body-worn cameras on different factors related to policing and police perceptions at one police agency.

Lum, Cynthia, Koper, Christopher, Merola, Linda, Scherer, Amber, and Reioux, Amanda. *Existing and Ongoing Body-Worn Camera Research: Knowledge Gaps and Opportunities. Report for the Laura and John Arnold Foundation*. Fairfax, Va.: Center for Evidence-Based Crime Policy, George Mason University, 2015. Comprehensive review of literature concerning existing body-worn camera research.

Ready, Justin, and Young, Jacob. "The Impact of On-Officer Video Cameras on Police-Citizen Contacts: Findings from a Controlled Experiment in Mesa, AZ." *Journal of Experimental Criminology*, 11, no. 3 (2015): 445-58. Examination of how body-worn cameras can impact encounters between the police and citizens.

White, Michael. *Police Officer Body-Worn Cameras: Assessing the Evidence*. Washington, D.C.: Office of Community Oriented Police Services, 2014. Review of literature regarding body-worn cameras.

See also Deadly force; Technology's transformative effect; Police brutality; Police civil liability; Police subculture; Resisting arrest; Use of force.

Booking

Definition: Police administrative procedure following arrest, during which suspects are identified and official records of arrests are made
Criminal justice issues: Arrest and arraignment; Probation and pretrial release
Significance: Booking records a suspect's official entry (or reentry) into the criminal justice system and moves the suspect from the jurisdiction of the police department to that of the courts.

Booking is one of many criminal procedures that suspects undergo following arrest. Police make an official record of arrest when a suspect is booked. This usually occurs at a police station or central booking facility and is managed by the arresting officer or booking personnel. Booking methods are guided by departmental Standard Operating Procedures and vary among law-enforcement agencies.

During booking, all suspects are searched, fingerprinted, and photographed. Evidence is documented, and reports are begun. Positive identification is made by cross-checking the suspects' Social Security numbers, driver's license numbers, and dates of birth, and their photographs may also be checked against those stored in various databases. Other law-enforcement agencies are then contacted to determine whether the suspects have outstanding warrants, often using the National Crime Information Center (NCIC), a computerized database of criminal justice information. Arrest reports list this infor-

Baltimore Central Booking and Intake Center. (By groupuscule, via Wikimedia Commons)

mation as well as the dates, times, locations, and circumstances of arrests. Separate uniform incident reports contain narratives describing the arrests and information pertinent to the crimes committed and offenses charged.

The entire booking process generally takes between one and two hours. If a maximum of forty-eight hours has elapsed, a person must either be charged with a crime or released. If charged, the defendant will be given a complaint summons. This document states the charges and the time and place to appear in court. Those arrested and booked for serious offenses or those eligible for bail but lacking financial resources must remain at a jail or holding facility until their initial appearance. People arrested for minor offenses are generally released on their own recognizance when booking is complete. The procedural treatment of defendants throughout the booking process is subject to judicial review. A suspect is booked pursuant to the commission of a crime, investigation, and arrest. Following booking, defendants move to the jurisdiction of the courts for their initial appearance before a magistrate.

Joel M. Caplan

Further Reading
Bannon, Mark E. *A Quick Reference Guide to Contemporary Criminal Procedure for Law Enforcement Officers: One Hundred Notable United States Supreme Court Decisions and Their Effect on Modern Policing in America.* Springfield: Thomas, 2003. eBook Collection (EBSCOhost). Web. 24 May 2016.
Cole, Simon A. *Suspect Identities: A History of Fingerprinting and Criminal Identification.* Cambridge: Harvard UP, 2001.
Feld, Bary C. *Cases and Materials on Juvenile Justice Administration.* St. Paul: West Publishing, 2000.
Loewy, Arnold H., and Arthur B. LaFrance. *Criminal Procedure: Arrest and Investigation.* Cincinnati: Anderson Publishing, 1996.
Simeone, Julie A.I. "Not So Legitimate: Why Courts Should Reject an Administrative Approach to the Routine Booking Exception." *New York University Law Review* 89.4 (2014): 1454-1487. *Legal Source.* Web. 24 May 2016.
Wertheim, Kasey E., and Kelly Badgett. "FBI-The FBI's National Data Exchange (N-Dex)." *FBI Law Enforcement Bulletin* (2015): 24. *MasterFILE Complete.* Web. 24 May 2016.

See also Arrest; Bail system; Computer information systems; Criminal procedure; Criminal records; Fingerprint identification; *Miranda v. Arizona*; National Crime Information Center; Police lineups; Suspects.

Border patrols

Definition: Units of the federal agency that oversees the 8,000 miles of coastal and land boundaries of the United States

Criminal justice issues: International Law; Law-enforcement organization; Terrorism
Significance: As a federal law-enforcement body under the aegis of the Department of Homeland Security, the U.S. Customs and Border Protection agency is responsible for controlling the entry of both people and substances into the United States.

The Customs and Border Protection (CBP) is one of the busiest law-enforcement agencies in the United States. On March 1, 2003, the Department of Homeland Security unified border personnel working in the immigration, customs, agriculture, and border patrol divisions under one agency. Formerly known as the U.S. Border Patrol under the Immigration and Naturalization Service, the border patrol was originally founded in 1924 after Congress passed strict limitations on legal immigration. With only several hundred agents on horseback, there were challenges in patrolling all the areas between inspection stations in the United States. Over the next eighty years, the border patrols evolved into a technologically advanced and increasingly sophisticated workforce with nearly ten thousand uniformed agents.

During the early twenty-first century, the CBP still maintained its primary mission to prevent the illegal entry of goods and immigrants into the United States. This duty, undertaken in cooperation with numerous other local and state law-enforcement agencies across the United States, resulted in approximately twelve million arrests between 1994 and 2004. This monumental task requires scrutiny from the land, air, and sea of more than 6,000 miles of international boundaries with Canada and Mexico and another 2,000 miles of coastal waters. Agents from twenty-one sectors across the United States work in all weather conditions and terrains, twenty-four hours a day, 365 days a year.

Twenty-first Century Priorities

During the 1980s and 1990s, Congress reacted to the increased flow of illegal immigrants and drugs across U.S. borders by providing for a significant increase in the number of agents and better technology to apprehend contraband and aliens. Drug seizures then became a major focus, with more than 18,500 pounds of cocaine and 1.1 million pounds of marijuana seized in 2001 alone by border patrol agents. Resources of equipment and personnel have typically been concentrated across the U.S.-Mexico border, where the majority of illegal entries have occurred. These initiatives in areas such as San Diego, California, resulted in illegal crossings decreasing by more than 70 percent during the late 1990's. Similar strategic plans to concentrate resources have been implemented in Arizona, New Mexico, and Texas under the National Border Patrol Strategy. These activities to curb illegal immigration have not occurred without controversy, as pro-immigration advocates and human rights groups have protested the arrest and return of detainees to their home countries.

In reaction to criticism of the border patrol's inability to render aid to illegal aliens in remote and isolated areas, the CBP began the Border Safety Initiative in 1998, in joint cooperation with Mexican authorities. This plan seeks to reduce injuries and deaths along the border between the United States and Mexico by sharing intelligence, conducting joint search-and-rescue training, and posting signs that warn of the dangers of unauthorized border crossings. By reducing dangerous crossings, rescuing illegal immigrants in trouble, identifying casualties, and tracking and recording data collected from this initiative, the CBP aims to make national borders safer and to reduce fatalities.

Immigration policies continue to be a considerable source of debate nationally, as some illegal immigrants are given asylum and others are deported back to their home countries. Laws passed by several presidential administrations have allowed for illegal immigrants to attain American citizenship. These laws have been applauded by advocates of various immigrant populations and denounced by others who back strict enforcement of immigration laws across the United States.

The most serious concern of the modern CBP since the terrorist attacks of September 11, 2001, involves intercepting terrorists who may be attempting to enter the United States, possibly with weapons of mass destruction. With the increased focus on homeland security, border defense and law enforcement have again become a hot topic on Capital Hill. The use of advanced military equipment such as the unmanned drone aircraft in mid-2004 in the American Southwest and other developments offer the CBP new tools to stop the flow of illegal persons and goods into the United States. Increased funding and enforcement proposals were likely to continue as terrorism prevention and the protection of its borders were considered a vital link in the safety of the United States.

According to the Congressional Research Service's April 2016 report "Border Security: Immigration Enforcement Between Ports of Entry," in 2014 the administration of President Barack Obama introduced executive actions to improve the immigration system. These measures included a revised security plan at the southern border of the United States.

Denise Paquette Boots

A CBP Border Patrol agent monitors the Canada-United States border. (By groupuscule, via Wikimedia Commons)

Border patrol car patroling on border. (By U.S. Fish and Wildlife Service, via Wikimedia Commons)

Further Reading

Argueta, Carla N. "Border Security: Immigration Enforcement Between Ports of Entry." *Congressional Research Service: Report* (2016): 1-33. *International Security & Counter Terrorism Reference Center*. Web. 24 May 2016.

Bohn, Sarah, and Todd Pugatch. "U.S. Border Enforcement and Mexican Immigrant Location Choice." *Demography* 52.5 (2015): 1543-1570. *Health Business Elite*. Web. 24 May 2016.

Byrd, Bobby, and Susannah M. Byrd, eds. *The Late Great Mexican Border: Reports from a Disappearing Line*. El Paso: Cinco Puntos P, 1996.

Crosthwaite, Luis Humberto, John William Byrd, and Bobby Byrd, eds. *Puro Border: Dispatches, Snapshots and Graffiti from La Frontera*. El Paso: Cinco Puntos P, 2003.

Krauss, Erich. *On the Line: Inside the U.S. Border Patrol*. New York: Kensington, 2004.

Mertz, Matthew A. "The Post-9/11 Evolution of the USBP." *Military Police* 16.1 (2016): 29. *MasterFILE Complete*. Web. 24 May 2016.

Moore, Alvin Edward. *Border Patrol*. Santa Fe: Sunstone P, 1991.

Nevin, Joseph. *Operation Gatekeeper: The Rise of the "Illegal Alien" and the Making of the U.S.-Mexico Boundary*. New York: Routledge, 2002.

Urrea, Luis Alberto. *The Devil's Highway: A True Story*. New York: Little, Brown, 2004.

Urrea, Luis Alberto, and John Lueders-Booth. *Across the Wire: Life and Hard Times on the Mexican Border*. New York: Doubleday, 1992.

Williams, Mary E., ed. *Immigration: Opposing Viewpoints*. San Diego: Greenhaven P, 2004.

See also Drugs and law enforcement; Homeland Security, U.S. Department of; Illegal aliens; Law enforcement; September 11, 2001, attacks; Vehicle checkpoints.

Boston police strike

The Event: Two-week work stoppage by the majority of Boston's uniformed police officers
Date: September 9-22, 1919
Place: Boston, Massachusetts
Criminal justice issues: Law-enforcement organization; police powers
Significance: This strike raised the question of how to balance public safety and the right of police officers to unionize, bargain collectively, and strike for economic justice.

The Boston police strike lasted from September 9 to September 22, 1919. Of the city's 1,544 policemen, 1,117 went on strike. Immediately after the policemen walked out, acts of violence broke out in the South End area of Boston. On September 11, Governor Calvin Coolidge brought in the state guard, which quickly established control over the city. On September 22, the police gave in, ending the strike, and the recruiting of new policemen began. None of the striking policemen was allowed to return to duty.

The Boston police strike was only one of many labor disturbances in 1919. During World War I, inflation had driven prices up, while unions had gained government backing for the right to organize and bargain collectively in exchange for wage concessions. In 1919, 4 million workers, or 22 percent of the workforce, engaged in strikes. In Boston, telephone operators and transit workers had gone on strike and succeeded before the policemen walked out.

Work conditions for policemen in Boston had deteriorated significantly over the decades. Their pay scale dated back to 1898, while prices had gone up 79 percent, city government had increased their obligations, promotion regulations were arbitrary, and the quality of police facilities was generally poor. When Mayor Andrew J. Peters and Police Commissioner Edwin Upton Curtis responded hesitatingly to the policemen's demands, offering only a two-hundred-dollar annual increase, they decided to organize and affiliate themselves with the American Federation of Labor (AFL). The Boston Police Union was part of a larger movement: By August of 1919, the police forces of thirty-seven large cities had unionized and affiliated themselves with the AFL. Commissioner Curtis suspended the nineteen policemen who had been elected officers of the new union, among them union president John F. McInnes. The bad pay and work conditions, along with the city officials' hostile response to their demands, convinced the policemen to strike: They voted 1,134 to 2 for the walkout.

From the perspective of the city officials, the policemen, by joining the AFL, had entered a conflict of interest. City government argued that policemen were officers of the state, bound to the impartial enforcement of the law. Any affiliation, then, with an outside group that represents only a part of the population would compromise police officers in the exercise of their duty. The policemen, on the other hand, could point to pay and work conditions that undermined their ability to carry out their mission effectively.

For police unions, the Boston strike had important consequences. Most police unions remained and remain independent. Those that are affiliated with the AFL-CIO carry a no-strike rule in their charters. The Boston policemen eventually reorganized as the Boston Police Patrolmen's Association in 1965. In 1968, the police officers arbitrated a labor contract with the city of Boston.

Thomas Winter

Further Reading
Russell, Francis. *A City in Terror: The 1919 Boston Police Strike*. New York: Penguin Books, 1977.
Wells, Donna M. *Boston Police Department*. Mount Pleasant, S.C.: Arcadia, 2003.

See also National Guard; Police.

Broken windows theory

Definition: A theory that posits a relationship between neighborhood disorder and serious crime.
Criminal justice issues: Civil rights and liberties; crime prevention; police powers; vandalism

Significance: Broken windows theory is the notion that unheeded petty crime and public disorder lead to more serious crime and neighborhood deterioration. The theory is the basis for several types of law enforcement models, most notably New York City's zero tolerance policing strategy that was launched in the 1990's.

Broken windows theory is a metaphor for the putative relationship between crime and disorder in urban environments. Introduced in a March 1982 Atlantic Monthly article by social scientists James Q. Wilson and George L. Kelling, the theory has provided the conceptual foundation for community policing (the prevailing model of policing in the United States since the 1980's) and its variants, including public order policing, quality-of-life policing, and zero tolerance policing. Neighborhood disorder consists of signs of physical decay (e.g., garbage, graffiti, unmown lawns, and abandoned buildings and cars) and social incivilities (e.g., public drinking, vandalism, littering, street prostitution, and gang activity). Such public nuisances adversely affect residents' perceptions of the safety of their streets, increasing their fear of crime and decreasing their interactions with their neighbors and their use of public places for shopping, recreation, and socializing.

Theoretical Underpinnings

Fewer people on the street renders neighborhoods less safe due to the absence of public guardians, and less socializing renders neighborhoods less safe due to a weakening in the informal social control mechanism (i.e., the capability of residents to maintain order in their own communities) and a diminution in collective efficacy (i.e., the belief that neighbors can act together to accomplish consensual goals). Informal social control is effectuated by residents who are the "eyes and ears" of the police, watching their streets for any signs of disorder, intervening to restore peace, and calling and cooperating with the police to stamp down on disruptions before they escalate into more serious misbehaviors.

The informal social control mechanism strengthens neighborhood solidarity. However, these can deteriorate reciprocally, culminating in greater hopelessness, helplessness, and despair among residents. A widespread belief in the fecklessness of residents perpetuates a cycle of urban decay and decline, eventually producing pockets of intergenerational poverty and a perpetual underclass. Residents who are able to move away from the growing social and economic blight and deteriorating conditions do so, weakening the social fabric, undermining the tax base, and causing businesses to flee as their customers dwindle. These conditions are the recipe for creating crime-ridden, impoverished communities that persist for decades and become focal points for gang shootings and homicides. This is exemplified by the conditions in Chicago's West and South Side neighborhoods, which contribute significantly to the city's alarming homicide totals (surpassing those of New York City and Los Angeles between 2012 and 2015).

At the core of the broken windows theory is the notion that unattended signs of decay in a community (i.e., laxities in policing) signal that the streets are being neglected and unmonitored, inviting increasing acts of destruction and abandonment and leading to the eschewal of the basic norms of community preservation. In the seminal *Atlantic Monthly* article, the authors describe a scenario in which an abandoned building with only a few visible broken windows encourages disruptive passersby to break more windows. Neglect begets further neglect until the building becomes a site for squatters and a variety of other antisocial behaviors. Neglect also reflects a climate of apathy and negligence, fostering disinvestment in the community and destroying interest in cultivating a spirit of well-being and the pursuit of the commonweal. Unless the initial occurrence of disorder is immediately contained, one broken window fosters more vandalism and a spiral of decay that engulfs more buildings, streets, and, inevitably, entire neighborhoods. This is the basis for the application of the broken windows theory to community crime prevention and policing programs.

Broken Windows and the New York Miracle

The broken windows phenomenon was first demonstrated by social psychologist Philip Zimbardo of Stanford University. His research in the Bronx, New York, and Palo Alto, California, showed that an abandoned car with minimal signs of damage was stripped of all its valuable parts and destroyed in both communities (in just one day, in the case of the Bronx). In Palo Alto, the car remained intact until Dr. Zimbardo dented it with a sledgehammer, after which the entire car was damaged and cannibalized. Left to be destroyed, the abandoned car (broken window) is a symbol of community decline and a reminder that no one cares or is in control. It is the impetus that encourages offenders to engage in criminal and disorderly behaviors with impunity.

At the heart of public order policing is the belief that deterrence of serious crime occurs when the police respond swiftly and consistently to minor crime and disorderly behavior. According to the broken windows theory, ignoring petty offenses creates an atmosphere of lawlessness that becomes the breeding ground for more serious crime. Officially announced in 1994 by Mayor Rudy Giuliani, the New York City Police Department's landmark zero tolerance law enforcement policy, which produced the so-called New York Miracle (massive reductions in city crime in every category), illustrates the implementation of broken windows policing. In fact, George Kelling began the testing of broken windows policing as a consultant to the New York City Transit Authority in the mid-1980's. These new policies involved the removal of all graffiti and garbage from the subway, the arrest of toll jumpers and subway vandals, the expedition of case processing, and background checks for all arrestees, including the perpetrators of minor crimes.

With William Bratton as Mayor Giuliani's police commissioner, these policies were implemented citywide and included the arrest of New Yorkers for public drinking and intoxication, public urination, living under bridges, panhandling, prostitution, and vandalism. The targeting of the infamous squeegee men epitomized the era of zero tolerance policing in New York City. At stoplights, the squeegee men would wipe clean the windshields of cars without the drivers' permission, aggressively demanding payment for their unsolicited services. The police clamped down harshly on criminals of every ilk (major and minor offenders alike), and so began the steady and unparalleled decline in the city's crime rate. Young men suspected of gang activity were arrested for loitering, flouting traffic laws, and driving without a license. The police instituted the widespread use of stop, question, frisk, and arrest practices as the modus operandi for law enforcement officers, employing these techniques writ large against anyone suspected of possessing a gun or drugs.

Criticisms

The broken windows theory and its related policing strategies have faced criticisms from various quarters, mostly along three lines. First, the contribution of broken windows policing to crime reduction in New York and other cities is largely unknown and likely exaggerated. In fact, crime was already declining steeply in New York City and other large jurisdictions before zero tolerance policing was implemented. During this time, the crack epidemic and its attendant violence were already subsiding, along with the wealth of disorders related to the street-corner drug market. In addition, the broken windows policy was accompanied by the introduction of a strategic reengineering of policing in New York City, including the use of computerized data to identify hot spots for police deployment (COMPSTAT) and the restructuring and decentralization of the department, which promoted a more visible police presence in neighborhoods. The concomitant declines in unemployment, the revitalization of midtown Manhattan, and the upturns as a result of gentrification throughout the city were also correlated with decreases in crime and disorder. Second, broken windows policing has led to public outcries against police overzealousness. In particular, analyses of the New York Civil Liberties Union have shown that aggressive police tactics were aimed disproportionately at people of color, leading to accusations of racial profiling and a plethora of lawsuits against the city. Third, empirical evidence has failed to consistently support the crime-reducing effects of broken windows policing in different jurisdictions.

Arthur J. Lurigio

Further Reading
Berk, R., and J. MacDonald. "Policing the Homeless: An Evaluation of Efforts to Reduce Homeless-Related Crime." *Criminology and Public Policy* 9 (2010): 813-40.
Harcourt, B. *Illusion of Order: The False Promise of Broken Windows Policing*. Cambridge, Mass.: Harvard University Press, 2001.
Kelling, G. L., and C. Coles. *Fixing Broken Windows: Restoring Order and Reducing Crime in Our Communities*. New York: Free Press, 1996.
Taylor, R. B. *Breaking Away from Broken Windows: Baltimore Neighborhoods and the Nationwide Fight against Crime, Grime, Fear, and Decline*. Boulder: Westview, 2001.
Weisburd, D., J. C. Hinkle, C. Famega, and J. Ready. *Legitimacy, Fear and Collective Efficacy in Crime Hot Spots*. Washington, D.C.: National Institute of Justice, 2012.
Wilson, J. Q., and G. L. Kelling. "Broken Windows: The Police and Neighborhood Safety."*Atlantic Monthly* 127 (March, 1982): 29-38.

See also Community-oriented policing; Neighborhood watch programs; Police powers; Problem-oriented policing.

Campus police

Definition: Law-enforcement departments based on college and university campuses
Criminal justice issues: Law-enforcement organization; Police powers
Significance: Long little more than campus custodians, campus security forces began evolving into modern police forces during the 1960s and now play important roles in law enforcement.

Campus police forces trace their origins back to 1894, when Yale University hired two New Haven, Connecticut, police officers to patrol university grounds. Those first two campus officers were hired simply as campus "watchmen," and their duties included patrolling the university grounds and watching for fire, water, or other damage.

Over the next half-century, as other universities throughout the United States followed Yale's example, the campus "watchman" system predominated. Most officers hired by university and college administrators had no formal law-enforcement experience and were typically people who had retired from other occupations. Rarely performing any true police or law-enforcement functions, they acted in a custodial capacity for their campuses.

A subtle transformation in the established watchman system occurred in campus policing in the 1930s and 1940s. During the late 1930s, campus watchmen were increasingly entrusted with additional duties, including some with true law-enforcement functions, as well as the enforcement of campus rules. However, while these quasi-police officers were still used primarily as campus custodians, they had the added responsibility of campus social control.

Emergence of Modern Campus Police

Modern campus police forces finally began to emerge during the 1950s, as American colleges and universities were entering an era of unprecedented growth in both student enrollments and campus sizes. During that period, university and college administrators began acknowledging the need for the full-time presence of law-enforcement officers on their campuses. Many chose to hire retired municipal police officers to act as campus security officers.

These newly hired campus security officers began the transformation of campus watchmen to full-fledged security officers and, finally, campus police officers. In an effort to become more professional and autonomous, campus security officers generally broke away from the traditional affiliations with physical plants and affiliated with upper administrations. However, despite the administrative and organizational changes occurring in campus policing during the 1950s, the primary duties of the officers remained custodial. They had no more power to police the behavior of students and campus visitors than any other ordinary citizen.

Until the 1960s, the legal doctrine of *in loco parentis* (in place of parents) guided the relations of campus security

Boston University Police Department. (Public domain, via Wikimedia Commons)

officers and students. This doctrinal basis created many unforeseen problems for campus security as well as administrations. Campus security officers might legally be able to detain troublesome outside visitors to their campuses, but enrolled students who caused problems were generally referred to campus administrators for disciplinary action. Moreover, campus security officers had to refer cases involving faculty or staff to local municipal police.

The last major shift in campus policing occurred during the era of campus social unrest as part of the counterculture of the 1960s. As student protests became increasingly unruly, college and university administrators were forced to admit that they had to create more efficient mechanisms to deal with the growing problem of campus strife. In conjunction with previously hired campus security officers, college administrators utilized the existing model of municipal law enforcement. As a result campus police started reorganizing along the lines of traditional paramilitary police hierarchies, complete with badges, police uniforms, and firearms.

Modern campus police have witnessed increases in the size of most departments, as college and university enrollments have grown. By the year 2005, 680 different institutions had their own campus police departments. These departments had an average of twenty-one full-time employees, including twelve sworn officers. Duties of campus police officers in the twenty-first century include routine patrols, building lockup, personal-safety escorts, and alarm monitoring. According to the Bureau of Justice Statistics in January 2015, during the 2011-12 school year there were almost 32,000 law enforcement employees serving four-year colleges and universities with 2,500

Campus police, Antelope Valley College. (By Rennett Stowe, via Wikimedia Commons)

or more students. A little more than two thirds of these institutions employed sworn police officers with full arrest powers.

As a result of decades of growth and professionalization, campus police forces have evolved from campus custodians and watchmen to the modern campus police forces seen on today's college and university campuses. As educational requirements for recruits have grown more rigorous, campus police have become increasingly similar to municipal law-enforcement agencies, and campus police work is now becoming an important law-enforcement career choice.

Wendy L. Hicks

Further Reading

Fisher, Bonnie, and John J. Sloan. *Campus Crime: Legal, Social, and Policy Perspectives*. Springfield, Ill.: Charles C Thomas, 1997.

McCarthy, Kara. "4-Year Colleges, Universities Had Nearly 32,000 Law Enforcement Employees; Nearly Half Were Sworn, Armed Officers." *Bureau of Justice Statistics*. Office of Justice Programs, US Dept. of Justice, 20 Jan. 2015. Web. 24 May. 2016.

Powell, John, Michael Pander, and Robert Nielsen. *Campus Security and Law Enforcement*. 2d ed. St. Louis, Mo.: Butterworth-Heinemann, 1994.

Reaves, Brian. "Campus Law Enforcement, 2011-12." *Bureau of Justice Statistics*. Office of Justice Programs, US Dept. of Justice, 20 Jan. 2015. Web. 24 May. 2016.

Rengert, George F. *Campus Security: Situational Crime Prevention in High-Density Environments*. Monsey, N.Y.: Willow Tree Publishing, 2001.

See also Community-oriented policing; Date rape; Law enforcement; Police; Private police and guards; School violence.

Civilian review boards

Definition: Official groups of citizens that examine the merits of complaints against police officers

Criminal justice issues: Government misconduct; police powers; professional standards

Significance: Civilian review boards have been instituted in various cities as a way to restore public confidence in police departments, some of which had been tainted by corruption scandals and charges of brutality.

One of the greatest potential threats to justice is corruption within law-enforcement organizations. Police corruption has been addressed historically through a variety of mechanisms, including internal affairs divisions, police commissions, political oversight agencies, and special investigatory bodies. Despite these mechanisms, complaints have persisted that charges of police corruption are sometimes ignored by governmental authorities. During the 1960s, experiments were conducted with civilian review boards (CRBs), groups of citizens from the community who would examine complaints against police officers and recommend further action. Police departments strongly opposed the establishment of these boards as a threat to police professionalism and morale. During the 1980's and 1990s, however, enthusiasm for CRBs increased, particularly in larger cities. A series of notorious cases of alleged police abuse of power, particularly against persons belonging to racial minority groups, fueled calls for civilian oversight.

CRBs seldom are empowered to make ultimate determinations on citizen complaints. Instead, their findings and recommendations are passed on to other authorities as well as made available to the general public.

However, one of the more recent trends comes from a recommendation from the Department of Justice's Community Oriented Policing Services. Based on one of their published reports, they suggest that an annual report should be compiled each year to provide an update of the events that have occurred and the changes in policies and practices that have developed over the year. In addition, the annual report should include the impact of these changes in policies and practices, on the community and the police. In particular, the first report (January 2015 to March of 2016), covered excessive use of force, strategies that the police can use to engage the public, as well as the impact (on the police and the community) of the events that occurred over the past year on policy and practice.

This effort can be seen as a way to increase visibility and transparency in a time when the police (and police administration) are not trusted. In Chicago, another effort helped develop new and more effective civilian oversight of police departments that have been plagued by brutality and perceived racial bias. By utilizing community members and consulting them on their views, the goal is to reduce their frustration. CRBs can be seen as a logical complement to the trend toward community-oriented policing, which was gaining popularity at the same time. The more citizens are involved in the investigatory process, the less critical they will be of law enforcement.

Steve D. Boilard
Updated by Gina M. Robertiello

Further Reading
Gallagher, E.H, Kim, J., Markovic J. and Spence, D. The State of Policing in the United States, Volume 1. Washington, D.C.: Office of Community Oriented Policing Services (2016)
McDevitt, J., Farrell, A., Andresen, W.C. Enhancing Civilian Participation in the Review of Complaints and Use of Force in the Boston Police Department. Institute on Race and Justice, Northeastern University, 2005.
National Research Council. *Fairness and Effectiveness in Policing: The Evidence.* Washington, D.C.: National Academies Press, 2003.
Ostrom, Elinor, R. Parks, and Gordon Whitaker. *Patterns of Metropolitan Policing.* New York: Praeger, 1978.
Prosecuting Police Misconduct: Reflections on the Role of the U.S. Civil Rights Division. New York: Vera Institute of Justice, 1998.
Skolnick, Jerome H., and James J. Fyfe. *Above the Law: Police and Excessive Use of Force.* New York: Free Press, 1993.
Wilson, S. "Civilian Review Boards." The Encyclopedia of Criminology and Criminal Justice, pp 1-5, 2014.

See also Community-oriented policing; Deadly force; King beating case; Knapp Commission; Noble cause; Police brutality; Police chiefs; Police corruption; Police ethics; Procedural justice; Victim-offender mediation.

Cold cases

Definition: Unsolved cases, usually involving homicide, on which active police work has ceased
Criminal justice issues: Homicide; Investigation; Technology
Significance: Unsolved homicides provide no closure to relatives or friends of the victims. In some instances, a homicide's going unsolved may allow an at-large killer to commit another homicide. Additionally, large numbers of open homicide cases can place a burden on detectives already struggling with high caseloads. These situations have led to the development of a specialized unit within the homicide division of certain police departments that deals specifically with "cold" cases.

Police departments are, at times, plagued with such high caseloads that their performance is adversely affected. For example, increased homicide rates leading to a backlog of cases could slow results from crime laboratories, autopsies, and medical examiners. Case overloads can be frustrating to detectives who may already be working in departments that are short-staffed. All of these factors can hurt police performance, while allowing homicide cases to remain unsolved.

Unsolved homicides are commonly referred to as "cold cases." The phrase "cold case" can apply to any unsolved crime but mainly refers to homicides because there is no statute of limitations on murder, and these cases, despite the passing of months, remain open. Police department policies vary regarding the length of time that passes before a case is considered cold. Depending on the size of the department and its number of homicide detectives, a case could become cold after three months or after one year.

An increase in cold cases resulted from the rise in homicides, generally attributed to gang- and drug-related murders. Such cases are among the most difficult to solve. Traditionally, murder victims and their killers usually had some kind of relationship. However, deaths involving illegal immigrants, homeless people, transients, unsolved police shootings, and prostitutes are less likely to be rooted in long-standing personal relationships; thus the cases have a greater likelihood of becoming cold.

The Development of the Cold Case Squad

Cold case squadrons are a viable solution for police departments that have a high number of unsolved homicides. A high volume of new cases may prevent regular homicide detectives from looking into old cases. The cold case squad originated in Washington, D.C., where the homicide rate had skyrocketed to the point at which overwhelmed detectives solved very few cases, and murders kept increasing. This situation left many cases unsolved, with no detectives to work on them.

The Washington, D.C., Metropolitan Police Department (MPD) needed to address this issue. In a joint effort with the Federal Bureau of Investigation (FBI), the Cold Case Homicide Squad or the Cold Case Squad (CCS) was formed. The squad, which would not respond to new homicide cases, worked exclusively on unsolved murders. Other law-enforcement agencies had formed similar squads in the past, but this was the first time the FBI contributed agents to assist in investigations.

Staffing

Personnel make up the most important element of a cold case squadron. Old cases are among the most frustrating to work on because evidence could have been lost and witnesses are missing or are now deceased. These are cases that, after all, one or several competent detectives have failed to solve. Only experienced, innovative, and resilient detectives are recommended for cold case investigations. These agents should have knowledge in investigating and prosecuting various types of homicides. Experience with violent crimes is also helpful in these types of cases as well as experience in gang- and drug-related homicides.

Most full-time cold case squads employ two to four investigators. Usually they also have a lieutenant supervisor from the homicide division or a sergeant who manages the squad. Some departments that are too small to carry a full-time cold case squad instead have a part-time squad made up of detectives who split their time between cold cases and their regular caseloads.

Process

A case is usually referred to a cold case squad by a homicide division supervisor or another homicide detective. Sometimes a prosecutor will decide to reopen an unsolved case and will request assistance from local law enforcement. Cases are then prioritized, usually being ranked by their likelihood of being solved.

After reviewing the case file, cold case detectives assess previously collected evidence for usability. Investigators then attempt to fill in any information missing from the original investigation. This includes speaking with the original case investigators, obtaining missing notes from the case file, and reinterviewing old witnesses.

One of the main challenges in a cold case investigation is locating and interviewing unknown or reluctant witnesses. These witnesses may be difficult to find or reluctant to speak, but the hope is that enough time has passed so that they are now willing to cooperate with the police. In this instance, the passage of time could aid, rather than hinder, detectives.

Once the process is completed, if no arrest is made or no viable suspect is identified, the detectives write a summary of their new investigation and recommend either further investigation or to close the case. A cold case can either be closed through an arrest or administratively. A case can also be considered closed if the suspect believed

$20,000 reward for information leading to an arrest in the Deanna Cremin unsolved murder investigation. (By GrfxDziner, via Wikimedia Commons)

to be guilty is deceased or is serving a life sentence for another crime. Ultimately, the effectiveness of a cold case squad is measured by the number of cases it clears.

Technology

A significant advantage possessed by modern cold case investigators is the benefit of improved technology. Advancements in forensic analysis and investigative techniques have improved investigators' capabilities; these resources were not available to previous examiners.

New technology can shed new light on previously unsolved cases. DNA analysis and new methods in fingerprint identification and biometric identification technology have been great tools in clearing cases. Cold case investigators have also been known to utilize external resources, such as assistance from the FBI and U.S. Marshals Service, medical officers, and coroners.

Mark Anthony Cubillos

Further Reading

Mallett, Xanthé, Teri Blythe, and Rachel Berry, eds. *Advances in Forensic Human Identification*. Boca Raton: CRC, 2014. Print.
Ramsland, Katherine. *The Science of Cold Case Files*. New York: Berkley, 2004.
Reavvy, Pat. "Deputy's Diligence Pays Off." *Deseret Morning News*, September 27, 2004, p. B4.
U.S. Department of Justice, Office of Justice Programs. *Using DNA to Solve Cold Cases*. Washington, D.C.: National Institute of Justice, 2002.
Walton, Richard H. *Practical Cold Case Homicide Investigations Procedural Manual*. Boca Raton: CRC, 2014. Print.

See also Autopsies; Bloodstains; Computer forensics; Coroners; Crime labs; Crime scene investigation; Criminal history record information; DNA testing; Fingerprint identification; Forensic accounting; Forensics; Medical examiners; Murder and homicide; Murders, mass and serial.

Community-oriented policing

Definition: Philosophy of law enforcement that encompasses aspects of social service as police officers work with members of the communities they serve to solve local problems

Criminal justice issues: Crime prevention; Law-enforcement organization

Significance: Community policing practices have been adopted in one form or another by a vast majority of police departments throughout the United States.

Formal policing is less than two centuries old, and a community-oriented approach is being advanced as the new philosophy of policing for the twenty-first century. Although the variety of roles police have played during the history of the United States is not well documented, an understanding of what is known will aid in understanding the concept of community-oriented policing.

Historical Background

At the turn of the twentieth century, American police officers performed duties that amounted to social services. Such activities included assisting the unemployed to find jobs, operating soup kitchens, and making police stations available as night shelters for the indigent. During the first decade of the twentieth century, the New York City police commissioner initiated a number of policies that facilitated community-oriented policing. The commissioner believed that the rank-and-file police officers held positions of social importance of great public value. The community-oriented policies should not only be considered for their benefits to the police but also as beneficial to the public. The New York City Police Department held that every police officer was accountable for the social condition on the beat that he patrolled.

Many disciplines in the social sciences now hold that employment is a deterrent to crime. The 1990s saw a verification of this theory: The United States had both a low unemployment rate and a low crime rate. Likewise, in the early twentieth century, the New York City police commissioner considered unemployment to be a major cause of crime, and beat officers were expected to distribute employment information and assist the unemployed in locating employment. One of the overall responsibilities of beat officers was to improve the safety of their beats.

Initiatives by the New York City Police Department in its early, community-oriented approach to policing included creating so-called play streets. Play streets were designated for youngsters in neighborhoods that had no playgrounds, parks, or safe open places. For several hours during the day, the police would close streets in specific neighborhoods by placing barricades to vehicle traffic.

The police also referred teenage boys who were involved in delinquent acts to social services agencies, such as the Young Men's Christian Association and Big Brothers. One more creative approach to community-oriented policing was the police department's communication with ethnic newspapers of that era. Greek-, Italian-, and Yiddish-language papers were encouraged to publish city ordinances, so that immigrants could read about the laws in their native languages.

Eras of Policing

Historians recognize that policing in the nineteenth century was primarily decentralized and neighborhood-oriented. The major problems of this policing model were inefficiency, police corruption, incompetence, and undue political influence on police officers. That era has been called the "political era," during which the police and politicians had close relationships. Meanwhile, as towns and cities were developing, policing was in its initial stages, under the control of local governments. In the cities, the politicians oversaw all police operations. Although the police were usually organized in centralized, semimilitary, and hierarchical structures, they generally did not function along those lines. Rather, they made up decentralized units, with each ward politician running the police department in his ward.

Around the turn of the twentieth century, the Progressive movement emerged as a voice that sought to improve city government. The Progressive movement reflected upper-middle-class values that emphasized honesty in government officials, and it ushered in uniform, well-defined police procedures and policies. This period of policing has been called the "reform era." It saw attempts to free the police from control by politicians. Civil service reforms in police departments led to decreased influence by politicians, who lost their power in the hiring and firing of police officers. The reforms in policing emphasized the law-enforcement functions of policing over their social service functions. Although some law-enforcement scholars have suggested different policing eras and models, the terms "political era" and "reform era" have become generally accepted as the names of the eras preceding the modern era of community-oriented policing.

Problem-Oriented Policing

The road to modern change may have been laid down in 1979, when Herman Goldstein published an article on problem-oriented policing that would greatly influence modern-day practices. Goldstein claimed that the reform approach to policing was not working. Police responded to citizens' calls to handle specific incidents then returned to their patrol cars. According to Goldstein, beat officers were responding to events that kept occurring over and over again. Goldstein recommended that the police address the cycles themselves by developing a problem-oriented approach in order to solve the underlying issues that lead to problems. The emphasis of problem-oriented policing, he said, should be on the police working proactively to resolve situations that generate the reactive calls for help from beat officers.

In community-oriented policing, as in problem-oriented policing, the police take an active role in problem solving, but the goal of community-oriented policing is for officers to develop partnerships with members of the communities they serve. Problem-oriented policing has been incorporated into community-oriented policing as an important tool. Police departments that have adopted the community policing philosophy refer to problem-oriented policing (POP) projects, in which beat officers are expected to be involved.

The literature of various police departments reveals that the philosophy of community-oriented policing has a variety of meanings. Some police administrators believe that community-oriented policing has always taken place in small towns, where police officers typically know everyone on a first-name basis. Some administrators equate problem-oriented policing with community-oriented policing. Still others equate community-oriented policing with specialized units that work in high-crime areas. Also, there are police administrators who tout community-oriented policing because they consider it the latest fad and have instituted it for public relations purposes. Community policing has become so fashionable that a vast majority of police departments are claiming they are doing it.

The Nature of Communities

Basically, community-oriented policing involves police working with people in the communities they serve as equal partners to solve local problems. The term "community" may refer to a specific geographical area, such as a neighborhood, precinct area, or a patrol beat. Different areas of the city or community typically have different problems, the solutions to which should be determined by the police officers assigned to these areas in partnership with the local residents. A major premise of community-oriented policing advocates that strategies to solve problems are developed in concert with the citizens, whether the community refers to neighborhood or beat.

What is the value of community-oriented policing? Will it produce safer communities? Will citizens be more willing to cooperate with and support the police? Will the police be willing to share decision-making when it comes to controlling and preventing crime within the community? At present, no definitive answers can be provided. Because of a lack of scientific evidence that community-oriented policing has been successful, supporters are stressing other benefits to the community that are easier to demonstrate, based on surveys of residents taken both before and after implementation of community-oriented policing strategies in their neighborhoods. These successes involve citizens' attitudes, specifically regarding their fear of crime, their evaluation of the police, and their satisfaction with their neighborhoods.

In addition, the distribution of police newsletters informing residents about crime prevention and police programs; community projects, such as cleanup campaigns, property identification, and "safe" houses for children are considered to be successful attributes of community policing. Other benefits that community-oriented policing offers include public scrutiny—the public has a close view of police practices—and accountability-community-oriented policing provides the public with greater control over the police and law enforcement. Obviously, because community policing is implemented by individual police departments throughout the United States, it

The Madison Police Department is a progressive agency committed to the philosophy of community-oriented policing. (By Cliff from Arlington, Virginia, via Wikimedia Commons)

should be expected that some communities will be further advanced than others in community-oriented policing.

The community-oriented policing philosophy is not completely new, but it represents a major break with the reform or crime control model of policing that dominated the United States for most of the twentieth century. Many of the strategies of community-oriented policing are based on concepts that have been used by police departments in the past. Community-oriented policing has adapted from police-community relations ideas that have been proposed since the 1960s. The team-policing concept adopted in the 1970s could be considered a forerunner to the philosophy of community-oriented policing. The strategy of directed patrol, or patrolling guided by analysis of crime patterns and directed toward the solution of specific neighborhood problems was used in the 1970s and is being used in community policing today.

In large part, community-oriented policing has been advocated because of the failures of previous crime control methods to prevent, solve, or reduce crimes substantially. The concept of community policing has a variety of definitions and meanings, but generally it includes a problem-solving, results-oriented, public-oriented approach which emphasizes collaboration and partnership with the members of the community. The police-community collaboration focuses on solving problems of crime, fear of crime, public disorder, and neighborhood decay. Although its effectiveness in preventing crime has not clearly been proven, community-oriented policing can have a positive effect on citizen attitudes, decreasing the fear of crime and increasing satisfaction with neighborhoods of residence. Community-oriented policing can also have a positive effect on the police, who gain a more positive image of the public, enjoy increased grassroots support, and see improved police morale. The Department of Justice's Office of Community Oriented Policing Services (COPS Office) has invested more than $14 billion in community policing, reflecting the importance placed on the policy by the US government.

Possible Problems

Potential problems with community-oriented policing might include actions by police to uphold local norms of order and respectability that go beyond the legal bounds, such as harassment of the homeless. Also, police strategies may selectively favor the affluent and powerful in the community at the expense of the less privileged. Officers could use their close ties with the community members for political ends or for corrupt personal gain; the police could also become too intrusive into the private lives of residents.

In addition, implementation of community-oriented policing may face several obstacles. Many aspects of the reform or traditional policing organization and culture should be expected to resist change. Even in departments that have had community policing for several years, there are officers who resist the community-oriented philosophy and want a return to traditional policing. Also, community support and involvement can be difficult to obtain. Reasons behind lack of support could range from lack of residents' time to commit to community-oriented programs to residents' mistrust of the police, fear of neighborhood criminals, or lack of infrastructure in high-crime neighborhoods. Community support has to be obtained by the police and should never be assumed by them.

Michael J. Palmiotto

Further Reading
Alpert, Geoffrey P., Roger G. Dunham, and Meghan S. Stroshine. *Policing: Continuity and Change.* Long Grove: Waveland, 2015. Print.
Bennet, W., and Karen Hess. *Management and Supervision in Law Enforcement.* 5th ed. Belmont: Wadsworth, 2007. Print.
De Guzman, Melchor, Aiedeo Mintie Das, and Dilip K. Das. *The Evolution of Policing: Worldwide Innovations and Insights.* Boca Raton: CRC, 2014. Print.
Miller, L., and Karen Hess. *Police in the Community: Strategies for the Twenty-first Century.* 3rd ed. Belmont: Wadsworth, 2002. Print.
Palmiotto, Michael J. *Community Policing: A Policing Strategy for the Twenty-first Century.* 2nd ed. Boston: Jones, 2005. Print.
Palmiotto, Michael J. "The Influence of 'Community' in Community Policing." *Visions for Change: Crime and Justice in the Twenty-First Century.* Ed. Roslyn Muraskin and Albert Robert. 4th ed. Upper Saddle River: Prentice, 2004. Print.
Palmiotto, Michael J., M. Birzer, and N. Unninthan. "A Suggested Curriculum for Police Recruit Training in Community Policing." *Policing: An International Journal of Police Strategies and Management* 23.1 (2000). Print.

See also Criminology; Neighborhood watch programs; Peace Officer Standards and Training; Police; Police academies; Police civil liability; Police ethics; Police powers; September 11, 2001, attacks; Strategic policing.

Crime analysis

Definition: Crime analysis is the use of methodological strategies for analyzing crime data and other data that are relevant to law enforcement authorities and their constituents.

Criminal justice issues: Crime prevention; crime statistics; technology

Significance: Crime-analysis techniques are considered by many as an integral part of the evolution of policing from reactive to proactive and preventative methods.

Many today view crime-analysis techniques as part of an ongoing paradigm shift in law enforcement towards more technologically sophisticated strategies used to counter crime. In a rudimentary form, however, crime-analysis techniques arguably date back to the origins of policing. Early police agencies as far back as the Metropolitan police in England and even before, used analysis to predict where crime will occur most or where a particular criminal will strike next. Indeed, on a general scale, crime-analysis techniques in their most basic form likely date back to the beginning of modern civilization.

More modern crime-analysis techniques can be traced back to the early 1960's to departments located in large urban areas and cities that had crime large enough to necessitate its use at the time. These techniques logically coincided with the increased focus on crime data and more sophisticated databases through which crime data were stored. At this time crime analysis was often basic with some departments using pen maps or other primitive methods to analyze crime and calls for service in their cities. It was not until the advancement of computers in the 1980's and 1990's that crime analysis began to transform into its current form. This evolution was expedited by government grants, a shift back towards community policing, and the reliance on other scientific techniques such as forensics.

Crime analysis today is a multifaceted strategy that involves not only techniques similar to crime mapping and statistical analysis, but, also includes techniques more suited for administrative concerns about placement of patrols based on these crime statistics. Crime-analysis techniques can be broken down by focus on long-term solutions as well as predictive policing and short-term decisions about where police should be focused based on crime trends. Crime analysis, however, is not entirely focused on crime problems in an area, but, also calls for service, resources used on manpower, and other related concerns of departments.

The job of crime analyst is quickly expanding today and the analyst's job description is often dependent on the type of agency that employs the crime analyst. For instance, it is becoming increasingly common for departments to hire civilian professionals with statistical and methodological backgrounds to handle crime-analysis techniques. Indeed, many large cities employ entire crime-analysis units to analyze their crimes and provide feedback and strategies for the department. These analysts may provide displays of crime broken down by neighborhood or precinct or even intelligence information. There are still many smaller departments, however, that simply devote only a percentage of a sworn officer's time to undertake crime analysis for the department. This has led to a fragmentation within U.S. departments where some departments use cutting-edge crime-analysis methods that employ sophisticated statistical software and multivariate techniques, while others use primitive databases and use only the most elementary of statistical approaches.

While crime analysis is part of a scientific revolution in law enforcement that has many proponents, there remain some detractors as well. Many critics of this modern strategy believe that while the statistical approaches and graphics involved in crime analysis today are sophisticated, they are built on an unstable foundation. One key argument is that law enforcement should focus more resources on improving existing crime data rather than improving on techniques that analyze unstable data. Accordingly, the very crime data that is being relied upon is highly questionable, with the "dark figure of crime" being only one of a myriad of problems with the data. Thus, it remains to be seen whether crime analysis will continue to move into the forefront of policing as have other scientific methods such as forensics.

Brion Sever

Further Reading

Cope, Nina. "Intelligence Led Policing or Policing Led Intelligence? Integrating Volume Crime Analysis into Policing." *British Journal of Criminology* 44 (2004): 188-203.

Ferreira, Jorge, Paulo Joao, and Jose Martins. "GIS for Crime Analysis: Geography for Predictive Models." *Electronic Journal Information Systems Evaluation* 15 (2012): 36-49.

Haley, K., J. Todd, and M. Stallo. "Crime Analysis and the Struggle for Legitimacy." In *Contemporary Issues, Applications, and Techniques in Crime Analysis*, M. Stallo and K. Haley, eds., 64-77. Acton, Mass.: Copley Custom Textbooks, 2004.

O'Shea, T., and K. Nichols. "Police Crime Analysis: A Survey of U.S. Police Departments with 100 or More Sworn Personnel." *Police Practice and Research* 4 (2003): 223-50.

Ribaux, O., S. Walsh, and P. Margot. "The Contribution of Forensic Science to Crime Analysis and Investigation: Forensic Intelligence." *Forensic Science International* 156 (2006): 171-81.

See also Geographic information systems; Predictive policing; Technology's transformative effect.

Crime scene investigation

Definition: Meticulous preservation of physical evidence at specific locations by use of photographs, sketches, and collection and preservation of crime-related evidence

Criminal justice issues: Evidence and forensics; investigation; technology

Significance: Securing the crime scene and meticulously protecting evidence contributes to successful prosecution. Crime scene procedures allow proper coordination among investigators, scientific laboratory personnel, and prosecutors; interagency cooperation is essential to exoneration of the innocent and conviction of the guilty.

The primary objectives of the first responding officers at a crime scene are to arrive safely and render aid to crime victims. The officers' next immediate task is to isolate, contain, and preserve the crime scene. Officers use barriers to create an exclusion zone and prevent unauthorized access. In most cases, the responding officers conducting the preliminary investigation release the crime scene to the follow-up investigators and the Crime Scene Investigation unit (CSI). The ultimate purpose of crime scene investigation is to maintain proper care, custody, and control of evidence. Well-delineated procedures result in competent, material, and reliable evidence for presentation in a criminal trial.

Crime Scene Coordination

Lead investigators coordinate logistical resources for crime scene investigation. Requests for technical CSI unit services—crime scene processing and a mobile crime laboratory-require approval of the senior investigator. CSI technicians process the crime scene; they do not conduct follow-up investigations or arrest suspects. The media, however, portray CSI roles inaccurately.

The CSI's primary role is to record the crime scene, including photographing it, and collect evidence. The CSI evidence team coordinates with forensic laboratory scientists and investigators. In smaller agencies with limited resources, state police or the State Bureau of Investigation (SBI) may assist local officers with the follow-up investigation.

The lead follow-up investigator establishes a systematic search plan at the crime scene. Officers estimate boundary determinations; inner and outer crime boundaries divide the scene. The investigator attempts to identify potential offender routes. For example, in a homicide, the inner crime scene might include the victim's home and immediate property. The outer crime scene may include several blocks or open fields. A wounded criminal may provide a travel pattern of blood trace evidence from the bedroom window, backyard, and to a specific vehicle. The vehicle, once traced to another location, may provide additional evidence. Additional locations to be investigated may include those of other crimes or dump sites. These areas may contain other evidence that will lead police to offenders.

Investigative service teams may assist in interviewing witnesses, recording statements, and canvassing neighborhoods or vehicles. Lead investigators conduct liaison activities with technical and investigative services personnel. Specialists in criminal investigative analysis and criminal profiling may assist in linking physical and psychological evidence. Criminal information is stored, collated, analyzed, and disseminated to appropriate agencies and personnel.

A Typical Crime Scene Application

Officers respond to a homicide call and discover the body of a young woman in the bedroom. After securing the scene, they set up the crime scene log, which controls all people having the right of access to the crime scene. The preliminary survey requires written notes, sketches, and identification of fragile evidence. Officers identify footprints outside the bedroom window. They alert investigators and CSI specialists to the location of fragile evidence.

Officers establish a pathway for medical personnel; this pathway prevents destruction of physical evidence. If emergency medical responders request assistance from the pathologist, the pathway allows such follow-up investigators opportunities to locate obvious physical evidence, for example, a weapon, blood, and footprints. The initial point-to-point search turns up additional evidence to be photographed.

Special attention to points of entry windows and exits will assist in identifying the offender's travel pattern. Officers locate broken glass near a damaged window and notice a bloody fingerprint below the putty line. This is a strong indicator that the offender pulled the broken glass from the window frame.

The corpse represents a secondary crime scene. The autopsy examination provides essential information on cause of death. There are three possible explanations for death crime scenes: accidental, suicide, or homicide. The case of death in this scenario is homicide. The autopsy report links trace evidence from the victim to the scene and offender.

Crime Scene Inspection

The basic rule of criminal investigation requires that evidence never be touched, altered, or moved before being photographed. The CSI team records the crime scene according to specific photography and videography procedures. Specialists such as fingerprint examiners, blood evidence technicians, and footprint technicians may gather fragile trace evidence. A sketch team further documents and measures the location of the physical evidence. Standard search methods ensure the successful collection of all crime scene evidence. The collection team secures, marks, and tags the evidence and initiates the chain of custody forms.

In the after-action briefing review, the investigative team and the CSI team share findings. Investigative teams compare preliminary notes for potential follow-up procedures. Discussions focus on essential evidence and its connection to primary suspects. The process identifies potential suspects and the need for laboratory examination to develop associative trace evidence.

The final survey is the last official step before the crime scene is released according to agency regulations or other legal requirements. Standing procedures require final inspection by the lead investigator and CSI team leader. The purposes of the final survey are to check for and collect uncovered evidence, police equipment, and dangerous materials.

In summary, crime scene reconstruction requires critical thinking and problem-solving strategies. Investigators apply scientific analysis to determine an accurate sequence of events and reconstruct what happened at a crime scene. Physical evidence determines the suspects and the manner in which the crime was carried out. Crime scene interpretation is the result of hypothesis formulation, experimentation, laboratory examination, and logical analysis.

Thomas E. Baker

Further Reading
Becker, Ronald F. *Criminal Investigation*. Gaithersburg, Md.: Aspen Publications, 2000. A handbook for use by crime laboratory personnel.
Gilbert, James N. *Criminal Investigation*. Upper Saddle River, N.J.: Prentice-Hall, 2001. Includes index and bibliography.
Ogle, Robert R. *Crime Scene Investigation Reconstruction*. Upper Saddle River, N.J.: Prentice-Hall, 2004.

See also Arson; Bloodstains; Chain of custody; Cold cases; Computer forensics; Crime labs; Evidence, rules of; Fingerprint identification; Forensic psychology; Forensics; Plain view doctrine; Police detectives; Psychological profiling; Shoe prints and tire-tracks.

Dallas and Baton Rouge police officer attacks (2016)

Definition: Two incidents of shooting against police officers. Shooters specifically targeted police, especially white police officers. The shootings were retaliation for earlier police shootings of black men.

Criminal justice issues: Civil rights and liberties; law enforcement organization; morality and public order; police powers; political issues; victims

Significance: The emerging concern of retaliation with regard to race-related deaths

Micah Xavier Johnson, an Army Reserve Afghan War veteran, ambushed and fired at a group of police officers in Dallas, Texas on July 7, 2016. The heavily armed Johnson started shooting at the end of a peaceful "Black Lives Matter" protest organized in solidarity against police shootings that occurred in preceding days, killing two black males, Alton Sterling in Baton Rouge, Louisiana, and Philando Castile in Falcon Heights, Minnesota.

Johnson claimed that he wanted to kill white people, especially white police officers, in retaliation over the police shootings of black men. The shooting killed five officers, injured nine other officers, and two civilians were wounded. After the shoot-out, Johnson fled inside one of the buildings on the El Centro College campus with the police on his trail. During the standoff that followed, Johnson claimed, falsely, that explosives were planted in the area and threatened to kill more police. Negotiations between the police officials and Johnson reached a dead end as he held off the police for hours in the parking garage. Subsequently, in the early hours of July 8, 2016, police killed Johnson with a bomb attached to a robot, a first for U.S. law enforcement (wherein a robot was used to kill a suspect).

During the standoff, Johnson, who was black, told police negotiators that "he was upset about the recent police shootings...was upset at white people....[and that] he wanted to kill white people, especially white officers."

Baton Rouge Police Officer Attacks (2016)

Gavin Eugene Long fired on six police officers, killing three of them, on July 17, 2016, at Baton Rouge, Louisiana. The gunman was a twenty-nine-year-old ex-marine from Kansas City, Missouri. He stalked, ambushed, and then killed the police officers.

Long arrived at Hammond Aire Plaza, a shopping complex on Airline Highway, in his rented sport-utility vehicle (SUV) on July 17, 2016, at around 8:40 a.m. and was reported to be carrying a gun near the Old Hammond Area. However, police officials were unable to act as a result of Louisiana's law that allows people to carry firearms, though they did notice him walking with "a coat and an assault rifle." He began his search for police officers and spotted a police patrol vehicle parked at "B-Quik," a convenience store. Long parked his SUV at the adjacent building, got out, and prepared to shoot. As the police vehicle was empty, he drove north a short distance and noticed a police officer washing his vehicle. This officer, however, left before Gavin Long could get close enough.

A few minutes later, shots were fired at around 9:00 a.m. near the Old Hammond Area resulting in the killing of three officers that included two Baton Rouge police officers and one sheriff's deputy. Gavin Long was killed in a shoot-out with police a short while after he had killed the first officer. The entire shoot-out between the police and Long lasted less than ten minutes.

Two days after the Dallas police officers' attacks, a friend who interacted with Gavin Long recalled that he had lavished praise for the Dallas shooter, Micah Xavier Johnson. Long was also reported to be upset over stories of black men being shot by police officers, and in this case, the death of Alton Sterling, his mother said.

Tania Sebastian

Further Reading

Achenbach, Joel, William Wan, Mark Berman, and. "Five Dallas Police Officers Were Killed by a Lone Attacker, Authorities Say." *The Washington Post.* https://www.washingtonpost.com/news/morning-mix/wp/2016/07/08/like-a-little-war-snipers-shoot-11-police-officers-during-dallas-protest-march-killing-five/.

Bloom, Julie, Richard Fausset, and Mike McPhate. "Baton Rouge Shooting Jolts a Nation on Edge." *The New York Times.* http://www.nytimes.com/2016/07/18/us/baton-rouge-shooting.html.

"Dallas Police Shooting: Five Officers Killed, Seven Wounded by Gunmen." http://www.bbc.com/news/world-us-canada-36742835.

Fernandez, Manny, Richard Perez-Pena, and Jonah Engel Bromwich. "Five Dallas Officers Were Killed as Payback, Police Chief Says, July 8, 2016." *The New York Times.* http://www.nytimes.com/2016/07/09/us/dallas-police-shooting.html?_r=0.

Karimi, Faith, Catherine E. Shoichet, and Ralph Ellis. "Dallas Sniper Attack: 5 Officers Killed, Suspect Identified." http://edition.cnn.com/2016/07/08/us/philando-castile-alton-sterling-protests/.

Levin, Sam, Amber Jamieson, Jesssica Glenza, Mathew Weaver, and Claire Phipps. "Dallas Police Shooting: Micah Johnson Was 'Lone Shooter'—As It Happened." *The Guardian.* https://www.theguardian.com/us-news/live/2016/jul/07/dallas-protest-police-shooting-live.

"US Police Officers Killed in Baton Rouge Shooting." http://www.aljazeera.com/news/2016/07/report-police-shot-baton-rouge-160717151137437.html.

See also Black Lives Matter Movement/Blue Lives Matter Movement; Deadly force; Ferguson, Missouri unrest amid police shooting of Michael Brown; Police powers; Reasonable force; Use of force.

DARE programs

Identification: Drug abuse prevention programs targeted at schoolchildren
Date: Founded in 1983
Significance: The DARE programs, designed to help youths make life-affecting decisions, represent a cooperative effort between the police and the local school systems.

Escalating drug abuse in the 1980s prompted the development of the Drug Abuse Resistance Education (DARE) program by the Los Angeles Police Department in 1983. The program's original goal was to focus on fifth- and sixth-grade elementary school children, helping them to build self-esteem and providing them with information about the detrimental effects of drug abuse, ideas for resisting peer pressure, and strategies for avoiding participation in gangs and violent activities. Instruction was provided in seventeen lessons by trained law-enforcement officers as part of the curriculum in public schools. The program was later extended and included in middle- and high school curricula.

By the late-1990s, the DARE program had been implemented in almost 80 percent of the school districts in

D.A.R.E. program. (Public domain, via Wikimedia Commons)

the United States, as well as in more than fifty-four countries throughout the world. Although it was a very popular program, results of numerous studies showed that DARE was not greatly effective in reducing substance abuse. In many cases, the program heightened the curiosity of its student participants about drug use, leading some to experimentation. The program also tended to alienate socially deviant youth. Further analysis of DARE revealed questionable objectives and content.

By 2004, a new DARE program was being implemented by many school districts in the United States. The number of lessons was reduced to ten, which focused on interactive, real-life, problem-based activities that emphasize decision-making skills. Lessons and related activities were being developed for elementary, middle-school, and high school curricula.

Alvin K. Benson

Further Reading

Bergin, Tiffany. *The Evidence Enigma : Correctional Boot Camps and Other Failures in Evidence-Based Policymaking*. Burlington: Routledge, 2013. eBook Collection (EBSCOhost). Web. 26 May 2016.

Greenwood, Peter W. *Changing Lives : Delinquency Prevention As Crime-Control Policy*. Chicago: U of Chicago P, 2006. eBook Collection (EBSCOhost). Web. 26 May 2016.

Lucas, Wayne L. "Parents' Perceptions of the Drug Abuse Resistance Education Program (DARE)." *Journal of Child & Adolescent Substance Abuse* 17.4 (2008): 99-114. SocINDEX with Full Text. Web. 26 May 2016.

Maran, Meredith. *Dirty: A Search for Answers Inside America's Teenage Drug Epidemic*. San Francisco: Harper, 2003.

U.S. National Institute of Justice. *The D.A.R.E. Program: A Review of Prevalence, User Satisfaction, and Effectiveness*. Washington, DC: U.S. Department of Justice, 1994.

See also Comprehensive Drug Abuse Prevention and Control Act; Drug courts; Drug Enforcement Administration, U.S.; Drug testing; Drugs and law enforcement; Juvenile Justice and Delinquency Prevention, Office of; Juvenile justice system; Peace Officer Standards and Training.

Deadly force

Definition: Killing of people by police officers through the use of choke holds, firearms, or other methods of physical control

Criminal justice issues: Homicide; Government misconduct; Police powers

Significance: Because of controversies about excessive, inappropriate, and discriminatory applications of force to citizens by police officers, fatalities caused by the police have been reduced through training programs, regulations, and court decisions.

To control crime and maintain order in society, law-enforcement officers have traditionally been granted the authority to use physical force to capture or gain control of people who violate the law. American police officers, unlike those in some other countries, carry firearms, and police throughout the country have used their guns to kill people in the course of seeking to enforce the law and maintain order. Police officers have also caused people's deaths through the use of choke holds around people's necks and blows to the head administered with nightsticks, flashlights, or pistols.

The Context of Police Deadly Force

Deaths caused by the police were not randomly distributed throughout the broad spectrum of society, but instead occurred most frequently among poor people and members of racial minority groups who lacked the political power to complain effectively about improper police behavior. Because criminal offenders have easy access to firearms in the United States, American police officers know that they risk being shot; therefore they sometimes overreact to persons whom they suspect of being armed and dangerous. The problem has been compounded throughout American history because of negative attitudes toward poor people and members of minority groups. Police officers have used guns, nightsticks, and choke holds more frequently in seeking to capture or gain control over people in inner-city neighborhoods. Lethal physical force was applied not only to people suspected of committing felonies but also sometimes to people who ar-

The Los Angeles Police Department has been known to use deadly force.. (By Jonathan McIntosh, via Wikimedia Commons)

gued with officers about parking tickets or failed to cooperate with the police about other relatively minor matters.

During the 1960s and 1970s, as African Americans became more assertive about gaining equal rights and American society became less tolerant of discrimination, many police departments came under sharp criticism for their harsh behavior toward members of minority groups. In the urban riots of the late 1960s, for example, most of the fatalities were caused by police officers' shooting of suspected looters and rioters. The actual nature and extent of police deadly force varied by city, depending on the training provided to officers and the guidelines developed by police departments for the use of firearms and other physical interventions. Deadly force was more likely to be applied by officers whose police chiefs saw their job as attacking criminal segments of society as opposed to serving the entire public in a professional manner.

Control of Police Deadly Force

Controversies over highly publicized killings by the police led many police departments to develop stricter rules about the use of force. Greater attention was given to the precise situations in which officers would be justified in firing their guns or hitting someone with a nightstick. Officers also received more training in crowd-control techniques and immobilizing holds that would not threaten the lives of resisting civilians. Most important, courts and juries increasingly found police officers and their departments liable for needlessly causing the deaths of citizens. The threat that a city might have to pay millions of dollars in damages to the family of a person killed by police created even greater incentives for police chiefs to address the deadly force issue through stricter guidelines, better supervision, and increased training. Such guidelines still permit officers to use their weapons against armed offenders who pose an immediate threat, but they significantly narrow the circumstances in which it is reasonable for potentially lethal force to be applied.

As a result of these changes, the number of people killed annually by police officers in major U.S. cities dropped from approximately 350 in 1971 to 170 in 1984. Yet the guidelines for officers had developed unevenly, and some states still permitted officers to shoot unarmed suspects if they were suspected of fleeing from the scene of a felony. In 1985, in *Tennessee v. Garner*, the U.S. Supreme Court provided a common national rule regarding the use of deadly force on fleeing felons. The Court declared that it was an unconstitutional violation of a person's rights to shoot at an unarmed suspect who is fleeing

Protest against police brutality. (By Fibonacci Blue, via Wikimedia Commons)

from the scene of a crime. Under the Fourth Amendment, such actions constituted an unreasonable use of force to seize people.

This ruling helped to clarify and standardize the application of deadly firearms force, but it could not solve the problem completely. Some police departments, including that of Los Angeles, faced further controversy and lawsuits over deaths that resulted from the use of choke holds—especially given that the holds appeared to be applied most frequently to members of minority groups.

In 1989, in *Graham v. Connor*, the U.S. Supreme Court established the "objective reasonableness" standard for use of force by police. Under this ruling, each application of force should be based upon a standard of objective reasonableness under the totality of circumstances. Three determinants were pivotal as to whether force used was reasonable: severity of the crime at issue, whether the suspect posed an immediate threat to the safety of officers or others, and whether the suspect actively resisted arrest or attempted to evade arrest through flight.

The issue of police use of deadly force, particularly against African American suspects, came to the fore again in 2014, when the Black Lives Matter movement protested the shooting of the unarmed Michael Brown by a police officer in Ferguson, Missouri, and the death of Eric Garner after being placed in a chokehold by police in New York City. The movement subsequently drew attention to a number of other instances of allegedly unwarranted use of deadly force against African Americans, including the deaths of Tamir Rice, Eric Harris, Walter Scott, Jonathan Ferrell, Samuel DuBose, and Freddie Gray. A number of police forces, including that of Ferguson, Missouri, have undertaken reforms to attempt to address this issue, but on a nationwide level, disproportionate use of force against members of minority groups has remained a problem. According to 2015 research by the *Guardian*, black suspects were subjected to deadly force by the police at the highest rates of any ethnic group in the United States, at a rate of 7.25 per million compared to 3.5 per million for Hispanic and Latino suspects, 3.4 for Native Americans, 2.9 for white people, and 1.3 for Asians and Pacific Islanders.

Christopher E. Smith

Further Reading

Alpert, Geoffrey, and Lorie A. Fridell. *Police Vehicle and Firearms: Instruments of Deadly Force*. Prospect Heights: Waveland, 1992. Print.

"The Counted: People Killed by Police in the US." *Guardian*. Guardian News and Media, 24 May 2016. Web. 26 May 2016.

Del Carmen, Rolando V. *Civil Liabilities in American Policing*. Englewood Cliffs: Prentice-Hall, 1991. Print.

Fyfe, James J., ed. *Readings on Police Use of Deadly Force*. Washington, D.C.: Police Foundation, 1982. Print.

Kappeler, Victor E. *Critical Issues in Police Civil Liability*. Prospect Heights: Waveland, 1993. Print.

Milton, Catherine H., et al. *Police Use of Deadly Force*. Washington, D.C.: Police Foundation, 1977. Print.

Reisig, Michael D., and Robert J. Kane. *The Oxford Handbook of Police and Policing*. New York: Oxford UP, 2014. Print.

Salter, Jim. *Deadly Force: Fatal Confrontations with Police*. New York: AP Editions, 2015. Print.

Skolnick, Jerome H., and James J. Fyfe. *Above the Law: Police and the Excessive Use of Force*. New York: Free Press, 1993. Print.

Stroud, Carsten. *Deadly Force: In the Streets with the U.S. Marshals*. New York: Bantam, 1996. Print.

Thrasher, Ronald. "Internal Affairs: The Police Agencies' Approach to the Investigation of Police Misconduct." Police Misconduct. Ed. Michael J. Palmiotto. Upper Saddle River: Prentice-Hall 2001. Print.

See also Arrest; Civilian review boards; Color of law; High-speed chases; MOVE bombing; Police brutality; Reasonable force; Special weapons and tactics teams (SWAT); *Tennessee v. Garner*; *Graham v. Connor*.

Discretion

Definition: Flexibility allowed to the police and the courts to make decisions such as whether to arrest and prosecute individuals and the severity of sentences to be imposed

Criminal justice issues: Courts; Legal terms and priniciples; Police powers

Significance: Public officials may employ conscience and good sense, not only the letter of the law, in the reasonable exercise of power; however, discretion, particularly judicial discretion, has many critics.

Discretion allows police to decide whether to arrest an individual. (By Keith Allison, via Wikimedia Commons)

Discretion is the ability of a public official to decide whether and how a law will be enforced. It allows a range of judgments to be made to fit particular circumstances while still maintaining the spirit of the law. Discretion exists in many areas of the criminal justice system, from the actions of the police to the sentencing of a criminal by a judge. Discretion is therefore a very important aspect of the system, and it is one reason that the law as written often differs from the law in practice. Regarding police actions, for example, a law may prohibit all incidents of public drunkenness, but police officers may arrest only certain violators of the law who are particularly disorderly or appear disheveled. Officers always have the power to decide whether or not to arrest a person at the scene of a disturbance or suspected crime. In addition, administrative discretion exists within the police department: The administration decides where and how to deploy what numbers of officers, and particularly in the case of large-scale disturbances, how much force officers should be instructed to use.

Various aspects of discretion in the courts apply to the prosecution, defense, and judge. Prosecutorial discretion comprises deciding whether to prosecute, what charges to bring, the method of conducting the trial, and the type of sentence requested. In defense of a matter, discretion permits counsel to choose to present a case under one of several equal provisions of the law. The discretion of the judge at the time of sentencing has been the most criticized aspect of discretion in the system. The judge typically weighs a number of factors, such as the convicted person's criminal history and character, in deciding how severe a sentence to pass within the guidelines of the law. A first-time offender may receive a suspended sentence or probation, while a person with many past convictions may receive the maximum sentence allowable. Reforms such as strict sentencing guidelines and mandatory sentencing laws (including "three-strikes" laws) have attempted to reduce the allowable amount of judicial discretion. Discretion exists even after sentencing, in the corrections system. For example, corrections officers have discretion in determining who will be eligible for parole and when.

Elizabeth Algren Shaw

Further Reading

Arrigo, Bruce A., ed. *Encyclopedia of Criminal Justice Ethics*. Thousand Oaks: Sage, 2014. Print.

Beckett, Katherine. "The Uses and Abuses of Police Discretion: Toward Harm Reduction Policing." *Harvard Law and Policy Review* 10.1 (2016): 77-100. Print.

Cady, Erin. "Prosecutorial Discretion and the Expansion of Executive Power: An Analysis of the Holder Memorandum." *Harvard Journal on Legislation*. Harvard U, 15 Oct. 2015. Web. 26 May 2016.

Tonry, Michael, and Richard Fraser. *Sentencing and Sanctions in Western Countries*. New York: Oxford UP, 2001. Print.

Walker, Samuel. *Taming the System: The Control of Discretion in Criminal Justice, 1950-1990*. New York: Oxford University Press, 1993. Print.

See also Aggravating circumstances; Arrest; Deadly force; Diversion; Lesser-included offenses; Mandatory sentencing; Mitigating circumstances; Model Penal Code; Parole; Plea bargaining; Presentence investigations; Preventive detention; Sentencing; Sentencing guidelines, U.S.

Drug Enforcement Administration, U.S. (DEA)

Identification: Federal agency responsible for enforcing federal laws and regulations concerning controlled substances

Date: Established as a branch of the Bureau of Internal Revenue in 1915; became the Drug Enforcement Administration in 1973

Significance: In carrying out its mission, the Drug Enforcement Administration brings to justice organizations involved in producing or distributing controlled substances destined for illicit traffic in the United States.

The Drug Enforcement Administration (DEA) proactively investigates and prosecutes major growers, manufacturers, and distributors of controlled substances. It also conducts drug awareness and abuse prevention programs targeted toward demand reduction in the domestic and international illicit drug markets.

The DEA, compared to other federal criminal justice agencies, has a brief history. Its origins are traceable to the Harrison Narcotic Drug Act of 1914; it was originally classified as a "miscellaneous division" of the Bureau of Internal Revenue in 1915. In its first year, the agency seized 44 pounds of heroin and produced 106 convictions. Major expansion and reorganization over the following decades resulted from the Narcotics Drugs Import and Export Act of 1922, legislation establishing the Federal Narcotics Control Board; the Marijuana Tax Act of 1937, which levied a fine of $100 per ounce on untaxed marijuana; and the Boggs Act of 1956, which made heroin illegal.

The Bureau of Narcotics and Dangerous Drugs (BNDD) was created in 1968 through a congressionally approved merger of the older Bureau of Narcotics and the Bureau of Drug Abuse Control. Congress then passed the Controlled Substances Act, known as Title II of the Comprehensive Drug Abuse Prevention and Control Act of 1970, legislation that established consolidated oversight of both narcotics and psychotropic drugs. Rapid growth in the BNDD's domestic and foreign operations and the rise of recreational drug use in the popular culture prompted the creation of the Drug Enforcement Administration in 1973.

The DEA engages casework and prepares for the prosecution of major violators of controlled substance laws. Its operations focus on disrupting and dissolving violent drug trafficking organizations. The agency also is responsible for maintaining a national drug intelligence program that collects, analyzes, and disseminates drug intelligence information. Additionally, the DEA serves as the U.S. liaison to the United Nations and Interpol and is responsible for the seizure and forfeiture of assets that are associated with criminal drug enterprises.

According to the DEA, in 2014 it had an annual budget of $2.882 million and 11,055 employees (5,249 special agents plus support staff) and operated 221 domestic field offices throughout the United States plus foreign field offices in 69 countries. In 2015, the DEA made 31,027 domestic drug arrests and, in 2014, seized nearly 33,770 kilograms of cocaine, 1,020 kilograms of heroin, 74,225 kilograms of marijuana, and 2,946 kilograms of methamphetamines.

During its brief history, the DEA has established a significant worldwide presence. The agency's primary mission of drug law enforcement involves coordination and cooperation with federal, state, and regional authorities on mutual drug law-enforcement efforts as well as nonenforcement methods such as crop eradication or substitution, drug resistance education, and awareness efforts.

Theodore M. Vestal

Further Reading

Belenko, Steven R., and Cassia C. Spohn. *Drugs, Crime, and Justice.* Thousand Oaks: SAGE, 2014. Print.

"DEA Statistics and Facts." *Drug Enforcement Administration.* DEA, 2015. Web. 31 May 2016.

Drug Enforcement Administration. *Tradition of Excellence: The History of the DEA from 1973-1998.* Washington: US Dept. of Justice, 1999. Print.

Machette, R. B. *Guide to Federal Records in the National Archives of the United States.* Washington: Natl. Archive and Records Administration, 1995. Print.

See also Attorney General, U.S.; Comprehensive Drug Abuse Prevention and Control Act; DARE programs; Decriminalization; Drug courts; Drug legalization debate; Drug testing; Drugs and law enforcement; Homeland Security, U.S. Department of; Justice Department, U.S.; National Narcotics Act; Opium Exclusion Act; Comprehensive Addiction and Recovery Act (CARA) (2015); Designer and date rape drugs; Opioid treatment breakthroughs.

Drugs and law enforcement

Criminal justice issues: Federal Law; Law-enforcement organization; Substance abuse

Significance: Drug abuse and drug enforcement are major concerns for law-enforcement agencies and the criminal justice system as a whole. Drug enforcement activities account for a large portion of federal and state law-enforcement budgets, and drug offenders are a growing population in both state and federal prisons.

At the turn of the twentieth century there was a growing concern on the part of many Americans regarding the use of so-called patent medicines, many of which contained opium. One of the most common of the numerous "cures" for various ailments was Laudanum, which was a mixture of opium and alcohol. At that time, drugs were considered a medical issue subject to control at the individual state level, and it was usually left to the determination of the medical community as to what constituted appropriate and inappropriate use. Drugs officially became a national law-enforcement issue in 1914 with the U.S. Congress's passage of the Harrison Narcotics Drug Act

The Harrison Act made drugs and drug abuse federal law-enforcement concerns with the creation of the Narcotics Division within the U.S. Treasury Department. In 1930, Congress's passage of the Porter Act created the federal Bureau of Narcotics under the direction of the Treasury Department; it became the predecessor to the modern Drug Enforcement Administration (DEA).

Throughout the twentieth century, drug enforcement efforts changed the focus from one drug of choice to another, and increased authority was granted to law enforcement in attempts to control the illicit importation and distribution of controlled substances. Some of the most significant legislative enforcement efforts include the Comprehensive Drug Abuse and Control Act of 1970 (also known as the Controlled Substances Act), the Omnibus Crime Control Act of 1984, the Violent Crime Control and Law Enforcement Acts of 1990 and 1994, the Homeland Security Act of 2002, and the Illicit Drug Anti-Proliferation Act of 2003. Each of these federal laws provided additional tools and authority for law enforcement to identify, apprehend, penalize, and incapacitate those involved in the trafficking and use of controlled substances.

Types of Drugs

In general, law-enforcement efforts in the United States focus primarily on five major categories of what are collectively known as "controlled substances": stimulants, depressants, narcotics, hallucinogens, and cannabis. Cocaine and methamphetamines are the two primary controlled stimulants that require law-enforcement action. Depressants include barbiturates, rohypnol ("roofies"), methaqualone, and gamma hydroxy butyrate (GHB).

Law-enforcement agencies are concerned with both natural and synthetic narcotics. Natural narcotics derive from the opium poppy and include heroin, morphine, and codeine. Synthetic narcotics, which are manufactured from chemicals in laboratories, include such substances as methadone, demerol, and oxyContin. Hallucinogens cover a wide range of naturally occurring substances such as peyote and psilocybin and synthetically produced substances such as lysergic acid diethylamide (LSD), phencyclidine (PCP), methylenedioxymethamphetamine (MDMA or Ecstasy), and ketamine. Finally, the cannabis category of drugs includes marijuana, hashish, and any other substance containing tetrahydrocannabinol (THC).

Drug Schedules

The federal Drug Enforcement Administration is charged with the responsibility of regulating the manufacture, distribution, and scheduling of controlled substances in the United States. Controlled substances are scheduled according to their potentials for abuse, propensities for user dependency, and levels of accepted medical use within the United States. Drugs are classified in five schedules.

Schedule I controlled substances have no currently accepted medical uses within the United States. They also have high potentials for abuse and lack accepted safety for use even under medical supervision. Examples include heroin, LSD,

Schedule II substances also have a high potential for abuse, but they differ from Schedule I substances in that they have accepted medical uses in the United States. Despite the latter fact, abuse of these substances can lead to severe physiological or psychological dependence. Schedule II substances include cocaine, methamphetamines, methadone, PCP, and oxyContin.

Schedule III substances have less potential for abuse than those on Schedules I and II and also have well-documented and accepted medical uses in the United States. They present low or moderate potentials for physical dependence but high potentials for psychological dependence. Drugs in this schedule include ketamine, codeine, many diet pills, and steroids.

Schedules IV and V controlled substances have a low potentials for abuse. They are well known as useful in medical treatments in the United States and present limited potential for either physical or psychological dependence.

Federal Drug Law Enforcement

The Treasury Department was originally tasked with enforcement of the Harrison Narcotic Drug Act because this act was a taxation measure and fell under the same jurisdiction as other taxation matters. The Federal Bureau of Narcotics was established within the Treasury Department in 1930 to focus specifically on controlled substances and narcotics violations. In 1968 jurisdiction was transferred from the Department of Treasury to the Bureau of Narcotics and Dangerous Drugs within the U.S. Department of Justice. In 1973 the Drug Enforcement Administration was created and charged with primary responsibility for drug and narcotics enforcement within the United States. In 2014 the DEA had an annual budget of $2.882 million and 11,055 employees (5,249 special agents plus support staff) and operated 221 domestic field offices throughout the United States plus foreign field offices in 69 countries. In 2015, the DEA made 31,027 domestic drug arrests.

Nogales Port director Guadalupe Ramirez speaks to the media regarding a major marijuana seizure. (By Customs Border Protection, via Wikimedia

In 1982, the Federal Bureau of Investigation (FBI) was given concurrent jurisdiction with the DEA on drug enforcement-related investigations. Since then, the FBI has focused mainly on organized crime's role in drug trafficking and has employed specific legislative enforcement tools in this effort. Continuing criminal enterprise (CCE) statutes and the Racketeer Influenced and Corrupt Organizations Act of 1970 (RICO) laws are two of the primary law-enforcement tools used by the FBI to combat organized crime's role in drug trafficking. The FBI established the Organized Crime Drug Enforcement Task Force (OCDETF) in 1983 to detect and prosecute large criminal organizations that traffic in drugs. The OCDEFT is a multiagency endeavor, with both state and federal participation, that boasts a highly successful record of apprehending and prosecuting large drug trafficking organizations and their associates.

Along with law-enforcement efforts to identify, apprehend, and prosecute drug users and distributors at the federal and state levels, federal agencies also focus on the interdiction of drugs prior to their entry into the United States and during their transportation from point of entry to distribution locations. Interdiction efforts attempt to prevent the entry of drugs into the United States by concentrating efforts on the supply routes on land, air, and sea.

The United States Coast Guard plays an active role in the identification and interception of drug smugglers on the oceans and in the coastal waters that surround the United States. The Coast Guard employs advanced intelligence systems and utilizes interdiction patrols on known smuggling routes to profile "mother ships" that may be loaded with drugs being shipped from one of the many source countries. The Bureau of Immigration and Customs Enforcement (ICE) is responsible for securing the nation's borders and transportation systems and is charged with the prevention of smuggling drugs, weapons, and instruments of terrorism across U.S. nation's borders or through the numerous ports of entry either by air or from the sea.

State and Local Drug Law Enforcement

State and local drug law enforcement is similar to the federal system in organization. However, most state and local law-enforcement agencies are heavily dependent on federal funding to support their enforcement activities. Drug investigations can be both personnel and time intensive and are often beyond the capability of small local agencies; they can even place severe strains on some state law-enforcement budgets. Federally sponsored multijurisdictional task forces and the involvement of the federal agencies in major cases are frequently utilized techniques at the state and local levels of drug enforcement.

A common method of effective drug investigations at both state and federal levels is drug interdiction. In drug interdiction, law-enforcement agencies attempt to intercept and seize illegal drugs during their transportation from their source locations to their intended distribution sites. Federal efforts focus on intercepting drugs before they enter the United States, while state and local efforts focus on intercepting drugs before, or while, they enter the individual states and before they reach their points of distribution.

Interdiction efforts at the state and local levels include highly visible efforts by uniformed officers on major interstates and major routes of travel between source cities and areas of distribution. Another effective interdiction strategy involves the interception of drugs that are being moved from source to distribution locations by means of public transportation, such as buses, railways, and public airlines.

Special Operations

A highly visible drug investigative effort that is viewed by the general population as an effective strategy is known as the fish net operation. This type operation is a planned and coordinated labor-intensive effort targeting both buyers and sellers of drugs at the street level. This strategy is used most frequently in open-air drug markets that are commonly located in inner cities. Known drug-selling locations are subjected to intense surveil-

A port security specialist stationed at the Maritime Safety and Security Team 91105, stands guard over more than 40,000 pounds of cocaine worth an estimated $500 million being offloaded from the cutter Sherman. (Public domain, via Wikimedia Commons)

lance in this type of operation. Individuals observed selling or purchasing drugs are contacted away from the sites of the sales and are arrested for possession or distribution of controlled substances. This technique is often enhanced by the use of undercover police officers making buys from targeted individuals.

As may be expected, these operations receive strong support from local communities and serve as effective public relations strategies for law-enforcement agencies. Fish net operations are effective in disrupting the flow of illegal drugs for short periods of time but have limited impact on long-term drug control or drug reduction strategies.

The most highly publicized drug enforcement investigative technique involves the use of undercover operatives to make purchases or to infiltrate drug trafficking organizations. There are two primary types of undercover operations employed at the state and local level. The first type involves the use of police officers in undercover roles; the second involves the use of informants to make undercover purchases or gather other evidence.

Each type of undercover operation has specific benefits and limitations. When utilizing police officers in undercover roles, the primary concern throughout the operations is focused on the safety of the officers. These operations must be well planned and coordinated with adequate surveillance and "cover" units in place to ensure the safety of the undercover officers. The value of using undercover police officers, instead of informants, is the level of confidence that is obtained in the details of the drug purchases and in the evidence obtained. Basically, judges and juries trust police officers more readily than informants.

The use of informants to make undercover purchases or obtain evidence for use in drug prosecution requires detailed efforts to "validate" the information obtained. Since many informants have less-than-credible pasts (some may even be currently involved in illegal activities), it is imperative that interviews and searches of the informants be conducted immediately before and after they make their drug purchases or collect their evidence. Consequently, a primary focus of undercover operations utilizing informants is on the credibility of the evidence the informants obtain. Informants must be kept under constant surveillance during and after their drug purchases to ensure that all collected evidence is recovered and that no evidence is "planted" or stolen by the informants. The primary benefit of using informants is in that they can often infiltrate organizations or gain the trust of individuals to which undercover law-enforcement officers would not have access.

Another form of undercover operation used by larger agencies and at the federal and state level is the so-called "reverse sting." In a reverse sting, the police are the individuals "selling" drugs. These operations are usually large in scale and target mid- and upper-level dealers who show a predisposition to drug trafficking activities. Reverse sting operations require detailed planning and coordination and can pose serious dangers to the officers involved.

There have been reported instances of individual law-enforcement agencies setting up reverse sting operations whose intended drug buyers were from other law-enforcement agencies. Such situations can hold dramatic and unfortunate outcomes when each agency involved believes the other side to be the "bad guy." Another issue of concern in the reverse sting is the defense of entrapment that is frequently presented at trial. It is important in this type investigation to establish the predisposition of the targeted individual prior to the actual conduct of the operation.

Summary

Law enforcement has been officially fighting the War on Drugs for more than four decades, and the battle still rages on. Strategies have changed over the years, as has the focus on the different types of drugs being smuggled into, or produced within, the United States. Although drug trafficking efforts continually evolve to meet the changing demand for the drugs of choice, law enforcement has rallied to meet this evolution with newer and more effective enforcement strategies. Although many critics of the War on Drugs believe that the war has already been lost, law-enforcement agencies at the federal, state, and local levels have neither surrendered nor retreated.

Michael L. Arter

Further Reading

Bagley, Bruce Michael, and Jonathan D. Rosen. *Drug Trafficking, Organized Crime, and Violence in the Americas Today*. Gainesville: UP of Florida, 2015. Print.

Brienen, Marten W., and Jonathan D. Rosen. *New Approaches to Drug Policies: A Time for Change*. New York: Palgrave, 2015. Print.

Gaines, Larry K., and Peter B. Kraska, eds. *Drugs, Crime, and Justice*. Prospect Heights: Waveland, 2003. Print.

Goode, Erich. *Drugs in American Society*. Boston: McGraw, 2005. Print.

Gray, James P. *Why Our Drug Laws Have Failed and What We Can Do about It*. Philadelphia: Temple UP, 2001. Print.

Lee, Gregory D. *Global Drug Enforcement: Practical Investigative Techniques*. Boca Raton: CRC, 2004. Print.

Lyman, Michael D. *Criminal Investigation: The Art and the Science*. Upper Saddle River: Prentice, 2002. Print.

Manning, Peter K. *The Narcs' Game: Organizational and Informational Limits on Drug Law Enforcement*. Prospect Heights: Waveland, 2004. Print.

See also Alcohol use and abuse; Comprehensive Drug Abuse Prevention and Control Act; Decriminalization; Drug courts; Drug Enforcement Administration, U.S.; Drug legalization debate; Drug testing; Entrapment; Federal Bureau of Investigation, U.S.; Homeland Security, U.S. Department of; Opium Exclusion Act; Organized crime; Racketeer Influenced and Corrupt Organizations Act; Victimless crimes; Comprehensive Addiction and Recovery Act (CARA) (2015); Designer and date rape drugs; Immigration and Customs Enforcement, U.S.; Opioid treatment breakthroughs; Recreational and medical marijuana movements.

Evidence-based policing

Definition: Evidence-based policing is an empirically based approach to crafting policing policies and implementing police practices that incorporates evaluations and objective data to promote best practices.

Criminal justice issues: Law enforcement organization; police powers; restorative justice

Significance: Consistent with movements in other disciplines to promote data-driven policy, evidence-based policing reforms continue to mold the way police undertake their responsibilities

The term evidence-based policing describes both a school of thought and a specific set of practices within the policing profession. As a theoretical construct, evidence-based policing maintains that police practices should be crafted based on objective data founded in empirical research. Evidence-based policing, as a set of practices, refers to a broad array of programs and policies that have been tested through evaluations and replication research. These specific practices derive from the theoretical construct, and both generally are perceived to be positive innovations for the policing profession.

Evidence-based policing promotes integration of research and data into police policies and procedures. Colloquially, it may be said that evidence-based policing promotes the ethos of "working smarter, not harder." As part of a larger movement that originated in medicine and has influenced a variety of social science fields, evidence-based policing promotes use of academic analysis in policing. Scientific evaluations of police practices generate recommendations for national and state policy and provide guidance for community-level practices. Often, development of evidence-based policies involves partnerships between police departments and academic institutions pursuant to which researchers periodically evaluate practices and make recommendations for improvement based on objective data derived from those evaluations.

Historically, policing was decentralized, with local police departments operating with autonomy. Police officers hailed from the communities that they protected, and there was a fair amount of cronyism. In the earliest years of the 1900's, August Vollmer established police science as an academic discipline. In the ensuing decades, police departments sought to mitigate corruption that so often plagued local, male-dominated, racially homogenous departments that often crafted their policies on gut instinct or traditions within the community. Evidence-based policing evolved as a means to provide objective data on how to run police programs. Rather than rely on local culture, personalities, or tradition for policy, police departments began to turn to science to determine whether what they were doing worked. Courses taught and research conducted within that discipline led to professionalization of policing, reduction of corruption, and promotion of best practices. Subsequent research examined effectiveness and consistency of police practices, injecting science into daily police operations. Compliance monitoring, periodic reviews, and controlled experiments continue to contribute to this growing body of knowledge.

Research on program efficacy has yielded significant results and changed the way police behave. For example, "Scared Straight" was lauded in the late 1970's as an effective means of deterring juveniles from engaging in crime by taking youthful offenders on tours of prisons and interviews with convicts. Pursuant to deterrence theory, these juvenile awareness programs hypothesized that juveniles would see how bad prison would be and desist from offending. After researchers conducted longitudinal studies of participants, the data revealed that Scared Straight actually increased the risk that juveniles would commit crimes in the future, perhaps because they became desensitized to threat of incarceration. Other police practices have been proven effective and enjoyed evidence-based improvements, including sobriety checkpoints, cognitive behavioral therapy, and restorative justice programs, all of which have been shown through academic analysis to decrease crime.

These types of data-driven programs allow police departments to highlight "what works," as first coined by Lawrence Sherman. They also allow departments to reform, reconsider, or eliminate programs that do not produce pro social results. Because evaluations of these programs generate data, they are more amenable to comparison across jurisdictions and across policies. Evidence-based policing is heralded as saving money because as evidence on effectiveness becomes available, police departments can reallocate resources to invest in successful programs.

Evidence-based policies also allow police departments to target spending appropriately, to promote transparency, to improve program integrity, and to increase accountability. These data generated through evaluations provide objective information upon which thoughtful debate can develop. They reduce the likelihood that policies and practices will be politically or culturally reactive. They contribute to a community's sense of procedural due process. They are more likely to survive public scrutiny. They enhance communication within departments and provide data for public dissemination. Finally, evidence-based programs promote ethical behavior and police legitimacy.

Problems persist with translating science into action. Practitioners regularly complain, with justification, that there is a translation gap. Police, like most professions, often resist outsiders (such as academics) injecting themselves into their daily professional operations, and they sometimes resent being treated as science experiments. Additionally, limitations on the usability and accessibility of these policies and programs persist. Advocates from within policing communities call for better presentations of research (in more accessible forms) that speak to specific practices rather than academic jargon.

Anne S. Douds

Further Reading

Evidence-Based Policing. Washington, D.C.: Police Foundation, 1998.

Lum, C., C. S. Koper, and C. W. Telep. "The Evidence-Based Policing Matrix."*Journal of Experimental Criminology* 7, no. 1 (2011): 3-26.

National Institutes of Justice. 2016. http://www.crimesolutions.gov/PracticeDetails.aspx?ID=4. Accessed November 26, 2016.

Sherman, L. W. "The Rise of Evidence-Based Policing: Targeting, Testing, and Tracking."*Crime and Justice* 42, no. 1 (2013): 377-451.

See also Broken windows theory; Community-oriented policing; Crime analysis; Law Enforcement Assistance Administration; Peace officer standards and training; Problem-oriented policing.

Federal Bureau of Investigation, U.S.

Identification: Primary investigative and enforcement arm of the federal government's Department of Justice

Date: Established in 1908; renamed the Federal Bureau of Investigation (FBI) in 1935

Criminal justice issues: Federal law; investigation; law-enforcement organization

Significance: As a division of the U.S. Department of Justice, the Federal Bureau of Investigation (FBI) has seen its investigative and other powers greatly expanded as Congress has gradually added one duty after another. The FBI has been engaged in combating many forms of interstate and international criminal activity. It has also strived to raise the standards of regional police units, which the FBI frequently assists in training.

The forerunner of the Federal Bureau of Investigation (FBI) was established in 1908 by U.S. attorney general Charles J. Bonaparte, who hired nine former Secret Service agents on a permanent basis in the U.S. Department of Justice. This investigative division was first funded from "miscellaneous expenses" without specific mandate from Congress. Bonaparte actually opposed legislation to specify this new investigative division's authority, assuring congressmen that personal and political activities would not be investigated but that the new division's responsibilities would focus on interstate commerce and antitrust violations.

History

The period of the attorney general's direct supervision was rather short. By 1910 the unit's dictate was to enforce

The FBI's Changing Names

Date	Official name
July, 26, 1908	(No official name)
March 16, 1909	Bureau of Investigation
July 1, 1932	U.S. Bureau of Investigation
August 10, 1933	Division of Investigation
March 22, 1935	Federal Bureau of Investigation (FBI)

the new Mann (White Slave Traffic) Act, which made it a federal crime to transport women across state lines for illicit purposes. Now, as personal and commercial activities increasingly projected themselves across state lines with the creation of nationwide transportation systems and national markets—together with the crimes that go with them—the investigative arm of the Department of Justice acquired an expanded role mandated by Congress, together with additional personnel and funds. Thus, in 1919, Congress passed the Dyer (Motor Vehicles Theft) Act to combat automobile theft, which the unit was assigned to investigate, while the Volstead Act, also of 1919, gave the "Feds" the power to investigate and prosecute violations of the Constitution's Eighteenth Amendment, prohibiting the manufacture, transportation, sale, import, and export of alcoholic beverages.

Even before that time, the early bureau was involved in internal security matters—at first because of the opposition to World War I, as well as possible espionage and sabotage. Thus, the agency had to investigate cases arising from the Espionage Act of 1917, the Selective Service Act (draft dodgers) of that same year, the Sedition Act of 1918, and the Immigration Act of 1918.

Simultaneously and thereafter, radicals of all kinds became the focus of the bureau's investigation: labor union leaders, members of the Socialist Party, those sympathetic to the Bolshevik (communist) Revolution in Russia in 1917, pro-Irish activists supporting the rebellion for independence from Britain (1916-1922), black militants such as Marcus Garvey, and others. The head of the antiradical alien enemy unit was J. Edgar Hoover, one of the architects of the 1920 Palmer Raids against suspected radicals and leftists during the so-called Red Scare.

Following that period, often viewed as one involving abuse of power and scandal (including the Teapot Dome scandal of 1923-1924), the bureau witnessed a few years of administrative reform and retrenchment coinciding with the early years of Hoover's directorship

450

(1924-1972). The New Deal era (1932-1939) was to see the naming of additional federal crimes, thus empowering the bureau. These included kidnappings—mostly involving Prohibition-connected gangsterism—and the use of the U.S. mail for extortion, the robbing of federally chartered banks, and, with the growth of fascism and Nazism, espionage. The bureau's detentive, wiretapping, and break-in powers were also extended.

By that time the bureau had become the FBI, and its agents were now authorized to carry weapons and to make arrests independently of state and local law enforcement. A broad surveillance program was instituted against subversives in 1936.

During World War II, curbing German espionage and communist activity became the FBI's major focus, and its internal security investigative powers grew even more. Especially with the passage of the McCarran (Internal Security) Act of 1950 and the Communist Control Act of 1954, during the Cold War period (1947-1991), the FBI sustained its emphasis on the containment of communism (especially during the witch-hunt orchestrated by Senator Joseph R. McCarthy of Wisconsin) and of various types of radical activism.

In the meantime, there was additional targeting of organized crime (and enlarged empowerment of the FBI) with the passage of such legislation as the Omnibus Crime Control and Safe Streets (OCCSS) Act of 1968 and the Racketeer Influenced and Corrupt Organizations (RICO) Acts of 1970 and 1986.

However, the Watergate scandal of 1972-1974 and legislative disclosure of abuse of power by several federal agencies, including the FBI, led to new guidelines, reorganization, and reform to make the agency more accountable to Congress and the general public. After the terrorist attacks of September 11, 2001, terrorism and counterterrorism have occupied center stage amid the concerns and activities of the FBI.

The dynamic nature of American society and its evolving views of crime—the new forms that it took, novel threats to internal security, and Congress's response to these—have, in part, accounted for the changing role and powers, even abuses of power, of the FBI. Another factor was the nature and character of the man with whom the agency had become so closely identified for much of its history: director J. Edgar Hoover. Hoover's obsession with "security" investigations helped to provide a particular bias to the agency's activities for much of his nearly fifty-year tenure.

To this day, the public is divided in its assessment of the FBI. Some recall the heroic role played by the "G-men," by "The Untouchables," immortalized by the media, while others dwell on the high-handed nature of some of the agency's operations and the autocratic nature and tactics of its best-known director.

Organization

The FBI is the principal investigative arm of the U.S. Department of Justice, headed by the attorney general, who is therefore the bureau's nominal head. It is a field-oriented organization in which eleven divisions and four offices at FBI Headquarters in Washington, D.C., provide program direction and support services to fifty-six field offices, some four hundred satellite offices known as resident agencies, four specialized field installations, and more than forty foreign liaison posts, each of which is headed by a legal attaché (legat) or legal liaison officer who works abroad with American and local authorities on criminal and civil matters within FBI jurisdiction—that is, on cases not assigned by law to another federal agency. Accordingly, the FBI has priority in such matters as national security, counterintelligence, counterterrorism, cybercrime, international and national organized crime or drug matters, and financial crimes. To implement these functions, the FBI is primarily charged with gathering and reporting facts, locating witnesses and alleged perpetrators, and compiling evidence in federal cases.

Among the services the FBI provides are fingerprint identification; laboratory examinations; police training; the Law Enforcement Online communications, information services for use by the law-enforcement community; and administration of the National Crime Information Center and the National Center for the Analysis of Violent Crimes (which contains the various Behavioral Analysis Units). Also, the bureau provides law-enforcement leadership and assistance to state and international law enforcement agencies.

The organization is headed by a director, now appointed by the U.S. president with the advice and consent of the U.S. Senate. The term is currently limited to ten years. There is a deputy director and thirteen assistant directors, who supervise deputy assistant directors. Each assistant is in charge of one of the eleven headquarters divisions, the Office of Congressional Affairs, and the Office of Professional Responsibility. The Office of the General Counsel is headed by the FBI's general counsel, while the Office of Equal Employment Opportunity is administered by the equal employment manager.

The FBI has about 11,400 special agents (diversified in every way but with a predominance of white males) and some 16,400 support employees, of whom about 10,000 are at FBI Headquarters. Nearly eighteen thousand are assigned to field installations. In 1911, the original bureau had eighty-one agents and thirty-three support staff members, with an appropriation of $329,984. During the early twenty-first century, the FBI had an annual budget of some $3.5 billion.

Programs

The FBI's programs include background checks on federal job applicants and appointees slated for sensitive federal agencies as well as those of presidential nominees to executive or judiciary positions. Other programs involve the investigation of civil rights violations, domestic terrorism, international terrorism, national foreign intelligence (foreign espionage and foreign counterintelligence within the United States), and drug trafficking by organized groups, as well as racketeering, violent crimes, kidnapping, sexual exploitation of children, extortion, bank robbery, consumer product tampering, crimes on Indian reservations, unlawful flight to avoid prosecution, and threats—or other harm to—the president, vice president, or members of Congress. Finally, the FBI's white-collar crimes program targets such criminal activity as money laundering, bank fraud and embezzlement, public corruption, environmental crimes, fraud against the government and health care, election law violations, and telemarketing fraud. The FBI's strategic plan prioritizes combating threats to national and economic security or to U.S. citizens and their property as well as criminal enterprises.

Notable FBI Cases

During the early years of the FBI's predecessors (1908-1924), high-profile cases involved violations of the Mann (White Slave Traffic) Act of 1910, focusing on the likes of Jack Johnson, a black heavyweight champion accused of eloping with and seducing a white woman, whom he later married. There was also the case of Edward Y. Clarke, at one time acting imperial wizard of the Klu Klux Klan. Under the authority of the Espionage and Sedition Acts of 1917 and 1918 during World War I, the bureau prosecuted the likes of William D. "Big Bill" Haywood of the Industrial Workers of the World (IWW, or Wobblies), Jacob Abrams, and Emma Goldman of the Union of Russian Workers, all held to be radicals, anarchists, or subversives.

The Hoover years opened with the tracking down of "bad guys," as the age of Prohibition-driven gangsterism and kidnappings, corruption, and rackets of all kinds had arrived. Cases involving the likes of Al "Scarface" Capone, John Dillinger, Clyde Barrow and Bonnie Parker (popularly known as Bonnie and Clyde), George "Machine Gun" Kelly, Alvin "Creepy" Karpis, Charles "Pretty Boy" Floyd, Louis "Lepke" Buchalter, and Willie "the Eel" Sutton catapulted the FBI and its director to fame.

Two famous kidnapping cases in that era were those of the twenty-month-old child, eventually found dead, of hero-aviator Charles Lindbergh (for which Bruno Hauptmann was executed in 1936) and of wealthy Oklahoma City oilman Charles F. Urschel. Most of the perpetrators ended up in prison or were killed in shoot-outs with the G-men, as agents were now known. Even more important, the favorable publicity moved Congress to empower the bureau to intervene in additional crimes formerly considered to be regional, or where local law enforcement proved itself unable to cope.

Even before World War II's outbreak in Europe in 1939, the FBI became involved in German espionage cases such as that of Guenther Gustav Rumrich and Frederick ("Fritz") Joubert Duquesne and in sabotage cases such as that involving George John Dasch and the Long Island (Nazi) Saboteurs. The Smith Act of 1940, outlawing advocacy of the violent overthrow of the government, had given the "Feds" additional authority to pursue radicals. Even before the Japanese attack at Pearl Harbor in 1941, the FBI was again responsible for locating draft evaders and deserters.

Overlapping these mandates was the ferreting out of communists and other leftists, increasingly emphasized after the advent of the Cold War in 1947. Thus, there was the case of the *Amerasia* journal and the trials of William Remington, Alger Hiss, and Judith Coplon. With the surrender of the tripartite Axis powers, communist espionage and subversion became a major issue. Witness the 1957 trial of Colonel Rudolf I. Abel, a Soviet Committee for State Security (KGB) intelligence officer, and most notably of the American "atomic spies," Julius and Ethel Rosenberg, executed in 1953 for giving the Soviet Union classified information.

There was then a recurrence of targeting organized crime, with the trials of Joseph P. Valachi (1963), who later cooperated with the FBI, and the Mafia (La Cosa Nostra). This was to continue through the 1970's, 1980's, and 1990's, with the Pizza Connection case, the Commission case, the Patriarca case, and that of John Gotti. Notorious crime "families" such as the Profacis, Luccheses, Genoveses, Bonannos, Trafficantes, Magaddinos, and Zerillis were not neglected.

Neither were civil rights cases such as those of Medgar Evers and the three civil rights workers Michael Schwerner, Andrew Goodman, and James E. Chaney, all murdered in Mississippi; of Viola Liuzzo, murdered in Alabama; and of Martin Luther King, Jr., murdered in Tennessee. The post-World War II years also involved a new crop of radicals such as Patricia Hearst and others of the Symbionese Liberation Army, and of Leonard Peltier of the American Indian movement.

The FBI was also involved in the militia cases (Randall "Randy" Weaver's Christian white supremacists at Ruby Ridge, Idaho, in 1992, and the Freemen at Jordan, Montana, in 1996) and cases involving religious groups (such as the Branch Davidians at Waco, Texas, in 1993). Last but not least was terrorism, whether by individuals such as Theodore J. Kaczynski, the Unabomber (1978-1996), or groups of Muslim fundamentalists at the World Trade Center in New York City (1993 and 2001).

Espionage cases also continued—not only those involving Soviet operatives but also U.S. government employees of agencies outside the FBI—for example, John A. Walker and Jonathan Jay Pollard, both of the U.S. Navy; Ronald Pelton of the National Security Agency; and Aldrich H. Ames of the Central Intelligence Agency. There were additional cases of double agents in the FBI itself.

Undoubtedly, with the advent of weapons of mass destruction—especially biological and chemical—the FBI will be involved, as it was in the anthrax scare on the East Coast in 2001. Since its origins, the FBI's investigations have intersected with major events and public issues in American life and have thus been equally controversial.

Moles and Double Agents

Even though there was considerable mumbling about director J. Edgar Hoover's supposed eccentricities and idiosyncrasies when it came to the behavior of his special agents—according to stories, true or apocryphal, he would not tolerate homosexuals or adulterers, mandated formal dress even before air-conditioning was available in district offices, had a phobia about overweight men or even those with sweaty palms—unquestionably, during his near half-century at the helm, there were extremely few cases of disloyalty, such as that of William G. Sebold in 1941. Things changed, however, after Hoover's death.

One of the most notable—indeed, notorious—cases of disloyalty within the agency was that of FBI special agent Robert Philip Hanssen. Hanssen's clearances allowed him to access classified information at the CIA, the National Security Agency, the White House, and the defense department. They also enabled Hanssen to check an FBI database that would show any possible investigation of himself by his employer. Hanssen, a computer whiz who had majored in chemistry, spoke Russian, had an M.B.A., and had helped the FBI create a database of Soviet intelligence officers, including their addresses, appearances, likes, and dislikes. He was also involved with anti-Soviet electronic bugs and video surveillance.

In 1979, Hanssen started working for the GRU (Soviet military intelligence), blowing the cover on Soviet double agent General Dmitri F. Polyakov. The latter, like several others who had worked undercover for the United States and were compromised by Hanssen, was executed in Russia. Back in New York in 1985 after a stint at FBI Headquarters, Hanssen returned to spying for the Soviets, this time for the more prestigious KGB. After that, he worked for the Russian SVR, the successor to the KGB's foreign intelligence unit, sporadically until 2001. But on February 18 of that year, Hanssen was arrested at a dead drop (a drop used for the clandestine exchange of intelligence information) in Foxstone Park, Vienna, Virginia, close to where he lived with his wife and six children. Another team of agents at a second drop site found $50,000 in $100 bills left for him.

The damage Hanssen had caused was incalculable. Over twenty-one years of spying for the Soviets and then for the Russians, he transferred to them six thousand pages of classified documents, twenty-seven computer discs cataloging secret and top-secret programs, including one on how to ensure the survival of the U.S. government in the event of a nuclear attack. Instead of the death penalty, which Attorney General John Ashcroft had sought for him, in exchange for continuing debriefings about Russian undercover operations and FBI countermeasures, Hanssen got a life sentence in prison without parole in July, 2001, and his wife was allowed to collect some of his pension. He admitted getting a kick from outwitting the intelligence communities, both the FBI and the KGB, because it gave him a sense of power, of control.

Peter B. Heller
Updated by Jenna M. Kieckhaefer

Further Reading

Churchill, Ward, and Jim Vander Wall. *The COINTELPRO Papers: Documents from the FBI's Secret Wars Against Dissent in the United States.* 2d ed. Cambridge, Mass.: South End Press, 2002. Purports to show through documentary evidence (including deletions) how the FBI in such case studies as that of the Puerto Rican Independence Movement was willing to sacrifice (according to the bureau's director) more than a small measure of American liberties in order to preserve the great bulk of them. Bibliography, index.

De Loach, Cartha "Deke." *Hoover's FBI: The Inside Story by Hoover's Trusted Lieutenant*. Washington, D.C.: Regnery, 1995. A sympathetic "insider" assessment by the bureau's number three man, including interesting reminiscences about the difficulties of trying to "terminate" Hoover's tenure. Bibliographical note, index.

Directors, Then and Now; https://www.fbi.gov/history/directors (accessed January 8, 2017).

Kessler, Ronald. *The Bureau: The Secret History of the FBI*. New York: St. Martin's Press, 2002. A critical assessment, especially during the "dirty years," of the FBI's abuse of power. Bibliography, index.

Mitgang, Herbert. *Dangerous Dossiers*. New York: Penguin/Primus, 1996. The FBI's secret war against prominent intellectuals, domestic and foreign, in all art forms. Bibliography, index.

Reebel, Patrick A., ed. *Federal Bureau of Investigation: Current Issues and Background*. New York: Nova Science, 2002. A series of essays to support the conclusion that the FBI is a "first-rate organization with a mission impossible." The case studies include those of the Oklahoma City bombing (1995), the Montana "Freemen" standoff (1996), and the Branch Davidian siege (1993). Exhaustive bibliography; author, title, and subject indexes.

Whitehead, Don. *The FBI Story: A Report to the People*. New York: Random House, 1956. A reporter refutes the frequent allegations that the FBI represented a shadowy menace to civil rights. Includes famous case histories, based on privileged access to selected FBI documents. Notes, chronology, index.

Whitnah, Donald R., ed. *Government Agencies*. Westport, Conn.: Greenwood Press, 1983. Includes a succinct history of the FBI. Chronology, genealogy, and other appendixes; index.

See also Attorney General, U.S.; Bureau of Justice Statistics; Crime index; Cybercrime; Drugs and law enforcement; Espionage; Hoover, J. Edgar; Justice Department, U.S.; Law enforcement; Motor vehicle theft; Organized crime; Skyjacking; Terrorism; Treason; Unabomber.

Frankpledge and watch system

Definition: An ancient system of public law enforcement that was a precursor to formal police organizations and community policing

Criminal justice issues: Law enforcement organization; morality and public order; police powers

Significance: This community-based system for managing public order in ancient England laid the foundation for professional police organization, geographic jurisdictional organization of police departments, and community policing.

Under the frankpledge, or peace pledge, systems in ancient England and Denmark, communities policed themselves under the auspices of an often absentee noble. Landowning men were assigned to groups of ten households, or "tything" for purposes of managing their communities' safety and security. The groups selected a leader, or "tythingman," who represented the group in communications with the nobility and royalty. These groups, or tythes, were responsible for maintaining the peace, also known as the frankpledge. The "watch" system developed as a complement to the frankpledge system as society grew and demanded greater formalization. Under the watch system, men were assigned to patrol their communities at night (and later throughout the day) as part of their obligations to the tythe. These systems have roots in Anglo-Saxon practices, but they gained traction during Norman times.

Before the frankpledge system, men were responsible for maintaining order among their kin. Relatives vouched for one another and ensured that they conformed to community norms. When William and his troops conquered England in 1066, they sought to exert greater control over the people. William wanted to dilute the power of family ties and promote leadership from among his allies. Thus, he and his retinue restructured the security systems and concentrated greater control in the hands of nobility. Nobles were not members of (or accountable to) the tythes, but the nobility did oversee the tythes. Common people who lived within nobles' jurisdictions served in their tythes. This system introduced the idea that neighbors should take responsibility for one another. The tythings largely governed themselves in their day-to-day affairs. They were required to report crimes committed by their members. If a member of the tythe was called to court, the other members of the tythe had to produce that man or swear that they did not know where he was and/or that they had not aided in the man's failure to appear. If the tythe members did not make this oath, they could be held liable for the missing man's misdeeds, including restitution and detention. Elements of the modern grand jury system can be seen in this tything process. It should be noted that the ancient word "tythe" as used in this system had nothing to do with "tithing" (giving money or assets) to a church.

Representatives of the king or nobility would conduct periodic "views of the frankpledge." Leaders would survey the communities to confirm that all appropriate men were participating in the frankpledge, and all men were required to take an oath of good conduct. In the early decades, these reviews included all men other than high-ranking nobility. In later years, only unfree and landless men were required to participate. In those times, it was assumed that men who owned land had a great enough stake in the community to ensure their compliance with the law.

Tythingmen worked as unsalaried representatives of the king who were required to execute the king's law. They located and detained suspects prior to trial, testified for or against members of their own tythes, and provided evidence or testimony in matters related to members of other tythes and people who resided outside the tythe system (usually unlanded paupers or indentured servants).

The frankpledge system slowly evolved in response to population growth, changes in royal leadership, and social forces. Social systems trended towards greater formalization. Tythes were grouped into "hundreds," or ten groups of ten. These hundreds were led by a constables who was appointed by the regional nobility. Later, those hundreds were organized into "shires," which were akin to counties. The shires were led by "shire reeve," whose title evolved into "sheriff" and who were appointed by the king.

By the thirteenth century, the frankpledge system faded from practice due to poor oversight and spotty law enforcement. The Statute of Winchester of 1285 (which was passed in the wake of multiple iterations of the Magna Carta) ushered in a new era of more neutral law enforcement. Policing activities migrated towards a professional force. Constables were appointed for a one-year term. They were not paid per se, but they wielded great power within their local communities. They also enjoyed the support of night watchmen who patrolled the communities and provided an on-call police force. Under this "watch system," the constables could issue a "hue and cry" to summon all watchmen in the event of crime or security issues. The watchmen were required to drop what they were doing and render aid to the constable.

The role of the justice of the peace appeared in the 1300's, and that position was superior to the constable and shire reeve. While the constables and shire reeves retained supervisory authority over their communities, the justices of the peace assumed roles resembling modern local judges or magistrates. They issued warrants, took suspects into custody, and ran the night watchman programs. These justices of the peace were full-time professional positions that purportedly provided detached law enforcement. In reality, the justices of the peace, and the subordinate shire reeves and constables, were beholden to the nobility and royalty. Corruption was common. The night watch system evolved into a formal policing system and provided early examples of shift work and patrol.

These practices persisted into modern times. The colonists carried remnants of these practices with them as they settled in North America, and modern American policing practices still carry stamps of their practices. Local law enforcement, sheriff's departments, and local justices of the peace exist today in forms that reflect the practices of ancient England. Principles of community policing can be traced to the watch system and its predecessor frankpledge system.

Anne S. Douds

Further Reading
Morris, W. A. *The Frankpledge System*, Vol. 14. New York: Longmans, Green, 1910.
Reynolds, E. A. *Before the Bobbies: The Night Watch and Police Reform in Metropolitan London, 1720-1830.* Palo Alto, Calif.: Stanford University Press, 1998.
Sheleff, L. S. *The Bystander: Behavior, Law, Ethics.* Lanham, Md.: Lexington Books, 1978.

See also Law enforcement; Neighborhood watch programs; Posse comitatus; Preventive patrol; Sheriffs.

Graham v. Connor (1989)

Definition: United States Supreme Court case where the Court held that cases claiming law enforcement used lethal or nonlethal excessive force should be analyzed under the Fourth Amendment's "objective reasonableness" standard rather than the "substantive due process" standard of the Fourteenth Amendment: Case cited as *Graham v. Connor*, 490 U.S. 386 (1989)

Criminal justice issues: Civil rights and liberties; constitutional protections; legal terms and principles; search and seizure

Significance: Following this decision, individuals suing law enforcement officers for excessive force claims under Section 1983 must now demonstrate that the officer's use of force was unreasonable for an officer in that specific situation. Under the previous Fourteenth Amendment substantive due process standard, the plaintiff had to show the officer's intent was malicious or sadistic and "shocked the conscience."

Facts of the Case

The petitioner, Dethorne Graham, had diabetes and began to feel the symptoms of a diabetic insulin reaction on November 12, 1984. He asked his friend William Berry to drive him to a nearby convenience store to purchase some orange juice, which would offset the reaction.

When Graham got to the store and saw the checkout line would take too long, he quickly left and asked Berry to take him to his girlfriend's house instead. According to an *amicus* brief filed on behalf of the respondent by the State of North Carolina, Graham hit the counter before he left. Officer Connor, a Charlotte, North Carolina police officer, was in his patrol car in the parking lot of that convenience store and saw Graham hurry into the store, then hurry out again. He testified that people near the store told him there was "a crazy man" inside.

Connor stopped Berry's vehicle about half a mile from the store to investigate. Graham began to feel more intense symptoms of the diabetic reaction, and he jumped out of the car and ran around it twice. Connor and Berry were able to get Graham to sit on the curb. Connor claimed Graham continued to kick at him, though Graham's argued he was sitting calmly. Other officers arrived to assist Connor. Graham was put in handcuffs and, according to Graham, his head was slammed onto the hood of the car. The backup officers claimed they were trying to get Graham into the back of a police car as he was kicking and struggling. Meanwhile, Connor spoke with the store clerk and determined that Graham had not done anything illegal. Graham claimed he repeatedly asked for orange juice or candy, but the officers refused.

When he returned from speaking with the clerk, Connor asked if Graham would like to go to the hospital. Graham said he just wanted to go home, so the officers took him home and allowed Berry to give Graham some juice. The officers then removed the handcuffs and left. Graham later received medical treatment for a broken foot, cuts on his wrist, a bruised forehead, and an injured shoulder. The Supreme Court didn't rule on whether those injuries had occurred during or after the incident, and instead viewed the facts in the light most favorable to the petitioner, in accordance with appellate procedure.

Graham filed a lawsuit against Connor and the other officers involved, arguing they had used excessive force during an investigatory stop in violation of his rights according to the Fourteenth Amendment and 42 U.S. Code, Section 1983, which allows individuals to bring a civil action against any person who, under color of any law, deprives others of any right, privilege, or immunity secured under the Constitution and laws.

Legal Analysis and Significance

After Graham presented his case to the District Court, the court ruled in favor of the officers. The District Court followed a four-factor "substantive due process" test from *Johnson v. Glick*, 481 F.2d 1028 (2nd Cir. 1973) to determine when excessive force gave rise to a cause of action under Section 1983. The four factors were:

1) the need for the application of force;
2) the relationship between that need and the amount of force that was used;
3) the extent of the injury inflicted; and
4) [w]hether the force was applied in a good faith effort to maintain and restore discipline or maliciously and sadistically inflicted for the very purpose of causing harm.

Applying that test to the facts, the District Court held that the amount of force used was appropriate under the circumstances and that the use of force was not applied maliciously or sadistically. The petitioner appealed to the Fourth Circuit arguing that the court applied the incorrect standard when it required proof of malicious or sadistic intent. The majority of the Fourth Circuit agreed with the District Court, and the petitioner appealed to the Supreme Court.

In an opinion written by Chief Justice Rehnquist, the Supreme Court explicitly held that not all excessive force claims brought under Section 1983 should be judged by a single generic standard. Many courts were applying the four-factor test from *Johnson v. Glick* to all excessive force claims, but according to the Court's analysis in footnote six, the *Johnson v. Glick* holding chose to focus on substantive due process rather than the specific constitutional standards of either the Eighth or Fourth Amendments because of the specific facts of that case. Furthermore, the Court held that Section 1983 simply provided a method for vindicating rights conferred elsewhere, and did not provide substantive rights itself. Therefore, it was more appropriate to judge Section 1983 claims based on the specific constitutional standards that governs the right that was infringed, as opposed to using an outside standard like substantive due process.

The Court went on to hold that as the facts here included the arrest or investigatory stop of a free citizen, it should be judged using the objective reasonableness standard of the Fourth Amendment. Based on jurisprudence from *Tennessee v. Garner*, 471 U.S. 1 (1985), and *Terry v. Ohio*, 392 U.S. 1 (1968), the Court also held that the objective reasonableness standard required a careful examination of the facts for each case, including "the severity of the crime at issue, whether the suspect poses an immediate threat to the safety of the officers or others, and whether or not he is actively resisting or attempting to evade arrest by flight." Furthermore, the "reasonableness" of an officer's actions must be judged from the perspective of a reasonable officer in that situation. The underlying intent or motivation of the officer does not come into question.

The Supreme Court reversed the judgment and remanded the case back to the Fourth Circuit for reconsideration using the proper Fourth Amendment objective reasonableness standard.

Subsequent Legal Developments

The *Graham Court* stated that the specific facts of each case should be considered, but it did not outline a specific test for balancing facts. While actions of the suspect are mentioned, such as attempts to flee or danger they present to others, possible counterbalancing actions of the officers are not discussed. After *Graham*, some federal courts tried to flesh out the holding by requiring the plaintiff to prove that a significant injury resulted directly from a use of force excessive to the need, which was objectively unreasonable. The most notable of these "significant injury" cases is *Johnson v. Morel*, 876 F.2d 477 (5th Cir. 1989). However, other courts have held that a serious injury is not essential for a Section 1983 claim, including the Seventh Circuit in *Titran v. Ackman*, 893 F.2d 145 (2d Cir. 1990). The Supreme Court has not ruled on this specific circuit split, though it did hold that a plaintiff did not need to prove a serious injury in an Eighth Amendment context in *Hudson v. McMillian*, 503 U.S. 1 (1992), and many legal scholars have applied this logic to Fourth Amendment claims as well.

Savanna L. Nolan

Further Reading

Bryan N. Georgiady. "An Excessively Painful Encounter: The Reasonableness of Pain and De Minimis Injuries for Fourth Amendment Excessive Force Claims." *Syracuse Law Review* 59 (2008): 123. Examines the "significant injury" circuit split and potential Supreme Court review post-*Hudson*.

Daniel J. O'Connell. "Excessive Force Claims: Is Significant Bodily Injury the Sine Qua Non to Proving a Fourth Amendment Violation?" *Fordham Law Review* 58 (March 1990): 739. Discusses how in following *Graham* some federal courts required plaintiffs to show significant injury as well as unreasonableness.

Eleanor G. Jolley, and Tim Donahue Sr. "A Cursory Overview to Section 1983 as It Applies to Violations of the Fourth and Eighth Amendments." *American Journal of Trial Advocacy* 39 (Spring 2016): 517. Discusses the legal history, essential elements, and standards of review for Section 1983 excessive force claims.

Jay Gold. "Contemporary Trends in Qualified Immunity Jurisprudence: Are Circuit Courts Misapplying *Graham v. Connor*?" *Utah Bar Journal* 28 (May/June 2015): 26. Examines recent cases and their application of *Graham*, which the author argues fails to consider the totality of the circumstances.

See also Deadly force; Discretion; King beating case; Nonviolent resistance; Police brutality; Police ethics; Police militarization; Police powers; Reasonable force; Resisting arrest; *Tennessee v. Garner*; Use of force.

High-speed chases

Definition: Vehicular pursuits by law-enforcement officers of suspected or known criminals or traffic law violators

Criminal justice issues: Police powers; Traffic Law

Significance: Police high-speed pursuits raise important legal and safety issues for both law-enforcement organizations and the public.

Vehicular pursuits have grown into a major social problem, as pursuit litigation costs taxpayers millions of dollars annually. In addition, such pursuits raise concerns regarding the safety of the officers involved and of the public. Officers' actions during a vehicular pursuit can have far-reaching implications for law-enforcement agencies as well as the individual officers involved. If an officer is found to have been negligent during the course of the pursuit, subsequent litigation can be financially devastating for both department and police officer.

Although the safety risk is not exorbitantly high, there is little doubt that high-speed chases can become dangerous quite quickly in some circumstances. Research has demonstrated that approximately half of all pursuit crashes occur within the first two minutes of a chase.

Despite varying rates of crashes, injuries, and fatalities, police pursuits have been supported by researchers and officers alike as a necessary component of police work. Police officers believe that felony offenses are the most likely to result in a high-speed chase. Officers have also indicated that their approval or tolerance for a pursuit increases in proportion to the seriousness of the crime committed. When asked about the abolishment of pursuits, officers generally respond that the police, as a law-enforcement institution, would suffer a loss of respect from the public as well as potential offenders. Most police officers have indicated a belief that the danger to the public would increase, as would crime in general, if pursuits were eliminated as an acceptable means of apprehending suspects.

During the early twenty-first century, the Chicago and Los Angeles police departments developed new written policies to aid officers in instances of high-speed pursuit in an effort to decrease threats to public safety. The policies prohibit pursuits following most routine traffic viola-

Motor vehicle accident following a vehicular pursuit. (Public domain, via Wikimedia Commons)

tions and place tighter controls on officers in unmarked vehicles. The more restrictive policies are designed to increase police accountability and public safety while simultaneously reducing the dangerousness of vehicular pursuits.

Data from the National Highway Traffic Safety Administration (NHTSA) and the Fatality Analysis Reporting Systems (FARS) have been used in an effort to come to terms with disparities observed among research studies concerning the precise number of fatalities occurring as a result of police pursuits. There have been discrepancies between many research endeavors and official data as to the exact number of individuals killed or injured as a result of police pursuits.

In spite of the perceived danger posed by pursuits, many scholars have noted a trend in the underreporting of police pursuits. A dramatic disparity between the official record of pursuits and those in which officers actually engage has emerged. It has been estimated that for every fourteen vehicular pursuits, as few as five are reported. This has been termed the "dark figure" of pursuits.

Legal Issues

Police pursuits have involved the legal system to a large extent. The Supreme Court, as well as district courts, has been called upon to rule on issues such as Fourth Amendment seizure considerations, Fourteenth Amendment concerns over due process, and the use of force in pursuits.

The Supreme Court refuses to detail specifically the circumstances under which a pursuit amounts to a Fourth Amendment seizure, but it has suggested that a pursuit communicates to reasonable persons that they are not at liberty to ignore the police and go about their business. Originally, the Court agreed with the district courts by stating that a pursuit alone did not constitute a seizure protected under the Fourth Amendment. Later, this decision was overturned as justices deemed a pursuit an actual seizure applicable under the Fourth Amendment.

Additionally, the Court has ruled on issues related to the guarantee of substantive due process laid out in the Fourteenth Amendment. Justices have decided that only arbitrary conduct shocking to the conscience and unrelated to the legitimate object of arrest satisfies the requirements of the Fourteenth Amendment's guarantee of due process of law.

Twenty-first Century Developments

Many police departments have experimented with strategies to reduce, and possibly eliminate, the need for high-speed vehicular pursuits. Aerial pursuit is a tactic used by many larger urban departments. Aircraft such as helicopters can hover and maneuver in ways that can safely track a suspect fleeing on foot or in a vehicle. The use of aircraft is an effective, albeit costly, method of pursuing suspects safely and with minimal danger to bystanders. Ideally, costs saved in decreasing litigation arising from vehicular chases could be put to good use in increased air patrol and pursuit.

Larger metropolitan agencies are also experimenting with "stop" techniques, such as so-called sticky foam, pulse guns, and road spikes, in an effort to decrease the need for lengthy vehicular pursuits in apprehending suspects. The added degree of safety to the general population has motivated departments to increase funding for these new tools, and many new devices have a great deal of potential in this regard. However, the use of devices such as spike strips bring controversies of their own, including the potential of causing an out-of-control crash and the danger posed to officers deploying them in a roadway.

Wendy L. Hicks

Further Reading
Alpert, Geoffrey, and Lorie A. Fridell. *Police Vehicles and Firearms: Instruments of Deadly Force*. Prospect Heights, Ill.: Waveland Press, 1992. Print.
Burns, Ronald, G., and Charles E. Crawford. *Policing and Violence*. Upper Saddle River, N.J.: Prentice-Hall, 2001. Print.
Kappeler, Victor E. *Critical Issues in Police Civil Liability*. Prospect Heights, Ill.: Waveland Press, 1993. Print.
Palacios, William, Paul Cromwell, and Roger G. Dunham. *Crime and Justice in America-A Reader: Present Realities and Future Prospects*. 2d ed. Upper Saddle River, N.J.: Prentice-Hall, 2001. Print.

Roberts, Albert, ed. *Critical Issues in Crime and Justice*. 2d ed. Thousand Oaks, Calif.: Sage, 2003. Print.

Wrobleski, Henry M., and Karen M. Hess. *Introduction to Law Enforcement and Criminal Justice*. New York: Wadsworth, 2003. Print.

See also Deadly force; Highway patrols; Hit-and-run accidents; Police; Police academies; Proximate cause; Supreme Court, U.S.; Traffic law; Vicarious liability.

Highway patrols

Definition: State government law-enforcement agencies whose primary responsibilities are traffic management and traffic law enforcement

Criminal justice issues: Law-enforcement organization; traffic law

Significance: The two kinds of primary state law-enforcement agencies, highway patrols and state police, represent a departure from the American tradition of local control of police.

Like state police, highway patrols are state government law-enforcement agencies that are responsible for policing the highways within a state. The principal duty of highway patrols is to support the safe and efficient use of the highways by enforcing traffic laws, investigating traffic crashes, directing and controlling traffic, and promoting traffic safety. Highway patrol officers, sometimes called state traffic officers or state troopers, are generally not responsible for investigating crimes and enforcing criminal laws, except for those offenses that occur in their presence, are encountered incident to the performance of their traffic responsibilities, or as may be specifically authorized by state statute.

State governments generally began to establish law-enforcement agencies during the early twentieth century as a result of concerns with urban police corruption, ineffectiveness of rural sheriffs' departments, and the inability or unwillingness of both municipal and rural police to deal with violent labor disputes. As automobile use increased and highway systems expanded in the 1910's and 1920's, the need for motor vehicle regulation and law enforcement became apparent, further influencing the development of state law-enforcement agencies.

The state of Maryland is credited with establishing the first "highway patrol" in 1914, when the state commissioner of motor vehicles was authorized to appoint "motorcycle deputies" to enforce the motor vehicle laws. Most state law-enforcement agencies created after 1920 were essentially highway patrols, and the authority of these agencies has been expanded over time beyond strictly motor vehicle law enforcement, with some being reorganized as state police agencies.

In 2000, there were fifteen primary state law-enforcement agencies officially named "highway patrol" and twenty-two called "state police," but other agencies are named "state patrol" and "department of public safety," so it is not always possible to determine the type of agency from its name alone.

The traffic safety mission of highway patrols is an important responsibility, and highway patrols prioritize the apprehension of persons who drive under the influence of alcohol or drugs, utilizing a number of tactics including sobriety checkpoints to identify impaired drivers. Speeding is a major contributing factor in traffic crashes, and speed limit violations are a top enforcement priority. Highway patrols use radar and laser speed detection devices, as well as aircraft and other visual methods of detecting speeders. Highway patrols also focus on hazardous moving violations, vehicle equipment violations, and driver license and vehicle registration violations.

In most states, highway patrols have been statutorily assigned additional responsibilities, such as commercial vehicle safety, auto theft investigation, and security of state officials and buildings. Some highway patrols may provide services such as radio dispatch, crime laboratory, and criminal history records systems for other law-enforcement agencies. After the terrorist attacks of September 11, 2001, highway patrols have often been assigned homeland security responsibilities.

Raymond L. Sparks

Further Reading

Bechtel, H. Kenneth. *State Police in the United States: A Socio-Historical Analysis*. Westport, Conn.: Greenwood Press, 1995.

Torres, Donald A. *Handbook of State Police, Highway Patrols, and Investigative Agencies*. Westport, Conn.: Greenwood Press, 1987.

See also High-speed chases; Hit-and-run accidents; Law enforcement; Mothers Against Drunk Driving; Police; Sobriety testing; State police; Traffic law.

Homeland Security, U.S. Department of

Identification: Federal cabinet-level department that coordinates the work of twenty-two separate agencies

Date: Established on March 1, 2003

Significance: The U.S. Department of Homeland Security encourages active communication and collaboration among its numerous agencies and organizations to meet the department's primary goal of improving the security of the United States against possible terrorist attacks and natural disasters.

After the terrorist attacks of September 11, 2001, in New York City, Washington, D.C., and Pennsylvania, a massive reorganization of 180,000 federal employees from twenty-two different agencies was proposed by President George W. Bush and authorized by the Homeland Security Act of 2002. This controversial restructuring unified a sprawling federal network of institutions and organizations into the Homeland Security Department in order better to protect against terrorist threats, as well as natural and accidental disasters throughout the United States and its territories. The enormous (FEMA), and Transportation Security Administration under a single cabinet-level department on March 1, 2003.

With a proposed budget in 2005 of more than $40 billion, the department was tasked with overseeing and managing the daily operations of protecting national targets, coordinating domestic intelligence, preparedness, research initiatives, and monitoring the flow of trade and legal immigration across all US ports of entry. Agencies in the Homeland Security Department are divided among four major divisions: Border and Transportation Security, Emergency Preparedness and Response, Science and Technology, and Information Analysis and Infrastructure Protection.

Borders, Transportation, and National Preparedness

The Homeland Security Department's Border and Transportation directorate oversees security and management of immigration, borders, and transportation operations in the United States. Its Citizenship and Immigration Services branch (USCIS) provides all services and benefits relating to immigration. Customs and Border Protection (CBP) serves as the enforcement agency and oversees the legal entry of goods, services, and persons into and out of ports of entry.

The Federal Protective Service is charged with protecting all federal buildings and installations. Another major responsibility of this directorate includes the monitoring of transportation systems by the Transportation Security Administration (TSA). With an estimated 11 million trucks, 2 million road cars, and 55,000 calls on ports per year, the TSA has the enormous task of protecting and monitoring all forms of transit, including air travel, across the country. Also working closely with other agencies in this directorate are the Animal and Plant Health Inspection Service, the Office of Domestic Preparedness, and the Federal Law Enforcement Training Center (FLETC).

Seal of the United States Department of Homeland Security. (Public domain, via Wikimedia Commons)

The federal Emergency Preparedness and Response directorate combines agencies from the Departments of Justice and Health and Human Services with Federal Emergency Management Agency (FEMA).

A central component of preparedness planning involves coordinating large-scale hypothetical disaster drills across communities to test their readiness for attacks using nuclear and biological weapons and attacks with weapons of mass destruction. Other agencies under this directorate focus on the stockpiling of drugs to treat biochemical assaults and training medical workers on how to treat victims. Domestic Emergency Response Teams and the National Domestic Preparedness Office work with FEMA and other agencies to develop comprehensive strategies for planning, prevention, response to and recovery from acts of terrorism and to assist when natural disasters strike.

Scientific Advancement and Threat Assessment

All available technological and scientific antiterrorism groups across the federal government were combined under the Science and Technology directorate of the Homeland Security Department. These organizations work together and provide states with federal guidelines regarding responses to weapons of mass destruction. By merging resources, labs, and scientific knowledge formerly scattered across the Departments of Energy, Agriculture, and Defense, the Homeland Security Department tries to assist local and state public safety officials in developing sound plans to monitor and defend their communities.

The final group included in the Homeland Security Department is that of the Information Analysis and Infrastructure Protection directorate. Its agencies gather and analyze information from many national agencies and then issue threat assessment warnings to US citizens and targets. The Homeland Security Advisory System issues these warnings to specific and general targets and encourages continuous public vigilance. The Advisory System also provides information to local and state authorities, the private sector, and international partners as intelligence is received.

A color-coded threat level system is used to communicate the perceived danger to the public and has been activated when threats have been discovered. These warnings attempt to protect important infrastructure systems that are most prone to attack, including food, water, health, emergency, and telecommunications systems. Using a federal television campaign, the Homeland Security Department has also encouraged Americans to make family emergency plans in the case of a terrorist attack or natural disaster. This system was phased out and simplified in 2011 as the National Terrorism Advisory System (NTAS). The NTAS now uses two tiers: bulletins and alerts. Bulletins announce general trends in threats to the American public, while alerts identify and warn against verified threats. These are issued to the media, posted to the Department of Homeland Security website, and the DHS's social media outlets.

Additional Agencies and Initiatives

In addition to Homeland Security Department's four directories, the US Coast Guard and Secret Service are also part of the Homeland Security Department. The Coast Guard monitors the coastal and interstate waters of the United States and its territories, assists other agencies in the prevention of the illegal entry of aliens and contraband, and provides rescue missions and aid to vessels in distress.

The Secret Service also remains intact under the Homeland Security Department and reports directly to the secretary of Homeland Security. First established in 1865, the Secret Service was initially created to protect against counterfeit currency. Perhaps the service's most visible role includes its responsibility for protecting former, current, and elected presidents and vice presidents, along with their immediate families. The service also protects major political candidates, visiting diplomats, and other high-ranking government officials. The Secret Service Uniformed Division has also guarded the grounds of the White House since 1860. Other initiatives of the department focus on potential threats to banking and finance systems, health and safety of citizens, and the monitoring of potential targets and intelligence across the world.

In an attempt to expand collaboration among federal, state, and local governments, as well as organizations in the private sector, the Homeland Security Department is building a coalition of organizations that are linked together by a computer-based counterterrorism communications network. In 2005, the Homeland Security Information Network linked agencies in more than fifty major cities, all fifty states, Washington, D.C., and five US territories through a state-of-the-art computer communication system. This system relays sensitive, nonclassified information to more than one hundred different agencies and approximately one thousand users who share a joint counterterrorism mission.

Future expansion of this project targets including smaller agencies at county levels and private businesses and sharing classified information among cleared parties. This system aims to offer real-time information across geographical regions and between public and private sectors in order better to identify, share, and respond to terrorist threats.

Future Challenges

With the massive integration of numerous agencies across departments, the transition of key personnel, services, and cross-authorized duties has not been accomplished without difficulties. Audits of the department's financial statements are used to determine what corrective measures are necessary to streamline government spending and identify potential wastes of taxpayer funds. Dramatic changes within the agencies consolidated into the department are expected to continue as the agencies are studied and redundant jobs and assignments are eliminated. Budgetary and human resource management has been a critical area of concern from the inception of the integration of so many independent agencies under one umbrella department.

The changing of employee benefits, the cutting of automatic overtime pay for personnel, the elimination of seniority and rank for those persons being adopted into new agencies, and the potential loss of trained employees to the private sector are all challenging issues that the department will address in the years to come. With so many important responsibilities concerning national defense, homeland security, disaster preparedness, and transportation and border protections resting on the shoulders of the Homeland Security Department, this fledgling department is expected to remain in the public eye and front and center on the war on terrorism in post-September 11, 2001, America.

Denise Paquette Boots

Further Reading

Brzezinski, Matthew. *Fortress America: On the Frontline of Homeland Security-An Inside Look at the Coming Surveillance State*. New York: Bantam, 2004. Print.
Flynn, Stephen. *America the Vulnerable: How Our Government Is Failing to Protect Us*. New York: HarperCollins, 2004. Print.
Kettl, Donald F. *Department of Homeland Security's First Year: A Report Card*. New York: Century Foundation, 2004. Print.
Mena, Jesus. *Homeland Security: Techniques and Technologies*. Hingham: Charles River Media, 2004. Print.
White, Jonathan R. *Defending the Homeland: Domestic Intelligence Law Enforcement and Security*. Stamford: Wadsworth, 2003. Print.

See also Attorney General, U.S.; Border patrols; Computer information systems; Deportation; Drugs and law enforcement; Law enforcement; Secret Service, U.S.; September 11, 2001, attacks; Skyjacking; Terrorism.

Intelligence-led policing

Definition: Intelligence-led policing (ILP) is a law enforcement management approach whereby data are used to help target crime-fighting resources to the areas of greatest need.

Criminal justice issues: Crime prevention; law enforcement organization; terrorism

Significance: In an era of finite law enforcement budgets and burgeoning online crime, ILP can help authorities pinpoint where law enforcement resources are most likely to have an immediate crime detection and control impact. ILP helps convert law enforcement from reactive to proactive.

Intelligence-led policing (ILP) is the process by which law enforcement managers use detailed crime data to identify and quantify those areas and suspects where policing resources can be most effectively applied. This is a critically important management approach when data are available and law enforcement budgets are limited. At its highest level, ILP can become the driving force for organizational design and strategy. These intelligence data allow more efficient and effective law enforcement.

ILP and Community Policing

ILP began in the days when police officers walked a beat. They knew the beat well. They knew every resident and merchant in the area where they walked the beat. And the officer on the beat knew instantly when something didn't seem quite right. "That alley door is always locked; why not tonight." "Those inside lights are never on this late at night." "That pedestrian isn't from around here." Those cops on the beat were gathering intelligence in real time and on a very small scale. They then used that intelligence to help them decide what law enforcement steps to take next.

More recently, in the community policing era, law enforcement agencies are affirmatively striving to reinsert themselves into the served communities. That close contact serves as the modern version of the cop on a beat, gathering intelligence gleaned from the officers' familiarity with the areas served and familiarity with the residents and merchants in those areas.

Today's ILP gathers all of that individual intelligence together to allow law enforcement managers to better target public safety resources to the areas of most need.

Geographic Information Systems (GIS) and ILP

Imagine a law enforcement agency with limited staff and other resources that can use existing calls for service and other police records to identify when and where crimes of certain types are committed. That information can be mapped to show the locations and times when those finite police resources can be best targeted to catch the offenders in the act or deter the offenders before they commit the act. A few dollars spent on GIS analysis and crime-mapping can multiply the value of an otherwise very limited police presence. Many agencies using GIS and crime-mapping also post their data online for citizen viewing and transparency.

COMPSTAT & ILP

COMPuter STATistics (COMPSTAT) was part of the natural evolution of ILP. It combines computerized crime statistics with accelerated response times and cross-departmental data sharing. Following its initial rollout within the New York Police Department, COMPSTAT's most salient features are ongoing collaboration and datasharing among officers within and between departments, but ILP is at COMPSTAT's core, providing the data fuel that drives COMPSTAT's analysis and targeting.

ILP and the Globalization of Crime

The digital age, at a grand scale, has fueled an explosion of interrelated and coordinated crime across the globe. Global crime consortiums bring together software specialists in Eastern Europe to aggregate digital data stolen from consumers accessing the Internet and other sites around the world, then sell the aggregated data to the highest bidder, fraudulently obtain credit with the stolen identities, or file fraudulent tax returns for refunds. At a far smaller scale, laptops, smartphones, and other digital devices are used to traffic or participate in child pornography across the globe. At a still smaller scale, criminals use cell phones to set up drug deals.

At each of these scales, from largest to smallest, while criminals' digital age devices enable them to coordinate their illegal activities, those same devices leave a constant trail of evidence behind: cell site locations, numbers called, locations visited, Internet Service Provider (ISP) information, and so on. When criminals develop expertise in the next digital technology, law enforcement must follow close on the criminals' heels and develop the ability to decode the digital evidence the criminals left behind.

Those digital data become part of the flow of intelligence that drives ILP. Perhaps the most obvious and far-reaching digital intelligence-gathering process plays out in the global War on Terror.

ILP, Homeland Security, and the Global War on Terror

In the United States, domestic and international anti-terrorism efforts are driven by intelligence. Some of that intelligence is gathered at the street level; other intelligence is gathered digitally and even internationally. Witness the NSA (National Security Agency) efforts to gather and warehouse cell phone metadata for subsequent use in ferreting out connections among terrorists and their funders and supporters. Or consider the use of data gathered at airports by the TSA (Transportation Security Administration) related to travel patterns, passports, no-fly lists, and the like. Or remember the intelligence-gathering efforts that followed the Boston Marathon bombing,

These antiterrorism and homeland security efforts extend far beyond national and international borders, as well. For example, when the Paris terror attacks occurred in 2015, Interpol and other national and international police and intelligence groups tracked connections to Belgium and beyond. After the 9/11 attacks on the World Trade Center and the Pentagon, digital and other intelligence allowed investigators to track the terrorists' travels, flight training, and funding sources across the globe. One major consequence of the globalization of crime and the global War on Terror is a vastly enhanced international coordination of intelligence gathering and sharing.

Thus, at local, national, and global levels, ILP has allowed law enforcement to use data gathered in the community and combine it with other data to yield a better assessment of risks and opportunities for crime detection and control. Intelligence-led policing, at its best, improves law enforcement's ability to evolve from merely reactive—answering calls for service—to proactive, using intelligence to efficiently and proactively target law enforcement efforts and resources.

Charles E. "Chuck" MacLean

Further Reading

Ratcliffe, J. H*Intelligence-Led Policing*. 2nd ed. London: Routledge: Taylor & Francis, 2016.

Schaible, L. M., and J. Sheffield. "Intelligence-Led Policing and Change in State Law Enforcement Agencies." *Policing: An International Journal of Police Strategies & Management* 35, no. 4 (2012): 761-84.

U.S. Department of Justice, Bureau of Justice Assistance. COMPSTAT: *Its Origins, Evolution, and Future in Law Enforcement Agencies*. Washington, D.C.: Police Executive Forum, 2013.

See also Community-oriented policing; Fusion centers; Geographic information systems; Paris terrorist attacks (2015); Terrorism; Wiretaps.

Internal affairs

Definition: Units within police departments that investigate charges of police misconduct

Criminal justice issues: Government Misconduct; Police powers; Professional standards

Significance: Internal affairs units provide citizens with avenues for reporting police misconduct and seeking redress.

Individuals and governments that have control over people are often abusive. The same may be said of police personnel. Since the inception of formalized policing during the first half of the nineteenth century, police misconduct and misbehavior have often occurred in policing agencies. The early decade of the twenty-first century does not appear to be any closer to eliminating this problem. This may be due to the very nature of police work. Police in American society have legal and recognized positions of authority and power. Their primary mission is to maintain social order through their legitimate authority.

However, police periodically misuse their authority and have confrontations with citizens. Confrontations can occur, for example, when citizens challenge police officers' authority or do not obey officers' commands as quickly as the officers would like. Confrontations between citizens and police may leave the impression that the police often overstep their authority in enforcing social order.

Human rights groups as well as many members of minority groups believe that the police have often denied citizens their civil rights. In actuality, American police officers have the responsibility to protect the constitutional rights of all citizens. However, there are police officers and officials who do not believe that their responsibility extends to all citizens equally.

The police have the responsibility to maintain the trust of the community. When there are reports of inappropriate behavior and actions performed by police officers, then citizens lose confidence in the police. If police even give the appearance of wrongdoing, citizens lose respect for them. Without community support, the police will have difficulties in maintaining order and solving crimes.

Police misconduct includes any wrongdoing by officers who commit acts that violate criminal laws or departmental regulations or policies. Actions such as excessive use of force, police corruption, use of drugs on duty, and rudeness to citizens are examples of behaviors that cannot be condoned. When police are charged with misconduct, the departmental branches responsible for investigating the charges are internal affairs units.

Purpose of Internal Affairs

The goal of internal affairs units is to protect both communities and their police departments from inappropriate police behavior by investigating citizen allegations of misconduct. Most departments have structured complaint procedures. Citizens can file their complaints in person, by telephone, or by mail. It is generally preferable that complainants identify themselves, as anonymous complaints lack the impact of identifiable complaints.

Ideally, all complaints, regardless of their nature, are impartially investigated. Most complaints are minor and are handled by supervisors. For example, a rudeness complaint—which is common—would be handled by the offending officer's immediate supervisor. Serious allegations are handled by the formal internal affairs units. Their investigations can lead to officers being reprimanded, suspended, or even terminated. In a formal investigation, all witnesses to the alleged misconduct are interviewed, and all relevant physical evidence is collected and examined. This evidence includes information submitted by the officers under investigation.

Investigations

Police officers under investigation may not wish to cooperate but are required to do so. When they are interviewed by internal affairs investigators, the investigators must follow guidelines established by the U.S. Supreme Court in its 1967 ruling in *Garrity v. New Jersey*. These guidelines include a statement that investigators read to officers under investigation that is known as the "Garrity warning." (It is also sometimes called the "Garrity law" or "Garrity rule.")

Similar to the Miranda warning that police officers read to suspects whom they arrest, the Garrity warning advises officers under investigation that they must answer all questions asked by investigators or face disciplinary action, including possible termination. However, the Garrity warning also requires that officers being questioned be advised that their responses to questions cannot be used in criminal prosecutions. Officers who may face criminal prosecution are informed that they are not required to answer the questions, but if they do, then their responses may be used against them in criminal proceedings.

Upon completion of internal affairs investigations, the findings are submitted to the departments' police chiefs or other high-ranking administrators. The investigations can have several possible outcomes. They may sustain the allegations or rule them "not sustained" for lack of evidence to prove or disprove the allegations. Exoneration is the finding in cases in which the investigators conclude that the alleged acts did occur but were justified, lawful, and proper. When investigators find sufficient evidence to conclude that the alleged misconduct did not occur, they rule the case closed, with "no finding."

When allegations against officers are sustained, disciplinary action is taken against the officers. Such discipline varies with the seriousness of the misconduct and the officers' prior service records. Punishment can range from formal letters of reprimand to suspensions from duty without pay and termination. Letters reporting the investigations' findings are sent to the complainants.

Michael J. Palmiotto

Further Reading

Bennet, W., and Karen Hess. *Management and Supervision in Law Enforcement*. 5th ed. Belmont: Wadsworth/Thomson Learning, 2007.

Fyfe, James, et al. *Police Administration*. 5th ed. New York: McGraw-Hill, 1997.

Palmiotto, Michael J. *Community Policing: A Policing Strategy for the Twenty-first Century*. 2d ed. Boston: Jones and Bartlett, 2005.

Thrasher, Ronald. "Internal Affairs: The Police Agencies' Approach to the Investigation of Police Misconduct. *Police Misconduct*. Ed. Michael J. Palmiotto. Upper Saddle River: Prentice Hall, 2001.

Walker, Samuel, and Charles M. Katz. *The Police in America: An Introduction*. 8th ed. New York: McGraw-Hill, 2013.

See also Bill of Rights, U.S.; King beating case; Knapp Commission; Miranda rights; Police brutality; Police civil liability; Police dogs; Police ethics.

Internal Revenue Service, U.S.

Identification: Federal agency responsible for enforcing income and excise tax laws, and investigating criminal violations of the Internal Revenue Code and related financial crimes

Date: Established in 1862

Significance: The Internal Revenue Service (IRS) is the only federal agency commissioned to investigate criminal violations of the U.S. Internal Revenue Code.

The IRS, a branch of the Department of the Treasury, was established in 1862 by President Abraham Lincoln to enact a tax to compensate for the expense of the Civil War. As a direct result of the IRS Restructuring and Reform Act of 1998, the IRS was reorganized into four major operating divisions, corresponding to various categories of taxpayers. The four divisions are the Wage and Investment division, the Small Business/Self-Employed division, the Large and Mid-Size Business division, and the Tax-Exempt and Government Entities division. There are three additional divisions: Communications and Liaison, Appeals, and Criminal Investigation. This discussion will focus on the Criminal Investigation division.

The predecessor of the Criminal Investigation division was created in 1919, when an IRS intelligence unit was assembled to investigate tax fraud. This unit attained much notoriety in the summer of 1930, when world-renowned gangster Al Capone saw his deviant career brought to an end by the IRS, not for his violent criminal activity but for income tax evasion. In 1978, the unit was named Criminal Investigation when its jurisdiction was expanded to include activities violating the Money Laundering Act and Bank Secrecy Act of 1970. This division is identified as the law-enforcement aspect of the Internal Revenue Service. From 1919 to 2004, the conviction rate for federal tax prosecutions was 90 percent or better, the highest among all federal law-enforcement agencies.

IRS Building in Washington D.C. (By Joshua Doubek, via Wikimedia Commons)

As of September 2015, the Criminal Investigation division comprises about twenty-five hundred special agents performing a combination of accounting and law-enforcement duties in the investigation of financial crimes. Its operations include surveillance and undercover work, intelligence, strike forces, and the organized crime drug task force. Six areas categorize financial crimes in a diverse combination of industries and professions for which this division is responsible: tax return preparer fraud, real estate fraud, automotive industry fraud, construction industry fraud, restaurant industry fraud, and medical fraud. In the wake of the, September 11, 2001 terrorist attacks on the United States, as well as myriad technological advancements in the use of computers to commit crime, the Criminal Investigation division has augmented its financial skills and law-enforcement resources to create several task forces to combat terrorism.

Lisa Landis Murphy

Further Reading

"Criminal Investigation (CI) At-a-Glance." *IRS*. IRS, 29 Sept. 2015. Web. 26 May. 2016.

Landolfi, Richard P. *The Internal Revenue Service : Selected Analyses of Issues And Improvement Strategies*. New York: Nova Science Publishers, 2014. *eBook Collection (EBSCOhost)*. Web. 26 May 2016.

Plan Your IRS Career. Washington, D.C.: U.S. Department of Treasury, Internal Revenue Service, 1997.

Schmalleger, F. *Your Criminal Justice Career: A Guidebook*. Englewood Cliffs, N.J.: Prentice-Hall, 2002.

Territo, L., J. B. Halsted, and M. Bromley. *Crime and Justice in America: A Human Perspective*. 6th ed. Englewood Cliffs, N.J.: Prentice-Hall, 2003.

See also Fraud; Money laundering; Tax evasion; Treasury Department, U.S.

Interpol

Identification: More formally known as the International Criminal Police Organization, the largest international police organization in the world

Date: Founded in 1923

Significance: The increasing internationalization of crime—particularly in the areas of drug trafficking, arms dealing, money laundering, human trafficking, high-tech crime, and terrorist activities—has heightened the importance of cooperation among police and law-enforcement officers around the world.

The International Criminal Police Organization, or Interpol, was founded in 1923 to facilitate cross-border police cooperation and in 2016 had a membership of 190 nations. Differences in cultures, languages, and legal systems can cause difficulties in cooperation among police of different nations. Interpol's mission is to help police and law-enforcement officers from around the world cooperate with one another to prevent and solve international crimes. Interpol addresses only international crimes involving two or more member countries, and thus much of its work is focused on crimes such as drug trafficking, arms dealing, money laundering, counterfeiting, human trafficking, information technology crimes, and-strongly emphasized-terrorism. Interpol does not engage in casework that is political, military, or religious in character.

Interpol Services and Organization

Interpol provides three basic services for member nations. First, its global communications system allows police from member nations to store and exchange information. Member countries are thereby connected and are able to access police information around the clock, including data regarding persons being sought by police forces worldwide. Second, Interpol makes its information available to law-enforcement agencies within numerous databases: Fingerprints, pictures, and even DNA profiles can be accessed by computer. Third, Interpol provides support for police operations throughout the world.

The General Assembly is Interpol's governing body and is composed of delegates appointed by the governments of member states. It meets once a year and decides issues of general policy, resources, programs, and operations. Each member country has one vote, and decisions are made by a simple majority in the form of resolutions. The General Assembly also elects the organization's Executive Committee, which supervises the execution of

ICPO-Interpol Headquarters in Lyon, France. (By Massimiliano Mariani, via Wikimedia Commons)

the decisions of the General Assembly and prepares the agenda for its sessions. The Executive Committee has thirteen members, a president, three vice presidents, and nine delegates. Interpol is funded from the member countries, with contributions based on each nation's ability to pay.

National Central Bureaus

Each member country has its own Interpol office, or National Central Bureau (NCB). These bureaus form a point of contact for any foreign agency or government wishing to exchange or gather information on international criminal activities. The U.S. National Central Bureau (USNCB) operates within the guidelines prescribed by the Department of Justice, in conjunction with the Department of Homeland Security. It is an office under the control and direction of the Department of Justice and Department of Treasury.

The threat of terrorist activities, the increasing internationalization of crime, and the large number of foreign nationals residing in or visiting the United States have increased the importance of the USNCB and its relationship to Interpol. USNCB assistance is given not only to authorities in Interpol member countries but also to all U.S. federal, state, and regional enforcement agencies. Each state has an Interpol contact, and numerous major metropolitan areas have direct access to Interpol's resources; in 2004, Seattle joined New York, Washington, D.C., Los Angeles, San Francisco, Chicago, Boston, San Diego, and Miami.

One important Interpol service is helping member countries' police communicate critical crime-related information to one another using Interpol's international notices, a system that helps the world's law-enforcement community exchange information about missing persons, unidentified bodies, and persons who are wanted in connection with serious crimes. These notices, color-coded to designate their purposes, are published at the request of a member country by the Interpol General Secretariat in the organization's four official languages. The NCB of a country receives the notices and distributes them among appropriate law-enforcement authorities. Ten different types of notices exist to communicate various kinds of criminal information.

Interpol's Role in Combating Terrorist Activities

In the wake of the terrorist attacks in the United States on September 11, 2001, Interpol underwent substantial change in order to combat terrorism better. New, more efficient systems of information exchange have been developed to facilitate international police cooperation in combating terrorist activities. Interpol has also attempted to avoid politically sensitive aspects of terrorism by focusing on such criminal aspects as murder, kidnapping, and illegal weapons trade. On May 6, 2004—in association with the U.S. National Central Bureau of Interpol, the U.S. Department of Justice, and the Interpol General Secretariat in Lyon, France-the U.S. Department of State announced that the United States was joining many other countries in providing current information on passports reported lost or stolen. This program was intended to contribute to worldwide travel document security and impede the movement of terrorists and other criminals across international borders.

Jerome L. Neapolitan

Further Reading
Anderson, M. "Interpol and the Developing System of International Police Cooperation." In *Crime and Law Enforcement in the Global Village*, edited by W. F. McDonald. Cincinnati: Anderson Publishing, 1997.
Bresler, F. *Interpol*. New York: Penguin Press, 1992.
Deflem, M. *Policing World Society: Historical Foundations of International Police Cooperation*. New York: Oxford University Press, 2002.
Imhoff, J. J., and S. P. Cutler. *Interpol: FBI Law Enforcement Bulletin* 67, no. 12. Chapel Hill, N.C.: Academic Search Elite, University of North Carolina Academic Affairs, 1998.
United States. Dept. of Justice. "About Interpol Washington." *Justice.gov*. US Dept. of Justice, 30 June 2014. Web. 26 May 2016.

See also Attorney General, U.S.; Computer information systems; Drug Enforcement Administration, U.S.; Federal Bureau of Investigation, U.S.; International law; Marshals Service, U.S.; Money laundering.

Justice Department, U.S.

Identification: Federal cabinet-level department that investigates, prosecutes, and punishes offenses against the United States, makes national criminal justice policy, and provides financial, training, and other forms of support to state and municipal law-enforcement agencies
Date: Established in 1870
Criminal justice issues: Federal law; law-enforcement organization
Significance: The largest and most influential law-enforcement entity in the U.S. criminal justice system, the federal Justice Department serves as a link between the court system and the executive branch of the federal government. It also brings suit against violators of federal law and defends the U.S. government against claims brought by persons, organizations, and local and state governments.

In 1789, the first U.S. Congress laid the foundations of the federal justice system by creating both the federal court system and the office of U.S. attorney general. The legislation creating the office of attorney general empowered the holder of that office to represent the United States in Supreme Court cases in which the United States was a party and to give advice and legal opinions as requested by the president or heads of any of the executive departments.

Working with only small staffs, the attorneys general conducted their duties without the aid of a bureaucratic department until 1870, when Congress established the Department of Justice. From that modest beginning, the department grew to its twenty-first century position as the largest investigative, prosecutorial, and punishment entity in the United States. In 2015, its budget was nearly $46.4 billion, and it employed almost 115,000 persons.

The mission of the Department of Justice is: To enforce the law and defend the interests of the United States according to the law, to ensure public safety against threats foreign and domestic, to provide federal leadership in preventing and controlling crime, to seek just punishment for those guilty of unlawful behavior, and to ensure fair and impartial administration of justice for all Americans.

Organization

The modern Justice Department has 41 separate component organizations that conduct a broad range of functions related to the criminal justice system. Its law-enforcement agencies include the Federal Bureau of Investigation (FBI), the Drug Enforcement Administration (DEA), and the Bureau of Alcohol, Tobacco, Firearms and Explosives (ATF). These agencies investigate crimes against the United States and threats to national security. They also coordinate with state and local law-enforcement offices and provide training and expertise in nonfederal cases.

The Justice Department also conducts all litigation—except as otherwise authorized by statute—in which the United States is a party. Its lawyers include U.S. attorneys and assistant U.S. attorneys, who represent the federal government within assigned districts, and so-called "main justice" prosecutors. Based in Washington, D.C., these prosecutors travel nationwide to handle cases throughout the nation. They present criminal matters to federal grand juries and prosecute criminal cases in federal court.

Justice Department lawyers also represent the federal government in appellate courts and before the U.S. Supreme Court. They may also testify in trials to present the government's views in cases to which the United States itself is not a party. They also handle international criminal matters on behalf of federal, state, or municipal governments and in cases in which foreign fugitives flee to the United States to avoid prosecution in other countries. In U.S. extradition cases, Justice Department lawyers represent the governments of the foreign nations involved.

The U.S. Marshals Service protects federal courts, parties to criminal cases, witnesses, and criminally used or obtained property forfeited to the United States. The department's Bureau of Prisons maintains custody of persons convicted of crimes against the United States. Finally, various offices within the Justice Department provide training, technical assistance, financial aid, and coordination to state and local investigative and prosecution offices.

Through several statutes, Congress specifically authorized the positions of attorney general, deputy attorney general, associate attorney general, solicitor general, twelve assistant attorneys general, and ninety-four U.S. attorneys. Congress also created the investigative, protective, and prison entities and directed that they be integrated into the Justice Department.

Distinctions Between Federal and State Offenses

Under the nation's federal system of government, responsibility to enforce the law is divided between the federal, state, and local governments. A crucial and primary distinction between the federal and state governments is that whereas the powers of the former are few and narrowly defined, those of the latter are both numerous and indefinite. The federal Justice Department can prosecute only offenses that violate federal law, such as statutes enacted by Congress. Some crimes are uniquely federal, some are uniquely subject to state jurisdiction, and some are concurrently proscribed by both state and federal law.

Uniquely federal crimes, which are prosecuted and punished only by the U.S. Justice Department, include such offenses as counterfeiting U.S. currency, treason, espionage and other national security related offenses, immigration fraud, federal tax offenses, federal program fraud, and other crimes that are directed solely against the interests of the national government. The Justice Department may also prosecute crimes within "the special maritime and territorial jurisdiction of the United States," which includes federal enclaves such as Army bases, as well as places and vessels outside the territorial jurisdiction of any state.

Criminal acts that are subject to the concurrent criminal jurisdiction of both state and federal authorities include the manufacture and distribution of drugs; kidnapping; firearm offenses and other crimes that also involve interstate activity; frauds in which instrumentalities of interstate or foreign commerce are used; and other crimes that harm federally protected institutions, such as robberies of banks that are federally insured.

The range of offenses exclusively under state jurisdiction, and in which the federal government may not prosecute is large. They include purely regional crimes that have no connections with interstate or foreign commerce or do not implicate instrumentalities or other legitimate interests of the federal government. Murder, for example, is ordinarily not a federal crime, but it may be prosecuted by the Justice Department when its victims are federal government officials or foreign diplomats or when it occurs on military bases or other federal property.

In the late twentieth century, federal law criminalized a broad range of conduct that traditionally had been addressed by state laws, in part because of congressional dissatisfaction with local prosecution efforts and state-ordered sentences on convicted offenders. The U.S. Supreme Court's 1995 decision in *United States v. Lopez* reinvigorated federal principles and rebuffed federal prosecutions of crimes that are subject to state jurisdiction and do not reflect constitutionally sanctioned federal interests.

Authority for the prosecution of federal offenses resides primarily with the U.S. attorneys, who are distributed throughout the country, and with "main justice," the assistant attorneys general who head the criminal divisions and their attorneys. Prosecutorial authority for tax, antitrust, and environmental matters is assigned to other divisions within the Justice Department. Those divisions are also led by presidentially appointed assistant attorneys general.

The Attorney General

The attorney general ordinarily does not appear personally in pending cases, though it is not unusual for one to argue a case before the U.S. Supreme Court. However, attorneys general and their subordinates have the power to set national priorities and to issue guidelines to Justice Department prosecutors on a broad variety of issues involving litigation. Attorneys general must also approve the issuance of federal grand jury or trial subpoenas.

Because attorneys general are political appointees who serve at the pleasure of the presidents, it is an inherent conflict of interest to grant the attorney general responsibility for investigating and prosecuting the president or other top executive branch officials. Accordingly, Congress created independent counsels, who are appointed by judges when it is necessary to conduct politically sensitive investigations. On June 30, 1999, the independent counsel statute expired, and investigations and prosecutions of top executive branch officials once again became the responsibility of the attorney general. In practice, attorneys general appoint "special prosecutors" to conduct such investigations or prosecutions when the attorney general are not able to do so.

United States Attorneys

Ninety-four U.S. attorneys work throughout the United States, Puerto Rico, the Virgin Islands, Guam, and the Northern Mariana Islands. Each U.S. attorney is appointed by the president, with the U.S. Senate's advice and consent, and serves at the pleasure of the president. Each attorney serves within one of the ninety-four congressionally established judicial districts, with the exception that a single U.S. attorney serves for the District of Guam and the District of the Northern Mariana Islands. The U.S. attorneys are the chief federal law-enforcement officers in their own districts. By law, the U.S. attorneys and assistant U.S. attorneys are empowered to prosecute federal criminal cases.

U.S. attorneys have considerable discretion in determining priorities and in deciding whether to present cases to federally impaneled grand juries and, when indictments are returned, to prosecute cases. They also have broad discretion in choosing and pursuing investigative and litigation techniques. However broad though, this discretion is not unlimited. The attorneys general set national priorities and retain the right to approve certain litigation and investigative decisions of the U.S. attorneys. The central office of the Department must authorize the initiation of criminal charges under the Racketeer Influenced and Corrupt Organizations (RICO) Act of 1970. Main justice must also approve requests for judicial orders conferring immunity on prospective witnesses when judicially conferred immunity is necessary to compel the witnesses to give evidence that might be self-incriminatory. U.S. attorneys may not appeal district court decisions without approval from the solicitor general in the Justice Department.

Congress can also restrict the discretion of U.S. attorneys by requiring approval by main justice of certain actions. For example, the federal wiretap statute requires that U.S. attorneys who seek judicial orders authorizing wiretaps or other electronic surveillance receive authorization from main justice.

Criminal Division and Other Enforcement Divisions

The Criminal Division of the Justice Department develops, enforces, and supervises the application of all federal criminal laws except those specifically assigned to other divisions in the Department. This division is responsbile for overseeing criminal matters as well as certain civil cases. The division prosecutes many high-profile cases of substantial nationwide significance. In addition to its litigation responsibilities, the Division formulates and implements criminal enforcement policy and provides advice and assistance on criminal matters prosecution authority. It comprises multiple sections, with particular responsibility for prosecuting several offenses including narcotics, organized crime, terrorism, money laundering, white-collar fraud, bribery of public officials and other forms of public corruption, computer crimes, criminal copyright offenses, violation of child exploitation and obscenity statutes, certain violent crimes, and alien smuggling.

The Criminal Division also operates as the central authority in international treaty issues that involve criminal law enforcement. Treaties for extradition and mutual legal assistance (the process by which the judicial or prosecution authorities in one country seek assistance in securing important evidence located in another country) generally are negotiated by attorneys of the Department of State and the Criminal Division. After treaties are negotiated, ratified, and entered into force, the Criminal Division makes and receives international requests for extradition or mutual legal assistance, even when fugitives or evidence are sought by state or local prosecutors.

Although the primary responsibility for criminal prosecutions lies within the Criminal Division, other litigation divisions within the department have limited criminal law-enforcement authority. For example, the Antitrust Division prosecutes criminal antitrust violations. The Tax Division prosecutes major tax offenses, such as the promotion of fraudulent tax shelters, and is also involved in the prosecution of terrorist financing cases. The Civil Rights Division prosecutes slavery, voter fraud, and criminal civil rights violations. The Environmental and Natural Resources Division prosecutes environmental offenses, such as criminal violations of the Clean Air Act of 1970.

The Federal Bureau of Investigation

Several agencies under the jurisdiction of the Justice Department have exclusively or primarily investigative functions. The FBI, the DEA, and the ATF are the primary investigative agencies. In addition, the department participates in international criminal investigations and cooperation, primarily through Interpol.

Established as the Bureau of Investigation in 1908, the Federal Bureau of Investigation has the broadest responsibility of all federal investigative agencies, authorized to investigate more than 180 federal crimes. In the early twenty-first century, its official top priority was counterterrorism. The FBI is also primarily responsible for the investigation of espionage, treason, and other related national security cases. In addition, the FBI has responsibility for investigating cybercrime and cyber-based attacks, public corruption, civil rights offenses, international national and national organized crime, white-collar crime, and major federal violent crimes.

The FBI also maintains a computerized database of fingerprint records in its Integrated Automated Fingerprint Identification System (AFIS), which provides information to several federal and state law-enforcement agencies. Its profiling unit and laboratories also assist in federal and state investigations and prosecutions. Thomas Harris's novel *Silence of the Lambs* (1988) and novels by author Patricia Cornwell have portrayed the profiling unit in some detail.

The FBI Academy in Quantico, Virginia, trains federal, state, local, and international police officers. The FBI's National Crime Information Center (NCIC) maintains databases with a wide variety of information; its databases are accessed approximately two million times a day by federal, state, and local police agencies.

The director of the FBI is appointed by the president, with Senate approval, for a term of ten years. His or her resignation can, however, be requested by the sitting president. The FBI has 35,000 employees and has fifty-six field offices in major cities throughout the United States and Puerto Rico and hundreds of satellite offices within the United States, and FBI legal attachés (called legats) in nearly 70 offices outside the United States support investigations and operations around the world.

U.S. Marshals Service

The Justice Department's U.S. Marshals Service (USMS) is the oldest of the U.S. law-enforcement agencies. The Marshals Service was created to provide security and protection for federal courts. The service now has myriad law-enforcement functions. Its protective functions include protection of courthouses and courtrooms and, as necessary, federal prosecutors, federal public defenders, and judges. The USMS also transports and maintains the security of federal witnesses and prisoners. It operates the federal Witness Protection Program, which protects, relocates, and provides new identities to people—and sometimes their family members—who are in jeopardy on account of their testimony in criminal trials. Since 1970, more than 18,000 people have participated in the program.

The U.S. Marshals Service also has a significant police function. It executes arrest warrants issued for fugitives who are accused of violating federal laws. In fact, federal marshals arrest more people than all other federal law-enforcement agencies combined. The service also is responsible for apprehending foreign fugitives sought for extradition and believed to be in the United States. It also is the primary agency for tracking U.S. fugitives charged by federal, state, or regional authorities when those fugitives are believed to have fled to areas outside the United States.

The USMS is responsible for the housing and transportation of persons charged with federal crimes (from point of arrest to the date of sentencing) and of internationally wanted fugitives. It houses more than forty-seven thousand federal prisoners (prior to conviction and sentencing) each day, in federal facilities or, through contract arrangements, in jails maintained by state and local authorities. It operates the Justice Prisoner and Alien Transportation System (JPATS), which transports prisoners and criminal aliens between judicial districts and correctional institutions and even to and from foreign countries. It manages and disposes of properties acquired by criminals through illegal activities after those properties have been seized and forfeited to the United States. Under the auspices of the Justice Department Asset Forfeiture Program, the Marshals Service in 2015 managed nearly $3.1 billion worth of property, proceeds of which are designed for federal, state, local, and foreign law-enforcement purposes. There are 94 US marshals. The USMS has 5400 employees at 218 offices within the United States and three foreign field offices.

Other Investigative and Protective Agencies

The Drug Enforcement Administration (DEA) enforces U.S. federal laws concerning controlled substances. It investigates organizations and persons involved in the importation, growth, production, and distribution of controlled substances in the United States. DEA agents are based throughout the United States as well as abroad, where they support investigations and international operations. The DEA currently has more than 10700 employees in 221 offices, organized into 21 divisions in the United States, and 86 foreign offices in 67 countries.

Formerly a branch of the U.S. Treasury Department, the Justice Department's Bureau of Alcohol, Tobacco, Firearms and Explosives (ATF) enforces federal firearms laws and investigates violent crimes involving firearms and explosives. The ATF also investigates offenses involving the smuggling of contraband untaxed alcohol and tobacco, but this is a relatively small part of its overall responsibility. The ATF has 4800 employees in 25 field offices in the United States, Puerto Rico, the Virgin Islands, and Guam. The ATF has been the subject of scrutiny and investigation over the years for controversial or failed actions such as the "fast and furious" gun-tracking operation, which was carried out between 2009 and 2010. In that failed operation, ATF lost track of nearly 2,000 assault rifles and other firearms that were smuggled into Mexico in an effort to trace them to drug cartels. Some of these firearms later reappeared at crime scenes near the US-Mexico border, including at the Arizona murder scene of a US Border agent in 2010. The House of Representatives, under control of the Republicans, condemned Attorney General Eric Holder and his top aides for the flawed program and found Holder in contempt for allegedly failing to fully answering questions pertaining to the operation.

The National Central Bureau (NCB) of Interpol, the International Criminal Police Organization that is headquartered in Lyon, France, is the U.S. point of contact for international law enforcement. The NCB facilitates U.S. participation in international law-enforcement cooperation by transmitting requests and information to and from Interpol member states and domestic law-enforcement agencies and coordinating information in international investigations. Among other key functions, Interpol facilitates efforts to locate internationally wanted fugitives and property that has been stolen and transported across national borders.

Federal Bureau of Prisons (BOP)

Offenders convicted of federal crimes and sentenced to prison terms are remanded to the custody of the Bureau of Prisons (BOP). The bureau has wide discretion to designate their places of imprisonment and then to regulate the conduct of the prisoners within that penal institution. The BOP has 41400 employees and operates 122 penal institutions, six regional offices, and 26 detention management field offices. The BOP is responsible for the custody and care of nearly 19600 federal offenders.

Loretta Lynch served as the 83rd Attorney General of the United States from 2015 through 2017. She was the second attorney general of the administration of President Barack Obama. Lynch succeeded Eric Holder, who served as Attorney General between 2009 and 2015 having previously served as United States Attorney for the Eastern District of New York. Her tenure as U.S. Attorney began in 2010, and she also held that position from 1999 to 2001. As U.S. Attorney for the Eastern District of New York.

One of the major recent issues for the Justice Department has been investigating of police-involved shootings of unarmed African American males throughout the United States, including an incident in Ferguson Missouri. The Civil Rights Division of the Justice Department investigated the Ferguson police department and uncovered several unconstitutional police practices. The report also found that the city focused its municipal operations on raising revenue, rather than public safety, resulting in practices that violate the constitutional rights of area residents.

On November 18, 2016, President elect Donald Trump nominated Alabama Senator Jefferson Sessions (R), to become Attorney General when the new administration assumes power in January 2017. Sen. Sessions was an early supporter of Donald Trump's candidacy for president and is one of the most conservative members of Congress. For example, Sen. Sessions has argued that prospective immigrants do not have constitutional protections, opposes federal sentencing reform, favors continuing an aggressive "war on drugs," and opposes legalization of marijuana.

Sara Criscitelli
Updated by Christopher Anglim

Further Reading

Clayton, Cornell C. *The Politics of Justice: The Attorney General and the Making of Legal Policy.* Armonk, N.Y.: M. E. Sharpe, 2015. Scholarly examination of the role of the attorney general in the shaping of national legal policies.

Cole, George F., and Christopher Smith. *American System of Criminal Justice.* 15th ed. Belmont, Calif: Thompson/Wadsworth, 2017. Standard textbook that covers all aspects of criminal justice in the United States, with extensive attention to the Justice Department and its branches.

Earley, Pete, and Gerald Shur. *WITSEC: Inside the Federal Witness Protection Program.* New York: Bantam Books, 2002. Inside view of the federal witness protection program, based on Shur's twenty-five-year career as a Justice Department attorney.

Johns, Margaret, and Rex R. Perschbacher. *The United States Legal System: An Introduction.* 4th ed. Durham, N.C.: Carolina Academic Press, 2016. Broad survey of the American justice system, with considerable attention to the Justice Department.

Kessler, Ronald. *The Bureau: The Secret History of the FBI.* New York: St. Martin's Press, 2003. Critical assessment of the Federal Bureau of Investigation that focuses on allegations that the bureau often abused its power.

Littman, Jonathan. *The Fugitive Game.* New York: Little, Brown, 1996. Inside look at the U.S. Marshals Service's work in tracking fugitives from justice.

Reebel, Patrick A., ed. *Federal Bureau of Investigation: Current Issues and Background.* New York: Nova Science, 2002. Collection of essays on the FBI with attention to some of its most publicized investigations, including those into the 1995 Oklahoma City bombing, the 1996 Montana "Freemen" standoff, and the 1993 Branch Davidian siege.

Stroud, Carsten. *Deadly Force: In the Streets with the U.S. Marshals.* New York: Bantam Books, 2012. Exploits of modern federal fugitive hunters.

See also Attorney General, U.S.; Criminal justice system; Federal Bureau of Investigation, U.S.; Marshals Service, U.S.; National Institute of Justice; Omnibus Crime Control and Safe Streets Act of 1968; Organized crime; Secret Service, U.S.

King beating case

The Event: Arrest and beating of Rodney King and subsequent criminal trial of the arresting officers
Date: March 3, 1991-June 1, 1994
Place: Los Angeles and Simi Valley, California

Significance: The trial of four white policemen following the arrest and beating of Rodney King, a black man, sparked a major investigation of police brutality in Los Angeles and violent race riots after a California court acquitted the police.

Following a high-speed chase along a Los Angeles highway that ended just after midnight on March 3, 1991, California Highway Patrol officers Timothy and Melanie Singer stopped driver Rodney Glen King and his two passengers, Bryant Allen and Freddie Helms, for questioning. More than twenty Los Angeles Police Department (LAPD) officers soon arrived on the scene in Los Angeles's Lake View Terrace neighborhood. Police sergeant Stacey Koon, assisted by officers Theodore Briseno, Laurence Powell, and Timothy Wind, took over the investigation. The police quickly subdued and handcuffed Allen and Helms without incident. Their encounter with King, however, caused a controversy with far-reaching legal and social consequences.

King's Arrest

According to the four white police officers who arrested Rodney King, a black man, King refused at first to leave the car and then resisted arrest with such vigor that the police officers had to apply two jolts from a Taser electric stun gun, fifty-six blows from aluminum batons, and six kicks (primarily from Briseno) to subdue King before they successfully handcuffed and cordcuffed him to restrain his arms and legs. The event probably would have gone unnoticed had not George Holliday, an amateur cameraman who witnessed the incident, videotaped the arrest and sold the tape to a local television station news program. The videotape became the crucial piece of evidence that the state of California used to charge the four LAPD arresting officers with criminal assault and that a federal grand jury subsequently used to charge the officers with civil rights violations.

Broadcast of Holliday's tape on national news programs elicited several responses from the LAPD. On March 6, 1991, the LAPD released King from custody and admitted that officers failed to prove that King had resisted arrest. On March 7, Los Angeles police chief Daryl Gates announced that he would investigate King's arrest and, if the investigation warranted it, would pursue criminal assault charges against the arresting officers. On March 14, a Los Angeles County grand jury indicted Sergeant Koon and officers Briseno, Powell, and Wind for criminal assault, and they subsequently pleaded not guilty.

Investigation of Police Brutality

Overwhelming public sympathy for King following the national broadcast of Holliday's videotape prompted Los Angeles mayor Tom Bradley to investigate charges that instances of police brutality motivated by racism were commonplace during LAPD arrest operations. On April 1, 1991, Mayor Bradley appointed a nonpartisan commission, headed by Warren Christopher (who had formerly served as the deputy secretary of state for President Jimmy Carter), to study the LAPD's past record of complaints regarding police misconduct. On April 2, Bradley called on Police Chief Gates, who had served on the LAPD since 1949 and had been police chief since 1978, to resign. In May, the LAPD suspended Sergeant Koon and officers Briseno and Powell without pay and dismissed officer Timothy Wind, a rookie, without tenure, pending the outcome of their criminal trial. King then filed a civil rights lawsuit against the city of Los Angeles.

Several significant developments occurred as the officers awaited trial. On July 9, 1991, the Christopher Commission released the results of its investigation and its recommendations to the five-member Los Angeles Police Commission. The Police Commission employed the police chief and was responsible for the management of the LAPD. The Christopher Commission found that the LAPD, composed of 67.8 percent white officers in 1991, suffered from a "siege mentality" in a city where 63 percent of the population were people of color. The commission also found that a small but significant proportion of officers repeatedly used excessive force when making arrests and that the LAPD did not punish those officers when citizens filed complaints. Finally, the commission recommended measures to exert more control over the LAPD's operations, including limiting the police chief's tenure to a five-year term, renewable by the Police Commission for one additional term only. After the release of the Christopher Commission report, Police Chief Gates announced his retirement, effective in April 1992 (which he later amended to July, 1992). On July 23, 1991, a California court of appeal granted the police defendants' request for a change of venue for the upcoming criminal trial.

The State of California Court Trial

The trial of the four officers began on March 4, 1992, in the new venue—the primarily white community of Simi Valley in Ventura County. The jury who heard the state of California's case against the four officers consisted of ten whites, one Latino, and one Asian. The officers' defense lawyers presented Holliday's videotape broken down into a series of individual still pictures. They asked the jury to judge whether excessive force—that is, force that was not warranted by King's "aggressive" actions—was employed at any single moment during the arrest. Referring often to the "thin blue line" that protected society from the "likes of Rodney King," the defense built a case that justified the police officers' actions. King's lawyer, Steven Lerman, a personal injury specialist, advised King not to testify at the trial out of concern that King's "confused and frightened" state of mind since the beating might impair his memory of events and discredit his testimony. The Simi Valley jury acquitted the four officers of all charges of criminal assault, with the exception of one count against officer Laurence Powell on which the jury was deadlocked.

Rodney King, years after he was beaten by LAPD Officers. (By Justinhoch, via Wikimedia Commons)

The acquittal of the four police officers on April 29, 1992, ignited widespread and destructive riots led by poor and angry black Angelenos. The Los Angeles riots affected areas throughout the city but particularly devastated parts of impoverished South Central Los Angeles. Fifty-three people died during the riots, which raged until May 2, and more than one billion dollars' worth of property was damaged. There had long been friction between Los Angeles's neighboring Korean and black communities, and the Korean American community bore the brunt of the rioters' destructive attacks.

The Federal Court Civil Rights Trial

On August 5, 1992, a federal grand jury indicted the four officers for violating King's civil rights. The grand jury charged Sergeant Koon with violating the Fourteenth Amendment, which obligated Koon, as the officer in charge of the arrest, to protect King while he was in police custody. Officers Briseno, Powell, and Wind were charged with violating the Fourth Amendment in using more force than necessary, and using that excessive force willfully, when they arrested King. King testified during the federal trial. On April 17, 1993, a jury of nine whites, two African Americans, and one Latino found Koon and Powell guilty and Briseno and Wind not guilty. On August 4, 1993, Koon and Powell were sentenced to two-and-one-half-year prison terms. In May 1994, a Los Angeles jury awarded King $3.8 million in compensatory damages in his civil rights lawsuit against the city, but on June 1, 1994, the jury denied King's request for additional punitive damages.

Karen Garner

Further Reading

Gooding-Williams, Robert, ed. *Reading Rodney King/Reading Urban Uprising*. New York: Routledge, 1993. Print.

Khalifah, H. Khalif, ed. *Rodney King and the L.A. Rebellion: Analysis and Commentary by Thirteen Best-Selling Black Writers*. Hampton: UB US Communications Systems, 1992. Print.

Koon, Stacey, with Robert Deitz. *Presumed Guilty: The Tragedy of the Rodney King Affair*. Washington, DC: Regnery Gateway, 1992. Print.

Owens, Tom, with Rod Browning. *Lying Eyes: The Truth Behind the Corruption and Brutality of the LAPD and the Beating of Rodney King*. New York: Thunder's Mouth, 1994. Print.

Roth, Mitchel P. *Historical Dictionary of Law Enforcement*. Westport: Greenwood, 2000. Print.

Thrasher, Ronald. "Internal Affairs: The Police Agencies' Approach to the Investigation of Police Misconduct." In *Police Misconduct*. Ed. Michael J. Palmiotto. Upper Saddle River: Prentice Hall, 2001. Print.

See also Change of venue; Civilian review boards; Double jeopardy; Due process of law; Internal affairs; Police brutality; Police ethics; Reasonable force.

Knapp Commission

Identification: Body established to investigate allegations of widespread corruption among New York City police

Date: Established in 1970; issued report in 1972

Significance: This commission investigated and substantiated unprecedented levels of police corruption, resulting in the dismissal and prosecution of police officers and a massive restructuring of New York City's police department.

Named after its appointed leader, Whittman Knapp, the Knapp Commission was charged with the responsibility of investigating allegations of extreme police corruption among officers within the New York City Police Department (NYPD). The commission was impaneled in 1970 by Mayor John Lindsay after he learned that *The New York Times* was preparing to publish a major exposé of rampant police misconduct in the city's police department. The newspaper's primary informants were NYPD officers Sergeant David Durk and Detective Frank Serpico, both of whom agreed to talk to the newspaper after their police supervisors and the mayor's office ignored their concerns about police corruption in the department.

The commission held public hearings to investigate the behavior of police officers alleged to be "dirty cops"; it also examined the organizational structure of the police department. The hearings were contentious, with police officers testifying against fellow officers about their involvement in bribery, prostitution, drug rings, and illegal gambling.

The commission eventually found that there was, indeed, widespread corruption within the police department. In its report, it classified corrupt officers as "meat-eaters" and "grass-eaters." The former were officers who aggressively sought out bribes or other corrupt activity; the latter were officers who accepted bribes or partook in unethical behavior when opportunities were presented to them.

The commission's findings led to a massive restructuring of the police department, dismissals of many officers and supervisors, and criminal prosecutions of dirty cops. In response to controversies surrounding the commission, the mayor abolished it in 1972. A year later, the problem of corruption in the NYPD received new national attention with the release of the film *Serpico*, which was based on Peter Maas's book about the Knapp Commission's star witness.

Rachel Bandy

Further Reading

Armstrong, Michael F. *They Wished They Were Honest: The Knapp Commission and New York City Police Corruption*. New York: Columbia UP, 2012. Print.

City of New York. *The Knapp Commission Report on Police Corruption*. New York: Braziller, 1972. Print.

Delattre, Edwin J. *Character and Cops: Ethics in Policing*. 4th ed. Washington, DC: Amer. Enterprise Inst., 2002. Print.

Serpico, Frank. "The Police Are Still Out of Control." *Politico*. Politico, 23 Oct. 2014. Web. 24 May 2016.

Sherman, Lawrence W., ed. *Police Corruption: A Sociological Perspective*. Garden City: Anchor, 1974. Print.

See also Civilian review boards; Internal affairs; Law enforcement; Police; Police corruption; Police ethics; Police powers.

Kyllo v. United States

The Case: U.S. Supreme Court ruling on warrantless searches
Date: Decided on June 11, 2001
Criminal justice issues: Search and seizure; substance abuse
Significance: This case established that government use of technology not commonly employed by the public to sense images, sounds, or smells coming from homes is a form of search and thus requires a warrant.

In 1991, Agent William Elliott of the U.S. Department of the Interior suspected that Danny Kyllo was growing marijuana in his Florence, Oregon, residence. Initially, Elliott believed that Kyllo resided with his estranged wife, Luanna, who had recently been arrested on drug charges. Additionally, known drug dealers occupied two of the units in the triplex in which Kyllo resided. Further, Kyllo allegedly advised a police informant that both he and his wife could supply marijuana. Elliott also reviewed Kyllo's electrical utility records and found that his home's power usage was unusually high.

Based on this information, Elliott and Dan Haas, a member of the Oregon National Guard, used an Agema Thermovision 210 thermal imager to scan the triplex in which Kyllo lived on January 16, 1992. The device was used to determine whether the amount of heat emanating from Kyllo's home was consistent with the amount of power used by the types of high-intensity lamps often associated with indoor marijuana growing. Within minutes, the scan revealed that the garage roof and one wall were noticeably hotter than the rest of Kyllo's home and the other parts of his triplex.

Producing the results of the scan, the information provided by the informant, and Kyllo's subpoenaed utility bills, Elliott obtained a warrant from a federal magistrate judge to search Kyllo's home. The search found weapons, illegal drug paraphernalia, and more than one hundred marijuana plants.

After he was indicted on a federal drug charge, Kyllo unsuccessfully moved to suppress the evidence seized from his home. He conditionally pleaded guilty to the charge of producing marijuana and was subsequently sentenced to five and one-half years in prison. The district court considering Kyllo's appeal decided that the warrantless thermal imaging scan of Kyllo's home was permissible under the Fourth Amendment. The court reasoned that the thermal imager did not reveal any intimate details of Kyllo's home, and that only the heat being emitted from the home was recorded. Additionally, the court concluded that there was sufficient probable cause to issue the search warrant.

Kyllo next appealed the district court's decision. Ultimately, an appeals court upheld the decision of the lower court, maintaining that use of the device revealed nothing more than the amount of heat rising from the home and that Kyllo had not attempted to conceal the heat.

The U.S. Supreme Court heard Kyllo's case on February 20, 2001, and released its decision on June 11, 2001. Five of the nine justices ruled in favor of Kyllo, thus reversing the decision of the appellate court. The opinion, delivered by Justice Antonin Scalia, stated that exploration of the details of the home that would have been "unknowable without physical intrusion" qualifies as a search and is unreasonable without a warrant.

Christine Ivie Edge

Further Reading
Katsh, M. Ethan. *Clashing Views on Controversial Legal Issues*. Guilford, Conn.: McGraw-Hill/Dushkin, 2004.
LaFave, Wayne R. *Search and Seizure: A Treatise on the Fourth Amendment*. 3d ed. St. Paul, Minn.: West Publishing, 1996.

See also *Chimel v. California*; *Illinois v. Krull*; *Maryland v. Buie*; Probable cause; Search and seizure; Search warrants; Stakeouts; Supreme Court, U.S.

Law enforcement

Definition: Component of the criminal justice system that is responsible for such functions as crime prevention and fighting, order maintenance, conflict management, and other services
Significance: American law enforcement encompasses approximately 17,500 different public agencies at the local, state, and federal levels of government that employ about 750,000 sworn officers. Primary law enforcement is performed at the local level, which includes cities, municipalities, and counties. State and federal law-enforcement officials enforce laws at their levels of government and also assist local law-enforcement agencies with their functions.

Depending on the local jurisdiction, law-enforcement officers may serve as police officers or deputy sheriffs. The United States has a mixture of police departments and sheriff offices/departments which serve a variety of different functions.

History

American law enforcement has its roots in English history. Modeled on the principles and structure of the London Metropolitan Police Force of the early nineteenth century, early American policing began in earnest during the mid-nineteenth century in response to the urban problems brought on by the Industrial Revolution, as increasing numbers of people lived and worked together in densely populated and racially and ethnically diverse communities. Early American policing was tainted by the significant influences of politics and local politicians who sought to gain control of the police for political purposes. Appointments and promotions were based largely on the value of individual officers to the local political authorities responsible for administering police departments. Corruption and political patronage were very common in departments.

From the mid-nineteenth century through the early twentieth century the functions of law enforcement in the United States included not only the traditional crime-fighting roles but also social services that complemented local social service agencies in assisting the poor and disadvantaged. As law enforcement entered the twentieth century and technology advanced, political pressures on police lessened, and departments became more professional. Among the changes taking place during this era of professionalization, or reform, included the adoption of motorized patrol using automobiles and motorcycles, the application of civil service system hiring processes, improved training, forensic science improvements, and a general increased profile with the public.

The Prohibition era of the 1920s elevated the influence of organized crime, placing the Federal Bureau of Investigation in the media spotlight and cementing the "crime-fighting" image of law enforcement for several decades. By contrast, the social turmoil of the 1960s soiled the reputation of local law enforcement as a result of direct confrontations between police and war protesters, civil rights demonstrators, and drug users. Many of these confrontations provoked police to use excessive force, thereby damaging their image among the citizens whom they were sworn to serve and protect. This era of policing resulted in a number of significant changes within the law-enforcement community.

In 1968, the US Congress enacted the Omnibus Crime Control and Safe Streets Act, which created the Law Enforcement Assistance Administration. This agency was created to improve police professionalism and increase the capacity to fight crime. It provided federal grants to local police to improve their crime-fighting technology and subsidize the education of police officers who wanted to make law enforcement their careers.

Efforts were also made to improve police-community relationships with the intent to forge partnerships with the community to fight crime and improve the quality of life. This eventually evolved into a philosophical change in policing from a primarily reactive response to problems to a combination reactive/proactive response in which problem solving became the primary focus of law enforcement through the implementation of a community policing strategy. This strategy has carried into the twenty-first century.

Organizational Structure

Law-enforcement agencies typically include operational and administrative, or support services, components. The offices of police chief, police commissioner, and police superintendent are generally separate components. Operational components usually include basic pa-

Drug Enforcement Administration special agent. (Public domain, via Wikimedia Commons)

trol operations and criminal-investigation branches. They often also include traffic enforcement and special operations divisions.

The administrative components typically encompass the more purely administrative, or "business," functions of the agencies, such as human resources offices, training divisions, crime laboratories, fleet management, information management, and other support services.

The offices of police chiefs normally include the chiefs' administrative staffs; internal affairs, or investigative, components; and inspections components, which handle internal audits. Public affairs, or media offices, are also placed under the chiefs' offices.

Local Police Functions

The primary functions of local law-enforcement agencies revolve around basic law enforcement and crime fighting. These functions include the enforcement of state laws and local ordinances and codes. Law-enforcement officers arrest violators and often testify in trials. Officers are also responsible for order and conflict management. They break up fights, intervene in violent domestic disputes, and other conflicts, which often include disagreements between landlords and their tenants and merchants and their consumers.

Local agencies' crime prevention responsibilities include helping to educate the public on how to reduce opportunities for crime and initiating local plans to prevent terrorist activities. The intelligence responsibilities of law enforcement require officers to gather information that may assist their agencies to reduce crime and improve the quality of life in the local communities.

Local agencies are also usually responsible for enforcing traffic laws and investigating accidents. Their mission is to help reduce both the frequency of traffic accidents and their severity through systematic evaluations of problem areas. Local law enforcement also provides a vast array of other services, which include investigating animal complaints and handling juvenile and administrative matters.

State and Federal Law-Enforcement Agencies

Every US state has a primary state law-enforcement agency. Most have similar responsibilities. All state law-enforcement agencies are committed to working with myriad local law-enforcement agencies within their jurisdictions. The cooperative relationships between state and local agencies typically include memoranda of understanding (MOU) that spells out the duties and functions of the state and local agencies.

Female police officer in NYC. (By Michele Ursino, via Wikimedia Commons)

State law-enforcement agencies coordinate statewide criminal investigations, provide statewide forensic services and crime laboratory assistance, and enforce traffic laws on interstate highway systems.

Well over one hundred different federal departments and agencies have their own law-enforcement services. Of these, by far the largest and best known are the Federal Bureau of Investigation, the US Secret Service, the Bureau of Alcohol, Tobacco, Firearms and Explosives (ATF), and the Drug Enforcement Administration (DEA). These agencies investigate specifically federal crimes, coordinate investigations with state and local law-enforcement agencies, and assist in homeland security activities.

Law-Enforcement Standards

During the 1970s, it was widely recognized that there was a need to improve professionalism of law enforcement in agencies throughout the United States. To help achieve that goal, four prestigious law-enforcement organizations came together and developed professional standards in law enforcement. These groups included the International Association of Chiefs of Police (IACP), the National Sheriffs Association (NSA), the National Organization of Black Law Enforcement Executives (NOBLE), and the Police Executive Research Forum (PERF). Their work led to the creation of the Commission for the Accreditation of Law-Enforcement Agencies (CALEA) in 1979. A private commission, it comprises private and public sector executives who are dedicated to improving law-enforcement services in the United States.

The standards defined by the new commission covered many critical areas in law enforcement, including the use of deadly force, high-speed pursuit driving, prisoner processing and detention, hiring practices, training, patrol and investigative procedures, and handling of juvenile matters. By 2015, almost nine hundred separate law-enforcement agencies in the United States had been accredited by the commission for meeting its standards. However, some are skeptical about the efficacy of CALEA accreditation, with a 2009 study by the public policy research center Cato Institute finding that CALEA-accredited agencies in fact had a slightly higher average of incidents of police misconduct than nonaccredited agencies.

Community Policing

The vast majority of law-enforcement agencies in the United States engage in some form of community policing. This philosophy of policing was initiated in the 1970s as a result of a fundamental evaluation of how law-enforcement services were being provided and how well they worked. A philosophical switch from reactive to reactive/proactive policing made its debut.

The fundamental emphasis in community policing is developing active partnerships with communities to enhance mutual trust. After relationships are developed, the emphasis switches to problem solving and improving the quality of life within the communities. In contrast to earlier eras, when police felt that they could handle crime problems without active community involvement, the modern community-oriented policing era emphasizes the mutual benefits to be gained by police-community cooperation.

Modern police officers train in police academies that encourage critical thinking and train officers to see themselves as "project managers" within their beats. It is no longer acceptable for officers to be simply "report writers" who place bandages on problems and are content to let the next shifts deal with the same kinds of problems at the same locations. Officers are encouraged to think more creatively and to solicit assistance in problem solving from other governmental agencies, community groups, private sector groups, and the media.

Challenges

Law enforcement faces many new challenges in the twenty-first century. A primary challenge comes from new threats of terrorism, especially since the terrorist attacks on the United States of September 11, 2001. Police in every jurisdiction must now be alert to the danger signs of possible terrorist training and activity and know how to deal with the new threats. The challenge of facing the terrorism threat cannot be overestimated.

Shrinking law-enforcement budgets present another serious challenge. Agencies must continuously look at ways to carry out their functions in the most cost-efficient manner possible. Likewise, the recruitment, retention, scheduling, and deployment of police officers will continue to require innovative thinking and approaches on the part of police executives.

In the 2010s there has been increased scrutiny of police brutality and other misconduct, especially excessive force used against African American suspects. As a result, many police departments have had to rethink their training processes and increase oversight of individual officers through methods such as body cameras.

As modern technologies continue to change and grow more complex, so, too, do the challenges to law enforcement to keep up with the changes. Computerization of all aspects of law enforcement and improvements in communication—especially in dispatching centers—are now permanent priorities. Modernizing forensic services, such as DNA analysis, is also a critical concern.

Finally, there is an unprecedented need for interagency communication and cooperation. With criminal mobility increasing at an unprecedented pace, police must develop significant relationships with all levels of law enforcement and allied agencies in order to improve information sharing.

Jay Zumbrun

Further Reading

"America's Police on Trial: The United States Needs to Overhaul Its Law-Enforcement System." *Economist*. Economist Newspaper, 13 Dec. 2014. Web. 7 Dec. 2015.

Balko, Radley. *Rise of the Warrior Cop: The Militarization of America's Police Forces*. New York: PublicAffairs, 2013. Print.

Lardner, James, and Thomas A. Reppetto. *NYPD: A City and Its Police: The Inside Story of New York's Legendary Police Department*. New York: Holt, 2000. Print.

Lee, Henry C., Timothy M. Palmbach, and Marilyn T. Miller. *Henry Lee's Crime Scene Handbook*. New York: Academic, 2001. Print.

Lesce, Tony. *Cops! Media vs. Reality*. Port Townsend: Loompanics, 2001. Print.

McElreath, David H., et al, eds. *Introduction to Law Enforcement*. Boca Raton: CRC, 2013. Print.

Morash, Merry, and Kevin J. Ford. *The Move to Community Policing*. Thousand Oaks: Sage, 2002. Print.

Packman, David. "Can Accreditation Affect Police Misconduct Rates?" *National Police Misconduct Reporting Project*. Cato Inst., 29 Nov. 2009. Web. 7 Dec. 2015.

Perlmutter, David D. *Policing the Media: Street Cops and Public Perception of Law Enforcement*. Thousand Oaks: Sage, 2001. Print.

Roth, Mitchel P. *Historical Dictionary of Law Enforcement*. Westport: Greenwood, 2000. Print.

Stevens, Dennis J. *Policing and Community Partnerships*. Upper Saddle River: Prentice, 2002. Print.

See also Campus police; Community-oriented policing; Criminal justice system; Federal Bureau of Investigation, U.S.; Highway patrols; Homeland Security, U.S. Department of; Marshals Service, U.S.; Police; Police chiefs; President's Commission on Law Enforcement and Administration of Justice; Sheriffs; Strategic policing; Women in law enforcement and corrections.

Law Enforcement Assistance Administration

Identification: Federal agency created to assist local law-enforcement bodies to combat civil unrest

Date: Created in 1968; abolished in 1982

Criminal justice issues: Federal law; law-enforcement organization; morality and public order

Significance: This short-lived federal agency was given responsibility for developing state and local law-enforcement agencies' riot control capabilities following massive urban riots during the mid-1960's, but the infusions of federal dollars were principally used for police equipment rather than broader programs to reduce violence.

The Law Enforcement Assistance Administration (LEAA) was created by Title I of the Omnibus Crime Control and Safe Streets Act of 1968. In response to a series of studies of urban violence in the 1960's and a growing fear of riots in more cities, the agency was established to provide federal funds and technical assistance to state and local law-enforcement agencies. Its mandates were to encourage state and local officials to adopt comprehensive plans to deal with the specific kinds of urban violence they might encounter and to build local capacities to respond effectively to the violence. In support of that activity, LEAA provided block grants to state and local law-enforcement agencies and undertook research on how to reduce the levels of violence and to improve the effectiveness of law-enforcement efforts. The clear priority in the grant program was to expand state and local capabilities in riot control, although relatively small amounts were also allocated to improve police-community relations and other programs to reduce racial conflict in some cities.

LEAA became a symbol of the "law and order" orientation of the federal government during the late 1960's and, later, of the ineffectiveness of that approach in reducing violence. Over the life of the agency, $5 billion was provided to state and local governments to respond to the threat of riots. The block-grant funding permitted local authorities to spend the money where they believed it was most needed, within the broad guidelines of the Omnibus Crime Control and Safe Streets Act. Most of the money was spent to improve policing capabilities rather than to address the causes of the violence or to reduce the level of tension between police and communities. In fact, so many local governments invested their LEAA grant money in police cars that the program was sometimes referred to as federal funding for "car buying." Money was also spent on communications equipment and weaponry for special weapons and tactics (SWAT) teams.

For the most part, the expenditures did little to reduce tension and violence. Subsequent studies of civil disorders even indicated that the police themselves tended to increase the levels of tension and often caused outbreaks of violence because of their poor training and insensitivity to community concerns. During the 1970's, studies by the Office of Management and Budget and other agencies severely criticized LEAA for not addressing the root causes of urban violence or improving relationships between police and other city officials and African American communities. The agency was eliminated in 1982.

William L. Waugh, Jr.

Further Reading

Button, James W. *Black Violence: Political Impact of the 1960's Riots*. Princeton, N.J.: Princeton University Press, 1978.

Connery, Robert, ed. *Urban Riots*. New York: Vintage Books, 1969.

Higham, Robin, ed. *Bayonets in the Streets: The Use of Troops in Civil Disturbances*. Lawrence: University of Kansas Press, 1969.

Report of the National Advisory Commission on Civil Disorders. New York: Bantam Books, 1968.

See also Law enforcement; Omnibus Crime Control and Safe Streets Act of 1968; President's Commission on Law Enforcement and Administration of Justice.

Marshals Service, U.S.

Identification: Oldest federal law-enforcement agency
Date: Created by the First Judiciary Act, September 24, 1789
Criminal justice issues: Federal law; law-enforcement organization
Significance: The Marshals Service has played a major role in the creation of law and order in the United States.

With the First Judiciary Act in 1789, Congress created the federal court system. As with most court systems, the enforcement arm associated with it provides security, serves court processes and generally enforces the orders issued by the court. To provide those services the First Judiciary Act also created the position of the United States marshal.

President George Washington appointed the first thirteen marshals within two days of the enactment of the act creating the position. By 1791, Washington had appointed the first sixteen marshals for the first sixteen federal judicial districts. The marshals played major roles in the growth and development of the United States. Their early duties included enforcing the Fugitive Slave Act, taking data for the national census, and helping create law and order in the American West.

Settling the West

The Marshals Service has a history of being a law-enforcement agency made up of generalists. This agency had the most broad law-enforcement powers and was used by the federal government and the courts to fill gaps that existed in the American federal judicial system. Prior to the Civil War and the creation of the Secret Service, marshals and their deputies were called upon to enforce laws against counterfeiting.

After the Civil War, famous Western lawmen served as deputy U.S. marshals. Among the most famous deputies were Bat Masterson and Wyatt Earp. The post-Civil War Oklahoma Territory was one of the deadliest places for deputy U.S. marshals to be assigned. It was in Oklahoma Territory that almost half of two hundred marshals and deputies were killed in the line of duty.

Beginnings of Modern Federal Law Enforcement

As the American justice system evolved, lawmakers created specialized federal law-enforcement agencies. By the mid-1920's, the Federal Bureau of Investigation (FBI), under the direction of J. Edgar Hoover, became what would be considered the premier federal law-enforcement agency. With the ascendancy of power and prestige for the FBI, and the quieting of the Wild West, the role of the United States marshal came to be reduced to one of bailiff for the federal courts. Marshals and their deputies called federal courts to order, maintained the peace in the courtroom, protected the judge, executed federal court orders, and transported federal prisoners.

After the passage of desegregation orders by the federal courts in the 1960's, U.S. marshals were called upon by then-attorney general of the United States, Robert Kennedy, to enforce the orders. With the passage of the Racketeer Influenced and Corrupt Organizations Act of 1970, there arose a need to protect witnesses who testified against organized crime figures. By 1971, witness security became a duty for the U.S. marshals.

In 1973, U.S. marshals were sent to Wounded Knee, South Dakota, to help quell violence on the Indian reservation there. During the 1970's, the marshals fulfilled a need for airport security created by a rash of skyjackings of commercial airliners. The marshals began profiling potential skyjackers and conducting weapons screening at airports. Eventually, the federal government created a permanent response to the threat of skyjacking by creating the "sky marshal" program within the Federal Aviation Administration. Although these agents are called

---

U.S. Marshals in the Movies

The 1993 film *The Fugitive*, directed by Andrew Davis, is about a distinguished surgeon (Harrison Ford) who is wrongly convicted of killing his wife. After escaping from incarceration, the surgeon attempts to find his wife's true killer. Meanwhile, a relentless U.S. marshal (Tommy Lee Jones) leads a team that tries to track him down. The marshall eventually comes to believe that his quarry is innocent, but that fact does not deter him from doing his duty.

Based on a long-running television series of the same title, *The Fugitive* highlights one of the roles played by a little-known branch of law enforcement: the U.S. Marshal Service. As the film reveals, marshals have responsibility for apprehending fugitives, as well as protecting witnesses and judges involved in federal cases. Other films about the U.S. Marshals include *U.S. Marshals* (1998), a sequel to *The Fugitive*, and *Out of Sight* (1998), in which Jennifer Lopez plays a marshal named Karen Sisco. The latter film also inspired the short-lived television series *Karen Sisco*.

Timothy L. Hall

"marshals," they are not associated with or part of the United States Marshals Service.

By the late 1970's, the marshals again began to establish themselves as the agency to track down and arrest fugitives. In 1984, the passage of the Comprehensive Crime Control Act permitted law-enforcement agencies at the federal, state, and municipal levels to use federal law to seize assets used in or gained through the trafficking in drugs. The U.S. marshals became the federal agency to seize, manage, and dispose of these assets according to the laws and the orders of the courts.

During the 1990's, the Marshals Service became the first federal law-enforcement agency to be accredited by the Commission for Accreditation of Law Enforcement Agencies (CALEA).

Twenty-first Century Roles

Among the duties of the modern United States Marshals Service are providing for the physical security of courtrooms, courthouses, and their occupants. Included in this charge is the personal protection of judges and prosecutors who may have been threatened in the course of their jobs. Marshals serve court orders, including restraining orders, writs of *habeas corpus*, summonses, subpoenas, warrants, and warrants in rem and writs of attachment for the court-ordered seizure of property. Marshals escort federal prisoners to and from court and also assist state and municipal agencies with international extradition and are involved in international prisoner exchanges.

U.S. marshals investigate fugitive cases for federal agencies without arrest authority—and for some agencies with arrest authority. The marshals have memoranda of understanding with both the U.S. Customs Service and the Drug Enforcement Administration to locate and arrest fugitives under their jurisdictions.

The Marshals Service helps the Department of State guard and protect foreign dignitaries while the General Assembly of the United Nations is in session in New York. Deputy marshals have been U.S. delegates to Interpol, the international police organization headquartered in France. It is through Interpol that the United States can share information on fugitives with other countries.

In 2004, U.S. marshals were appointed by and served at the pleasure of the president, and there were ninety-four United States marshals. Each federal judicial district has a marshal. The position of deputy U.S. marshal is a civil-service position which involves a competitive hiring process. In order to be deputized, individuals must compete for openings by taking a written test, undergoing an interview, and passing stringent physical exams as well as background investigations. The deputy select must then pass a rigorous training program at the Federal Law Enforcement Training Center in Brunswick, Georgia.

Gerald P. Fisher
Updated by Timothy L. Hall

Further Reading

Calhoun, Frederick S. *Hunters and Howlers: Threats and Violence Against Federal Judicial Officials in the United States, 1789-1993.* Arlington, Va.: U.S. Department of Justice, 1998. History of the U.S. Marshals Service by an agency historian.

Sabbag, Robert. *Too Tough to Die: Down and Dangerous with the U.S. Marshals.* New York: Simon Schuster, 1992. Examination of the modern marshals that follows the exploits of some of the more colorful deputies.

Stroud, Carsten. *Deadly Force: In the Streets with the U.S. Marshals.* New York: Bantam Books, 1996. Exploits of modern federal fugitive hunters.

See also Attorney General, U.S.; Bailiffs; Bench warrants; Justice Department, U.S.; Law enforcement; Parole; Prison escapes; Probation, adult; September 11, 2001, attacks; Skyjacking; Parole Commission, U.S.; Witness protection programs.

MOVE bombing

The Event: Attempt to evict illegal squatters that killed eleven people and destroyed sixty-one homes
Date: May 13, 1985
Place: Philadelphia, Pennsylvania
Criminal justice issues: Government misconduct; police powers
Significance: One of the most controversial government actions of modern times, the Philadelphia city government's use of a bomb to evict squatters was widely condemned and raised questions about the limits of government power.

MOVE, founded in 1972 by Vincent Leaphart, who adopted the name "John Africa," was a group of "back-to-nature" activists with an unusual and inconsistent philosophy. Although they advocated going back to nature, they were an urban movement. They shunned modern technology but used an elaborate loudspeaker system to bombard neighbors with their views. They decried pollution but littered property with their garbage and human waste.

The origin of the name "MOVE" is unclear. Not an acronym, it is generally believed to be merely a shortened form for the term "movement." MOVE first received media attention in 1978, when Philadelphia police clashed with members when police tried to evict them from an illegally occupied house. One police officer was killed, and eight officers and firefighters were wounded. Nine MOVE members were convicted of murder.

After failing to win the release of their imprisoned colleagues, MOVE members barricaded their new residence in a middle-class neighborhood, hooked up an elaborate sound system, and bombarded their neighbors for twelve hours per day with their profanity-laced speeches. This continued for more than two years, despite repeated appeals to the city by neighborhood residents. Philadelphia Mayor Wilson Goode, that city's first African American mayor, chose to ignore the appeals of local residents. At one point, Mayor Goode announced that he preferred "to have dirt and some smell than to have death." The denouement, however, included dirt, smell, and death.

After local residents held a press conference on May 1, 1985, criticizing the city's inaction, city officials decided to take aggressive action. On May 13, 1995, Police Commissioner Gregore Sambor told MOVE members to vacate their two-story row house. Tear gas was fired into the house, and a gun battle commenced. Twelve hours later, MOVE members still occupied the house. Police officials requested and received Goode's permission to drop a satchel filled with explosives onto the roof of MOVE's house. The goal was to dislodge a rooftop bunker; the result, however, was a fire that quickly got out of control. By the time the fires were controlled, eleven MOVE members, including four children, were dead. Only one thirty-year-old woman and one thirteen-year-old boy escaped alive. In addition to the deaths, two city blocks were destroyed, and sixty-one homes were reduced to embers.

Aftermath

Newspapers across the nation and throughout the world condemned the mayor's decision to drop the bomb, but a majority of local residents, both black and white, supported Goode and the police department. By the mid-1990's, the MOVE bombing had cost Philadelphia $30 million, and legal action was still pending. The city rebuilt the sixty-one destroyed homes, paid settlements to residents for lost belongings, and paid damages to the families of slain MOVE members. A 1986 citizens' commission concluded that Goode and the police and fire commissioners had "exhibited a reckless disregard for life and property." Goode was reelected to another four-year term in 1987.

Darryl Paulson

Further Reading
Anderson, John, and Hilary Hevenor. *Burning Down the House: Move and the Tragedy of Philadelphia*. New York: John Wiley & Sons, 1990.
Assefa, Hizkias, and Paul Wahrhaftig. *The MOVE Crisis in Philadelphia: Extremist Groups and Conflict Resolution*. Pittsburgh, Pa.: University of Pittsburgh Press, 1990.
"MOVE Plaintiffs Awarded $1.5 Million in 1985 Bombing." *Jet*, July 15, 1996.
Wagner-Pacifici, Robin. *Discourse and Destruction: The City of Philadelphia Versus MOVE*. Chicago: University of Chicago Press, 1994.

See also Deadly force; King beating case; Police powers.

National Guard

Identification: Military force with the dual mission of being on call to serve as state militia units and acting as a reserve force of the U.S. Army and Air Force during war time and in federally declared emergencies
Date: Authorized under the Militia Act of 1903
Criminal justice issues: Federal law; law-enforcement organization; military justice
Significance: Organized, equipped, and trained for combat as part of the federal military, and to respond to state emergencies such as riots and natural disasters.

In the early twentieth century, the National Guard replaced the old organized militia as well as the regiments that the individual states had raised for federal service during wartime. The National Guard became the vehicle for continued state participation in federal war efforts. However, when the National Guard is not performing its federal military missions, its units are controlled by state governments for local law-enforcement and disaster relief missions.

State and Federal Origins

The modern National Guard originated during widespread labor strikes in the coal industry in 1877. State militia units then in existence were either unable or unwilling to confront the strikers. As a result, state and business leaders supported the idea of increased federal support for militia in the form of the National Guard. The National Guard's first complete mobilization occurred during World War I, when the entire National Guard entered

National Guard troops maintaining a safe pathway for African American students to enter Little Rock's Central High School during the 1957 integration crisis. (Library of Congress)

the Army of the United States, thus leaving the states without organized militias.

A need for state militia arose during the two years following the war, when new labor and racial unrest often overwhelmed police forces. When the Boston police went on strike in 1919, Massachusetts mobilized its own state guard, which it had formed to replace the National Guard as the state militia to maintain order during the war. However, most states did not have replacements for their National Guard forces. Use of the National Guard in modern major military conflicts has varied. National guardsmen comprised only a tiny percentage of combat troops in Vietnam. In fact, National Guard service was seen by many as a way to fulfill military service requirements while avoiding combat deployment. By contrast, National Guard troops comprised roughly 15% of troops deployed to Afghanistan and Iraq during the first six years following the attacks of September 11, 2001. Because the vast majority of National Guardsmen serve in a part-time "citizen soldier" capacity unless activated or mobilized, lengthy deployments can place significant strains on them, their families, employers, and communities. Since September 2001, the National Guard has played the key role in homeland defense.

Posse Comitatus

Under the Posse Comitatus Act of 1878, federal military forces are not permitted to perform civil law-enforcement duties. Although the National Guard is primarily a federal military force, its units are not inhibited by the Posse Comitatus Act while acting under state authority. State governors can therefore employ their National Guard units for law enforcement without the restrictions that would be placed on the same troops in federal status.

Prior to the creation of state police forces between the world wars, the National Guard provided many of the services later provided by state police. However, because National Guard units are organized, trained, and equipped primarily for military combat, National Guard leaders encouraged the development of state police, allowing guard units to distance themselves from controversial civilian disturbances, such as strike breaking, which had cost the guard the support of organized labor.

The Civil Rights and Antiwar Movements

The late 1950s and 1960s saw new civil disorders with the rise of the Civil Rights movement and widespread opposition to the Vietnam War, and the guard again became involved with civil law enforcement. For political and global strategic reasons, few National Guard units were sent to Vietnam. In Tennessee and Kentucky, the guard provided credible service in protecting black students entering what had been white-only public high schools. The attempt by Arkansas governor Orville Faubus to use the National Guard units to prevent black students from attending Central High School in Little Rock in 1957 moved President Dwight D. Eisenhower to federalize Arkansas's National Guard. A small number of Arkansas National Guard troops, supported by U.S. Army soldiers, ensured that the black students were able to enter the school safely.

The National Guard was also called up during episodes of urban rioting. In 1965, for example, California's National Guard responded to rioting in the Watts section of Los Angeles. Two years later Michigan called out its National Guard to restore civil order in Detroit. As a result of the evident shortcomings in the guard's performance during the Detroit riots, guardsmen received additional training and equipment to deal with civilian law-enforcement missions. In 1968, the National Guard responded to riots in twenty-seven states and the District of Columbia. Many of these disturbances followed the assassination of civil rights leader Martin Luther King, Jr., in April of that year.

Opposition to the Vietnam War also brought increased use of the guard in domestic police actions during the 1960s and early 1970s. The most infamous incident occurred on Kent State University in Ohio. On May 4, 1970, a clash between protesters and a company of the National Guard ended when guardsmen opened fire on the protesters. Four civilians were killed and another nine were injured, after almost sixty guardsmen had been injured by rocks and bottles thrown at them. After the Kent State incident, guardsmen received more training in riot control; however, governors became increasingly hesitant to use the guard for similar missions.

Of particular significance to criminal justice is the military criminal jurisdiction over National Guard troops. When federalized, the federal Uniform Code of Military Justice applies; when in state status, the state's military justice system, if the state has one, applies. Actions by troops in state status in a state with no military justice code are subject to the state criminal code applicable to civilians.

Barry M. Stentiford
Updated by Eric Merriam

Further Reading

Doubler, Michael D. *I Am the Guard: A History of the Army National Guard, 1636-2000*. Washington, D.C.: Army National Guard, 2001. Official history of the Army National Guard, with emphasis on the period since World War II.

Higham, Robin, ed. *Bayonets in the Streets: The Use of Troops in Civil Disturbances*. Lawrence: University of Kansas Press, 1969. History of the use of both federal and state soldiers during riots and other periods of civil unrest.

Mahon, John K. *History of the Militia and the National Guard*. New York: Macmillan, 1983. Part of the Macmillan Wars of the United States series. Especially valuable for its coverage of the nineteenth century militia.

Preiss, Robert A. *The National Guard and Homeland Defense, Joint Force Quarterly*, Vol. 36, Dec. 2004. Explanation of National Guard's role in homeland defense and military support to civil authorities.

Stentiford, Barry M. *The American Home Guard: The State Militia in the Twentieth Century*. College Station: Texas AM Press, 2002. Study of state militia units not part of the National Guard. Emphasizes the inability of the National Guard to perform state functions during full federal mobilizations.

See also Boston police strike; Homeland Security, U.S. Department of; Martial law; Military justice; Right to bear arms; State police.

Neighborhood watch programs

Definition: Community programs designed to reduce local crime and fear of crime and help restore a sense of community

Criminal justice issues: Crime prevention

Significance: Since the 1970s, citizen involvement in crime prevention has increased, but questions about the effectiveness of citizen participation in reducing crime remain unanswered.

The modern movement of community crime prevention grew out of the realization that government institutions represented by the police and courts were failing in their efforts to reduce crime and restore social order. During the late 1960s and early 1970s, the neighborhood watch movement began as a grassroots effort to reduce burglaries in residential homes, it quickly became linked with other urban police programs.

Neighborhood watch programs are grounded in two theoretical crime prevention models: informal social

Neighborhood watch sign in Memphis, Tennessee. (By Thomas R Machnitzki, via Wikimedia Commons)

control and opportunity reduction. Informal social control assumes that maintaining public peace is not the primary responsibility of the police. Order should be maintained by unconscious networks of voluntary controls and standards among members of communities and enforced by the people themselves. The opportunity reduction model emphasizes the value of deterrence through modifying physical environments to improve security and maintain an informed group of citizens who adapt certain techniques to reduce criminal victimization.

Neighborhood watch programs involve small groups of people connected by their neighborhoods who share information provided by local law-enforcement agencies on local crime problems. Block meetings are organized by police officers who are trained in crime prevention techniques. The meetings offer training in crime strategies, surveillance, home security surveys, internal communications, and property markings or signage.

Neighborhood residents help provide surveillance by becoming the "eyes and ears" of the police, to whom they report suspicious activities. They also establish communication networks by setting up telephone trees with which to disseminate information quickly, utilizing computer communications, and holding periodic meetings. Individual residents improve their own home security by creating written, photographic, and electronic records of their assets. Residents participating in the programs post permanent signs in their yards advertising the fact that neighborhood watch programs are at work.

Effectiveness of the Programs

Citizen involvement in crime prevention began increasing rapidly during the mid-1990s. Neighborhood watch programs have forged partnerships between the police and communities and helped to reduce the isolation and fear that criminal activity fosters within communities. However, questions remain whether the programs are effective tools in reducing crime. Two types of empirical studies have been used to support the concept of neighborhood watch; neighborhood surveys on citizen participation, and reactions to crime and the evaluation of crime prevention programs.

Neighborhood watch studies have garnered varied responses. Some studies have confirmed that citizen participation and informal social control mechanisms such as neighborhood watch can be implanted in communities where they do not already exist. However, some researchers find that citizen participation is a middle-class phenomenon and that neighborhood watch programs do not work in poor neighborhoods.

Tracie L. Keesee

Further Reading

Garofalo, James, and Maureen McLeod. *Improving the Use and Effectiveness of Neighborhood Watch Programs.* Washington, DC: Natl. Inst. of Justice, 1988. Print.

Hawkins, Janet. "Long Live Neighborhood Watch!" *Sheriff* 66.6 (2014): 42-45. Print.

Mann, Stephanie, and M. C. Blakeman. *Safe Homes, Safe Neighborhoods: Stopping Crime Where You Live.* Berkeley: Nolo, 1993. Print.

Monson, Thomas N., et al. *Community Watch Administration Manual.* 3rd ed. Medford: Crime Prevention Resources, 2003. Print.

Tonry, Michael, and David P. Farrington. *Building a Safer Society: Strategic Approaches to Crime Prevention.* Chicago: U of Chicago Press, 1995. Print.

See also Citizen's arrests; Community-based corrections; Community-oriented policing; Community service; Law enforcement; National Crime Information Center; National Institute of Justice; "Not-in-my-backyard" attitudes; Police; Strategic policing; Youth gangs.

Noble cause corruption

Definition: A form of illicit police behavior that ignores procedural guidelines in order to achieve an outcome the officer considers just.

Criminal justice issues: Government misconduct; morality and public order; professional standards

Significance: Police officers are charged with enforcing substantive law according to specific procedural guidelines. When such guidelines are ignored in pursuit of law enforcement, the constitutional rights of suspects are curtailed and the legitimacy of the police, and by extension the law itself, is jeopardized.

Noble cause corruption is best understood as a moralistic form of corruption. Typically, police corruption is described in terms of pecuniary ends: An officer is corrupt if he abuses his position for monetary gains. Noble cause corruption, however, begins with an explicitly morally good goal in mind: to achieve justice and retribution, at least as understood by the officer. This good and just end is the noble cause; the corruption is determined by the means the officer employs to arrive at this noble end. Noble cause corruption is often described as accepting unjust means to achieve just ends. Examples of noble cause corruption range from lying in court to planting evidence to secure a conviction.

It is useful to consider noble cause corruption in light of the social contract. The idea of a social contract implies that both the government and the governed assume specific responsibilities in exchange for the provision of services and obligations. In a very real sense, the police are the literal manifestation of the state's obligation under the social contract to enforce the law. In exchange, the body politic agrees to limit their own use of force in pursuit of justice, relying on the state to do so, while concomitantly agreeing to follow the law. When one party fails in their part of the contract, they free the other party of their obligations. Thus when a civilian commits a crime, police can abridge their freedom of movement through arrest.

Importantly, this legal action by the police is directed by specific procedural guidelines. Such guidelines are themselves a part of the social contract. When procedure is ignored, the government has broken its part of the social contract, leaving the populous to ignore its obligations, as well. In this sense, noble cause corruption, while noble in principle, undermines the very fabric of American law and order as framed by the social contract.

Theoretical Advances

Noble cause corruption is largely an atheoretical concept. In many respects, our understanding of noble cause corruption was born out of observing the behavior of the police in tandem with trying to understand how the police approach their job. There has been very little discussion concerning the actual etiology underlying this behavior. One of the earliest discussions of noble cause corruption by this name came from the philosopher Edwin DeLattre (although it had been discussed descriptively for several decades prior to DeLattre's volume) who approached the topic ethically.

Cooper did attempt to explicitly theorize noble cause corruption. Drawing from the work of Katz and Kahn, he suggested that noble cause corruption occurs as a result of role conflict. Namely, the police have an opposing role. As agents of the state, they must follow due process, but as protectors, they must safeguard the innocent. These two roles are inherently in conflict. Following the work of Carl Klockars, Cooper suggested that when faced with such a role conflict, officers will engage in behavior associated with the role that is most compelling. In this case, he argues that the role of protector is the most compelling. Due process is therefore ignored to meet a noble end.

Empirical Status

Little work has been done to explore noble cause corruption empirically. It largely remains a philosophical discussion couched in the language of ethics. What research has been done has suggested that noble cause corruption is, in fact, a measurable phenomenon. As a phenomenon, attempts to measure its frequency have been impeded by the large variety of ways it manifests in tandem with the irregularity with which police officers seemingly apply it. In other words, noble cause corruption is not unidimensional in any positivist sense; to this end, "noble cause corruption" is perhaps best employed as an umbrella term to describe a suite of behaviors. Keeping operational concerns in mind, and setting aside the fluid nature of noble cause corruption, research has found that as a moralistic form of corruption, noble cause corruption occurs less frequently than its economic counterpart. Key to moving forward in the empirical discussion of noble cause corruption is the realization that it is best understood as a part of the behavior of public organizations generally, rather than being uniquely attributable to the police.

Jonathon A. Cooper

Further Reading

Crank, John P., and Michael A. Caldero. *Police Ethics: The Corruption of Noble Cause.* New York: Routledge, 2011. Full elaboration on the characteristics and consequences of noble cause corruption among police.

DeLattre, Edwin J. *Character and Cops: Ethics in Policing.* Washington, D.C.: The AEI Press, 2006. Comprehensive volume on the ethics of policing, including a large section on noble cause corruption.

Ivkovic, Sanja K. *Fallen Blue Knights: Controlling Police Corruption.* New York: Oxford University Press, 2005. A general resource on police corruption, focused mostly on economic corruption but with important nods to moral corruption.

Klockars, Carl B. "The Dirty Harry Problem." *The Annals of the Academy of Political and Social Sciences* 452 (1980): 33-47. A classic article on the nature and etiology of noble cause corruption.

Muir, William K. Jr. *Police: Streetcorner Politicians*. Chicago: The University of Chicago Press, 1977. Seminal work on the nature of policing, including that of noble cause corruption.

See also Due process of law; Internal affairs; King beating case; Knapp Commission; Police brutality; Police ethics; Police subculture; Racial profiling.

Peace Officer Standards and Training

Identification: State programs establishing training and performance standards for law-enforcement officers
Date: First programs begun in 1959
Significance: Professional training and standards play a critical role in the quality and quantity of services delivered by the police, who are a major component of the American criminal justice system.

One criterion of any profession is that it defines minimum standards of performance and minimum amounts of training or preparation for its practitioners. Peace officers, or police or law-enforcement officers as they are more frequently called, throughout the criminal justice system in the United States all now claim professional status.

Development

By the middle of the nineteenth century, most large northeastern cities in the United States had some type of police, but there were no recognized standards or professional training for them. The idea that the police should have training and display the best of ethics had originated in 1829 in Great Britain's capital, London, where Sir Robert Peel created the Metropolitan Police Service. In 1893, the International Association of Chiefs of Police was formed in the United States, and it began advocating the training of police officers. However, it was not until 1960 that this association was to develop minimum training standards and promote them to the fifty states.

In 1929, President Herbert Hoover created the National Commission on Law Observance and Enforcement, which became known as the Wickersham Commission. It was the first major body to look into the workings of what would later become known as the American criminal justice system; it was also the first federal assessment of law enforcement throughout the United States. The commission's final reports on the police were highly critical, highlighting the lack of training and standards. The commission's official report made many recommendations, but as they were only recommendations, police around the nation were slow to change and adopt new ways.

Mid-Twentieth Century Progress

In 1953, the American Bar Association drafted a *Model Police Training Act* that sought to provide a model for those involved in or monitoring police training. During the mid-1960s, for the first time in the history of public-opinion polling, crime became the leading concern of Americans. President Lyndon B. Johnson created the President's Commission on Law Enforcement and Administration of Justice, and numerous blue-ribbon panels were appointed to study the problem. In 1968, the presidential commission published *The Police*, which made many recommendations for improving police training and education. *The Police* also recommended that each state establish a police officers standards and training body.

In 1959, California and New York became the first states to establish Peace Officer Standards and Training agencies. Over the next twenty-five years, the remaining states established their own agencies. Some states use different names for their offices, which makes for some confusion; however, California was the first with the name "Police Officers Standards and Training," and most police forces now simply use the term POST.

POST personnel serve as liaisons between government policy and lawmakers and law-enforcement agencies. They work with law-enforcement and police officers in general and with the heads of police academies and police training divisions, in particular.

Functions and Benefits

POST agencies work to increase the efficiency and effectiveness of the police by improving the quality and increasing the quantity of their training. Since police officers perform as they are trained, improved training helps to improve their performance. Systematic training also helps to make police work more uniform and more predictable within the state offering the training and lends an air of enhanced professionalism to the police.

Studies of police departments have found an inverse correlation between the numbers of hours of training that officers receive and the numbers of lawsuits that are brought against the departments. Training is perhaps the best insurance a law-enforcement agency can have against litigation. POST bodies closely monitor lawsuits against police departments because they point to areas in which additional training is needed. POST agencies function to assist police departments in reducing their liabilities.

If training appears not to affect how police and the public interact, then the POST agency must question whether the training being given is relevant to the work of the police. POST must take account of what the public expects and the nature of problems the police are facing. POST agencies function to keep training and standards current by ensuring that policing meets the needs and expectations of current conditions, in contrast to the desires of the police clique. As POST agencies work to improve the quantity and quality of training, society enjoys the benefits of more effective delivery of police services and increased public safety.

The beginning of the twenty-first century saw police standards and training being taken to higher levels. British and American police have long been the two models of modern policing for the rest of the world. During the 1990s, the U.S. State Department began work that led to the creation of four international law-enforcement academies. They are located in Roswell, New Mexico; Budapest, Hungary; Gaborone, Botswana; and Bangkok, Thailand. The concept of Peace Officer Standards and Training now serves to promote democracy and represent U.S. foreign policy worldwide.

Vic Sims

Further Reading

Charles, Michael. *Police Training: Breaking All the Rules*. Springfield: Charles C Thomas, 2000.

Guthrie, Edward. "Higher Learning and Police Training." *Law and Order* (December, 2000): 124.

Kenny, Dennis J., and Robert P. McNamara, eds. *Police and Policing: Contemporary Issues*. 2d ed. Westport, Conn.: Praeger Publishing, 1999.

Morash, Merry. *The Move to Community Policing: Making Change Happen*. Thousand Oaks, Calif.: Sage Publications, 2002.

Office of the United Nations High Commissioner for Human Rights. *Human Rights Standards and Practice for the Police*. New York: United Nations, 2004.

See also Community-oriented policing; DARE programs; Law enforcement; Police; Police academies; Police ethics; Wickersham Commission.

Police

Definition: Officers of municipal law-enforcement agencies whose primary mission is to protect their assigned communities from crime and general threats to public safety and well-being

Criminal justice issues: Law-enforcement organization; Police powers

Significance: Municipal police are the only segment of government that normally has the authority to use coercive force. As such, they represent a potentially coercive power of government. They have many responsibilities, but because it is they decide whom to arrest and take into custody based on current local, state, and federal laws, they are often considered the gatekeepers of the criminal justice system. Law enforcement agencies nationwide made 11.2 million arrests, excluding traffic violations, in 2014. During an average twenty-four-hour period, police make about forty thousand arrests—a fact that contributes to the United States having the highest incarceration rate in the world.

After the turn of the twenty-first century, almost one-half million uniformed and armed municipal police officers were employed by about 13,000 separate police departments to provide a variety of services to citizens. Before the terrorist attacks on the United States of September 11, 2001, municipal police were in the process of rapidly changing their philosophies to adopt more of a service orientation. This movement has continued; however, the threat of terrorism has renewed emphasis on law enforcement.

Police in a Changing Society Balancing the rights of individuals against the needs of society is always difficult but especially so in democracies. Municipal police do much more than enforce the law. The fact that most of them are armed and uniformed makes them the most visible representatives of government, and this, in turn, makes them lightning rods for individual and public woes.

Modern police have come to realize that their tasks are far more difficult and sometimes even impossible to accomplish without the cooperation and assistance of the public. As public ideas of what the police should do evolve, and as other variables come into play, the only obvious conclusion appears to be that the police are changing at an unprecedented rate. In the early twenty-first century, some police watchers suggested that US police departments had changed more in the previous ten years than they had in the previous century. Several things have contributed to the changes that define modern municipal police.

Some of the changes have been driven by the recognition of a vast gulf between what police officers actually do and what the public thinks they do. For example, while the public long believed that municipal police spent most of their time investigating and solving crimes, arresting suspects, and enforcing laws, research has shown that most officers now spend 20 percent or less of their time in such efforts. Most of their time is spent responding to calls for other types of service.

In contrast to the manner in which working police distribute their time, basic police training in police academies has historically devoted at least 80 percent of training to crime and law-enforcement functions and the remainder of the time to miscellaneous services. Modern police training is changing to reflect the tasks that police actually do, but task-analysis research focusing on the police is woefully lacking.

The federal Violent Crime Control and Law Enforcement Act of 1994 was the most far-reaching piece of anticrime legislation in US history. Among other things, it provided for the hiring of 100,000 new police officers—an approximately 25 percent increase nationwide. Many of the new officers were hired under the Police Corps program that was funded by the 1994 law and were four-year college graduates.

Changing Face of Police

The 1994 federal law changed the face of modern policing in several ways but perhaps none more profound than its injection of the college-educated into police roles. A 2015 study suggested that the higher the level of education, the less likely police officer will use force against citizens. A 2006 report by *USA Today* noted that in the state of Florida, 75 percent of all disciplinary actions were against police officers who held only high school diplomas. Officers with four-year degrees accounted for 11 percent of the disciplinary actions in that state. In 2003, about 25 percent of all adult Americans were college graduates—roughly the same percentage that was found among municipal police officers. At the same time, a higher percentage of American police chiefs had four-year college degrees. The relatively rapid influx of leaders with a college education into a profession as traditionally conservative and static as policing has helped to make municipal police more sensitive and responsive to society's changing needs.

A rapid increase in the number of women in policing has also contributed to changing the face of modern policing. According to Johnson (2015), only about 11 percent of police officers nationwide are women, it appears, however, that a critical mass has been reached, and the numbers of women police will rise. Research and replicated studies point to several attributes women bring to policing.

Although both men and women enter policing because of a desire to help people, they also appear to be attracted to the profession for different reasons. Men tend to be drawn to the potential for excitement and action, while women tend to have more of a service orientation. Women officers are far less likely than men to be involved in cases involving police brutality or police violence. At the same time, female officers initiate far more non-police contacts than male officers. This alone seems to cause increased interaction between the police and individuals members of the community. Male officers are far quicker to employ force than female officers, but research has shown that female officers do not hesitate to use force when it is clearly necessary. Women are also better than men at handling certain types of cases, such as sexual assaults and problems involving female victims or complainants in lower-income housing.

Standards and Training

The training of municipal police has improved significantly in both quantity and quality since the mid-1990s, and this development has improved delivery of police services. Some of this improvement can be quantified. Municipal governments have had to pay out millions of dollars in settlements with plaintiffs who have sued their police departments, and police now realize that improved training of officers is the best defense against future litigation. The availability of government funding has always been a powerful incentive. The move to community policing and the endless desire on the part of the police to improve and professionalize also played roles in increasing the hours and quality of training for municipal police

Boston police officers. (By Piotrus, via Wikimedia Commons)

New York City police officers. (By Cocoaguy, via Wikimedia Commons)

officers. The increasing complexity of police work contributed to the necessity of additional training.

Every state has a Police Officers Standards and Training, or POST, office that oversees municipal police departments and offers guidelines for training officers. The states now mandate minimum numbers of training hours for new officers; these requirements range from a low of 320 hours to a high of more than 1,200 hours—the equivalent of thirty forty-hour weeks of training. After officers complete the initial training, they must spend several additional months working under the supervision of field training officers. Only after both phases of their training are complete are the new officers allowed to work without supervision, and even then, most new officers remain on probationary status for several months more. Finally, many states now require all officers to continue their training with minimum numbers of in-service hours.

According to the *Washington Post* in 2016, the United States experienced 987 fatal shootings by on-duty police officers in 2015. In early 2016, police chiefs from across the United States met to discuss restructuring use-of-force procedures and training policies with the intent of decreasing the number of annual citizen fatalities caused by police officers. The forum was organized in the wake of intense and sometimes violent citizen protests following the well-publicized deaths of young, black males at the hands of police officers, namely Michael Brown in Furguson, Missouri, and Freddy Grey in Baltimore, Maryland. While many criticized organizers of the forum for being motivated solely by the increased media scrutiny during the Ferguson and Baltimore protests, organizers themselves pointed out that police departments must enact proactive change in policy before controversial fatalities occur.

Technology and Equipment

Municipal police have profited greatly from advances in technology. Police cruisers, for example, were traditionally sedans, most notably the Ford-produced Crown Victoria. As of 2012, when Ford ceased to manufacture that model, many police departments across the United States replaced the sedan with new technology-filled sport utility vehicles (SUVs). These new cruisers were equipped with all-wheel, four-wheel, or front-wheel drive and were more roomy than sedans to accommodate prisoners, police gear, and police equipment. Many included backup cameras, in-dashboard touchscreen computers, Bluetooth connectivity, and engines that alternate between four and eight cylinders in order to save fuel. Many police SUVs are rated for speeds reaching over 130 miles-per-hour.

Despite the advances in motorized technology that supports police departments across the United States, police mountain bicycles are still considered effective tools in law enforcement. Many officers find them effective for their versatility, cost efficiency, and accessibility to crime and medical emergencies. Bike patrol, as it is often referred to, allows police to remain mobile and visible in myriad situations and environments. The average cost of a police mountain bike in 2015 was $1,200, which is a fraction of the cost of a fully-equipped SUV.

The refinement and sophistication of small portable radios and cell phones have freed field officers from dependence on patrol cars, while permitting them to remain in constant communication with their departments as they become far more accessible to the public. Virtually all municipal police departments now make extensive use of computers, and all large-city police departments enjoy the benefits of geographic information systems, which are used for crime mapping. Geographic information systems enable community policing to change the focus from the individual criminal to the areas where the crimes are committed, thus striking more closely at the roots of problems. Three-fourths of municipal police officers have access to in-field computers, and more than one-half have Internet access. Such technology greatly increases information sharing among different agencies.

Scholarly research on policing did not begin in earnest until the 1970s, and it was another two or three decades until replication studies were used to implement and institutionalize scholarly research findings into police practice and policy in the field. Through those years, research-based policing gradually replaced policing driven by emotions and tradition. Fewer police officers overlooked the law and proper procedures for the sake of expediency or custom. The quality of police services improved noticeably because research-based policing proved far more effective than traditional policing.

Community-Oriented Policing

Of all the changes in municipal policing around the turn of the twenty-first century, none was as well known or had an impact as great as the adoption of the new philosophy of community-oriented policing. Community policing has been defined in many ways, but as is the case with many complex subjects, it seems to defy precise definition. In general, community policing attempts to move municipal police ever closer to the ideal of the early nineteenth century founder of London's metropolitan police, Sir Robert Peel, that the people are the police, and the police are the people.

The most successful community policing efforts and programs have been those that have resulted in closer permanent working relationships between police and individual citizens. The idea that the police are the experts and always know what is best for a city quickly has given way to the understanding that more can be accomplished when everyone works together to solve serious problems with long-range solutions, rather than applying quick fixes to the symptoms of the problems. Community-oriented policing involves community leaders who are often better equipped than police to engage fresh challenges and transform problems into opportunities.

During the 1990s, community policing reached a point of critical mass when the U.S. Congress passed the Violent Crime Control and Law Enforcement Act, which made billions of federal dollars available to municipal police departments to adopt community policing. Much of the funding was used to recruit a new breed of police officers, who quickly made their presence felt. At the same time, a new generation of college-educated police chiefs provided leadership that helped municipal policing to reach an unprecedented level of effectiveness.

The United States has always been an energized, dynamic society, and the terrorist attacks of September 11, 2001, served to renew the country's commitment to improve and strengthen itself. As society changes, so do the police. In 2002, the International Association of Chiefs of Police adopted a resolution that recognized that the country's most powerful intelligence source is its citizenry and that community policing is the best means of tapping into that intelligence.

Vic Sims

Further Reading

Beiser, H. Dan. "Police Agencies Find It Hard to Require Degrees." *USA Today.* Gannett, 18 Sept. 2006. Web. 15 June 2016.

Dunham, Roger G., and Geoffrey P. Alpert. *Critical Issues in Policing.* 7th ed. Long Grove: Waveland, 2015. Print.

Gaines, Larry, and Victor Kappeler. *Policing in America.* 8th ed. Waltham: Elsevier, 2015. Print.

Henion, Andy, and William Terrill. "Do Cops Need College?" *MSU.* Michigan State University, 5 Feb. 2015. Web. 15 June 2016.

Johnson, Kevin. "Women Move Into Law Enforcement's Highest Ranks." *USA Today.* Gannett, 2 Dec. 2015. Web. 15 June 2016.

Lardner, James, and Thomas A. Reppetto. *NYPD: The Inside Story of New York's Legendary Police Department.* New York: Henry Holt, 2000. Print.

Lesce, Tony. *Cops: Media vs. Reality.* Port Townsend: Loompanics, 2001. Print.

Lowery, Wesley. "Police Chiefs Consider Dramatic Reforms to Officer Tactics, Training to Prevent So Many Shootings." *Washington Post.* Washington Post, 29 January 2016. Web. 15 June 2016.

Morash, Merry, and Kevin J. Ford. *The Move to Community Policing.* Thousand Oaks: Sage, 2002. Print.

Peak, Kenneth. *Policing in America: Methods, Issues, Challenges.* 5th ed. Upper Saddle River: Pearson, 2006. Print.

Schultz, Paul D. "The Future Is Here: Technology in Police Departments." *Police Chief.* International Association of Chiefs of Police, June 2016. Web. 20 June 2016.

Stevens, Dennis J. *Policing and Community Partnerships.* Upper Saddle River: Prentice Hall, 2002. Print.

Walker, Samuel, and Charles M. Katz. *The Police in America: An Introduction.* 8th ed. New York: McGraw-Hill, 2013. Print.

See also Campus police; Community-oriented policing; Highway patrols; Police academies; Police brutality; Police chiefs; Police civil liability; Police corruption; Police ethics; Police powers; Sheriffs; Special weapons and tactics teams (SWAT); State police; Women in law enforcement and corrections.

Police academies

Definition: Training schools for police recruits

Criminal justice issues: Law-enforcement organization; Professional standards

Significance: For almost all new police recruits, police academies provide the only formal training they receive before they begin their initial police assignments.

Before the establishment of the first state-accredited police training academies, local police departments had little assistance in the training of their recruits. Many recruits were simply handed badges and guns and then expected to learn all they needed to know in the course of their work. Now, however, training for new officers is both intense and nearly universal in the United States. Most police officers must undergo from 400 to 800 hours of training before they take up their duties. Instructors at police academies are mostly police officers, either retired or active. Experts in their fields, instructors often bring to bear many real-life examples from their own field experience.

The atmosphere in police academies has traditionally been paramilitary and autocratic. Since the 1980s, however, increasing numbers of academies are emphasizing educational training, while relaxing some of their paramilitary traits, such as rigid dress codes. A traditional emphasis on weapons training, handling of suspects, and physical aspects of police work has not greatly changed, but it has been supplemented by training in other areas. For example, modern police academies' curricula may include courses on the criminal justice system in the United States and the role of police within it; constitutional law, particularly due process issues and police civil liability; ethics; cultural diversity issues; and interaction with such "special needs" groups as persons with mental disabilities, the elderly, and victims of rape and domestic violence.

In addition to their formal curricula, police academies help recruits adjust to the culture of police service. As trainees hear the firsthand experiences of veterans, they come to think of themselves as part of a brotherhood whose members must band together and constantly be on guard against unforeseen perils. Such perils may come from civilians they encounter in their work, regardless of age or sex. An element of professionalism is another by-product of academy training, as recruits learn about proper dress and appearance, acceptable behaviors in public, and the importance of having a network of respectable friends.

Negative Aspects of Academies

Along with their positive characteristics, police academies sometimes foster, directly or indirectly, questionable views and behaviors among recruits. For example, careful studies of academies have documented sexist attitudes and comments among both recruits and instructors that reflect a lack of confidence among male police officers that female officers are capable of meeting the physical demands of police work, such as handling weapons and violent suspects. In its grossest manifestations, antifemale bias takes the form of sexual harassment during academy training and later in the field.

Although police academies do not officially sanction such bias, researchers have documented "hidden" curricula that may actually encourage it. Examples include the use of exclusively male pronouns by instructors in references to law-enforcement personnel, including the re-

The Police Academy of the New York Police Department. (By Beyond My Ken, via Wikimedia Commons)

cruits themselves; uses of exclusively male examples when discussing matters related to police work methods and dress; and established male "zones" of casual conversation and activities that female recruits are discouraged from entering. Instructors occasionally perpetuate assumptions that women are less able than men to fight and handle weapons and that it is dangerous for officers to have female partners in physically challenging situations.

In the guise of "protecting" women by treating them more gently, academy instructors and recruits sometimes reinforce stereotypes about feminine fragility. It has also been charged that the images of women used in academy training materials sometimes portray women as weak sex objects. This in turn sometimes leads male recruits to pay less serious attention to aspects of their training relating to domestic violence and rape intervention. There is also some evidence indicating that female academy instructors are treated with less respect than their male counterparts.

Another dark side in the development of a police culture in academy training is drinking behavior. Some research indicates that the amount of time that recruits spend drinking with their relatives and friends decreases significantly after they have spent six months in academies, while the amount of time they spend drinking with other recruits increases significantly. There are also increases in the overall frequency and quantity of drinking.

A survey of Australian police recruits on this problem found that nearly one-half of the recruits felt some pressure to drink more during their training. Moreover, the increased drinking that began during their training did not decrease during their first six months as officers in the field. These patterns develop despite the fact that more than 90 percent of the recruits reported receiving some alcohol education during their academy training.

While clearly there are areas for improvement in academy policies and procedures, one aspect of their rapid growth has been the incorporation of new forms of technology in training curricula. Grants have enabled police departments to develop advanced simulation labs, with exercises on such matters as defensive driving, handling suspects, and searching buildings. Moreover, academy coursework has made increasing use of computers and the Internet. Future technological vistas include academies "without walls"—a distance-learning approach that may in turn pave the way for internationalization of police training. In an era of increased globalization of types of crime, including terrorism, international training should assist law enforcement to develop new and more effective crime-fighting approaches.

Eric W. Metchik

Further Reading

Baker, Thomas. "Computer Technology in Police Academy Training." *Law and Order* (August, 2002): 107-110.

Charles, Michael. *Police Training: Breaking All the Rules.* Springfield: Charles C Thomas, 2000.

Guthrie, Edward. "Higher Learning and Police Training." *Law and Order* (December, 2000).

Ness, J. J. "The Relevance of Basic Law Enforcement Training: Does the Curriculum Prepare Recruits for Police Work—A Survey Study." *Journal of Criminal Justice* 19, no. 2 (1991): 181-193.

Prokos, Anastasia, and Irene Padavic. "'There Oughtta be a Law Against Bitches': Masculinity Lessons in Police Academy Training." *Gender, Work and Organization* 9, no. 4 (2002): 439-459.

See also Community-oriented policing; Criminal justice education; Law enforcement; Peace Officer Standards and Training; Police; Police chiefs; Police civil liability; Police ethics; Special weapons and tactics teams (SWAT); Women in law enforcement and corrections.

Police brutality

Definition: Abuses of authority that amount to serious and divisive human rights violations involving the excessive use of force that may occur in the apprehension or retention of civilians

Criminal justice issues: Government misconduct; Police powers; Professional standards

Significance: Persistent and pervasive patterns of abuse and the enduring obstacles to justice in American policing have contributed to increasing international scrutiny since 1999, when the United States was placed on the Human Rights Watch list of major human rights abusers, along with such countries as Rwanda, Cambodia, and Zimbabwe. Although the impact of cases of police brutality and the disparities in criminal justice in the United States represent substantial threats to institutional legitimacy, it is important to note that the incidence of police use of force is in fact quite rare given the large numbers of contacts between police and members of the large and diverse American public.

Article 3 of the United Nations (UN) Code of Conduct for Law-Enforcement Officials states that the legitimate use of force is only that which is "strictly necessary" to subdue persons under the circumstances confronting officers. The UN Basic Principles on the Use of Force and Firearms by Law Enforcement Officials restricts the use of force and firearms to situations in which the "use of force and firearms is unavoidable." Meanwhile, law-enforcement officials are expected to "exercise restraint in such use and act in proportion to the seriousness of the offense and the legitimate objective to be achieved." Definitions and justifications for "reasonable" and "necessary" force provided by US law have varied throughout history. The proper use of force by the police maintains the substance of the US Constitution and is fundamental to legitimacy because the police hold a virtual monopoly over the power to exercise lethal force against citizens.

Background

Excessive and lethal force have always been major sources of conflict between members of minority groups and the police in the United States. Despite substantial improvements in race relations, race remains central to police brutality in the United States. A vast body of multidisciplinary literature on the use of force by the police has revealed that members of minorities face a significantly higher risk than other citizens of becoming victims of police violence, and that members of racial and ethnic minorities are more likely to be incorrectly fired at by police, regardless of the race or ethnicity of the officer.

Incidents of police violence against members of ethnic and religious minorities and immigrants have reinforced the public perception that some citizens are subjected to harsher treatment and greater bias than others. Incidents in which real or perceived abuses are made public often spark civil unrest that results in costly and violent uprisings and reinforces public distrust. In 1968, the National Advisory Commission on Civil Disorders, also known as the Kerner Commission, concluded that abusive policing tactics had contributed significantly to the widespread civil disorder of the 1960s.

Later investigatory commissions came to the same conclusions. These include the Christopher Commission, which was appointed to investigate the Los Angeles riots that had followed the acquittal of police officers who had beaten Rodney King; the 1992 St. Clair Commission on excessive force in Boston; and the Mollen Commission on police misconduct in New York. The reports of all these commissions revealed the same patterns that were evident in the Kerner Commission report and reached essentially the same conclusions. Nevertheless, the recommendations made by these commissions remain unrealized.

In August 2014, violent protests erupted and continued for days and then months after a white police officer, Darren Wilson, shot and killed an unarmed black man, Michael Brown, in Ferguson, Missouri, during an altercation related to a recent theft. After more than three months and amid continued verbal and physical protests and unrest in Ferguson, the St. Louis County grand jury decided not to indict Wilson on any charges. The entire country became involved in the emotions and issues raised by the incident, and Wilson ultimately resigned from his position without severance in late November. Additionally, President Barack Obama proposed a new plan to fund a program to institute the use of body cameras for police forces. The subsequent deaths over the next year of a number of young black men, including Akai Gurley, Tamir Rice, Freddie Gray, and Samuel DuBose, at the hands of police officers generated a continued public outcry. The police shot and killed over 680 people in 2015; 6 percent of white suspects who were shot were unarmed, while 14 percent of black victims were.

Law-enforcement institutions implement their charges through the complex signaling relationships among the various branches of government. Police must try to balance responsiveness to the law, responsiveness to electoral institutions, and responsiveness to the public with the demands of keeping the peace. The impact of "law and order" candidates on both the law and the executive direction of bureaucratic agencies, such as police departments, has been tremendously influential on the history of police brutality. For example, President Richard M. Nixon's White House chief of staff H. R. Haldeman once noted that "President Nixon emphasized that you have to face the fact that the whole problem is really the blacks. The key is to devise a system that recognizes this without appearing to." Given the rampant criminality of the Nixon administration itself, political leadership lacking credible commitments to the public perpetuate institutional legacies that define classes of people who are deemed unworthy of protection by the police.

In addition, the "tough on crime" attitude that pervades public opinion is another element that makes it such that those deemed unworthy of constitutional protections are further disadvantaged, as they are perceived to fail to contribute in valuable ways to society. Citizens who are targets of policy are more likely to be victims of police brutality because they are likely to have more interactions with the police. Moreover, they are less likely to have access to avenues of recourse when they are victimized, and they are not likely to be supported by institutions of justice or the public. Consequently, whether the police respond to the law, politics, or the public, police brutality can be understood at least in part as a reflection of the intolerance of American society.

Prevalence

Although incidents of improper use of force by officers are actually statistically rare, individual cases have tre-

---

The Abner Louima Case

In one of the most infamous cases of police brutality on public record, Haitian immigrant Abner Louima was brutally beaten and sodomized by officers of the New York Police Department (NYPD) while under arrest in 1997 for a scuffle outside a nightclub. Louima suffered severe internal injuries requiring several surgeries to repair. He also claimed that while he was in custody, he was walked past several officers in the NYPD's 70th Precinct building while his pants were down around his ankles before he was tortured in the bathroom.

NYPD officer Charles Schwartz was convicted of holding down the handcuffed Louima, as fellow officer Justin Volpe rammed a wooden stick into Louima's rectum and then forced it into Louima's mouth, breaking his teeth. Volpe was sentenced to thirty years in prison for violating Louima's civil rights, but the convictions of Charles Schwartz, Thomas Wiese, and Thomas Bruder were overturned by the Second Circuit Court of Appeals in 2002. Michael Bellomo, charged with lying to cover up the incident, did not agree to testify until two years after the incident.

After the brutality incident was publicly exposed, the disorderly conduct charges against Louima were dropped, and the city of New York settled a civil suit that paid him $8.7 million. The involvement of five white officers using racial epithets during the beating and engaging in obstruction of justice during the criminal investigation of the assault on Louima provoked widespread protest regarding police practices and accountability. The Louima case continues to be a source of mistrust and undermines police-community relations.

mendous implications for social cohesion. A nationwide study conducted by the National Institute of Justice (NIJ) in 1999 found that officers used force in slightly less than 1 percent of their encounters with the adult public. There are obviously a number of methodological issues related to this study. First, there is no universal definition of what constitutes "reasonable" and "necessary" force in a given situation. Second, the NIJ study did not address police interactions with juveniles, and there is no indication as to what amounts to excessive force against a child. Third, compliance and discretion in reporting vary considerably. In a 2008 survey, the Bureau of Justice Statistics reported that among those who had come into contact with the police that year, around 1.4 percent had force used or threatened against them.

Rates of the use of force by the police vary widely and are significantly impacted by both departmental policies and state laws as well as the compliance of statutes and policies with U.S. Supreme Court guidelines. By 2004, approximately thirty states had laws on their books allowing police officers to use all means necessary to effect arrests, including arrests of unarmed citizens suspected of nonviolent crimes. The Supreme Court's 1985 ruling in *Tennessee v. Garner* outlined the boundaries of the police use of force such that permissive statutes, such as the fleeing felon rule, are considered unconstitutional. *Garner* has been shown to have reduced fatal shootings by the police. However, between that 1985 ruling and 1990, only four states had changed their laws to bring them into compliance with the constitutional rule.

Ultimately, the elemental task of law enforcement, the application of lawful force to protect society, creates a dilemma in which social cohesion is both preserved through and threatened by force. The prevalence of police brutality is profoundly affected by expectations in ways that are self-reinforcing. Given the history of police brutality in the United States and the self-perpetuating nature of reputations, distrust between members of minority communities and the police are not likely to change without affecting expectations.

The dilemma of forced peace makes it such that society cannot expect to eliminate all cases of brutality against the public. Therefore, implementing effective analysis of what is reasonable and necessary force and what are credible commitments by the police to all members of society is essential to affecting the prevailing patterns of police brutality. In addition, credibility must be earned and commitments are likely to be tested.

Responsible leadership committed to reducing the prevalence of police brutality requires at least the following conditions:
- establishing and using a reputation that reinforces the notion that police protect all members of society
- making it costly to the careers of individual officers to violate their commitments to the public
- investing in incremental changes
- employing mandatory negotiating agents such as external complaint collection and automatic civilian review

The principal of "rule of law" should protect citizens from arbitrary power, and the legitimacy of democratic policing is integrally linked to police compliance with legal standards. The exercise of discretion by the police is fundamental to the duty of police to protect and facilitates their ability to serve the public. Excessive use of force is a federal crime that makes it criminal for an individual acting under the color of the law, including private and contracted security personnel, to deprive any citizens of their civil rights. Concerns about arbitrary police power and racial bias represent a significant threat to the principles of the US Constitution. Therefore, transparency and accountability are essential to the fair and effective pursuit of justice.

Investigation

Addressing brutality is a matter of political will. In many cases, organizations are in place to counter such behavior effectively, but the parties responsible for oversight operate in hostile environments or are themselves unwilling to engage in preventive or retributive actions. Limits on effective oversight and organizational leadership that is designed to protect officers, rather than the public, magnify shortcomings and contribute to a climate wherein officers are aware that punitive actions are unlikely.

There are three primary obstacles to effective oversight: lack of public accountability and transparency, failure to investigate and prosecute incidences of brutality, and obstructionism. The first of the three, lack of accountability and transparency, enables the others. One approach to monitoring police accountability is through internal review, which is a formal bureaucratic process that is often referred to as internal affairs (IA).

Most internal mechanisms designed to investigate incidences of abuse operate with secrecy and often allow officials to refuse to furnish the public with relevant information regarding investigation. This institutional secrecy manifests itself even in cases in which such information is supposed to be publicly available. The provision and availability of data and systematic analysis of the use of force by the police at the local, state, and federal levels rely on voluntary compliance and are inconsistent at best. Furthermore, the data collected by the Federal Bureau of Investigation and held by the Department of Justice do not include injuries that fall short of death and also are known to be inaccurate.

One of the inherent difficulties in internal monitoring is that the police do not always recognize their own violations. Although departments are required to train their officers to deal with citizen claims regarding brutal treatment, myriad problems pervade the process of compiling information from the public regarding interactions with the police. The vast majority of citizens who feel they have been mistreated by the police do not attempt to address the issue formally, primarily out of fear of retribution. Police efforts to dissuade members of the public from making complaints are widespread and persistent.

Citizens who express interest in filing complaints against police may be threatened with the notorious "trilogy" of disorderly conduct, resisting arrest, and assaulting an officer. Scholar James J. Fyfe has dubbed this phenomenon "contempt of cop," citing a small percentage of officers who repeatedly file such charges because they are offended by citizens' demeanor without a legitimate law-enforcement purpose. Complainants may face civil countercharges as well. Since the 1990s, there has been a trend in which police officers have filed suits against plaintiffs and attorneys after unsuccessful litigation, alleging defamation, malicious prosecution, or abuse of process. It should also be kept in mind that police deal regularly with people motivated to make claims against police that might diminish their own culpability.

Civilian review is another approach to oversight that constitutes independent, external review of police activities. Citizen oversight bodies are often created in response to demands for external accountability and take a number of different forms. Because demands for citizen oversight tend to occur in communities in which police use of excessive force is consistently a divisive issue between the police and public, and because of the political bargaining that takes place in the formation of civilian review boards, evidence on the effectiveness of citizen participation in this form is limited. Public participation in this form does, however, afford the police some relief from the occupational demands that characterize police work, in that civilian review can inform police departments and share the responsibility that comes with broadly defined objectives and authority.

The increased relative risk to minorities and the relative inability of personnel diversity to affect police killings make external institutional checks on authority an investment rather than a cost. A considerable amount of scandal that can undermine legitimacy arises from incidents in which police officers kill suspects. Departments spend a substantial amount of time and resources dealing with situations in which lethal force is used. Additionally, officers involved in killings often experience trauma that necessitates counseling services to deal with situations in which they have used lethal force, they may have their careers interrupted, and their reputations can be damaged by such incidents. Instituting structural mechanisms that influence the likelihood of excessive or deadly force also means that officers will not have to experience this form of violence either.

Prosecution

There are essentially two paths to exacting justice for unlawful use of force by the police: criminal and civil prosecution. Criminal prosecution may occur at the local, state, and federal levels. At the local level, prosecutors can bring criminal charges against officers under state laws regarding such violent offenses as assault, battery, murder, and rape. A few states have laws that specifically address excessive police force. Federal prosecutors also have the authority to bring charges against officers under relevant federal laws, and federal and state grand juries also have the power to investigate and indict officers for the alleged criminal use of force. However, less than 1 percent of cases reported to the US Department of Justice actually lead to prosecution.

Criminal prosecution is an extremely limited mechanism of accountability. Judges and juries tend to afford considerable deference to police testimony, making conviction incredibly difficult and ultimately making successful prosecution less likely. In addition, criminal prosecution does not address the systematic organizational, leadership, political, and policy problems that contribute to the abuse of power by officers.

Most states do not compile data on rates of prosecution, conviction, and sentencing, but there is substantial evidence for concluding that criminal prosecution for police use of excessive force is extremely rare. The lack of support by public officials, the need for good working relationships between police and prosecutors, and the low probability of conviction contribute to a reluctance to bring charges against officers. There are also few referrals from internal affairs. Moreover, the standard of proof that requires prosecutors to demonstrate that officers had "specific intent" to deprive citizens of their civil rights represents a significant obstacle to convictions.

Civil liability is another potential vehicle for achieving justice in cases of police brutality. The necessary elements of proof and legal standards vary widely from state to state. Although the law permits plaintiffs to recover both monetary damages and equitable relief, civil suits alleging excessive force are exceedingly difficult to win. On the other hand, the amounts awarded in civil cases of excessive force have risen steadily since the 1970s, and large settlements for police brutality have strained the resources of some city governments. Nevertheless, potential financial burdens have not served as effective deterrents to excessive force, primarily because civil suits provide little incentive for individual officers to cease using excessive force. Civil suits also fail to influence systemic change in organizational culture, departmental policies, unfair institutional structures, and patterns of political bias.

Punishment

The avenues for addressing police brutality include, but are not necessarily limited to, criminal conviction, civil litigation leading to job loss, early warning systems that expect supervisors to impose penalties for misuse of power, exacting additional education and training requirements for officers exhibiting contempt, and victim-offender mediation. The reality, however, is that none of these avenues is regularly or consistently utilized.

Institutional bias within police departments often favors officers and can include such protections as police officer bills of rights. Although most bureaucrats are required to give up some of their individual civil liberties for the privilege of government work, strong police unions and professional associations afford exceptions for the police. Exceptions for officers allow for the purging of instances of abuse from officers' personnel files and negotiated contracts that can prevent the disciplining and dismissal of officers when appropriate. Moreover, because police officers rely on one another for their own personal physical safety, the use of lethal force to protect fellow officers is central to cohesion among officers. Finally, the high degree of isolation inherent in police work contributes further to the organizational culture known as the "blue wall of silence." All these factors insulate the police from both necessary and unnecessary punitive measures.

Addressing police brutality requires an understanding of the character of the law, the history of disparities in criminal justice in the United States, and the fundamentally paradoxical nature of police work. Justice is an abstract idea that is never perfectly actualized from all possible perspectives. Punitive measures are not only extremely unlikely, but also are often unsatisfactory and insufficient means for restorative justice. Punitive measures do not prevent police brutality in the future, nor do they provide any means for re-establishing the trust that underlies the authority of the state, the legitimacy of police power, and mutually beneficial community relations.

Holona L. Ochs
Updated by Kuroki M. Gonzalzles

Further Reading

Balko, Radley. *Rise of the Warrior Cop: The Militarization of America's Police Forces.* New York: PublicAffairs, 2013. Print.
Chaney, Cassandra, and Ray Robertson. "Racism and Police Brutality in America." *Journal of African American Studies* 17.4 (2013): 480-505. Print.
Greenwald, Anthony G., Mark A. Oakes, and Hunter G. Hoffman. "Targets of Discrimination: Effects of Race on Responses to Weapons Holders." *Journal of Experimental Social Psychology* 39 (2003): 399-405. Print.
Human Rights Watch. *Shielded from Justice: Police Brutality and Accountability in the United States.* New York: Human Rights Watch, 1998. Print.
Lawson, Tamara F. "Powerless against Police Brutality: A Felon's Story." *St. Thomas Law Review* 25.2 (2013): 218-43. Print.
Lingan, John. "Copping To It." *Pacific Standard* 8.6 (2015): 18-9. Print.
Mauer, Marc. "Race, Class, and the Development of Criminal Justice Policy." *Review of Policy Research* 21.1 (2002): 79-91. Print.
Middlewood, Erin. "The Education of Jesse Hagopian." *Progressive* 79.10 (2015): 22-6. Print.
National Research Council. *Fairness and Effectiveness in Policing: The Evidence.* Washington, DC: National Academies, 2003. Print.
Nuwer, Rachel. "When Cops Lose Control." *Scientific American Mind* 26.6 (2015): 44-51. Print.
Ostrom, Elinor, R. Parks, and Gordon Whitaker. *Patterns of Metropolitan Policing.* New York: Praeger, 1978. Print.
Prosecuting Police Misconduct: Reflections on the Role of the U.S. Civil Rights Division. New York: Vera Inst. of Justice, 1998. Print.
Skolnick, Jerome H., and James J. Fyfe. *Above the Law: Police and Excessive Use of Force.* New York: Free, 1993. Print.
Smith, Rogers. *Civic Ideals: Conflicting Visions of Citizenship in U.S. History.* New Haven: Yale UP, 1997. Print.
Tennenbaum, A. N. "The Influence of the Garner Decision on Police Use of Lethal Force." *Journal of Criminal Law and Criminology* 85 (1994): 241-60. Print.
Walker, Samuel. *Police Accountability: The Role of Citizen Oversight.* Belmont: Wadsworth, 2001. Print.

See also Assault and battery; Civilian review boards; Confessions; Deadly force; *Graham v. Connor*; Internal affairs; King beating case; Police; Police corruption; Police ethics; Reasonable force; Special weapons and tactics teams (SWAT); *Tennessee v. Garner*; Wickersham Commission.

Police chiefs

Definition: Top officers in urban police departments
Criminal justice issues: Law-enforcement organization; Police powers; Professional standards
Significance: Establishment of the office of chief of police is crucial to enabling the successful operation and underpinnings of a police department.

The history of police chiefs can be traced to the mid-nineteenth century, when the highest-ranking police officers in American cities were called "superintendents." The duties of modern police chiefs, like those of their predecessors, are varied and are functions of the composition of the departments in which the chiefs work. For example, a small-town chief of police may be the town's only salaried law-enforcement officer, assisted by numerous volunteers. By contrast, a police chief in a large metropolitan area may command thousands of sworn officers, along with thousands of civilian employees. In direct contrast to sheriffs, who are usually elected county officials, police chiefs are commonly appointed by mayors or police commissions. In some jurisdictions, police commissioners also serve as police chiefs.

The main function of any chief of police is to perform administrative and managerial functions directly related to supervising the activities of the police department. In addition, the chief also acts as the main facilitator in the enforcement of all city statutes and state laws for which the police department is held accountable.

In 1893, the International Association of Chiefs of Police (IACP) was formed as a professional organization designed to facilitate exchanges of information and experiences among police administrators throughout the world. One of the most influential chiefs of police was August Vollmer, who became the first police chief of the newly created police department of Berkeley, California, in 1909. Vollmer pioneered the use of automobiles in patrols, established the first police training school, served as president of the IACP in the 1920s, and created the first academic criminology curriculum in the United States in 1939. Vollmer has been dubbed by many as the founder of modern professional policing because of his countless innovations in the establishment of police professionalism.

Lisa Landis Murphy

Further Reading

Bennet, W., and Karen Hess. *Management and Supervision in Law Enforcement*. 4th ed. Belmont: Wadsworth, 2004. Print.
Johnson, Kevin. "Amid Heightened Scrutiny, It's 'a Precarious Time' for US Police Chiefs." *USA Today*. USA Today, 24 May 2016. Web. 27 May 2016.
Jones, Phill. "August Vollmer: Police Reformer." *History Magazine* 12.5 (2011): 12-13. Print.
Miller, L., and Karen Hess. *Police in the Community: Strategies for the Twenty-first Century*. 3rd ed. Belmont: Wadsworth, 2002. Print.
Schmalleger, Frank. *Criminal Justice Today: An Introductory Text for the Twenty-first Century*. 8th ed. Upper Saddle River: Pearson, 2005. Print.

See also Civilian review boards; Law enforcement; Police; Police academies; Police ethics; Sheriffs.

Minneapolis Police Chief Tim Dolan. (By Calebrw, via Wikimedia Commons)

Police civil liability

Definition: Police officers' obligations to refrain from acts within the course of duty that may cause undue harm to another
Criminal justice issues: Government misconduct; Immunity; Police powers
Significance: Police officers may be held financially responsible in civil court for on-duty conduct that harms a civilian. Lawsuits against officers have increased markedly, making it necessary for police departments to consider ways to reduce the threat of potential liability.

Police officers come into contact with the public in a variety of difficult situations, some of which give rise to civil liability cases. Lawsuits against the police had sharply increased by the end of the twentieth century. Considering the tendencies of juries to award large monetary settlements in police civil liability cases, government officials took notice of public concern and began exploring ways to minimize the prevalence of lawsuits against their departments.

In response to the need to develop better methods of protecting the public, many police departments have realized that the threat of civil liability cannot be eradicated but can be reduced. Attempts to do so include implementation of better policies regarding hiring, retention, and supervision of officers. These policies include tougher screening processes for police recruits, better education, and stricter disciplinary measures for misconduct.

Tort Claims

Many lawsuits against police officers involve intentional torts, or private wrongs against a person or property. Wrongful-death lawsuits arise when officers directly cause a person's death or fail to prevent the death of a person. These suits often involve pursuits, shootings, or handling of prisoners. Police officers are also subject to lawsuits for battery if they use unlawful force to effect an arrest or perform an improper search of a suspect. Officers may also incur liability for false arrest if they detain someone without probable cause or other legal justification.

Police officers are also sometimes sued for negligence. In order to be found liable for negligence, an officer must have had a duty to act which went unfulfilled or was performed without reasonable care. Claims in this area of law are most often made for failure to operate a vehicle safely or for failure to protect persons who need assistance, such as a motorist on the side of the road or a suspect in the rear of a patrol car. Police supervisors can be held liable for the acts of their subordinates if they fail to supervise adequately or to investigate claims of misconduct.

Federal Claims

A type of lawsuit that may be brought against police officers involves a violation of a person's civil rights, under Title 42 of the United States Code, Section 1983. Such claims are federal and must involve the deprivation of a right provided by the U.S. Constitution. For a Section 1983 claim to be sustained, officers must have been acting in their official capacity, which is referred to as "acting under color of law."

Lawsuits brought against the police for First Amendment violations involve some action by the officers that prevent people from exercising their freedom of speech, religion, or peaceful assembly. This issue most often arises when police break up protests. Fourth Amendment claims arise when officers effect an unreasonable search or seizure that is not based on probable cause. Police officers may also be held liable for depriving suspects of their Fifth Amendment rights, such as failing to recite the Miranda rights prior to custodial interrogation, if a statement made by the suspect is later used at trial.

Many lawsuits are brought against the police for excessive force, under several different legal theories. Lawsuits based on the Fourth Amendment require showing that the force used was unreasonable. Lawsuits based on the Eighth Amendment by convicted offenders require showing that the force used inflicted "cruel and unusual punishment." Lawsuits based on the Fourteenth Amendment require showing that the force used "shocks the conscience." Although each amendment requires a different level of proof, claims of excessive force often include combinations of these amendments.

Defenses

Because police officers must continue to protect the public regardless of the threat of civil liability, the criminal justice system has built-in controls to make sure that only cases that appear to have merit will be allowed to proceed. Otherwise, police officers would not be able to do their jobs out of fear of being sued. The defense to the crime that is available to an officer depends upon the type of lawsuit involved.

Police officers facing a lawsuit involving an intentional tort can attempt to show that their acts were unintentional or, alternatively, that no actual harm was suffered. An officer facing a negligence suit can attempt to show that the action taken was not unreasonable or that any damage resulting from the alleged act was brought about by something other than the officer's conduct.

In federal lawsuits, an officer may seek qualified immunity from the court. Qualified immunity is an affirmative defense that will completely bar a plaintiff from recovery. To establish qualified immunity, an officer must have been performing a discretionary act, one which requires judgment. The court will then determine whether there was a clearly established constitutional right involved. If the law was not clearly established, or if it was clearly established but the officer's conduct was objectively reasonable, qualified immunity applies, and the lawsuit will be dismissed.

Kimberly J. Belvedere

Further Reading
Gaines, Larry, and Victor Kappeler. *Policing in America*. 4th ed. Cincinnati: Anderson, 2002.

Kappeler, Victor. *Critical Issues in Police Civil Liability*. 3d ed. Prospect Heights: Waveland, 2001.

Peak, Kenneth. *Policing in America: Methods, Issues, Challenges*. Upper Saddle River: Prentice-Hall, 1997.

Ross, Darrell. *Civil Liability in Criminal Justice*. 3d ed. Cincinnati: Anderson, 2003.

Worrall, John. "Administrative Determinants of Civil Liability Lawsuits Against Municipal Police Departments: An Exploratory Analysis." *Crime and Delinquency* 44, no. 2 (1998): 295-313.

See also Color of law; Community-oriented policing; Immunity from prosecution; Internal affairs; Police; Police academies; Police corruption; Police ethics; Reasonable force; Vicarious liability.

Police corruption

Definition: Unethical, dishonest, and other criminal conduct or deviant behaviors by police officers that involve abuses of their authority for personal gain
Criminal justice issues: Government misconduct; Police powers; Professional standards
Significance: Police corruption, which may take the form of soliciting, taking, or offering bribes; selling favors; accepting gifts; abusing authority; and aiding and abetting criminal behavior, is anathema to the repository of public trust in institutions that are entrusted with protecting citizens from crime and bringing criminals to justice. In a nation that regards democracy and justice as cardinal values, the investigation, prosecution, and punishment of corrupt police officers are crucial for preservation and advancement of social order, as well as efficacy of the criminal justice system itself.

Police corruption poses a dilemma for the criminal justice system because of the unique trust that the public has in police to stamp out crime and bring criminals to justice. Police corruption puts courts at odds with their supposed primary ally in the pursuit of justice. Although corrupt officers constitute a small percentage of sworn officers, corruption is a serious matter that needs to be addressed to maintain police morale and retain public confidence in the police.

History

Corruption among police is as old as the profession of policing. In fact, prevention of crime and elimination of bribery were two of the major reasons why the first police force was established in London in 1829. In colonial America, corrupt practices and official recklessness punctuated the history and development of law enforcement. Citizen groups exercised responsibility for law and order in their small and homogeneous communities through the watch, or vigilante, system. Over time, new immigration and industrialization transformed small settlements into large communities until many of them became true towns and cities.

Although the watch system persisted into the twentieth century in many communities, it became obvious that it could no longer effectively police crime in heterogeneous societies. In frontier communities, especially in the Far West, corrupt and dishonest bounty hunters, similar to private police agents called thief takers in eighteenth century England, were often hired by private citizens for debt collection and the apprehension of felons. Vigilantism and bounty hunting were riddled with corruption, particularly as they were sometimes used to extract money from both honest citizens and criminals at the same time.

County sheriffs were officially the most important law officers. They were charged with keeping the peace, crime fighting, tax collection, and election supervision. For their services, they were paid by the fee system, an outdated practice in which peace officers kept percentages of the taxes they collected and received fixed amounts for every arrest they made. With time, it became obvious to many that tax collection and graft were more lucrative than crime fighting, so those pursuits consumed much of the time of early law officers. Meanwhile, burgeoning cities looked toward the successful London type of policing to deal with their own spiraling crime problems.

In 1838, the first formal police department in the United States was created in Boston. New York followed in 1854. Between the 1840s and the 1890s, corruption spurred by political patronage permeated the newly established police departments. Some officers had to pay bribes for promotions or assignments in areas offering opportunities for graft. The roles and functions of early police departments were ill defined; they were utilized primarily as enforcement arms of the reigning political powers and concentrated on controlling European immigrants and protecting private property. Later, many of the corrupt practices of this early system carried over into the more professional police departments of the twentieth century, and some have remained fixtures of city police departments into the twenty-first century.

Types of Corruption

The most prevalent forms of police corruption are accepting gratuities, selective enforcement of laws, outright theft and burglary, bribery and extortion, and internal corruption. Other forms include aiding and abetting criminal behavior, abuse of authority, perjury, favoritism, and brutality.

A gratuity is any type of payment received by the police in the form of gifts made with the expectation of later receiving favors in return. Some police departments have strict guidelines prohibiting acceptance of any form of gift from citizens.

A cartoon by William Allen Rogers entitled "The Big Chief's Fairy Godmother', published in Harper's Weekly in 1902; a caricature of New York City Police Chief William Stephen Devery.. (Public domain, via Wikimedia Commons)

Selective enforcement occurs when officers exercise legitimate discretion in deciding what action to take but for improper reasons. An example would be letting a criminal act go unpunished in exchange for something of value.

Theft and burglary involve active criminality by sworn officers. Examples include an officer keeping part of the money seized during a drug bust or taking money from suspects arrested for public drunkenness who are unlikely to remember how much cash they should have. A petty form of police theft, called "shopping," is the police taking small items, such as gum, candy, and cigarettes, from stores that are left unlocked after business hours. Some police also actively engage in premeditated and outright burglary that involves forced entry into business places for the sole purpose of robbery. Police burglary rings have been uncovered in such major American cities as Atlanta, Chicago, Cleveland, Nashville, and Reno.

Other categories of police theft include shakedowns and stealing money, drugs, and other property from department evidence rooms and unguarded business premises. "Shakedown" is a corrupt police practice of extorting expensive items for personal use while responding to emergency calls for break-ins or burglaries and attributing the resulting losses to the burglars.

Bribery is the voluntary offer of something of value to a police officer aimed at influencing the officer's duty performance. For an offense to qualify as bribery, citizens must initiate the offer, such as by offering officers money in return for not being arrested. Extortion differs from bribery in being initiated by officers who use their power to demand money, services, or goods from criminal suspects in return for favors. A typical example is an officer who refrains from arresting a drug dealer in return for cash payments.

Bribery and extortion take a variety of forms. For example, the "pad" is a regular weekly, biweekly, or monthly payoff by a criminal enterprise to police, usually in exchange for protection against arrest and interference. A "score" is a one-time payment solicited by an officer from a violator to avoid ticketing or arrest. "Mooching" involves the acceptance of gifts such as liquor or even donuts from retail establishments in exchange for such favors as ignoring city code violations by the establishments. "Chiseling" is a demand made by an officer for price discounts or free admission to events not connected to police duty.

Police who commit perjury intentionally lie while under oath in court, usually for the purpose ensuring the conviction of a defendant or to cover up for a fellow officer caught in unlawful activity. Favoritism is the selective favoring of one citizen or group at the expense of another. An example is giving immunity to friends or relatives from citations for traffic violations.

Police officers who aid criminal behavior are present at the scenes of crimes and render assistance to the perpetrators without personally taking part in the crimes. By contrast, abetting involves constructive presence during the commission of crimes or assisting or encouraging others to commit crimes without directly participating in their commission.

Police brutality encompasses the use of abusive language, unnecessary use of force or coercion, threats, and harassing searches while dealing with suspects. Police brutality is considered a form of corruption because it entails abuse of authority. An incident in 2014 elicited public outcries when a black man in New York died after being placed in a controversial choke hold by a white police officer; the officer was ultimately not indicted on any charges, prompting further public protest.

Internal corruption involves corruption at the departmental level. For example, in some police departments, promotions and favorable assignments are sold to the highest bidders. The Knapp Commission that investigated the New York City Police Department during the early 1970s noted that systematic payoffs permeated the entire departmental apparatus. Investigators even found a chart listing the selling prices of every police rank.

Departmental corruption can be classified in three categories: rotten apples and rotten pockets, pervasive unorganized corruption, and pervasive organized corruption. A "rotten apples and rotten pockets" department is one in which a minority of officers use their positions for personal gain. When there is no organized effort by other members of the force to institutionalize such behavior, the culpable officers can usually be identified and flushed out. Pervasive unorganized corruption develops in departments in which the corruption of a few officers goes unchecked, and other officers join them. The main difference between this and the previous form of department corruption is the numbers of officers involved. Pervasive organized corruption is found in departments in which large numbers of officers practice organized corruption with the cooperation of their administrators, as was found in New York City by the Knapp Commission.

Prevalence

Police corruption is still a serious problem in the twenty-first century, and the police departments of the largest cities tend to be most prone to the problem. As the largest and one of the oldest American police departments, the New York City Police Department has a long history of pervasive corruption, but New York is not the only American city that has faced the problem. Most big cities have had similar cases of official corruption.

During the early years of the twenty-first century, an investigation into the Los Angeles Police Department found that officers in its Rampart Division had persistently engaged in such active criminal pursuits as bank robbery, false imprisonment, theft of drugs, planting evidence on victims, and outright brutalizing of arrestees. The investigation led to the indictment of several officers on charges ranging from drug dealing and framing of innocent people to using torture to force confessions and murder.

In Cleveland, forty-nine police officers and jail guards were convicted of accepting bribes to protect drug shipments. In Detroit, the city's first black police chief was convicted of diverting nearly $1.3 million of departmental money to his own personal use. In Miami, Florida, police officers were convicted of active burglary of private homes and the theft of two million dollars worth of cocaine. In an unrelated case, four Miami officers were convicted of stealing thirteen million dollars worth of cocaine from a drug-smuggling boat. Two separate

The Los Angeles Police Department (LAPD) has also been involved in a number of controversies, mostly involving racial animosity and police corruption. (By Cliff, via Wikimedia Commons)

suspicious deaths have also been linked to two Miami police officers. Other cases include the disappearance of $150,000 from a police department safe.

A much different kind of case of police corruption occurred in Tulia, Texas. There it was found that the convictions of forty-three persons on drug charges in 1999 had been based on the uncorroborated evidence of one corrupt undercover officer who framed all of them. That same officer had earlier fled from his previous law-enforcement job to avoid theft charges. These and other examples of corrupt practices in different states suggest that police corruption is a pervasive problem.

Investigation

Three major ways of controlling police corruption and brutality include establishing rules and regulations, initiating civil liability lawsuits, and prompting investigative processes. Rules and regulations are written departmental policies that inform all officers of expected standards of behavior, thereby establishing clear grounds for easy supervision and discipline of erring officers. Such rules also communicate to the community what standards to expect from their officers. Civil liability lawsuits are tort actions designed to make erring officers and their departments pay compensatory damages to litigants for personal harm resulting from the officers' unreasonable actions.

The third method of controlling corruption is through investigative processes. In directed efforts to restore public trust and confidence in the police, most big cities have instituted police administrative and civilian review boards to reduce police control by special interests and stem corruption. These boards are assigned the responsibility of appointing police administrators and overseeing police affairs, including investigations of all allegations of corruption. Additionally, most large city departments have established internal affairs units.

Internal affairs units are committees made up of officers within departments that investigate allegations of corruption and brutality by members of their departments. These bodies generally involve high-ranking officers in their investigations. After they complete fair and impartial evaluations of complaints, they can take any of four actions: unfound the allegations, exonerate the accused, declare the allegations not sustained, or declare the allegation as sustained. "Unfounded" rulings are issued when the evidence is insufficient to be sure the alleged incidents have actually taken place. Exonerations are issued when investigations find the accused officers' conduct to have been both lawful and justified. "Not sustained" rulings are issued when investigations lack sufficient evidence to proceed with the cases. Allegations are "sustained" when there is sufficient evidence to prove them and thereby justify disciplinary actions against the accused officers.

Civilian review boards are independent tribunals made up of leading members of the civilian community. These boards review internal affairs recommendations on grievances leveled against the police, especially in brutality and corruption cases. Civilian review boards serve as independent oversight agencies and tend to be most popular in jurisdictions that practice community policing. In such communities, police departments generally go out of their way to accommodate diverse interests and maintain cordial relations with members of the community to clear all doubts about their officers' conduct.

Special commissions have frequently been created to investigate charges of police corruption. One of the most famous was created in May 1970, by New York City's Mayor John V. Lindsay, in response to an article in *The New York Times* charging widespread corruption in the city's police department. To investigate the allegations, Lindsay appointed the Knapp Commission, which issued its report in August 1972. The document was a massive indictment of the New York City Police department. New York is generally regarded as having the highest levels of police corruption of any American city. Since the 1880s, its police have been investigated by special commissions an average of once every twenty years. The Knapp Commission itself was preceded by the Gross Commission of 1954 and followed by the Mollen Commission of 1994.

By the turn of the twenty-first century, the focus of police corruption investigations was shifting to drug-related offenses and publicized cases of police involvement in illegal drug trafficking, especially in New York, Miami, Chicago, and Philadelphia. During the 1990s, for example, the Mollen Commission found serious incidents of drug trafficking and related corruption in the New York City Police Department. Officers in some precincts were caught selling drugs and beating suspects. The Mollen Commission found the worst examples of police corruption and brutality in neighborhoods with large minority populations. The commission also found that vigilante justice and power were additional factors influencing drug-related police corruption.

Prosecution

During the 1990s, police corruption remained sufficiently pervasive to cause serious concern in political circles and government. Corruption in this sense also encompasses police brutality because it involves police abuse of its legitimate authority. Persistent incidents, especially drug-related corruption, attracted so much media attention that the US House of Representatives, through the US General Accounting Office (GAO), commissioned an investigation into drug-related police corruption. The commission's 1998 report found wide-scale police involvement in drug-related corruption, particularly in eleven major cities.

In 1995, six Atlanta police officers were convicted on drug-related crimes, and another five were suspended though not charged. During the following year, seven Chicago police officers were indicted for robbery and extortion of money and narcotics from known drug dealers, and another three officers were arrested in 1997 for conspiracy to commit robbery and sale of illegally confiscated narcotics. In 1998, forty-four officers from local police, sheriff, and corrections departments were charged with taking money to protect cocaine traffickers. In another incident in 1991, nine Detroit police officers were prosecuted on charges of conspiracy to aid and abet the distribution of cocaine, attempted money laundering, and other crimes.

Other prosecutions have included twenty-seven Los Angeles County sheriff's deputies and one officer of the city of Los Angeles's elite narcotics unit being convicted in 1994 for hiding drug money. During that same year, eleven New Orleans police officers were convicted for receiving more than $100,000 from Federal Bureau of Investigation (FBI) undercover agents posing as cocaine suppliers. Similarly, more than one hundred Miami police officers were convicted and punished for drug-related offenses during the 1980s.

The results of FBI-led investigations into police corruption and convictions between 1993 and 1997 indicate that indictments and convictions for police corruption were on an upward trend. In 1993, there were 129 convictions of law-enforcement officers for corruption throughout the United States; 59 of the convictions were for drug-related offenses. In 1994, 1995, and 1997 the numbers of convictions exceeded 135 each year, and the proportions of drug-related convictions were similar to the 1993 figures.

The National Police Misconduct Statistics and Reporting Project released its Police Misconduct Statistical Report in 2010, finding that 6,613 sworn law enforcement officers were involved in reported acts of misconduct that year, with 7.2 percent of the officers reported engaging in acts of theft, fraud, and robbery. In 2013, fifty-three drug convictions were dropped by a federal court after it was learned that the cases had been corrupted by a veteran police officer of Philadelphia's narcotics unit. The following year, the city of Tulsa, Oklahoma, was still settling lawsuits filed by individuals wrongfully convicted of drug crimes after an investigation had led to the conviction of four officers in the Tulsa Police Department accused of corruption crimes such as perjury. Also in 2014, two San Francisco police officers were convicted of conspiracy, theft, and wire fraud by a federal court; a surveillance video had been released by a public defender in 2011 that had shown the officers stealing property during raids of single room occupancy apartments.

Punishment

Two major methods of punishment have been used to discipline officers convicted of corruption: administrative and judicial processing. Possible forms of administrative punishments for convicted officers include departmental warnings, suspensions of pay and from duty, relief of command especially for commanders, demotions in rank, referrals for criminal prosecution, and outright dismissals from departments. Typical judicial outcomes are warnings, fines, and incarceration.

Emmanuel C. Onyeozili

Further Reading

Alexander, Michelle. "Why Police Lie Under Oath." *New York Times*. New York Times, 2 Feb. 2013. Web. 5 Feb. 2015.

Corsianos, Marilyn. *The Complexities of Police Corruption: Gender, Identity, and Misconduct*. Lanham: Rowman, 2012. Print.

Gaines, Larry, and Victor Kappeler. *Policing in America*. 4th ed. Cincinnati: Anderson, 2002. Print.

Katz, Charles M. *The Police in America: An Introduction*. 5th ed. New York: McGraw, 2005. Print.

The Knapp Commission Report on Police Corruption. New York: Braziller, 1972. Print.

Langworthy, Robert H., and Lawrence F. Travis III. *Policing in America: A Balance of Forces*. 3rd ed. Upper Saddle River: Prentice, 2003. Print.

Lardner, James, and Thomas A. Reppetto. *NYPD: A City and Its Police-The Inside Story of New York's Legendary Police Department*. New York: Holt, 2000. Print.

Palmiotto, Michael J. *Community Policing: A Policing Strategy for the Twenty-first Century*. Gaithersburg: Aspen, 2000. Print.

Sherman, Lawrence W., ed. *Police Corruption: A Sociological Perspective*. Garden City: Anchor, 1974. Print.

Siegel, Larry J., and Joseph J. Senna. *Essentials of Criminal Justice*. 4th ed. Belmont: Wadsworth, 2004. Print.

Walker, Samuel, and Charles M. Katz. *The Police in America: An Introduction*. 5th ed. New York: McGraw, 2005. Print.

See also Bounty hunters; Civilian review boards; Discretion; False convictions; Knapp Commission; Miscarriage of justice; Perjury; Police; Police brutality; Police civil liability; Police ethics; Police powers; Political corruption; September 11, 2001, attacks; Wickersham Commission.

Police detectives

Definition: Police officers who specialize in criminal investigations

Criminal justice issues: Evidence and forensics; Investigation; Police powers

Significance: Trained detectives increase the effectiveness of police efforts to solve crimes. As specialists in the art and science of criminal investigation, they help to ensure professional and thorough responses to serious crimes.

Glorified in fiction and essential in fact, detectives are both common and crucial figures in American law enforcement. Although full-time police detectives are not nearly as numerous as uniformed patrol officers, they can be found in almost all large and medium-sized police departments. Although the popular image of police detectives is of plainclothes officers assigned full time to criminal investigative work, almost all police officers perform at least some detective work in the course of their routine duties.

History

The development of professional police detectives is closely linked to crimes that could not be prevented or deterred by uniformed patrol officers. When the first American police departments began forming in the early nineteenth century, they consisted only of uniformed patrol officers. Over time, it became obvious that crimes were continuing to occur despite the work of routine police patrols and that methods of investigating crimes after they occurred was necessary.

In England and France, criminals known as "thief catchers" were used by police forces to help catch other criminals, as it was believed that only criminals themselves could know enough about the habits of criminals to solve crimes. However, that method of crime detection failed—primarily because of the dishonesty of the thief catchers themselves—so agencies began experiments using sworn police officers as investigators of crimes. The London Metropolitan Police pioneered the use of plainclothes detectives in the mid-nineteenth century. These detectives were stationed in a London building that had been formerly used by Scottish royalty, and their work was closely followed by the press and by the novelist Charles Dickens, who wrote positive articles about the detectives who came to be known as "Scotland Yard," or "the Yard," after their headquarters. In addition to writing about the detectives' heroic work, Dickens coined the term "detective" in his 1853 novel *Bleak House*.

In the United States, detectives began appearing in police departments during the 1840s, most notably in Boston, Chicago, and New York City. By the end of the Civil War, in 1865, nearly all large American cities had detective units. Many of them were kept busy by a postwar crime wave and problems of urban overcrowding brought on by new waves of European immigration. Some detectives became well known as newspapers closely followed their exploits.

New York City's Inspector Thomas Byrnes promoted the theory of modus operandi (MO), which was based on the principle that individual criminals tend to use the same methods of operation in their crimes and that recognizing those distinctive methods can help identify the perpetrators of crimes. In 1886, Byrnes published a book detailing the methods of hundreds of felons then active along the East Coast.

In contrast to those in Europe, American private detectives rivaled public detectives in popularity and effectiveness. Allan Pinkerton emerged as the country's foremost private detective, setting an example that was copied by many police investigators. In addition to establishing a series of highly profitable private detective branch offices across the country, Pinkerton also served as Chicago's first public detective and headed the US Secret Service during the Civil War.

During the twentieth century, the development of motor vehicle transportation and the rise of statewide crime rings promoted the creation of state police and highway patrols with detective units of their own. Meanwhile, a number of specialized federal offices of criminal investigation arose during the late nineteenth and early twentieth centuries. In addition to the Secret Service, these included the US Customs Service, the Bureau of Investigation-which later became Federal Bureau of Investigation (FBI)-and the Internal Revenue Service (IRS).

Types of Detectives

The largest numbers of full-time, plainclothes detectives are found in local law-enforcement agencies. In 2004, approximately 10 percent of all sworn police officers were detectives, almost 60,000 of whom were working in city and county agencies. An additional 30,000 to 40,000 worked at the state and federal levels. The New York City Police Department had the largest number of detectives of any single agency, with nearly 4,000; the FBI had the most federal investigators, with nearly 12,000. In 2015, according to the Bureau of Labor Statistics, there were 106, 580 detectives and criminal investigators working at state, local, and federal law-enforcement agencies, illustrating the continued need for these professionals in the modern criminal landscape.

Most city, county, and state detectives are selected from among officers already working in regular patrol divisions. Unlike many European police departments that allow college graduates to begin their police careers as investigators, most American agencies regard patrol work to be an invaluable part of the maturing and learning process that officers should have before becoming detectives. Although some federal criminal investigators have prior patrol experience, it is not required for federal special agent positions.

In addition to sworn police officers, thousands of other government investigators and private detectives also do detective work in the United States. Investigators who assist public defenders' offices and coroners, and other government employees who perform state and federal background applicant checks, are also numerous. The numbers of private detectives vary considerably from state to state, with more than thirty thousand employed throughout the country in 2015, according to the Bureau of Labor Statistics..

Police Detective Duties

Crime cases come to the attention of police agencies through three channels: victim and witness reporting, patrol observation, and initiatives undertaken by investigators. The majority of cases are reported by the general public. After they are reported, cases are assigned to individual detectives either through systems of rotation or because of the detectives' investigative specialties. Although most detectives are able to investigate all types of crime, individual detectives tend to specialize. Some concentrate on violent crimes, others on serial crimes, high-loss property offenses, or cases involving unidentified perpetrators.

Criminal investigations are typically divided into three phases: preliminary investigations; continuing, or follow-up, investigations; and concluding investigations. Preliminary investigations focus on processing crime scenes and the initial interviewing of victims and witnesses. Often completed by regular patrol officers, the preliminary investigations serve as case foundations.

In larger police agencies, continuing and concluding investigations are undertaken exclusively by detectives. Continuing investigations seek to establish the identities of suspects, find new victims and witnesses, and coordinate evidence processing with crime laboratories. During the concluding phase, decisions must be made whether to suspend the cases or prepare them for prosecution.

Success rates of detective work vary with the types of crimes. The FBI reported that in 2014, 47.4 percent of violent crimes and 20.2 percent of property crimes were cleared by arrest.

Traits of the Detective

Certain personality traits appear to be important to successful detective work. For example, an ability to reason logically and objectively is essential. Deductive and inductive reasoning are both commonly employed in detective work. Detectives employing the deductive method form their general conclusions before all facts are explained and then use additional facts to modify or verify those conclusions. Detectives using the inductive method wait for all relevant facts and information to emerge before drawing any conclusions. The inductive method is most commonly used in complex white-collar crimes and drug cases involving many suspects.

Other traits essential to proper detective work include strong organizational ability, heightened observational skills, ability to communicate with a wide variety of people, advanced search and seizure legal knowledge, and a thorough understanding of forensic science capabilities.

James N. Gilbert

Further Reading

Corwin, Miles. *Homicide Special: On the Streets with the LAPD's Elite Detective Unit*. New York: Holt, 2003. Print.

Douglas, John. *The Anatomy of Motive: The FBI's Legendary Mindhunter Explores the Key to Understanding and Catching Violent Criminals*. New York: Pocket, 2000. Print.

Gilbert, James N. *Criminal Investigation*. New York: Prentice, 2004. Print.

Micheels, Peter. *The Detectives: Their Toughest Cases in Their Own Words*. New York: Pocket, 2003. Print.

"Occupational Employment and Wages, May 2015: Detectives and Criminal Investigators." *Bureau of Labor Statistics*. Bureau of Labor Statistics, 30 Mar. 2016. Web. 27 May 2016.

"Occupational Employment and Wages, May 2015: Private Detectives and Investigators." *Bureau of Labor Statistics*. Bureau of Labor Statistics, 30 Mar. 2016. Web. 27 May 2016.

Sanders, William. *Detective Work*. New York: Free, 1980. Print.

US Dept. of Justice, Federal Bureau of Investigation. *Crime in the United States, 2014*. Washington, DC: US Dept. of Justice, FBI, 2015. PDF file.

See also Cold cases; Crime labs; Crime scene investigation.

Police dogs

Definition: Dogs used by law-enforcement professionals to help find missing persons and criminal suspects and to sniff out controlled substances

Criminal justice issues: Investigation; Police powers

Significance: Police dogs are now trained in more varied and diverse missions than ever before.

Dogs' work in law enforcement began in Belgium in 1899, with the deployment of Belgian sheepdogs, and quickly spread through the law-enforcement agencies around the world. Police dogs were first used in the United States by the New York City Police Department in 1907. The growth in the police dog service has been explosive; Jim Watson, director of the North American Police Work Dog Association, estimated that there were more than fifty thousand police dogs serving law-enforcement agencies in the United States in 2010. These dogs are referred to as K-9 (shorthand for canine) officers.

Different breeds of dogs have been trained for police work. Trainers find that a dog needs to have a distinct set of characteristics for police work. These traits include intelligence, loyalty, an excellent sense of smell, and natural aggression. The breeds most often chosen are Belgian sheepdogs, German shepherds, Doberman pinschers, and a variety of hounds and beagles. The last two groups are used primarily for tracking and smell detection. Non-neutered male dogs are used for their natural aggression.

During the early twenty-first century with heightened awareness of terrorism, the role of police dogs and their

Police dog. (Public domain, via Wikimedia Commons)

companion officers expanded dramatically. A dog's sense of smell is fifty times more acute than that of its human companion. Dogs can smell substances present in trace amounts of less than 1 gram, and some are 70 percent more effective than odor detection machines. These olfactory skills are put to use searching for explosives, drugs, and people.

The use of police dogs has seen challenges to its legality. When a large, well-trained dog attacks and bites a suspect, the question of reasonable force can arise. The US Supreme Court has heard two cases that address this issue of deadly force. In 1985, *Tennessee v. Garner* reviewed the Fourth Amendment and the use of deadly force. In 1989, *Graham v. Connor* discussed the "reasonableness" of the use of force by a police dog. In 2013, the Supreme Court held in its ruling in *Florida v. Harris* that a drug-detection dog's alert to an officer provides probable cause for officers to conduct a warrantless search of a vehicle, without requiring any other evidence of the dog's reliability so long as it has been certified. At the appellate court level, almost all circuits have heard cases discussing the deployment of police dogs, their training, and what constitutes reasonable force.

Robert Stewart

Further Reading
Albrecht, Kathy. *Lost Pet Chronicles: Adventures of a K-9 Cop-Turned-Pet Detective*. New York: Bloomsbury, 2004. Print.
Balko, Radley. "Federal Appeals Court: Drug Dog That's Barely More Accurate than a Coin Flip Is Good Enough." *Washington Post*. Washington Post, 4 Aug. 2015. Web. 27 May 2016.
Condon, Stephanie. "Supreme Court Rejects Distinct Limits on Drug Dog Searches." *CBS News*. CBS Interactive, 19 Feb. 2013. Web. 27 May 2016.
Ingraham, Christopher. "The Surprising Reason More Police Dogs Are Dying in the Line of Duty." *Washington Post*. Washington Post, 20 Nov. 2015. Web. 27 May 2016.
Johnson, Glen R. *Tracking Dog: Theory and Methods*. 4th ed. Mechanicsville: Barkleigh, 1999. Print.
Schillenberg, Dietmar. *Top Working Dogs: A Training Manual—Tracking, Obedience, Protection*. Rev. ed. Oslo: I.D.I., 1994. Print.

See also Deadly force; Police civil liability; Reasonable force; Trespass.

Police ethics

Definition: Written and unwritten rules of acceptable conduct by law-enforcement personnel within their agencies, in their dealings with other agencies, and in their dealings with the public
Criminal justice issues: Civil rights and liberties; Confessions; Interrogation; Professional standards
Significance: The conceptualization of what constitutes "proper" behavior in a wide variety of law-enforcement situations has heavily influenced both public attitudes toward police and the legal system's response to allegations of unethical police conduct.

The parameters defining acceptable and unacceptable police behavior are as old as law enforcement itself and have evolved continuously. Police ethics touch on many issues, such as intentional deception in investigations and court proceedings, the use of deadly force, corruption, and selective law enforcement.

The development of formalized codes of police ethics in the United States can be traced back to O. W. Wilson's work with the Wichita, Kansas, police during the late 1920s. However, the first statewide ethics code was developed in California in 1955. Two years later, the International Association of Chiefs of Police (IACP) adopted it as the Law Enforcement Code of Ethics. With minor revisions drafted in 1989 and unanimously adopted in 1991, along with a newly prepared Law Enforcement Code of Conduct, the IACP's ethics code has served as the model for many police departments. Central elements of the code include a statement of the officer's basic service mission, the obligation to "respect the constitutional rights of all to liberty, equality, and justice," and a charge that one's private life and public actions exemplify honesty and integrity. The code also enjoins officers to enforce the law without any biases arising from "personal feelings, prejudices, political beliefs, aspirations, animosities, or friendships"; to avoid unnecessary force; and to reject bribes and other forms of corruption.

Police ethics codes serve multiple purposes. They assure the public that officers who are granted unique powers to further their investigative work are nonetheless required to behave in ways that meet at least minimal acceptable standards. They may seen as providing a "moral compass" that guides officers' decision making in uncertain situations, while contributing to the development of a police culture and a cohesive work environment. Having such codes can improve the public image of police and serve as an alternative to external review and regulation, although this is true only to the extent that such codes are publicly seen to be rigorously and consistently enforced.

Interrogations

While ethics codes provide laudable blueprints for police behavior, the actual everyday work experiences of officers present many stressful ethical challenges. One broad category that invites unethical behavior is the use of deception during interrogations of suspects. The courts have clearly outlawed physical abuse of suspects, and the Supreme Court has ruled that police officers must read suspects their Miranda rights before any interrogation; however, deceptive behaviors are handled on a case-by-case basis.

Police may employ a variety of deceptive tactics during interrogations. For example, some officers try to convince suspects that they are not really being held in custody and that their interrogations are merely "interviews." Adoption of this tactic may officially relieve the officers from having to issue Miranda warnings to the suspects, even though the officers' actual agendas may be to elicit confessions so that they can commence arrest procedures.

Sometimes police read the Miranda warnings to suspects in such a perfunctory manner that the suspects mistakenly conclude that they can waive their rights without serious consequences. Another tactic is for police to attempt to lessen the actual severity of offenses in murder suspects' eyes by leading them to believe that one or more murder victims are still alive and able to testify. At other times, police may try to increase the perceived severity of offenses so that suspects will admit to lesser offenses. Yet another tactic is for officers to pretend to be investigating one crime while actually gathering information about another. Officers also sometimes express sympathy toward suspects, while trying to convince them that confessing is the best way for them to resolve matters. Promises of more lenient judicial treatment after confessions cannot be guaranteed, but they often produce confessions.

Confronting suspects with falsified evidence pointing toward their guilt is another frequently used tactic for eliciting confessions during interrogations. Confessions resulting from deceptive interrogation techniques are a major ethical concern and must be balanced against their usefulness in finding and convicting guilty suspects. Deceptive tactics may also undermine police credibility.

Prospects for the Future

During the early years of the twenty-first century, it was expected that the movement toward community-oriented policing and the escalating fight against terrorism were likely to influence the development of police ethics. For example, a central tenet of community policing is the empowerment of foot-patrol officers by assigning them to "quality of life" community projects. However, their increased power may cause them to lose some of their sensitivity to civil liberties in police-citizen interactions. Similarly, a national concern with preventing future terrorist acts in the United States has already led to a reduction in civil liberties, exemplified most prominently by the USA PATRIOT Act that was enacted shortly after the terrorist acts of September 11, 2001.

While the ends in both cases may be noble, they cannot be used to justify the reduction of individual liberties. Community policing poses new moral challenges that will need attention. For example, closer interactions with members of the community may lead police to discover law violations committed by their new "citizen partners." The police will then have to decide whether such violations should be vigorously prosecuted and thus imperil police-citizen collaboration. On the other hand, as citizens become more involved in law-enforcement practices, should they have a greater voice regarding police responses to violators? Will citizens want to take justice more in their own hands, through vigilante-type actions? Finally, what is the proper police reaction if their associated citizen groups adapt racist or otherwise unacceptable agendas? Twenty-first-century law-enforcement personnel must take specialized intensive training programs to best confront all types of traditional and new ethical dilemmas.

Eric W. Metchik

Further Reading

Albanese, Jay S. *Professional Ethics in Criminal Justice: Being Ethical When No One Is Looking.* 4th ed. Boston: Pearson, 2016. Print.

Braswell, Michael C., Belinda R. McCarthy, and Bernard J. McCarthy, eds. *Justice, Crime, and Ethics.* 8th ed. New York: Routledge, 2015. Print.

Close, Daryl, and Nicholas Meier. *Morality in Criminal Justice: An Introduction to Ethics.* Belmont: Wadsworth, 1995. Print.

Goodman, Debbie J. *Enforcing Ethics: A Scenario-Based Workbook for Police and Corrections Recruits and Officers.* 4th ed. Boston: Pearson, 2013. Print.

Pollock, Joycelyn M. *Ethical Dilemmas and Decisions in Criminal Justice.* 8th ed. Belmont: Wadsworth, 2014. Print.

Souryal, Sam S. *Ethics in Criminal Justice: In Search of the Truth.* 6th ed. New York: Routledge, 2015. Print.

United States. Dept. of Justice. Office of Justice Programs. Bureau of Justice Assistance. *Police Chiefs Desk Reference: A Guide for Newly Appointed Police Leaders.* 2nd ed. Boston: McGraw, 2008. International Association of Chiefs of Police. Web. 3 June 2016.

See also Civilian review boards; Community-oriented policing; Internal affairs; Miranda rights; Peace Officer Standards and Training; Perjury; Police; Police brutality; Police civil liability; Police corruption; Police powers; Racial profiling.

Police lineups

Definition: An investigative tool used by police to identify possible suspects of a crime

Criminal justice issues: Evidence and forensics; investigation; witnesses

Significance: Police may be useful tools in police investigations, but they have serious drawbacks and are often performed improperly they often violate suspects' rights and lead to false identifications by witnesses.

Police investigators use lineups as an analytical tool based on the premise that eyewitness testimony is the strongest evidence to use in the investigation of crime, a premise that is highly debatable The purpose of police lineups is to check the veracity of eyewitness statements for the purpose of identifying a suspect.

Unlike what most people think from the movies or TV, there are essentially three forms of police lineups. The photographic lineup can be done exclusively with the use of photographs (or "mug shots") in which a photograph of the suspect can be placed within an array of other photographs. A more common form of lineup is to have a suspect stand in a room with other people, known as foils, who look similar. Sometimes a lineup consists only of foils. Police may also make use of showups, in which one suspect appears before a victim or witness. Showups have been questioned and many legal experts see them as highly unreliable. They are restricted by many legal restraints. Some investigators prefer to use a combination of these techniques, such as first requesting a photographic lineup and then later a regular police lineup or showup.

Investigators are bound by constitutional requirements concerning the use of lineups. As in all other investigative procedures, police cannot violate the suspect's due process rights; thus, in some cases the accused must be provided with counsel during the lineup procedure. The U.S. Supreme Court ruled in *Kirby v. Illinois* (1972) that a person at a lineup or showup is entitled to counsel if the investigative procedure is held at or after the time that criminal proceedings have begun. However, if the lineup is conducted before the beginning of criminal proceedings, a suspect is not entitled to counsel. Counsel is also not required for photographic lineups. A defendant may request a waiver of rights to have counsel at a lineup or showup provided that the defendant is made aware of the procedure and the fact that the purpose of the procedure is for the identification of a criminal suspect.

The Problem of Misidentification

The issue of the possibility of misidentifications in police lineup procedures has been debated both by the Court and by scholars. In *Neil v. Biggers* (1972), the Court opined that five factors should be used to detect misidentification. The factors include the opportunity of the witness to view the criminal at the time of the crime, the witness's degree of attention, the accuracy of the witness's prior description of the criminal, the level of certainty demonstrated by the witness at the confrontation, and the length of time between the crime and the confrontation.

Further, scholars suggest that misidentification could be reduced by using either double-blind police lineups or sequential lineups. The double-blind procedure is based on a premise posited by several scholars that police officers who know the identity of the suspect may influence the decision of the eyewitness. The double-blind procedure thus prevents this by having the supervising police officer of a lineup unaware of who the possible suspect is. Sequential lineups require that eyewitnesses view potential suspects one at a time, rather than all at once. The sequential lineup procedure is based on the belief that eyewitnesses may be prone to make relative judgments and thus choose a suspect who looks most like the perpetrator when all of the suspects are viewed at once. Many police departments have begun utilizing both of these procedures in recent years.

D. Scott Canevit
Updated by Frank Salamone

Further Reading

Loftus, Elizabeth F. *Eyewitness Testimony*. Cambridge, Mass.: Harvard University Press, 1979.

Technical Working Group for Eyewitness Evidence. *Eyewitness Evidence: A Guide for Law Enforcement*. Washington, D.C.: U.S. Department of Justice, Office of Justice Programs, National Institute of Justice, 1999.

Bartol, Curtis R and Anne M. Bartol Introduction to Forensic Psychology: Research and Application 4th ed. Edition, 2015.

See also Booking; Counsel, right to; Due process of law; Eyewitness testimony; False convictions; Police; Police ethics; Suspects.

Police militarization

Definition: Police agencies have increasingly obtained military-style equipment to employ in meeting their local law enforcement duties.

Criminal justice issues: Law enforcement organization; police powers; political issues; professional standards; terrorism; violent crime

Significance: As police agencies obtain surplus military equipment to assist them in their daily crime-fighting efforts and their new antiterrorism role, some perceive that apparent militarization as the driving force for increased excessive use of force by officers and an increased interpersonal gulf between the officers and the communities they serve.

Police, driven by the global growth of terrorism, well-armed drug dealers, and cast-off surplus military equipment, have become much more militarized in the twenty-first century. When the criminals have better body armor and more powerful weaponry than the police, the officers want to improve their equipment to compete. This trend has been exacerbated during the War on Terror as more and more of the intelligence-gathering and public safety roles must be played by local and state law enforcement officials who find themselves, too often, outgunned by terrorists in their local communities.

Government Surplus Equipment

The United States Congress in its 1990-1991 National Defense Authorization Act authorized the federal Department of Defense, via the 1033 program, to transfer surplus military-grade equipment to federal, state, and local law enforcement agencies to assist in the War on Drugs. The equipment was provided to law enforcement free of charge although the local agencies were obligated to pay transportation and maintenance costs on the free equipment. The equipment included Humvees, automatic weapons, personnel carriers, body armor, and other military-grade equipment.

The local agencies, with limited budgets and facing, at times, heavily armed drug dealers, lined up to obtain the military surplus equipment. As of 2015, over $5 billion worth of military surplus equipment had been given to law enforcement agencies under the 1033 program.

Some attribute the rapid growth in the 1033 program and police militarization, in part, to the facts that law enforcement in the United States is frequently staffed with military veterans and many law enforcement agencies are top-down and paramilitary in organizational design with top officers labeled as commanders, captains, and lieutenants, and street cops labeled as officers and corporals.

Ferguson, Missouri: War Zone on Main Street

In August, 2014, Ferguson, Missouri erupted with street protests and violence after an unarmed young African-American man, Michael Brown, was shot to death by a White Ferguson police officer. During the demonstrations that followed, many commentators noted that when the police arrived at the scene, it looked much more like a war zone than a neighborhood. This was due, in large part, to the military-style equipment that Ferguson law enforcement had obtained through the 1033 program. To many Ferguson locals, the officers' militarization had served only to increase the officers' propensity toward violence and decrease the trust of the locals in their local law enforcement officers and agencies.

The War on Terror and Militarization

The global War on Terror has disseminated terror across the globe and to many cities and towns. In Boston, there was the Marathon bombing. In Paris, the Bataclan. In London, the subway bombing. In New York, the World Trade Center. In Washington, D.C., the Pentagon. As the reach of terrorism has grown, so too have the burdens on federal law enforcement to respond. But a substantial part of the federal response is to partner with local and state law enforcement agencies as their eyes and ears, but also as frontline "soldiers," as it were, in the War on Terror. That enhanced local role, coordinated through regional Fusion Centers, has perhaps inadvertently accelerated the militarization of local law enforcement as they equip to meet the terrorist threat.

Militarization and Public Confidence

Civilian confidence in local law enforcement grows when the officers act ethically, ensure procedural justice, and are more like guardians than warriors. Unfortunately, the War on Terror and the rise of violence in some communities has caused some officers and agencies to feel under siege, needing military-grade equipment to keep pace and keep the peace. Many commentators suggest that militarization has led more officers more often to use excessive force. Still others believe that militarization has resulted in less—not more—civilian confidence in the police. Although many law enforcement agencies are striving to become softer and more community policing-oriented, the countervailing impact of increased militarization has driven a wedge between civilians and their local police in some communities.

As a result, elected officials and commentators have called for demilitarization and a reduction of the 1033 program. And limits have been placed on that program such that at least some of the most lethal military-grade equipment is no longer provided to local agencies.

The tension between militarization of local law enforcement on the one hand and community policing on the other will continue to play out in major communities throughout the United States.

Charles E. "Chuck" MacLean

Further Reading

American Civil Liberties Union. *War Comes Home: The Excessive Militarization of American Policing.*
Balko, R. *Rise of the Warrior Cop: The Militarization of America's Police Forces.* New York: Public Affairs, 2013a.
Balko, R. (2013b). "The Militarization of America's Police Forces." *Cato's Letter—* 11, no. 4 (2013b): 1-7.
Department of Justice. *Report Regarding the Criminal Investigation into the Shooting Death of Michael Brown by Ferguson, Missouri Police Officer Darren Wilson.* March 4, 2015.
Wofford, T. "How America's Police Became an Army: The 1033 Program." *Newsweek*, August 13, 2014.

See also Drugs and law enforcement; Ferguson, Missouri unrest amid police shooting of Michael Brown; MOVE bombing; Police brutality; Reasonable force; Terrorism.

Police powers

Definition: Authority conferred on law-enforcement officers to enforce the law
Criminal justice issues: Police powers; Professional standards
Significance: Police officers must balance their right to enforce the law and the discretion inherent in their profession with the judgments of their peers, supervisors, and members of the community.

Public perception of police officers' exercise of powers is difficult to characterize in general terms, as it differs among individuals based on their personal circumstances and, on a broader scale, typically shifts in response to current events. While American police gained both new respect and expanded powers after the terrorist attacks of September 11, 2001, subsequent high-profile cases involving the deaths of members of minority groups at the hands of police—such as the 2014 shooting death of unarmed African American teenager Michael Brown in Ferguson, Missouri—have led to increasingly public criticism of police officers for being too often overzealous, biased, or even corrupt in the exercise of their powers. Over the years, there have been many investigations into the behavior of police officers, especially with regard profiling, a potentially effective but controversial tool for identifying possible suspects.

Police power is generally understood as the lawful exercise of the sovereign right of government to promote order, safety, and security. It has also been referred to as a right of the government itself to regulate personal conduct. However, the state may limit this activity for the good of all the people. In general, the authority to preserve order and peace is subject to constraints by the US Constitution. In fact, the concept of police power became important after ratification of the Fourteenth Amendment in 1868, in particular the clause that states, "No state shall make or enforce any law which shall abridge the privileges or immunities of citizens of the United States; nor shall any state deprive any person of life, liberty, or property, without due process of law; nor deny to any person within its jurisdiction the equal protection of the laws."

In the past, the US Supreme Court has justified police power to intrude into citizens' lives. For example, officers have been allowed to question persons who fit the "profile" of drug couriers by entering or exiting areas known for drug activity and carrying one-way airplane tickets and no luggage. In *Florida v. Royer* (1983), the Court ruled that police could approach and ask questions of such individuals on the street or in any public places without violating the Fourth Amendment. Although this type of profiling appears logical and may contribute to apprehending drug couriers, it can also appear to be racially or ethnically motivated and therefore biased. In addition, even though the stated profile of a drug courier is not racially specific, a police officer's assessment of who fits this profile may be influenced by unconscious racial or ethnic biases, resulting in a disproportionate number of members of minority groups being targeted even in situations where the officers in question did not explicitly intend to do so.

Racial Profiling

While criminal or offender profiling is a long-established technique used in law enforcement, over the years the racial aspect of profiling has come under increased criticism. Criminal profiling attempts to describe the type of offender who is most likely to have committed a particular crime, including characteristics such as age, gender, and race; racial profiling takes this one step further, either intentionally or unintentionally prioritizing race above other factors and, by extension, making the implicit assumption that people of a particular race or ethnicity are inherently more likely to commit certain crimes.

State police have been criticized for stopping disproportionate percentages of drivers who are members of racial and ethnic minorities. The practice has given rise the slang phrase "driving while black," describing cases in which drivers who are members of minority groups, usually African Americans, are stopped by police when they are doing nothing wrong—or, in some cases, committing infractions for which white drivers are far less likely to be stopped, such as not wearing a seat belt—because their actions are viewed as inherently more suspect. A common example given is that a black man driving an expensive car is far more likely to be stopped on suspicion of having stolen the car.

Numerous studies have shown that police often do disproportionately target members of minority groups in traffic stops. One such study, published by the American Civil Liberties Union (ACLU) in January 2016, found that in the state of Florida in 2014, black drivers were stopped and issued citations for not wearing seat belts at nearly twice the rate as white drivers—1,821 citations issued per 100,000 resident black drivers, compared to 970 citations per 100,000 resident white drivers. This disparity cannot be explained by actual rates of seat-belt usage

Racial profiling is a police power. (By longislandwins, via Wikimedia Commons)

among the two groups, as calculations of usage showed only a 5 to 6 percentage point difference (85.8 percent of black drivers and passengers versus 91.5 percent of white drivers and passengers). Other studies have similarly shown that race does influence the likelihood of officers using force in encounters with suspects. Notions such as the assumption that typical drug-law offenders are young, male African Americans reflect racial stereotypes and are discriminatory. Although this type of profiling can be useful to pick out actual offenders, it also stigmatizes all young black males, and any benefits it provides should be weighed carefully against the very real harm it causes.

Since the 2001 terrorist attacks, police officers have been trained to look for the typical characteristics of foreign terrorists in order to help in the protection of the United States. The result has been a renewed emphasis on profiling that focuses on people of Middle Eastern origin or descent. Although erring on the side of caution may enhance public safety, such profiling has the result of unfairly treating an entire group of people. The news media has published many accounts of mistakes made by police attempting to profile suspects that have led to unnecessary delays at airports, airplane rerouting, and forced landings, as well as more serious human-rights violations such as unjustifiable detentions and arrests. Such mistakes have the potential to ruin or even end an innocent person's life.

Crime Control versus Due Process

While some amount of police power is necessary for police to effectively do their jobs, this power must be balanced against the due process rights of the accused. This is not an easy task, as decisions made in the exercise of police power are rarely "cut and dried." Often, the lowest-ranking police officers have the most discretion because they are often alone on the street, sometimes with potentially dangerous suspects, and have much power to act as they see fit. Additionally, members of historically oppressed communities often regard officers on patrol as their enemies and distrust their motives.

While some members of the public are primarily concerned with the rights of the accused, others believe that crime control should be more important, and these individuals tend to expect police to use their power to intrude despite legal restrictions. It can be difficult to please both sides. Officers who use their power to enforce the law based on their experience and on-the-job training may not find support from the more conservative observers; officers who use their power to enforce the law based on the letter of the law may not find support from more liberal observers. Consequently, police may feel vast pressures on them and believe that their powers are limited by politics, precedents, and various interpretations of the law.

Reasonable Suspicion

What gives an officer the power to intrude? Case law has set precedents for proper police behavior on the streets. Regardless of the amount of discretion police have, they are bound by the law. There are different levels of intrusiveness possible by the police, such as encounters as serious as a search-and-seizure based on probable cause, a stop-and-frisk initiated on reasonable suspicion, or encounters in which police and citizens are simply engaging in verbal interaction.

Under the Fourth Amendment to the Constitution, police may arrest and take suspects into custody with probable cause. Probable cause means that arresting officers believe, based on the circumstances and facts at hand, that crimes have been or are about to be committed. In *Terry v. Ohio* (1968), however, the US Supreme Court ruled that police could act on less than probable cause, or what is called reasonable suspicion. This case set a precedent that justified police action without probable cause. Instead, a lower standard of proof can be used to justify a stop-and-detention if officers reasonably believe that suspects are committing or are about to commit crimes. Previously, officers could not act unless they believe their own lives were in danger. Yet while reasonable suspicion allows police to make the initial "stop," frisking, or patting down, is legally allowed after a stop only when the evidence discovered elevates an officer's level of suspicion.

Citizen Perceptions and Police Ethics

Modern police and police administrators have increasingly incorporated public perceptions into their decision making. Community-oriented policing and civilian police academy programs are among the new efforts being made to coordinate community views into the roles police should play.

Policing research has been focused on educating laypersons about the role of police while determining the role that citizens want police to play. The difficult next step has been to train police to place themselves in the citizens' place to determine how the power they use may be interpreted by the public. Balancing their legal rights against the strict scrutiny of others is a challenging task. However, to take away police power or to limit their discretion could have disastrous consequences. The main reason police have so much discretion is that often no clear-cut responses to street encounters are known.

Part of the problem with entrusting police with so much power is that individual officers handle their power differently. Discretion may work well in the hands of fair, ethical, and moral officers. However, some officers do not adhere to the same standard and thus exercise their power in unfair, prejudicial, and inequitable ways. It may be that only time will tell if efforts to improve police-citizen relations will close the gap in perceptions of legitimate uses of police power.

Gina M. Robertiello

Further Reading

American Civil Liberties Union. *Racial Disparities in Florida Safety Belt Law Enforcement.* N.p.: Author, 2016. American Civil Liberties Union. Web. 8 June 2016.

Barnett, Randy E. "The Proper Scope of the Police Power." *Notre Dame Law Review* 79.2 (2004): 429-95. Web. 1 June 2016.

Barnett, Randy E. *Restoring the Lost Constitution: The Presumption of Liberty.* Updated ed. Princeton: Princeton UP, 2014. Print.

Dunham, Roger G., and Geoffrey P. Alpert, eds. *Critical Issues in Policing: Contemporary Readings.* 7th ed. Long Grove: Waveland, 2015. Print.

Gaines, Larry K., and Victor E. Kappeler. *Policing in America.* 8th ed. Waltham: Anderson, 2015. Print.

Morash, Merry, and J. Kevin Ford, eds. *The Move to Community Policing: Making Change Happen.* Thousand Oaks: Sage, 2002. Print.

Robertiello, Gina. *Police and Citizen Perceptions of Police Power.* Lewiston: Mellen, 2004. Print.

Stevens, Dennis J., ed. *Policing and Community Partnerships.* Upper Saddle River: Prentice, 2002. Print.

Travis, Lawrence F., III, and Robert H. Langworthy. *Policing in America: A Balance of Forces.* 4th ed. Upper Saddle River: Prentice, 2008. Print.

See also Color of law; Community-oriented policing; Knapp Commission; Police; Police corruption; Police ethics; Racial profiling; Reasonable suspicion; Search and seizure; Search warrants; Special weapons and tactics teams (SWAT); Stop and frisk; *Terry v. Ohio.*

Police psychologists

Definition: Professionally trained psychologists who work in law enforcement
Criminal justice issues: Interrogation; Law-enforcement organization; Medical and health issues
Significance: Police psychologists play a significant role in many aspects of law enforcement.

The social science discipline of psychology is utilized by law enforcement in a variety of different ways. For example, police psychologists are involved in the interviewing and testing processes relating to the hiring of new police officers. Virtually all candidates for police officer vacancies undergo psychological testing to determine if they are emotionally stable and free of mental illness. Police psychologists are also used in the interviewing of both witnesses and victims of crimes, as well as the interrogation of suspects. Psychologists' skills assist law enforcement in the calming of victims and the accurate representation of the facts from witnesses of a crime.

Police psychologists also perform the critically important function of offering psychological therapy to police officers and their families. The daily stress of law enforcement can influence the emotional health of officers and their families. Psychologists play an especially important role in providing counseling intervention to officers following traumatic and dangerous duty experiences, such as the horrific events of September 11, 2001.

Police psychologists are also utilized in criminal investigations. Perpetrators of violent crimes against other persons often provide psychological clues in the commission of their crimes. For example, those who commit sexual assault and lust homicide typically do so to fulfill their intrinsic psychological needs, which reflect mental health or personality disorders. Police psychologists analyze the specific characteristics of victims and the specific manners in which the crimes are performed. The information they collect provides them with psychological profiles of the offenders that aid the officers investigating the crimes.

A hypothetical case provides an example of how a police psychologist works. If a prepubescent girl were to be found sexually assaulted and suffocated, a police psychologist in the case would probably suggest that the unknown perpetrator is afflicted with the sexual paraphilia known as pedophilia. The suspect would thus be likely to experience recurrent and intense episodes of sexual arousal around prepubescent children, in this case, preadolescent girls. The police psychologist would advise investigating officers that the perpetrator is likely to be found loitering around locations frequented by young girls. This knowledge helps to delineate the suspect group and orients the criminal investigation. This process is commonly referred to as "profiling."

Duane L. Dobbert

Further Reading
American Psychiatric Association. *The Diagnostic and Statistical Manual of Mental Disorders.* 4th ed. Washington, DC: Amer. Psychiatric Assn., 2000. Print.
Dobbert, Duane L. *Halting the Sexual Predators Among Us: Preventing Attack, Rape, and Lust Homicide.* Westport: Praeger, 2004. Print.
Kirschman, Ellen, Mark Kamena, and Joel Fay. *Counseling Cops: What Clinicians Need to Know.* New York: Guilford, 2014. Print.
Kitaeff, Jack, ed. *Handbook of Police Psychology.* New York: Routledge, 2011. Print.
Petherick, Wayne. *Profiling and Serial Crime: Theoretical and Practical Issues.* 3rd ed. Cincinnati: Anderson, 2014. Print.

See also Forensic psychology; Pedophilia; Police ethics; Polygraph testing; Psychological profiling; Psychopathy; Victimology.

Police subculture

Definition: Widely shared attitudes, values, and norms within certain police officers
Criminal justice issues: Law enforcement organization; police powers; government misconduct
Significance: Police subculture affects police departments and the behavior of police officers. Police subculture plays a crucial role in contemporary police management, as well as identifying and controlling police misconduct.

Researchers have studied police culture for over four decades. In 1996, Chan noted that police culture undoubtedly plays a critical role in American policing and policing worldwide. Findings of previous research on police culture are fruitful but inconsistent. Researchers Dean and Goldsmith claim that police culture has a negative influence on policing reform); while Chan and Manning argue that police culture has a positive influence, such as helping police officers deal with strains and training new police officers.

It is inevitable that new police officers will initially contact "real" police culture in the police academy and smoothly internalize that culture later in their field training. Importantly, police officers and researchers are not the only two parties who recognize the existence of police culture. The public, in general, has a fragmented, if not unreal, view of police culture through images created and spread by the mass media for a long time. Therefore, considering media's ambiguous relationship with the police, the public usually has a misguided view of police culture and whether police culture is of value.

Definitional Issues

One of the biggest challenges of studying culture or subculture is to define the terms culture or subculture. Generally speaking, the term "culture" is viewed more neutrally than the term "subculture." According to Paoline in 2001, culture represents widely shared attitudes, values, and norms within a certain population. Subculture represents a group of people from a certain population, but their attitudes, values, and norms are seen as different from mainstream culture.

However, most policing textbooks do not distinguish culture and subculture and use them interchangeably. Indeed, the traditional understanding of police culture presents police officers as pure outsiders from society. One of the main features of police officers is that they usually hold "we vs. them" attitudes toward the public. While this statement may have been true previously, contemporary policing management strategies have partially, if not completely, changed the situation. For example, most police departments in the United States now claim they have adopted some form of community-oriented policing (COP). It is plausible that at least some COP officers no longer have a negative attitude toward the public. Meanwhile, police attitude toward the public is still an important component of studying policing. However, it is not appropriate to treat the study of police officers' attitudes toward the public the same as the study of police culture since a variation exists among police officers; rather, studying police officers' attitudes toward the public is a part of studying police subculture.

Another challenge of studying police subculture is to determine whether it is a study of organizational culture or occupational culture. Organizational culture, by definition, must be studied at an organizational level. Currently, there are more than 17,000 police departments in the United States. Most of them are relatively small police departments with less than 100 sworn police officers. Theoretically speaking, no two police departments are alike. Therefore, studies on organizational culture may be limited to several super-large police departments, and the generalizability can be greatly questioned. On the other hand, occupational culture is related to the nature of police work. Police officers from different police departments are exposed to different circumstances, but factors used to measure circumstances are similar. Therefore, it may be more valuable (and promising) to study police occupational subculture than organizational culture.

Factors

Although it seems Paoline's typology of police officers is not well-accepted by academia, his idea presents an interesting approach to overcoming the difficulty of measuring police occupational subculture. The following factors are common indicators of circumstances that police officers may encounter: the public, supervisors, legal restrictions, role orientation, policing tactics, change, group and loyalty to peers, and danger. Some of the factors are unique to police work (e.g., policing tactics); while others may also be applied to other occupations (e.g., danger).

Many researchers have held the belief that police officers typically have a negative attitude toward the public. Sparrow, Moore, and Kennedy state that police officers tend not to trust the public and believe help provided by the public is useless. However, studies from Moon and Zager in 2007, Paoline in 2001, and Worden in 1993 show that police officers' attitudes toward the public vary and some variables, such as neighborhood characteristics and the gender of police officers, are related to the variation. In contrast to traditional beliefs that police officers typically have negative attitudes toward the public, studies from Engel and Worden in 2003, Paoline in 2001, and Sun in 2002 show that these attitudes tend to vary among police officers. The media usually shape the image of police officers as frequently ignoring department policies and stepping over legal restrictions. However, empirical studies by Eterno, Paoline, and Sun and Chu demonstrate that police officers' attitudes toward legal restrictions vary. For example, compared to male police officers, female police officers are more likely to obey legal restrictions in situations involving weapons.

The public usually treats and views police officers as crime fighters. Police officers tend to see themselves in this manner as well. However, according to Paoline in 2001 and Sun and Chu in 2006, with police education and training an increasing number of police officers, especially young police officers, also accept their role as service providers. Also, with police education and training, more and more police officers choose to use nonaggressive tactics. However, the issue of police brutality still appears frequently on social media websites. The development of technology, on the one hand, helps the police do their jobs. For example, many police departments now adopt social media websites to distribute information and interact with the public. On the other hand, some police officers, especially traditional officers, may be resistant to new technology.

Group solidarity and the loyalty to peers also shape the public image of police officers. One of the products from group solidarity and loyalty is the code of silence—police officers tend not to report others' misconducts. However, in a recent study by Loyens in 2013, police officers will report others' misconducts if the risk of being charged with complicity is high. Additionally, group solidarity and loyalty are partially products of "perceived danger." Particularly, police officers are taught to prepare for dangerous situations on a constant basis from multiple sources including the media, the police academy, and other experienced police officers.

Shortcomings

Studying police subculture is important to understanding police behavior, including police misconduct. However, studying police subculture is difficult. One of the biggest issues, as described previously, is the operational definition of police subculture. Although researchers may be able to apply factors that have been discussed above to investigating police subculture, data collection is the second issue. Police subculture is a relatively sensitive topic. Very few police departments will allow researchers to collect data directly. Researchers may hide their questions on police subculture into other nonculture-related questionnaires. Doing so, however, has a potential risk of destroying good relationships with police departments. Last but not least, even if police departments support research on police subculture, police officers may refuse to take surveys. To sum up, it takes a great effort for researchers to study police subculture.

Xiaochen Hu
Zahra Shekarkhar

Further Reading

Chan, J. "Changing Police Culture." *British Journal of Criminology* 36, no. 1 (1996): 109-34.
Dean, G. "Police Reform: Rethinking Operational Policing." *Journal of Criminal Justice* 23, no. 4 (1995): 337-47.
Eterno, J. A. "Gender and Policing: Do Women Accept Legal Restrictions More Than Their Male Counterparts?" *Women & Criminal Justice* 18, nos. 1-2 (2006): 49-78.
Engel, R. S., and R. E. Worden, R. E. "Police Officers' Attitudes, Behavior, and Supervisory Influences: An Analysis of Problem Solving." *Criminology* 41, no. 1 (2003): 131-66.
Goldsmith, A. "Taking Police Culture Seriously: Police Discretion and the Limits of Law." *Policing & Society* 1, no. 2 (1990): 91-114.
Loyens, K. "Why Police Officers and Labor Inspectors (Do Not) Blow the Whistle: A Grid Group Cultural Theory Perspective." *Policing: An International Journal of Police Strategies & Management* 36, no. 1 (2013): 27-50.
Manning, P. K. "The Police Occupational Culture in Anglo-American Societies." In *The Encyclopedia of Police Science*, edited by William Bailey, 472-75. New York: Garland, 1995.
Moon, B., L. J. Zager. "Police Officers' Attitudes toward Citizen Support: Focus on Individual, Organizational and Neighborhood Characteristics Factors." *Policing* 30, no. 3 (2007): 484-97.
Paoline, E. A. *Rethinking Police Culture: Officers' Occupational Attitudes.* New York: LFB Scholarly Publishing LLC, 2001.
Sparrow, M. K., M. H. Moore, and D. M. Kennedy. *Beyond 911: A New Era for Policing.* New York: Basic Books Inc., 1990.
Sun, I. Y. "Police Officer Attitudes toward Peers, Supervisors, and Citizens: A Comparison between Field Training Officers and Regular Officers." *American Journal of Criminal Justice* 27, no. 1 (2002): 69-83.

See also Law enforcement; Noble cause; Police brutality; Police corruption; Police ethics; Police powers; Warrior versus guardian.

Posse comitatus

Definition: Group of people pressed into service to help civilian officials enforce the law
Criminal justice issues: Law-enforcement organization; Police powers
Significance: The *posse comitatus* concept requires able-bodied adults to assist civilian law-enforcement officials when requested to do so; under federal law, the principle specifically exempts military involvement.

Posse comitatus means "the entire power of the county" from which the sheriff can draw able-bodied adults to help quell civil disturbances. The name derives from ancient Roman times, when traveling government officials were accompanied by their retainers, a practice known as *comitatus*. The *posse comitatus* can be traced to the *jurata ad arma* of the feudal kings of England, whereby all freemen over fifteen years of age were required to own weapons and to be available for the king's defense. Eventually this civilian force became known as the *posse comitatus*, or simply posse.

The issue of who should be allowed to be in a posse has long been scrutinized. Except in extreme circumstances, the *posse comitatus* is composed of civilians under civilian authority. In English tradition, this separation of civil from military law enforcement can be traced to King John's signing of the Magna Carta in 1215. In the United States, the Posse Comitatus Act of 1878 stated that military personnel were not to be included in posses.

Passed in response to post-Civil War complaints of southerners that federal troops were being used to enforce civilian laws during Reconstruction, the Posse Comitatus Act instituted the separation between civilian forces under a civil control from martial forces under military control and proscribed the use of the military to quell civilian disturbances. Although the Navy and Marines are not specifically governed by the act, those branches of the military adhere to the act's prohibitions as a matter of policy. The Air Force was included in later amendments to the act.

The 1981 amendments to the act eroded its stand against the involvement of the military in law enforcement. These amendments, enacted in response to the increased power of drug smugglers, whose organizations and equipment rivaled those of some countries' military forces, delineated the military's role in civil law enforcement. In theory, the separation between civil and military law enforcement is still intact, but the 1981 amendments allow the military to supply civilian law-enforcement authorities with equipment, information, and facilities. They do not allow direct involvement of military personnel in civilian law enforcement.

The familiar posse of the American frontier was used to apprehend felons. Members of the community were deputized by sheriffs and federal marshals to chase rustlers and others who breached the peace. Sometimes the formation of posses led to abuses and vigilantism under the color of law, including abuses by groups such as the Ku Klux Klan. In modern times, the name "Posse Comitatus" was taken by an antitax vigilante group. This Posse Comitatus, a militant, armed survivalist group founded in the 1960's, believes in a reading of the U.S. Constitution that excludes all amendments beyond the first ten.

Paul Albert Bateman

Further Reading

Abrahams, Ray. *Vigilant Citizens: Vigilantism and the State*. Cambridge, England: Polity Press, 1998.

Buttaro, Andrew. "The Posse Comitatus Act of 1878 and the End of Reconstruction." *St. Mary's Law Journal* 47.1 (2015): 135-186. PDF file.

Kopel, David. "The Posse Comitatus and the Office of Sheriff: Armed Citizens Summoned to the Aid of Law Enforcement." *Journal of Criminal Law & Criminology* 104.4 (2015): 761-850. PDF file.

Neely, Richard. *Take Back Your Neighborhood: A Case for Modern-Day "Vigilantism."* New York: Penguin USA, 1990.

Sharum, Jerald A. "The Politics of Fear and Outsourcing Emergency Powers: The Death and Rebirth of the Posse Comitatus Act." *Lincoln Law Review* 37 (2009): 111-48. PDF file.

See also Criminal justice in U.S. history; National Guard; Patriot Act; Police powers; September 11, 2001, attacks; Sheriffs; Terrorism; Vigilantism.

Predictive policing

Definition: Analysis of data from a variety of sources and using the results to anticipate and deploy resources to locations where crime is expected to occur

Criminal justice issues: Criminal justice issues: Crime prevention; crime statistics; law enforcement organization

Significance: Predictive policing uses various techniques to predict and therefore reduce crime. These techniques use information, computer models, and intervention models based on evidence, as well as other techniques to reduce crime.

The goal of predictive policing is to reduce crime and improve public safety. A more proactive approach is a better means of solving the problem of crime prevention. This approach helps predict crime and lets law enforcement focus on crime-fighting resources more effectively. Computer models help anticipate where crime is most likely to occur and help mobilize preventive measures appropriately. These models are based on crime reports (major and minor), algorithms, and various other data. Typically, the underlying algorithm produces, in real time, graphically displayed areas for patrol. This methodology also can locate police bias and support efforts to combat it.

Allocating law enforcement resources to areas predicted to have increasing crime and disorder can be laden with ethical trapdoors. For example, intensive policing of young parolees and probationers in poor neighborhoods may be a recipe for deteriorating police-community relations. Moreover, civil liberties groups are not convinced that these efforts are benign and geared to stop crime. They argue that predictive policing is just another means for justifying efforts against minorities. The argument is that this method is based on bad statistics and, therefore, gives a false legitimacy to bias against minorities. There is a danger of violations of privacy. Also, there is the fact that distinguished scientists have stated that at best there is only a small gain over current methods.

Predictive policing goes back at least to 1931 and the book of Clifford R. Shaw and Hendry D. McKay, The Natural History of a Delinquent Career. It was not until recently that computers could deal with the large data sets necessary for predictive policing. The greatest contribution of predictive policing is providing situation analysis, pointing out where and how crime may be commited, and how best to combat or prevent crime.

There is the matter of the expense of the tools required for predictive policing. These vary from zero to astronomical, depending on the material purchased. Developers must be aware of the financial limitations that law enforcement agencies face and should consider regional cost-sharing agreements for the most sophisticated systems.

Predictive policing must not be considered a replacement for already existing good crime prevention techniques. They are, rather, supplements for them. Moreover, predictive policing should not be used to reinforce stereotypes or continue practices that single out minorities.

Frank A. Salamone

Further Reading

Brantingham, Jeffrey. *Research Brief: Predictive Policing, Forecasting Crime for Law Enforcement*. Santa Monica, Calif.: RAND Corporation, 2013.

Casady, Tom. "Police Legitimacy and Predictive Policing." *Geography and Public Safety* 2, no. 4 (2011): 1.

McInnis, Brian, Carter C. Price, John S. Hollywood, and Susan C. Smith. *Predictive Policing: The Role of Crime Forecasting in Law Enforcement Operations*. Santa Monica, Calif.: RAND Corporation, 2013.

Police Executive Research Forum. *Future Trends in Policing*. Washington, D.C.: Office of Community Oriented Policing Services, 2014.

Portland State University. *Criminology and Criminal Justice Senior Capstone: Predictive Policing: A Review of the Literature*. Portland, Ore.: Portland State University, 2012. http://pdxscholar.library.pdx.edu/cgi/viewcontent.cgi?article=1004&context=ccj_capstone.

See also Computer information systems; Reasonable suspicion; Stop and frisk; Technology's transformative effects.

Preventive patrol

Definition: A policing strategy dependent on officers' visible presence in communities to serve as a deterrent to street-level crimes

Criminal justice issues: Criminal justice issues: Crime prevention; law enforcement organization; police powers

Significance: Preventive patrol is a form of community policing that seeks to eliminate, or at least reduce, the opportunity for crime. Basically, it includes walking or driving in an area to watch out for problems. Increasing visible police presence is expected to deter crime.

Preventive patrol is part of what is termed the five core operational strategies of community policing. These are: preventive patrol, routine incident response, emergency response, criminal investigation, and problem solving. Preventive patrol seeks to deter crime; catch law violators; meet the public need for services and plans dealing with crime; aid the need for public confidence in law enforcement and their feelings of safety; and return stolen property to its rightful owners. Routine patrols do not lead to a reduction of crime in public areas. However, according to research by Larry Sherman and David Weisburd, targeted preventive activities do lead to such a reduction.

Preventive patrolling entails paying attention to major problems in the area being patrolled. It means being aware of the neighborhood or area in which patrolling occurs. The best way to deal with a problem is to find ways to prevent them in the first place. That requires knowing the area under patrol and the people in the area. It focuses on means for relating to people and preventing law breaking through dealing with situations before problems occur.

Those who object to prevention patrols usually point to two experiments. The Kansas City Preventive Patrol Experiment of 1972 and 1973 is generally cited as evidence that patrols do not affect the amount of crime in an area or the feeling of security in an area. The Newark Foot Patrol Experiment, conducted between 1978 and 1979, is the second experiment opponents cite. The results indicate that foot patrol may not reduce crime but it does reduce fear of crime. Citizens feel safer when they can get to know police and they know that the police know them and their area. Other studies have tended to uphold and refine these studies.

There is clear evidence that preventive patrol in conjunction with the other four elements of community policing can have an impact on the incidence of crime. The 2009 Philadelphia Experiment saw a decrease of about 23 percent. The notion of knowing the area being patrolled makes intrinsic sense and leads to more efficient use of personnel. It not only harkens to the good old days, but the fact is clear that when people get to know each other and work together crime can be reduced. Police presence can aid in reducing crime. People who trust police will aid them in doing their jobs. Simply put, it is a two-way street paved with trust. Knowing where and when danger is present can lead to its prevention. Consistency of presence is also a deterrent to rule breaking.

Frank A. Salamone

Further Reading

Braga, Anthony. "The Effects of Hot Spots Policing on Crime." *The Annals of The American Society of Science* 578 (2001): 104-25.

Larson, Richard C. "What Happened to Patrol Operations in Kansas City? A Review of the Kansas City Preventive Patrol Experiment" *Journal of Criminal Justice* 3(1975): 267-97.

Mazerolle, L., E. Antrobus, S. Bennett, and T. R. Tyler. "Shaping Citizen Perceptions of Police Legitimacy: A Randomized Field Trial of Procedural Justice." *Criminology* 51, no. 1 (2013): 33-63.

McGarrell, Edmund, Steven Chermak, Alexander Weiss, and Jeremy Wilson. "Reducing Firearms Violence Through Directed Police Patrol." *Criminology and Public Policy*, no. 1 (2001): 119-48.

Sherman, Lawrence W., and David Weisburd. "General Deterrent Effects of Police Patrol in Crime 'Hot Spots': A Randomized, Controlled Trial." *Justice Quarterly* 12 (1995): 625-48. http://renegadenoble.com/weblog/evaluating-the-effectiveness-of-random-preventive-patrol/.

Weisburd, David, and Cynthia Lum. "The Diffusion of Computerized Crime Mapping Policing: Linking Research and Practice." *Police Practice and Research* 6 (2005): 433-48.

Weisburd, David, and J. Thomas McEwen, eds. *Crime Mapping and Crime Prevention*. Monsey, N.Y.: Criminal Justice Press, 1997.

Weisburd, David, Lisa Maher, and Lawrence Sherman. "Contrasting Crime General and Crime Specific Theory: The Case of Hot Spots of Crime." *Advances in Criminological Theory*, Vol. 4. New Brunswick, N.J.: Transaction Press, 1992.

Weisburd, David, Stephen Mastrofski, and Rosann Greenspan. *Compstat and Organizational Change*. Washington, D.C.: Police Foundation, 2001.

See also Community-oriented policing; Law enforcement; Police; Problem-oriented policing.

Private police and guards

Definition: Nongovernment security personnel who provide protective services that supplement law-enforcement protection

Criminal justice issues: Crime prevention; Law-enforcement organization

Significance: Private security personnel make a valuable contributions to the criminal justice mission of safeguarding lives and property by supplementing the work of government law enforcement; however, their contributions are limited by restrictions on their enforcement powers and by the lack of training that many of them receive.

As American society has developed and the challenges of crime have become more formidable, private policing and security services have increased. Public or governmental policing has the primary responsibility to ensure that lives are protected and property is safeguarded, but individual corporations, private persons, and residential communities have turned to private security agencies to supplement the governmental services provided by government police. Since the mid-nineteenth century, the growth of private security agencies and private police has been tremendous. As of May 2015, it was estimated that over one million private security personnel were working in the United States. That figure was more than double the number of public law-enforcement officers.

History

The earliest significant private security services in the United States were offered by the Pinkerton National Detective Agency that began in Chicago in 1850. Allan Pinkerton, the founder of the agency, contributed the term "private eye" to the English language by creating a logo that placed the company's slogan, "We never sleep," under a picture of a human eye that came to symbolize private detective work. The development of the Pinkertons, as they were called, and other private detective and security agencies was directly related to railroad security, counterfeiting investigations, and other property-related crimes. Eventually, the private security business took on investigations of violent crimes in the United States.

Growth of the Private Security Industry

The growth of private security and loss prevention agencies has been fueled by a number of factors, such as the limited budgets of government police agencies. As governmental law-enforcement agencies have had to do more with less, pressure has grown on corporations and residential communities to look to the private security industry to provide needed protective services such as building security, armored car guards, asset protection, personnel protection, and general increased security presence.

Another factor has been the increasing specialization of security services. As society becomes more complicated with improved technology and special needs, public police resources are more strained. This trend has prompted the need for the employment of specialized pri-

Private security guard. (By Todd Huffman, via Wikimedia Commons)

vate security services that can be employed quickly and efficiently. For example, a corporation detecting signs of internal theft can quickly respond by employing the services of a private security company that specializes in such problems. If the corporation opted to seek the services of local police, it would be competing with the many other priorities and budget constraints of the police. The alternative, private security arrangements, might serve as an ongoing initiative to reduce long-term corporation losses.

Another example of a special problem focus might be threats against a top corporation official by a terrorist group. By employing the protective services of a private security agency, the targeted official would receive around-the-clock protection that few public law-enforcement agencies would be able to provide.

Private police and guards sometimes offer the additional advantage of being able to act without the same legal restraints placed on government agencies. The US Constitution holds public law-enforcement officials to high standards of accountability, particularly in matters of search and seizure and interrogation of suspects. Private security officials are not held to the same standards and may engage in some actions that are not allowed to police. For example, corporations may require their employees to submit to polygraph (lie detector) testing conducted by private security officials and use negative results as justification for terminating employees. Public police officials cannot become involved in such matters, except in cases in which they are specifically targeting suspects in investigations and the suspects consent to be tested.

Challenges to the Private Security Industry

The growth of private policing brings with it a wide variety of challenges and issues. These challenges will increase as public police budgets come under closer scrutiny and public demands for private services increase. One major challenge is finding and training qualified personnel. Demands for private security personnel are increasing in a world in which crime is becoming increasingly high tech, and in which domestic and international terrorism are growing threats. Attracting, training, and retaining qualified personnel is an ever-present concern in the private security industry. Whereas public police have defined standards of training and certification to meet government mandates, the private security industry is lagging in this regard.

The global dimensions of crime require public and private security professionals to engage in ongoing dialogues and cooperative partnerships in their efforts to prevent, detect, and investigate crime. For example, local public police may reach out to their private security counterparts to gain information concerning investigations that only the private security personnel may have. Conversely, private security personnel may seek the assistance of the public police in complicated criminal investigations, particularly in situations in which eventual criminal prosecution is likely.

One of the personnel trends in private security is the hiring of off-duty public police officers. Although this practice allows private security firms to benefit from the services of well-trained and experience law-enforcement officers, it also has the potential of creating problems relating to identifying who is liable for the actions of such personnel.

Jay Zumbrun

Further Reading

Cunningham, William, John Strauchs, and Clifford Van Meter. *The Hallcrest Report II: Private Security Trends, 1970-2000.* McLean, Va.: Hallcrest Systems, 1990. Private security industry assessment of trends in the industry over the last decades of the twentieth century.

Holder, Philip, and Donna Lea Hawley. *The Executive Protection Professional's Manual.* Boston: Butterworth-Heinemann, 1997. Detailed guide to all aspects of corporate security for both professionals in the field and corporations that use their services.

Horan, James D. *The Pinkertons.* New York: Bonanza Books, 1967. Popular history of the famous Pinkerton Detective Agency founded in the mid-nineteenth century.

June, Dale L. *Introduction to Executive Protection.* Boca Raton, Fla.: CRC Press, 1998. How-to guide for persons interested in becoming executive security guards. Written by a veteran in the security field, the book offers many insights into the nature of private security work.

Nemeth, Charles P. *Private Security and the Law.* 2d ed. Cincinnati: Anderson Publishing, 1995. Comprehensive textbook on all the legal issues relating to private police and guards.

See also Campus police; Citizen's arrests; Law enforcement; Police; Polygraph testing; Women in law enforcement and corrections.

Problem-oriented policing

Definition: A model of policing focused on proactively identifying and combating specific crime and societal disorders through means beyond those typically used in traditional policing.

Criminal justice issues: Criminal justice issues: Crime prevention; investigation; law-enforcement organization

Significance: Problem-oriented policing allows for law enforcement agencies to engage with certain types of crime and social disorder in a proactive manner.

Problem-oriented policing is an alternative model of policing whereby law enforcement agencies work to proactively prevent specific types of crime and social disorder as opposed to the standard model of policing, which focuses on responding to particular instances of crime after said instances have occurred.

Standard Model of Policing

To properly understand problem-oriented policing, and its significance, one must first grasp the concepts underlying the standard model of policing.

Under the standard model of policing, law enforcement agencies act in a reactive fashion. Traditionally, policing requires an instance of criminality significant enough to warrant a report being made to law enforcement. Following such a report, the agency then proceeds into action. This action typically begins with a period of information gathering by way of interviewing victims, witnesses, suspects, and offenders as well as collecting physical evidence where applicable. Thereafter, the information gathered is used in the course of the criminal justice process wherein an attempt is made at proving that an individual is (or individuals are) responsible for the particular instance of criminality such that conviction is warranted. Finally, to determine the effectiveness of the standard model of policing, those evaluating it must look to criminal statistics related to the type of crime in question. While the standard model of policing is not the only means by which any particular law enforcement agency operates, it is the primary means for most agencies.

The standard model of policing has certain drawbacks, most notably its after-the-fact implementation. Additionally, under this model, those pursued and potentially punished for their actions are limited to particular actors. However, the pursuit and punishment of particular individuals is not guaranteed to deter others who may consider engaging in the same or similar acts of criminality. It is because of these drawbacks posed by the standard model of policing that academics, law enforcement agencies, and policymakers decided to pursue an alternative manner of policing.

The Origins of Problem-Oriented Policing

In the late 1970's, as researchers became more aware of the limitations posed by the standard model of policing, a movement to establish an alternative model arose. At the forefront of this movement was University of Wisconsin-Madison professor Herman Goldstein. In his seminal 1979 article entitled "Improving Policing: A Problem-Oriented Approach," Goldstein pointed to the trend whereby law enforcement agencies were becoming increasingly concerned with the means by which they operated as opposed to the ends of such operation under the standard model of policing. Goldstein argued that this means-focused approach detracted from the effectiveness of law enforcement. For that reason, Goldstein called for the increased use of programs that focus on a more holistic approach to law enforcement—an approach he named "problem-oriented policing."

Implementing Problem-Oriented Policing

Problem-oriented policing is a means by which to increase the effectiveness of police operations by engaging with the underlying concerns which give rise to those instances of criminality and social disorder to which law enforcement agencies typically respond.

The implementation of problem-oriented policing often involves the use of a method known as the "Scanning, Analysis, Response, and Evaluation (SARA) Problem-Solving Model." The first step in the SARA Model, scanning, requires law enforcement agencies to pinpoint particular issues present in their jurisdiction and to prioritize those issues. Next, the law enforcement agencies must perform the analysis phase of the SARA Model. During this phase those matters identified during through scanning are analyzed to determine relevant information (i.e., the time at which problems typically arise, actors commonly engaging in the problem activities). Thereafter, the law enforcement agency undertakes the third phase of the SARA Model-response. During the response phase the agency develops and engages in intervention techniques that directly address those matters previously identified and analyzed. Finally, the agency engages in the evaluation phase wherein it determines the effectiveness of its strategy.

Given that problem-oriented policing is designed to proactively counteract broad areas of problems—as opposed to the standard model of policing's reactive responses to individual acts of criminality and social disorder—its implementation provides certain unique opportunities in implementation and evaluation. With regards to implementation, problem-oriented policing provides the opportunity for individuals other than officials—such as frontline officers and even members of the public—to share insight and develop strategy, thereby providing a more well-rounded plan of action. As for analysis, given the fact that it has a broader focus than the standard model of policing, problem-oriented policing allows for evaluation by means such as poverty and housing statistics—in addition to the criminal statistics traditionally used—which allows for a more thorough analysis which, in turn, helps to better law enforcement moving forward.

Reception of Problem-Oriented Policing

Studies have repeatedly shown a positive impact stemming from law enforcement agencies engagement in problem-oriented policing. As a result of its positive impact, problem-oriented policing has garnered a great deal of support from policymakers who encourage its use through generous grant funding. Conversely, problem-oriented policing has elicited negative responses from groups who believe it detracts from the structural guidelines necessary for effective policing.

Overall, given its continued successful implementations and the increased financial support, problem-oriented policing is likely to continue to grow in use alongside the standard model of policing.

John W. Klinker

Further Reading

Goldstein, Herman. "Improving Policing: A Problem-Oriented Approach." *Crime and Delinquency* 25 (1979): 236.

Spelman, William, and John E. Eck. *Problem-Oriented Policing.* National Institute of Justice: Research in Brief. Washington, D.C.: Department of Justice, 1987.

See also Law enforcement; Crime analysis; Geographic information systems.

Procedural justice

Definition: Procedural justice is the degree of due process guaranteed to every criminal suspect under the United States Constitution.

Criminal justice issues: Constitutional protections; legal terms and principles; morality and public order; professional standards

Significance: There is, at times, a natural tension for law enforcement officers, between doing the right thing, procedural justice, and getting the job of public safety done, even if that means cutting a procedural justice corner or two. That reduces the quantum of justice for everyone and reduces public confidence in law enforcement.

The American criminal justice system is imperfect. After all, it is a human system at every level. Victims, eyewitnesses, police officers, prosecutors, judges, and juries are all subject to human frailties, including prejudices and biases that can compromise the constitutional rights of a criminal suspect. At the frontline of public safety, it is law enforcement's job to ensure than the procedures, practices, and policies that guide law enforcement officer behavior will ensure due process and procedural fairness for all suspects. Unfortunately, some officers are sometimes willing to cut corners and bypass or short circuit some procedural fairness to make the bust and protect public safety—in other words, to protect and serve, some officers are occasionally willing to look the other way. When officers fail to ensure procedural justice, public confidence in law enforcement is diminished.

What Process Is Due?

The United States Constitution's first ten amendments, the Bill of Rights, contain most of the rights guaranteed to all criminal defendants. The Fourth Amendment guarantees the right to be free from unreasonable searches and seizures. The Fifth Amendment guarantees due process and the right against compelled self-incrimination. The Sixth Amendment guarantees rights to a fair and speedy jury trial, to cross-examine one's accusers, and to the assistance of counsel during all critical phases of a criminal investigation and prosecution. The Eighth Amendment protects criminal suspects from cruel and unusual punishment and excessive fines. Each of these constitutionally guaranteed rights can be violated by an uninformed or overzealous law enforcement officer. Sometimes, those officers violating suspects' constitutional rights believe that they are in the right because only they stand on the thin blue line between chaos and a vulnerable public. That is sometimes referred to as warrior mentality or the corruption of noble cause.

It is relatively easy for an unscrupulous officer to plant drugs on an innocent suspect to improve arrest rates or to arrest the suspect this time that got off on a technicality last time. An officer focused only on public safety and not on procedural justice could conduct an illegal search; profile suspects based on race, religion, or ethnicity; threaten a suspect into confessing; or refuse to make an attorney available to a suspect upon demand. All these features of procedural justice can only be delivered to civilians and suspects in police encounters when good, honest, fair, ethical, and well-trained officers elevate procedural justice to its rightful place of honor. Even laudable public safety and law enforcement ends do not justify unethical and unjust means.

When Officers Bypass Procedural Justice

Civilians, who rely on law enforcement to protect and serve, lose confidence in their local law enforcement when the officers bypass procedural justice. This impact is particularly acute for each civilian when the officer bypassed procedural justice rights belonging to that civilian. Indeed, even when an interaction with law enforcement results in arrest or criminal charges, it does not materially diminish that arrestee's confidence in local law enforcement so long as the officers treated that civilian in a manner that protected the civilian's procedural justice.

Less important perhaps, but still critical to public safety, inasmuch as law enforcement depends upon civilians for funding, information, tips, cooperation, and the like, when officers fail to protect procedural justice, civilians stop cooperating. When that happens, the entire community becomes less safe, secure, and protected.

How Agencies Optimize Procedural Justice

Many individual law enforcement decisions happen in relative secrecy between an officer patrolling alone and the civilian that officer encounters. It is not feasible for chief law enforcement officials to observe all of their junior officers' behavior. However, law enforcement agencies can organize to optimize procedural justice by having chiefs and senior officers who model ethical behavior, training officers who teach ethical decision-making, hiring and recruiting approaches that select for ethics and moral fiber, discipline methods that identify and retrain errant officers, advancement approaches that promote for ethics and procedural fairness, and policies and procedures that compel ethical behavior and encourage or require officers to report unethical behavior by other officers. Law enforcement managers must create a culture of ethics where the blue code of silence (officers covering for each other's ethical misconduct), does not hide, support, and propagate poor ethics.

Civilian confidence in local law enforcement is shaped in large measure by the degree to which those local officers honor procedural justice and adhere to the rule of law. And when evidence or confessions are unconstitutionally obtained, procedural justice requires that the improper evidence or confessions be suppressed at trial. That perceived procedural justice, in turn, leads civilians to also perceive law enforcement and the entire criminal justice system as legitimate and fair.

Charles E. "Chuck" MacLean

Further Reading

Caldero, M. A., and J. P. Crank. *Police Ethics: The Corruption of Noble Cause*. 3rd ed., revised. London: Routledge-Taylor & Francis Group, 2015.

Mazerolle, L., E. Sargeant, A. Cherney, S. Bennett, K. Murphy, E. Antrobus, and P. Martin. *Procedural Justice and Legitimacy in Policing*. Switzerland: Spring International Publishing, 2014.

See also Community-oriented policing; Due process of law; Discretion; Equal protection under the law.

Racial profiling and criminal justice

Definition: Police practice of using race or ethnicity as a primary reason for stopping, questioning, searching, or arresting potential suspects

Criminal justice issues: Civil rights and liberties; Government misconduct; Police powers; Search and seizure

Significance: Increasingly recognized as a major problem in the United States, racial profiling is damaging to everyone it touches—from its victims to the police officers who employ it and society as a whole.

Criminal profiling is a recognized technique of law enforcement that is used to help identify and apprehend criminal suspects. Police investigators establish "profiles" of typical offenders of specific crimes and then try to find suspects who match those profiles. The more variables the police consider in building a profile, the greater the probability that the profile is accurate. A central problem with racial profiling is that it is based on race, or ethnicity, and only a small number of other variables, such as sex and age.

Racial profiling is based on the assumption that members of certain racial and ethnic groups are more likely than other people to commit certain types of crime. An example of a particularly common assumption is that because many young African American men commit drug crimes, young African American men in general are more likely to commit such crimes. Acting on that assumption, law-enforcement officers who see young African American men in neighborhoods known to be centers of drug crime might feel justified in stopping and questioning them, simply because they appear to fit a drug-dealer "profile." Such stops may sometimes actually help police apprehend drug dealers who might otherwise escape arrest. However, officers practicing racial profiling also stop many entirely innocent young black men whose only offense is being black.

The central problem with racial profiling is that it tends to stigmatize whole groups of people, even though most members of the stigmatized groups are law-abiding citizens. As a consequence, members of the stigmatized groups may go through their lives feeling that they are something less than full members of society and that they are always in danger of being scrutinized and distrusted.

During the 1990s, the practice of racial profiling gained so much national attention that it became an issue of public debate. Public opinion turned against the practice, which seemed unfair, undemocratic, and perhaps even un-American. Finally, in the first state of the union address of the twenty-first century, a US president publicly spoke out against the practice. On February 27, 2001, President George W. Bush declared before a joint session of Congress that racial profiling was wrong and that it should be abolished in the United States. His message moved members of both parties to take action on the problem. The following June, a bipartisan bill, the End Racial Profiling Act of 2001, was presented to Congress.

However, in September, before Congress completed action on the bill, something happened that turned public opinion on racial profiling upside down. On September 11, Middle Eastern terrorists hijacked four American airliners and killed thousands of people in attacks on New York City and Washington, DC. Because the terrorists involved in the attacks were Muslim Arabs, a cloud of suspicion of all Middle Easterners and Muslims—as well as many other immigrants and Americans of foreign descent—descended over the United States. In the new, post-September 11 atmosphere of fear, national sentiment swung back in favor of allowing law-enforcement officers to detain and arrest suspicious-looking people on the basis of evidence as limited as their physical appearance. As a result, the End Racial Profiling Act of 2001 was never passed.

The Problem

Numerous studies have shown that police in many jurisdictions stop and question or initiate investigations of members of racial minorities at rates fare greater than the minorities' representation in the general population would suggest is appropriate. Statistical evidence from across the country points to the conclusion that racial profiling, or racially biased policing, is a measurable and real phenomenon.

An example of racial profiling on a large scale occurred in the California in 1999, when the state's Highway Patrol conducted a drug interdiction program called Operation Pipeline. The program utilized a profile provided by the federal Drug Enforcement Administration to make more than 34,000 traffic stops, only 2 percent of which resulted in drug seizures. Meanwhile, well over 33,000 motorists-most of whom were members of racial minorities-were detained and temporarily deprived of their rights.

In 2000, a federal General Accounting Office (GAO) study of the practices of the US Customs Service revealed evidence of racial profiling by federal agents. The GAO study found that during 1998, individual white women entering the United States carried with them contraband goods at a rate that was twice that of black women. Nevertheless, the black women were X-rayed for contraband at a rate nine times greater than the rate for white women. A general finding of the study was that the rates at which women and members of minorities were selected by customs officials for intrusive searches was inconsistent with the rates at which members of the same groups were found to be carrying contraband.

Studies conducted by the US Department of Justice on law-enforcement treatment of suspects have found similar patterns and inconsistencies. For example, one study found that African American drivers were 20 percent more likely than white drivers to be stopped by police and that individual African American drivers were 50 percent more likely than white drivers to have been stopped more than once. Moreover, among all drivers who were stopped by police, African Americans and Hispanics more than twice as likely as whites to be searched.

Effects of Racial Profiling

Individual citizens, communities, police forces, and society in general all suffer when racial profiling occurs. Individuals subjected to racial profiling can be injured in a variety of ways. They may experience anxiety, anger, humiliation, cynicism, fear, resentment, or combinations of these responses. Racially biased policing can cause psychological trauma and racial profiling can violate an individual's constitutional rights.

Racial profiling affects communities in several ways. The faith of communities in their local police tends to decline when the police engage in racial profiling because it humiliates and degrades all minorities. Profiling also degrades the legitimacy of the criminal justice system by breeding distrust between minority communities and the police.

The police tend to lose their effectiveness when the communities they are entrusted to protect lose confidence in them. Even when racial profiling is practiced only by a minority of police officers, the public is apt to lose confidence in the entire force.

One reason that racial profiling exists is that it reflects deeper societal attitudes about race. In fact, it tends to reflect the attitudes of members of *all* races about race. Support for this observation can be found in studies undertaken in the general population. In one such study, for example, subjects were shown two similar pictures. The first picture was of two young African American men, both in unkempt clothing, standing on street corner in a run-down neighborhood. One man was pointing a pistol at the other man. The second picture was exactly the same, except for the fact that both men were white.

When asked what was happening in the first pictures, most subjects—both white and black—thought that the man with the gun was either holding up the other man or was about to kill him. By contrast, when asked about the second picture, most subjects—both white and black—thought that the man with the gun was an undercover police officer. Tests such as that one show that the assumptions about race underlying racial profiling go well beyond police departments.

Progress

By mid-2004, nine states had passed legislation prohibiting racial profiling. Meanwhile, in February, 2004, Senator Russ Feingold of Wisconsin and Representative John Conyers of Michigan introduced the End Racial Profiling Act of 2004 in both houses of the US Congress. The new bill was designed to do five things:

- prohibit racial profiling by all federal agencies
- require state and local police agencies applying for federal assistance to have policies that discourage racial profiling
- offer grants to local and state law-enforcement agencies to create programs that ensure racially neutral administration of justice
- require all government law-enforcement agencies to submit data to the U.S. attorney general data on the racial composition of the persons whom the agencies stop, investigate, or arrest
- require the US attorney general to process the data collected and submit to Congress annual summaries on the use of racial profiling throughout the United States

This bill was never passed, but found its way to Congress several times. The most recent reintroduction of the bill was in 2015, after the unrest in Ferguson and a spate of cases of unarmed black victims being shot by white police officers brought racial profiling in law enforcement to the

---

> **The Mathematics of Racial Profiling**
>
> The seductive appeal of a racial profile lies in the belief that if members of group X are disproportionately more likely to commit a particular crime than other people, it makes sense to focus attention on group X. However, if only a tiny percentage of group X members commit the crime, then such a focus may be ethically questionable, as it would burden the overwhelming majority of law-abiding members of group X. It is instructive to consider the mathematics of profiling.
>
> If a particular crime that is committed by only 0.1 percent of the general population is committed by 1.0 percent of the members of group X, then any individual member of group X is ten times more likely to commit the crime than a member of the general population. However, 99 percent of the members of group X are law-abiding with respect to this crime. Moreover, if all the members of group X constitute less than 10 percent of the total population, then fewer than half of the people who commit the crime in question are actually members of group X.

forefront of the national consciousness. As of June 2016, no decision has been made on the bill.

Vic Sims

Further Reading

Cole, David. *No Equal Justice: Race and Class in the American Criminal Justice System*. New York: New Press, 1999. Introduction to the problems of racism in the American criminal justice system.

Davis, Kelvin R. *Driving While Black: Coverup*. Cincinnati: Interstate International Publishing, 2001. First-person account of a man who was unfairly arrested and eventually incarcerated because of racial profiling.

Harris, David. *Profiles in Injustice: Why Police Profiling Cannot Work*. New York: New Press, 2002. Powerful critique of racial profiling that may be the best general overview of the subject yet published.

Harris, David A. "Driving While Black: Racial Profiling on Our Nation's Highways." *American Civil Liberties Union*. American Civil Liberties Union, June 1999. Web. 1 June 2016.

Meeks, Kenneth. *Driving While Black: What to Do If You Are a Victim of Racial Profiling*. New York: Random House, 2000. Critique of racial profiling that offers practical advice to victims and potential victims.

Mutual Respect in Policing: Lesson Plan. Washington, D.C.: U.S. Department of Justice, Office of Community Oriented Policing Services, 2001. Federal government report on the progress made in ending racial profiling.

"Restoring a National Consensus: The Need to End Racial Profiling in America." *Leadership Conference*. Leadership Conference, March 2011. Web. 1 June 2016.

See also Equal protection under the law; *Illinois v. Wardlow*; Police civil liability; Police ethics; Police powers; Probable cause; Psychological profiling; Search and seizure; Stop and frisk; *Whren v. United States*.

Reasonable force

Definition: Amount of physical force that police officers may use while making arrests
Criminal justice issues: Arrest and arraignment; Legal terms and principles; Police powers
Significance: It is understood that police must sometimes use force to arrest suspects; however, excessive force is sometimes applied, and legal remedies exist for such cases.

Police officers are legally allowed to use the amount of force that is reasonably necessary to make an arrest. Courts should not substitute their own judgment for the judgment of the police officer in the field when the latter's discretion is exercised reasonably and in good faith. Nevertheless, the courts examine allegations of excessive force as potential violations of the due process of law that is guaranteed under the US and state constitutions. Moreover, excessive force can generate civil liability under tort law and the civil rights laws, and it can itself be a crime.

The standard used for evaluating the use of force is whether an "ordinary, prudent man under the circumstances" would condone the use of force. This is a question of fact for the jury's deliberations. Factors to be considered include the need for force, the relationship between the need and amount of force applied, the extent of injuries caused by the use of force, and whether the force was used in a good faith effort to effect the arrest. In addition, courts consider whether the application of force violates accepted standards of decency. Deadly force may generally be used only when the officer fears for his safety or the safety of others, and force used by a police officer to punish (rather than restrain) is strictly prohibited.

The US Supreme Court has made a number of rulings regarding what constitutes reasonable force. In *Tennessee v. Garner* (1985), the Supreme Court found a statute that authorized the use of deadly force to prevent the escape of a fleeing suspects to be a violation of the Fourth Amendment . In the majority opinion, Justice Byron R. White wrote, "Where the suspect poses no immediate threat to the officer and no threat to others, the harm resulting from failing to apprehend him does not justify the use of deadly force to do so. . . .Where the officer has probable cause to believe that the suspect poses a threat of serious physical harm, either to the officer or to others, it is not constitutionally unreasonable to prevent escape by using deadly force." In *Graham v. Connor* (1989), the Supreme Court ruled that "the reasonableness of a particular use of force must be judged from the perspective of a reasonable officer on the scene, rather than with the 20/20 vision of hindsight. The calculus must embody allowance for the fact that police officers are often forced to make split-second judgments—in circumstances that are tense, uncertain and rapidly-evolving—about the amount of force that is necessary in a particular situation." In *San Francisco v. Sheehan* (2015), the Supreme Court heard a case in which a woman with a history of mental illness was shot by police officers after she approached them wielding a knife while they attempted to arrest her. She then sued the officers alleging that they had failed to reasonably accommodate her disability as required by the Americans with Disabilities Act. The Court rejected this argument and held that "knowledge of a person's disability cannot foreclose officers from protecting themselves, the disabled person, and the general public."

Gwendolyn Griffith

Further Reading
Alpert, Geoffrey, and Lorie A. Fridell. *Police Vehicle and Firearms: Instruments of Deadly Force.* Prospect Heights: Waveland, 1992. Print.
Geller, William, and Hans Toch, eds. *Police Violence: Understanding and Controlling Police Abuse of Force.* New Haven: Yale UP, 1996. Print.
Panditharatne, Mekela. "When Is the Use of Force by Police Reasonable?" *Atlantic.* Atlantic Monthly Group, 17 July 2015. Web. 31 May 2016.
Susman, Tina, and Maria L. La Ganga. "Police Killing, Beating of Civilians Raise Issue of Reasonable Force." *Los Angeles Times.* Los Angeles Times, 16 Nov. 2014. Web. 31 May 2016.

See also Arrest; Deadly force; King beating case; Police brutality; Police civil liability; Police dogs; Self-defense; Special weapons and tactics teams (SWAT); *Tennessee v. Garner*; *Graham v. Connor* (1989).

Resisting arrest

Definition: Crime arising out of the preventing of law-enforcement officers from detaining or arresting suspects
Criminal justice issue: Arrest and arraignment
Significance: The statutory crime of resisting arrest is unusual in that it can occur only during confrontations between suspects and police officers attempting to make arrests on other charges.

Resisting arrest is a statutory crime of seeking to prevent an officer from taking a person into custody. A person may be taken into custody for the purpose of an arrest or a brief questioning. A police officer need not obtain a warrant to arrest or detain a defendant in a public place. Police officers may arrest a person for misdemeanors committed in their presence or if such misdemeanors qualify as a breach of the peace. Probable cause is the legal standard for arresting a defendant. Resisting arrest is a separate crime from the underlying offense.

Even if the underlying offense proves to be without cause or the arrest is illegal, a defendant may be liable for the separate offense of resisting arrest. A police officer has the authority to conduct a warrantless search of vehicles provided there is probable cause that a crime was committed. A person preventing a police officer from detaining the defendant or seized property may be charged with the crime of resisting arrest. A person who injures a police officer in the course of resisting arrest may be charged with more serious offenses such as aggravated assault or attempted murder. A police officer is permitted to use reasonable force in detaining a criminal suspect.

Michael L. Rustad

Further Reading
Loewy, Arnold H., and Arthur B. LaFrance. *Criminal Procedure: Arrest and Investigation.* Cincinnati: Anderson Publishing, 1996.
Quick, Bruce D. *Law of Arrest, Search, and Seizure: An Examination of the Fourth, Fifth, and Sixth Amendments to the United States Constitution.* Rev. ed. Bismarck, N.Dak.: Attorney General's Office, Criminal Justice Training and Statistics Division, 1987.

See also Arraignment; Disorderly conduct; King beating case; Nonviolent resistance; Police; *Tennessee v. Garner*.

Secret Service, U.S.

Identification: Federal law-enforcement agency that performs both investigative and protective tasks
Date: Founded in 1865
Significance: With their dual responsibilities of protecting federal government officials and investigating financial and other federal-government-related crimes, the men and women of the Secret Service are central figures in US law-enforcement work.

During the US Civil War, more than seven thousand varieties of paper currency circulated in the United States. Confusion over these currencies allowed counterfeiting to flourish. After the war, the federal government responded by creating the Secret Service to prevent the counterfeiting and dissemination of fake treasury notes and currencies. President Abraham Lincoln signed the bill creating the agency on April 14, 1865—the same day on which he was to be shot by John Wilkes Booth. The new agency fell under the auspices of the Department of the Treasury.

Throughout the rest of the nineteenth century, government currency remained in disarray, and money markets were rife with corruption and illicit activity. At one point, every individual state had its own coin and paper currency. Meanwhile, more than one-third of all paper currency in circulation in the United States was believed to be fake.

Through its first few decades of operation, the Secret Service shut down hundreds of illegal money operations throughout the country. However, the agency was also re-

U.S. Secret Service agents. (Public domain, via Wikimedia Commons)

quired to investigate many cases that fell outside its narrow investigative realm. For example, presidents directed the Secret Service to investigate persons associated with the Teapot Dome scandal during the 1920s, frauds committed by members of the government, and various people who might pose threats to the government and the citizens of the United States. The most frequently targeted groups by the Secret Service were members of groups that exhibited antigovernment sentiment, such as the Ku Klux Klan

Responsibilities

The primary investigative responsibility of the Secret Service has been and continues to be counterfeiting and other financial crimes. Along with hundreds of support personnel, special agents are assigned to carry out these investigations. During the early 1980s, Congress began expanding the investigative responsibilities of the Secret Service. The agency's responsibilities now encompass credit card fraud; crimes involving specific types of forgery; fraud stemming from false identification; cybercrime; all crimes relating to US financial institutions; certain crimes relating to terrorism, especially issues of school violence and domestic hate groups; certain types of money laundering; and major identity theft cases. In fact, the Secret Service is the only federal agency that has explicit federal investigative power over identity theft cases.

By a tragic irony, President Lincoln was shot the same day that he signed the bill creating the Secret Service, which would later take on the task of protecting presidents. Outraged citizens petitioned Congress to find ways to protect future presidents. However, Congress waited thirty-six years before it responded. Meanwhile, two more presidents would be assassinated: James A. Garfield in 1881 and William McKinley in 1901.

In 1906, five years after McKinley's assassination, Congress passed a law giving the Secret Service responsibility for protecting presidents. In 1917, Congress expanded on this protection by making verbal and written threats against presidents and members of their families federal offenses. This law was further broadened in 1951 to protect vice presidents and their families.

The protective responsibilities of the twenty-first century Secret Service have grown exponentially. Two divisions of Secret Service personnel are responsible for various protective assignments. The first are special nonuniformed agents who act as personal bodyguards for governmental dignitaries. Many years of guided training are required before agents are assigned to special protective duties.

The second division consists of uniformed Secret Service officers who carry out their duties much like regular police officers. Created by President Warren G. Harding in 1922, the uniformed officers provide a visible security presence in places such as the White House, the vice president's residence, buildings in which presidential offices are located, all US Treasury buildings, all foreign embassies in Washington, DC, and other federal facilities throughout the United States that the president deems necessary to protect.

The Secret Service Today

As of 2016, the Secret Service employed approximately 7,000 people in field offices in both the United States and overseas. Approximately 1,300 of these people are uniformed officers assigned to protect federal facilities affiliated with the president, vice president, foreign embassies, and the Treasury Department. Most facilities that these officers are assigned to protect are located in the metropolitan District of Columbia area.

An additional 3,200 employees are special agents who are assigned to investigative and protective duties in Washington DC, throughout the continental United States, and overseas. Special agent are trained for both protective and investigative capacities and are expected to be able to perform the duties and responsibilities of both roles at any time and any place.

Paul M. Klenowski

Further Reading

"Frequently Asked Questions." *US Secret Service*. US Dept. of Homeland Security, n.d. Web. 30 May 2016.
Melanson, Philip H., and Peter F. Stevens. *The Secret Service: The Hidden History of an Enigmatic Agency*. New York: Carroll, 2002. Print.
Motto, Carmine J. *In Crime's Way: A Generation of Secret Service Adventures*. Boca Raton: CRC, 1999. Print.
Petro, Joseph, and Jeffrey Robinson. *Standing Next to History: An Agent's Life Inside the Secret Service*. New York: Dunne, 2005. Print.
Seidman, David. *Secret Service Agents: Life Protecting the President*. New York: Rosen, 2003. Print.

See also Counterfeiting; Cybercrime; Homeland Security, U.S. Department of; Identity theft; Justice Department, U.S.; Money laundering; Treasury Department, U.S.

Sheriffs

Definition: Chief law-enforcement administrators of counties who are usually elected officials

Significance: As chief county law-enforcement administrators, sheriffs are responsible for maintaining public order within their jurisdictions.

In addition to maintaining public order, the duties of sheriffs may also include the execution of the mandates and judgments of criminal and civil courts, the delivery of writs, the summoning of juries, and the maintenance of county jails. The responsibilities of sheriffs are often so vast that sheriffs' offices are the largest employers of law-enforcement personnel in many areas of the country. Around 1990, more than one in five law-enforcement officers served in sheriffs' departments. In states that legally require sheriffs, the duties and responsibilities of the office vary widely as do the requirements for holding the office. It is not unusual in many states for individuals to be elected who possess little or no educational training in law enforcement.

Sheriffs in England

The office of sheriff originated in England prior to the Norman Conquest of 1066. Each shire, or county, was administered by a representative of the king known as a reeve. The appointed reeve was usually a baron who was an ally of the king. These officials had nearly absolute power within their jurisdictions. Eventually the title "shire reeve" evolved phonetically into "sheriff." The sheriff in the English countryside collected taxes, commanded the militia, delivered writs, and served as judge and jury in all criminal and civil cases. After the reign of William the Conqueror (r. 1066-87), the sheriff's power and status were dramatically diminished. Under King Henry II (1154-89) the position assumed a law-enforcement role. By the end of the Protestant Reformation in England, specifically during the reign of Queen Elizabeth I (1558-1603), most of the duties and powers once reserved exclusively for the sheriff had been assumed by the newly created offices of constable and justice of the peace.

Early American History

The English settlers of colonial America referred to their first law-enforcement officials as constables, as they had responsibilities very similar to those of their English namesakes. However, the governor of colonial New York appointed sheriffs who functioned in much the same manner as they had in England, exercising considerable power in their respective counties. The sheriff in colonial New York was also responsible for the total oversight of elections, which led to widespread claims of corruption and abuse of power. The office of sheriff was stripped of much of its power following the American Revolution (1775-83) and sheriffs as the law-enforcement agents of frontier justice did not emerge until after the American Revolutionary War.

Prior to the Civil War of the early 1860s, American sheriffs were typically appointed to their positions by state, territorial, or city governments, and they exercised wide-ranging powers. Their many duties included maintaining order, collecting taxes, apprehending criminals, conducting elections, and maintaining local jails. Frontier sheriffs led particularly dangerous lives. They were poorly trained and often ill-equipped to deal with the hardships required of their office.

In the Western territories of California, Oregon, Utah, New Mexico, Colorado, Nevada, and Texas they were called upon to travel great distances to apprehend criminals and perform other duties. When granted the authority, sheriffs also appointed deputy sheriffs to assist them in carrying out the duties of their office, especially the apprehension of fleeing criminals. It was not uncommon for sheriffs to "deputize" dozens of volunteers when circumstances required, especially during emergency situations. As the former Western territories achieved US statehood, sheriffs increasingly became elected officeholders.

The Modern Sheriff

By 1900 population shifts in many states from the countryside to the cities required the creation of new law-enforcement agencies, such as city and state police departments. These new agencies assumed much of the work and duties performed by sheriffs' offices. The complexities of organized crime and other developments, especially the automobile and the expanding highway system, necessitated the creation of highly trained and skilled state and federal police agencies capable of dealing with the challenges of modern criminal activity. Most sheriffs, generally popularly elected, did not have the training or professional qualifications to deal with the modern criminal, who could move rapidly from one jurisdiction to another.

Another often-heard complaint was that the sheriffs in many communities were nothing more than servants of the local elites. In 1940 sheriffs around the country who were concerned about the level of professionalism and expertise needed to survive in the ever-changing field of criminal justice began organizing what evolved into the National Sheriffs' Association (NSA). The NSA offers training, information, and other services to sheriffs, deputies, and other personnel throughout the United States, allowing law-enforcement professionals to network and share information about trends in law enforcement and policing. In 1972 the National Sheriff's Institute (NSI) was established by the NSA to provide sheriffs and their administrative staffs with high-quality, low-cost training and programs. Jail administration, liability issues, crime prevention, and public relations are but a few of the many concerns addressed by NSI classes. The NSA also publishes the *Sheriff* magazine, *Community Policing Exchange*, *Sheriff Times*, and several other periodicals.

According to the Bureau of Justice Statistics, as of the 2008 census, there were more than 3,000 sheriffs' departments in the United States, which serve as a critical part of the modern law-enforcement community. Issues of concern for modern sheriffs as they enter the twenty-first century include funding, community policing, coping with law-enforcement stress, and rising medical costs. In many sparsely populated and unincorporated areas of the United States, the locally elected sheriff is still the primary source of law-enforcement protection. Alaska and New Jersey are the only states that do not maintain sheriffs' offices. As of 2016, sheriffs are elected in forty-six states, and most states require that all law-enforcement personnel, including sheriffs, undergo training before acting in their capacity as law-enforcement officers.

Donald C. Simmons, Jr.

Further Reading

Cohn, Paul, and Shari Cohn. *Careers in Law Enforcement and Security*. New York: Rosen, 1990. Print.

Daniels, Bruce C., ed. *Town and Country: Essays on the Structure of Local Government in the American Colonies*. Middletown: Wesleyan UP, 1978. Print.

Duncombe, Herbert Sydney. *Modern County Government*. Washington, DC: Natl. Assn. of Counties, 1977. Print.

Keith-Lucas, Bryan. *The History of Local Government in England*. New York: Kelly, 1970. Print.

Prassel, Frank R. *The Western Peace Officer: A Legacy of Law and Order*. Norman: U of Oklahoma P, 1971. Print.

Rosa, Joseph G. *The Gunfighter: Man or Myth?* Norman: U of Oklahoma P, 1969. Print.

US Bureau of Labor Statistics. *Census of State and Local Law Enforcement Agencies, 2008*. Washington, DC: BLS, 2011. PDF file.

See also Highway patrols; Law enforcement; Marshals Service, U.S.; Police; Police chiefs; *Posse comitatus*; Vigilantism.

Slave patrols

Definition: Summoned bodies of citizens charged with enforcing laws restricting the activities and movement of slaves in the antebellum South

Criminal justice issues: Civil rights and liberties; Law-enforcement organization

Significance: Slave patrols provide an example of the piecemeal, militia-style law enforcement of the pre-Civil War South and served as a blueprint for the vigilante groups of the postbellum South.

The British American colonies began to establish informal slave patrols during the late seventeenth and early eighteenth centuries in reaction to public fears of slave rebellion. South Carolina, with its majority black population, was the first colony to establish formal slave patrols in 1704, followed by Virginia in 1727 and North Carolina in 1753. By the end of the eighteenth century, slave patrols existed in every state where slavery was legal. The patrols' makeup and the extent of their activities varied from state to state and often from locality to locality according to the size of the slave population and the threat of runaways and insurrection. Patrollers were typically white men between the ages of sixteen and sixty, chosen from militia and tax rolls to serve terms that varied in length.

Slave patrols usually worked at night in small groups, looking for slaves wandering from their home plantations without permission, evidence of unlawful slave assemblies, and other illegal activities. Patrollers were assigned broad authority to act as police, judge, and jury, including the right to enter plantations without a warrant, search slave quarters and other plantation property, and arrest or summarily punish slaves at will. Brutality, vindictiveness, and other abuses of power were common under this system; just as common, however, were complaints of laxity and ineffectiveness on the part of the patrols in suppressing slave assemblies and reducing the number of runaway slaves. Slave patrols operated sporadically in many locations, especially those in which slaves were relatively few in number. In some areas, they were little more than loosely organized posses activated in the event of real or perceived threats.

Evidence indicates that public attitudes toward slave patrols were mixed and that many southerners simply considered them a necessary evil. Nonslaveholders often bore most of the burden of patrolling, leading to resentment and abuses of power leveled against both slaves and their owners. Men with the means to avoid patrol duties by hiring substitutes or simply paying the fines for not serving often did so. Nevertheless, few southerners advocated doing away with the patrols, which continued to exist until slavery was abolished. Over time, slave patrols assumed other law-enforcement duties in many localities, becoming de facto police forces in some southern towns and cities.

Slave patrols intensified their activities during the Civil War, often joining forces with local militias. Although they ceased to operate after the war, slave patrols provided the inspiration for the activities of the Ku Klux Klan and other "night riders" who terrorized southern blacks during the Reconstruction era.

Michael H. Burchett

Further Reading
Hadden, Sally E. "Slave Patrols." *New Georgia Encyclopedia*. Georgia Humanities Council, 10 Jan. 2014. Web. 25 May. 2016.
Hadden, Sally E. *Slave Patrols: Law and Violence in Virginia and the Carolinas*. Cambridge, Mass.: Harvard University Press, 2001.
Iyamah, Jackie. "Slave Patrols and the Origins of Policing." *Ella Baker Center for Human Rights*. Ella Baker Ctr. for Human Rights, 6 Nov. 2015. Web. 25 May. 2016.
Stampp, Kenneth M. *The Peculiar Institution: Slavery in the Antebellum South*. New York: Vintage Books, 1989.
Wyatt-Brown, Bertram. *Southern Honor: Ethics and Behavior in the Old South*. New York: Oxford University Press, 1983.

See also Corporal punishment; Criminal justice in U.S. history; Lynching; Marshals Service, U.S.; Vigilantism.

Special weapons and tactics teams (SWAT)

Definition: Specialized police units designed to resolve dangerous crises
Criminal justice issues: Morality and public order; police powers; violent crime
Significance: Nearly every major municipal police department in the United States now includes some type of SWAT unit, and these tactical units are gradually moving from acting as urban-emergency response teams to performing more routine police duties, such as drug-interdiction, marijuana eradication, and police training, among other similar activities.

Special weapons and tactics teams, or SWAT teams as they are better known, were first established by the Los Angles Police Department in response to the Watts riot of 1965. The brainchild of future Los Angeles police chief Daryl Gates, SWAT teams were designed as paramilitary units to counter urban insurgencies regular police officers were not trained or equipped to handle. In fact, many modern SWAT teams now get much of their equipment, weapons, and training directly from the U.S. military.

The units were originally called "special weapons attack teams," but the name was changed to make the units sound more technical and less aggressive. More American cities began creating SWAT teams after an incident in Austin, Texas, in 1966, when a sniper named Charles Whitman barricaded himself in a university tower and began randomly firing upon people below. That incident brought to national attention the idea of training and equipping specialized police units to deal with exceptionally dangerous situations.

The first SWAT teams were especially designed to deal with situations involving hostages and barricaded suspects. However, they were soon used to control violent political groups such as the Black Panthers and the Symbionese Liberation Army.

SWAT teams place a high emphasis on teamwork and set high standards for their members. Candidates for SWAT team placement are carefully selected and must meet strict qualifications. They must have good service records, meet certain physical requirements, and demonstrate that they can react quickly in stressful situations. The criteria are strict because SWAT members are involved in highly volatile situations and carry weapons that can cause a great amount of damage.

In the twenty-first century, SWAT teams are being used in everyday police situations and are no longer limited to responding to hostage and barricaded suspect situations. Their current responsibilities now include serving search warrants to high-risk suspects (and in many cases low-risk suspects as well), especially those believed to possess firearms. SWAT teams also often participate in drug raids, riot control, and in some areas are used to stabilize violent domestic disputes and vicious animals.

The use of SWAT teams in everyday policing has been controversial. Some critics argue SWAT teams are increasing the militarism of police forces, thereby eroding the line between domestic law enforcement and martial law. Peter Kraska, the leading academic researcher on police militarization, cites several aspects of the militarization of the police as concerning: 1) the erosion of the Posse Comitatus Act, 2) multi-level cooperative relationships between US military and civilian police related to training and equipment and information sharing, 3) increased use of SWAT raids modeled after military operational tactics, 4) increasing US civilian police reliance on a military model of rational and operations to guide police operations, and 5) defining criminality as "insurgency". Additionally, in October of 2014, Kraska testified at the Senate Hearing on Police Use of Military Equipment, that it is also problematic that police officers are increasingly trained to adopt a "survivalist" mindset, by which they are taught to perceive all situations as potentially life-threatening scenarios. Such a mindset is thought to translate into more aggressive styles of policing being used in generally non-life threatening situations. Overall, Kraska contends the central importance of studying the increasing militarization of US police forces (including changes in the nature and use of SWAT teams) is because this change, "signals a historic shift in the nature of the state, how it secures (or attempts to secure) compliance, and the overall character of modern social control". Finally, also concerning are SWAT operations which have resulted in the loss of innocent lives and injuries. For example, one botched SWAT raid executed in Georgia left an 18-month old toddler with facial and torso burns and a collapsed lung after an officer threw a flash-bang grenade into the toddler's pack-and-play.

Critics have highlighted such problems as reasons why SWAT teams should not be used.

The militarization of the police (and simultaneously the use of SWAT teams in the United States) became a national and public issue in 2014 after Officer Darren Wilson killed Michael Brown in Ferguson, Missouri. After rioting started, police officers arrived in military/SWAT uniforms equipped with armored vehicles and assault rifles, which led many critics to state the police were treating the streets as a "warzone". Law enforcement's response to the Ferguson protest brought national attention to the U.S. Departments of Defense's 1033 program, which supplies law enforcement agencies across the U.S. with excessive military-grade weapons and equipment not needed by the military. Through the 1033 Program, roughly 13,000 law enforcement agencies have historically been able to receive Humvees, high-powered weapons, infrared imaging systems, military assault vehicles, and night-vision goggles; in 2012 local law enforcement agencies received defense surplus weapons and equipment valued at $546 million. In response to these criticisms, President Barak Obama signed Presidential Executive Order 13688—Federal Support for Local Law Enforcement Equipment Acquisition, which placed some restrictions on the types of equipment law enforcement agencies can acquire through the DOD's 1033 program. The order essentially limited law enforcement's ability to procure bayonets and grenade launchers.

Proponents of SWAT teams counter, however, that dangerous situations will always arise that police officers cannot control. Proponents also note that the increasing number of violent criminals in American society and the growing threat of terrorism will continue to make SWAT teams necessary, and that in the long run, SWAT teams will save many more lives than they cause to be lost. Indeed, future developments and research on the nature and use of SWAT teams in the United States (and their ties to militarism) will be watched closely by both critics and proponents alike.

Mark Anthony Cubillos
Updated by Allen Copenhaver

Further Reading
Bennett, K. (2015). 365 days and 605 armored military vehicles later: Police militarization a year after Ferguson. Retrieved from https://www.aclu.org/blog/speak-freely/365-days-and-605-armored-military-vehicles-later-police-militarization-year-after
Goranson, Christopher D. (2003). *Police SWAT Teams: Life on High Alert.* New York, NY: Rosen.

Kiker III, C.R. (2015). From Mayberry to Ferguson: The militarization of American policing equipment, culture, and mission. Washington & Lee Law Review, 71(4/5), 282-298.

Kraska, P. B. (2007). Militarization and policing—Its relevance to 21st century police. Policing,1-13. doi:10.1093/police/pam065

Kraska, P.B. (2001). The military-criminal justice blur: An introduction. In P.B. Kraska (Ed.), Militarizing the American criminal justice system (3-13). Boston, MA: Northeastern University Press (see pg. 11 specifically for quote referenced above).

Lynn, A., & Gutman, M. (2014). Family of toddler injured by SWAT 'grenade' faces $1m in medical bills. Retrieved from http://abcnews.go.com/US/family-toddler-injured-swat-grenade-faces-1m-medical/story?id=27671521

Peralta, E., & Eads, D. (2015). White House ban on militarized gear for police may mean little. National Public Radio, 21. Retrieved 10/11/2016 from http://www.npr.org/sections/thetwo-way/2015/05/21/407958035/white-house-ban-on-militarized-gear-for-police-may-mean-little

Potter, G. (2013, December 19). A bullet for Barney: The DOD and small town police forces. Retrieved from http://uprootingcriminology.org/blogs/bullet-barney-dod-small-town-police-forces/

Snow, Robert L. (1996). SWAT Teams: Explosive Face-offs with America's Deadliest Criminals. Cambridge, MA: Perseus Books.

See also Criminal justice system; Criminals; Deadly force; Drugs and law enforcement; Law Enforcement Assistance Administration; No-knock warrants; Police; Police brutality; Police ethics; Police powers; Reasonable force; Terrorism.

Stakeouts

Definition: Tactical deployments of law-enforcement officers to specific locations for the purpose of surreptitiously observing criminal suspects to gather information or to stop crimes from occurring

Criminal justice issues: Crime prevention; investigation; technology

Significance: Stakeouts are frequently high-profile tactical operations that can present risks to officers, offenders, and bystanders alike. As forms of police intervention, they may involve armed and violent criminal suspects. To avoid exposure and to minimize risks, stakeouts require careful tactical planning and complex team efforts.

The action-packed portrayals of police stakeouts that are often presented in novels, films, and television shows are misleading. The fictional kinds of stakeouts, in which cops sit in vehicles for an hour or so and then arrest multiple suspects, would rarely succeed in real life. Real stakeouts tend to be undramatic, tedious, and personally demanding.

Stakeouts take two basic forms: temporary and planned. Temporary stakeouts tend to be impromptu actions, undertaken as unexpected situations develop. They can also be high-risk operations. Most temporary or impromptu stakeouts result when officers are in the preliminary stages of investigations or discover pending criminal activity that requires immediate action.

To succeed, surveillance and stakeout teams must blend into neighborhoods to avoid being detected themselves. Fictional stakeouts often show officers sitting in their cars for hours in the suspects' neighborhoods. However, occupied vehicles parked for prolonged periods rarely go unnoticed. If investigators fail to be in harmony with their surroundings, they are likely to be identified, or—in stakeout jargon—"burned" or "made." The best results in temporary stakeouts occur when they are conducted from fixed and secure positions, such as buildings.

Planned stakeouts are more complex operations, whose success results from team efforts, not lone detective improvisation. Stakeout operations may offer opportunities to interrupt serial offenses, such as robbery, drug deals, and other offenses. For example, a crime analyst studying convenience-store robberies who discovers patterns in the methods of the robberies and trademark behaviors of the robbers would have reason to suspect that the robberies are part of a series. Moreover, the analyst might even see something in the patterns to suggest that certain stores are likely to be hit next. Drawing on the analyst's conclusions, a police lieutenant would organize a surveillance team to stake out the threatened stores. A major operation might have teams working both inside and outside the stores, so that careful coordination of their efforts would have be planned in advance.

Thomas E. Baker

Further Reading

Adams, James A., and Daniel D. Blinka. *Electronic Surveillance: Commentaries and Statutes.* Notre Dame, Ind.: National Institute for Trial Advocacy, 2003.

Lyman, Michael D., and Gary W. Potter. *Organized Crime.* Upper Saddle River, N.J.: Prentice-Hall, 2004.

Monmonier, M. S. *Spying with Maps: Surveillance Technologies and the Future of Privacy.* Chicago: University of Chicago Press, 2002.

Rossmo, D. Kim. *Geographic Profiling.* Boca Raton, Fla.: CRC Press, 2000.

See also Electronic surveillance; *Katz v. United States*; *Kyllo v. United States*; *Olmstead v. United States*; Privacy rights; Stop and frisk; Surveillance cameras; Wiretaps.

State police

Definition: Law-enforcement organizations that operate directly under the authority of state governments, rather than under municipalities

Criminal justice issues: Law-enforcement organization; Police powers; Traffic Law

Significance: State police carry out certain specific functions, principally highway safety and criminal investigations.

The US Constitution assigned to the states the responsibility for maintaining law and order. Until 1900, however, the states entrusted policing mainly to local communities. In case of riots or other serious disorders, governors called out the militia. In Texas, the Rangers, a mounted militia, kept the peace in isolated areas in addition to fighting Native Americans and patrolling the Mexican border.

Early State Police Forces

During the 1890's, the United States underwent rapid industrialization and grew more interdependent, its parts connected by a vast network of railroads. Crime became more mobile and complex, challenging the resources of local police. At the dawn of the twentieth century there was a pressing need for more specialized, better-trained police at the state level.

The first state to meet that need was Pennsylvania. Like many other newly industrialized areas of the Northeast and Midwest since the Civil War (1861-1865), Pennsylvania suffered chronically from severe social unrest, especially among workers in its coal mines and factories. A fierce, lengthy strike in the anthracite mines in 1902 aroused public opinion to demand that other, more civilized means be found of calming industrial disputes than the indiscriminate clubbing of mine workers by private police. This outcry set in motion a reform movement led by Governor Samuel W. Pennypacker to create a state police. The governor sent John C. Groome, a former officer in the Philippine Constabulary, to Ireland, where he studied the Royal Irish Constabulary. In 1905 Groome organized the Pennsylvania State Police, recruiting 228 men with military backgrounds, some of whom had also been officers in the Philippine Constabulary. They were given rigorous training and then deployed in four units in western Pennsylvania, where they proved to be impartial and effective at quelling disorder.

Fourteen states established police forces over the next twenty years, the eastern states generally following Pennsylvania's example. Western states, such as Nevada and Colorado, created forces that were extremely brutal and partial to the interests of wealthy absentee employers, especially in the mining industry. During the 1920's, modern highways spread out across the United States, creating a new task for state police: traffic control. This required a new approach to policing. Persons wealthy enough to own or drive automobiles were likely to be prosperous merchants and professionals rather than foreign-born coal miners. Police had to be recruited and trained who could deal civilly with middle-class taxpayers, offering traffic safety programs and mildly enforcing traffic regulations.

At the same time, the expense of installing the technology to fight crime led many states to establish bureaus of criminal identification. By 1940 highway patrols or state police were at work in more than 80 percent of the states. They had earned reputations as "elite lawmen." Since World War II, state police have continued to be concerned mainly with traffic control, while assuming a more significant role in criminal investigation. State police agencies are characterized by their narrow, specific mandates, reflecting public distrust of centralized policing in the European tradition.

Organization of State Police

The term "state police" is broadly understood to refer to the various agencies of law enforcement that function directly under the authority of the governments of the states, in contrast to county and local police agencies and federal police agencies. This broad definition of state police includes highway patrols, state police forces, and a variety of state investigative agencies. In 1993 there were 87,000 state police in the widest sense of the term, which amounted to 9.7 percent of all sworn law-enforcement personnel in the United States. In contrast, there were 110,000 federal, 173,000 county, and 465,000 municipal police. All U.S. states except Hawaii have state policing agencies. Twenty-six states have highway patrols and twenty-three have state police agencies. Thirty-five states have investigative agencies that are separate from highway patrols or state police. There are, in addition, a great number of specialized investigative bodies, such as fire marshals and fish and wildlife agents. All state law-enforcement entities derive their authority to investigate wrongdoing or enforce the law from the state legislatures, from which they receive most of their funds.

State law enforcement is organized differently from state to state. In some states several agencies are centralized in one department. The Iowa Department of Public

Safety, which is headed by a commissioner who reports to the governor, oversees the divisions of state patrol, criminal investigation, fire marshal, capitol security, communications, and administrative services. In other states, law-enforcement agencies are organized in various departments. The California Highway Patrol, for example, is organized in the Business, Transportation, and Housing Agency while the state's investigative agencies are grouped together in the Division of Law Enforcement under a director appointed by the state attorney general. Some state police agencies are controlled by commissions and others by state governors.

A Ford Expedition used by the Pennsylvania State Police. (By Niagara, via Wikimedia Commons)

State Police Powers

State police in the narrow sense, in contrast to highway patrols, have state-wide powers to arrest persons suspected of both criminal and traffic offenses. Most state police agencies have plainclothes and uniformed agents. They provide the auxiliary services of record-keeping, training, communications, and forensics. Pennsylvania has the largest state police agency and Idaho the smallest.

State highway patrols are usually limited to enforcing traffic regulations, but they are empowered to assist any law-enforcement officer upon request. The investigation of crime is generally left to separate state investigative agencies. California has the largest highway patrol and Wyoming the smallest.

Investigative agencies with statewide authority to arrest have primary jurisdiction in certain crimes. Criminal investigative personnel are plainclothes officers who provide a variety of auxiliary services. They are distinguished from other state investigative agents, such as fish and game inspectors, whose powers are limited to a particular area of enforcement. Florida has the largest state bureau of investigation and North Dakota and South Dakota the smallest.

Role of State Police Broadly Considered

All state law-enforcement agencies require that applicants be US citizens and state residents. Most state police agencies provide a basic course of instruction and training, usually at police academies, and in-service training. The minimum educational requirement is usually a high school diploma or equivalent. The investigative agencies of California and several other states require that applicants must have completed two or more years of college, concentrating on police sciences.

Regardless of how differently state police systems are organized, they share common functions within law enforcement. They investigate certain crimes as prescribed by state law and provide forensic and other technical services to local police. They also provide specialized investigators, such as narcotics squads, to assist investigations by local agencies. State police enforce, with the power of arrest, state traffic laws and laws pertaining to certain criminal offenses. Usually state constitutions assign to county and municipal police the general responsibility for enforcing state laws and keeping the peace. If rural or unincorporated areas are unwilling or unable to perform these functions, they may contract or arrange for service by state police, as is the case in Alaska, Rhode Island, and Connecticut

On rare occasions state governments may call upon their police to temporarily assume law-enforcement duties in municipalities, as in New York City in 1935 and Trenton, New Jersey, in 1983. With a few exceptions, the state police's authority to carry arms and to arrest is limited to the areas within state borders. States may enter into mutual agreements with one another that allow their respective police to cross borders in pursuit of fugitives.

State police forces provide information to themselves, to local police within their states, and to other state and federal agencies. Every state has access to the National Crime Information Center of the Federal Bureau of Investigation (FBI). They all have computer information systems for processing criminal records. The effectiveness of communication is improved by regional cooperation, as in the New England State Police Compact, under which police forces share resources in the investigation of organized crime. In most cases state law-enforcement agencies are responsible for collecting, transmitting, and publishing states' crime statistics. State law-enforcement agencies also supply forensic services to their own personnel and to other criminal justice agencies. For the most part, the employees of states' forensic institutions are civilians.

Examples of State Police Forces

Established in May 1905, the Pennsylvania state police was the first state police force in the United States. It is also the largest. Its organization is centralized under a commissioner, who is appointed by the governor and has the rank of colonel. Reporting directly to the commissioner is the Bureau of Professional Responsibility, the Office of General Counsel, the Office of the Budget, and Public Information. A chief of staff responsible for several bureaus of technical and administrative services also reports to the commissioner. A deputy commissioner responsible for a bureau of highway patrol, a bureau of criminal investigation, and five area commands also reports to the commissioner. In addition to the main forensic laboratory in Harrisburg, there are four regional crime laboratories serving local police. The Bureau of Criminal Investigation includes divisions of general investigation, organized crime, fire marshal, and drug-law enforcement.

Recruits to the Pennsylvania state police must be US citizens, state residents, and high school graduates, and they must meet certain physical requirements. Cadets undergo a twenty-week trooper course at the training academy in Hershey followed by field training and periodic in-service instruction.

Founded in 1929, the California Highway Patrol has grown to be the largest agency of its kind in the United States that focuses on traffic control. Situated in the Business, Transportation, and Housing Agency, it is led by a commissioner, who is appointed by the governor. It is one of two primary state law-enforcement agencies, the other being the California Division of Law Enforcement, which is responsible for criminal identification and investigation and forensic and other technical investigative services. The California Highway Patrol requires its recruits to be US citizens, holders of valid California driver's licenses and high school graduates. Moreover, they must meet certain physical and legal requirements. Recruits undergo a basic training course of twenty-two weeks at the academy in Yolo County.

Charles H. O'Brien

Further Reading
Bechtel, Kenneth H. *State Police in the United States: A Socio-Historical Analysis.* Westport, Conn.: Greenwood Press, 1995.
Fisher, Scott M. *Courtesy, Service, Protection: The Iowa State Patrol.* Dubuque, Iowa: Kendall-Hunt, 1993.
Johnson, David R. *American Law Enforcement: A History.* St. Louis, Mo.: Forum Press, 1981.
Smith, Bruce. *The State Police: Organization and Administration.* Montclair, N.J.: Patterson Smith, 1969.
Stark, John. *Troopers: Behind the Badge.* West Trenton: New Jersey State Police Memorial Association, 1993.
Stephens, Donna M. *Soldiers of the Law: Oklahoma Highway Patrolmen During the Early Years, 1937-1964.* Philadelphia: Xlibris Corporation, 2003.

Torres, Donald A. *Handbook of State Police, Highway Patrols, and Investigative Agencies.* Westport, Conn.: Greenwood Press, 1987.

See also Criminal justice system; Highway patrols; National Guard; Police; Sheriffs; Sobriety testing; Traffic fines; Traffic law.

Sting operations

Definition: Undercover police operations in which officers pose as criminals in order to trap law violators
Criminal justice issues: Government misconduct; police powers
Significance: Sting operations are now a major law-enforcement tactic, especially in dealing with drug trafficking, prostitution, and property theft crimes. Undercover sting operations can be effective law-enforcement tactics in combating crime. However, even for such cases prosecutors must be careful to apply fair-play and constitutional standards in their pursuit of criminals.

In typical sting operations, police officers pose as would-be purchasers ("fences") of stolen property; when criminals attempt to sell them stolen goods, the officers arrest them. Sting operations also often involve officers posing as buyers of illegal drugs to catch pushers. Studies have shown that sting operations are also effective against career burglars and motor vehicle thieves. However, studies of the effectiveness of sting operations in combating illegal drug activities have been inconclusive.

Sting operations are often criticized as unethical or even illegal forms of entrapment. They raise a host of issues not relevant to routine catch-the-crook-red-handed police work. For example, the police are not allowed to entrap people by inducing them to commit criminal acts that they are not otherwise predisposed to commit. Presenting predisposed criminals with apparent opportunities to commit a crime is the goal of sting operations, and it in itself does not constitute entrapment. However, there is often a thin line between a successful sting operation and illegal entrapment.

Recognizing the need to separate legal sting operations from illegal entrapment, the Federal Bureau of Investigation (FBI) has issued detailed descriptions of acceptable and unacceptable operations to its agents. A document with eighteen single-spaced pages, the FBI guidelines have been criticized as so overly complex and technical that they are likely to be violated frequently in real-life sting operations.

> **Two Big-Time Sting Operations**
>
> One of the most successful sting operations in modern history was conducted in Washington, D.C., from 1974 to 1980. Local police joined with agents of the Federal Bureau of Investigation and the Treasury Department to pose as members of the "New York Mafia." During a five-month period, the federal officers purchased some $2.4 million worth of stolen property for only $67,000 and arrested a total of 180 sellers.
>
> In 1988, the FBI operated a high-tech electronic store in Miami that was used by drug traffickers to purchase electronic equipment, such as beepers, cell phones, and computers. Based on leads generated by these sales, the FBI arrested 93 drug traffickers in one seventeen-month period.

Another controversial area in sting operations is the use of intermediaries. In the Abscam scandal that involved U.S. Congress members during the 1970's, the FBI was criticized because its operation drew on the help of known criminals. Another issue is the belief by many that the mere existence of sting operations may lead innocent citizens to live in fear that "Big Brother" is watching them all the time.

Cliff Roberson

Further Reading

Dempsey, John. *An Introduction to Policing.* 2d ed. Belmont, Calif.: Wadsworth, 1999.

Miller, Linda, and Karen M. Hess. *The Police in the Community: Strategies for the Twenty-first Century.* Belmont, Calif.: Wadsworth, 2002.

See also Asset forfeiture; Defenses to crime; Drugs and law enforcement; Entrapment; Gambling; Political corruption.

Strategic policing

Definition: Style of police management that relies on an assessment of performance goals and allocates resources to meet those goals most efficiently

Criminal justice issues: Law-enforcement organization; police powers; professional standards

Significance: The move to strategic policing changed the view of police administration from one of cost-of-service, response-based policing to one of outcome-oriented performance. This can be thought of as a shift in central focus from one of "what one does" to "what one is trying to accomplish."

A major push to "reinvent" government began in the federal bureaucracy during the early 1990's, central to which was a move toward smarter, more efficient operation of government programs. As the federal government began to administer its agencies based on this new way of thinking, state governments followed suit. Not long after, county and municipal administrations instigated similar changes. As government agents, many police chiefs and county sheriffs saw the expectations of their governments changing and so began embracing strategic policing as a way to meet the expectations of this new brand of management.

Strategic policing is a method of police administration and management that is outcome- and performance-focused, rather than output- and accounting-focused. During the Reform and Professional eras of American policing, many police departments had adopted output-related management styles, in which accounting practices were brought to bear on information about the tasks police undertake. Police departments established their annual goals and budget requirements based on output-based indicators, such as the numbers of traffic citations, arrests, motorists assisted, and the like. Departments' success was judged based on how well they met or exceeded their output goals.

Under the move to strategic policing, police administrators shifted focus from outputs to outcomes. While a traffic-related output assessment might count the things police do, such as number of citations issued, a traffic-related outcome assessment might count the things police officers try to affect, such as number of fatal crashes. Rather than judging a department to be successful based on their output goals, departments are rewarded for having a meaningful impact on the community and for meeting their outcome goals.

The move to strategic policing has been important for fundamental reasons. While output goals were traditionally established based on accounting projections and other scientific methods, strategic policing ensures that agencies seriously evaluate their outcome expectations. Often this involves closely working with all members of the department, as well as members of the community. Working together, the department establishes service priorities and then constructs outcome measures that will assess whether or not the department is adequately addressing those priorities. If the community agrees that traffic fatalities are a serious problem, the department may establish the number of fatal crashes as an outcome-related measure. While the number of traffic citations is an informative gauge, it does not measure the thing police are interested in changing—crashes.

Timothy M. Bray

Further Reading

Brady, T. V. *Measuring What Matters, Part One: Measures of Crime, Fear, and Disorder.* Washington, D.C.: National Institute of Justice, 1996.

Bureau of Justice Statistics. *Performance Measures for the Criminal Justice System.* Washington, D.C.: Bureau of Justice Statistics, 1993.

Langworthy, R. H. *Measuring What Matters: Proceedings from the Policing Research Institute Meetings.* Washington, D.C.: National Institute of Justice, 1999.

National Institute of Justice. *Measuring What Matters, Part Two: Developing Measures of What the Police Do.* Washington, D.C.: National Institute of Justice, 1997.

See also Community-oriented policing; Law enforcement; Neighborhood watch programs; Police.

Tennessee v. Garner

The Case: U.S. Supreme Court ruling on police use of deadly force
Date: Decided on March 27, 1985
Criminal justice issues: Arrest and arraignment; police powers
Significance: This case significantly limited the power of police officers to use deadly force in effecting arrests.

Most arrests do not entail problems, but occasionally the accused will resist arrest or flee. There are also occasions when law-enforcement officers must make an instantaneous decision on the severity of any threat posed to the officers. The common law developed the rule that law-enforcement officers could use all necessary and reasonable force, including deadly force, to arrest a suspected felon, regardless of whether the suspect committed an act of violence or posed a threat to the arresting officers.

The common-law rule became increasingly controversial during the 1960's and 1970's, but courts adhered to it. There were numerous objections of constitutional, legal, and humanistic natures. The main objection was that, in essence, the rule allowed police officers to become judge, jury, and even executioner. Indeed, many jurisdictions that did not use capital punishment allowed officers to use deadly force through "fleeing felon" statutes modeled after the common law.

In *Tennessee v. Garner*, a fifteen-year-old boy, Edward Garner, broke a window and entered an unoccupied residence in suburban Memphis on the night of October 3, 1974. A neighbor called the police. Two police officers responded and intercepted the minor as he ran from the back of the house to a six-foot cyclone fence in the backyard. By shining a flashlight on the suspect, the officers could tell that the suspect was a youth and apparently unarmed. There was therefore no indication that the boy had committed a felony involving violence, nor did he pose an apparent threat to the officers' safety. The suspect ignored the officers' directive to stop. Instead, he tried to escape. One officer took aim and fatally shot the suspect in the back as he climbed over the fence. The officer had acted in accordance with his training, the Tennessee fleeing felon statute, and police department policy. The deceased had ten dollars worth of money and jewelry in his possession, stolen from the house.

The decedent's father brought suit against the officers, their superiors, and the city under the federal civil rights statute to recover damages for wrongful death caused by violation of the decedent's constitutional rights. The lawsuit was filed in federal court in a successful attempt to circumvent the common law. The Supreme Court overturned the common-law rule in a 6-3 decision. Justice Byron White delivered the majority opinion, which held that deadly force may be used to effectuate an arrest only in cases where it is necessary to prevent the escape of the suspect and the officer has probable cause to believe that the suspect poses a significant threat of death or serious physical injury to the officer or others. The Court noted that most major police departments had forbidden the use of deadly force against nonviolent suspects. The practical effect of *Tennessee v. Garner* was that lawsuits involving wrongful-death causes of action against state law-enforcement officers will be brought in federal courts and will invoke federal constitutional law.

Denis Binder

Further Reading

Alpert, Geoffrey, and Lorie A. Fridell. *Police Vehicles and Firearms: Instruments of Deadly Force.* Prospect Heights, Ill.: Waveland Press, 1992.

Del Carmen, Rolando V. *Civil Liabilities in American Policing.* Englewood Cliffs, N.J.: Prentice-Hall, 1991.

Fyfe, James J., ed. *Readings on Police Use of Deadly Force.* Washington, D.C.: Police Foundation, 1982.

Skolnick, Jerome H., and James J. Fyfe. *Above the Law: Police and the Excessive Use of Force.* New York: Free Press, 1993.

See also Arrest; Deadly force; Discretion; Police brutality; Police dogs; Police ethics; Reasonable force; Supreme Court, U.S.; Wiretaps.

Treasury Department, U.S.

Identification: Primary federal agency tasked to promote the prosperity and stability of the US economy by assisting in regulating financial institutions and markets and enforcing laws dealing with money, taxes, and related matters
Date: Established in 1789
Significance: The Department of Treasury works to create a prosperous capitalist economy by regulating federal laws dealing with economic matters throughout the United States. This objective is also linked to the world economy, as the Treasury also works to assist and promote a healthy and vibrant economy for the many nations of the world.

In 1789, the US Congress created the Treasury Department of the United States and outlined and prescribed all the new department's duties and responsibilities for maintaining, protecting, and assisting in the growth of the nation's economy. The modern Treasury Department is the main federal agency tasked with maintaining and securing the economic safety of the United States.

The Treasury Department's duties include a wide range of activities—from advising the president on any and all economic issues, to enhancing and creating corporate governance in financial institutions, assisting other nations to build a stable world economy, predicting and preventing global economic crises, and regulating and protecting the economy of the United States by enforcing the economic laws and tax laws needed to regulate appropriate growth and stability of the national economy.

Organization of the Department

The Treasury Department is organized in two major components: the departmental offices and the operating bureaus. The departmental offices are responsible for the formulation of policy and management for the entire department. The operating bureaus carry out the specific tasks assigned by the department and employ 98 percent of the department's personnel. Different bureaus are tasked with numerous different responsibilities; however, they share a central mission: protecting and maintaining the United States economy.

The basic functions of the Treasury Department as a whole include producing postage stamps, US currency, and coinage; managing all federal finances, collecting federal taxes, duties, and all other moneys owed to the government; paying all bills that the United States owes to other nations; supervising national banks and credit institutions; advising other branches of the government, including the president, on financial and tax-related policies and issues; enforcing federal finance and tax laws; and investigating and prosecuting persons who counterfeit US currency and persons who evade paying taxes on regulated goods and services.

Before 2003, four other bureaus operated under the auspices of the Treasury Department. However, under the Homeland Security Act, in 2003 those bureaus were transferred to other departments and given revised investigative and protective missions. The four bureaus are the Bureau of Alcohol, Tobacco, Firearms and Explosives (ATF), the Federal Law Enforcement Training Center, the US Customs Service, and the US Secret Service

The four remaining Treasury Department bureaus with enforcement and investigative responsibilities are the Alcohol and Tobacco Tax and Trade Bureau, the Internal Revenue Service, the Financial Crimes Enforcement Network (FinCEN), and the Office of the Inspector General.

Alcohol and Tobacco Tax and Trade Bureau

The Homeland Security Act of 2002 divided the Treasury Department's Bureau of Alcohol, Tobacco, and Firearms into two bodies with separate missions. The core of ATF was moved to the new Homeland Security Department, and the remainder of it was reconstituted within the Treasury Department as the Alcohol and Tobacco Tax and Trade Bureau (ATTB). The Homeland Security Act called for the tax collection functions to remain with the ATTB under the Department of the Treasury. The ATTB now collects alcohol and tobacco taxes owed to the federal government and works to ensure that alcoholic beverages are produced, labeled, advertised, and marketed in accordance with federal law. These duties date back to 1789, when Alexander Hamilton, the first Treasury secretary, suggested that under the new US Constitution, Congress should impose a tax on imported spirits to help pay the Revolutionary War debt.

Internal Revenue Service

The largest of the Treasury bureaus, the Internal Revenue Service (IRS) is responsible for determining, assessing, and gathering internal revenue in the United States.

The IRS deals directly with more Americans than any other institution, public or private, in the United States. It also is one of the world's most efficient tax administrators and collects more than two trillion dollars in taxes every year.

A major goal of the IRS is to ensure that all Americans understand and carry out their tax obligations to the government. This is not an easy task to accomplish. To ensure that all federal tax laws are carried out and administered fairly and justly, the IRS maintains a criminal investigation unit that employs about twenty-nine hundred special agents. They investigate violations of tax, money laundering, and Bank Secrecy Act laws. Although the IRS shares the jurisdictions of money laundering and Bank Secrecy Act violations with other federal agencies, it is the only agency that has sole investigative jurisdiction over criminal violations of the Internal Revenue Code.

The special agents who make up the law-enforcement arm of the IRS are some of the most elite financial investigators in the world. Individual financial investigations may take hundreds of hours and require the scrutiny of many thousands of financial records and tax statements. The agents focus their investigative efforts on legal-source tax crimes, illegal-source financial crimes, and narcotics and terrorist-related financial crimes. Agents also investigate public and governmental corruption, tax evasion, health care fraud, telemarketing fraud, money laundering, and other forms of financial fraud. IRS agents have one of the highest conviction rates among federal law-enforcement agencies, and many of the people whom they help to convict pay severe fines; some are awarded lengthy prison sentences.

Financial Crimes Enforcement Network (FinCEN)

The Financial Crimes Enforcement Network (FinCEN) is tasked with bringing people and information together to fight the complex crime of money laundering, which is now considered to be the third-largest business in the world. FinCEN was established by the Treasury Department in 1990, and since its inception it has worked to maximize information sharing and gathering among all branches of law enforcement and its other partners in the regulatory and financial sectors.

FinCEN's network system encourages cost-effective methods to combat money laundering both domestically and globally. FinCEN has been designated by the Department of the Treasury as one of the principal agencies to establish, oversee, and implement policies to detect and prevent money laundering, terrorist financing, and inter-

US Treasury Department in Washington, D.C. (By Don-vip, via Wikimedia Commons)

national organized crime financial activities. FinCEN's primary goals are to support law-enforcement investigative efforts, foster interagency and global cooperation against domestic and international financial crimes, and provide U.S. policymakers with strategic analyses of domestic and worldwide money laundering developments, trends, and patterns. FinCEN officials try to accomplish these goals through information collection, analysis, and sharing, as well as technological assistance and innovative, cost-effective implementation of the Bank Secrecy Act and other Treasury authorities. FinCEN offers online access to both national and international law-enforcement agencies who are deeply involved in the fight against money laundering.

FinCEN's staff includes approximately two hundred employees, many of whom are intelligence research specialists from both law-enforcement and financial communities; law-enforcement support staff; and law-enforcement and legal analysts. In addition, at any given moment about forty long-term detailees from twenty different law-enforcement and regulatory agencies around the United States work in the bureau. As members of a collective bureau, these individuals are tasked with connecting the links among the individuals and financial institutions who engage in the illegal act of money laundering. This task is quite arduous; however, FinCEN maintains and operates one of the largest repositories of information on money laundering activities available to law enforcement nationally and internationally.

Office of Inspector General

The Department of the Treasury's Office of Inspector General (OIG) was established in 1989 by the secretary of the treasury. The OIG is led by an inspector general who is appointed by the president of the United States with the consent of the US Senate. The inspector general reports indirectly to the secretary of the treasury through the deputy secretary and provides the secretary with independent and unbiased reviews of all department operations.

The inspector general is also required to keep both the secretary and the entire Congress up to date on all problems and concerns relating to the administration of Treasury Department programs and operations. Serving with the inspector general is a deputy inspector general, who is responsible for assimilating all current bureau reports and investigations. In addition to the inspector and deputy, the office keeps a staff of one hundred full-time civil servants who are responsible for record keeping, external auditing, report writing, and internal investigations.

In regard to investigations, it is vital that all erroneous or criminal behavior be dealt with at once. Audits and investigations that indicate any form of specious or suspected criminal activity are usually passed on to the Department of Justice for further investigation and appropriate action. It is the main goal of the office of the inspector general to act as an internal investigation mechanism for the Department of the Treasury so that a fiduciary environment in which the US economy can grow and prosper can be maintained.

One of the main tasks of the civil servant staff is to create and submit semiannual reports on the activities and investigations of the inspector's office. Disclosures of problems, abuses, and deficiencies in the Treasury Department are highlighted and brought to the attention of the Congress and the secretary of the treasury. The reports also offer recommendations of what the department should do with regard to corrective action plans when particular abuses and deviancies are reported. Overall, the office of the inspector general plays an integral role for the Department of Treasury by making sure that all operations of the twelve bureaus are carried out efficiently and without corruption or deceit.

Paul M. Klenowski

Further Reading

Berson, Susan A. *Federal Tax Litigation*. New York: Law Journal, 2004. Print.

International Business Publications USA. *U.S. Department of Treasury Handbook*. 2nd ed. Washington, DC: Intl. Business, 2001. Print.

Johnson, David. *Illegal Tender*. Washington, DC: Smithsonian Inst., 1995. Print.

Melanson, Philip H., and Peter F. Stevens. *The Secret Service: The Hidden History of an Enigmatic Agency*. New York: Carroll, 2002. Print.

The Use and Counterfeiting of U.S. Currency Abroad. Washington, DC: US Dept., of the Treasury, 2003. Print.

Yancey, Richard. *Confessions of a Tax Collector: One Man's Tour of Duty Inside the IRS*. New York: HarperCollins, 2004. Print.

See also Alcohol, Tobacco, Firearms and Explosives, U.S. Bureau of; Counterfeiting; Forgery; Fraud; Internal Revenue Service, U.S.; Money laundering; Secret Service, U.S.; Tax evasion; Telephone fraud.

Use of force

Definition: Law enforcement officers must, at times, use force to ensure compliance and make arrests.

Criminal justice issues: Constitutional protections; government misconduct; legal terms and principles; police powers

Significance: The degree of force an officer uses must be reasonable, necessary, and proportional. Agencies often assess use of force on a continuum varying the degree of force permitted commensurately with the quantum of the perceived threat or public or officer safety needs.

When tragedy strikes, we expect our law enforcement officers to run toward, not away from, the scene. We expect our officers to stand bravely between civilians and threats to their lives and property. To help officers meet those demands, statutes allow officers to use force that is "necessary" to protect themselves and others, protect property, and arrest offenders.

To guide officers in assessing the degree of force the officers may use in given situations, many agencies have adopted a use-of-force continuum. That continuum arrays the officer's permitted force from none on one extreme—when the officers' mere presence is sufficient to quell any unrest or defuse any threat—to lethal force when the officer or a civilian is threatened with deadly force and must respond in kind.

When an officer uses force greater than that justified under the circumstances, that is, greater than the use of force continuum would prescribe, that is deemed an excessive use of police force (sometimes called police brutality). Although no exhaustive national databases exist at present that track excessive force and officer-involved shooting incidents, as this volume goes to press there have been a series of very well-publicized cases of apparent or actual excessive use of police force, particularly with regard to young persons of color.

Recent High-Profile Excessive Force Cases

In the 1980's and 1990's, a few particularly heinous excessive use of police force cases stand out. An African-American man, Abner Louima, was brutalized and sodomized by New York police officers when he was in their custody in 1987. Another African-American man, Rodney King, was viciously beaten by Los Angeles police officers in 1991 when the officers stopped King after a high-speed vehicle pursuit.

More recently, police officers in the United States killed over 1,000 people in a single year, 2015. In and around that period, a string of unarmed young African Americans have been killed while in police custody or otherwise in police encounters. In 2014: Michael Brown (age 18) was shot to death by a Ferguson, Missouri police officer; Tamir Rice (age 12) was fatally shot by Cleveland, Ohio officers as he played in a park with a bb gun; Eric Garner (age 43) died as police were apprehending him in New York City; and Jerame Reid (age 36) was shot by police during a traffic stop in New Jersey. In 2015: Walter Scott (age 50) was shot in the back as he fled a traffic stop in North Charleston, South Carolina; and Freddie Gray (age 25) was injured in a police transport vehicle and later died from his injuries. In 2016: Alton Sterling (age 37) was shot and killed in Baton Rouge, Louisiana; and Philando Castile (age 32) was fatally shot in St. Anthony, Minnesota. Although commentators and researchers have evaluated the disparate racial impact of police use of excessive force, the question remains whether these recent killings of unarmed, young, Black males are an aberration or trend.

Self-Defense and *Tennessee v. Garner*

In every American jurisdiction, people have the right to defend themselves when they reasonably believe they are confronted with an imminent and unlawful force and that responsive force is necessary. Similarly, deadly force may be used when the threatened imminent and unlawful force was deadly force. In all cases, the self-defensive response must be proportional to the threat.

Law enforcement officers, in most jurisdictions, are given a bit more leeway, but officer use of force in self-defense and defense of others still must be necessary and proportional to the threat. Nonetheless, in many jurisdictions, procedures and practice once appeared to allow officers to use deadly force to apprehend a fleeing felon; that rule fell far short of the imminent unlawful threat required for self-defense. In 1985, the United States Supreme Court in *Tennessee v. Garner* reset that bar by holding that police officers can use lethal force to apprehend a fleeing felon or prevent escape only if that suspect posed an ongoing and "significant threat of death or serious physical injury to the officer or others."

Although we rely on law enforcement officers to protect us—to go toward the danger when civilians run the other way—officers still must adhere to reasonable use of force requirements as circumscribed by *Tennessee v. Garner* and the use-of-force continuum, ensuring that force is necessary and that the quantum of force used is proportional to the threat faced.

Charles E. "Chuck" MacLean

Further Reading

Cole, G. F., C. E. Smith, and C. DeJong. *Criminal Justice in America*. 8th ed. Boston: Cengage Learning, 2014.

Hyland, S. S., L. Langton, and E. Davis. *Police Use of Nonfatal Force, 2002-11*. November 14, 2015. http://www.bjs.gov/index.cfm?ty=pbdetail&iid=5456.

National Institute of Justice. *The Use-of-Force Continuum*. 2016. http://www.nij.gov/topics/law-enforcement/officer-safety/use-of-force/pages/continuum.aspx.

Pollock, J. M. *Ethical Dilemmas and Decisions in Criminal Justice*. 5th ed. Belmont, Calif.: Thomson Wadsworth, 2007.

Robert F. Kennedy Human Rights Global Justice Clinic, New York University School of Law. *Excessive Use of Force by the Police against Black Americans in the United States*. February 12, 2016. http://rfkcenter.org/media/filer_public/7d/84/7d8409c1-588f-4163-b552-1f6428e685db/iachr_thematic_hearing_submission_-_excessive_use_of_force_by_police_against_black_americans.pdf.

Tennessee v. Garner, 471 U.S. 1 (1985).

See also Body-worn cameras; Deadly force; *Graham v. Connor*; Police brutality; Police militarization; Police powers; Reasonable force; Resisting arrest.

Vehicle checkpoints

Definition: Stoppages of motorists by police for such purposes as apprehending criminals, preventing criminal behavior, and obtaining information

Criminal justice issues: Crime prevention; investigation; search and seizure; traffic law

Significance: Vehicle checkpoints have been proven to be effective tools in law enforcement, but their use has raised constitutional challenges that have won court decisions that limit their use.

One of the most publicly visible and useful tools in law enforcement is the use of vehicle checkpoints, in which police officers stop traffic passing through certain locations in order to question drivers and passengers and to perform quick visual inspections of vehicles. The specific purposes of individual checkpoints vary. Some are set up to apprehend criminal fugitives in emergencies, and others are set up on holidays to check for drunk drivers and to discourage drunken driving by their mere presence. Vehicle checkpoints take at least five different forms:

- ✓ general crime control checkpoints
- ✓ border patrol checkpoints
- ✓ driver's license checkpoints
- ✓ sobriety checkpoints
- ✓ informational checkpoints.

Despite their frequent usefulness in deterring crime and apprehending criminals, the use of vehicle checkpoints has raised legal challenges because of their perceived infringement on civil liberties. For example, general crime control checkpoints, including those set up to search for illegal drugs, have been ruled constitutionally unreasonable in several landmark decisions of the U.S. Supreme Court. On the other hand, the Supreme Court has upheld them as legal, under certain circumstances, in a number of cases. For any type of vehicle checkpoint to be considered reasonable and constitutional, there is a fine balancing act between the public interest the stop serves and the right of individuals to be free from governmental interference.

The Fourth Amendment of the U.S. Constitution gives citizens the right to be secure in their persons, houses, papers, and effects against unreasonable searches and seizures. The individuals in some Supreme Court cases claimed that their Fourth Amendment rights were violated when they were stopped at vehicle checkpoints. Although the amendment has been interpreted to permit informational vehicle checkpoints, the crimes about which information is sought must be serious. Under court rulings, such checkpoints must be narrowly tailored to the investigative purpose. Moreover, all checkpoint stops must be brief and systematic. Arbitrary stops are unconstitutional.

Informational Checkpoints

Informational checkpoints are used by police to ask motorists if they have information about recent crimes and other matters. They can be useful tools, especially when they succeed in finding witnesses to crimes who might otherwise not come forward. In 2003, the Supreme Court heard the case of *Illinois v. Lidster*, which challenged the constitutionality of vehicle checkpoints for informational purposes. A bicyclist had been struck and killed by a vehicle at approximately the same time of day as the checkpoint was being conducted. Police were stopping individual vehicles for only about ten to fifteen seconds each, in order to hand drivers flyers to ascertain if they had been witnesses to the fatal hit-and-run. The officers did not ask motorists for their names or any other information. The police roadblock was set up purely for informational purposes.

When a motorist named Robert Lidster approached the vehicle checkpoint, a police detective smelled alcohol on his breath and noticed that Lidster's speech was slurred. He asked Lidster for his driver's license and insurance card and directed him to a side street, where another officer performed a sobriety test. After Lidster failed the test, he was arrested and charged with driving under the influence of alcohol. Later, Lidster argued that the checkpoint was unconstitutional because he was seized without suspicion. Lidster said that his Fourth Amendment rights were being violated, and he motioned to suppress the evidence of his offense.

In the trial that followed, Lidster was found guilty of driving under the influence of alcohol, despite his argument that he successfully completed all of the roadside sobriety tests. Afterward, he appealed his conviction, arguing that the hindrance to drivers that the checkpoint created outweighed its possible usefulness in obtaining information. An Illinois appellate court agreed and reversed the trial court's decision, but the case later reached the U.S. Supreme Court, which upheld the trial court's original ruling.

Other Checkpoint Cases

Another U.S. ruling bearing on vehicle checkpoints, *Brown v. Texas* (1979), originated in a Texas case in which police officers stopped two men in a neighborhood with a high incidence of drug traffic merely because they looked suspicious. One man refused to identify himself and was arrested. The Supreme Court ruled that this violated the man's Fourth Amendment rights. The Court's decision ruled that a Texas statute requiring individuals to identify themselves to police violated the Fourth Amendment because it could be applied when officers lacked any reasonable suspicion to believe that suspects were engaged in criminal conduct.

The Supreme Court's ruling in *Indianapolis v. Edmond* (2000) involved a vehicle checkpoint system that had been established by the city of Indianapolis in 1998 to intercept unlawful drugs. Secondary purposes of the system were to keep impaired drivers off the road and to verify motorists' license and registration information. Police stopped selected vehicles at a checkpoint and spent less than five minutes per vehicle searching for signs of driver impairment, conducting open-view examinations of the vehicles, and leading a drug-sniffing dog around the vehicles.

Later, two motorists, James Edmond and Joell Palmer, filed a class-action suit in a federal district court, claiming that the vehicle stop violated their rights under the Fourth Amendment and Indiana's own constitution. When their case reached the U.S. Supreme Court, the Court ruled that a checkpoint program was unconstitutional if its only purpose was to uncover "ordinary criminal wrongdoing."

Heidi V. Schumacher

Further Reading
Hall, John Wesley. *Search and Seizure*. 3d ed. Charlottesville, Va.: LEXIS Law Publishing, 2000. Textbook focusing on issues surrounding search and seizure, including vehicle checkpoints.
LaFave, W. R. *Search and Seizure: A Treatise on the Fourth Amendment*. 3d ed. St. Paul, Minn.: West Publishing, 1995. Comprehensive overview of search and seizure with special attention to the constitutional issues that the subject raises.
McWhirter, Darien A. *Search, Seizure, and Privacy*. Phoenix, Ariz.: Oryx Press, 1994. Book written to make subjects such as search and seizure, the exclusionary rule, and privacy rights interesting for high school and undergraduate college students.
Miller, Marc L., and Ronald F. Wright. *Criminal Procedures: The Police: Cases, Statutes, and Executive Materials*. New York: Aspen Law & Business Publishers, 1998. Discussion of both police-citizen interactions and appeals processes in the U.S. justice system.
Wetterer, Charles M. *The Fourth Amendment: Search and Seizure*. Springfield, N.J.: Enslow, 1998. Discussion of various aspects of search and seizure law and how the courts have interpreted the Fourth Amendment.

See also Automobile searches; Border patrols; Consent searches; Drunk driving; Plain view doctrine; Probable cause; Search and seizure; Sobriety testing; Speeding detection.

Warrior versus guardian mentality

Definition: Police officers with a warrior mentality view themselves as warriors, willing to fight for the citizens they protect. Police officers with a guardian mentality view themselves as protectors of the public, due process, and procedural fairness.

Criminal justice issues: Civil rights and liberties; law enforcement organization; police powers; professional standards

Significance: Some commentators argue that officers with warrior mentalities are more prone to use violence more quickly and with more ferocity, while officers with guardian mentalities are more likely to excel at community policing, combatant mediation, and de-escalation while they optimize procedural fairness and justice for all.

Police officers self-select for the profession. Those who become officers, in the main, are prone to be servants, protectors, and fighters, willing to defend civilians from all risks. Those who chose careers as line law enforcement officers, are willing—even anxious—to meet threats on behalf of others. Thus, viewed through that lens, those with warrior mentalities and a strong sense of justice and rule enforcement are quite likely to become law enforcement officers.

Conversely, inasmuch as the criminal justice system benefits when officers use force wisely and are as focused on safeguarding procedural justice and due process as they are in catching "the bad guys," perhaps the system would be better served by hiring more officers with a guardian mentality and fewer with a warrior mentality. Juxtaposed against this preference for peaceable guardians rather than warriors are the realities of the risks of modern law enforcement and the global War on Terror.

Warrior Officers Control Their Communities

Warrior officers strive to control those around them. They are more likely to impose directives than to elicit cooperation. They are more prone to use their voices and strength to take control and impose their will on the communities they were hired to serve. They do not hesitate to step into the breach and confront danger or absorb risk, but they are more likely to control by intimidation and less willing to negotiate and interact, tactics that warrior officers are likely to see as weak or beneath them.

Warriors see the served community as filled with threats that must be controlled and subordinated by force. They favor militarization, military-style equipment, and special weapons and tactics (SWAT) training. They believe that the best start for every citizen interaction is for the citizen to immediately perceive that the warrior is, without question, in charge, and the citizen's obligation is to bow to the guardian's will.

Guardian Officers Serve Their Communities

Guardian officers are peacekeepers, problem solvers, and negotiators. They know how to defuse and de-escalate tensions. They insert themselves, because that is their preference, into the communities they serve.

Guardian officers are ideal for roles in community policing and school liaison initiatives.

Guardian officers build alliances with the served community, more like in an earlier time of cops who walked a beat. That familiarity breeds trust, confidence, and cooperation in a two-way relationship between these guardians and the citizens they serve.

Guardians see their served communities as filled with potential allies. They begin each citizen interaction seeking to understand the needs and concerns of the citizen and offering to play a role in helping each citizen meet their needs and address their concerns. These guardians are far more likely to ask questions than to bark commands.

The Irony of Guardians as Superior Law Enforcement

At first glance, one might think it wiser to staff a law enforcement agency with warriors rather than guardians, but research does not support that hypothesis. On the contrary, guardian officers are more likely to yield a safer and less crime-ridden community. Guardian officers are more likely to create confidence and cooperation among those they serve, who are more likely to imbue the local guardian officers and therefore the local law enforcement agency with legitimacy and trust.

Warrior officers may be too confrontational and abrasive to create confidence and calm. They may approach each officer-citizen encounter adversely, using their commands, presence, voice, and strength to compel acquiescence through fear rather than cooperation. Civilian acquiescence in law enforcement is a far cry from civilian confidence in law enforcement. The former yields resentment and fear; the latter breeds confidence and trust.

Gender and the Guardian Mentality

Some researchers and criminal justice commentators have opined that when agencies strive to break through the historic preference for male law enforcement officers and open the ranks to females, as well, one spin-off benefit is that the force is, on average, more predisposed to exhibit a guardian mentality and more likely to use conversation skills to cajole and persuade than to use brute force to compel and command.

Although ironic at first blush, the community-policing era, which embedded guardian officers into their served communities to meet and greet and breed familiarity, seems to create safer communities than inserting warrior officers into communities to assert their will on the citizens they were hired to protect and serve. In law enforcement, in many areas, the guardian era is on the rise and the warrior era is receding. In other areas, the warrior mind-set still prevails.

Charles E. "Chuck" MacLean

Further Reading
Balko, R. *Rise of the Warrior Cop: The Militarization of America's Police Forces.* New York: Public Affairs, 2013.
Rahr, S., and S. K. Rice. *From Warriors to Guardians: Recommitting American Police Culture to Democratic Ideals.* Harvard Kennedy School, New Perspectives in Policing. April, 2015. https://www.ncjrs.gov/pdffiles1/nij/248654.pdf.
Stoughton, S. "Law Enforcement's 'Warrior' Problem." *Harvard Law Review Forum* 128(2015): 225.

See also Due process of law; Police academies; Police ethics; Police militarization; Police powers; Police subculture; Procedural justice.

Wickersham Commission

Identification: Commission appointed by President Herbert Hoover to examine the enforcement of laws throughout the United States
Date: Created in 1929; issued final report in June, 1931
Criminal justice issues: Government misconduct; law-enforcement organization; professional standards
Significance: The first federal study of the administration of justice, the Wickersham Commission placed crime on the national public policy agenda.

Formally known as the National Commission on Law Observance and Enforcement, the government commission chaired by George Wickersham from 1929 to 1931 was created to conduct an objective, scientific study of the administration of justice because of public concern and distrust of the justice system that arose during the Prohibition era. The commission examined the police, courts, and corrections, and published its findings in a series of thirteen official reports.

The commission's findings of widespread official corruption and lawlessness, including a special condemnation directed at police for the use of the "third degree" or torture in interrogations, ignited intense public discussions and led to a series of Supreme Court decisions protecting the rights of those in custody. Identification of other critical problems—such as inadequate recruitment standards and inadequate training in law enforcement, inept and corrupt management, and invasive political influence—spawned the movement for professionalization of police.

The Wickersham Commission advocated a systems approach to criminal justice; endorsed probation, parole, and rehabilitation programs for offenders; and endorsed the development of a national system for collecting statistical data on crime. The commission's *Report on the Causes of Crime* held the seeds for sociological approaches to the study of crime and juvenile delinquency. Its analysis of the effects of inadequate enforcement of Prohibition and its encouragement of organized crime became the foundation for modern discourses on drug policies.

The commission's work is one of the most important events in the history of the American criminal justice system. The long-term effects of its recommendations continue to shape public policy and criminal justice procedures in the twenty-first century.

Susan Coleman

Further Reading

Calder, James D. *The Origins and Development of Federal Crime Control Policy*. Westport, Conn.: Praeger, 1993.

Friedman, L. M. *Crime and Punishment in American History*. New York: Basic Books, 1993.

Walker, Samuel. *Popular Justice: A History of American Criminal Justice*. 2d ed. New York: Oxford University Press, 1997.

See also Criminal justice in U.S. history; Organized crime; Peace Officer Standards and Training; Police brutality; Police corruption; Political corruption; Prohibition; Uniform Crime Reports.

Women in law enforcement and corrections

Definition: Women who work as police officers, corrections and probation officers, and security guards, and in other related fields

Criminal justice issues: Civil Rights and liberties; Professional standards; Women's Issues

Significance: Women first entered law enforcement and corrections work in the United States during the early nineteenth century, but significant numbers of women were not given the full responsibilities and opportunities available to men until after the passage of federal civil rights legislation in the late twentieth century. The numbers of women in law enforcement and corrections then grew dramatically, only to level off as women in those professions encountered workplace discrimination and harassment.

Introduction

The roles and scope of women in law enforcement and corrections have changed significantly since the beginning of the twentieth century. Women began working in policing during the mid-nineteenth century, but their duties confined them primarily to clerical work and to working with other women and children. Since the U.S. Congress passed the Civil Rights Act of 1964 and the Equal Opportunity Employment Act of 1972, women have entered police patrol work and have become police officers with job functions similar to their male counterparts.

In the early nineteenth century, the reformatory movement in corrections opened new avenues of employment for women as matrons in prisons because they were viewed as having the abilities necessary to redirecting female offenders to the types of lives they were expected to live after their release. As in policing and other law-enforcement positions, however, women now enter and work in the same kinds of corrections jobs-with the same security, benefits, and salaries, as their male counterparts. Finally, with the rise in the use of security officers in the private sector, increasing numbers of women are finding employment as security personnel in restaurants, shopping malls, and other locations.

Policing

In 1845, the New York City Police Department became the first department officially to employ women. However, the women it hired served as matrons and were essentially social workers who assisted the women and children with whom the department dealt. Their hiring met opposition from male police officers and citizens, but by 1885, other cities were also beginning to utilize women officers as matrons.

In 1893, the mayor of Chicago officially appointed Marie Owens, the widow of a Chicago police officer, as the first woman "patrolman" with powers of arrest. Seventeen years later, Los Angeles made Alice Stebbins Wells the first woman to be classified as a "policewoman." Wells, who had previously worked as a social worker, was initially appointed for prevention and protection principles related to youth. Although she was later given powers of arrest, her duties were limited to enforcing laws in places such as dance halls, movie theaters, amusement parks and arcades, and other places of recreation frequented by women and children. It would be many years before limitations placed on women in policing would be eased through US Supreme Court decisions and legislation.

US Customs and Border Protection (CBP) officers going aboard a ship to examine cargo. (By Don-vip, via Wikimedia Commons)

The 1970s was the decade that set in motion the modern era for women in policing. In *Reed v. Reed* (1971), the Supreme Court ruled that police departments that discriminated on the basis of sex were in violation of the equal protection clause of the Fourteenth Amendment. The Equal Rights Amendment and its subsequent Equal Opportunity Employment Act of 1972 provided for the advancement of women in policing and other law-enforcement positions. In 1972, two women successfully completed Federal Bureau of Investigation (FBI) training, New York City's police began hiring and training women for patrol duty, and Pennsylvania's state police began giving women increased duties.

After the 1970s, the numbers of sworn female police officers increased dramatically from a handful across the United States to more than 82,000 in 2011. However, despite these advances, the total number of women in law enforcement remains small, and their progress has been slow. Although women constituted 58 percent of the nation's workforce in 2011, they held only about 12 percent of sworn law-enforcement positions in the country. Moreover, the progress that women were making toward the end of the twentieth century actually regressed slightly. According to the Feminist Majority Foundation's National Center for Women and Policing's annual survey, women are not promoted as often as men, and they hold only about 7.5 percent of top command decision-making positions and only 9.6 percent of supervisory positions. Another indication of the lack of overall progress being made by women is a statistic from the National Association of Women Law Enforcement Executives as reported in 2015 by *USA Today*: of the over 14,000 police agencies nationwide, there were just 219 women holding department-head jobs. An exception to this statistic in the District of Columbia where seven notable federal and local agencies, such as the Drug Enforcement Administration (DEA), the DC Metropolitan Police Department, and US Marshals Service, are headed by women. However, the barrier popularly known as the "glass ceiling" is especially evident in the majority of law enforcement agencies and departments.

Studies spanning decades have shown, however, that increasing the numbers of women in police departments would significantly decrease police violence, use of excessive force, and the escalation of potentially violent situations. Researchers have found that these outcomes are expected because women behave less aggressively than men, are more prone to use dialogue before resulting to force, and view police work as a public service rather than a position of control and authority.

Barriers to Women in Policing

Possible explanations for the low numbers of women found in law-enforcement positions, especially those of higher rank, may be rooted in the continuing problems of disparate practices concerning societal gender bias, work assignments, and sexual harassment. Once on the job, women in law enforcement often face discrimination, harassment, and intimidation from their male colleagues, especially as they move up the ranks.

Despite more than a century of evidence showing that women are as capable of police work as men, widespread bias in recruitment policies, selection practices, hiring, and promotions keep their numbers disproportionately low. Although discriminatory size requirements were discarded during the early 1970s, modern entrance tests continue to bar qualified women from entering policing. Many mandatory physical agility tests have a significant negative effect on the representation of sworn female officers, as most departmental entry exams overemphasize physical strength, thereby disqualifying many suitable female applicants.

Another obstacle is the stereotype of policing as a male job because of its association with crime and danger. The prevailing attitudes of policing styles have focused on use of force with emphasis on paramilitary environments. In these conditions, male officers perceive their female counterparts as weak and unimposing, unable to carry out the duties required by their positions. Thus, the primary obstacle that women must overcome is the attitudes of male officers. However, despite negative male ideas about women police officers, time and experience have shown that male and female officers are equally effective in their activities—as measured by productivity on patrol, commitment to law-enforcement organizations, and performance evaluations.

Women employed in policing often encounter hostile workplaces, facing sexual harassment on the job. Despite legislation and departmental policies prohibiting sexual harassment in the workplace, women in law enforcement face such problems in many agencies across America. Found mainly in smaller departments, the "good old boy" system exemplifies stereotypical attitudes and often allows such misconduct. One of the major reasons cited for the high turnover rate found among female officers is sexual harassment

Notwithstanding the barriers that female officers confront, they bring to policing a style that relies more on communication skills than physical force. The citizenry they serve sees them as more respectful, and by using tactics and techniques that defuse potentially violent situations, female officers often successfully resolve situations that might otherwise lead to serious injury or death. Finally, because of their emphasis on communication, female officers are also able to respond more effectively to cases of domestic violence, which represent almost one-half of all violent crime calls to police agencies.

Corrections Work

The advancement of women into policing jobs was actually established by female correctional matrons. Between 1822 and 1832, the first women were hired as jail matrons and prison guards, thus paving the way for female police officers by legitimizing women working within the criminal justice field.

The background and history of women working in corrections is similar to that of women in policing. Impacted by women's reform groups, such as the Women's Christian Temperance Union and the American Female Moral Reform Society, female jail and prison matrons were essentially social workers who were interested in the morality of women arrested and detained for prostitution and other forms of commercial vice, as well as wayward juveniles. Matrons were intended to serve as role models who could influence female inmates and young women in the "ways of being a lady." Their work often required them to lead classes on such domestic skills as cooking, cleaning, and sewing.

From the beginning, as with policing, women in corrections were relegated to lower positions of authority. Female correctional officers did not hold the same pay grades as men in similar positions, and the facilities in which they served were often below the standard of those used by men. The pay of correctional matrons was similar to that of domestic servants. Like domestic servants, they worked long shifts with few days off. Moreover, they often lived and worked alongside the inmates they were charged to supervise.

As the reformatory movement in corrections rose and fell in the early twentieth century, women worked as correctional officers for the same pragmatic reasons as men. No longer focused on the ideals of reform, women went into corrections for job security and steady paychecks. Female corrections officers were not concerned with reforming their charges. Instead, they became custodial employees whose main duties revolved around prevention of violence within, and escape from, jail and prison facilities.

Corrections has historically been the most sex-segregated and male-dominated component of the criminal justice system. However, since the late twentieth century, and because of the same laws and decrees that affected police, correctional staffs have become more gender integrated. Now, female officers are allowed to work in prisons for both women and men. This advancement is not without problems, however. As with policing, male colleagues often do not take female officers seriously. Consequently, female officers feel a constant need to prove their abilities and often confront sexual harassment by inmates and male officers alike.

Work in corrections also presents problems of cultural differences. Corrections officers often work mostly in rural environments where most lockup facilities are located, and they supervise inmates from urban areas with whom they share little in common. Correctional work is particularly difficult for working mothers, as the shifts are long and often rotating, and involuntary overtime work is common. Correctional officers cannot easily leave their jobs for personal emergencies, especially as most correctional facilities operate shorthanded or with minimal staff supervision.

Many women work in the subfield of corrections known as "intermediate sanctions," which is better suited to their schedules. This field includes the supervision of all persons in the correctional pipeline who instead of being incarcerated in jails or prisons are housed in halfway houses, boot camps, and the like. The most common jobs for women in this field are as probation officers who monitor the conduct and behavior of criminal offenders (both juvenile and adult) serving probation terms in lieu of incarceration. Some jurisdictions combine probation with parole, requiring officers to monitor the reintegration of criminal offenders into communities during their conditional release from prison.

As in policing, many correctional experts have observed that female corrections officers have better listening and communication skills than men. They can have a calming effect on prisoners, are less confrontational, and are better than men at exercising control without using force.

Security Work

A variety of private police services, including the private detective and security businesses, have arisen to compete with traditional law enforcement. Moreover, the US Department of Labor reports that this twelve-billion-dollar-a-year industry, which employs more than ten million men and women in such protective services as store detectives, undercover investigators, and security guards, is rapidly growing to meet increasing demand. This is also an area of law enforcement in which women are more welcome than in the traditional areas of policing and corrections, as women have a greater ability than men to "blend in with the crowd" with which they work.

Conclusion

Most modern agencies attempt to recruit women, and all positions are at least theoretically open to them. The adage that "everything old is new again" now applies, as law-enforcement recruiters are returning to the traditional sources of female officers from the nineteenth century, attempting to attract social workers and other caregivers from whom the first police matrons were drawn in the early nineteenth century.

However, the numbers of women in general policing or corrections or in supervisory roles has not increased significantly, as these occupations remain traditionally filled by men with women having to continually prove themselves in their everyday work experiences. For women in law enforcement, the "glass ceiling" remains firmly in place, and until women are fully integrated into the profession, incidents of sexual harassment and obstacles in employment, promotions, and other advancements will likely remain in place.

Pati K. Hendrickson

Further Reading
Gall, Gina. *Armed and Dangerous: Memoirs of a Chicago Policewoman*. New York: Tom Doherty Associates, 2001. Memoirs of a female police officer with sixteen years of experience in Chicago.
Horne, Peter. "Policewomen: Their First Century and the New Era." *Police Chief*. International Association of Chiefs of Police, Sept. 2006. Web. 20 June 2016.
Johnson, Kevin. "Women Move Into Law Enforcement's Highest Ranks." *USA Today*. Gannett Satellite Information Network, 2 Dec. 2015. Web. 21 June 2016.
Martin, Susan E., and Nancy C. Jurik. *Doing Justice, Doing Gender: Women in Legal and Criminal Justice Occupations*. 2nd ed. Thousand Oaks: Sage, 2007. Print.
Muraskin, Roslyn. *It's a Crime: Women and Justice*. 5th ed. Upper Saddle River: Prentice Hall, 2012. Print.
Scarborough, Kathryn E., and Pamela A. Collins. *Women in Public and Private Law Enforcement*. Boston: Butterworth-Heinemann, 2002. Print.
Spillar, Katherine. "How More Female Police Officers Would Help Stop Police Brutality." *Washington Post*. Washington Post, 2 July 2015. Web. 21 June 2016.

See also Criminal justice system; Law enforcement; Parole officers; Police; Police academies; Prison and jail systems; Prison guards; Private police and guards.

Courts

Acquittal

Definition: Formal legal certification of the innocence of a defendant who has been charged with a crime

Criminal justice issue: Convictions; trial procedures; verdicts

Significance: Acquittals automatically follow determinations through legal processes that defendants are innocent of the crimes for which they are tried.

An acquittal can result when the jury finds a defendant not guilty, when a judge determines that there is insufficient evidence in a case, or by dismissal of indictments by the court. Once an accused person has been acquitted of crimes, that person may not be lawfully prosecuted a second time for the same crime. If such prosecution were to take place, it would place the defendant in double jeopardy of losing life, liberty, or property, which is in violation of common law and of the U.S. Constitution and state constitutions.

Typically, protection against double jeopardy extends to any prosecution associated with the same act or acts. For example, if an individual has been acquitted of a charge of using a weapon to commit murder, the defendant cannot be retried for any assault committed on the alleged victim. However, when a trial is terminated because of a procedural defect, the defendant is not protected by the rule against double jeopardy. Thus, the defendant can be prosecuted again on the same charge or on related charges. In most states, no degree of procedural error on the part of the state can justify acquittal of a suspect whose conviction is sure based on the evidence. In addition, no evidence can be excluded for reasons of procedural error provided that the procedural error does not affect the confidence that can be safely vested in the evidence.

A motion for a judgment of acquittal can be made prior to submission of the case to the jury, at the close of all the evidence presented before the jury, or after the jury has been discharged. If the evidence is insufficient to produce a conviction, the defendant or the court may request a judgment for acquittal before the case is turned over to the jury. If a motion for judgment of acquittal is made at the close of all the evidence, the court can choose to reserve a decision on the motion, submit the case to the jury, and decide on the acquittal either before or after the jury returns a verdict. After the jury returns a verdict of guilty or is discharged without having returned a verdict, a motion for judgment of acquittal may be made or renewed within a specified time frame (usually fourteen days) after the jury is discharged. In order to make a motion for judgment of acquittal after the jury has rendered its verdict, it is not necessary that a motion was made prior to the submission of the case to the jury.

Alvin K. Benson

Further Reading

Abramson, Jeffery. *We, the Jury: The Jury System and the Ideal of Democracy.* Cambridge, Mass.: Harvard University Press, 1994.

Del Carmen, Rolando V. *Criminal Procedure: Law and Practice.* 6th ed. Belmont, Calif.: Thomson/Wadsworth, 2004.

Emanuel, S. L. *Criminal Procedure.* Aspen, Colo.: Aspen Publishing, 2003.

See also Convictions; Criminal law; Dismissals; Double jeopardy; Principals (criminal); Trials; Verdicts.

Amnesty

Definition: General pardon made by government to persons who have been convicted of crimes

Criminal justice issue: Pardons and parole; Immunity; Convictions

Significance: Often based on political considerations, the granting of amnesty is often controversial.

Amnesty is a government action that grants immunity from prosecution to an identified group of people for a specified criminal offense. The term is derived from the Greek word meaning "oblivion," which is appropriate, because amnesty involves the "forgetting" of an offense. Although accused individuals do not have to exchange

Kids hold signs in front of Los Angeles City Hall, demanding general amnesty for all immigrants. (By Jonathan McIntosh, via Wikimedia Commons)

The Vietnam War generated unprecedented levels of public protest. Many young men who opposed the war refused to serve in the armed services, and some fled to Canada to avoid the draft. After the United States pulled out of the war, the federal government faced the problem of how to deal with tens of thousands of draft evaders. President Gerald Ford resolved the matter by declaring a general amnesty. (Library of Congress)

information or testimony to receive amnesty, they are expected to abide by all laws in the future. In some cases grants of amnesty are conditional, requiring a loyalty oath or community service. The difference between amnesties and pardons is not well defined, but amnesties are typically granted to persons before prosecution has taken place, while pardons are usually granted to persons after their trial and conviction.

In the United States the power to grant amnesty usually resides in the chief executive. Governors usually possess the power to grant amnesties for violations of state law. At the federal level, both the president and Congress can grant amnesties. The president's authority derives from Article II, section 2 of the U.S. Constitution, which gives the president the "Power to grant Reprieves and Pardons for Offenses against the United States, except in cases of Impeachment." Congress may grant amnesties under the terms of the "necessary and proper" clause found in Article I, Section 8 of the Constitution. The U.S. Congress does not have the power to limit or place conditions on any presidential amnesties.

Presidents have generally granted amnesties in situations involving actions undertaken in protest against government policies. In 1795 President George Washington granted amnesty to participants in the Whiskey Rebellion, which was essentially a revolt against excise taxes. In 1865 President Andrew Johnson offered most ex-Confederates amnesty if they agreed to take a loyalty oath to the Union. These examples reveal the intent behind most amnesties: to end divisive conflicts within American society in order to achieve reconciliation and domestic tranquillity.

President Gerald R. Ford's decision to offer amnesty to individuals who had refused to serve in the Vietnam War illustrated both the confusion surrounding the meaning of the term "amnesty" and the political calculations involved in granting it. As late as March, 1974, Ford declared that draft evaders had to be tried in the nation's courts. However, upon succeeding President Richard M. Nixon as president the following August, Ford was advised by his cabinet officers that an amnesty program would speed the nation's recovery from the war. In addition, the American public would regard Ford as a conciliator, which would improve his political standing. Later that same month, Ford announced that draft evaders would have the opportunity to earn their reentry into American society. He called his proposal clemency rather than amnesty on the grounds that draft evaders would be required to perform some form of alternative nonmilitary service to the nation. Ford's action, commonly regarded as an example of conditional amnesty, was intended to appease Americans who opposed the unconditional pardon of persons who refused to perform military service during the Vietnam War.

Thomas Clarkin

Further Reading

Davis, John Martin, and George B. Tremmel.*Parole, Pardon, Pass and Amnesty Documents of the Civil War : An Illustrated History*. Jefferson: McFarland, 2013.*eBook Collection (EBSCOhost)*. Web. 23 May 2016.

Freeman, Mark.*Necessary Evils : Amnesties and the Search for Justice*. Cambridge: Cambridge UP, 2009.*eBook Collection (EBSCOhost)*. Web. 23 May 2016.

Gioglio, Gerald.*Days of Decision: An Oral History of Conscientious Objectors in the Military During the Vietnam War*. Trenton: Broken Rifle, 1989. Print.

Levi, Margaret.*Consent, Dissent, and Patriotism*. New York: Cambridge UP, 1997. Print.

Moore, Kathleen Dean.*Pardons: Justice, Mercy and the Public Interest*. New York: Oxford UP, 1989. Print.

See also Appellate process; Clemency; Pardons.

Appellate process

Definition: Process through which higher courts review the decisions of subordinate courts

Significance: The appellate process provides checks on the criminal justice system by ensuring that errors do not adversely affect the fairness of trial processes and the rights of defendants.

The United States has a dual court system, made up of state and federal courts. Each of these two systems encompasses two or three "tiers," or levels, of courts. The lowest level is made up of trial courts, which hear evidence and reach decisions based upon that evidence. The next tier, or tiers, is made up of appellate courts. These courts do not hear evidence but review the records of what has taken place in the trial courts. Some states have two appellate tiers, consisting of an intermediate appellate court and a court of "last resort." In other states, there are only two tiers: the trial courts and the courts of last resort.

The federal court system has three tiers, but few cases ever proceed to the highest federal court—the U.S. Supreme Court. There are also some situations in which the Supreme Court hears appeals from state courts of last resort.

Appellate courts do not automatically review every case handled by trial courts and assume jurisdiction over only cases that are appealed to them by aggrieved parties. There are usually fairly stringent time limits for making appeals, and it is common for appellate courts to require that appeals be brought within thirty days of the decisions being appealed. However, after the appellate court is given notice that an appeal has been filed, it may take several months for the record to be assembled at the trial court level and forwarded to the appellate court for review. Assembling the record often requires that court reporters transcribe testimony taken at the trial, which can be time-consuming. After the records are delivered to the appellate court, the parties prepare briefs containing their arguments and the applicable law. Sometimes the parties are asked to argue their cases in person before the appellate court so that the court can ask questions about the issues.

Unlike trial courts, which are usually presided over by lone judges, appellate courts usually have panels of judges. In court systems with two appellate levels, panels of the intermediate courts are small—usually only three or five judges, while the courts of last resort typically have nine members—as does the U.S. Supreme Court. Judges who serve on appellate courts of last resort are usually called "justices," as are the members of the U.S. Supreme Court.

After an appeal is heard, one member of a panel is usually assigned to write an opinion representing the majority position of the panel. Sometimes the panel cannot reach a unanimous decision, and members who disagree write opinions known as dissents.

In reviewing lower-court decisions for error, appellate courts usually limit their reviews to errors that are brought to the attention of the trial courts, through either objections or some sorts of motions. This process is known as preserving an error, or making a record. If an error is not properly preserved, the appellate court reviews a case only if it raises a matter of fundamental importance or if it has actually caused prejudice to the complaining party.

Appellate Court Decisions

Appellate courts issue their decisions in documents called opinions or memorandum decisions. Written decision of the courts include reasons for the decisions and the facts on which the decisions are based. At the conclusion of an opinion, the court explains whether it agrees with the trial court's decision or believes that the trial court has made some type of error. When the court's opinion agrees with that of the trial court, the opinion

---

A Hollywood Reversal

Considering the legal expertise behind the making of film *Reversal of Fortune* (1990), it is surprising how inaccurately the film depicts the appellate process. The film is based on Harvard law professor Alan Dershowitz's book about the real-life murder case of Claus von Bulow, who was convicted of assault with intent to murder his wife.

In the film, Dershowitz (played by Ron Silver) represents von Bulow (Jeremy Irons) after von Bulow's wife (Glenn Close) dies under suspicious circumstances and von Bulow is convicted. Dershowitz assembles a team of students to help him appeal von Bulow's case. They eventually locate new evidence that is favorable to von Bulow and persuade an appeals court to consider this evidence. The appeals court subsequently reverses von Bulow's conviction and orders him to be tried again. At the new trial, he is acquitted of all charges.

The film errs badly in having the new evidence taken directly to the appeals court. Appellate courts do not consider new evidence and use it as a basis for overturning prior verdicts. A lawyer who uncovers new evidence favorable to a client would first approach the trial court and ask to have the evidence considered and, possibly, have a new trial ordered. If the trial court unreasonably refuses to consider the evidence, then an appeals court might be asked to overturn its decision. However, the appeals court would never be the initial forum in which the new evidence is presented, as is depicted in *Reversal of Fortune*.

Timothy L. Hall

states, "affirmed." If the opinion disagrees with that of the trial court, it may state, "reversed" or "reversed and remanded." When as case is reversed or remanded, the court explains why it thinks the original decision was wrong and instructs the trial court to modify its result or rehear the case.

Appellate courts follow a doctrine known as *stare decisis*, which requires courts to adhere to their own prior decisions and those of the courts above it. This principle lends certainty and predictability to the law and provides a framework for the decision-making processes of individual judges. Although judges may be otherwise swayed by the equities of particular cases, they are bound to follow prior law—or "precedent" — in reaching their decisions. Occasionally, courts decide to depart from their prior decisions and "overrule" them. From that moment, the new decisions govern.

The U.S. Supreme Court is the highest court in the federal system but does not always hear appeals from the intermediate federal courts, known as courts of appeal. Only a small class of federal cases are automatically entitled to appeals to the Supreme Court. The remainder are only heard if they present particularly novel or important issues. This discretionary type of appeal is known as *certiorari* appeal. The Supreme Court also has the authority to hear *certiorari appeals of state court decisions when they are state courts of last resort and they raise issues of federal constitutional law. It is estimated that the Supreme Court hears only about 3 percent of the cases for which certiorari* appeals are sought.

Sharon K. O'Roke

Further Reading

Bowie, Jennifer Barnes, John J. Szmer, and Donald R. Songer. *The View from the Bench and Chambers: Examining Judicial Process and Decision Making on the U.S. Courts of Appeals*. Charlottesville: U of Virginia P, 2014. eBook Collection (EBSCOhost). Web. 24 May 2016.

Chapper, Joy. *Understanding Reversible Error in Criminal Appeals*. Williamsburg: Center, 1989. Print.

Coffin, Frank M. *On Appeal: Courts, Lawyering, and Judging*. New York: Norton, 1994. Print.

Greenberg, Ellen. *The Supreme Court Explained*. New York: Norton, 1997. Print.

Wasserman, David T. *A Sword for the Convicted: Representing Indigent Defendants on Appeal*. Westport: Greenwood, 1990. Print.

See also Amnesty; Certiorari; Criminal justice system; Criminal procedure; False convictions; *Habeas corpus*; Harmless error; Judicial review; Judicial system, U.S.; Miscarriage of justice; Opinions; Reversible error; Scottsboro cases; *Stare decisis*; Suspended sentences.

Argersinger v. Hamlin

The Case: U.S. Supreme Court ruling on right to counsel
Date: Decided on June 12, 1972
Criminal justice issue: Defendants; trial procedures
Significance: Defendants have the right to counsel at criminal trials whenever they may be imprisoned for any offense, whether it be classified as a felony or misdemeanor.

The police arrested Jon Richard Argersinger for carrying a concealed weapon. The potential punishment was up to six months in jail and/or a fine of one thousand dollars. Being indigent, Argersinger was unable to afford counsel. He was convicted and sentenced to serve ninety days in jail. At that time the Florida courts did not provide counsel, except for nonpetty offenses punishable by more than six months in jail. In a *habeas corpus* petition to the Florida Supreme Court, Argersinger argued that because he was poor and had not been provided with counsel, the charge against him could not effectively be defended. The Florida appellate court rejected the claim, and the U.S. Supreme Court agreed to hear the case.

In a unanimous decision, the Court ruled that the right to counsel applied not only to state defendants charged with felonies but also in all trials of persons for offenses serious enough to warrant a jail sentence. Prior to *Argersinger*, some doubt had existed as to whether the constitutional right to appointed counsel applied to any misdemeanor prosecutions. In *Gideon v. Wainwright* (1963), the Court had established a right to counsel only in felony prosecutions.

The Court in *Argersinger* held *Gideon* to be applicable to all misdemeanor defendants who could be sentenced to a jail term. The Court rejected the state's contention that the Sixth Amendment's right to counsel should not apply to petty offenses even when a jail sentence might be imposed. Nothing in the history of the right to counsel, the Court said, suggested a retraction of that right in petty offenses; conversely, the common law previously did require that counsel be provided.

The problems associated with petty offenses often require the expertise of counsel. The legal questions involved in a misdemeanor trial, or in a guilty plea, are not necessarily less complex simply because the jail sentence would not exceed six months. Indeed, petty misdemeanors may create a special need for counsel because the great volume of such cases may provide a tendency for speedy dispositions regardless of the fairness of the results.

Since the defendant had been sentenced to jail, the Court found it unnecessary to rule on the defendant's right to appointed counsel where "a loss of liberty was not involved." The opinion laid the foundation for distinguishing between cases involving sentences of imprisonment and those in which only fines are imposed. The Court noted the special qualities of imprisonment, "for however short a time," including its possible serious repercussions affecting the defendant's career and reputation.

Argersinger v. Hamlin established that, under the Sixth and Fourteenth Amendments to the U.S. Constitution, without a knowing and intelligent waiver, no person may be imprisoned for any offense, whether classified as petty, misdemeanor, or felony, unless represented by counsel at trial.

Susan M. Taylor

Further Reading
Smith, Christopher E. *Courts and the Poor*. Chicago: Nelson-Hall, 1991.
Taylor, John B. *Right to Counsel and Privilege Against Self-Incrimination: Rights and Liberties Under the Law*. Santa Barbara, Calif.: ABC-Clio, 2004.
Tomkovicz, James J. *The Right to the Assistance of Counsel: A Reference Guide to the United States Constitution*. Westport, Conn.: Greenwood Press, 2002.

See also *Brown v. Mississippi*; Counsel, right to; Criminal procedure; Felonies; *Gideon v. Wainwright*; *Powell v. Alabama*; Public defenders.

Arraignment

Definition: First stage of the criminal trial process, when defendants are formally informed of the charges brought against them and are expected to respond by entering pleas

Significance: To meet their burden under the Sixth Amendment of providing due process to defendants, courts are required formally to arraign defendants before trying them.

After criminal defendants are arrested, their first appearances in court are arraignments. The Federal Rules of Criminal Procedure specify that at the arraignment hearings, defendants are read in open court the formal criminal complaints against them. These complaints should outline the crimes of which the defendants stand accused. Defendants are then required to enter a plea to the charges. If the defendants are without attorneys, they may request the opportunity to secure them. If they cannot afford attorneys, they may request that the court appoint attorneys for them.

If the defendants wish to wait to enter pleas because they have not yet consulted with attorneys or if they refuse to enter pleas, the judges may enter pleas of "not guilty" on their behalf. Defendants may also enter preemptory pleas, which explain why the trials cannot legally go forward. When defendants plead not guilty, trial dates may be set at the arraignments.

Defendants have the right to be present at their own arraignments. They also have the constitutional right to be arraigned within twenty-four to forty-eight hours after they are arrested. If they are arrested without previously issued warrants, they have the right to be arraigned within forty-eight hours to allow time for judicial determinations of probable cause for their arrests. Failures to follow any of these procedures or rules may be considered violations of the defendants' Sixth Amendment rights under the US Constitution.

Rachel Bandy

Further Reading
Ackerman, Alissa, and Meghan Sacks. *Introduction to Criminal Justice: A Personal Narrative Approach*. Durham: Carolina Academic, 2016. Print.
Federal Criminal Code and Rules. St. Paul: West, 2003. Print.
Loewy, Arnold H., and Arthur B. LaFrance. *Criminal Procedure: Arrest and Investigation*. Cincinnati: Anderson, 1996. Print.

See also Arrest; Bail system; Competency to stand trial; Counsel, right to; Criminal procedure; Due process of law; Hearings; Manhattan Bail Project; Misdemeanors; *Nolo contendere*; Plea bargaining; Pleas; Preliminary hearings; Resisting arrest.

Attorney ethics

Definition: Ethical rules and norms under which attorneys are expected to operate

Significance: Defense attorneys and prosecutors largely control the presentation of evidence in criminal proceedings, as well as the conduct of plea bargaining. Thus, the ethics of how they perform these functions are critical to the criminal justice system.

Attorneys in criminal proceedings are both officers of the court and zealous advocates. These obligations may conflict, generating difficult ethical dilemmas that attorneys must resolve. As prosecutors and defense lawyers play distinct roles in the criminal justice system, ethical obligations differ between the two.

Ethical Obligations of Prosecutors

Prosecutors, as representatives of the state or the people, operate under specific ethical constraints. In general terms, a prosecutor must act to further the public interest. As a result, a prosecutor is not only an advocate but also an agent of justice. It is often said that the role of a prosecutor is to see that justice is done, not to obtain convictions. Thus, prosecutors are ethically bound to protect the rights of accused persons.

Even prior to pressing formal charges, prosecutors must make reasonable efforts to ensure that a suspect is appropriately advised of the right to counsel. The prosecutor must not seek to have an unrepresented suspect waive pretrial rights. While prosecutors have discretion about when and if to press charges, such power—usually nonreviewable by the courts—must be exercised with extreme care and fairness. In legal terms, prosecutors can bring charges only when there is probable cause to do so. Moreover, given that defense attorneys are not present at grand jury proceedings, prosecutors must present evidence in such proceedings without generating subjective bias against a defendant.

Once charges have been filed, prosecutors must operate under more rigorous ethical constraints than defense attorneys. Foremost among these constraints are constitutional, statutory, and ethical requirements mandating that prosecutors disclose to defendants all information or evidence that tends to negate a defendant's guilt or mitigate an offense. This duty usually extends to sentencing. A failure to make appropriate disclosures may be grounds for the defendant to appeal a conviction.

While all attorneys must adhere to some limitations in extra judicial statements about a case, prosecutors tend to be subject to the greatest scrutiny in this regard. It is unethical for prosecutors to make extrajudicial statements that will prejudice observers or heighten public condemnation of an accused.

Unethical Movie Attorneys

In director Richard Marquand's film *Jagged Edge* (1985), a lawyer (Glenn Close) defending a husband (Jeff Bridges) accused of murdering his wife begins an affair with her client. After her client is acquitted, the lawyer discovers evidence of his guilt and confronts him. When he attempts to kill her, she defends herself and shoots him dead. Despite its melodrama, the film realistically illustrates the adverse effect on attorneys' professional performances when they have affairs with their clients. Although such affairs are seldom specifically prohibited by the ethics rules for attorneys, lawyers can find themselves reprimanded, suspended from the practice of law, or even disbarred when such affairs cause them to provide inadequate representation to their clients.

In director Martin Scorsese's 1991 film *Cape Fear*, a remake of a 1962 film, an ex-convict played by Robert De Niro sets out to terrorize and exact revenge upon his former attorney (Nick Nolte) for having not adequately represented him. He claims that the attorney concealed evidence that might have saved him from going to prison. At first, the attorney tries to use the law to protect his family, but when the law proves to be—in the words of one character—"slow and suspicious," he hires a private investigator to protect him. The investigator, in turn, hires thugs to beat up the ex-con. After this plan fails, the attorney eventually fights hand-to-hand against the ex-con to protect his family.

Cape Fear poses intelligent questions about the nature of attorney obligations to clients. However, in dealing with the ethical difficulties into which its attorney lands after agreeing to the hiring of thugs to beat up his nemesis, the film strays from reality. Moreover, contrary to a suggestion made in the film, the American Bar Association does not grant attorneys the right to practice law or disbar attorneys who behave badly. Instead, each state has a bar association responsible for such matters.

Timothy L. Hall

Ethical Obligations of Defense Attorneys

Like prosecutors, defense attorneys are officers of the court. In contrast, however, the primary role of a defense counselor is to advocate zealously on behalf of a client. There tend to be fewer ethical constraints upon the performance of defense counselors than on that of prosecutors.

Nonetheless, several ethical issues are particularly applicable to criminal defense attorneys. While all lawyers, including prosecutors, must adhere to rules regarding conflicts of interest, it is nearly always unethical for an attorney to represent more than one criminal defendant in the same matter because the risks of conflicts between or among codefendants are so grave. Moreover, ethical rules prohibit attorneys from establishing contingent fee arrangements in criminal cases because of the corrupting influence that such fees could have on the administration of criminal justice. This rule, although well established, has sometimes been the subject of criticism.

Finally, ethical rules prohibit the sale of media or literary rights by a client to an attorney prior to the conclusion of the representation. The reason for this prohibition is that an attorney's interest in generating publicity or going to trial in order to increase the value of such rights might conflict with a client's interests in, for example, a speedy plea bargain.

Apart from these specific rules, two other ethical issues are of paramount importance when considering criminal defense counsel. First, defense attorneys have an obligation to zealously represent their clients, even those clients whom the attorney believes to be guilty. This principle has several justifications. A primary one is that defense attorneys have a role to play in administering justice and that role does not extend to the power to determine guilt or innocence—a power vested solely in judges and juries.

The Problem of Perjury

Perhaps the most celebrated ethical issue confronting criminal defense counsel is the so-called client perjury problem. This issue arises when a criminal defense attorney knows that a client intends to commit perjury or already has committed perjury. Criminal defense attorneys, like all attorneys, cannot knowingly offer false evidence and are obligated to correct the record when they later learn that a piece of evidence presented was false.

Some courts and jurisdictions have modified this principle in the criminal context in light of constitutional protections afforded an accused. What is or is not ethical in such circumstances varies and remains subject to vigorous debate. Some of the answers that have been proposed include having an attorney seek withdrawal from representation, mandating that an attorney refuse to elicit perjured testimony and, if necessary and if the client continues to insist on the perjury, disclose the proposed perjury to the court or to the prosecution, allowing a client to present perjured testimony in narrative form or permitting an attorney to elicit the testimony as an attorney normally would. Virtually all authorities agree, however, that as an initial matter, an attorney is ethically bound to try to dissuade a client from committing perjury.

Robert Rubinson

Further Reading

ABA Standards for Criminal Justice: Prosecution and Defense Function. 3rd ed. Washington: American Bar Association, 2014. Print.

Freedman, Monroe H., and Abbe Smith. *Understanding Lawyers' Ethics*. 5th ed. Durham: Carolina Academic Press, 2016. Print.
Hall, John Wesley, Jr. *Professional Responsibility of the Criminal Lawyer*. 2nd ed. Deerfield: Clark Boardman Callaghan, 1996. Print.
Wolfram, Charles. *Modern Legal Ethics*. St. Paul: West, 1986. Print.

See also *Brady v. United States*; Counsel, right to; Cross-examination; Defense attorneys; District attorneys; Effective counsel; Moral turpitude; Police ethics; Public defenders; Prosecutorial abuse.

Attorney General, U.S.

Definition: Cabinet-level head of the U.S. Department of Justice and chief federal law-enforcement officer
Criminal justice issue: Federal law; law-enforcement organization; political issues
Significance: As the chief law-enforcement officer in the United States, the attorney general occupies a position of unique influence on the criminal justice system.

The attorney general of the United States is appointed by the president of the United States and confirmed by a majority vote in the U.S. Senate. As leader of the Department of Justice, the attorney general is a member of the president's cabinet but is the only cabinet position not called a secretary. The Office of the Attorney general represents the United States in legal cases and counsels the president and other executive officials on various legal issues. The attorney general represents the U.S. government before the U.S. Supreme Court in important cases; however, the U.S. solicitor general is the Justice Department representative who usually argues cases when the United States is party to legal disputes.

History of the Office

In 1789, the newly formed U.S. Congress passed the Judiciary Act, which created the basic structure of the federal court system. The same legislation also created the position of attorney general, which was originally conceived as a part-time position for only one person. The position was not initially a cabinet-office rank, but President George Washington requested that his attorney general be present at all cabinet meetings because legal issues were frequently discussed.

Over the years, the attorney general's office grew into a vast bureaucracy that employed a large number of private attorneys and legal assistants. From 1790 until 1819, both the Congress and the presidents received legal advice from attorneys general. However, in 1819, the attorney general's role as legal counsel for Congress ended because the workload of the position had increased dramatically. In 1870, Congress created the Department of Justice as an official cabinet position within the executive branch and the attorney general assumed leadership of the cabinet post, but the office's duties and responsibilities did not change in any material way.

During the past few decades, the list of those who have served as Attorney General has become much more diverse. Although the first Jewish Attorney General was Edward Levi, serving from 1975 to 1977, all who had held that office into the 1990s had been white males. This changed when Janet Reno was appointed to the position in 1993, serving until 2001. She was followed by John Ashcroft who was followed by Alberto Gonzalez, 2005-2007, the first Hispanic appointed to that position. He was followed by the second Jewish Attorney General, Michael Mukasey (2007-2009). In 2009, Eric Holder was the first African-American appointed to be Attorney General (2009-2015), and was followed by Loretta Lynch (assumed office in 2015), who is the first African-American woman to hold the post.

As the head of the Department of Justice, the attorney general's office controls a variety of operating agencies within the executive branch such as the Bureau of Alcohol, Tobacco, Firearms, and Explosives; the Drug Enforcement Administration; the Federal Bureau of Investigation; and the Bureau of Justice Statistics. In 2016, the department had an operating budget of over $26 billion and employed more than 113,000 people.

New Tasks for Post-9/11 Attorney Generals

With the War on Terror beginning with the attacks on September, 11, 2001, many new issues and responsibilities were laid on the Attorney General's desk. Among these were the powers granted to federal law enforcement in the Patriot Act of 2001. What previously would have been illegal searches or wiretaps had been made permissible. Broader powers were given in the pursuit of possible terrorists, and once captured, in their interrogation. The desire by the President, the Congress, and the general public to insure that no further attacks occurred on American soil, pressured the Justice Department, and others, to make use of these extensive powers. The result was that those opposed to these new powers attacked both the incumbent Attorney General and the legal opinions issued. Rulings by federal courts, in response to lawsuits filed on these issues, have had mixed results, upholding some new powers as constitutional while overturning others.

Ashcroft, the Attorney General in 2001, was the first to implement the Patriot Act. The expansive search capabilities granted by the law, and made possible with twenty-first century technology, were the target of most of the criticism directed against him. Having overseen the federal investigation into the intelligence failures which allowed the tragedy to happen, Ashcroft strongly supported this increased surveillance. Other governmental actions did not become visible until Gonzalez was in office. Gonzalez issued a legal opinion justifying "enhanced interrogation techniques," what opponents considered torture. He also upheld the warrantless surveillance of American citizens by the National Security Agency, a major concern for civil rights advocates. Mukasey's confirmation was delayed due to the fact he would not criticize the Justice Department's ongoing support for "enhanced interrogation techniques." While Holder withdrew some of the Justice Department's support for the ongoing use of the "enhanced interrogation techniques," new issues arose for him, such as the use of drones in the War on Terror. The death of a United States citizen in a drone strike in the Middle East raised the issue of not only the general use of drones, but whether the American's death was essentially an execution without a trial. Holder also desired to move jurisdiction for the trials related to 9/11 to civilian courts in New York. However this was blocked by Congress, resulting in the continued use of a military tribunal as the venue in which to try the defendants. Lynch has pushed the use of "hate crime" statutes against Americans who undertake, or plan to undertake, actions against a variety of classes of citizens. The past decade and a half has been a difficult time for all the Attorney Generals, as they have tried to help the nation clarify the fine line between civilian and military responsibilities and operations in the semi-nebulous War on Terrorism.

Other Recent Responsibilities

Since 2005 not all AG activity has been directed toward the War on Terror. Gonzalez oversaw steps to combat sexual predators, especially online. Mukasey moved to change the sentencing for crack cocaine to be similar to other forms of the drug. Holder oversaw the largest one day arrest of alleged organized crime members in history. He also pushed his prosecutors to seek penalties commiserate with the crime, not to get as many years as possible in each trial. He also strongly supported civil rights cases, including deciding not to offer a defense when the Defense of Marriage Act was being challenged. Lynch instituted a review of sentences for drug offenders, when the sentencing commission recommend retroactive changes. As an advisor to the president, the Attorney General has always been at least partially a political post. As a result, the priorities of those serving in this office generally reflect the basic beliefs of the president who appointed the AG, although there is a necessary separation between the two offices in the Department of Justice's role in the investigation of cases and in the decision as to whether there are grounds for taking a person, or legal entity, to court.

Scott P. Johnson
Updated by Donald A. Watt

Further Reading

Ashcroft, John, and Gary Thomas. *On My Honor: The Beliefs That Shape My Life.* Nashville, Tenn.: Thomas Nelson, 2001. This book reveals Attorney General Ashcroft's personal beliefs on various issues related to the criminal justice system.

Braun, Eric. *Loretta Lynch: First African American Woman Attorney General.* Minneapolis: Gateway Biographies, 2016. This is a brief biography of Lynch.

Clayton, Cornell C. *The Politics of Justice: The Attorney General and the Making of Legal Policy.* Armonk, N.Y.: M. E. Sharpe, 1992. Scholarly examination of the role of the attorney general in the shaping of national legal policies.

Dash, Samuel. *The Intruders: Unreasonable Searches and Seizures from King John to John Ashcroft.* New Brunswick, N.J.: Rutgers University Press, 2004. Historical overview of violations of the Fourth Amendment guarantee against unreasonable searches and seizures and the danger of the recently passed Patriot Act.

Holder, Eric. "Office of the Attorney General: Selected Publications." U.S. Department of Justice. Washington: United States Department of Justice, 2016. Web. 3 October 2016. This website contains letters and reports by Holder regarding counterterrorism and criminal matters.

Kleindienst, Richard. *Justice: The Memoirs of Attorney General Richard Kleindienst.* Ottawa, Ill.: Jameson Books, 1985. Autobiography of the attorney general appointed by President Richard Nixon in 1973. Kleindienst was forced to resign along with other members of the Nixon administration during the Watergate scandal in 1974, after it was revealed that he had lied during the Senate hearings on his confirmation.

See also Attorneys general, state; Criminal prosecution; Deportation; Drug Enforcement Administration, U.S.; Federal Bureau of Investigation, U.S.; Homeland Security, U.S. Department of; e Interpol; Justice Department, U.S.; Marshals Service, U.S.; National Institute of Justice; Patriot Act.

Attorneys general, state

Definition: Chief legal officers of the states, who serve as counselors for state government agencies, legislatures, and the citizenry

Criminal justice issue: Law-enforcement organization; prosecution

Significance: Attorneys general provide legal advice and legal representation for state agencies and the public on diverse matters such as drug abuse, the environment, business regulation, and criminal appeals.

The development of state attorneys general in the United States can be traced to England. The king of England had specially designated lawyers to represent his legal interests. The attorney general of England served as legal adviser to the king and all government departments and was responsible for all litigation. During the American colonial era, the attorney general provided legal advice to the king and governance over the colonies. After the revolution, American officials adapted the English version of the office of attorney general to govern their own legal interests. Constitutional provisions were enacted to create the office of the attorney general to have jurisdiction of legal affairs of the federal government. As the new nation grew, the states also adopted the office of attorney general, and many had constitutional provisions for the office.

Attorneys general are popularly elected in forty-three states, appointed by the governors in five states and six jurisdictions, appointed by the state supreme court in Tennessee, and selected by the state legislature in Maine. New legislation and conceptions of the office have significantly expanded the powers and duties of the state attorneys general. There is much diversity in the role of the attorney general from state to state.

In response to needs identified by governors and legislatures, attorneys general have become active in areas of consumer protection, antitrust law, toxic waste, child-support enforcement, organized crime, and many other areas. The most common duties of the attorney general involve controlling litigation concerning the state, serving as chief legal officer, writing opinions that clarify law, acting as public advocate, enforcing criminal law, and investigating issues of public interest.

Public advocacy is a growing field for attorneys general in nearly all states. In addition to providing legal service in such areas as consumer protection and child-support enforcement, relatively new areas of concern for states' chief legal officers include utility regulation and advocacy regarding the provision of services to crime victims. These new areas of interest put attorneys general in the position of being the initiator of legal action, or plaintiff, which is a role reversal that provides a new opportunity to implement and interpret public policy. One of the most important functions of the state attorney general is writing opinions. Opinions clarify law for the executive and legislative branches. Attorneys general use their opinions to identify legislative oversight that is in need of correction and to resolve issues that are not likely to be solved through litigation.

Donna Echols Mabus

Further Reading
National Association of Attorneys General, Committee on the Office of Attorney General. *Powers, Duties, and Operations of State Attorneys General*. Raleigh, N.C.: Author, 1977.
Ross, Lynne M., ed. *State Attorneys General: Powers and Responsibilities*. Washington, D.C.: Bureau of National Affairs, 1990.

See also Attorney General, U.S.; District attorneys; Public prosecutors.

Australia's "Reintegrative Shaming" approach

Definition: Reintegrative shaming promotes the idea that informal, disapproving reactions from people with whom an offender has a meaningful bond, when followed by gestures of reacceptance and support, are more likely to be reintegrative and discourage reoffending than formal criminal justice reactions, which are retributive and stigmatizing.
Criminal justice issue: Rehabilitation; restorative justice
Significance: Reintegrative shaming, and its application in restorative justice conferencing, offers an innovative approach to responding to crime, one that has attention for the victims' and offenders' interests and does not rely on retribution, as opposed to the dominant criminal justice system, which has been criticized for failing to meet victims' and offenders' concerns as well as to prevent reoffending.

Criminal justice systems around the world tend to rely on retribution and punishment to respond to offending and encourage future compliance with the law. This approach has been widely criticized, by scholars in NorthAmerica and Europe, for failing to meet victims' concerns for reparation and healing and offenders' concerns for rehabilitation as well as for failing to prevent crime and reoffending. The argument that punishment does not only cause pain to the offender but also ignores the crime victim's interests inspired John Braithwaite to look into whether informal responses to delinquency might be more effective. In his influential work entitled *Crime, Shame and Reintegration*, published in 1989, Braithwaite describes the emotional and interpersonal dynamics that are set in motion when someone who has committed a crime is faced with the reaction from the person they harmed as well as from the people with whom they have a meaningful bond (such as a partner, parent, sibling, close friend, etc.).

Braithwaite explains that people close to the offender commonly react by shaming the offender for his or her harmful actions. Shaming is defined by Braithwaite as the expression of disapproval that might result in remorse in the person being shamed. Such disapproval is painful for the offender, but has the potential to encourage the offender to do better. In order for shaming to promote desistance from crime, the harmful act and the person of the offender should be uncoupled: It should be made clear that the act is reprehensible, irresponsible and wrong, but not the offender as a person. In addition, shaming should be followed by gestures of reacceptance and efforts to reintegrate the offender into the community. Put differently, when shaming focuses on the offense, and not on the offender, and when it is followed by efforts from the offender's community of care to support the offender, it is likely to have a reintegrative impact and discourage reoffending. Braithwaite argues, when shaming focuses on the offender and is not followed by support for the offender it tends to shade into stigmatizing the offender, which is counterproductive and likely to result in more offending.

He continues that, given that entails expressions of support and tightening of bonds, ultimately then, reintegrative shaming might prevent reoffending because it inspires self-regulation. More particularly, it is argued that an offender will want to avoid disappointing his or her supporters again and as such refrain from offending behavior in the future. Loss of respect from those we care about would be more important as a deterrent, or discouragement, from reoffending than disapproval expressed by a judge in court in the form of a conviction and/or a formal sentence.

The reintegrative shaming theory provides theoretical backing for restorative justice (RJ) practices. Restorative justice is being used worldwide in response to both violent and nonviolent crime committed by young and adult offenders. Restorative responses do not necessarily replace criminal justice responses—often they merely complement them. Restorative justice is characterized by (face-to-face, written, or mediated) communication between the victim and offender of a particular crime, who voluntarily agree to participate in this intervention, in search of conciliation and maybe even reparation. A restorative intervention takes place outside of the courtroom in a more informal setting and is prepared and guided by a trained facilitator. Scholars who have extensively studied RJ practices, including Joanna Shapland, emphasize that good RJ practice provides a safe and confidential setting in which each participant feels safe to speak and express their concerns. One example of RJ practices is called restorative conferencing. This practice has strong roots in Australia's RJ developments. In a restorative conference, the victim and offender of a particular crime, who are accompanied by their respective supporters (i.e., people they feel connected to and care about such as a partner, parent, sibling, or friend) and, often, a police or community representative, are brought together by a trained facilitator to talk about the crime and its consequences. The offender and his supporters then draft a reparative plan that addresses the harm incurred by the victim (for instance, an apology or a voluntary agreement to [financially, materially, or symbolically] repair the damage) as well as steps towards the offender's reintegration into the community. Restorative conferencing thus puts in practice the conditions conducive to reintegrative shaming described above.

The potential of reintegrative shaming mechanisms in restorative conferencing to reduce reoffending was specifically measured in the Reintegrative Shaming Experiments study (RISE), which was done by Lawrence Sherman, John Braithwaite, Heather Strang, and Geoffrey Barnes. It compared offender experiences with police-run restorative conferencing and traditional court hearings in Canberra between 1995 and 2000. The Canberra police referred cases of drunk driving, juvenile property crime, juvenile shoplifting and violent crime by offenders up to age twenty-nine to the RISE study. Cases were then randomly assigned to be treated either in a restorative conference (which involved face-to-face communication between the offender, the victim, and their supporters, with the aim of addressing the consequences and causes of the offence) or in a traditional court hearing (which was overseen by a magistrate and did not allow room for communication between offender, victim, and their supporters, and tended to be very brief). The offenders and victims involved in the cases assigned to conferencing were free to refuse to participate and opt for a traditional court hearing instead. As is highlighted in the various publications resulting from the RISE study, none of the conference-assigned property or violent offenders opted out of conferencing and most of the offenders who were randomly assigned to conferencing completed the conferencing procedure. The conference was set up to be diversionary—this means that upon successful completion, charges against the offender would be dropped. Offenders in the study sample were interviewed and police data on reoffending was collected for up to two years following participation in the court hearings or restorative conferences. Offenders who reported experiences that could be categorized as reintegrative shaming, whether these resulted from court hearings or conferencing, demonstrated increased perceptions of legitimacy of the law (i.e., acceptance of and respect for the law) and compliance with the law-this effect was maintained in the long term. Finally, findings from the RISE study also suggest that conferences are more likely to produce reintegrative shaming than traditional criminal justice procedures.

Restorative conferencing is being used worldwide. When implemented correctly, it might be a better way to deal with crime than formal criminal justice responses and punishment. Although this is not a consistent finding in all research projects, many empirical research studies offer encouraging findings to support the positive impact of participation in a restorative intervention on reduction of reoffending. One particularly interesting explanation for this observation is presented by desistance scholars Gwen Robinson and Joanna Shapland: They suggest that offenders who agree to participate in RJ (after all, participation in a restorative intervention is, and should always be, voluntary) display strong intentions to desist from crime. By capitalizing on the offender's meaningful bonds and by facilitating a dialogue between the offender and the victim, RJ might just help to consolidate these intentions.

Tinneke Van Camp

Further Reading

Barnes, G. C., J. M. Hyatt, C. M. Angel, H. Strang, and L. W. Sherman. "Are Restorative Justice Conferences More Fair Than Criminal Courts? Comparing Levels of Observed Procedural Justice in the Reintegrative Shaming Experiments (RISE)." *Criminal Justice Policy Review* 26, no. 2 (2015): 103-30.

Braithwaite, J. *Crime, Shame and Reintegration*. New York: Cambridge University Press, 1989.

Braithwaite, J. "Encourage Restorative Justice."*Criminology & Public Policy* 6, no. 4 (2007): 689-96.
Braithwaite, J., and S. Mugford. "Conditions of Successful Reintegration Ceremonies: Dealing With Juvenile Offenders." *British Journal of Criminology* 34, no. 2 (1994): 139-71.
Robinson, G., and J. M. Shapland. "Reducing Recidivism." *British Journal of Criminology* 48, no. 3 (2008): 337-58.
Shapland, J. "Implications of Growth: Challenges for Restorative Justice." *International Review of Victimology* 20, no. 1 (2014): 111-27.
Sherman, L. W., J. Braithwaite H. Strangand G. C. Barnes.*Reintegrative Shaming Experiments (RISE) in Australia, 1995-1999*. College Park: University of Maryland, 2001.
Tyler, T. R., L. Sherman, H. Strang, G. C. Barnes, and D. Woods. "Reintegrative Shaming, Procedural Justice, and Recidivism: The Engagement of Offenders' Psychological Mechanisms in the Canberra RISE Drinking-and-Driving Experiment." *Law & Society Review* 41, no. 3 (2007): 553-86.

See also Diversion; Juvenile justice system; Prison and jail systems; Rehabilitation; Restorative justice; Victim-offender mediation; Victimology; Peacemaking criminology; Scandinavia's prison experience; Victims services; Victim recovery stages; Victimization theories; History of incarceration; Victim impact statements.

Bail system

Definition: System that allows individuals accused of criminal offenses to be released prior to their court appearances by securing funds to ensure their appearances in court

Criminal justice issue: Criminal justice issue: Probation and pretrial release; Defendants; Arrest and arraignment

Significance: This highly debated practice has been criticized for discriminating against poor and minority arrestees; it has also been criticized for the practice of preventive detention, which uses exorbitant bail to keep accused offenders from committing crimes while awaiting trial.

The United States bail system operates on the premise that some individuals can be released prior to their appointed court date by leaving an amount of money with the court. Individuals are expected to return for their subsequent court appearance to have the amount of bail returned to them. Many argue that this practice discriminates against poor arrestees who cannot afford a monetary bail and thus must remain incarcerated while awaiting trial.

Tradition in English Law

The bail system in the United States is rooted in the traditional court systems of England. In feudal England (prior to the Battle of Hastings in 1066), law was dispensed by judges who would travel from county to county. Sheriffs would typically keep accused offenders in local jails with the promise to turn the offender in when the judge returned. As the number of offenders increased and jail space became limited, offenders were occasionally entrusted to the custody of a friend or relative who would ensure their appearance. In some cases, these individuals were required to sign a bond promising a specific sum of money to the king if the accused failed to appear when the judge next visited the area.

Over time (and eventually in the American colonies), the practice of having an individual step forward for an accused was replaced by the use of financial security, or monetary bail. In exchange for freedom prior to trial, the accused would deposit a certain amount of money with the court, which would be returned following appearance. Even before the colonization of America it was recognized that the practice discriminates against individuals who cannot afford to leave a monetary bail. Arrestees who could not afford to leave bail were frequently incarcerated until their appearance at trial, a time period that could encompass years. Thus, the first formal regulations governing the use of bail were written in England in the year 1275. These statutes set forth specific conditions under which bail could be imposed, defining which crimes were "bailable" and which were not. That is, they specified for which crimes bail must be denied and the accused must be incarcerated prior to trial. Laws forbidding excessive bail eventually appeared in England, but not until they were included in the English Bill of Rights in 1688.

History of the American Bail System

Like the English system, early Americans also protected against excessive bail. The Eighth Amendment to the U.S. Constitution begins with the phrase, "Excessive bail shall not be required." The meaning of this phrase, however, has not been successfully decided by the U.S. Supreme Court. For example, does excessive bail refer to the defendant's ability to pay, or does it relate to the seriousness of the crime committed? In addition, is there a constitutional right to bail?

The Judiciary Act of 1789 gave offenders a right to bail unless arrested for a capital offense. For a capital offense, maximum penalties can consist of life imprisonment or death. Assuming that these offenders may be likely to flee, considering the severity of punishment, bail is typically denied. Thus, every defendant in a noncapital case was guaranteed to receive bail. The appropriate amount of bail was not discussed in the Judiciary Act of 1789.

Bail bond business. (By Daniel Schwen, via Wikimedia Commons)

A recommended or appropriate amount of bail was not dealt with in the United States until 1951, when the Supreme Court, in *Stack v. Boyle*, decided that bail must be of sufficient amount to ensure the defendant's appearance at trial. In other words, the amount of bail must be enough to assure the defendant's appearance, but it cannot be more than that amount, or else it would be considered excessive. The vagueness of this decision has left many experts speculating about the appropriate amount of bail.

Bail Reform

During the 1960s, it became apparent that the United States bail system was not operating as it was designed. Judges were accused of having an excessive amount of discretion in setting amounts for bail. In addition, judges were responsible for setting bail based on which defendants were at high risk for flight and which were not. These decisions were supposed to be based on criminal characteristics, such as the seriousness of the crime committed and prior appearance history. It became clear, however, that among the factors taken into account in the assessment of flight risk were race and sex. Thus, judges' decisions were discriminatory against certain racial groups and against male offenders.

Another form of discrimination emerged in the practice of pretrial detention. Although the primary purpose of bail is to assure a defendant's appearance at trial, there is another purpose. Preventive detention is the practice of holding arrestees prior to trial so that they cannot commit crimes during the time between their arrests and court appearances. If a defendant is deemed to be a danger to the community during the pretrial period, a high amount of bail might be set in order to keep the arrestee locked up. Judges are responsible for making the determination regarding the "dangerousness" of an offender. Again, it was found that these decisions were influenced by noncriminal characteristics such as sex and race. Thus, the type of discrimination that appeared when assessing risk of flight also occurred when judges attempted to assess how likely an offender was to commit a crime while awaiting trial.

In the face of these problems, the first bail reform movement developed. Beginning during the early 1960s, bail came to the forefront as a serious problem within the criminal justice system. The Bail Reform Act of 1966 was an attempt to limit judicial discretion and remove discrimination from the bail process. There were two important developments that came from the Bail Reform Act of 1966. First, judges were expected to release all defendants on their own recognizance unless the judge had some good reason to set bail. In other words, the judge had to have solid grounds for setting bail. Second, "pretrial service agencies" were created to collect information about defendants, thus allowing the judge to have more-and more correct-information about each defendant.

Although preventive detention was a reality in the bail system, there were no laws in the United States stating that it was legal. The second bail reform movement occurred during the early 1970s, and it focused on the issue of legalizing preventive detention. In 1970, the District of Columbia enacted a law that authorized the detention of arrestees without bail if they were deemed a danger to the community. This was the first statute to set standards for the detention of arrestees for preventive reasons.

The issue of preventive detention was not a legal one until the year 1984. In this year, the United States bail system was a central focus of the Comprehensive Crime Control Act of 1984. The Bail Reform Act of 1984 legitimated two federal judicial practices that were informally used before 1984. First, this act gave judges the power to assess defendants on their level of "dangerousness" to the community if released. It gave federal judges the legal right to use preventive detention. While the District of Columbia had its own provisions for preventive detention in 1970, it was not until 1984 that federal judges were given that right. Second, judges were given the right to deny bail in certain circumstances. Traditionally, bail was denied to offenders arrested for capital crimes; the Bail Reform Act of 1984 permitted judges to deny bail to those offenders who were judged to be at extremely high risk for nonappearance. Most notable in this group of offenders were drug traffickers, who were usually able to make extremely high bail and then flee the country.

The Bail Reform Act of 1984 was challenged in 1987, when *United States v. Salerno* was heard before the Supreme Court. This case challenged the idea of preventive detention, arguing that incarcerating alleged offenders violates their right to due process of law. Opponents of preventive detention argue that incarcerating offenders because of *potential* threat violates the presumption of innocence to which every arrestee is entitled. The Supreme Court did not agree with Salerno and upheld the judicial right to preventive detention. As long as judges have convincing evidence that the offender is likely to commit a crime while awaiting trial, they may set bail at a level higher than the typical amount.

Types of Bail

Judges must make a decision for every offender regarding the likelihood that the offender will appear for trial. They take several factors into account in making this decision, usually including prior arrest record, whether the defendant has appeared at previous hearings, stable family ties, and steady employment. After judges weigh these factors, they make a determination about how likely the defendant is to appear at trial. If offenders are classified as good risks—that is, if they are likely to appear for trial—they are typically released on their own recognizance. Release on recognizance (ROR) allows offenders to remain free before trial with the expectation that they will appear at the appropriate time.

Not all offenders are judged as good risks for appearance. For those expected to be bad risks, or those who are unlikely to appear at trial, some type of bail is usually required. While bail itself involves leaving some type of financial security with the court, the type of security can vary. The most obvious type of bail is typically called a cash bond, and this occurs when the defendant turns over money in the exact amount of bail to the court. Money is not the only type of bail that a defendant can leave with the court. In some cases, a defendant can post a property bond instead, which entails leaving property (personal possessions) with the court to ensure appearance. If the defendant does not appear for the next court appearance, all money and property are forfeited to the court.

Courts are aware that not everyone has the financial ability to post the exact amount of bail or to put up a substantial amount of property. For these individuals, a deposit bond is available. In a deposit bond, the accused offender deposits only a portion of the full bail amount to the court. If the defendant fails to appear, the deposit is kept by the court. If the defendant appears for trial, the

Sign of bail bond business. (By Darylosswald, via Wikimedia Commons)

majority of the bond is returned, with a small percentage kept by the court to cover court costs.

Finally, the most common type of bail is a surety bond. In this arrangement, a third party (not the court nor defendant) promises the court that if the defendant does not appear, they will turn over the amount of bail to the court. In exchange for this service, the defendant pays a fee to the third party. Usually, this third party is a bail bondsman.

Bailbondsmen

When defendants are required to pay bail prior to release, they may enlist the aid of a bailbondsman in securing funds. Bondsmen are independent businessmen who loan bail money to defendants with only a small amount of cash used as a fee. Bondsmen typically require 10 percent of the amount of bail for the fee. They use part of this fee to purchase a surety bond from an insurance company, which actually pays the bail if the defendant does not appear. In addition, bondsmen usually require some collateral as assurance that the defendant will not default on the loan. Many bond businesses also serve as pawn shops in their spare time, selling the collateral left by those who jump bail. Not all defendants will qualify for a bondsman's services. If defendants have a prior history of jumping bail, they will most likely be denied the bondsman's service.

Even those defendants judged as good risks for the bondsman's service sometimes jump bail. When a defendant fails to appear for trial after securing a bondsman, the bailbondsman has legal authority to retrieve the defendant. The bondsman hires individuals referred to as "bounty hunters" or "skip tracers," people who search for those who jump bail. These skip tracers have virtually unlimited discretion in apprehending the defendant. Unlike state and local police officers, skip tracers are allowed to cross state lines to retrieve individuals who jump bail and are allowed to enter a residence without an arrest warrant.

A major criticism of the bailbondsman trade is the ease with which corruption can flourish. Officers of the court, for example, are sometimes paid by bondsmen to refer defendants to their offices. These officers are typically given kickbacks for each defendant referred to the bondsmen. Judges are not immune from inappropriate behavior—some judges may set unreasonably high bail so that defendants are forced to utilize the bondsman's services. In return for these "referrals," judges are paid by the bondsman. Finally, the bondsman trade also discriminates against indigent offenders, as most poor people cannot afford the fees.

Trends and Statistics

Approximately half of all defendants are held prior to trial, according to 1991 statistics. This figure includes individuals who do not make bail (44 percent of all defendants) and those who are held without bail (9 percent of all defendants). Only about 18 percent are released on their own recognizance. The amount of bail also varies across individuals and is usually dependent on the seriousness of the crime committed and prior criminal record. Property offenders are likely to receive lower bail (under $2,500), while violent offenders are more likely to receive high bail (sometimes over $20,000). The World Prison Brief and Institute for Criminal Policy Research reported in June 2014 that, as of May 2014, there were about 480,000 pretrial/remand prisoners in the United States, a rate of 153 pretrial/remand inmates per 100,000 people, compared to a rate of 40 pretrial/remand inmates per 100,000 people worldwide.

Of those who are released prior to trial, about one-fourth fail to appear for trial. Drug offenders are most likely to jump bail, and public order offenders are most likely to appear for trial. There also appears to be a relationship between the type of bond and rates of appearance. For example, offenders who are released on their own recognizance and offenders who leave a deposit bond have the highest rates of failure to appear. Offenders who use a bondsman are most likely to appear at their appointed court date.

Christina Polsenberg

Further Reading

Bureau of Justice Statistics. *Sourcebook of Criminal Justice Statistics*. Washington, DC: U.S. Government Printing Office.

"Close to Three Million People in Pre-Trial Detention Worldwide, New Report Shows." *World Prison Brief*. WPB, Institute for Criminal Policy Research, 18 June 2014. Web. 24 May. 2016.

Flemming, Roy B. *Punishment Before Trial: An Organizational Perspective of Felony Bail Processes*. New York: Longman, 1982.

Goldfarb, Ronald. *Ransom: A Critique of the American Bail System*. New York: Harper Row, 1965.

Thomas, Wayne H., Jr. *Bail Reform in America*. Berkeley: U of California P, 1976.

Walker, Samuel. *Taming the System: The Control of Discretion in Criminal Justice, 1950–1990*. New York: Oxford UP, 1993.

See also Arraignment; Arrest; Bench warrants; Bill of Rights, U.S.; Booking; Bounty hunters; Criminal procedure; Criminal prosecution; Discretion; Due process of law; Manhattan Bail Project; Preventive detention; Speedy trial right; Suspects.

Bailiffs

Definition: Minor court official charged with duties designed to keep order in the courtroom
Criminal justice issue: Courts; trial procedures
Significance: Bailiffs have primary responsibility for maintaining security and order within courtrooms and ensuring that courtroom procedures are followed.

The term "bailiff" has been used since the Middle Ages to designate an administrative official of the courts. Although contemporary bailiffs have fewer duties and less power than their medieval counterparts, they nonetheless serve an important function in courtroom operations. A bailiff is usually a deputy sheriff with police authority whose main jurisdiction is the courtroom. The duties of the bailiff can be divided into two major categories: courtroom management and process serving.

Bailiffs are responsible for a host of courtroom duties. They provide security for the court, including searches before hearings to ensure there are no weapons present; they evict unruly spectators from the courtroom; they escort judges into courtrooms. They are also responsible for transporting defendants to court. Once there, they must control and guard defendants. Further, it is the bailiff who provides defendants with food. Bailiffs also ensure that the people in the court room act with decorum. For example, it is the bailiff who announces the entry of the judge and requests all present to stand. Bailiffs are responsible for the smooth running of court procedures by handling the docket—the order in which cases are heard.

An important function of bailiffs is the protection of the jury. Bailiffs escort juries in and out of the courtroom. Sometimes juries must be kept isolated during a trial so that they are not influenced by others outside the court. This procedure is called "sequestering." When a jury is sequestered, it is the responsibility of the bailiff to guard jurors and to arrange their food, lodging, and transportation.

The second major category of a bailiff's duties is process serving. In Louisiana, for example, bailiffs may be responsible for typing and serving subpoenas and other papers ordered by the court. In Ohio, bailiffs serve papers that include, among other things, criminal warrants, garnishment, and judgment executions. By so doing, the bailiff helps to enforce judgments made by the court.

Requirements for becoming a bailiff vary from state to state. Generally, a bailiff must be at least twenty-one years old, be a citizen of the United States, and have at least a high school diploma or the equivalent. Some states require additional training. In Missouri, for example, bailiffs who have not been certified as peace officers in other capacities must undertake sixty hours of basic training in a state-certified training course.

There are a number of skills bailiffs must have in order to do their jobs well. Some of these include typing, handling paperwork efficiently, knowing courtroom procedures, operating alarm systems, and having familiarity with the jails from which they transport prisoners. In addition, some states set minimal physical requirements for bailiffs. That is, bailiffs must be able to lift at least thirty pounds, sit and stand for long periods, and have good eyesight.

Diane Andrews Henningfeld

Further Reading

Meyer, J. F., and D. R. Grant. *The Courts in Our Criminal Justice System.* Upper Saddle River, N.J.: Prentice-Hall, 2003.

Neubauer, D. W. *America's Courts and the Criminal Justice System.* 7th ed. Belmont, Calif.: Wadsworth, 2002.

See also Criminal justice system; Jury sequestration; Marshals Service, U.S.; September 11, 2001, attacks.

Barker v. Wingo

The Case: U.S. Supreme Court ruling on speedy trials
Date: Decided on June 22, 1972
Criminal justice issue: Constitutional protections; probation and pretrial release; trial procedures

Significance: In this case for the first time, the Supreme Court gave substantive content to the Constitution's guarantee of a speedy trial.

In 1958 Silas Manning and Willie Barker were arrested for the murder of an elderly Kentucky couple. Kentucky had a stronger case against Manning, and the state decided to try him first. If Manning were convicted, then he could be required to testify against Barker. Kentucky sought and obtained the first of what would be sixteen continuances of Barker's trial.

Meanwhile, the prosecution had great difficulty in getting a conviction against Manning. The first trial ended in a hung jury, and a second trial, at which Manning was convicted, was annulled because of the admission of illegally seized evidence. Barker finally objected to additional delay when the state requested a twelfth continuance. Even after Manning's conviction—after a third trial—became final, the Kentucky court granted a further continuance because of the illness of the former sheriff, who had been the investigating officer in the case. Barker finally came to trial in 1963, more than five years after his arrest. During ten months of that period he had been held in jail. He moved to dismiss the charge on the ground that his right to a speedy trial had been violated. After several unsuccessful appeals, Barker asked the U.S. Supreme Court to review his claim.

In an opinion for a unanimous Supreme Court, Justice Lewis F. Powell, Jr., held that Barker's right to a speedy trial had indeed been violated. Justice Powell pointed out that the notion of a "speedy" trial is slippery because there is no clearly definable standard. The circumstances of each case are likely to determine whether any postponements are reasonable. Powell saw two possible alternatives. The first would be to set a rigid time period and to apply it to every case. This the Court rejected because it would amount to law making, a function reserved to the legislature. The second alternative would be to restrict the speedy trial right to defendants who demand it. Justice Powell rejected that solution because it would amount to waiving constitutional rights except for those who ask for them. That would be inconsistent with the Court's general approach to constitutional liberties.

The Court adopted a "balancing test" in which the conduct of both the prosecution and the defendant is considered. This approach requires courts to approach speedy trial issues on an *ad hoc* basis, but once the defendant has asserted the right to a speedy trial, the state must move forward expeditiously. Among the factors that courts must consider are the reasons for any delays, the strength and frequency of the defendant's objections, if any, and the length of any pretrial incarceration defendants have suffered.

The *Barker v. Wingo* balancing test did not prove satisfactory in practice, and the federal government and many states passed statutes to establish rigid time limits for trial. Typically, if no continuances are at the defendant's request, trial must proceed within ninety to one hundred days or the charges against the defendant must be dismissed with prejudice.

Robert Jacobs

Further Reading

Garcia, Alfredo. *The Sixth Amendment in Modern American Jurisprudence.* Westport, Conn.: Greenwood Press, 1992.

Lewis, Thomas T., ed. *The Bill of Rights.* 2 vols. Pasadena, Calif.: Salem Press, 2002.

See also Bill of Rights, U.S.; Criminal procedure; Speedy trial right.

Batson v. Kentucky

The Case: U.S. Supreme Court decision on juries
Date: Decided on April 3, 1986
Criminal justice issue: Civil rights and liberties; juries
Significance: This Supreme Court ruling held that the equal protection clause of the Fourteenth Amendment forbids prosecutors from using peremptory challenges to remove potential jurors because of their race.

On the surface, *Batson v. Kentucky* was one of a long string of Supreme Court efforts to eliminate discrimination from the U.S. judicial system. It departed from the Court's 1965 holding in *Swain v. Alabama*, in which the Court first considered the use of the peremptory challenge for discriminatory purposes.

In *Swain*, when asked whether the equal protection clause of the Fourteenth Amendment prevented the total exclusion of African Americans from juries, the Court declared that the "presumption in any particular case must be that the prosecutor is using the State's challenges to obtain a fair and impartial jury.... [even if] all Negroes were removed because they were Negroes." To overcome the presumption, the Court ruled, a defendant would have to demonstrate that the state followed a consistent pattern of discrimination in "case after case."

Swain prevailed until 1986. Challengers were unable to meet the standards of systematic exclusion established in the decision. State and federal courts alike refused to countenance presentation of evidence from only cases that involved black defendants. Over the repeated objections of Justice Thurgood Marshall, the Supreme Court waited to allow "states to serve as laboratories in which the issue receives further study before it is addressed by this Court" again. Marshall called the experimentation cruel, noting that "there is no point in taking elaborate steps to ensure Negroes are included in venires [pools of prospective jurors] simply so they can be struck because of their race by a prosecutor's use of peremptory challenges."

The reconsideration came in *Batson v. Kentucky*. Batson's counsel asked the Court:

> In a criminal case, does a state trial court err when, over the objection of a black defendant, it swears an all-white jury constituted only after the prosecutor had exercised four of his six peremptory challenges to strike all of the black veniremen from the panel in violation of constitutional provisions guaranteeing the defendant an impartial jury and a jury composed of persons representing a fair cross section of the community?

James Kirkland Batson had been charged with burglary and the receipt of stolen goods. The prosecutor used four of his six peremptory challenges to create, in his words, an "all-white jury." The defense counsel's motion to discharge the panel before it was sworn in on grounds that the panel did not represent a cross-section of the community and that to use it would be a denial of equal protection was denied by the trial judge. Tried and convicted, Batson appealed to the Kentucky Supreme Court, which upheld the conviction in 1984, based on the *Swain* doctrine. The U.S. Supreme Court disagreed. Reversing the conviction, it held that the impaneling of the jury resulted in a denial of equal protection. It ruled that when objection is lodged against an alleged racially discriminatory use of the peremptory challenge, the trial court must examine the validity of the claim.

Thus, for the first time, a federal court agreed that attorneys can be forced to explain their reasons for invoking peremptory challenges. In the process, the Court created a second category of peremptory challenges: those that must be explained.

Ashton Wesley Welch

Further Reading

Barak, Gregg, Jeanne M. Flavin, and Paul S. Leighton. *Class, Race, Gender and Crime: Social Realities of Justice in America.* Los Angeles: Roxbury, 2002. Broad overviews of justice issues.

Jonakait, Randolph N. *The American Jury System*. New Haven, Conn.: Yale University Press, 2003.

Schwartz, Victor E., et al. *Safeguarding the Right to a Representative Jury: The Need for Improved Jury Service Laws*. Washington, D.C.: National Legal Center for the Public Interest, 2003.

See also Equal protection under the law; Jury system.

Bench warrants

Definition: Documents issued by judges demanding that specific defendants be arrested and brought before the court without unneeded delay

Criminal justice issue: Judges; probation and pretrial release; trial procedures

Significance: The increasing frequency with which defendants skip their scheduled court dates has serious implications for future policy on pretrial release and bail.

Defendants released prior to trial do not always appear in court as mandated. Consequently, a judge issues a bench warrant, or *capias*, to retrieve them. Unlike an arrest warrant, which is requested by police officials and based on probable cause, a bench warrant is issued solely on failure to appear at a required legal proceeding. Leading to custody for the defendant, a bench warrant has other ramifications: Bail is forfeited, and the defendant is subject to a separate charge of bond jumping, which incurs additional penalties.

A 2000 Bureau of Justice Statistics study of the seventy-five largest U.S. jurisdictions reports that bench warrants for failure to appear were issued for 22 percent of released defendants. This percentage remained relatively stable from 1990 to 2004. Statistical data on bench warrants, however, should be read with caution. Percentages can vary greatly from study to study depending upon how the researcher defines "failure to appear." For example, during the early 1970's, Detroit's courts were under pressure to keep pretrial release to a minimum, thus a defendant only a minute late was said to be skipping. On the other hand, a city hoping to expand pretrial release may be more liberal, allowing a day or two for defendants to report before issuing a bench warrant.

Defendants who fail to appear do not always do so intentionally. In fact, failure-to-appear rates are strongly associated with court practices. A large percentage of defendants miss court dates because they are not given clear notice of when to appear next. In some jurisdictions, notification is simply an oral statement at the end of a proceeding. Considering the noise and confusion in the courtroom, as well as the strangeness of legal proceedings themselves, it seems logical that a defendant would fail to appear under these circumstances. Further, considering that defendants are often transients and courts keep only the last known address, delivery by mail of notices to appear may also be ineffective. Last, the court's consistent and lengthy delays seem to increase failure-to-appear rates.

Amy I. Cass

Further Reading

Clarke, Stevens, Jean Freeman, and Gary Koch. *The Effectiveness of Bail Systems: An Analysis of Failure to Appear in Court and Rearrest While on Bail*. Chapel Hill, N.C.: Institute of Government, University of Carolina, 1976.

Eskridge, Chris. *Pre-trial Release Programming: Issues and Trends*. New York: Clark Boardman, 1983.

Goldkamp, John, Michael Gottfredson, Peter Jones, and Doris Weiland. *Personal Liberty and Community Safety: Pre-trial Release in the Criminal Court*. New York: Plenum Press, 1995.

See also Arrest warrants; Bail system; Bounty hunters; Marshals Service, U.S.; No-knock warrants; Plain view doctrine; Search warrants.

Bifurcated trials

Definition: Proceedings in which two or more separate hearings or trials are held on different issues of the same cases

Criminal justice issue: Legal terms and principles; trial procedures

Significance: Bifurcated trials are often employed in complicated criminal cases to ensure efficiency and due process.

Frequently utilized in civil cases, the bifurcated trial process is also applied to criminal cases that require judges or juries to rule on certain issues before other issues are addressed. For example, a case in which a criminal defendant claims insanity or diminished capacity is typically decided by bifurcated trials. The guilt or innocence of the defendant is determined in the first phase, and the defendant's sanity is determined and sentence or treatment is imposed in the second phase. In cases involving juries, separate juries are often convened at each stage of the trial process.

Bifurcated trials are most frequently employed in capital murder cases and other cases in which defendants are eligible for the death penalty. During the 1970's, many states passed laws providing for bifurcated capital murder trials after the U.S. Supreme Court mandated that states wishing to impose the death penalty must enact procedural reforms to ensure higher standards of due process for capital defendants. A bifurcated capital murder trial consists of a guilt phase in which a jury decides whether the defendant is guilty and a penalty phase in which a judge or jury determines whether the convicted defendant is to be sentenced to death or to a lesser penalty, usually life without possibility of parole. The penalty phase allows judges and juries to evaluate evidence of aggravating or mitigating circumstances connected with the crime and to hear testimony from victims.

Michael H. Burchett

Further Reading

Bedau, Hugo A. *The Death Penalty in America: Current Controversies.* New York: Oxford University Press, 1997.

Roberts, Albert R., ed. *Critical Issues in Crime and Justice.* Thousand Oaks, Calif.: Sage, 2003.

See also Aggravating circumstances; Capital punishment; Death qualification; Diminished capacity; Due process of law; *Gregg v. Georgia*; Insanity defense; Mitigating circumstances; Sentencing; Trials.

Bill of particulars

Definition: Detailed document itemizing charges against a defendant

Criminal justice issue: Defendants; prosecution; trial procedures

Significance: Defense attorneys file motions to obtain bills of particulars for their clients so they will know all the details of the charges against their clients and be better prepared to organize their defenses.

A bill of particulars amplifies the charging document, which can be a complaint, information, or indictment, depending on the jurisdiction. Charging documents typically contain minimal information. In such cases, defense attorneys file formal motions for, or informally request—depending on the jurisdiction—bills of particulars. The prosecution must then give the defense documents providing additional details about the charges listed in the complaints.

A bill of particulars is essential to defendants in cases in which multiple offenses, or multiple counts of the same offense, are charged, as the information they contain prevents later surprises and thereby helps ensure fair trials. For example, a sexual assault offense occurring over a period of years may be generally charged as a continuing course of conduct. A defendant against such a charge should request a bill of particulars to learn the specific dates, times, and places of the alleged offenses.

Defendants who have detailed information of the charges against them can intelligently prepare their defenses against the charges. While having the same general purpose as discovery—requested by either the prosecution or the defense, used to produce evidence that will be used at a trial—a bill of particulars differs from discovery in that it is not designed to produce evidence that will be used at a trial.

Jennifer C. Gibbs

Further Reading

Emanuel, S. L. *Criminal Procedure.* Aspen, Colo.: Aspen Publishing, 2003.

Garner, Bryan A., ed. *Black's Law Dictionary.* 8th ed. St. Paul, Minn.: Thomson/West, 2004.

Schiller, N. *Criminal Procedure for the Criminal Justice Professional.* Eagan, Minn.: West Publishing, 2001.

See also Criminal procedure; Indictment; Information; United States Statutes at Large.

Blended sentences

Definition: Types of sentences in which judges simultaneously impose both juvenile and adult sanctions on juvenile offenders

Criminal justice issue: Criminal justice issue: Sentencing; Juvenile justice; Convictions

Significance: A relatively new form of sentencing, blended sentences allow juvenile courts to impose penalties on youthful offenders that can move them directly into the adult correctional system when they reach the age of maturity.

Trends indicating increases in violent juvenile crimes such as aggravated assault and robbery captured the attention of the criminal justice system during the late 1990s and the first years of the twenty-first century. In response to those trends, about one-half of state legislatures have enacted blended sentencing (also called "blended jurisdiction") statutes directed at the growing numbers of serious youthful offenders. Blended-sentencing laws allow courts to impose either juvenile or adult correctional sanctions, or a combination of the two, on

Cook County Juvenile Detention Facility & Court. (By Zol87, via Wikimedia Commons)

violent juvenile offenders whose cases are adjudicated in juvenile courts or convicted in criminal courts.

Major justifications for the use of blended sentencing include making juveniles who commit serious or violent crimes more accountable for their actions and promoting the rehabilitation of young criminals. In the matter of choosing whether to invoke blended sentencing, most statutes direct courts to consider three significant criteria: the seriousness of the offenses and need to protect communities; the maturity of the juvenile offenders; and the amenability of the offenders to treatment and rehabilitation while in the juvenile justice system.

Juvenile offenders who are given blended sentences are adjudicated as delinquents and sentenced as adults at the same time, for the same offenses. However, their adult sentences are suspended through the time they spend completing the conditions of their juvenile sentences. When they reach the age at which they pass from the juvenile justice system to the adult justice system, the courts can decide whether to impose what remains of the adult sentences that have hitherto been suspended.

Pati K. Hendrickson

Further Reading

Barrington, Richard. *Juvenile Court System*. [N.p.]: Rosen Publishing Group, 2015. *eBook Collection (EBSCOhost)*. Web. 24 May 2016.

Champion, Dean John. *The Juvenile Justice System: Delinquency, Processing, and the Law*. 4th ed. Upper Saddle River: Prentice-Hall, 2003.

Clarke, E. E. "A Case for Reinventing Juvenile Transfer." *Juvenile and Family Court Journal* 47, no. 1 (1996): 3–21.

Cox, Steven M., John J. Conrad, and Jennifer M. Allen. *Juvenile Justice: A Guide to Theory and Practice*. 5th ed. New York: McGraw Hill, 2003.

Howell, James C., John J. Wilson, and Mark W. Lipsey. *A Handbook for Evidence-Based Juvenile Justice Systems*. Lanham: Lexington Books, 2014. *eBook Collection (EBSCOhost)*. Web. 24 May 2016.

See also Indeterminate sentencing; Juvenile waivers to adult courts; Restitution; Juvenile courts.

Brady v. United States

The Case: U.S. Supreme Court ruling on plea bargaining
Date: Decided on May 4, 1970
Significance: In this decision the Supreme Court first acknowledged the validity of plea bargaining, asserting that it offered a "mutuality of advantage" for both the defendant and the state.

In 1959, Robert M. Brady, a defendant in a kidnapping case that involved the death of the victim, changed a plea of innocent to guilty when a codefendant in the case pleaded guilty and became available as a witness against him. Before admitting the new plea, the judge twice asked Brady if his plea was voluntary. Brady was convicted, but in 1967 he sought a reversal of his conviction in the U.S. District Court for the District of New Mexico, arguing that his guilty plea had not been voluntary. The petitioner argued that the death-penalty provisions of the Federal Kidnapping Act had coerced his plea. The district court denied Brady relief, upholding the constitutionality of the federal statute and arguing that Brady changed his plea because of his codefendant's confession. The Court of Appeals for the Tenth Circuit affirmed the lower court's finding.

On *certiorari*, the U.S. Supreme Court concurred. In the various opinions issued by the Court, it was argued that an earlier case, *United States v. Jackson* (1968), which struck down the section of the Federal Kidnapping Act under which Brady had originally been tried, did not mandate that every guilty plea previously entered under the statute be deemed invalid, even when the threat of death was a consideration. It was further argued that a guilty plea was not a violation of the Fifth Amendment protection against self-incrimination when it was entered to ensure a lesser penalty than the maximum provided for by a criminal statute. It was also noted that the Fifth Amendment did not bar prosecutors or judges from accepting pleas of guilty to lesser, reduced, or selected charges in order to secure milder penalties. Brady's guilty plea was held to have been made voluntarily, despite the fact that it was influenced by the death-penalty provision of the statute that *United States v. Jackson* later declared unconstitutional.

The formal recognition of plea bargaining as a valid procedure for obtaining criminal convictions was very important because plea bargaining has been widely used in the United States, despite the fact that there is no statutory or constitutional basis for it. In fact, almost four-fifths of all convictions in serious state and federal criminal cases are obtained through guilty pleas made to secure either reduced charges or milder punishments. Although the procedure has its critics, it is a practical way of speeding up justice and clearing court dockets. It also mitigates against long pretrial imprisonment and anxiety and protects the public from the criminal activities of habitual offenders who would be free on bail for indefinite periods.

John W. Fiero

Further Reading

Dripps, Donald A. "Guilt, Innocence, and Due Process of Plea Bargaining." *William & Mary Law Review* 57.4 (2016): 1343-1393. *Academic Search Complete*. Web. 24 May 2016.

Fisher, George. *Plea Bargaining's Triumph: A History of Plea Bargaining in America*. Stanford: Stanford UP, 2003.

Hawkins, Eric. "A Murky Doctrine Gets a Little Pushback: The Fourth Circuits Rebuff of Guilty Pleas in *United States v. Fisher*." *Boston College Law Review* 55.6 (2014): 103-114. *Legal Collection*. Web. 24 May 2016.

Rosett, Arthur I. *Justice by Consent: Plea Bargains in the American Courthouse*. New York: Lippincott, 1976.

Vogel, Mary E. *Coercion to Compromise: Social Conflict and the Emergence of Plea Bargaining, 1830-1920*. Rev. ed. New York: Oxford UP, 2005.

See also Attorney ethics; Kidnapping; Plea bargaining; *Rummel v. Estelle*; *Santobello v. New York*; Self-incrimination, privilege against.

Capital punishment

Definition: Execution of defendants convicted of capital crimes

Criminal justice issue: Criminal justice issue: Punishment; Capital punishment

Significance: Capital punishment has been one of the most debated topics in criminal justice policy in the United States, which at the beginning of the twenty-first century was one of the few remaining Western democracies still to employ the death penalty.

While the use of capital punishment as a criminal justice policy has been substantially reduced or eliminated in many countries around the world—as of 2015, 101 countries had abolished the death penalty and another 33 had not executed anyone in the past ten years—in other countries the death penalty continues to be used as the ultimate punishment for criminal behavior.

Between 1608 and the year 2004, the number of people legally executed in what is now the United States has been estimated to be between 20,000 and 22,500. From January, 1977, to July, 2004, alone, 921 executions were carried out in the United States. By the end of 2004, more than 3,400 convicted felons were being held on death rows across the United States. Ten years later, the Death Penalty Information Center reported that 1,394 people had been executed in the United States since 1976. However, the Legal Defense Fund of the National Association for the Advancement of Colored People reported that the known number of inmates on death row had dropped to 3,002 as of fall 2015. By that time, thirty-one states, the federal government, and the US military had laws permitting the use of capital punishment. Although a small portion of states account for the majority of executions, seven of the jurisdictions—including the US military—conducted no executions at all between 1972 and 2003. Of the thirty-one states with the death penalty, many also permit the sentencing of offenders to life in prison without the possibility of parole.

Although the specific circumstances of death-eligible cases vary from jurisdiction to jurisdiction, few states authorize the use of capital punishment for offenses other than murder. At the federal level, the death penalty can be sought in aggravated murder cases, as well as in four offenses that may not involve homicide: treason, espionage, large-scale drug trafficking, and attempted murder of officers, witnesses, or jurors in cases involving continuing criminal enterprises.

The majority of capital cases involve adult male offenders, but a small percentage have involved women and, in the past, juvenile offenders. Women represent a small percentage of death-row inmates and felons who are actually executed. According to the Death Penalty Information Center, women accounted for over forty executions in the United States over one hundred years. Only sixteen women were executed between 1976 and 2015, and fifty-nine women awaited execution in 2014.

Also representing a small proportion of past death-row populations and numbers of executions were juvenile offenders. Twenty-two executions of offenders who committed their crimes when they were under the age of eighteen account for less than 2 percent of all executions carried out between 1976 and 2004. In 2004, seventy-two offenders on death rows in twelve states were considered juvenile offenders. The following year, the execution of people under the age of eighteen at the time of the crime was deemed illegal through the ruling in the case of *Roper v. Simmons*.

Capital Punishment in History

The history of capital punishment in America dates back to early colonial times. Early settlers were influenced by their British counterparts, whose laws mandated the death penalty for more than 150 separate crimes. While the laws on death sentencing varied from colony to colony, its practice was dramatically reduced in comparison to Britain. Massachusetts had one of the strictest laws on the books, with twelve crimes that were considered "death-eligible."

In contrast, colonies dominated by Quakers were more lenient in their use of executions. They restricted the death penalty to cases of treason and murder. However, decisions to execute sparingly were not made solely for philosophical reasons, but because of the colonies' need for able-bodied workers.

The number of executions in the United States increased significantly during the nineteenth century. However, the rate of executions reached its peak during the 1930s, when more than sixteen hundred people were put to death in the country.

Methods of Execution

Just as the policies on capital punishment have evolved from colonial times, so, too, have the methods by which executions are carried out. Early methods, such as burning at the stake and beheading, have since been ruled as unconstitutional on the grounds that they violate the Eighth Amendment's protection against cruel and unusual punishment. Death by hanging is the only early method that has stood the test of time; it has been responsible for the greatest number of executions. A few US states still permit hanging, but methods such as electrocution, firing squads, and lethal gas are now either rarely used or have been declared unconstitutional.

By the early twenty-first century, lethal injection had become the primary method of execution in most states with death penalties. It was created in an effort to provide a more humane and socially acceptable method of execution. Lethal injections generally use three drugs: sodium thiopental sedates the convicted felon; pancuronium bromide provides a total muscle relaxant; and potassium chloride induces cardiac arrest, which results in death.

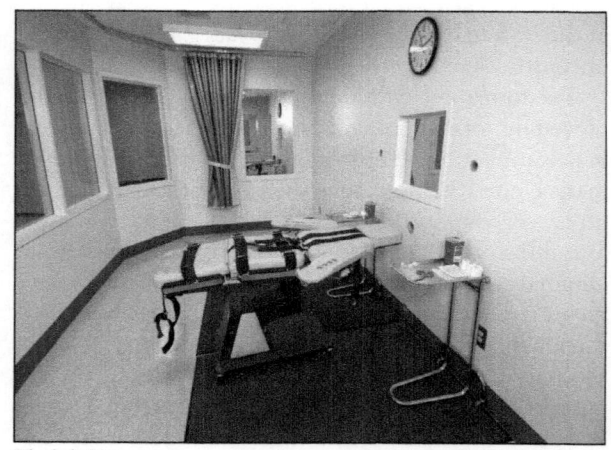

The lethal injection room at San Quentin State Prison. (Public domain, via Wikimedia Commons)

In 2014, a shortage of the drugs used for lethal injection (due in part to the European Union's refusal to export them to the United States) began to be a problem in many states, leading to three botched executions involving experimental drug combinations in Ohio, Arizona, and Oklahoma. Many executions scheduled for 2015 were postponed until the state could acquire a fresh supply of drugs.

Opposition to Capital Punishment

As executions surged during the nineteenth century, an anti-death-penalty movement also began to develop. During that period, several changes were made to the policies and practices of capital punishment that abolitionists viewed as progress toward its elimination in the United States. First, states began to change the processes by which death sentences were handed down. Up until that time, all the states utilized mandatory death sentencing for specific offenses. That practice changed in 1838, when Tennessee became the first state to change its capital sentencing policy to allow discretion in sentencing. The modern US Supreme Court has declared mandatory death sentences as unconstitutional.

The second nineteenth-century change came when several states limited the number of offenses that were considered death-eligible. Southern states expanded the use of capital punishment for slaves, but the majority of states limited its use to crimes of murder and treason. In 1846, Michigan became the first state to abolish the death penalty for all crimes, with the exception of treason.

A third change was the transformation of executions from public to private events. Previously, hangings had traditionally been held in public squares in order to deter criminal activity, and religious readings and prayers provided a foundation for the occasions. However, public executions often created public disorder as a result of public drunkenness, botched executions, and rioting. In 1834, Pennsylvania became the first state to remove executions from public view. The last public execution in the United States was conducted in 1937. Now, public attendance at executions is limited to small numbers of citizens. Access by journalists is also limited, and legal efforts to televise executions to the public have failed.

In addition to policy changes that limited the use of capital punishment, several states began to abandon the practice in its entirety during the late nineteenth and early twentieth centuries. In 1852, Rhode Island became the first state to eliminate the use of the death penalty for all crimes. Since then, several states have abolished the death penalty, only to reinstate it at later dates in response to political or public pressures. In 2015, nineteen states and the District of Columbia did not have any death penalty statutes, according to Amnesty International.

Supreme Court Decisions

A primary legal issue relating to capital punishment is whether the death penalty violates the Eighth Amendment's protection against cruel and unusual punishment. Before reviewing the constitutionality of the death penalty as a practice, the US Supreme Court addressed the question of how to define cruel and unusual punishment. In 1878, the Court ruled specific forms of torture as unconstitutional in its *Wilkerson v. Utah* decision. That ruling was explicit in specifying what types of execution procedures were cruel and unusual, but the Court's later rulings were less specific.

In *Weems v. United States* (1910), the Court argued that decisions on what constitutes cruel and unusual punishment are not immutable and limited by the beliefs of the framers of the Bill of Rights. Rather, definitions should be subject to interpretation and change. The Court's 1958 *Trop v. Dulles* ruling elaborated on this point, arguing that the definition of cruel and unusual should come from the evolving standards of decency as defined by modern society.

After the *Trop* ruling, measuring the evolving standards of decency led to several changes in death-penalty policy. In 1972, in *Furman v. Georgia*, the Supreme Court overturned state statutes on capital punishment nationwide in a 5–4 vote. The Court found that then-current laws violated the cruel and unusual clause of the Eighth and Fourteenth Amendments. As other justices in the past had debated on the definition of cruel and unusual punishments, so, too, did the *Furman* Court. Justices William J. Brennan and Thurgood Marshall argued that the death penalty itself was inherently cruel and unusual, Justices William O. Douglas, Potter Stewart, and Byron R. White argued that the statutes themselves constituted cruel and unusual punishment as they were arbitrary and were implemented with wide degrees of discretion. With the *Furman* ruling, the death sentences of all the prisoners awaiting execution on death rows throughout the nation were invalidated.

After the Supreme Court's *Furman* decision, legislators looked for ways of ensuring that capital punishment could be administered fairly and equitably, so that the death penalty could be reinstated. Newly written state statutes passed constitutional muster in several 1976 Supreme Court decisions, the most notable of which was *Gregg v. Georgia*. These new Court rulings reopened the floodgates for executions to continue.

The new state laws were designed to set standards for judges and juries in capital cases. First, a bifurcated process was to be conducted for all death-penalty trials, in which the guilt/innocence phases would be separated from the sentencing phases. Second, presentation of information on mitigating and aggravating factors was allowed during the sentencing phases, in which aggravating circumstances had to outweigh the mitigating circumstances before the death penalty could be awarded. Third, all death sentences became subject to automatic reviews by the states' supreme courts. Finally, the states were required periodically to conduct studies of proportionality to determine whether disparities in sentencing were developing.

The conditions outlined in *Gregg* passed the constitutional requirements of the Court in 1976, but the Court's justices continue to argue whether capital punishment itself represents cruel and unusual punishment. Later Court decisions continued to apply the criteria of the evolving standards of decency to limit which offenders may be subjected to capital punishment. In *Penry v. Lynaugh* in 1989, the Court held that the execution of the intellectually disabled did not constitute cruel and unusual punishment. However, the Court overturned this decision in 2002 in *Atkins v. Virginia* (2002). In its latter decision, the Court found that a national consensus had developed against the practice of executing the intellectually disabled and held that such a practice violates Eighth Amendment protections. Meanwhile, as of 2015, there were no restrictions against the execution of the severely mentally ill, though the American Psychiatric, Psychological, and Bar Associations have all recommended against it.

The *Atkins v. Virginia* ruling opened the possibility of other challenges to capital punishment. One example is the execution of juvenile offenders. In 1988, the Court held in *Thompson v. Oklahoma* that offenders under the age of sixteen at the time they commit their crimes are not eligible to receive death sentences. In 2002, four justices voted to hear the case of Kevin Nigel Stanford, who was seventeen at the time of his crime. Their dissenting opinion indicated that not only did they wish to revisit the issue of the juvenile death penalty, they were prepared to declare it as an unconstitutional practice. The state of Kentucky granted clemency to Stanford and commuted his death sentence to life in prison without the possibility of parole, but the US Supreme Court was still left with the issue of the juvenile death penalty.

In 2003, Missouri's supreme court, drawing largely on the rationale set forth in *Atkins*, declared juvenile executions unconstitutional. The Missouri court referenced public and professional opinion, as well as declining legislative support for capital punishment in its decision. On March 1, 2005, the US Supreme Court upheld the Missouri court ruling in a 5–4 decision. Writing for the majority, Justice Anthony Kennedy stated that to extinguish a juvenile's life before he attains the maturity to understand his own humanity would be cruel and unusual punishment.

Arguments for and Against Capital Punishment

Death-penalty supporters argue that capital punishment should be retained on the basis of retribution and deterrence. Most people who support the death penalty favor it because of the principle of retribution. Retribution is often described by the concept of *lex talionis*, or "an eye for an eye"—a principle holding that punishments must be proportionate responses to crimes. *Lex talionis* is also often associated with the concept of revenge. Retribution is also characterized as just deserts, holding that offenders deserve to be punished for their actions.

Supporters of the death penalty argue that for justice to be served and for order to be restored to the community, society requires the execution of offenders as payment for their crimes. In contrast, death-penalty opponents argue that criminal justice policies should not be based on a retributive position because revenge is an emotional, rather than a reasonable, response. They further argue that the death penalty is a disproportionate response when compared to other sentencing philosophies, as the American system does not rape rapists or steal from thieves.

In contrast to the emotionally laden concept of retribution, deterrence is viewed as a more rational and scientific argument for capital punishment. Proponents are quick to argue that the death penalty provides for both specific and general deterrence. Not only do executions prevent convicted murderers from killing again, but the belief is that if murderers are executed, other potential murderers will think twice before committing murder, for fear of losing their own lives. However, deterrence theory assumes that offenders are thinking individuals who rationally consider the potential consequences of their actions before engaging in them.

Opponents to the death penalty argue that deterrence can be achieved by incarcerating offenders for life without the possibility of parole. Additionally, they argue that if the death penalty were, in fact, an effective deterrent, murder rates would increase when it is abolished and decline when it is restored. Proponents counteract this argument by stating that the death penalty as it is currently administered in the United States may not provide a deterrent effect because the average length of time that persons sentenced to death spend awaiting their executions is overly long. Based on FBI data on murder rates by state, states without the death penalty consistently have lower murder rates than states with the death penalty.

Additionally, a botched lethal injection given to an inmate on death row in Oklahoma attracted an especially large amount of national—and international—attention to the United States' capital punishment standards and procedures in 2014. This event, combined with another chaotic execution performed in Ohio earlier in the year, raised further concerns and questions regarding the types of drugs used as well as the definition of "cruel and unusual" punishment.

Wrongful Convictions

Between 1973 and 2015, 156 inmates were released from death row after new evidence demonstrated that they had been wrongfully convicted. Their releases seemed to refute arguments presented by supporters of capital punishment that only the guilty are sentenced to death row. In the state of Illinois, thirteen death-row inmates were exonerated between 1977 and 2000, while twelve others were executed. Illinois's Governor George Ryan, previously a strong supporter of the death penalty, expressed concern that the system of handing out death sentences in his state may have allowed executions of the innocent, so he declared a moratorium on executions in

> ### A Mixed Movie Message About Capital Punishment
>
> The 2003 film *The Life of David Gale* makes a curious case against capital punishment. Kevin Spacey plays the title character, a philosophy professor, who is convicted of murder and sentenced to death for killing a woman (Laura Linney) who had participated in anti-death penalty activism with him. Shortly before Gale's scheduled execution, he invites a reporter (Kate Winslet) to hear his story. When the reporter later comes into possession of a videotape showing that the woman's death was a suicide, she tries unsuccessfully to deliver this new evidence to authorities before the professor is executed. Afterward, she discovers that the professor and his alleged victim voluntarily cooperated in the latter's death with the specific intent of having the professor wrongfully executed. The conspirators wanted his wrongful conviction to be discovered too late to stop his execution, hoping that these circumstances would promote public opposition to the death penalty. In other words, both the professor and his alleged victim sacrifice their lives in the cause of ending capital punishment.
>
> The final plot development in *The Life of David Gale* confuses the film's anti-death penalty message. An innocent man is convicted, to be sure, and the possibility of such convictions is a key argument against the death penalty. However, the fact that the innocent man deliberately manipulates the justice system to ensure his own execution makes it difficult to take from the film any clear lesson about the criminal justice system.
>
> — Timothy L. Hall

2000. Following a two-year investigation by a commission appointed by Ryan to review capital sentencing procedures, the commission made eighty-five recommendations on the processing of capital cases to ensure a system of fair, equitable, and accurate sentencing. Illinois incorporated some of those recommendations, but many, such as the immediate appointment of counsel, remained to be implemented. Meanwhile, following reviews of Illinois's death-row population, Governor Ryan commuted the sentences of 156 inmates awaiting execution to life in prison without parole.

The use of DNA testing has played an increasingly important role in proving wrongful convictions. The Death Penalty Information Center has claimed that by 2014, DNA identification was a prominent factor in dropping murder charges and releasing prisoners from death row in twenty different cases. Those who were eventually exonerated still spent an average of eleven years behind bars.

Proponents of capital punishment disagree with the argument that it is administered in a discriminatory fashion. In 2014, about 43 percent of the prisoners held on death rows were classified as white and 41 percent were black, according to the Legal Defense Fund. However, while the majority of inmates and executions have involved white offenders, such statistics do not take into account the proportion of population demographics. Opponents argue that the death penalty is disproportionately applied to African Americans, who constitute only 13 percent of the entire population. A 2014 study from the University of Washington of criminal trials in that state found that jurors were three times more likely to recommend the death sentence for a black defendant than a white defendant accused of a similar crime.

While the role of race in capital punishment sentences remains a subject of debate, a review of post-*Furman* executions provided additional evidence for opponents of capital punishment. As of 2015, 77 percent of all execution cases involved white murder victims, even though white victims constitute only about 50 percent of all murder victims nationwide. In Louisiana, the odds of a defendant receiving the death penalty in a case with a white victim were 97 percent higher than in cases where the victim was black. In California, a perpetrator who had killed a white person was three times more likely to be sentenced to death than one who had killed a black person, and four times more likely than one whose victim was Latino. In North Carolina, a white victim made the death sentence 3.5 times more likely than a victim of any other race. Issues of discrimination are also raised on the variable of class, as poor defendants are unable to obtain the resources to provide an adequate defense

Some critics of capital punishment charge that the death penalty is applied randomly, without concern for legal criteria. While proponents contend that the death penalty is applied in an equitable fashion, opponents disagree. Because the death penalty is actually invoked in only a small number of death-eligible cases, two different offenders who commit similar crimes may receive dramatically different sentences: death versus life imprisonment. Additionally, evidence demonstrates that the death penalty is subject to significant jurisdictional differences, as the majority of post-*Furman* executions have been carried out by southern states. Texas alone accounted for more than one third of all executions between 1972 and 2004. By 2015, Texas still topped the list in terms of total executions conducted.

Conclusion

Even as capital punishment remains a subject of debate, raising issues such as deterrence, retribution, innocence, and discrimination, it remains a component of the American criminal justice system. Questions of who should be executed, for what crimes, and by what methods have been addressed throughout American history and continue to be debated. Recent decisions to limit the application of the death penalty, to declare moratoriums against executions, and to declare the practice in itself as unconstitutional indicate that support for capital punishment may be fading. Regardless of the future of the death penalty, it has sealed its place in history as the ultimate punishment philosophy in criminal justice policy.

Stacy L. Mallicoat

Further Reading

Banner, Stuart. *The Death Penalty: An American History*. Boston: Harvard UP, 2003. Print.

Bedau, Hugo Adam, and Paul Cassell. *Debating the Death Penalty: Should America Have Capital Punishment? The Experts on Both Sides Make Their Best Case*. Oxford: Oxford UP, 2003. Print.

Berman, Mark. "What It Was Like Watching the Botched Oklahoma Execution." *Washington Post*. Washington Post, 2 May 2014. Web. 13 Jan. 2015.

Bohm, Robert M. *Deathquest: An Introduction to the Theory and Practice of Capital Punishment in the United States*. Cincinnati: Anderson Publishing, 2003. Print.

Death Penalty Information Center. *Facts about the Death Penalty*. Washington, DC: Author, 2015. PDF file.

Goo, Sara Kehaulani. "5 Facts about the Death Penalty." *Pew Research Center*. Pew Research Center, 28 May 2015. Web. 2 Nov. 2015.

Johnson, Robert. *Death Work: A Study of the Modern Execution Process*. Belmont: Wadsworth, 1998. Print.

National Association for the Advancement of Colored People Legal Defense and Educational Fund. *Death Row U.S.A. Fall 2014*. New York: NAACP Legal Defense and Educational Fund, 2014. Web. 13 Jan. 2015. PDF file.

Prejean, Helen. *Dead Man Walking: An Eyewitness Account to the Death Penalty in the United States*. New York: Vintage, 1993. Print.

Radelet, Michael L., Hugo Adam Bedau, and Constance E. Putnam. *In Spite of Innocence: Erroneous Convictions in Capital Cases*. Boston: Northeastern UP, 1994. Print.

State of Illinois. *Report of the Former Governor Ryan's Commission on Capital Punishment*. April, 2002. Print.

Vollum, Scott, et al. *The Death Penalty: Constitutional Issues, Commentaries, and Case Briefs*. 3rd ed. Boston: Anderson, 2015. Print.

See also Antiterrorism and Effective Death Penalty Act; Bureau of Justice Statistics; *Coker v. Georgia*; Cruel and unusual punishment; Death qualification; Deterrence; Execution, forms of; *Ford v. Wainwright*; *Furman v. Georgia*; *Gregg v. Georgia*; *McCleskey v. Kemp*; Murders, mass and serial; Punishment; Sentencing guidelines, U.S.; Supreme Court, U.S.; Treason; *Roper v. Simmons* (2005); Deterrence; Incapacitation.

Case law

Definition: Body of past legal decisions that serve as binding authority for judges to issue rulings in cases

Criminal justice issue: Courts; judges; trial procedures

Significance: The use of case law requires judges, in most cases, to craft legal opinions consistent with history and tradition, thus promoting stability and efficiency in the court system.

The U.S. legal system is actually two largely separate systems. One is the federal system, which is composed of district courts at the trial level, circuit courts for appeals, and the U.S. Supreme Court as the highest authority. The second comprises state systems. Each state has different names for the courts within its system, but, at a minimum, every state has trial courts, appellate courts, and a high, or supreme, court.

The primary way in which judges make decisions in all U.S. courts is through the use of case law. Derived from the English common law, case law is a body of prior legal decisions that form the rule of law to be applied to cases before the courts. This concept of using prior decisions to regulate future decisions is more commonly referred to as the doctrine of *stare decisis*, a Latin phrase meaning "to stand by precedent."

A primary purpose of case law is to ensure that judges do not issue rulings based on their own personal opinions. This approach to judicial decision making creates consistency in the legal system and promotes fairness by making sure that people in the same jurisdiction are not treated differently, especially when their cases may be factually similar.

An important limitation to the use of case law is that prior decisions are binding upon courts only when they have been issued by higher courts within the same system. Therefore, a state court decision would not be binding on a federal court. Likewise, a decision made at the trial level in either system would not be binding on an appellate or supreme court within the same system. Decisions that are not binding on courts are known as "persuasive authority." When no binding authority exists on a particular legal question, parties may try using persuasive authority to persuade judges to decide cases in their favor.

Occasionally, past decisions are inconsistent with present societal norms. When this occurs, judges may issue rulings contrary to case law, thus establishing new binding authorities for future courts. A noteworthy historical example of this occurred when slavery was legal in the United States. Early judicial decisions found slavery to be constitutional. Once attitudes changed, the Supreme Court declared slavery unconstitutional, thus overruling its own well-established precedent. Consequently, it can be said that the use of case law in the judicial decision-making process is not absolute.

Kimberly J. Belvedere

Further Reading

Johns, Margaret, and Rex R. Perschbacher. *The United States Legal System: An Introduction.* Durham, N.C.: Carolina Academic Press, 2002.

Rehnquist, William H. *The Supreme Court.* New York: Alfred A. Knopf, 2001.

See also Common law; Discretion; Due process of law; Harmless error; Judges; Judicial review; Opinions; Precedent; *Stare decisis*; Trials.

Cease-and-desist orders

Definition: Order from court or agencies prohibiting certain persons or entities from continuing certain conduct

Criminal justice issue: Courts; judges

Significance: A cease-and-desist order provides a nonstatutory legal remedy to a situation in which one is giving offense but not breaking any specific law.

A cease-and-desist order is a judicial option used to prevent or halt behavior which may not, by itself, be illegal according to statutory law but which could lead to harm if not stopped. The order generally includes a notice of the right to a hearing, and usually there is at least an allegation of a statutory violation, with the appropriate law being cited. Law requires that the order be delivered either through the marshal's office or via registered mail. Tangible evidence of the order's issuance must be stored by a third party, often an attorney.

The issuance of a cease-and-desist order can be beneficial to individuals and to society as a whole. It puts an immediate halt to behavior or activity which could result in measurable harm if the slow-paced justice system were left to move at its usual speed. Such an order could prevent a wrong from occurring for which there is no totally appropriate remedy and no way to satisfy the aggrieved party.

Cease-and-desist orders may also have negative consequences. They have been used to stop reporters or whistle-blowers from exposing corporate wrongs. Issues of jurisdiction sometimes arise, as federal, state, and local judges are capable of issuing the orders. The clarity and uniformity of the various laws impacting the issuance are also questioned at times. Cease-and-desist orders undeniably give courts an effective tool for controlling individual behavior.

Thomas W. Buchanan

Further Reading

Garner, Bryan A., ed. *Black's Law Dictionary.* 8th ed. St. Paul, Minn.: Thomson/West, 2004.

Janosik, Robert J., ed. *Encyclopedia of the American Judicial System.* New York: Scribner, 1987.

See also Judges; Judicial system, U.S.; Jurisdiction of courts; Psychopathy; Restraining orders; Trespass.

Certiorari

Definition: A writ of *certiorari* is a discretionary procedure employed by appellate courts—including the U.S. Supreme Court—to review lower court decisions

Criminal justice issue: Appeals; constitutional protections; courts; legal terms and principles

Significance: Writs of *certiorari* are the legal mechanisms through which the U.S. Supreme Court accepts almost all cases it decides. The principle gives the Court almost complete discretion in the choice of which cases it hears.

Derived from a Latin word meaning to be "informed," writ of *certiorari* is a legal term that goes back to the early history of English courts. A writ of *certiorari* is a discretionary order issued by an appellate court. When appellate courts want to review decisions of lower courts, they issue writs of *certiorari*. Such writs require the lower courts to deliver their findings to the appeals courts for review. The procedure enables higher courts to review lower court decisions for possible judicial errors that might justify overturning those decisions.

The term *certiorari* is most commonly used in reference to the process by which the U.S. Supreme Court selects the cases that it reviews. *Certiorari* controls almost all appellate access to the Court. The Supreme Court reviews only the cases that it chooses, which are those that raise the most significant constitutional issues.

In selecting a case for review, four of the Supreme Court's nine justices must agree that it presents an issue that raises a significant constitutional question. After four justices agree (the "rule of four"), the Court issues a writ of *certiorari* to the lower appellate court ordering that its appellate record be brought before the Supreme Court for review. The Supreme Court then reviews the lower court's finding and renders its decision. The Court can dismiss the case, reverse the lower court's decision and send it back for further review or a new trial, or uphold the findings of the lower court.

Lawrence C. Trostle

Further Reading
McGuire, Kevin. *Understanding the U.S. Supreme Court*. New York: McGraw-Hill, 2002.
Wood, Horace G. *A Treatise on the Legal Remedies of Mandamus and Prohibition: Habeas Corpus, Certiorari, and Quo Warranto*. 3d ed. Revised and enlarged by Charles F. Bridge. Littleton, Colo.: Fred B. Rothman, 1997.

See also Appellate process; *Gideon v. Wainwright*; *In forma pauperis*; Supreme Court, U.S.

Chain of custody

Definition: Procedure which documents the transfer of physical evidence collected at a crime scene from station to station, such as from the preliminary investigation scene to the evidence room, laboratory, and courtroom

Criminal justice issue: Evidence and forensics; investigation; legal terms and principles

Significance: The chain of custody secures and protects the competency of evidence for courtroom presentation and ensures that the evidence remains untainted.

The following hypothetical situation will demonstrate a chain of custody. Police officers arrive at the scene of a bank robbery. During the preliminary investigation, a bank teller discloses information. He provides a bank robbery note from the robber. The note contains the following instructions: "This is a robbery! Follow my instructions and all will go well." The officer carefully collects the document and forwards it to the evidence custodian for storage.

The officer initiates the process by placing his initials and the time and date on the outside of a plastic evidence envelope. This lock-seal envelope will enclose the evidence. An evidence tag and chain-of-custody form are printed on one side of the transmittal envelope.

The investigator records pertinent information before placing the document inside and is careful not to alter the document or place any writing indentation marks on the surface. The reverse side of the envelope is clear plastic, which allows investigators to view the writing without compromising trace evidence or fingerprints. In cases where biological evidence or fluids are involved, envelopes are not appropriate; refrigerator containers are used instead.

Evidence Tag

The evidence tag generally lists the following information: case and control number, date and time, description of the evidence, location, victim/incident, remarks, special handling instructions, test results, and red tags which indicate the presence of blood or other biological fluids that require refrigeration. In addition, red tags indicate the need for special safety precautions. This information may appear on the transmittal envelope or on a white sticker or an attached card.

Chain of Custody Form

The primary purpose of chain-of-custody reports is to identify all handlers by signature. All those who assume authority over the bank robbery note sign to document their handling. The chain-of-custody form also contains the following information: case and control number, receiving agency, location, description, name of person who recovered the evidence, victim's name, name of person who sealed the evidence envelope, name of person who released the evidence, name of person who received the evidence, and purpose of transfer. In this hypothetical investigation, the first person to sign the chain-of-custody form is the bank teller. The investigator's signature is next, followed by those of the evidence custodian and laboratory examiner. The evidence custodian signs the chain-of-custody form, and the investigator signs the form before transporting the evidence to court. The chain-of-custody list is limited to a few handlers and signatures; this prevents gaps or breaks in the chain.

Thomas E. Baker

Further Reading
Gilbert, James N. *Criminal Investigation*. Upper Saddle River, N.J.: Prentice-Hall, 2001.
Swanson, Charles R., Neil C. Chamelin, and Leonard Territo. *Criminal Investigation*. New York: McGraw-Hill, 2003.

See also Computer forensics; Crime scene investigation; Criminal procedure; Evidence, rules of; Fingerprint identification; Sobriety testing.

Change of venue

Definition: Relocation of a trial from one jurisdiction to another

Criminal justice issue: Juries; jurisdictions; media; trial procedures

Significance: The importance of impartiality in the court system is demonstrated by court procedures such as change of venue.

A change of venue is a change in the location of a trial. Criminal trials are usually conducted within the jurisdictions in which the crimes being tried take place. Trials can be moved to other jurisdictions because of concerns about jurors being biased because of local media coverage, dangers of violence, or racial prejudice. Initiatives for changing venues are often taken by defense attorneys who ask judges to relocate their trials because they believe different locations will provide more impartial juries for their clients. Prosecutors often object to changing venue because they believe they are more likely to win convictions in the communities in which the crimes take place.

Judges make the decisions to move trials to different parts of the state, due in part to the amount of media attention that cases receive. A judicial decision to change the venue of a trial can impact the outcome of that trial. Moving a trial from its original jurisdiction may locate it in an area where potential jurors are resentful of the media attention it brings to their community. However, choosing not to relocate a high-profile trial can provide the basis for an appeal at the conclusion of the trial.

Jenifer A. Lee

Further Reading

Meyer, J. F., and D. R. Grant. *The Courts in Our Criminal Justice System.* Upper Saddle River, N.J.: Prentice-Hall, 2003.

Neubauer, D. W. *America's Courts and the Criminal Justice System.* 7th ed. Belmont, Calif.: Wadsworth, 2002.

See also Court types; Defendants; Judges; Jurisdiction of courts; King beating case; Presumption of innocence; Trial publicity.

Citations

Definition: Printed documents issued by an officer that serve as an official summons, demanding the presence of the offender at the court on a specified time and date

Criminal justice issue: Criminal justice issue: Traffic law; Arrest and arraignment

Significance: Citations are written for the court's administrative purposes: to give an alleged violator notice of a date and time to appear at court, and to contain a law-enforcement officer's notes of the incident at the time the citation is issued.

Citations may be issued by court officials, such as prosecutors, but they are usually issued by law-enforcement officers in conjunction with their daily duties. Citations are usually associated with traffic and parking violations, although they may be written for infractions, misdemeanors, or felonies.

Violators of the law are issued citations in lieu of being taken forthwith before the court, a judge, or a justice of the peace. By signing citations, alleged violators are not admitting guilt to the offenses; rather, they are promising to appear in court at the times and dates specified. By signing citations, alleged violators are, in essence, releasing themselves on their own recognizance. A refusal to sign the citation is not seen by the court as an admission of guilt, but in most jurisdictions failure to sign will result in the arrest of the alleged offender. The failure to sign the citation is thus a failure to acknowledge the mandated court date. The alleged violator is then taken either to a judge or justice of the peace, or if one is not available the violator is held at a local jail facility until a hearing before the court can be arranged. When a citation is written for a parking violation, the offending driver need not sign the citation.

In some misdemeanors and felonies, citations are written and submitted to the prosecutor in conjunction with a report prepared by a law-enforcement officer. In these cases, citations merely serve as an administrative charge-filing reminder. Citations also serve another administrative function for law-enforcement officers and courts: Officers frequently write field notes on citations at the time they are written as a reminder of the circumstances surrounding the citing. Courts recognize such notes, and officers may use them when testifying on the merits of the citation. If such notes exist, the defendant has legal access to view the citation and attendant notes.

Charles L. Johnson

Further Reading

Bannon, Mark E. *A Quick Reference Guide to Contemporary Criminal Procedure for Law Enforcement Officers : One Hundred Notable United States Supreme Court Decisions and Their Effect on Modern Policing in America.* Springfield: Thomas, 2003. eBook Collection (EBSCOhost). Web. 24 May 2016.

Brown, David W. *Beat Your Ticket : Go to Court & Win.* Berkeley: NOLO, 2013. *eBook Collection (EBSCOhost).* Web. 25 May 2016.

Loewy, Arnold H., and Arthur B. LaFrance. *Criminal Procedure: Arrest and Investigation.* Cincinnati: Anderson Publishing, 1996.

Pretrial Justice Inst. "Citation in Lieu of Custodial Arrest." *Pretrial Justice Institute.* PJI, 2014. Web. 25 May. 2016.

Whitcomb, Debra, Bonnie Lewin, and Margaret J. Levine. *Citation Release.* Washington, D.C.: U.S. Department of Justice, National Institute of Justice, 1984.

See also Arrest; Arrest warrants; Court types; Defendants; Jaywalking; Misdemeanors; Plain view doctrine; Speedy trial right; Traffic courts; Traffic law.

Civil commitment

Definition: Civil commitment statutes allow the involuntary hospitalization and treatment of a person with mental illness who is dangerous to him- or herself (or others).

Criminal justice issue: Constitutional protections; courts; mental disorders

Significance: Involuntary civil commitment, like criminal incarceration, involves significant deprivation of liberty and raises due process concerns. Although there are some differences among states, civil commitment standards require objective evidence of both dangerousness and severe mental illness. Patients who are civilly committed must have access to high-quality treatment that includes meaningful community reentry services and support.

Freedom, liberty, and autonomy are cherished values in a free society, and loss of these values raises due process concerns. Civil commitment statutes allow the involuntary hospitalization and treatment of a person with mental illness who is a danger to him- or herself (or others). These statutes reflect two primary legal principles that date back to Aristotle: parens patriate (parent of the country) and police power. *Parens patriate* refers to the role of the state as a sovereign authority to intervene on behalf of citizens who are unable to care for themselves, whereas police power refers to the state assuming responsibility to maintain order and public safety. The core purpose of civil commitment is protecting the safety of the public and/or the person with mental illness. The state's overarching interest in maintaining public safety, however, may come at the expense of restricting the liberties of certain individuals. Individuals may be hospitalized after conviction for a crime, either immediately or after conviction, in lieu of a prison sentence, or upon completion of a prison sentence. Involuntary civil commitment, like criminal incarceration, involves significant deprivation of liberty and raises due process concerns. Arguably, due process concerns are more implicated in civil commitment than criminal proceedings, given that civil commitment may continue for a lifetime. The circumstances under which a person can be involuntarily committed remain a complex legal and clinical issue.

Although there are some differences among states, civil commitment standards require objective evidence of both dangerousness and severe mental illness. In a landmark case, *O'Connor v. Donaldson*, the U.S. Supreme Court articulated that the state cannot confine a nondangerous mentally ill person against his will who is capable of surviving safely in the community. The patient in this case, Kenneth Donaldson, while visiting his parents had claimed that someone was putting poison in his food. He had a history of mental illness and hospitalization. His father fearing that his son was having another episode petitioned a commitment hearing. Mr. Donaldson was diagnosed with paranoid delusions and admitted to a state hospital where he was held for nearly fifteen years. Throughout the hospitalization, he never posed a danger to himself or others, nor was he ever suicidal or suspected of injuring himself. However, he was confined in a locked room with sixty beds and his treatment was custodial at best. He did not receive meaningful treatment for the illness that he was being held for. He repeatedly requested release to friends who agreed to care for him but his pleas were dismissed. Courts held that involuntary commitment by virtue indicated that the person was incompetent to make meaningful decisions. His continued confinement was justified under the pretext of suffering from paranoid delusions and refusing treatment, which mainly consisted of medication and electroshocks. This case was significant in setting standards to protect the due process and the rights of civilly committed individuals.

The decision on *O'Connor v. Donaldson* established the basis that mental illness, in and of itself, was not enough to keep a person civilly committed indefinitely. A finding of danger to oneself or others was needed to meet the due process requirement. What constitutes dangerous behavior, however, remains an abstract construct that is hard to define and measure. Mental health and legal experts define and assess dangerousness differently from each other and within their own professions. Another major limitation on the assessment of dangerousness was that early assessments of violence and dangerousness, often based on unsubstantiated beliefs of individual psychiatrists and psychologists, were found to be inaccurate, leading to some researchers likening such predictions to "flipping a coin." This was especially evident when their opinion was grounded in unstructured interviews, intuition, and professional discretion. Prominent researchers saw the need to increase predictive accuracy of dangerousness, leading the prediction of future dangerousness to shift toward evidence-based risk assessment; this has advanced the field considerably. To date, mental health experts with competent knowledge of risk assessment, rely on empirically validated risk factors to estimate the likelihood of recidivism and use objective instruments that are designed for specific settings, populations, and types of violence.

After *O'Connor v. Donaldson*, another issue that the courts had to address was whether proof of dangerousness alone was sufficient for continued commitment. Could an individual deemed dangerous as a result of mental illness and criminality be kept against his will? Interpreted broadly, would this include contract killers, gang members, drug dealers, and other dangerous offenders whose criminal behaviors are motived by pursuit of personal goals? In *Foucha v. Louisiana*, another seminal case on civil commitment, the Supreme Court ruled that dangerousness alone, without the presence of a serious and severe mental illness, was not enough to support civil commitment. In 1984, Mr. Foucha was charged with aggravated burglary and a firearm offense. The trial court found that at the time of committing the above offenses, he was unable to distinguish right from wrong and was thus insane. He was committed to a state hospital until such time that his sanity was restored. Four years later, he was found to have regained his sanity but still considered dangerous. His continued dangerousness, however, was attributed to the presence of antisocial personality disorder (a condition that was comorbid, but arguably independent of the condition that had impaired his ability to distinguish right from wrong). Although antisocial personality disorder is a codified Diagnostic and Statistical Manual of Mental Disorders (DSM) mental illness, the Supreme Court ruled that antisocial personality disorder was not a severe mental illness to support continued commitment. Since *Foucha v. Louisiana*, the connection between mental illness and dangerousness has generated considerable debate and there are conflicting opinions on this issue.

Overrepresentation of people with mental illness in the criminal justice system has led some states to enact laws and policies to distinguish between civil vs. forensic commitments. In California, for example, patients who are admitted from criminal courts for a crime linked to their mental illness are referred to as forensic patients, whereas patients admitted from civil courts who are a danger to themselves or others are referred to as civil commitment patients. Among the most prominent differences between forensic vs. civil commitment are that forensic commitments do not require a recent overt act, occur after an offender has served his term of incarceration, and may include personality disorders. This distinction between forensic vs. civil patients has brought greater awareness to the commitment process, treatment needs and planning, discharge, and supervision of these patients. One major emphasis has been recognizing the unique needs of these populations, and balancing rehabilitative goals with meaningful forensic outcomes. Another interest is the right to treatment in the least restrictive setting that is consistent with risk level and clinical needs. Finally, patients who are civilly committed must have access to high-quality treatment that includes meaningful community reentry services and support.

Allen Azizian and Charles Broderick

Further Reading

Dolan, M., and M. Doyle. "Violence Risk Prediction." The British Journal of Psychiatry 177, no. 4 (2000): 303-11.

Ennis, B. J., and T. R. Litwack. "Psychiatry and the Presumption of Expertise: Flipping Coins in the Courtroom." California Law Review 62, no. 3 (1974): 693-752.

Fazel, S., J. P. Singh, H. Doll, and M. Grann. "Use of Risk Assessment Instruments to Predict Violence and Antisocial Behaviour in 73 Samples Involving 24,827 People: Systematic Review and Meta-analysis." BMJ: British Medical Journal 345, no. 7868 (2012): 1-12.

Foucha v. Louisana, 504 U.S. 71 (1992).

Gendreau, P., C. Goggin, and M. Law. "Predicting Prison Misconduct." Criminal Justice & Behavior 24 (1997): 414-31. doi:10.1177/0093854897024004002.

Grove, W. M., D. H. Zald, B. S. Lebow, B. E. Snitz, and C. Nelson. "Clinical versus Mechanical Prediction: A Meta-Analysis." Psychological Assessment 12, no. 1 (2000): 19.

Hart, S. D., and C. Logan. "Formulation of Violence Risk Using Evidence-Based Assessments: The Structured Professional Judgment Approach." In Forensic Case Formulation. Edited by P. Sturmey and M. McMurran. Chichester, UK: John Wiley & Sons, Ltd. doi:10.1002/9781119977018.ch4.

Meyer, R. G., and C. M. Weaver. Law and Mental Health: A Case-based Approach. New York: Guilford Press, 2006.

Monahan, J. The Clinical Prediction of Violent Behavior. Northvale, N.J.: Jason Aronson, 1995.

Monahan, J., and H. J. Steadman. "Toward a Rejuvenation of Risk Assessment Research." Violence and Mental Disorder: Developments in Risk Assessment (1994): 1-17.

O'Connor v. Donaldson, 422 U.S. 563 (1975).

See also Mental illness; Prison and jail systems; Psychopathy; Punishment; Rehabilitation; Solitary confinement; Criminal law; Criminal justice system; Competency to stand trial; Community-based corrections.

Clemency

Definition: Power of an executive authority to pardon convicted criminals and to commute sentences
Criminal justice issue: Appeals; pardons and parole; restorative justice
Significance: Clemency generally serves as a last-ditch effort to secure justice for convicted individuals.

In each of the fifty American states, convicted defendants may appeal their sentences or punishments through a proscribed appeals process. When all steps of the appeals process have been exhausted, the sentences stand unless an executive body grants clemency. In rare instances, clemency may be granted at any step of the legal procedure, even prior to arraignment on charges.

Clemency may take several forms. Pardons nullify punishments and sentences, and all rights of the individual are restored as though no wrongdoing had ever occurred. By contrast, commutation of sentences acts as an exchange of the punishments originally ordered by courts with other sentences, usually sentences that are less severe. For example, a governor may commute a death-penalty sentence to life imprisonment, or a ten-year prison sentence may be commuted to deportation.

Executive bodies may issue clemency in the form of reprieves from sentences, that is, temporary postponements. Reprieves are most often used for death-penalty cases in which proponents of the convicted inmates seek to keep the inmates from being put to death, while simultaneously hoping to bring forward new evidence that will reverse prior appeals decisions.

Because many states have adopted mandatory sentencing for certain criminal convictions, the courts are occasionally required to impose sentences that seem out of proportion to the crimes when all the facts, exigencies, and personalities are taken into account. The possibility of clemency thus allows for restorative justice in such instances.

Taylor Shaw

Further Reading
Burnett, Cathleen. *Justice Denied: Clemency Appeals in Death Penalty Cases.* Boston: Northeastern University Press, 2002.
Carter, Linda E., and Ellen Krietzberg. *Understanding Capital Punishment Law.* Newark, N.J.: LexisNexis, 2004.
Novak, Andrew. Comparative Executive Clemency: The Constitutional Pardon Power and the Prerogative of Mercy in Global Perspective. New York, N.Y.: Routledge, 2016.

See also Amnesty; Pardons; Parole; Probation, adult; Rehabilitation.

Clerks of the court

Definition: Elected or appointed officer of the court who performs a multitude of legal processing, courtroom, and judicial support duties
Criminal justice issue: Criminal justice issue: Courts
Significance: Acts as the sole custodian of the records of all criminal and civil cases.

Clerks of the court (also referred to as county clerks) are also known as the keepers of the records, as they play a vital role in serving the interests of justice. They are responsible for the maintenance and preservation of all court pleadings for criminal and civil cases. Clerks of the court attend court hearings, motions, and trials in order to log information onto court records. They are responsible for the recording system in the courtroom and transcribing the information onto docket sheets. They maintain the judges' calendars, prepare files for docket, and coordinate the flow of documents necessary for court assignments. During trials, the clerks of the court receive, mark, and assume custody of evidence presented. They also serve as liaisons between judges and a wide variety of agencies throughout the county.

In some states, as determined by a judge, clerks of the court may be afforded limited judicial duties, such as preparing and issuing warrants, subpoenas, and other official documents on behalf of the court. They may also prepare jury pools, swear in witnesses and jurors, file jury charges and verdicts, and record jury service and compensation due jurors. Lastly, clerks of the court may serve as probate judges, becoming responsible for the administration of numerous issues regarding probate estates.

Lisa Landis Murphy

Further Reading
Dileo, A. M., and A. B. Rubin. *Law Clerk Handbook: A Handbook for Federal District and Appellate Court Law Clerks.* Washington, D.C.: Federal Judicial Center, 1977.

Schmalleger, Frank. *Criminal Justice Today: An Introductory Text for the Twenty-first Century.* 8th ed. Upper Saddle River, N.J.: Pearson/Prentice-Hall, 2005.

See also Court types; Criminal justice system; Summonses; Trials.

Coker v. Georgia

The Case: U.S. Supreme Court ruling on capital punishment
Date: Decided on June 29, 1977
Criminal justice issue: Capital punishment; sex offenses
Significance: In this case, the Supreme Court held that capital punishment for the crime of rape is an excessive and disproportionate penalty, and therefore contrary to the prohibition against cruel and unusual punishments in the Eighth and Fourteenth Amendments.

While serving sentences for murder, rape, kidnapping, and other crimes, Erlich Anthony Coker escaped from a Georgia prison in 1974. That same evening he entered the private home of a couple, tied up the husband in the bathroom, raped the wife, and then forced her to leave with him in the car belonging to the couple. Apprehended by the police, Coker was tried and convicted on charges of rape, armed robbery, and kidnapping. Based on procedures that had been approved by the U.S. Supreme Court in *Gregg v. Georgia* (1976), the jury found Coker guilty of rape with aggravating circumstances and sentenced him to death. After the Georgia Supreme Court upheld the conviction and sentence, the U.S. Supreme Court accepted the case for review.

The Supreme Court limited its review to the single question of whether capital punishment for rape is a cruel and unusual punishment that violates the Eighth and Fourteenth Amendments. Ruling 7 to 2 in the affirmative, the Court reversed Coker's death sentence and remanded the case to the Georgia courts for a new sentencing.

Writing the majority opinion, Justice Byron R. White argued that the sentence of death for the crime of rape is unconstitutional because it is an excessive and disproportionate punishment. As evidence that the public judgment agreed with this conclusion, White pointed to the fact that Georgia was the only state to authorize the death penalty for the rape of an adult woman. Although the crime of rape deserved serious punishment, it was disproportionate to inflict the defendant with a more severe punishment than he inflicted on his victim. Although rape was not equivalent to the unjustifiable taking of a human life, the crime of deliberate murder in Georgia was not a basis for the death penalty except where there were aggravating circumstances. White wrote that it was disproportionate to punish a rapist more severely than a deliberate killer.

As in other cases dealing with capital punishment, the justices expressed a variety of views. Two concurring justices opposed all use of capital punishment, while two dissenters would have allowed it for rape. One justice, Lewis F. Powell, Jr., joined the majority because the rapist did not inflict great brutality or serious injury on the victim.

The *Coker* decision underscored the extent to which the Court had accepted the view that the Eighth Amendment prohibited excessive and disproportionate punishments. It appeared that the Court would not approve the use of the death penalty for any crime other than deliberate murder, but it was not certain how the Court would react to capital punishment for rape with excessive brutality or when the victim sustained serious injury. Some observers noted that *Coker* appeared to indicate that the Court was becoming more reliant upon the doctrine of substantive due process.

Thomas Tandy Lewis

Further Reading
Bohm, Robert M. *Deathquest: An Introduction to the Theory and Practice of Capital Punishment in the United States.* Cincinnati: Anderson Publishing, 2003.
Carter, Linda E., and Ellen Krietzberg. *Understanding Capital Punishment Law.* Newark, N.J.: LexisNexis, 2004.
Latzer, Barry, ed. *Death Penalty Cases: Leading Supreme Court Cases on Capital Punishment.* 2d ed. Burlington, Mass.: Butterworth Heinemann, 2002.
Sarat, Austin. *When the State Kills: Capital Punishment and the American Condition.* Princeton, N.J.: Princeton University Press, 2001.

See also Capital punishment; Cruel and unusual punishment; Rape and sex offenses.

Competency to stand trial

Definition: Determination of whether defendants are mentally able to understand the charges against them and to understand trial proceedings
Criminal justice issue: Criminal justice issue: Defendants; Mental Disorders; Trial procedures

Significance: A long-standing American and English legal tradition holds that mentally incompetent persons should not be subjected to criminal trials.

The idea that a person judged to be incompetent should not be forced to stand trial on criminal charges has its basis in English common law. In the United States it has been considered a constitutional principle since the Supreme Court case *Drope v. Missouri* (1975). Part of the rationale is that if an accused party does not have the capacity to participate in the trial, then the American adversarial system of justice cannot be fairly applied, and the accused will therefore not receive due process of law.

Dusky v. United States (1960) established that the standard of incompetency for federal trials was to be whether the accused has "sufficient present ability to consult with his lawyer with a reasonable degree of rational understanding" and could have a rational and factual understanding of court proceedings. To be legally competent, a person must be able to confer with a lawyer, testify coherently, and follow evidence that is presented. State courts generally follow this standard as well, although the wording of state statutes varies. Although the federal incompetency statute refers to mental incapacitation, some cases of severe physical incapacitation have been held to constitute incompetency.

Determining competency involves three stages: initiating an inquiry, making a preliminary determination as to competency, and, if there is sufficient evidence, holding a competency hearing. An inquiry is usually initiated by counsel, either prosecution or defense. Generally a psychiatric evaluation is then mandatory. If the examination indicates that the defendant may be incompetent, a competency hearing is mandatory. The hearing is adversarial in nature; the main witness is usually the psychiatrist who conducted the psychiatric evaluation, but other witnesses may also be called. The trial judge usually rules on the defendant's competency, and the judge may consider the defendant's appearance and demeanor as well as the witness's testimony. A finding of incompetency does not mean that the person has been judged not guilty. Traditionally, a person found incompetent would be committed to a psychiatric institution, and there were no restrictions on how long such confinement could be. In *Jackson v. Indiana* (1972), however, the Supreme Court ruled that indefinite commitment is unconstitutional and that the length of commitment cannot exceed "the reasonable period of time necessary to determine whether there is a substantial probability that he will attain competency in the foreseeable future."

Elizabeth Algren Shaw

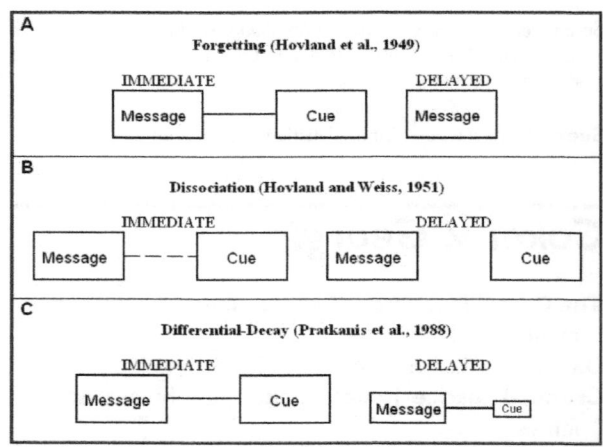

The sleeper effect, part of a psychological evaluation. (Public domain, via Wikimedia Commons)

Rorschach inkblot test, used in psychological evaluations. (Public domain, via Wikimedia Commons)

Further Reading

Bardwell, Mark C., and Bruce A. Arrigo. *Criminal Competency on Trial: The Case of Colin Ferguson.* Durham: Carolina Acad., 2002. Print.

Huckabee, Harlow M. *Mental Disability Issues in the Criminal Justice System: What They Are, Who Evaluates Them, How and When.* Springfield: Thomas, 2000. Print.

Perlin, Michael L. *A Prescription for Dignity: Rethinking Criminal Justice and Mental Disability Law.* Surrey: Ashgate, 2013. Print.

Schopp, Robert F., et al., eds. *Mental Disorder and Criminal Law: Responsibility, Punishment and Competence.* New York: Springer, 2009. Print.

Slobogin, Christopher. *Minding Justice: Laws That Deprive People with Mental Disability of Life and Liberty.* Cambridge: Harvard UP, 2006. Print.

Zapf, Patricia A., and Ronald Roesch. *Evaluation of Competence to Stand Trial.* New York: Oxford UP, 2009. Print.

See also Arraignment; Common law; Criminal intent; *Ford v. Wainwright*; Forensic psychology; Insanity defense; Malice; Mental illness.

Concurrent sentences

Definition: Sentences for separate convictions that an offender serves at the same time
Criminal justice issue: Judges; legal terms and principles; punishment; sentencing
Significance: Judges determine whether defendants serve their sentences concurrently or consecutively based on factors related to the specific crimes and the offenders.

When defendants are convicted of more than one crime at the same time, the judges in their cases have the option of deciding whether the sentences for the individual crimes should run consecutively (one after the other) or concurrently (at the same time). When judges choose to order defendants to serve their sentences concurrently, the total time that the offenders serve-barring other complications—is equivalent to the lengths of their longest sentences.

Concurrent sentences sometimes arise out of plea-bargain agreements. Additionally, judges may decide to be more lenient on particular offenders or may view the crimes of which defendants are convicted as being so closely related to one another as to amount to a single crime. However, state laws may set the conditions under which judges can decide to have sentences run concurrently. Typically, state laws require judges to impose consecutive sentences, instead of concurrent sentences, when the crimes, or purposes behind the individual crimes, are distinct.

A major criticism of the principle of concurrent sentences is that offenders who serve their sentences concurrently spend only as much time in prison as they would if they were convicted of only the most serious charges brought against them. They thus go unpunished for their additional crimes, while other defendants who commit the same combinations of crimes may serve longer sentences.

Sheryl L. Van Horne

Further Reading
Demleitner, Nora V., Douglas A. Berman, Marc L. Miller, and Ronald F. Wright. *Sentencing Law and Policy: Cases, Statutes, and Guidelines*. New York: Aspen Publishers, 2003.

Tonry, Michael. *Sentencing and Sanctions in Western Countries*. New York: Oxford University Press, 2001.

United States Sentencing Commission. *Federal Sentencing Guidelines Manual 2003*. St. Paul, Minn.: West Publishing, 2004.

See also Convictions; Defendants; Judges; Mandatory sentencing; Plea bargaining; Prison and jail systems; Sentencing.

Contempt of court

Definition: Conduct that obstructs a court's administration of justice or undermines its dignity
Criminal justice issue: Courts; punishment; trial procedures
Significance: Citing persons who disrupt court procedures or disobey court orders with contempt of court can be a powerful tool for maintaining order and decorum within courtrooms, and judges can use contempt of court to send offenders to jail without the help of police or trials.

Just as law-enforcement officers use discretion in deciding whom to arrest, judges use discretion when deciding to hold persons in contempt of court. However, just as police officers do not issue tickets to all motorists who exceed posted speed limits, judges do not cite all those who disrupt court proceedings with contempt. Judges typically reserve contempt citations for those who they believe are creating the most serious disorders and for situations in which they wish to set examples for other persons present in their courtrooms.

Contempt of court can also be used as a prosecutorial tool for imprisoning wrongdoers without trials. For example, prosecutors might call certain witnesses to testify, knowing that they are likely not to cooperate and then be jailed for contempt of court. In fact, everyone who fails to comply with subpoenas or other court orders can be punished with contempt. In addition, those who disobey gag orders can also be held in contempt of court. Those who are found in contempt of court can be subjected to fines, jail time, or both, depending on the decisions of the judges holding the offenders in contempt. Those held in jail can be kept there without trial until they comply with the original court orders.

A justification for the courts' power to punish those guilty of contempt of court is deterrence. The sanctioning of individuals with contempt of court may deter others from being disruptive in court or from disobeying court orders. It can be especially useful in persuading news reporters to obey gag orders.

Jenephyr James

Further Reading

Neubauer, D. W. *America's Courts and the Criminal Justice System*. 7th ed. Belmont, Calif.: Wadsworth, 2002.

Rabe, Gary A., and Dean John Champion. *Criminal Courts: Structure, Process and Issues*. Upper Saddle River, N.J.: Prentice-Hall, 2002.

See also Deterrence; Discretion; Fines; Gag orders; Judges; Obstruction of justice.

Convictions

Definition: Legal process through which judges and juries establish the guilt of criminal defendants

Criminal justice issue: Convictions; defendants; prosecution; verdicts

Significance: The focus of all criminal trial proceedings is the prosecution's efforts to obtain convictions by proving defendants guilty and the defendants' efforts to avoid convictions.

Convictions may be established in several ways: Defendants may enter pleas of guilt, they may enter pleas of *nolo contendere*, or they may be found guilty at trial. In each instance, the courts enter final judgments, in which the factual and legal allegations are sustained, and orders of conviction. Upon entry of the orders, the courts may then proceed to the sentencing phase. The combined process of entering judgments, convictions, and penalties are known as the judgment and sentence phase.

A conviction may only be entered when the legal and factual allegations reach the appropriate level of proof. In all criminal matters, the level of proof required is beyond a reasonable doubt. This is the level of factual certainty in which no mere skeptical condition of the mind exists but in which the evidence may fall short of absolute proof beyond all doubt. It means simply that the proof must be so conclusive and complete that all realistic doubts of the facts are removed from the minds of ordinary persons.

After Convictions

The legal status of defendants changes substantially once they are convicted. Convictions bring with them restrictions and losses of certain due process and other rights. The most significant loss is that of the defendants' freedom, which may be ordered as part of the sentences. In addition, convictions confer the status of having been found guilty of crimes. In some instances a conviction may also terminate or limit personal rights, such as the ability to own firearms, vote, be bonded, serve in the U.S. military, or obtain professional licenses, such as those of attorneys, medical doctors, or accountants.

Convictions are generally considered permanent parts of the defendants' criminal records. A person who has multiple convictions—especially for the same or similar crimes—may receive an enhanced punishment for the later offenses. For example, in most states conviction of the felony crime of burglary carries penalties of from one to seven years in the states' penal systems. Second and subsequent convictions generally increase punishments up to life in prison. Similar crimes carry similar punishments, which may be enhanced based on the type or number of prior convictions.

In instances in which more than one crime is charged against a defendant, each conviction may affect the penalties for any other convictions. In such instances, the courts tend to treat the companion cases either as separate crimes requiring individual punishments or as parts of a larger group of crimes.

The courts may run sentences concurrently or consecutively, depending on how they wish the individual convictions to be treated. Concurrent sentences are served and completed at the same time. For example, a person convicted both of driving under the influence of alcohol (DUI) and of manslaughter (both arising from the same set of facts), may be punished for both convictions at the same time. Thus, if a court were to order the defendant to serve a one-year sentence for the DUI conviction and a two-year sentence for the manslaughter conviction, the defendant would serve both sentences at the same time and spend a total of only two years in prison. By contrast, if a defendant were convicted of the exact same pair of crimes and instead received one- and two-year sentences to be served consecutively, the defendant would spend a total of three years in prison.

Convictions may also be used to prove conduct in civil cases as well. The burden of proof in criminal cases is higher than that required in civil actions. This means that once the burden is met for a criminal case, as proven through existence of the conviction, the burden will also be met for the civil action. The key is that the facts leading to the conviction must be the same as those used in the civil case. Thus, defendants who are convicted of driving under the influence of alcohol may find themselves civilly liable for car crashes arising from the same set of facts.

One must be careful when associating convictions with a jury trial. The duty of the jury is to determine the facts in a case. It is always the duty of the judge to determine the given law. A conviction can only be entered when both facts and law combine to prove the elements of the particular crime. While a jury may reach a verdict as to the facts, it is only the judge that may enter a conviction as part of the final judgment.

Carl J. Franklin

Further Reading
Christianson, Scott. *Innocent: Inside Wrongful Conviction Cases.* New York: New York University Press, 2004. Investigative reporter's account of forty-two wrongful conviction cases.
Connors, E., T. Lundregan, N. Miller, and T. McEwen. *Convicted by Juries, Exonerated by Science: Case Studies in the Use of DNA Evidence to Establish Innocence After Trial.* Alexandria, Va.: National Institute of Justice, 1996. Close examination of some of the first cases of false convictions that were overturned by DNA evidence.
Hanson, Roger A. *Federal Habeas Corpus Review: Challenging State Court Criminal Convictions.* Washington, D.C.: U.S. Department of Justice, Bureau of Justice Statistics, 1995. Statistical study of *habeas corpus* petitions in eighteen federal district courts in nine states.
LaFave, Wayne. *Criminal Law Hornbook.* 4th ed. Belmont, Calif.: West Publishing, 2003. Detailed treatise of criminal law with lengthy explanations and references to cases.
LaFave, Wayne R., Jerold H. Israel, and Nancy J. King. *Criminal Procedure.* 4th ed. St. Paul, Minn.: Thomson/West, 2004.

See also Acquittal; Aggravating circumstances; Burden of proof; Concurrent sentences; Criminal records; Double jeopardy; Execution of judgment; False convictions; Mitigating circumstances; Plea bargaining; Pleas; Presentence investigations; Recidivism; Sentencing; Verdicts.

Corporal punishment

Definition: Infliction of physical pain or discomfort as the means to punish behavior that violates established rules, including criminal laws
Criminal justice issue: Confessions; interrogation; medical and health issues; punishment
Significance: Although corporal punishments were once commonly applied, they were eliminated from the American justice system as the United States moved toward exclusive reliance on fines and restrictions on freedom, such as probation and incarceration, as methods of criminal punishment.

In seventeenth and eighteenth century Europe and colonial America, people routinely received physical punishments for violating society's rules. These corporal punishments included branding, whipping, cutting off ears, fingers, hands, or tongues, and placing people in stocks—wooden structures in a town square into which a person's head, arms, or legs could be locked. These corporal punishments were legacies of religious beliefs that had also encouraged torture, burning people at the stake, and public executions for a variety of offenses, both serious and minor. A basic belief that underlay these physical punishments of people's bodies was an assumption that people who misbehaved were possessed by the devil and therefore unable to conform their behavior to God's rules for society.

During the Enlightenment period of the late eighteenth century, the emphasis on corporal punishment in Europe began to be displaced by reforms intended to rehabilitate offenders. Instead of branding or whipping them, various localities began to incarcerate them with a Bible or make them work in prison shops in the hope that they would discover God and self-discipline and thereby become good people.

Punishment in the United States

During the colonial and postrevolutionary periods, the United States employed many of the corporal punishments that had been brought from Europe, including whipping, branding, and placing in stocks. The movement away from corporal punishments in favor of incarceration occurred during the nineteenth century.

In the southern United States, corporal punishments of the most vicious kinds, particularly whipping, branding, and dismemberment, were applied against African American slaves as punishment for escapes or any other infractions as defined by slave owners. Local law-enforcement officials and courts reinforced the institution of slavery by actively supporting these forms of punishment.

After the Civil War, corporal punishments began disappearing as formal punishments for crimes, but their use still flourished on an informal basis. Police in many localities throughout the country utilized beatings and even torture as a means to punish people informally and to obtain confessions. While corporal punishment was used successfully to obtain many confessions, these confessions often came from innocent people who had simply been selected for victimization by unethical police officers. Such abusive behavior by police officers became less common in the twentieth century as policing began to be-

Whippings and other forms of corporal punishment that did not interfere with slaves' productivity were frequently inflicted on American slaves before the Civil War. (Library of Congress)

come a profession with training, and as judges scrutinized the activities of police.

Corporal punishment was used in prisons and jails until the 1960's. Prisoners in some states were beaten, locked in small compartments, and otherwise physically coerced into obeying orders. Officials sometimes permitted inmates to abuse other inmates in order to force prisoners to perform labor under harsh conditions. These practices were outlawed by federal judges as a result of lawsuits in the 1960's and 1970's.

Corporal Punishment and the Law

By 1969, all but two states had abolished whipping as a punishment for prison inmates. The final two states were effectively barred from further use of corporal punishment when a U.S. court of appeals decision said that Arkansas's continuing use on prisoners of the "strap"—a leather whip attached to a wooden handle—violated the prohibition on cruel and unusual punishments (*Jackson v. Bishop*, 1969).

Beginning in the 1970's, prison officials, like police officers, could not use corporal punishments. They could, however, use physical force for self-defense and for gaining control over people who were fighting, threatening, or disruptive. Despite the prohibition on corporal punishments, occasional lawsuits are still filed against police officers and corrections officials who have beaten criminal defendants and inmates.

The formal abolition of corporal punishment in the criminal justice system did not mean that corporal punishment no longer existed in the United States. Parents are permitted to apply corporal punishment to their children as long as that punishment does not cause injuries or break laws against child abuse. In addition, corporal punishment is permitted in schools in many states. In 1978, the Supreme Court decided that the Eighth Amendment's prohibition of cruel and unusual punishments did not apply to disciplinary corporal punishments in schools (*Ingraham v. Wright*, 1978). Thus many schools continued to use corporal punishments, most frequently paddling with a wooden paddle, as a means to punish misbehaving students. As of today, thirty one have banned corporal punishment, while in a lot of other states, parental permission is required. New Mexico was the latest state to abolish corporal punishment in schools in 2011.

In 1994, public debates resumed concerning the desirability of corporal punishment when Singapore sentenced Michael Fay, an American teenager, to six lashes with a bamboo cane for committing acts of vandalism. Although the U.S. government protested on Fay's behalf that the punishment ("caning") was barbaric, leaders in many American local communities seized on the issue to advocate the reintroduction of corporal punishment as a cheaper and more effective punishment for juvenile offenders. Corporal punishment was not reinitiated, but the debate demonstrated that many Americans still consider corporal punishment to be an effective deterrent to misbehavior by young people.

The Committee on the Rights of the Child in its Forty Second session under The Convention on the Rights of the Child in the General Comment spoke about the Rights of the Child to Protection from Corporal Punishment and Other Cruel or Degrading Forms of Punishment speaks about eliminating violence against children, especially in the nature of corporal punishment.

Christopher E. Smith
Updated by Tania Sebastian

Further Reading
Berkson, Larry. *The Concept of Cruel and Unusual Punishment.* Lexington, Mass.: Lexington Books, 1975. Examination of the legal aspects of corporal and other forms of punishment.
Foucault, Michel. *Discipline and Punish: The Birth of the Prison.* Translated by Alan Sheridan. New York: Vintage Press, 1995. Traces the history of punishment from brutal public events to subtle exertions of power over individuals in everyday life.
Garland, David. *Punishment and Modern Society.* Chicago: University of Chicago Press, 1990. General overview of punishment.
Genovese, Eugene D. *Roll, Jordan, Roll: The World the Slaves Made.* New York: Pantheon Books, 1974. Discusses the use of whipping and other corporal punishments of slaves in the antebellum South.
Hyman, Irwin A., and James H. Wise, eds. *Corporal Punishment in American Education: Readings in History, Practice, and Alternatives.* Philadelphia: Temple University Press, 1979. Examination of the debates over corporal punishment in schools.
Rothman, David J. *The Discovery of the Asylum: Social Order and Disorder in the New Republic.* Boston: Little, Brown, 1971. Broad history of punishment in the U.S.
Straus, Murray A. and Donnelly, Denise A. *Corporal Punishment of Adolescents by American Parents* (1993) available at: http://files.eric.ed.gov/fulltext/ED354443.pdf
Newman G. *Just and Painful: A Case for the Corporal Punishment of Criminals* (Harrow and Heston Publishers, New York, 2nd edition, 1995)
Glenn, Mayra C. *Campaigns against Corporal Punishments: Prisoners, Sailors, Women and Children in Antebellum America* (State University of New York Press, Albany, 1st edition, 1984).
Kilimci, Songul. *Teachers' Perceptions on Corporal Punishment as a Method of Discipline in Elementary Schools,* 2 (8) the Journal of International Social Research (2009) 242.

See also Auburn system; Bill of Rights, U.S.; Cruel and unusual punishment; Police brutality; Punishment; Rehabilitation; Post-traumatic stress disorder.

Counsel, right to

Definition: Entitlement provided for criminal defendants by the U.S. Constitution to receive representation by an attorney during criminal proceedings
Criminal justice issue: Attorneys; constitutional protections; defendants
Significance: An essential aspect of the American adversary system of justice employed is the principle that criminal defendants receive professional representation in order to protect their constitutional rights and prevent the conviction of innocent people.

American legal proceedings employ an adversary system of justice which assumes that the truth will emerge through the clash of professional advocates who oppose each other in the courtroom. In criminal cases, the permanent advocate for the government is the prosecutor. If individuals accused of crimes did not have professional advocates to represent them, there would be grave risks that the prosecution would automatically overwhelm the average citizen-defendant in the courtroom and thereby obtain convictions, whether justified or not. Defendants who have sufficient funds can hire their own attorneys, but poor people who are accused of crimes cannot afford to secure their own professional representation. In order to increase the fairness of legal proceedings and provide protection for criminal defendants' rights, the U.S. Supreme Court gradually interpreted the words of the U.S. Constitution to provide a broad right to counsel for people who otherwise could not afford to hire an attorney on their own.

Constitutional Law

The Sixth Amendment to the U.S Constitution includes various rights intended to ensure that criminal defendants receive fair trials. One of those rights is the right "to have the Assistance of Counsel for his defense." For most of American history, the application of this right to counsel was limited for two reasons. First, until the middle of the twentieth century, the Bill of Rights was regarded as protecting people only against the federal government. Thus the Sixth Amendment applied only to federal criminal cases, which are a tiny proportion of the total criminal cases processed each year. Second, the right to counsel was interpreted to mean that people could not be prevented from having an attorney if they could afford to hire one. It did not mean that an attorney would be provided for people who could not afford to hire their own.

The Supreme Court began to alter its interpretations of the Sixth Amendment in the 1930's. In a case concerning several unrepresented African American youths convicted of rape and sentenced to death in a lynch-mob atmosphere in Alabama (*Powell v. Alabama*, 1932), the Supreme Court declared that poor defendants facing the death penalty must be provided with attorneys. In *Johnson v. Zerbst* (1938), the Supreme Court said that all defendants facing felony charges in federal court must be provided with attorneys if they are too poor to hire their own. During the 1940's, the right to appointed counsel was expanded to cover poor state felony defendants who needed professional representation because of "special circumstances" such as illiteracy or mental retardation.

During the 1950's and early 1960's, state legislatures, state supreme courts, and local state judges began to require that poor defendants be supplied with attorneys in criminal cases. By 1963, seven states still did not ensure that defense attorneys were provided for all felony defendants. The Supreme Court brought the entire country into line in 1963 with its decision in *Gideon v. Wainwright* (1963), which applied the Sixth Amendment to all state courts by requiring that poor defendants be given attorneys in felony cases. In subsequent decisions, the Supreme Court expanded the right to counsel to cover initial appeals after conviction (*Douglas v. California*, 1963) and misdemeanor cases in which the defendant faces the possibility of incarceration for less than one year in jail (*Argersinger v. Hamlin*, 1972). The Supreme Court also applied the right to counsel to pretrial processes by declaring that the Sixth Amendment required that defense attorneys be made available during police questioning of suspects, during preliminary hearings, and at identification line-ups after a defendant has been charged with a crime.

Limitations on the Right to Counsel

Under the Supreme Court's interpretations of the Sixth Amendment, the right to counsel applies only when a criminal defendant faces a charge that might result in incarceration. If a defendant faces only a small fine, then the county or state government is not required to supply a defense attorney unless mandated by that state's laws.

The right to counsel does not apply at all to civil cases. Poor people who want to file lawsuits usually must obtain their own attorneys, unless they qualify for free representation through the Legal Services Corporation, a federal government agency.

The right to counsel for criminal defendants does not guarantee that the defense attorney supplied by the state will take the case all the way to trial or will do an outstanding job in representing the defendant. Whether the state chooses to supply defense attorneys for poor people through state-salaried public defenders or through assignments to private attorneys who receive a small sum for each case, most attorneys work to obtain plea bargains for their clients. If the defendants are unhappy with their court-appointed attorney or public defender, there is little that they can do about it. It is difficult to prove that an attorney's performance was so bad that it violated the Sixth Amendment by providing "ineffective assistance of counsel." Thus there is often distrust and dissatisfaction evident in the relationships between poor defendants and the attorneys provided for them by the state.

Christopher E. Smith

Further Reading

Lewis, Anthony. *Gideon's Trumpet*. 1964. Reprint. New York: Vintage, 1989. History of the right to counsel in American jurisprudence built around the story of the *Gideon v. Wainwright* case, which expanded the right to counsel to all state courts.

Smith, Christopher E. *Courts and the Poor*. Chicago: Nelson-Hall, 1991. Examination of the special problems of poor defendants in the criminal justice system, with special attention to the issue of the right to counsel.

Taylor, John B. *Right to Counsel and Privilege Against Self-Incrimination: Rights and Liberties Under the Law*. Santa Barbara, Calif.: ABC-Clio, 2004.

Tomkovicz, James J. *The Right to the Assistance of Counsel: A Reference Guide to the United States Constitution*. Westport, Conn.: Greenwood Press, 2002.

Wishman, Seymour. *Confessions of a Criminal Lawyer*. New York: Penguin, 1982. First-person account of the work of a criminal defense attorney.

See also *Argersinger v. Hamlin*; Arraignment; Arrest; Attorney ethics; Bill of Rights, U.S.; Constitution, U.S.; Defendant self-representation; Defense attorneys; *Gideon v. Wainwright*; *Massiah v. United States*; *Minnick v. Mississippi*; *Miranda v. Arizona*; *Powell v. Alabama*; Public defenders.

Court reporters

Definition: Courtroom employees who are responsible for recording all testimony and utterances that take place during legal proceedings

Criminal justice issue: Courts

Significance: Court reporters are an integral component of the court system as their main function is preservation of spoken testimony.

The inception of this career began more than two thousand years ago, when a scribe recorded speeches during the Roman Senate. In 2004 there were approximately fifty thousand court reporters across the United States. It is expected that this number will continue to soar throughout the next several decades. Court reporters play a fundamental role in the criminal justice system by ensuring the preservation of the spoken word as a legible written transcript. Their main function is to record testimony, speeches, judges' rulings, judges' instructions to juries, attorneys' objections, and comments by attorneys, verbatim, during all court proceedings.

Court reporters assist judges and attorneys in the retrieval of information for official records, including reading back all or any portion of the court record, as requested. Court reporters edit the translation to correct grammar, identify proper names and places, and prepare written transcripts to file with the clerk of the court. In addition, court reporters are also expected to have knowledge of real-time technology, to enable them to provide closed-caption services and translating for the deaf where required.

The most common method by which court reporting is administered is stenotyping. This employs the use of computer-aided transcriptions (CAT) to translate combinations of letters that represent words and phrases into complete and legible transcripts. Because maintaining a high degree of accuracy is essential, coordination, concentration, and strong grammatical skills are required.

Lisa Landis Murphy

Further Reading

Knapp, M. H., and R. W. McCormick. *The Complete Court Reporters Handbook.* 3d ed. Englewood Cliffs, N.J.: Prentice-Hall, 1998.

Schmalleger, Frank. *Criminal Justice Today: An Introductory Text for the Twenty-first Century.* 8th ed. Upper Saddle River, N.J.: Pearson/Prentice-Hall, 2005.

See also Court types; Criminal justice system; Testimony; Trials.

Court types

Definition: Courts of narrow and broad functions
Criminal justice issue: Appeals; Courts; Jurisdictions; Military justice

Significance: The judicial system in the United States is complex. Each state has courts of specialized, limited, and general jurisdiction. A separate hierarchy of federal courts parallels the fifty state judiciaries. In many states efforts have been made to reduce the number of court types.

In contrast to Japan and many European countries, the United States has a highly complex network of courts. In nations with unitary political systems, such as France, there is a single judicial hierarchy. Because of federalism, however, there are two sets of trial and appellate courts in the United States, one state and the other federal. At the state level many courts of original jurisdiction can hear only a single type of case, such as that dealing with wills (probate courts) or claims for small amounts of money. Courts differ also in whether jury trials are possible, in what types of procedures are used and in what types of remedy judges can provide complaining parties. Selecting the correct court in which to file a complaint is so complicated that most law schools offer students a course called "Conflict of Laws" to help them make the right choice.

Types of Jurisdiction

There are a number of fundamental characteristics that distinguish one court from another. Jurisdiction is the power, or authority, of a particular court to hear a case. Courts of original jurisdiction, or trial courts, hear cases for the first time. Courts of appeal review the decisions of trial judges to determine if they made any reversible errors. Courts of common law can provide monetary compensation to injured plaintiffs in civil suits. Equity courts, or chancery courts, issue injunctions, which are orders to act or to refrain from acting in a particular way, such as polluting a river. The right to trial by jury can be exercised in common law and criminal courts but not in equity courts. Courts of specialized jurisdiction can hear only one type of case. Courts of limited jurisdiction hear several kinds of cases but not all.

The most important state trial courts are the civil and criminal courts of general jurisdiction, which can hear and determine any case. State courts hear cases involving state law, while federal courts determine legal disputes arising under the U.S. Constitution or federal laws. There are circumstances, however, in which a state court can hear a case that requires the interpretation of federal law and in which a federal court can determine controversies arising under state legislation. In the former type of case, the losing party may appeal to the U.S. Supreme Court af-

New York City Family Court. (Public domain, via Wikimedia Commons)

ter the state supreme court has rendered its decision. Criminal courts try cases in which the government seeks punishment of a defendant for violating the law. Civil courts resolve disputes between private parties in which a complainant alleges harm as a result of a defendant's failure to fulfill a legal duty. A court of record is a trial court whose determinations of fact are final.

Criminal Courts

States have established a variety of judicial tribunals to handle criminal cases. Municipal courts are trial courts of limited jurisdiction with the authority to determine misdemeanor cases. Other names for criminal courts of limited jurisdiction are justice or general sessions courts. Night court, or police court, is available in many large urban areas to process cases in which defendants are charged with petty offenses, such as public drunkenness. Police forces in populous cities issue citations ordering drivers caught breaking the law to appear in traffic court. In rural areas, justices of the peace often hear cases involving minor criminal charges. Municipal courts preside over preliminary hearings to determine if evidence is sufficient to hold over felony defendants for trial in superior court. Felonies are prosecuted in criminal courts of general jurisdiction, often called superior or county courts. It is in these courts that most jury trials occur. Other names for such bodies are circuit, district, or criminal courts.

Civil Courts

Trial courts of limited and general criminal jurisdiction in most states have the power to determine civil controversies. Municipal courts may hear legal disputes in which the amount of compensation requested is relatively low, usually under $30,000. County and superior courts hear civil cases in which the monetary amount in dispute exceeds that. Most states have established a court of specialized jurisdiction, or small claims court, to make the civil courts more accessible to ordinary citizens. In these courts parties typically are not represented by lawyers, the filing fees are low, and the waiting period before trial is relatively short. The jurisdiction of small claims courts is typically confined to cases not exceeding $5,000.

Probate courts exercise jurisdiction over wills, estates, and guardianship questions. Probate judges determine how the assets of deceased persons are to be allocated and who is legally responsible for frail elderly or mentally incompetent persons. Family law courts, or domestic relations courts, process divorce cases and resolve often contentious issues of child custody, visitation, child support, alimony, and the division of property. Family law court judges have broad equitable powers. Youths charged with delinquency or youths in need of protection appear in family law or juvenile courts. Juvenile courts are civil courts; they do not mete out punishment, but rather provide treatment. In mediation court, or conciliation court, judges help parties negotiate mutually acceptable compromises rather than impose solutions to conflicts. In states with unified judicial systems, such as California, the trial court of general jurisdiction, the superior court, may sit as a probate court, juvenile court, family law court, and conciliation court.

Appellate Courts

While trial courts consist of a single judge, appellate courts are collegial bodies with three or more judges. They review trial courts' decisions at the request of losing parties. A reversible error is one that is so egregious that a trial judge's decision must be overturned. In general, appellate courts can reverse only a trial judge's interpretation of the law and not the trial court's determinations of fact. This rule exists to prevent appellate judges from undermining the jury system. In the United States, each loser in a trial has the right to one appeal. A consequence of this tradition is that some appellate courts have no control over their dockets. They must hear and decide every appeal that is filed.

The final court of appeal is the state supreme court (known in New York as the Court of Appeals). If a case involves matters of state law only, the decision of a state supreme court cannot be further appealed. In many states, the state supreme court is the only appellate court. In twenty-five states, however, there are intermediate courts of appeal. In these states the state supreme court enjoys discretion over the cases it wishes to review. Some states have separate intermediate courts of appeal for criminal and civil cases.

Several states, including New Jersey, Virginia, and California, have taken steps to simplify their judicial hierarchy. Their goal is to establish an integrated judicial pyramid embracing only a few kinds of trial courts and a single type of intermediate appellate court.

Federal Courts

Article III of the U.S. Constitution authorizes Congress to establish trial and appellate courts to determine cases arising under federal law, cases involving foreign ambassadors, and suits between citizens of different states. The federal courts of general trial jurisdiction are the ninety-four U.S. district courts. Federal jury trials occur in the district courts. They have both civil and criminal jurisdiction. Federal law requires that judges give preference to criminal over civil cases when scheduling trials.

There are a number of federal trial courts of specialized jurisdiction. Each district court has a bankruptcy unit. Bankruptcy courts determine whether petitioners can be relieved of the obligation to repay debts. Magistrate judges handle misdemeanor trials and many of the procedural disputes that must be resolved before a trial in the district court can begin.

Appeals of district court decisions are made to one of the thirteen U.S. courts of appeals. The judges sit in panels of three. They also hear appeals from the decisions of federal administrative agencies, such as the National Labor Relations Board (NLRB) and the Federal Communications Commission (FCC). The courts of appeal must accept for review all appeals. A specialized federal court is the U.S. Court of International Trade. It reviews the rulings by federal customs inspectors governing tariffs on imported goods.

When a federal question is at issue, appeals of decisions of the U.S. courts of appeals and the state supreme courts may be filed with the U.S. Supreme Court. The U.S. Supreme Court has complete discretion and only grants review to approximately 1 percent of the cases that are filed before it. All nine justices of the U.S. Supreme Court participate in the decision of every case accepted for review.

From time to time the U.S. Congress has established tribunals to assist administrative agencies in the performance of their adjudicative functions. U.S. Tax Court, for example, was set up to hear taxpayers' appeals of decisions of the Internal Revenue Service (IRS). Such so-called Article I courts differ from their Article III counterparts in the judges' tenure. Article I judges serve for a limited number of years while Article III judges are appointed for life. There are four other federal legislative courts: the U.S. Court of Federal Claims, the U.S. Court of Military Appeals, the U.S. Court of Veterans Appeals, and territorial courts.

The Court of Federal Claims adjudicates plaintiffs' claims for compensation from the federal government. The Court of Military Appeals is a body of civilian judges who hear appeals from military courts-martial. The Court of Veterans Appeals reviews decisions of the Board of Veterans Appeals denying benefits to former military personnel. Appeals from the Court of Federal Claims, the Court of International Trade, and the Court of Veterans Appeals must be filed with the U.S. Court of Appeals for the Federal Circuit. The federal territories Guam, the Virgin Islands, and the Northern Mariana Islands have territorial courts, which can hear matters involving both local and federal law. Because Puerto Rico has its own set of local courts, the territorial court in Puerto Rico has the same jurisdiction as a U.S. district court.

Kenneth M. Holland

Further Reading

Abraham, Henry. *The Judicial Process: An Introductory Analysis of the Courts of the United States, England, and France.* 7th ed. New York: Oxford UP, 1998. Print.

Banks, Lenore. *The Judicial Maze: The Court System in New York State.* Albany: League of Women Voters, 1988. Print.

BNA's Directory of State and Federal Courts, Judges, and Clerks. Washington: BNA, 1997. Print.

Corley, Pamela C., Artemus Ward, and Wendy L. Martinek. *American Judicial Process: Myth and Reality in Law and Courts.* New York: Routledge, 2016. Print.

Rennison, Callie Marie, and Mary Dodge. *Introduction to Criminal Justice: Systems, Diversity, and Change.* Thousand Oaks: SAGE, 2016. Print.

State Justice Institute. *Improving the Quality of American Justice, 1987-1997.* Alexandria: State Justice Inst., 1997. Print.

Want's Federal-State Court Directory 1998: All Fifty States and Canada. New York: Want, 1997. Print.

See also Change of venue; Citations; Clerks of the court; Court reporters; Criminal justice in U.S. history; Criminal justice system; Judicial system, U.S.; Jurisdiction of courts; Juvenile delinquency; Night courts; Supreme Court, U.S.; Trials.

Criminal prosecution

Definition: Area of legal practice that involves the charging and trying of persons for criminal offenses

Criminal justice issue: Courts; Prosecution; Trial procedures

Significance: Criminal prosecution, or the work of criminal prosecutors, is an integral part of the criminal justice system.

The U.S. criminal justice system is an adversarial system based on the model of two opposing sides presenting their best cases to an impartial fact finder—either a jury or a judge. The side presented by the government in an effort to prove beyond a reasonable doubt that defendants committed the offenses for which they have been charged is presented in criminal cases by the prosecution.

The work of criminal prosecution in the United States is wider than simply presenting a case to a fact finder. Criminal prosecutors sometimes assist law-enforcement authorities in the investigation of suspected crimes, assess the strength of evidence, and make critical decisions about whom—if anyone—to charge with criminal offenses and what charges to bring. They often present these charges to a grand jury in order to have the grand jury weigh the evidence of a suspected crime and—if it is sufficient—return an indictment, or a statement of charges. Prosecutors handle hearings and arguments in court following the formal institution of charges and deal with questions such as bail or the suppression of evidence under the exclusionary rule. The vast majority of criminal charges in the United States that result in convictions never go to trial but are resolved through plea bargaining.

The prosecutor, as the representative of the government's position in legal cases, is the principal player in this process. If a case goes to trial, the prosecutor tries it and attempts to convince the fact finder that the defendant is guilty as charged. Finally, whether a case is resolved through negotiation or trial, if a conviction is handed down, the prosecutor presents the government's recommendation for sentencing. In many jurisdictions, the prosecutor's sentencing recommendation is weighed heavily by the judge. In jurisdictions in which sentencing is constrained by guidelines, such as in federal court and an increasing number of states, the prosecutor's charging decision before the case ever reaches court can have a dramatic impact on sentencing. Throughout this wide range of responsibilities, the prosecutor's discretion in these matters is virtually unconstrained.

Systems of Prosecutors

There are three distinct levels of prosecution in the United States, each of which focuses on different offenses. Local prosecutors, often called district attorneys, handle prosecution of criminal offenses in state court for a particular county or judicial district, which may span several counties. Local prosecutors are usually elected, although some are appointed, and they may be employees of the county or state. They primarily prosecute crimes against persons or property or drug offenses. They may prosecute very serious offenses such as murder, but most of the important events and facts surrounding the offenses they prosecute generally occur within their local jurisdictions. The national organization of local district attorneys is the National District Attorneys Association.

State prosecutors, usually under the supervision of a state attorney general, represent the state in state and federal courts. The state attorney general is often elected, although sometimes this is an appointed position. State prosecutors handle criminal appeals (defending the validity of convictions on appeal) and the prosecution at the trial level of certain types of more complex criminal offenses, which are often committed in several counties or districts or even several states. These types of more complex offenses involve environmental crimes, consumer fraud, civil rights violations, and securities offenses. The organization of state attorney generals is the National Association of Attorneys General.

Finally, federal prosecutors are located in each federal judicial district, which is either a state or in more populous regions a portion of a state. Federal prosecutors, called U.S. attorneys, operate under the control of the U.S. attorney general, an officer in the cabinet of the president of the United States. The attorney general runs the U.S. Justice Department, which has hundreds of prosecutors handling the prosecution of different types of federal crimes in its "criminal division." The attorney general also supervises U.S. attorneys, who are responsible for the local prosecution of offenses in the federal court in their judicial districts. U.S. attorneys are appointed by the U.S. president. Besides these systems of prosecutors, there are also military prosecutors, who handle cases arising under military law.

State and Local Prosecutors

State and local prosecutors in the United States are spread over more than two thousand offices. According to the 2007 statistics from the U.S. Justice Department's Bureau of Justice Statistics, there were 2,330 offices of state prosecutors employing about 78,000 lawyers, investigators, and support personnel. Slightly more than 10 percent of these offices, or 254, were concentrated in major metropolitan centers with populations over 250,000 people. About 60 percent of the prosecutors' offices in

District Attorney Vance at February 2011 Press Conference. (By Saffie 55, via Wikimedia Commons)

the United States served cities and towns with populations under 100,000 people. About 15 percent of the country's prosecutor's operated only part-time offices.

State and local prosecutors' offices and procedures vary widely from jurisdiction to jurisdiction. Some have particular units to prosecute particular types of offenses, such as drug crimes, sex offenses, or homicides. Others organize their staffs according to the particular courts in which they practice. In most jurisdictions prosecutors review criminal charges before they are filed. One of the most important functions of the prosecutor is to screen prospective cases and identify those that present the most significant violations, for which the public benefit from prosecution will be greatest.

Federal Prosecutors

The U.S. Justice Department is responsible for the prosecution of federal crimes in federal court. In each federal judicial district, the local U.S. attorney's office handles federal prosecutions. From its main office in Washington, D.C., the Justice Department also centrally investigates and prosecutes violations of criminal laws and laws that may carry criminal penalties, such as civil rights violations, antitrust offenses, and consumer fraud offenses. These investigations often span more than a single federal district. The agency responsible for investigating and assisting in the prosecution of federal offenses is the Federal Bureau of Investigation (FBI).

The U.S. attorney is the lawyer who represents the federal government in each judicial district. A U.S. attorney is appointed by the president of the United States with the advice and consent of the U.S. Senate in each of the ninety-four federal judicial districts in the country and in U.S. territories. U.S. attorneys serve four-year terms. The U.S. attorney is the chief federal law-enforcement officer in a federal judicial district and is assisted by assistant U.S. attorneys. U.S. attorneys have extensive discretion over their staffs, resources, and prosecutorial efforts. Different districts characteristically have different focuses of investigation and prosecution. Major financial and securities cases, for example, are characteristically brought in large urban areas—particularly the southern district of New York—which includes the financial area of Wall Street in Manhattan. Drug prosecutions are brought in virtually every district and are the most common cases heard in federal court. Prosecutions for drug offenses are particularly common in the border areas of the southern districts of Florida and Texas.

The Role of the Prosecutor

The job of prosecutors is to seek justice. This is different from the role of lawyers representing accused persons. Although prosecutors represent the government, they are also charged with representing the public interest and seeing that justice is done. The prosecutor, for example, has the authority to bring and to dismiss charges. This responsibility, a public trust, has been formalized in standards of practice for prosecutors prepared by the American Bar Association (ABA), the largest bar association in the United States. First published in 1968, these Standards for Criminal Justice set forth guidelines for effective and ethical conduct by both prosecutors and defense lawyers.

The ABA standards explain that "the duty of the prosecutor is to seek justice, not merely to convict." This means that prosecutors not only must pursue the most compelling cases for conviction but also must pursue them properly, within the applicable legal and ethical rules. They must disclose to defendants' lawyers any evidence suggesting that defendants are innocent.

Prosecutorial Discretion

Prosecutors in the United State wield extraordinary power. Their discretionary decisions concerning the investigation, charging, prosecution, and disposition of cases are largely unreviewable. This is a uniquely American phenomenon, for which several explanations have been offered. Criminal codes are the products of political processes; many offenses appear in criminal codes not necessarily because they are common problems but because legislatures seek to declare their public abhorrence of them. Sufficient evidence is not present in every potential case, and prosecutors must make hard judgments not only about the public importance of particular cases but also the likelihood of conviction. As prosecutorial resources are limited, they must be put to the most efficient use possible. Finally, justice must be done in every case for every offense, and some defendants are better candidates for informal types of sanctions or penalties (often called "diversion") than for formal criminal prosecution.

David M. Siegel

Further Reading

American Bar Association. *Standards for Criminal Justice: Prosecutorial Investigations*. 3d ed. Washington, DC: ABA, 2014.

Barnes, Patricia G. *CQ's Desk Reference on American Criminal Justice: Over 500 Answers to Frequently Asked Questions from Law Enforcement to Corrections*. Chicago: University of Chicago Press, 2000.

Jacoby, Joan E. *The American Prosecutor: A Search for Identity*. Lexington, Mass.: Lexington Books, 1980.

Perry, Steven W., and Duren Banks. "Prosecutors in State Courts, 2007—Statistical Tables." *2007 National Census of State Court Prosecutors*. Bureau of Justice Statistics, Office of Justice Programs, US Dept. of Justice, Dec. 2011. Digital file.

Schmalleger, Frank. *Criminal Justice Today: An Introductory Text for the Twenty-first Century*. 14th ed. Boston: Pearson, 2017.

Senna, Joseph J., and Larry J. Siegel. *Introduction to Criminal Justice*. 15th ed. Boston:Cengage, 2016

Stewart, James B. *The Prosecutors:Inside the Offices of the Government's Most Powerful Lawyers*. New York: Simon & Schuster, 1987.

See also Antitrust law; Attorney General, U.S.; Bail system; Criminal justice system; Dismissals; District attorneys; Exclusionary rule; Eyewitness testimony; Grand juries; Harmless error; Jurisdiction of courts; Plea bargaining; Pleas; Presumption of innocence; Sentencing; Speedy trial right; Statutes of limitations; Trials.

Cross-examination

Definition: Procedure in which witnesses testifying in trials and depositions are questioned by attorneys representing opposing sides

Criminal justice issue: Attorneys; Interrogation; Trial procedures; Witnesses

Significance: The fact that unexpected revelations from witnesses can upset the development of cases makes cross-examinations one of the most dramatic—and sometimes perilous—parts of the judicial process.

In trial testimony, attorneys try to establish the credibility of their own witnesses through direct examinations. When they complete their questioning, the opposing attorneys then cross-examine the same witnesses and try to undo their credibility. In the popular mind and media, cross-examination offers the appealing prospect of a clever interrogator—such as Erle Stanley Gardner's fictional Perry Mason, or one of his innumerable imitators—uncovering deception and establishing guilt.

For legal experts as well, cross-examination is at the heart of judicial proceedings. John Henry Wigmore, a famous early twentieth century theorist of the law of evidence, said of the matter:

"If we omit political considerations of broader range, then cross-examination, not trial by jury, is the great and permanent contribution of the Anglo-American system of law to improved methods of trial procedure."

The Sixth Amendment to the U.S. Constitution guarantees the right of defendants to confront witnesses brought against them. Cross-examination gives defendants—through counsel—the opportunity to put their opponents' evidence to the test. However, within the adversarial format of the American judicial system, emphasis in cross-examination is often less on testing the truth of claims than on discrediting inconvenient witnesses.

Many standard cross-examination techniques involve rhetorical maneuvers designed to capitalize on favorable concessions and to minimize the impact of unfavorable testimony on juries. The first question that trial counsel face is whether to cross-examine at all. Legal lore is replete with stories of attorneys who asked one question too many and elicited unanticipated answers that damaged, instead of helped, their cases.

The primary aim of cross-examination is to impugn the veracity of witnesses and thereby lessen the weight of the evidence supporting the opposing side. In practice, achieving that goal involves suggesting—if not actually proving—that a witness's testimony is incorrect or incomplete. Witnesses seem less believable to juries if they are shown to be biased, to have interests in the outcomes of cases, to be generally careless with the truth, or to lack the ability or opportunity to secure the knowledge they claim to possess.

For reasons well known to psychologists, judges, attorneys and, witnesses, even eyewitnesses, are often mistaken in their claims about who did what to whom. Members of juries, however, are less likely to be sophisticated about such matters, so one purpose of cross-examination is to alert them to the natural and inevitable limitations of testimony.

Witnesses in special categories, such as court-recognized experts, or children, require special treatment. In general, however, the basic object of cross-examination is to attack witnesses' credibility, without alienating judges or-especially-juries.

Edward Johnson

Further Reading
Brodsky, Stanley L., and Thomas G. Gutheil. *The Expert Expert Witness: More Maxims and Guidelines for Testifying in Court*. Washington, DC: American Psychological Association, 2016. *eBook Collection (EBSCOhost)*. Web. 26 May 2016.
Johnson, James A. "Cross-Examination." *Maryland Bar Journal* 48.4 (2015): 20-25. *Legal Source*. Web. 26 May. 2016.
Lamb, Michael E., and John R. Spencer. *Children and Cross-Examination: Time to Change the Rules?*. Oxford: Hart Publishing, 2012. *eBook Collection (EBSCOhost)*. Web. 26 May 2016.
Mauet, Thomas A. *Trial Techniques*. 6th ed. New York: Aspen Publishers, 2002.
Wellman, Francis L. *The Art of Cross-Examination*. New York: Macmillan, 1936. Reprint. New York: Simon and Schuster, 1997.

Wigmore, John Henry. *Evidence in Trials at Common Law*. 2d ed. Boston: Little, Brown, 1961.

See also Attorney ethics; Depositions; Due process of law; Effective counsel; Expert witnesses; Eyewitness testimony; Hearsay; *Maryland v. Craig*; Perjury; Testimony; Witnesses.

Cruel and unusual punishment

Definition: Treating convicted offenders in unnecessarily abusive ways
Criminal justice issue: Convictions; Government misconduct; Medical and health issues; Punishment
Significance: The U.S. Constitution prohibits cruel and unusual punishment, and the courts are responsible for interpreting the meaning of that provision.

The Eighth Amendment to the U.S. Constitution forbids the use of cruel and unusual punishments. The words are not complex, but exactly what they prohibit is not obvious. In 2004, much debate surrounded arguments about whether the death penalty violates the Eighth Amendment. Some legal scholars argue that the Eighth Amendment should be read to mean exactly what it meant to the founders and that they did not intend to restrict the use of death itself as a punishment.

Critics claim that capital punishment, because it treats a human life as disposable, is inherently cruel and therefore unconstitutional. Others look to the framers of the Constitution and assert that they had no qualms about capital punishment. They cite the Fifth Amendment's guarantee that no one should be deprived of *life*, liberty, or property without due process of law. It is possible to read that guarantee as meaning that deprivation of life is permissible if due process has been followed. Likewise, the Fifth Amendment's restriction on double jeopardy, providing that no one should twice be forced to risk *life* or limb, could imply that life is an acceptable stake if one only has to risk it once.

When the Constitution was written during the late eighteenth century, "cruel and unusual punishment" was a familiar phrase taken from the English bill of rights. Many states included similar wording in their constitutions. The terminology involved the ideas that punishments should be proportionate to crimes and that punishments not authorized by law were prohibited. The founding generation had vivid memories of gruesome punishments devised by kings for retribution against their enemies. The founders wished to avoid such creative use of unusual sanctions by placing the authority to codify crimes and punishments in the hands of the people's representatives, the legislatures. In deciding how and when to apply the legislated punishments, the courts and the executive branch enjoyed wide latitude.

The Eighth Amendment could be read to forbid punitive measures that were unnecessarily painful or too oppressive. Exactly how those characteristics were to be defined was based on the notion that the sensibilities of a republic placed a high value on human dignity. In a society where all free citizens were believed to share inalienable rights, punishments should not purposely degrade but should be severe enough only to accomplish a social purpose.

Ultimately, the responsibility for defining "cruel and unusual" rests with the courts, especially the U.S. Supreme Court. For more than a century after the Constitution was written, the justices considered only a few cases that addressed the issue. The idea that the death penalty itself might be unconstitutional because it violated the Eighth Amendment was not brought before the Court until the middle of the twentieth century. The Court, for the most part, assumed that the forbidden cruel and unusual punishments were the obvious tortures and barbaric cruelties that offended modern, civilized communities. They did not need to rule that boiling in oil or drawing and quartering would not be permitted under the U.S. Constitution. They did, however, rule that two less dramatic but still violent means of execution did not violate the Eighth Amendment.

Although hanging remained the most widely used form of capital punishment in the United States throughout the nineteenth century, the leaders of the Utah Territory preferred death by firing squad. As the territory was settled, largely by Mormons who believed in blood atonement for the crime of murder, being shot by riflemen was considered more theologically correct than being swung from the gallows. Use of the firing squad was challenged as cruel and unusual punishment in *Wilkerson v. Utah* (1878). In that case, the Court ruled that shooting was a traditional method of execution, long favored by the military. Utah and Idaho still offered condemned prisoners the choice of a firing squad or lethal injection in the twenty-first century. Another innovation in capital punishment techniques came in 1890, when the Supreme Court decided that death by electrocution was not a violation of the Eighth Amendment. Its ruling *in re Kemmler* held that, even though no human being had yet been put to death in the electric chair, the method would produce "instantaneous, and therefore, painless death."

House District Committee on abolishing capital punishment in 1926. (Library of Congress)

Aside from recognizing that there were outer limits to the humane treatment of offenders, in the nineteenth century the Court avoided most discussion of capital punishment, believing its methods and application were matters for the individual states to decide.

Eighth Amendment Cases

In 1910, the Supreme Court made a significant Eighth Amendment ruling in a case that did not concern the death penalty. *United States v. Weems* involved an American official in the Philippines who was sentenced to fifteen years of hard labor for forging a minor document. Weems challenged his punishment as cruel and unusual, and the Court agreed, holding that the sentence was so disproportionate to the crime as to be a violation of Weems's constitutional rights.

Almost a half century later, in *Trop v. Dulles* (1954), the justices revisited the Eighth Amendment and added the concept that cruel and unusual should be measured against contemporary public beliefs and attitudes. The case involved Army private Trop, who had left his unit for one day in 1944 during World War II. Trop thought better of going absent without leave and was voluntarily returning to his base when he was stopped by the military police. He was convicted of desertion, sentenced to three years at hard labor, and given a dishonorable discharge. Eight years later, when Trop applied for a passport, he learned that a dishonorable discharge for wartime desertion had resulted in the loss of his American citizenship. The Court examined the law that deprived a person of citizenship for desertion and found it unconstitutional. It spelled out one of the major premises of modern Eighth

Amendment jurisprudence: It held that the words "cruel and unusual" must draw their meaning from "the evolving standards of decency that mark the progress of a maturing society."

Thus, the Court provided a new test for determining whether a punishment violated the Constitution. The criteria were dynamic. As ideas about human dignity evolved and changed, the attitudes about what constituted acceptable treatment of offenders would presumably become more refined.

Virtually every Eighth Amendment and capital punishment case that followed *Trop v. Dulles* invoked the concept of "evolving standards of decency" and wrestled with how to measure and apply those standards. The National Association for the Advancement of Colored People (NAACP) was one group who brought cases during the 1950s and 1960s challenging the application of the death penalty on Eighth Amendment grounds. They raised the claim that racial bias in capital sentencing violated the evolving standards and was therefore unconstitutional. They developed and presented social science research on racial bias and the arbitrariness with which the death penalty was applied. In 1972, the Supreme Court heard *Furman v. Georgia*, an attempt by the NAACP to win from the Court a statement that capital punishment violated the Eighth Amendment.

Furman v. Georgia

In 1972, the Court heard three death-penalty cases grouped under the title *Furman v. Georgia*. Furman was a black man who had shot a white homeowner, apparently by accident, during a robbery. The other two cases, from Georgia and Texas, involved rapes in which the offenders were black and the victims were white. No injury, aside from the rape, had occurred in either case. All three defendants were sentenced to death. Each justice wrote a separate opinion, and although a majority of five members of the Court found that the death penalty, as administered, was unconstitutional, the explanations for the justices' holdings varied widely. The four dissenting justices found no constitutional flaws with the system of capital punishment. All nine justices argued that evolving standards of decency were the measure of cruel and unusual punishments. They differed over what those standards were.

Those who voted to uphold the death sentences believed that the only objective ways to assess contemporary standards were through the actions of legislatures and the decisions of juries. Neither had found capital punishment per se to be cruel and unusual—and therefore unconstitutional. Without that endorsement from lawmakers and jurors, the four dissenting justices held that the Court could not move on the issue. On the other side, Justice William Brennan argued that the death penalty was, by definition, unconstitutional. In this view, degrading punishments were not only those that caused pain, but also included those that dehumanized people and treated them as disposable objects. He maintained that even vile criminals retained their humanity and dignity.

Brennan's fellow opponents believed that capital punishment failed every constitutional test. It was unusually severe. There was a strong possibility of its arbitrary and biased use. It was substantially rejected by every modern democratic society, and it accomplished no greater purpose than less severe punishments. From this perspective, standards of decency had already evolved to the point where the death penalty was unacceptable. It remained only for the Court to formalize that position by declaring it unconstitutional on Eighth Amendment grounds. Thurgood Marshall, the first African American justice on the Supreme Court, reiterated that the "cruel and unusual" clause must be reexamined continually in the light of changing human knowledge. He asserted that if citizens were fully informed about the injustices inherent in the death penalty, they would find it unacceptable and reject it.

Justices taking a middle position in *Furman* identified the problem that the death penalty was being applied in an "arbitrary and capricious" manner, that death sentences were cruel and unusual "in the same way that being struck by lightning is cruel and unusual." In other words, it was the randomness in the application of capital punishment that made it cruel and unusual. *Furman* thus suspended executions until state legislatures could devise new laws that met the constitutional objections. The new legislation would be measured by its conformity with evolving standards of decency.

Gregg v. Georgia

The Court had found the laws at issue in *Furman* arbitrary and capricious, allowing too much discretion to juries and permitting the consideration of unacceptable factors such as race. North Carolina was one state that tried to meet those concerns by making the death penalty mandatory for certain offenses. To the majority of the Supreme Court in *Woodson v. North Carolina* (1976), this approach violated contemporary standards of decency and was therefore considered cruel and unusual under the Eighth Amendment.

On the same day as *Woodson*, however, the Court upheld the new Georgia capital statute again invoking contemporary standards of decency in their analyses of the death penalty. The majority in *Gregg v. Georgia* (1976) read the eagerness of thirty-five states to create new death-penalty laws as significant evidence that the punishment itself did not violate public sensibilities. They determined that a death sentence could serve to express a community's belief that because certain crimes were so reprehensible, only death was an adequate response. They also deferred to the theory of federalism, holding that each legislature can best evaluate the moral consensus in its state, determining what its constituents find cruel and unusual.

Gregg was a 7-2 decision. Since then, the Court has operated on the assumption that the death penalty itself is not cruel and unusual punishment and does not violate the evolving standards of decency. The justices have constructed an elaborate structure of law around the death penalty, providing for a process of guided discretion to choose who will die. Many of those decisions have employed the notion of evolving standards of decency to define the meaning of cruel and unusual punishment as it applies to specific crimes or to categories of defendants.

Evolving Standards

Just one year after *Gregg*, the Court ruled that the punishment of death for the rape of an adult woman violated the Eighth Amendment. In *Coker v. Georgia* (1977), they reasoned that execution was disproportionate for a crime in which the victim did not lose her life. On several occasions, the Court considered whether an accomplice to a crime, who did not actually commit murder, could be put to death without violating the ban on cruel and unusual punishments. In *Enmund v. Florida* (1982), the justices found the death penalty too severe for someone who participated in a crime but did not kill nor intend to kill. Five years later, however, in *Tison v. Arizona* (1987), the Court seemed to reverse itself and allowed for the execution of defendants whose recklessness allowed a murder to occur. *Coker*, *Enmund*, and *Tison* all attempt to measure whether punishment by death for those who did not take a life violates evolving standards and is therefore cruel and unusual punishment. Rather than drawing a bright line, the Court seems to have linked its judgment with the degree of the defendant's responsibility.

In other cases, the Supreme Court has ruled on whether the Eighth Amendment is violated if certain categories of defendants—the mentally ill, the developmentally disabled, juveniles, or the factually innocent—are executed. In *Ford v. Wainwright* (1986), they found it would offend basic standards of humanity to put a mentally ill person to death. The Court has not decided, however, whether a state may medicate inmates to make them "sane" enough for the death penalty to be carried out. In 2002, the justices ruled that there was a national consensus that executing the developmentally disabled violated standards of decency and was cruel and unusual punishment in *Atkins v. Virginia*. The ruling left it up to the states to determine who met the criteria as mentally retarded. In a 1989 case, *Stanford v. Kentucky*, the Court held that executing a juvenile who was sixteen years old at the time of his crime did not violate the Eighth Amendment. Since that ruling, the majority of states have raised the age of eligibility for the death penalty, and virtually every country in the world has outlawed the execution of juveniles. On March 1, 2005, the Supreme Court overturned its 1989 decision by ruling that executions of juveniles constituted cruel and unusual punishment.

The Supreme Court has not been clear with respect to whether it violates the Eighth Amendment when an innocent person is punished with death. In *Herrera v. Collins* (1993), the majority of the justices held that the Herrera had a fair trial, that he was not denied due process, and that if he were truly innocent, he should ask the governor for clemency. Therefore, he was not permitted to introduce new evidence of innocence in court. Five justices wrote separately that executing an innocent person would be constitutionally intolerable, but the Court has not ruled officially on the subject.

More Noncapital Issues

Citing the doctrine against cruel and unusual punishment, the Court required prisons to end the policy of whipping inmates in the 1960s. However, the justices have also ruled that prison officials cannot be sued for excessive use of force unless it is proved that they used force maliciously and sadistically and that they intended to cause harm. Thus, although inmates are theoretically protected from violent punishments, the remedies for such violations are difficult for those inside prison walls. Likewise, if corrections facilities fail to meet humane standards in food, housing, or health care, prisoners must prove the conditions were caused by the officials' deliberate indifference. The Supreme Court has also ruled that the Eighth Amendment applies only to convicted offenders. Therefore, people held in jail awaiting trial are not covered by the ban on cruel and unusual punishment. Nor do the provisions apply to children in public schools.

The Court has been unwilling to view school officials who beat or paddle students as violating the students' constitutional rights.

Mary Welek Atwell

Further Reading

Banner, Stuart. *The Death Penalty: An American History.* Cambridge: Harvard UP, 2002. Print.

Bedau, Hugo Adam, ed. *The Death Penalty in America: Current Controversies.* New York: Oxford UP, 1997. Print.

"Cruel and Unusual Punishments before the Supreme Court." *New York Times.* New York Times, 13 Oct. 2015. Web. 25 May 2016.

Hood, Roger, and Carolyn Hoyle. *The Death Penalty: A Worldwide Perspective.* 5th ed. New York: Oxford UP, 2015. Print.

Irons, Peter. *A People's History of the Supreme Court: The Men and Women Whose Cases Have Shaped Our Constitution.* New York: Penguin, 1999. Print.

Kaufman-Osborn, Timothy V. *From Noose to Needle: Capital Punishment and the Late Liberal State.* Ann Arbor: U of Michigan P, 2002. Print.

Latzer, Barry, ed. *Death Penalty Cases: Leading Supreme Court Cases on Capital Punishment.* 2nd ed. Burlington: Butterworth, 2002. Print.

Lifton, Robert Jay, and Greg Mitchell. *Who Owns Death? Capital Punishment, the American Conscience, and the End of Executions.* New York: Perennial, 2002. Print.

Sarat, Austin. *When the State Kills: Capital Punishment and the American Condition.* Princeton: Princeton UP, 2001. Print.

Stevenson, Bryan A., and John F. Stinneford. "Common Interpretation: The Eighth Amendment." *Constitution Center.* Natl. Constitution Center, 14 Sept. 2015. Web. 25 May 2016.

See also Bill of Rights, U.S.; Capital punishment; *Coker v. Georgia*; Corporal punishment; Execution, forms of; *Ford v. Wainwright*; *Furman v. Georgia*; *Gregg v. Georgia*; *Harmelin v. Michigan*; Miscarriage of justice; *Robinson v. California*; *Rummel v. Estelle*; *Solem v. Helm*; Solitary confinement; *Stanford v. Kentucky*; Supermax prisons; Three-strikes laws; *Tison v. Arizona*; *Roper v. Simmons (2005)*.

Death qualification

Definition: Procedure used in selecting jury members to try death-penalty cases

Criminal justice issue: Capital punishment; convictions; juries

Significance: The screening process in which prospective jurors are questioned about their views on capital punishment tends to exclude anti-death-penalty candidates. Critics argue that the juries, when finally chosen, are more likely to convict as a result of the screening.

Death qualification refers to a process in a capital case whereby potential members of the jury (the venire) are asked whether they will be able to consider death as a possible punishment during the penalty phase should the defendant be convicted of the capital crime.

During voir dire (oral questioning of jurors) both the prosecution and the defense seek to determine whether prospective jurors can consider death as a possible punishment after they have decided on guilt and heard aggravating and mitigating factors. The law, as developed by the U.S. Supreme Court in *Witherspoon v. Illinois* (1968), *Adams v. Texas* (1980), *Wainright v. Witt* (1985), *Morgan v. Illinois* (1992), and *Uttecht v. Brown* (2007) is meant to guide trial courts in determining whether jurors will be open to considering the death penalty. In Witherspoon, the Court ruled that a prospective juror could not be removed for cause solely on the basis of general objections to the death penalty or conscientious or religious opposition to its application. Even so, a prosecutor could remove such jurors through use of one of its peremptory challenges (excusing a venireperson without providing a reason). *Adams v. Texas* provided further clarification of the standard, stating that the juror could be excused for cause if his views would "prevent or substantially impair the performance of his duties as a juror in accordance with his instructions and his oath." *Wainwright v. Witt* held that determining a prospective juror's biases should largely rely on the trial judge's sense of his demeanor and credibility. In other words, appeals courts would be unlikely to overrule a trial court's decision about any juror's death qualification. This same principle was upheld in *Uttecht v. Brown* where the Supreme Court restated the need for deference to the local judgement. *Morgan v. Illinois* deals with a slightly different issue, the right of the defendant to have any juror who would always impose the death penalty excused.

There is a strongly held belief by some in the criminal justice system that, simply by being exposed to this death qualification process, the entire jury becomes "conviction-prone." In other words, because jurors have been probed at length by the judge and the attorneys about their death-penalty views, jurors have been given the clear impression that this case is more serious than most and that this defendant is very dangerous. Some research supports the notion that jurors going through this process go into the guilt phase of the case with a bias against the defendant before any evidence has been heard.

William L. Shulman
Updated by Mary Welek Atwell

Further Reading

Bohm, Robert M. *Deathquest II.* Cincinnati: Anderson, 2011.

Latzer, Barry and David McCord, eds. *Death Penalty Cases: Leading U.S. Supreme Cases on Capital Punishment*. 3rd ed. Burlington, Mass: Butterworth Heinemann, 2011.

Rivkind, Nina, and Steven Shatz. *Cases and Materials on the Death Penalty*. St. Paul, Minn.: West Publishing, 2001.

See also Bifurcated trials; Capital punishment; Jury system; *Voir dire*; *Witherspoon v. Illinois*.

Defendant self-representation

Definition: Situations in which criminal defendants reject professional legal counsel and represent themselves

Criminal justice issue: Attorneys; defendants; trial procedures

Significance: Defendant self-representation is a right of criminal defendants that has been recognized by the U.S. Supreme Court. However, that right sometimes comes into conflict with the right of defendants to counsel and their right to have fair trials.

The Judiciary Act of 1789, which expressly allows the accused to represent themselves in federal criminal cases, essentially codified common longstanding practice. Anglo-American jurisprudence has long recognized a Defendant's right to represent him or herself

The practice was widely engaged in for both most crimes in the British tradition and in the American colonies prior to the Revolutionary War. First recognized by the U.S. Supreme Court in *Gideon v. Wainwright* (1963), the right of criminal defendants to counsel is now a cornerstone of the criminal justice system. The recognition of that right has generated questions about what rights, if any, criminal defendants have to waive counsel. The Supreme Court also found that criminal defendants have a right to represent themselves, under the Sixth Amendment of the US Constitution, in *Faretta v. California* (1975). The basis of this decision rests on the principle that personal autonomy means that counsel cannot be foisted on unwilling defendants. However, the right to self-representation raises a number of difficult practical and legal issues.

In Faretta, the Court concluded that the defendant was "literate, competent, and understanding, and that he was voluntarily exercising his informed free will. The Court also found that the defendant's "technical legal knowledge, as such, was not relevant to an assessment of his knowing exercise of the right to defend himself."

Faretta seems to be saying that it is necessary for the defendant to competently and knowingly exercise his right to defend himself, but did not further explain the necessary requisites of competence or mental state that is needed. The fundamental principle at the basis of Faretta is to preserve the defendant's autonomy.

Scope of Self-Representation

Defendants who choose self-representation are allowed to control the organization and control of the defense, to offer motions, to make legal arguments, to participate in jury selection, to question witnesses, and address the judge and jury at appropriate times in the proceedings (*McKaskle v. Wiggins* [1984]). Defendants representing themselves, however, must follow applicable rules of evidence and criminal procedure. Generally, they are not permitted to object that their own defense represented "ineffective assistance of counsel" if the trial results in a conviction. Thus, a defendant who voluntarily waives his right to counsel assumes the plain and obvious risks that accompany such a decision.

Limitations on the Right to Self-Representation

As a practical matter, virtually no judge wants criminal defendants to represent themselves. Even otherwise well-educated defendants who lack legal training almost inevitably inhibit the smooth functioning of courts because they lack knowledge of criminal procedures, the norms and rules governing pretrial proceedings, and the trial proceedings themselves. Defendant self-representation almost always makes for lengthier and more laborious proceedings. Moreover, criminal defendants who represent themselves raise difficult questions about the degree to which judges should intercede on their behalf when they neglect to make motions or raise objections that competent lawyers would.

Despite these unresolved issues, courts must acknowledge the right to self-representation recognized in the Supreme Court's *Faretta* ruling. They do so, first, by advising defendants of their right to counsel, and then, by trying to ensure that the defendants' decisions are unequivocal, voluntary, and intelligently made. This second step almost always includes a recitation of the dangers and disadvantages of not having lawyers. In addition, most courts inquire as to whether requests for defendant self-representation are made to delay the proceedings, in which cases judges will not grant the requests. Many in the legal community, including some members of the Court, believed that the Faretta decision was poor jurisprudence in areas such as the right to counsel provision and the Sixth Amendment's history, and in its obliviousness to the chaos it could cause in the courtroom. The majority, however, insisted that honoring criminal defendants' autonomy outweighed these concerns. The defendant's right to self-representation, however, is not absolute.

The Issue of Competence

The most difficult and controversial issues surrounding exercise of the right to self-representation involve whether such an exercise is "voluntary and intelligent." In 2008, the Supreme Court ruled in *Indiana v. Edwards* that just because defendants are mentally competent to stand trial when represented by counsel does not mean they are sufficiently mentally competent to represent themselves at trial. The Court described these individuals as "grey-area defendants". In affirming the lower court's decision, the Supreme Court reasoned that allowing the defendant to self-represent, given his uncertain mental state, would lead to a humiliating spectacle and the defendant's lack of capacity could undercut the basic constitutional objective of providing a fair trial. Edwards seemed to be a departure from the Supreme Court's earlier decision, in *Godinez v. Moran* (1993), which held that mental competence to stand trial is sufficient to ensure the right to waive the right to counsel in order to plead guilty. A reasonable interpretation of Godinez's reasoning is that that the state is not constitutionally permitted to force counsel on a defendant who is competent to stand trial and voluntarily and intelligently waives the right to self-representation. The Godinez and Edwards decisions vested the trial judge with broad-ranging discretion in deciding whether a person with mental illness who is competent to stand trial may represent herself. These decisions also suggest, intentionally or not, how judges should exercise this discretion. One school of thought believes that Edwards, vis-a-vis is that it is an attempt to mitigate Godinez's occasionally harsh impact. As applied in the lower courts, the Godinez had sometimes permitted clearly disturbed individuals to make a mockery of the trial process and their own case. Edwards was the Court's attempt to assure trial judges they are authorized to prevent that result.

One of the major difficulties in the self-representation issue is that while the American criminal justice system has a well-established standard to determine whether a criminal defendant is competent to stand trial, the system does not currently have a well-established standard to determine a given defendant's level of competence to defend himself.

Often a criminal defendant suffering from a mental disorder seeks to exercise the right to self-representation. Such circumstances raise profound and troubling issues. When do defendants' autonomy and personal choice become so tainted by their mental disorders that the state should not permit them to pursue paths that are almost certainly more likely to result in their convictions and harsher sentences? Is it possible that the right of self-representation in such circumstances might conflict with the defendants' right to receive fair trials? How should these rights be balanced?

The so-called "insanity defense" is sometimes the most powerful defense available to a criminal defendant. However, a characteristic of some mental disorders is the inability of afflicted persons to recognize that they have the disorders. Defendants with mental disorders may not want their counsel to present evidence concerning their mental status and run into conflicts with their attorneys who believe that such evidence might be the most effective evidence available. In such situations, defendants may demand to represent themselves. How to handle these questions becomes all the more difficult in light of how challenging it is to draw definitive conclusions about the nature or even existence of mental illness.

Two cases illustrate the difficult of these issues. The first involves the "Unabomber" Theodore Kaczynski, who was tried during the late 1990's for a series of bombings. Kaczynski vigorously tried to prevent his attorneys from presenting evidence about his mental status but failed. The court then denied his request to represent himself. Faced with a choice between an inquiry into his mental status and a guilty plea, he chose the latter, and later unsuccessfully appealed his conviction on the grounds that his plea was "involuntary." What makes Kaczynski's case especially difficult is continuing debate about what mental illness afflicted him, or even whether he suffered from mental illness at all.

The second case involved Colin Ferguson, a man accused of shooting nineteen people on a commuter train and killing six. He successfully requested that he represent himself at trial. While virtually all commentators agreed that an insanity defense would be Ferguson's best hope at trial, he chose to argue that another assailant committed the murders after stealing his gun, thus contradicting the testimony of numerous witnesses. Ferguson's defense itself might well have been an example of psychosis. The bizarre trial that ensued ended in Ferguson's conviction.

The Kaczynski and Ferguson cases—both controversial and both representing different decisions as to whether criminal defendants should represent themselves—demonstrate the extraordinary challenges faced by the criminal justice system in reaching principled approaches in such cases.

In late 2016, Dylan Roof, the white supremacist accused of shooting nine African-American parishioners attending a Bible study at the historically African-American Emanuel Methodist Episcopal Church in Charleston, South Carolina in June 2016 was granted his request to act as his own attorney. Roof had earlier been found competent to stand trial. The court found that Roof had a constitutional right to represent himself under the Sixth Amendment as interpreted in Faretta. The earlier competency ruling appeared to form much of the basis for the court to find that Roof was competent to represent himself. Roof will have "standby" attorneys to assist him if Roof needs them to take over the case. According to Faretta, the participation of standby counsel should not "be allowed to destroy the jury's perception that the defendant is representing himself. The presence of standby counsel, however, does not violate the defendants Sixth Amendment's rights when it serves the basic purpose of assisting the defendant comply with routine courtroom procedures and protocols and thereby relieving the trial judge of these responsibilities. Judges may appoint standby counsel even if the Defendant's objects to this decision, both to be readily available if the defendant needs assistance or if the judge determines that the Defendant's self-representation should end.

Despite the Sixth Amendment's right to counsel and self-representation, the defendant does not have a right to hybrid representation, in which the defendant and attorney would essentially be presenting the case as co-counsel. A trial court, however, may allow for this type or representation.

Robert Rubinson
Christopher Anglim

Further Reading

Bardwell, Mark C. *Criminal Competency on Trial: The Case of Colin Ferguson*. Durham, N.C.: Carolina Academic Press, 2002. Full description of the Ferguson case.

Marcus, Paul. *The Rights of the Accused Under the Sixth Amendment: Trials, Presentation of Evidence, and Confrontation*. Chicago: American Bar Association, 2012.

Mello, Michael. *The United States of America Versus Theodore John Kaczynski: Ethics, Power, and the Invention of the Unabomber*. New York: Context Books, 1999. Description of the Kaczynski case by an attorney who assisted Kaczynski's appeal.

Rhode, Deborah L. *Access to Justice*. New York: Oxford University Press, 2004

Rhode, Deborah L., and David Luban. *Legal Ethics*. 7th ed. St. Paul Foundation Press, 2016. Casebook that excerpts portions of judicial opinions in the Kaczynski case, asks pointed questions about the conduct of the case, and provides additional citations to other commentators and sources.

Sabelli, Martin, and Stacey Leyton. "Train Wrecks and Freeway Crashes: An Argument for Fairness and Against Self-Representation in the Criminal Justice System." *Journal of Criminal Law and Criminology* 19 (2000): 161-235. Examination of the importance of mental illness evidence and the right of self-representation.

Scheb, John M. *Criminal Law and Procedure*. Belmont, CA: Wadsworth Cenage Learning, 2011,

See also Attorney ethics; Counsel, right to; Effective counsel; *Faretta v. California*; *Gideon v. Wainwright*; Habeas corpus; Insanity defense; Mental illness; Psychological profiling; Psychopathy; Unabomber.

Defendants

Definition: Persons or organizations who are formally accused of crimes; litigants in lawsuits

Criminal justice issue: Constitutional protections; defendants; trial procedures

Significance: The American criminal justice system is designed to pit litigants against one another in virtual fights for justice. Criminal justice procedures attempt to balance defendants' rights and government's interests in speedy and efficient trials with the desire for justice. The rules of criminal procedure are therefore designed to ensure that defendants' rights are protected.

The Sixth Amendment to the U.S. Constitution grants to all defendants the right to speedy and public trials decided by impartial juries in the states and districts in which the crimes are alleged to have been committed. The Sixth Amendment also grants accused persons the right to be informed of the nature and cause of the accusations against them, to be confronted by witnesses against them, to present witnesses of their own to testify on their behalf, and to consult with attorneys.

The Fifth Amendment to the Constitution grants defendants the right not to be tried more than once for the same crimes (the double jeopardy clause), the right not to testify against themselves (self-incrimination clause), and the right to established courses of judicial proceedings designed to protect the legal rights of citizens (due process clause). These are all federal constitutional protections that states can supplement but cannot take away.

> ### Realistic Fiction
>
> In Joyce Carol Oates's 1989 novel *American Appetites*, Ian and Glynnis McCullough are a longmarried couple who get into a drunken quarrel over the wife's suspicions that her husband has been unfaithful. As the quarrel turns into a brawl, Glynnis accidentally falls through a plateglass window and is fatally injured. Afterward, Ian is tried for second-degree murder. During the trial, the prosecution's evidence eventually appears so weak that the prosecutor reduces the charges against Ian to manslaughter. However, the jury acquits Ian of even that charge.
>
> The novel is a generally realistic depiction of how the criminal process might affect a middleclass citizen who becomes a defendant. It is a suburban variant of a similar setting in Tom Wolfe's *The Bonfire of the Vanities* (1987). One of the more interesting dynamics in Oates's book involves the continued insistence of Ian's lawyer to him that nothing will come of the police investigation, the grand jury consideration of his wife's death, and so forth. In reality, attorneys must walk a careful line between encouraging their clients and seeming to be in control of matters, on one hand, and accurately conveying to their clients the possibilities of an adverse conclusion, on the other hand.
>
> *Timothy L. Hall*

Defendants are subject to criminal or civil procedures depending on whether they are accused of violating criminal or civil statutes. The rules of criminal procedure differ from those of civil procedure because criminal and civil proceedings have different objectives and results. Criminal cases involve violations of criminal law, while civil cases involve violations of tort law, such as negligence and wrongfulness. In criminal cases, the states bring the suit against defendants and must prove guilt beyond a reasonable doubt. By contrast, in civil cases, private citizens and organizations bring the suits against defendants, and they are required only to show that the defendants are liable by a preponderance of the evidence.

Allison M. Cotton

Further Reading

Abramson, Leslie, with Richard Flaste. *The Defense Is Ready: Life in the Trenches of Criminal Law*. New York: Simon and Schuster, 1997.

Acker, J. R., and D. C. Brody. *Criminal Procedure: A Contemporary Perspective*. 2d ed. Sudbury, Mass.: Jones and Bartlett, 2004.

Ingram, Jefferson L. *Criminal Procedure: Theory and Practice*. Upper Saddle River, N.J.: Prentice-Hall, 2005.

See also Change of venue; Criminal procedure; Criminals; Double jeopardy; Due process of law; Equal protection under the law; Indictment; Mitigating circumstances; Plea bargaining; Pleas; Presumption of innocence; Public defenders; Self-incrimination, privilege against; Suspects; Verdicts; *Voir dire*.

Defense attorneys

Definition: Attorneys who are engaged to represent criminal defendants and are paid by the clients
Criminal justice issue: Attorneys; defendants; pleas
Significance: Private attorneys are essential to fair defenses in criminal cases.

Private defense attorneys engage in the representation of persons charged with crimes in local, state, federal, or tribal courts. Unlike public defenders, private defense attorneys are engaged and paid by their clients, rather than by the state.

Criminal defense lawyers must be members of the bar in good standing in the jurisdiction in which they practice. A law student wishing to become a criminal defense lawyer will usually take (in addition to the courses in criminal law generally required in law school) specialized courses preparing them for criminal trial work, including advanced criminal law, trial practice, criminal procedure, and negotiation. Many defense lawyers begin their career as prosecutors in local district attorney offices and go into private practice after receiving some criminal trial experience.

The defense lawyer's task is to represent the client zealously, regardless of any personal feelings about the defendant or the crime. If the client has not yet been charged, the defense attorney's job is to advise the client on communicating with the grand jury, to accompany the client to meetings with police and prosecutors, and to advise the client as to evidence. Once the client is arrested, the defense attorney will represent the client at bail hearings and arraignment. The defense attorney will often try to "build a Chinese wall" around the client, denying the police and prosecution access to the client and regulating the prosecution's access to evidence to the extent possible. The defense attorney is entitled to any information the prosecution has on the crime and defendant prior to trial, and the defense attorney will often use a private investigator to evaluate this information and discover new information. At trial, the criminal defense lawyer will seek to exclude damaging evidence, or at least minimize its impact, and will present evidence to introduce a "reasonable doubt" in the jury's mind as to guilt. If a defendant is convicted, a criminal defense attorney may participate in filing an appeal, but a different attorney will usually represent the defendant on appeal.

While criminal defense lawyers often take cases to trial, they also spend considerable time negotiating plea bargains for their clients. A plea bargain is an agreement between the prosecutor's office and the defendant for the latter to plead guilty to a particular charge in exchange for a predetermined sentence. A defense lawyer must be prepared to offer a plea bargain to a prosecutor, evaluate any offer of a plea bargain by the prosecuting attorney, make sure that the client understands any offer, and help the client decide either to take the offer or to go to trial. It is, however, ultimately the client's responsibility (not the lawyer's) to decide whether to make or accept a plea-bargain offer.

Gwendolyn Griffith

Further Reading

Clehane, Dianem, and Nancy Grace. *Objection! How High-Priced Defense Attorneys, Celebrity Defendants, and a 24/7 Media Have Hijacked Our Criminal Justice System.* New York: Hyperion, 2005.

Neubauer, David W. *America's Courts and the Criminal Justice System.* 8th ed. Belmont, Calif.: Thomson/Wadsworth, 2005.

Wishman, Seymour. *Confessions of a Criminal Lawyer.* New York: Penguin, 1982.

Wolfram, Charles. *Modern Legal Ethics.* St. Paul, Minn.: West Publishing, 1986.

See also Attorney ethics; Counsel, right to; Criminal justice system; Defendant self-representation; District attorneys; Effective counsel; Public defenders; Public prosecutors; *Voir dire.*

Deportation

Definition: Forcible expulsion of foreign visitors from a host nation, usually back to their home nations

Criminal justice issue: Espionage and sedition; international law; terrorism

Significance: Traditionally a tool for ridding countries of ordinary criminals and other foreign undesirables, deportation can also be used to remove political radicals or suspect terrorists.

The nations of the world have long used deportation as a criminal sanction. In U.S. history, however, deportation has tended to be regarded not so much as a judicial process involving punishment but as an administrative process to aid in shaping the composition of the national population. Indeed, in one of the Chinese exclusion cases, *Fong Yue Ting v. United States* (1893), the U.S. Supreme Court formally declared that deportation was an administrative process for removing undesirable and unwelcome resident aliens from the United States in the interest of "public welfare." With that ruling, due process provisions for deporting aliens persons were severely curtailed since deportation was not considered to pose a risk of "punishment."

Nevertheless, deportation was still deemed a serious matter that could significantly affect a person's future and required administrative hearings in order to be handled fairly. To that end, government interpreters have long been made available to aliens facing possible deportation. However, the services that such interpreters rendered to aliens during the early twentieth century were questionable, as the interpreters often took liberties in translating. In some deportation cases, the interpreters were provided by government prosecutors and occasionally even testified against the people for whom they were interpreting.

Aliens facing deportation also had a right to counsel. However, the significance of that right was often not made clear to them, and many chose not to utilize it. Moreover, even in cases in which aliens chose to use counsel, their attorneys sometimes had serious conflicts of interest, such as being employees of the Department of Justice or acting on primarily mercenary interests.

Federal Laws

One of the earliest deportation laws enacted in the United States was the Alien Act of 1798, which empowered the president of the United States to deport persons considered dangerous. The Immigration Act of 1903 permitted deportations in response to the social and economic changes accompanying late nineteenth century industrialization. After these laws came the Deportation Acts of 1917 and 1918, which made it easier for the federal government to deport anarchists. Sweeping immigration reforms in 1996 facilitated the deportation of resident aliens with criminal convictions, including those serving sentences for offenses as serious as first-degree murder.

In the twenty-first century, deportation remains an administrative tool for the removal of undesirable aliens from the United States. Reasons for deportation include entering the country improperly; violating the terms of admission or conditional residency; certain criminal convictions—in either the United States or abroad—including most serious felonies and "moral turpitude"; membership in a forbidden organization, such as a known terrorist

The black nationalist movement of Marcus Garvey was dealt an irreparable blow during the 1920's, when the federal government deported Garvey back to his homeland, Jamaica. In 1923, Garvey was convicted on a trumped-up mail-fraud charge and sent to a federal prison. Four years later, President Calvin Coolidge commuted Garvey's sentence, only to have him deported immediately. Garvey was never allowed to return to the United States. (Library of Congress)

group; certain cases in which immigrants become government dependents within five years of arriving in the country as the result of conditions that preceded their entry into the United States. Post 9/11, deportation is also seen as a mechanism to prevent terrorism and has the added aid of the Department of Homeland Security and the Homeland Security Act, 2002.

Stopping Deportations

Deportation proceedings can be stopped under the terms of the Immigration and Nationality Act of 1952, the first comprehensive federal immigration law that consolidated previous immigration laws into one coordinated statute. That law, and its many amendments, remains the basic federal immigration and nationality statute. The law empowers the U.S. attorney general to issue cancellations of departure, working through immigration judges or successful appeals of immigration court decisions to the Board of Immigration Appeals.

Cancellations of deportations can take several forms. One is a waiver of deportability in which an alien demonstrates that deportation would lead to unusual hardships for a parent, spouse or child who is a U.S. citizen or a permanent resident of the United States. Another form is a cancellation of removal for aliens who have been classified as permanent residents for at least five years and have resided in the United States continuously for at least seven years without any convictions for aggravated felonies.

Aliens can also get deportation orders cancelled when they can show that they have been in the United States continuously for ten years, while exhibiting good moral character and not engaging in document falsification, security violations, criminal activities, or marriage fraud. They must also show that their deportation would result in exceptional hardships to parents, spouses, or children who are U.S. citizens or permanent residents. Aliens resident in the United States for only seven years who otherwise meet the same qualifications can have their deportation orders suspended.

Political factors are also considered in suspending deportation orders, as when aliens can demonstrate that returning to their countries of origin would result in their persecution because of their race, religion, political opinions, nationality, or membership in certain groups.

Recent Trends

The US Immigration and Customs Enforcement (ICE) statistics indicate that deportations for the year 2015 have continued to decline, and are the lowest since 2006, including deportations of criminals. Till early 2016, ICE has completed 168,781 deportations, a slight decline from 2015. Majority of these deportations (72%) are border crossers, initially arrested by the Border Patrol or port of entry officers and turned over to ICE for deportation. Most of the rest are aliens who were arrested in the interior. Regarding criminal deportations, ICE has completed 43,005 deportations of criminals, a number that has fallen over the year, essentially a 60% decline from 2011.

Camille Gibson
Updated by Tania Sebastian

Further Reading

Cassese, Antonio. *International Criminal Law*. New York: Oxford University Press, 2003. A readable introduction to international criminal law examining the substantive aspects of the law and the procedural dimensions of state practice.

Panunzio, Constantine M. *The Deportation Cases of 1919-1920*. New York: Da Capo Press, 1970.

Preston, William. *Aliens and Dissenters: Federal Suppression of Radicals, 1903-1933*. Cambridge, Mass.: Harvard University Press, 1963.

Rush, George E. *The Dictionary of Criminal Justice*. 5th ed. New York: Dushkin/McGraw-Hill, 2000.

Hagan, Jacqueline Maria; Rodriguez, Nestor and Castro, Brianna, Social effects of mass deportations by the United States government, 2000-10 34 (8) Ethnic and Racial Studies (August 2011) 1374.

Johnson, Kevin R., Opening the floodgates—Why America needs to rethink its Borders and Immigration Law (NYU Press, 2007, 1st edition, USA).

Boza, Tanya Maria Golash, Immigration Nation: Raids, Detention and Deportation in Post 9/11 America (Paradigm Publishers, 2011, 1st edition, Colarado).

ICE Weekly Departures and Detention Reports, June 20, 2016, available at: http://cis.org/Immigration-Enforcement-Deportations-Decline-2016 and https://oversight.house.gov/hearing/recalcitrant-countries-denying-visas-to-countries-that-refuse-to-take-back-their-deported-nationals/

See also Attorney General, U.S.; Diplomatic immunity; Extradition; Homeland Security, U.S. Department of; Illegal aliens; Moral turpitude.

Depositions

Definition: Out-of-court statements from persons involved in cases

Criminal justice issue: Courts; legal terms and principles; witnesses

Significance: Depositions can provide attorneys with valuable information prior to trials and be useful during the trial process.

The formal and informal exchange of information between prosecutors and defense attorneys is called "discovery." One of the most common methods of discovery involves depositions, which are out-of-court statements given under oath by people involved in cases. They usually consist of oral examinations, followed by opposing attorneys' cross-examinations. Most states permit both prosecutors and defense attorneys to take depositions, and both sides have the right to be present during oral depositions.

Information collected through depositions can be used at trial or during the preparations for trials. The chief benefit of depositions is that they allow both prosecution and defense to know in advance what witnesses will say at the trials.

Depositions can take the form of written transcripts, videotapes, or both. There are instances in which information can be gathered prior to trial by either side by submitting sets of questions to the opposing side. This procedure requires that the questions be answered in writing and under oath.

In addition to depositions being taken so that attorneys are aware of what witnesses will say at trial, they also serve the purpose of questioning the credibility of witnesses' testimony. At the conclusion of a deposition, both sets of attorneys are provided with transcripts of the statements. This is a particularly useful function of the deposition when a witness's testimony at trial differs from what is offered in the deposition.

Depositions can also be taken to obtain testimony from important witnesses who cannot appear during trials, due to death or other reasons. When this is the case, testimony from depositions is read into evidence.

In contrast to testimony during trials, in which there are strict standards regarding what types of questions can be asked, questions asked during depositions are not held to such restrictions. Attorneys from either side have much wider latitude in the questions they may ask witnesses about different facets of the issues at hand.

Another obvious benefit of depositions is that they help preserve witnesses' recollections while the information is still fresh in their minds. This is especially important when long periods of time separate events and trials. Moreover, it sometimes happens that in the process of collecting depositions and reviewing all information collected, opposing attorneys find compromises that allow them to avoid the expense and time of trials.

Jenifer A. Lee

Further Reading

Meyer, Jon'a F., and Diana R. Grant. *The Courts in Our Criminal Justice System*. Upper Saddle River, N.J.: Prentice-Hall, 2003.

Rabe, Gary A., and Dean John Champion. *Criminal Courts: Structure, Process, and Issues*. Upper Saddle River, N.J.: Prentice-Hall, 2002.

See also Cross-examination; Discovery; Privileged communications; Subpoena power; Testimony; Witnesses.

Deterrence

Definition: Notion that harsh punishments discourage individuals from future involvement in criminal conduct
Criminal justice issue: Crime prevention; legal terms and principles; punishment
Significance: Prevention of crime is a major public issue; if punishments could indeed be shown to deter crime, the finding would be of considerable importance to numerous public policy questions.

There are two categories of deterrence, specific (or simple) and general. Both involve the idea that the threat of punishment will influence individuals not to commit crimes. Specific deterrence focuses on the individual and rests on the assumption that if the punishment imposed on a specific offender is severe enough for a crime, the offender will not commit crimes in the future. General deterrence focuses on society and is based on the idea that potential offenders will be deterred by seeing others being punished, and therefore experience the fear of being punished themselves. Both categories of deterrence are based on the assumptions that potential offenders are rational and will perceive the possible punishment for crime as painful.

Does punishment, in fact, deter? Although many people would intuitively argue that it does, scholarly studies have not proven with certainty that punishment, or the fear of it, deters. There are several problems with the notion that punishment or fear of punishment will prevent crimes in the future.

A major assumption of deterrence theory is that people are rational and will consider the costs of committing a crime before committing the act. While this may be true in some cases, many crimes are unplanned events resulting from chance and opportunity. Further, some individuals lack the ability to reason (due to mental incapacity, immaturity, or impulsivity problems).

Another assumption of deterrence theory is that swift punishment proportional to the seriousness of an offense will deter. In the American criminal justice system, however, many offenders are provided with the opportunity for numerous delays prior to trial. Moreover, many cases end in plea bargains that call for punishment for less than the actual offense.

Both specific and general deterrence theories rest on the notion that most offenders fear being caught. Critics of deterrence policies, however, note that many potential offenders do not believe that they will be caught and prosecuted. Victimization surveys reveal that fewer than half the crimes committed in the United States are known to law-enforcement authorities. Violent crimes are the crimes most frequently reported to the police, yet studies reveal that fewer than 47 percent of all violent crimes are reported. Fear of punishment is further mitigated by the fact that fewer than 5 percent of all crimes reported to police are ultimately prosecuted.)

A final argument used to bolster deterrence theory is the assertion that potential offenders will avoid criminal activity because they fear the pain associated with punishment. Yet some studies have shown that although substantial portions of the offender population in prisons acknowledge that prison is recognized as a cost of criminal activity, many offenders do not consider it an especially painful experience. Even with regard to crimes that carry the potential for the death penalty, most studies reveal, few criminals fear the pain of punishment prior to the crime because they do not believe that they will ever receive such a punishment.

Recent efforts to reduce gun violence have focused on the implementation of a blended deterrence strategy, by identifying risk factors and the causes of violent gun injury problems. Research suggests that combining the efforts of law enforcement, social services and the community, can help deter or change offender behavior, and reduce or prevent violence.

Although politicians and the public often clamor for stiffer penalties as a solution to rising crime rates, few scholars would argue that such remedies are likely to prove very effective.

Interestingly, there are still conflicting studies as to which conditions need to exist in order for sanctions to deter offender. Some research shows support for the hypothesis that those with high moral beliefs are more likely to be deterred from offending. Yet, other research shows that deterrence is more effective in preventing offending among those with low moral beliefs.

Robert R. Wiggins
Updated by Gina Robertiello

Further Reading
Colvin, M. *Penitentiaries, Reformatories, and Chain Gangs: Social Theory and the History of Punishment in the Nineteenth Century.* New York: St. Martin's Press, 1997.
Foucault, Michel. *Discipline and Punish: The Birth of the Prison.* Translated by Alan Sheridan. New York: Vintage Press, 1995.
Friedman, Lawrence M. *Crime and Punishment in America History.* New York: Basic Books, 1993.

Tonry, Michael, and Richard Fraser. *Sentencing and Sanctions in Western Countries.* New York: Oxford University Press, 2001.

Braga, A.A., and Weisburd, D.L. (2015). Focused Deterrence and the Prevention of Violent Gun Injuries: Practice, Theoretical Principles, and Scientific Evidence. Annual Review of Public Health, 36: 55-68.

Piquero, A.R., Bouffard, J.A., Piquero, N.L., & Craig, J.M. (2016). Does Morality Condition the Deterrent Effect of Perceived Certainty Among Incarcerated Felons? Crime and Delinquency, 62 (1) 3-25.

Svensson, R. (2015). An Examination of the Interaction Between Morality and Deterrence in Offending: A Research Note. Crime and Delinquency, 61 (1) 3-18.

See also Capital punishment; Community-based corrections; Contempt of court; Crime; Fines; Incapacitation; Just deserts; Prison and jail systems; Punishment; Punitive damages; Rehabilitation; Australia's "Reintegrative Shaming" approach; Medical model of offender treatment; Pennsylvania system of corrections; Scandinavia's prison experience; Schools of criminology; Victimization theories; History of incarceration; Auburn System.

Discovery

Definition: Court process that requires prosecution and defense attorneys to share the information they gather

Criminal justice issue: Attorneys; Legal terms and principles; Prosecution; Trial procedures

Significance: An overriding goal of the criminal justice system is fairness and impartiality in all phases of trial processes, and the principle of discovery helps achieve that goal.

American courts operate under an adversarial system in which opposing legal teams attempt to further their versions of the truth while being overseen by neutral judges. This system is based on the premise that adversarial proceedings provide the best way to uncover the truth and determine the facts in a case. Another premise of the system is that the accused must be presumed innocent until proven guilty. It is thus the task of prosecutors to prove beyond a reasonable doubt that defendants have committed the crimes of which they are accused. To do so, prosecutors submit evidence and testimony in support of their case. In contrast, the role of defense attorneys in the adversary system is to contest the criminal allegations made against the defendants and dissuade the courts or juries from concluding that the defendants are guilty.

Purpose of Discovery

When preparing for trial, both prosecutors and defense attorneys need to examine all available evidence that has been collected by police investigators, results of any tests that have been conducted, and information about who is to be called to testify at the trials. American courts insist that both sides have equal opportunities to present complete cases, so that one side does not have an unfair advantage over the other. Discovery ensures that both sides to have equal access to the same information.

Discovery involves both the formal and informal exchange of information between prosecutors and defense attorneys. The types of information considered "discoverable" vary from state to state. Items that are particularly likely to be considered discoverable include laboratory reports, fingerprint results, ballistic test results, witness statements, defendants' confessions, psychiatric reports, and police reports.

The implementation of discovery tends to focus on the actions of prosecutors more than on defense attorneys because prosecutors have greater access to investigators (usually police officers), laboratory technicians, and advanced equipment for the analysis of evidence. If prose-

---

Vinny's Discovery

In the popular 1992 film *My Cousin Vinny*, Joe Pesci plays a cocky self-taught Brooklyn attorney whose first trial experience comes when he defends his cousin and a friend in a murder case in Alabama. Much of the film's humor emerges from Vinny's bumbling attempts to comply with formal courtroom procedures. Although he has passed the New York bar exam, he is a complete novice in a southern courtroom. There are many holes in Vinny's legal education, and one of the most glaring is exposed midway through the trial.

While Vinny takes smug satisfaction in persuading the prosecutor (Lane Smith) to give him copies of his files in the murder case, his girlfriend (Marisa Tomei) learns—from browsing through a legal textbook—that the prosecution is required to do just that. The girlfriend's revelation of that fact to Vinny generates powerful comic tension, but it also touches on a central feature of modern criminal practice: Prosecutors are required to reveal any evidence to the defendants that might possibly exonerate them.

In *My Cousin Vinny*, the prosecutor agrees to give Vinny copies of his files while the two men are out hunting during a break in the trial. Such fraternization between opposing attorneys is unusual during trials, but the film reflects another reality about attorneys: They may be fierce opponents inside a courtroom but cordial professional acquaintances outside.

Timothy L. Hall

cutors were to restrict access to such information, it would jeopardize the right of defendants to fair trials. Defense attorneys therefore depend on strong discovery rules to secure their defendants' rights. Allowing defense attorneys to learn what the prosecutors know, or possess in the form of evidence, may spare defense attorneys from the difficult task of attempting to force their clients to voluntarily disclose information that they are reluctant to admit.

In addition to the formal process of discovery, there is an informal process. Informal prosecutorial disclosure operates under the long-held theory that providing defense attorneys with advance viewings of prosecutors' cases encourages guilty pleas and plea bargains. Because prosecutors believe that defendants tell their attorneys only part of the story, informal disclosure allows defense attorneys to be armed with the same information possessed by the prosecutors. The defense attorneys can use the evidence to confront their clients with more complete pictures of the events, which often leads both defendants and their attorneys to conclude that they would be better served by entering guilty pleas.

Informal and Reciprocal Disclosure

The process of discovery does not require that only prosecutors turn over their evidence to defense attorneys. Defense attorneys must reciprocate by disclosing all relevant materials in their possession. If trials are to be conducted fairly, both sides must start on a level playing field and be prevented from presenting surprise evidence.

As with many issues in state courts, reciprocal-disclosure requirements vary from state to state. Some jurisdictions require defense attorneys to file notices of alibi defense—claims that their clients were elsewhere when the crimes with which they are charged were committed—along with lists of witnesses to be called to support the alibis. Such pretrial notices allow prosecutors to investigate witnesses before they testify in court so they can counter the claims of the defendants. Some jurisdictions require similar pretrial disclosures from defense attorneys that an insanity defense will be entered or that expert witnesses will be called. Some states require defense attorneys to turn over to prosecutors the names, addresses, and statements of the witnesses they plan to call at trial.

The process of discovery is meant to ensure that the trial process results in a verdict based on all available evidence. The process achieves that goal when no side in a case is permitted to ambush the other with surprise evidence or witnesses because both sides have exchanged all relevant information.

Jenifer A. Lee

Further Reading

Champion, Dean John, Richard D. Hartley, and Gary A. Rabe. *Criminal Courts: Structure, Process, and Issues.* 3rd ed. Upper Saddle River: Prentice, 2012. Print.

Hancock, Barry W., and Paul M. Sharp, eds. *Criminal Justice in America: Theory, Practice, and Policy.* 3rd ed. Upper Saddle River: Prentice, 2004. Print.

Neubauer, David W., and Henry F. Fradella. *America's Courts and the Criminal Justice System.* 11th ed. Belmont: Wadsworth, 2014. Print.

Stolzenberg, Lisa, and Stewart J. D'Alessio, comps. *Criminal Courts for the 21st Century.* 3rd ed. Miami: Dept. of Criminal Justice, Florida Intl. U, 2010. Print.

See also Bill of particulars; Criminal procedure; Depositions; Due process of law; Subpoena power; Testimony; Trials; Witnesses.

Dismissals

Definition: Formal terminations of legal proceedings
Criminal justice issue: Legal terms and principles; prosecution; trial procedures; verdicts
Significance: Dismissals end judicial proceedings in legal matters without the completion of trials and generally without conclusive findings of law or facts.

In the broadest sense of the term, a dismissal is simply the termination of a legal proceeding. In criminal law it is the cancellation of an indictment, information, complaint, or charge. A dismissal may be done with or without prejudice to the refiling of a subsequent complaint. A dismissal without prejudice means the prosecution may seek new charges either through indictment, information, or complaint. However, a dismissal with prejudice does not allow the prosecution to file the same charge against a defendant again at a later time.

Dismissals may be voluntary, as in cases when the prosecution chooses to stop pursuing a matter, or involuntary. In cases of voluntary dismissals, the prosecution usually has tactical or legal reasons for its actions. Tactical reasons for dismissal may include the absence of key witnesses or the need to take more time to process important evidence. So long as the relevant statute of limitations on filing a charge does not expire, a prosecutor may choose to dismiss the original complaint and refile at a later time when the case is better prepared.

> ### Vinny Wins a Dismissal
>
> In the 1992 film *My Cousin Vinny*, Joe Pesci plays the title character, an inexperienced New York lawyer who defends his young cousin and a friend in an Alabama murder trial. Although Vinny has trouble coping with unfamiliar trial procedures, he eventually casts so much doubt on the prosecution's eyewitnesses and so thoroughly discredits the prosecution's expert witness on a key point of evidence that the prosecutor finally agrees that his case has no merit and dismisses all charges against the defendants. This is the appropriate action for a prosecutor to take in the circumstances, but it is unlikely that a real-life prosecutor would dismiss a case on the spot, as the film's prosecutor does. A prosecutor would probably use an evening recess to consider the new developments in the case before taking a step that is, by its nature, irrevocable. If he later discovers that he has made a wrong decision, he can not recall the defendants and try them again.
>
> *Timothy L. Hall*

Strict due process rights are common reasons that for dismissing cases for legal reasons. Once a criminal charge is brought against someone, due process rights attach and place a heavy burden on the prosecution to move forward. Any failure to proceed with a case in a timely fashion may subject the matter to either voluntary or involuntary dismissal. One example would be the use of evidence obtained without probable cause or a search warrant. Prosecutors who recognize that their cases rest on such evidence may voluntarily dismiss the cases in the hope of finding supported evidence later. If they do not dismiss at that time, they run the risk that courts will dismiss their cases later, possibly with prejudice, when defenses make motions or raise the troublesome issues at trial.

In circumstances in which dismissals are involuntary, courts generally make decisions as to the prejudice or harm caused to the parties. An involuntary dismissal does not always mean that it is with prejudice to the refiling. Involuntary dismissals are generally used when the interests of justice mandate the judicial action. One example is found in cases in which the defendants' affirmative defenses are sustained by the court. For example, when defendants can prove their alibis, then the prosecutors or the judges, upon proper motions, may enter dismissals based on the perfected defenses.

It is important to recognize that dismissals do not include rulings or judgments on the issues at trial. In most instances, dismissals occur prior to trial, and in almost all instances before verdicts or judgments are rendered. Thus, the dismissals are not legal determinations in the truest sense. Nevertheless, they may have impact similar to those of judgments. For example, dismissals with prejudice have the same weight in preventing subsequent charges for the same offense that findings of "not guilty" have at trial.

Another important point in criminal cases is that dismissals prior to the start of jury trials do not necessarily violate the concept of double jeopardy. This means that a dismissal at any time up to the point of picking a jury or beginning the trial does not restrict the later prosecution of the same case, unless prejudice has been ordered by the court.

Carl J. Franklin

Further Reading
Acker, J. R., and D. C. Brody. *Criminal Procedure: A Contemporary Perspective*. 2d ed. Sudbury, Mass.: Jones and Bartlett, 2004.
Del Carmen, Rolando V. *Criminal Procedure: Law and Practice*. 6th ed. Belmont, Calif.: Wadsworth, 2004.
LaFave, Wayne R., Jerold H. Israel, and Nancy J. King. *Criminal Procedure*. 4th ed. St. Paul, Minn.: Thomson/West, 2004.

See also Acquittal; Criminal prosecution; Hung juries; Trials; Verdicts.

District attorneys

Definition: Prosecuting attorneys for local government
Criminal justice issue: Attorneys; prosecution
Significance: District attorneys are responsible for pursuing charges against persons accused of violating state criminal laws.

In many cities the chief prosecutor responsible for enforcing state criminal laws is called the district attorney and is often referred to as the DA. In some places these officials are called county prosecutors or state's attorneys. They make decisions about which people will be charged with crimes, which charges will be filed, and which plea agreements will be accepted for presentation to a judge.

Duties of District Attorneys

District attorneys work closely with local police officials to identify suspects and crimes that should be investigated. They often must approve police officers' requests for search warrants and arrest warrants before those requests are presented to judges in order to obtain the actual warrants. After a suspect is arrested, DAs and their assistants often make arguments to the court about setting bail or other conditions for the pretrial release of individual defendants. They must also represent the government in preliminary hearings, in which judges may consider whether there is sufficient evidence to move a case forward. District attorneys determine which charges will be filed against each defendant based on an evaluation of the evidence gathered by the police. They have the authority to drop charges and have suspects released if they believe there is insufficient evidence to pursue a case. District attorneys are not obligated to prosecute every suspect arrested by the police. Even if the prosecutor believes that the suspect might be guilty of a crime, the district attorney has a professional obligation to pursue only those cases in which there is sufficient evidence to justify initiating criminal charges.

Many cases conclude after either a plea agreement or a trial. In the plea-bargaining process the district attorney determines whether any concessions will be made, such as dropping or reducing charges, in order to gain a guilty plea from the defendant. If a defendant agrees to plead guilty, the district attorney often agrees to recommend that the judge impose a sentence less than the maximum possible punishment for the crime. If no plea agreement is arrived at after discussions between the district attorney and defense attorneys representing the defendant, then the case will go to trial. The district attorney is responsible for organizing the available evidence and then preparing and presenting evidence and arguments in court before a judge or jury. After a defendant is convicted, the district attorney may represent the government in opposing any appeals filed by the convicted offender.

Selection of District Attorneys

District attorneys must be law school graduates who have passed their state's bar exam and have become licensed to practice law. In most places lawyers must run for election in order to become district attorneys. Successful efforts to gain election to local office usually require that attorneys be active in a political party and have the support of local political party leaders. Successful election campaigns also require that candidates raise money and gain public visibility.

The electoral process may pose problems for district attorneys. There are risks that reelection campaigns may take up so much time that they interfere with the effective fulfillment of the district attorney's prosecutorial responsibilities. In addition, some observers fear that the process of raising money from supporters and gaining favor with politicians make district attorneys unable to

> **"District" vs. "State's Attorneys"**
> The terms "state's attorney" and "district attorney" are often used interchangeably; however, they are not synonymous. A district attorney may be an officer of a municipality, a district, or a state, while a state's attorney represents only a state. Both types of government attorneys are called prosecuting attorneys. A district attorney for a particular federal district is known as a United States attorney. Special prosecutors, or United States attorneys, may be appointed to investigate possible criminal activities of the executive branch of the federal government.

make fair and equitable decisions if financial supporters or political colleagues become suspected of wrongdoing. A few states attempt to avoid such problems by having the state attorney general or chief state prosecutor appoint and supervise local prosecutors.

After a lawyer is elected district attorney, the lawyer must hire and train assistant DAs. In small cities there may be only one assistant, but in major metropolitan areas there may be hundreds of assistants under the supervision and direction of the district attorney. The district attorney must also attempt to establish policies for determining which cases will be prosecuted and which kinds of plea agreements will be acceptable. Assistant district attorneys often have substantial freedom to make decisions about what will happen in their own cases, but they must generally follow guidelines developed by the district attorney so that there is an element of consistency in the processing of criminal cases within a particular city.

Key Relationships

As the central figure in the criminal justice process, the district attorney must develop and maintain relationships with various court actors and constituents. The district attorney must cooperate with the police in order to prosecute cases effectively. The DA relies on the police to gather evidence properly and to serve as witnesses for many criminal cases. The district attorney must also work well with victims and witnesses from among members of the public. These people must be questioned with sensitivity and care, and they must be informed about the court processes and questions they will encounter in preliminary hearings and trials.

The district attorney must develop good relationships with defense attorneys and judges. The plea-bargaining process can operate smoothly if the prosecutor and defense attorney do not permit personal animosity to develop. Instead, both lawyers must recognize that they are likely to meet together repeatedly over the years as they discuss the possibility of concluding criminal cases without undertaking the time and expense of a trial.

Plea bargaining is not always adversarial, because both the prosecution and defense may gain benefits from a quick plea bargain that saves court time and seals a conviction while permitting the offender to avoid the strongest possible sentence. Similarly, district attorneys are likely to appear before the same judges year after year. Thus, there is a strong incentive to become well-acquainted with the judge and the judge's preferences for sentencing. The district attorney does not want to waste the court's time by, for example, recommending sentences in plea agreements that are known to be unacceptable to the presiding judge. Instead, the district attorney must often talk regularly with judges to gain an understanding of their values and philosophies about punishment and the criminal justice system.

District attorneys also seek to maintain good relationships with the news media and political parties. Such relationships are essential in efforts to gain reelection to office at the end of a term in office. These contacts also help if DAs seek higher office, because many DAs subsequently seek election to judgeships and legislatures. Thus, district attorneys often hold press conferences and submit to interviews with reporters. Typically, they attempt to portray themselves as being very tough on criminals in order to impress the voters with their effectiveness in combating crime. Relationships with political party officials are important for most district attorneys, because DAs need the parties to mobilize campaign workers and voters at each election.

Christopher E. Smith

Further Reading

Carter, Lief. *The Limits of Order*. Lexington, Mass.: Lexington Books, 1974. Examinations of the work of local prosecutors.

Heilbroner, David. *Rough Justice: Days and Nights of a Young D.A.* New York: Pantheon Books, 1990. Presents perspectives of actual district attorneys on their jobs.

McDonald, William. *The Prosecutor*. Beverly Hills, Calif.: Sage, 1979. Broad presentation of topics concerning prosecutors in the United States and other countries.

Neubauer, David. *Criminal Justice in Middle America*. Morristown, N.J.: General Learning Press, 1974.

Parrish, Michael. *For the People: Inside the Los Angeles District Attorney's Office, 1850-2000*. Santa Monica, Calif.: Angel City Press, 2001.

Rowland, Judith. *The Ultimate Violation*. New York: Doubleday, 1985.

See also Attorney ethics; Attorneys general, state; Criminal prosecution; Defense attorneys; Inquests; Plea bargaining; Preliminary hearings; Public prosecutors; Trials; *Voir dire*.

Diversion

Definition: Decision that may be made at several stages of the juvenile justice process to avoid formal court processing

Criminal justice issue: Legal terms and principles; Juvenile justice

Significance: Diversion is a pretrial practice commonly employed in juvenile justice that allows youthful offenders to avoid formal court processing, receive therapeutic interventions, and reconcile with victims while also preserving judicial resources and reducing court case loads.

Diversion is a pretrial practice commonly employed in juvenile justice and through specialty courts that allow offenders to avoid formal court processing, receive therapeutic interventions, and reconcile with victims while also preserving judicial resources and reducing court case loads.

Diversion is a blanket term used to describe a collection of alternatives to traditional criminal court processing that allow participants to resolve criminal charges against them. Traditionally, diversion has been used as a term to refer to programming afforded youthful offenders. However, in recent decades, concepts of diversion have expanded to include alternative processes for all offenders. Diversion programs can take several forms, but they have a common goal of diverting offenders away from courts that often impose punitive sanctions and into more therapeutic environments. Grounded in rehabilitation and labeling theory, diversion responds to the reality that formal responses to youth crime, such as arrest and referral to court, are not always in the best interests of young offenders or the communities in which they live. Rehabilitation theory holds that offenders who receive therapeutic interventions instead of punishments are more likely to desist from offending. Labeling theory, which maintains that the repeated processing of youth by juvenile justice agencies may lead to additional deviance by those labeled as delinquents. This typically happens when youths began to see themselves as deviants or delinquents, and the opportunities of youths to engage in law-abiding behaviors are limited because they have been labeled as delinquents. Diversion is typically reserved for behaviors that do not seriously threaten public safety, and diversion decisions are typically limited by police department and juvenile court policies. Diversion programs require offenders to participate in counseling, substance abuse treatment programs, community reintegration programs, anger management programs, and restorative justice programs. As the scientific community hones its understanding of mental health and psycho-social correlates of offending, diversion programs adapt and incorporate responsive therapies.

Diversion consists of true diversion (radical nonintervention), referral to a diversion program, or referral to a diversion court. True diversion occurs when police officers or other authorities decide to warn, counsel, or release offenders to parents or guardians without making arrests or formal court referrals. Referrals to diversion programs occur when offenders, and perhaps their families, are referred to community programs in lieu of making court referrals or taking formal court actions. Diversionary courts, also called specialty courts, problem solving courts, drug courts, veterans courts, housing courts, mental health courts, reentry courts, or therapeutic courts. Some scholars observe distinctions between conventional diversion and contemporary diversion. Conventional diversion involves formal processes of some sort, either through police, prosecutor, or court action, and usually entails a documented agreement, probation agreement, or suspended plea. Contemporary diversion circumvents all formal processes and involves police informally supervising offenders in community based programs or in collaboration with families.

Efforts designed to spare youth from the potentially negative consequences of formal court processing have existed since colonial times. Diversion gained popularity in the 1970s and has witnessed a resurgence in the 2010s. Efforts designed to divert some offenders from formal court processing are now common throughout the United States. The biggest area of growth in diversionary programming can be seen among specialty courts. All states host at least one form of specialty court, and new forms of these diversionary courts are being introduced each year. Data are mixed on whether diversion programs are effective. Some forms of diversion appear to help offenders stay connected to their communities, develop prosocial ties, and refrain from criminal or delinquent behaviors. Other diversion programs appear to be associated with recidivism because participants revert to bad behaviors once the protective factors (such as police supervision or heightened community support) are removed. Researchers also observe a net widening effect pursuant to which more offenders are brought under the auspices of criminal justice supervision. Diversion is not used to treat those who were already in the system; instead, it is used to bring in offenders who otherwise would not have warranted supervision or intervention.

Diversion also responds to the criminal justice field's growing awareness of the needs of victims. Offenders who participate in diversion programs often are required to apologize to, and reconcile with, people whom they have hurt through their offenses. Research suggests that these restorative or ameliorative justice programs are useful to victims' recovery.

Preston Elrod and Anne S. Douds

Further Reading
Champion, Dean John. *The Juvenile Justice System: Delinquency, Processing, and the Law.* 4th ed. Upper Saddle River, N.J.: Prentice-Hall, 2003.
DeMatteo, D., LaDuke, C., Locklair, B. R., & Heilbrun, K. (2013). "Community-based alternatives for justice-involved individuals with severe mental illness: Diversion, problem-solving courts, and reentry." *Journal of Criminal Justice,* 41(2), 64-71.
Elrod, Preston, and R. Scott Ryder. *Juvenile Justice: A Social Historical and Legal Perspective.* Gaithersburg, Md.: Aspen, 1999.
Lundman, Richard J. *Prevention and Control of Juvenile Delinquency.* 3d ed. New York: Oxford University Press, 2001.
Mears, D. P., Kuch, J. J., Lindsey, A. M., Siennick, S. E., Pesta, G. B., Greenwald, M. A., & Blomberg, T. G. (2016). "Juvenile Court and Contemporary Diversion." *Criminology & Public Policy,* 15(3), 953-981.
Schwalbe, C. S., Gearing, R. E., MacKenzie, M. J., Brewer, K. B., & Ibrahim, R. (2012). "A meta-analysis of experimental studies of diversion programs for juvenile offenders." *Clinical Psychology Review,* 32(1), 26-33.

See also Criminal records; Discretion; Juvenile delinquency; Juvenile Justice and Delinquency Prevention Act; Juvenile justice system; Australia's "Reintegrative Shaming" approach; Medical model of offender treatment; Realignment (PSR) policy; Scandinavia's prison experience.

Drug courts

Definition: Recently developed alternative to traditional prosecution of drug-related offenses that focuses on ending offenders' drug habits while integrating them into their communities
Criminal justice issue: Courts; Crime Prevention; Medical and health issues; Substance abuse
Significance: Drug courts are a new component of the criminal justice system that tries to remove, at least temporarily, cases of drug offenders from traditional criminal processing and to place them in less formal

hearings in which judges, prosecutors, public defenders, case workers, and the defendants themselves work together as teams to correct the offenders' drug and alcohol problems.

Drug and alcohol abuse tend to make people more likely to commit crimes for many reasons. Placing drug addicts and alcoholics on probation or incarcerating them in prisons typically does nothing to address the fundamental problems of their substance abuse. Drug courts combine accountability to the criminal justice system and protection of the public with treatment for alcoholism, treatment for addiction, and treatment for related mental health problems. The first US drug court was established in Miami, Florida, in 1989. By 2014, more than three thousand drug court programs were in operation throughout the United States.

Drug Court Processes and Characteristics

The drug court process begins when defendants are arrested for drug possession or offenses related to drug or alcohol use, such as committing thefts to buy drugs. After suspects are arrested, prosecutors screen their cases to determine if they are eligible for adjudication in drug courts. In some cases, defendants are not screened until after they are convicted of crimes or they violate the terms of their probation. Drug court participants are usually long-term users of more than one drug.

After defendants are classified as being eligible for drug courts, the requirements of the drug court program are explained to them. Depending on how far the judicial processing of their cases has developed, defendants can benefit by having the prosecution, adjudication, or sentencing of their cases postponed until after their successful completion of the drug court program. Defendants who "graduate" from drug court are typically rewarded by having the charges against them dropped, their cases dismissed, or their probation ended.

Drug courts differ from traditional criminal justice in many ways. For example, they incorporate drug testing into case processing. Participants in the programs may be subjected to random urine testing as often as three times a week. Those who test positive or miss tests may be subject to such penalties as weekend jail stays, increased testing, or restrictions on their freedom to leave their homes. Participants who do well may receive such rewards as gifts, tokens, or advancement to the next phase in their treatment. Most often, however, successful participants are rewarded merely by praise from the judges at their court hearings and applause from fellow participants in the programs.

Relationships between participants and the courts are nonadversarial. The courts sees their mission as assisting participants to recover from alcohol or drug addiction. They try to identify defendants in need of treatment and refer them to treatment as soon as possible after their arrests, rather than having them wait several months for trials and sentencing.

Participants in drug court programs are provided with extensive mental and physical health services, job skills training, education, and housing services to help them stay clean, sober, and out of trouble. Participants are usually required to attend meetings of Alcoholics Anonymous or Narcotics Anonymous.

The Team Approach

Judges, prosecutors, public defenders, probation officers, and treatment case managers (usually social workers or counselors) work as teams to monitor and assist participants. They try to reach consensus on how to reward participants who comply with their programs and penalize those who do not.

Drug court judges see individual participants as often as every week at court sessions attended by all participants. Every participant is called to the bench by the judges; together, they review their fellow participants' progress. Judges commend those who are doing well and may warn or penalize those who are not doing well. These proceedings all take place in open courts, before other participants and all members of the drug court teams.

Drug court teams seek to continually evaluate their programs' progress against their goals. They also work to incorporate innovations in substance abuse treatment, the technology of monitoring participants, and lessons learned from the experiences of other drug courts. Drug courts work in partnership with local government, community agencies, businesses, churches, and health professionals.

Effectiveness of Drug Courts

Several studies have suggested that drug courts are effective in reducing drug use, retaining participants, reducing repeat offending, and costing taxpayers less money than such alternative programs as incarceration. However, these findings must be treated with caution. Many of these studies are not scientifically rigorous, and even the studies that use sound methods shed little light on *how* drug courts achieve their positive results. Until more research is done, it will not be clear which components of the drug court model, such as drug testing and weekly court appearances, are essential to the court's success.

Yet there is a growing body of evidence that these programs have positive effects. A ten-year study of the Multnomah County drug court in Portland, Oregon, published in 2007, evaluated the impact of five different factors—age, gender, race, number of prior arrests, and participation in the drug court program—on the incidence of recidivism in the five years following an arrest that led to drug court. While the most statistically significant predictor of recidivism was the number of prior arrests, participation in the program was also statistically significant, as were age and race. Integrating this information into the data analysis showed that participation in the drug court program reduced the incidence of rearrest in the subsequent five years by approximately 29 percent, and recidivism of participants was significantly reduced for up to fourteen years after entry into the program. In addition, the drug court program cost significantly less per person compared to traditional prosecution for drug offenses; the study calculated that the program saved around $13,609 per person, or approximately $88.5 million over ten years.

Issues and Concerns

At the start of the twenty-first century, jurisdictions were launching new drug courts at an amazing rate. However, it was expected that some of these new programs either would not or could not implement the drug court model fully, as the model requires local jurisdictions to abandon their "business as usual" practices and become open to innovation. As jurisdictions move to adapt the drug court model to use with the juvenile justice system and the parents of children who have been abused and neglected, these issues will intensify.

Despite their apparent success, drug courts still reach only a small percentage of offenders who might benefit from their programs. Many early drug courts began their operations with the help of generous federal and state grants. However, some local jurisdictions may lack either the will or the means to continue operating their drug courts after their grant money is exhausted.

Although drug courts face numerous challenges, they show great promise as alternatives to "revolving door" justice in which the same offenders are repeatedly processed. In some criminal justice circles, the growth of drug courts is referred to as a "movement," and one that reflects the enthusiasm about this new way of dealing with crime and addiction.

Jerome McKean

Further Reading
Cole, David. "Doing Time—in Rehab." *Nation* 20 Sept. 1999: 30-31. *Academic Search Complete*. Web. 26 May 2016.
"Drug Courts." *National Institute of Justice*. Dept. of Justice, 13 May 2016. Web. 31 May 2016.
Finigan, Michael W., Shannon M. Carey, and Anton Cox. *The Impact of a Mature Drug Court over 10 Years of Operation: Recidivism and Costs*. Portland: NPC Research, 2007. *National Criminal Justice Reference Service*. Web. 31 May 2016.
Gaines, Larry K., and Janine Kremling, eds. *Drugs, Crime, Justice: Contemporary Perspectives*. 3rd ed. Long Grove: Waveland, 2014. Print.
Goode, Erich. *Drugs in American Society*. 9th ed. Dubuque: McGraw, 2014. Print.
Gray, James P. *Why Our Drug Laws Have Failed and What We Can Do about It: A Judicial Indictment of the War on Drugs*. 2nd ed. Philadelphia: Temple UP, 2012. Print.
United States. Dept. of Justice. Office of Justice Programs. Bureau of Justice Assistance. *Defining Drug Courts: The Key Components*. 1997. Washington: Author, 2004. *National Drug Court Institute*. Web. 26 May 2016.

See also Alcohol use and abuse; Community-based corrections; DARE programs; Decriminalization; Drug Enforcement Administration, U.S.; Drug legalization debate; Drug testing; Drugs and law enforcement; Mandatory sentencing; Recidivism; Victimless crimes; Violent Crime Control and Law Enforcement Act; Addiction; Comprehensive Addiction and Recovery Act (CARA) (2015); Designer and date rape drugs; Opioid treatment breakthroughs.

Effective counsel

Definition: Legal representation of clients by fully qualified attorneys who are committed to providing their clients with the best possible defense
Criminal justice issue: Attorneys; constitutional protections; professional standards
Significance: All persons charged with the commission of crimes have a constitutional right to have lawyers who are qualified and competent to represent them.

Everyone accused of a crime in the United States is entitled under Sixth Amendment of the U.S. Constitution to have a lawyer represent them, because legal representation is essential to ensure that the Defendant (one accused of a crime) has a fair trial. The Defendant's right to legal representation greatly improves the likelihood that the trial will be fair and that the adversarial system will function properly in convicting the guilty persons and exonerating the innocent. The presence of an attorney, however, ensures the fairness of the trial only if the lawyer is qualified and competent. Thus, the right to counsel is the right to the effective assistance of counsel. *McMann v. Richardson* (1971).

The Sixth Amendment of the U.S. Constitution, thus, guarantees not merely the assistance of a lawyer, but that this legal representation be competent. The lawyer must have loyalty to the client that is undivided and without undue restriction. Courts will view this representation as "effective" assistance of counsel, while viewing representation that fails to legal meet this standard as "ineffective." If persons are convicted of a crime and their lawyers were constitutionally ineffective, these defendants are entitled to have their convictions set aside and be granted new trials.

Scope of the Effective Right to Counsel.

There are two key aspects to the right of effective assistance of counsel. The first is that a court may not restrict the defense counsel in representing the accused. The second is that a defense counsel's lack of competence or preparation can deprive a defendant of the effective representation that is necessary to ensure a fair trial and a just outcome.

The Constitutional Right to Effective Counsel

The American criminal justice system is an adversarial one. Under this system, both the prosecution and defense attorneys vigorously present their interpretations of the law and the facts. If a lawyer fails to competently represent the client', so as to impair the likelihood of a fair trial or a just outcome, that lawyer is said to have provided "ineffective representation," and the persons they represent have been denied their constitutional right to effective assistance of counsel.

The guarantee of effective assistance of counsel most often applies to criminal cases, because it is only in criminal (and very few civil) cases that persons have a right to be represented by a lawyer. Note that both the right to a lawyer and standards of effective assistance of counsel apply to civil cases such as those involving deportations and the termination of parental rights In cases where the criminal defendant cannot afford to hire a lawyers, the court will appoint a lawyer to represent him or her. Even if a defendant has an appointed attorney, that defendant still has the legally recognized right to be represented by effective legal representation.In such cases, the Court has ruled that the government may not prosecute a defendant whose counsel, appointed or retained cannot defend him fully and faithfully. *Cuyler v. Sullivan* (1980).

How Counsel Can Be Ineffective

Ineffective assistance of counsel occurs in any of three general ways. First, the defense lawyer can be ineffective because of a conflict of interest—an issue that prevents them from fully and zealously representing the interests of their clients. Second, lawyers can be ineffective if a judge restricts their ability to be effective—by preventing them from fully and zealously advocating on behalf of their clients the trial court may not restrict defense counsel in carrying out their duties to represent their clients). Third, lawyers can be ineffective through lack of competence or preparation to handle particular cases.

Lawyers are ethically obligated to fully and zealously advocate for the interests of their clients. Sometimes lawyers can have conflicting interests—for example, by representing more than one client in a case when the defendants are known to have potentially conflicting interests. If a lawyer is forced to choose between advancing the interests of one client or another, the client whose interests did not receive preferential treatment may have received ineffective assistance of counsel. In addition to making the lawyer ineffective, conflicts of interest violate ethical rules of the bar association and can be a basis for sanctions or penalties against lawyers engaging in such behavior. Conflicts may result in lawyers' negligent performance of professional responsibilities and can make the lawyer civilly liable to his client for malpractice.

The Supreme Court has found that trial court judges also have denied effective legal representation to defendants—for example, by preventing lawyers from making closing arguments in bench trials (nonjury trials decided by judges alone), in *Herring v. New York* (1975), or by appointing lawyers for indigents shortly before trial and forcing them to proceed with their defense despite inadequate preparation. These practices have been found to render the legal' assistance provided in such circumstances to be ineffective. Courts must appoint attorneys for these defendants in a way that allows for effective assistance in the preparation and trial for the case.

Effective Counsel and Unsuccessful Outcomes

While conflicts of interest and court interference with a lawyer's' work can render a lawyer's' assistance ineffective, the most controversial area of ineffective assistance concerns incompetent or unqualified counsel. Incompetence can lead to mistakes, such as inadequate investigation of a case, failure to call certain witnesses, or inadequate presentation of evidence. Not all mistakes made by a lawyer, however, render his or her work ineffective.

> ### A Truly Ineffective Movie Lawyer
>
> In director Sidney Lumet's 1993 film *Guilty as Sin*, an attorney played by Rebecca De Mornay agrees to represent a client (Don Johnson) accused of murdering his wife. The attorney eventually becomes convinced of her client's guilt. Concerned that he might not be convicted otherwise, she plants evidence designed to incriminate him. However, the client himself produces a surprise witness who lies to provide the client with an alibi that prevents the jury from convicting him. Afterward, the client attempts to kill the attorney.
>
> The defense attorney in this film is unrealistically bad on several levels; she is a bad attorney when she initially believes her client is innocent and becomes even worse as she comes to believe that he is guilty. For example, the prosecution's key evidence against her client consists of statements written and made by the murdered wife that appear to implicate the client. In real life, a competent attorney would categorically object to the introduction of this evidence because it violates the rule against hearsay evidence. This rule of evidence provides that testimony intended to prove the truth of some matter normally cannot be offered by a witness who is not present in court to be cross-examined. Thus, evidence from the dead wife tending to prove that her husband has killed her should not be admitted because the woman herself cannot appear in court.
>
> Later in the film, when the attorney comes to believe that her client is, in fact, a murderer, she violates an even more fundamental rule. Attorneys are obligated to represent their clients diligently, whether they are innocent or guilty.
>
> *Timothy L. Hall*

The U.S. Supreme Court has held that the U.S. Constitution guarantees defendants the right to have a lawyer who is competent but does not guarantee a successful outcome. The Constitution guarantees only a fair trial, and if lawyers are competent, despite losing the case, are considered constitutionally effective. In defining competent representation, the Court has articulated standards of a level of general professional performance for lawyers representing a defendant. In defending a client, lawyers do not need to be the most expert lawyers in a given field or be those with the most resources available to pursue the case.

The Supreme Court has rejected restrictions on representation imposed during the trial as unconstitutional interference with the defense counsel's representation of a client. For example, the Court in *Geders v. United States* (1976), held that a trial judge's order that prevented a defendant from consulting with his counsel during an overnight recess between direct and cross-examination intended to prevent the "tailoring of evidence" deprived the defendant of his right to counsel and was invalid

The Strickland Standard

In the 1984 case of *Strickland v. Washington*, the U.S. Supreme Court articulated a general Sixth Amendment standard for adequacy of legal representation. The Strickland test looks for two major factors: 1) deficient representation and 2) resulting prejudice so serious that it calls into doubt the outcome of the trial. The test of deficient representation is an objective standard of reasonableness "under prevailing professional norms" that considers "all the circumstances" and evaluates conduct "from the counsel's perspective at the time." The court, however, did not provide any detailed rules or guidelines for adequate representation, deeming these as inappropriate and unduly difficult considering the many aspects involved in the lawyer's work in defending the client.

The Court explained that the reasonableness standard is equally applicable to a claim that counsel did not discover something he should have. In other words, counsel has a duty to make reasonable investigations or to make a reasonable decision that makes particular investigations unnecessary This duty accompanies the same "heavy measure of deference to counsel's judgment" required in all ineffectiveness cases. Strickland requires an objective standard requiring that counsel's performance be compared to a hypothetical reasonable attorney.

Because even the most highly competent attorneys might choose to defend a client differently, judicial "scrutiny of counsel's peformance must be highly differential. The lawyer's obligation is a general one, which is to operate within the wide range of legitimate, lawful, and reasonable conduct. Strategic "choices made after a thorough investigation of relevant law and facts" cannot be successfully challenged as it is "a reasonable decision that makes particular investigations unnecessary, or a reasonable decision reflecting which issues to raise on appeal. In the Strickland case, the allegation of ineffective assistance was rejected. The Court held that the defense attorney's decision to not enter character and psychological evidence in a capital murder sentencing proceeding to avoid rebuttal evidence of the defendant's criminal history was based on the lawyer's "reasonable professional judgment."

Defense attorneys, however, have a general duty to investigate a defendant's background, and limiting investigation and the presentation of mitigating evidence must be supported by reasonable efforts and judgment. Also, even though deference to counsel's choices may seem appropriate in a given case, an accused, in considering the plea, is clearly entitled to the advice of counsel on the prospect of conviction at trial and the extent of punishment that might be imposed. Therefore, in *Lafler v. Cooper* (2012), the prosecution conceded that the deficient representation part of the Strickland test was met when an attorney erroneously advised the defendant during the plea negotiations that the facts in his case would not support a conviction for attempted murder.

What constitutes prejudice from attorney error, the second Strickland requirement, has been the more difficult issue to determine. To show prejudice under Strickland, the defendant "must show that there is a reasonable probability that, but for counsel's unprofessional errors, the result of the proceeding would have been different. A reasonable probability is a probability sufficient to undermine confidence in the outcome." Defendants often fail to prove the prejudice requirement, with Court viewing it as a threshold matter and failing to find how other representation would have made a significant difference.

Ensuring Effective Assistance of Counsel

A challenge to lawyers' effectiveness usually comes only after the case has ended and the defendant has been convicted. Determining whether a lawyer was competent requires another trial, at which testimony and evidence are presented on the lawyer's work on the case. In such proceedings, lawyers are often the principal witnesses. These proceeding are civil rather than criminal cases, even though they concern the representation in criminal trials. They can be held in either federal or state courts if the conviction originally occurred in state court (as most convictions do) and can result in the issuance of a writ of *habeas corpus* (a writ permitting prisoners to challenge wrongful convictions) if the reviewing court finds that lawyers' assistance was ineffective. A 1995 U.S. Department of Justice study of approximately half of all petitions for writs of *habeas corpus* in federal courts found that the largest percentage of such petitions, 25 percent, involved claims for ineffective assistance of counsel. A very large majority claims of ineffective assistance, however, are unsuccessful.

David M. Siegel
Updated by Christopher T. Anglim

Further Reading

American Bar Association. *Annotated Model Rules of Professional Conduct and Code of Judicial Conduct.* 6th ed. Chicago: American Bar Association, 2007. Compilation of the codes establishing rules of ethics for lawyers. See also the ABA's *Code of Professional Responsibility and Judicial Conduct* (Chicago: American Bar Association, 1979).

Freedman, Monroe H., and Abbe Smith. *Understanding Lawyers' Ethics.* 5th ed. Durham, N.C.: Carolina Academic Press, 2016. A concise treatment of lawyer's ethics, including chapters on prosecutors' ethics and the client perjury problem.

Taylor, John B. *Right to Counsel and Privilege Against Self-Incrimination: Rights and Liberties Under the Law.* Santa Barbara, Calif: ABC-Clio, 2004.

Tomkovicz, James J. *The Right to the Assistance of Counsel: A Reference Guide to the United States Constitution.* Westport, Conn.: Greenwood Press, 2002.

Wolfram, Charles. *Modern Legal Ethics.* St. Paul, Minn.: West, 2004. A treatise on legal ethics that addresses ethical obligations of prosecutors and defense attorneys in some detail.

See also Attorney ethics; Cross-examination; Defendant self-representation; Equal protection under the law; *Habeas corpus*; Public defenders.

Execution, forms of

Definition: State-sanctioned ending of a condemned prisoner's life
Criminal justice issue: Capital punishment; Medical and health issues; Punishment; Technology
Significance: As the legality of capital punishment in the United States drew increasing criticism during the twentieth century, technological innovations were sought in order to carry out executions in more humane and dignified manners.

Executions were once conducted in public and in ways intended to be both brutal and disrespectful of the accused. Burnings, crucifixions, and dismemberments sought not only death but also the total annihilation of the condemned through the destruction of the body. Societies of the past two centuries have shown increasing concern for the dignity of the individual, extending this concern even to those convicted of heinous crimes.

Where capital punishment remains a part of the legal regime, the state has faced the issue of how to take a convict's life in a way that is different from—and morally superior to—the crime for which the prisoner stands condemned. Resolution of this question has involved searching for a method of execution that inflicts a minimum of physical pain upon the condemned and that respects human dignity by avoiding spectacle and disfigurement of the body. This concern also extends to execution team members who perform the act of terminating a life and to the community at large, in whose name the execution will be carried out. Critics charge that this has been a futile pursuit and that the only way human dignity can be honored is by eliminating capital punishment altogether.

Hanging and Firing Squads

Death by the hangman's noose was the dominant form of execution in colonial America, and it remained the most common method used until the turn of the twentieth century. Hangings could be conducted at the local level of government. At first, they were elaborately staged public events. The execution process included a ritualized procession from the jail to the nearby gallows, speeches by local officials, and a sermon on the depravity of human nature and the wages of sin from the local clergy. The condemned was offered a chance to make a public statement, with the expectation of a demonstration of contrition, although not all prisoners performed according to script.

Finally, the condemned would be hooded and the noose affixed to the neck. A trap door was sprung from beneath the prisoner, causing him to drop until his fall was arrested by the rope. Death came through the severance of the spinal cord and was thought to be fast and painless. However, all executions involve some risk of error. Calculating the proper drop of the prisoner turned out to be an imperfect science, and botched executions were common. Too short a drop produced a slow death by strangulation, with its accompanying struggle, while too long a drop resulted in decapitation of the prisoner. Largely for this reason, states began to remove hangings from public view, and by the late nineteenth century, they were more often carried out behind prison walls by a centralized and professional state bureaucracy. In 2004, hanging was an option in only three states, and only three state-sanctioned hangings were conducted from 1977 to 2004.

Death by shooting has played a minor role in American executions because of its inevitable disfigurement of the body and the significant possibility of botched executions. Only two state-sanctioned executions between 1977 and 2004 were by firing squad.

Twentieth Century Innovations

The possibility of botched executions and a growing public discomfort with capital punishment in general led states to seek more technologically advanced methods of execution that promised to be fast, painless, and reliable. They turned to electricity and chemistry.

New York carried out the first electrocution in 1890, and the electric chair was soon found throughout the United States. Prisoners were strapped to wooden chairs,

A display at the Penitentiary of New Mexico, showing the only electric chair used in New Mexico. (By Ken Piorkowski, via Wikimedia Commons)

and current was passed through their bodies in sufficient quantities to cause death by cardiac arrest. This technology was expensive and required expertise in the new science of electricity, resulting in the further centralization of executions. Later conducted indoors, usually at night, deep within state penitentiaries and at the hands of a professional bureaucracy, the public in whose name executions were carried out was by now insulated from the process. The few witnesses permitted by officials continued to report gruesome errors, however, and it became apparent that electrocutions did not guarantee a speedy and painless death as had been promised.

Nevada, in 1921, became the first state to employ lethal gas. The condemned was secured to a seat inside a small, airtight chamber. Pellets of sodium cyanide were dropped into a small container of sulfuric acid, producing cyanide gas. The gas blocked the ability of the body to absorb oxygen, producing unconsciousness followed by death from asphyxiation. Even when carried out properly, prisoners were frequently observed to struggle, sometimes violently, as they reacted to the gas. This method never spread beyond a small number of western and southern states. Eleven executions between 1977 and 2004 were by lethal gas.

The current mode of execution dates from 1982, when Texas carried out the first lethal injection. Its apparent effectiveness in delivering a humane execution resulted in its rapid spread, and lethal injection was in 2004 the sole method of capital punishment in most states and the preferred option in the rest, except for Nebraska. The condemned is strapped to a gurney, and deadly chemicals are injected intravenously. Sodium thiopental, a fast-acting sedative, is typically administered first, followed by pancuronium bromide, which paralyzes the muscles and causes the collapse of the lungs. Finally, potassium chloride is administered to stop the prisoner's heart. Death comes within minutes, and the convict does not struggle, whether because of the loss of consciousness or because of paralysis. The procedure is clinical, even to the point of applying alcohol to the prisoner's skin before inserting the needle, to avoid infection.

However, beginning in 2011, Hospira, the only manufacturer in the country approved by the Food and Drug Administration (FDA) to make sodium thiopental, stopped producing the anesthetic following a warning regarding contamination. While some correctional facilities resorted to buying the drug from overseas and other local buyers who had managed to get their hands on a supply by various means, others were forced to experiment with alternative drugs in order to continue performing executions. Some states, such as Oklahoma, settled for administering pentobarbital, made by the company Lundbeck, instead. Though it proved to be a suitable substitute, Lundbeck eventually issued distribution controls to prevent middlemen from selling the pentobarbital to prisons due to pressure from activist groups against the death penalty. Other states had begun using the sedative midazolam, reporting that it was effective despite claims from some experts that the drug could not guarantee the state necessary to be free from pain. The concern over the use of this drug escalated after the highly publicized botched execution in Oklahoma of convict Clayton Lockett in 2014, during which the prisoner was in visible agony and took a longer amount of time to die. Several executions had been delayed on account of the struggle to adjust to the shortage of sodium thiopental, and other executions involving experimental cocktails had also been botched, furthering the debate and concerns around the procedure. In March 2015, as a backup option, the state of Utah passed a bill reinstating the firing squad as a means of execution.

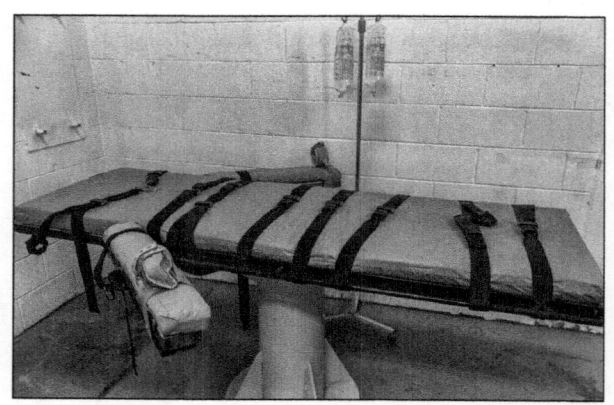

Table used to administer lethal injection, a form of execution. (By Ken Piorkowski, via Wikimedia Commons

Whether death by injection is, in fact, painless is also hotly contested, as observers have no way of knowing. Critics charge that the process is meant to cloak the killing of the prisoner in the trappings of medicine—to anesthetize a society no longer comfortable with state-sanctioned homicide—yet risks silent suffering by the condemned. It has not escaped their notice that several states that employ lethal injection to execute prisoners forbid the use of pancuronium bromide by veterinarians to euthanize pets.

John C. Hughes

Further Reading

Banner, Stuart. *The Death Penalty*. Cambridge: Harvard UP, 2002. Print.
Bohm, Robert M. *Deathquest*. Cincinnati: Anderson, 2003. Print.
Constanzo, Mark. *Just Revenge*. New York: St. Martin's, 1997. Print.
Crair, Ben. "Lethal Entanglements." *New Republic* June 2015: 42-47. Print.
Johnson, Robert. *Deathwork*. Belmont: Wadsworth, 1997. Print.
Stern, Jeffrey E. "The Cruel and Unusual Execution of Clayton Lockett." *Atlantic*. Atlantic Monthly Group, June 2015. Web. 25 May 2016.

See also Capital punishment; Cruel and unusual punishment; Punishment; *Stanford v. Kentucky*; *Roper v. Simmons (2005)*; Technology's transformative effect.

Execution of judgment

Definition: Process of carrying into effect the orders, judgments, or decrees of courts
Criminal justice issue: Convictions; courts; judges; sentencing

Significance: In criminal law, after defendants are convicted and sentenced, the execution of judgment is the crucial stage at which the court's decisions are actually implemented.

In civil law, the execution of judgment affords winning parties the benefit of the final judgments or decrees. For example, in a personal injury matter in which a plaintiff prevails, the execution of judgment includes payment of damages to cover costs or loss from injury.

In criminal matters, execution of judgment typically refers to the successful completion of court punishment orders. Execution of judgment in such cases may include payments of ordered fines, defendants reporting to prison to serve sentences, or in capital-punishment judgments, the actual execution of the defendants. In the broader sense, "execution" refers to the process required to carry forth the order of the court contained in the decree or judgment.

The execution of judgment may be deferred or suspended by a court. In each instance the actual completion of the sentence is delayed or in some way altered rather than carried forth. For example, defendants convicted of felony crimes may find their sentences to include set periods of incarceration in prison. Their sentences may also be suspended pending lawful conduct of the defendants under specific rules or conditions of probation. In such instances, the execution of judgment is limited or in some cases completely postponed so that defendants may complete the conditions of their probation. Upon successful completion of probation, the sentences may then be permanently set aside with no formal execution of the original sentence.

Carl J. Franklin

Further Reading

Allen, Harry E., Clifford E. Simonsen, and Edward J. Latessa. *Corrections in America: An Introduction.* 10th ed. Upper Saddle River, N.J.: Pearson Education, 2004.

LaFave, Wayne R., Jerold H. Israel, and Nancy J. King. *Criminal Procedure.* 4th ed. St. Paul, Minn.: Thomson/West, 2004.

United States Sentencing Commission. *Federal Sentencing Guidelines Manual 2003.* St. Paul, Minn.: West Publishing, 2004.

See also Convictions; Probation, adult; Punishment; Restitution; Suspended sentences.

Expert witnesses

Definition: Qualified witnesses, considered experts in their fields, provide scientific, technical, medical, or other specialized testimony

Criminal justice issue: Witnesses; Technology; Trial procedures

Significance: Testimony by expert witnesses can aid jurors in comprehending complex evidence; however, there are also risks that jurors may overvalue such testimony because of the professional positions of the witnesses or will completely dismiss the testimony because of its complexity.

In the second half of the twentieth century, case complexity within criminal and civil trials dramatically increased. As a result, reliance on expert witnesses and their role in the court system has also greatly increased. Within the adversarial trial system, the objective of expert testimony is to explain or clarify scientific, technical, or medical evidence for the benefit of the jury. Product liability, medical malpractice, antitrust, and many other issues arise in cases that require the testimony of an expert witness.

Rules and guidelines place limits on the types of witnesses who may be considered experts. It is the judge's responsibility to decide, first, if the testimony of the expert will assist the jury in understanding the evidence or in determining a fact that is at issue. Second, guidelines help judges ensure that any testimony heard is from a witness who is appropriately qualified to speak on the subject. As more expert witnesses are brought into courtrooms to comment on various complex subjects, concerns arise that experts are merely "hired guns."

Private Versus Court-Appointed Experts

One important issue to consider is how an expert witness is selected. Due to the adversarial nature of trials, each side may present an expert witness of its own choosing. Privately appointed experts have the potential of being biased in favor of the attorney who hired them. In addition, attorneys also have the opportunity to shop around until they find an expert who agrees to or is willing to present testimony in their favor. Privately appointed experts can be quite expensive, meaning that those with greater wealth may have an advantage in affording a helpful expert witness over those who lack financial resources.

An alternative to the privately appointed expert is the court-appointed expert. Although court-appointed experts are more common in other countries, some venues within the United States, such as family court in Texas, use them extensively. The benefit associated with using a court-appointed expert is that the witness is known to hold an objective position and is not perceived as having a hidden agenda.

Although approved of by judges and experts themselves, research has shown that attorneys are the least likely to favor using court-appointed experts. Not only do attorneys fear losing control over the trial process, there is also relatively less communication between court-appointed experts and attorneys. Court-appointed and privately retained experts both have their benefits and drawbacks; however, privately retained experts are most likely to be used in the criminal justice system in the United States. The next important issue to consider is how jurors perceive and evaluate expert witnesses and their testimony.

The Influence of Expert Testimony on the Jury

Once the judge has ruled on the admissibility of expert witness testimony, it becomes the jury's responsibility to weigh and evaluate the testimony. An important issue that continues to arise is the potential confusion of jurors that may result from a "battle of the experts."

Many court actors express apprehension at how the jury may interpret expert witness testimony. Some claim the intellectual incompetence of jurors will interfere with their ability to understand most expert testimony. This juror incompetence is said to result in one of two outcomes. In the first, jurors may simply rely on the superficial characteristics or credentials of the expert, taking the testimony for fact and not critically evaluating the testimony. In the second, the expert testimony and evidence may be too complex for jurors, and they will simply disregard it. In other words, there is a perception that jurors will either undervalue or overvalue the expert testimony.

Research has been able to assuage many of the concerns regarding jurors' interpretations. Although studies have revealed that jurors do have difficulty understanding complex expert testimony, research has also shown that jurors not only critically evaluate the quality of an expert's testimony, but also critically evaluate the credentials of the witness. In addition, difficulty in understanding and adequately evaluating expert testimony has been linked more often to the poor presentation of the evidence and testimony than to intellectual inadequacies among jurors.

Jurors themselves have revealed that they are not passive receptors, simply accepting expert testimony and complex evidence in an uncritical manner. To the contrary, jurors actively and critically evaluate and discuss complex evidence and testimony. Although there always stands a risk that jurors will misunderstand or undervalue complex expert testimony, it has been established that jurors take their responsibility quite seriously and adequately evaluate and integrate complex expert testimony. As science, medicine, and technology continue to advance, the role of the expert witness will continue to be relied upon to assist jurors in adequately comprehending important yet complex evidence.

Erin J. Farley

Professor John Campbell giving expert testimony. (By Extraordinary Chambers in the Courts of Cambodia, via Wikimedia Commons)

Further Reading

Anderson, Patrick R., and Thomas L. Winfree, Jr. *Expert Witnesses: Criminologists in the Courtroom*. Albany: State University of New York Press, 1987.

Billings, Paul R., ed. *DNA on Trial: Genetic Identification and Criminal Justice*. Plainville, N.Y.: Cold Spring Harbor Laboratory Press, 1992.

Freeman, Michael D. A., and Helen Reece. *Science in Court: Issues in Law and Society*. Brookfield, Vt.: Ashgate/Dartmouth, 1998.

Huber, Peter W. *Galileo's Revenge: Junk Science in the Courtroom*. New York: Basic Books, 1991.

Smith, Roger, and Brian Wynne. *Expert Evidence: Interpreting Science in the Law*. New York: Routledge, 1989.

See also Cross-examination; Evidence, rules of; Eyewitness testimony; False convictions; Subpoena power; Testimony; Trials; Witnesses.

Eyewitness testimony

Definition: Accounts given by persons who have directly observed crimes or actions related to crimes

Criminal justice issue: Evidence and forensics; witnesses

Significance: The description of criminal activities by an eyewitness has long been accepted by judges and juries as convincing. Psychological tests have repeatedly shown, however, that human perception and memory are flawed and that testimony is not always reliable. In this way, innocent people are sometimes incorrectly identified and convicted.

An eyewitness to an event is someone who has observed that event directly and is one form of evidence acceptable in court. Accounts by eyewitnesses are given special importance in criminal trials. Frequently, such testimony is the single largest determinant of a trial's outcome. Research by psychologists, however, suggests that testimony describing crimes and identifying perpetrators can be flawed by limitations in human perception and memory. Since psychologist Hugo Munsterberg began staging mock robberies in 1908, hundreds of crimes have been simulated for the purpose of psychological experiments. Such experiments have demonstrated that people, in remembering events they have witnessed, can unwittingly distort facts, resulting in mistaken testimony.

Perceiving and Remembering

Perception of any event can be influenced by the perceiver's expectations. Many aspects of a street crime, for example, make accurate identification of the offender difficult: The crime occurs quickly, the offender has probably never before been seen by the witness, the witness is under great stress, and distracting stimuli (such as a gun) are often present. In addition, studies have shown that a witness is less likely to notice identifying features of an offender whose race is different from that of the witness.

Folk wisdom and the law both assume that memories are stored like photographs and that somewhere in the brain lie exact images of past events, which can be later retrieved. This assumption is inaccurate. Experimental work by psychologist Elizabeth Loftus has documented how easily incidents occurring after an event are incorporated into memories of that event. For example, she introduced to children totally fictitious stories of being lost in a supermarket. These stories are later accepted by some of the children as personal memories. She modified memories of a video-presented traffic accident by introducing into her inquiry vivid words like "crash" and found that damage from the accident is thereafter remembered as more severe. Loftus cautioned that people's memories of a real crime can easily be modified as media accounts, suggestions by police officials, or imagined distortions that slip into one's memories of the original event. Such effects can be magnified with the passage of time. It was Loftus, however, who also made eyewitnesses testimony as the most persuasive form of evidence and legitimized the study of eyewitnesses in the minds of psychological scientists.

Retrieving One's Memory of the Crime

The retrieval task typically presented to witnesses after a crime is to try to identify the offender from a book of suspects' photographs or from a police lineup. An assumption common among witnesses is that the offender is among those in the lineup staged by the police. This subtly transforms the identification task into the multiple-choice quiz of selecting from the lineup whatever option is most similar to that stored in memory. If the police have erred by apprehending a suspect with superficial similarities to the real offender, the witness's choice will confirm the police error. Police officials may subtly, or sometimes explicitly, reinforce the witness's choice by their reaction. Even initially hesitant witnesses may become convinced of the accuracy of their memories and, by the time of the trial, exude confidence. Most studies have found little relationship between the accuracy of testifying witnesses and the confidence they project.

Special retrieval problems are presented by witnesses testifying about such activity as sexual abuse that occurred during their childhood. While children rarely concoct detailed descriptions of such abuse without a basis of fact, child witnesses are particularly susceptible to suggestive questioning by adults. Testimony by adults based upon repressed memories from their childhood and later "recovered" in therapy is particularly suspect of having been contaminated by suggestion.

Impact on the Justice System

Mistaken eyewitness identification by confident witnesses has been shown to be the

---

Eyewitness Testimony and False Convictions

The film 1988 film *The Thin Blue Line* is a documentary about Randall Dale Adams, who was wrongly convicted of killing a police officer. As a result of public attention raised by the documentary, and the evidence developed in the course of making it, a Texas criminal court ordered Adams released pending a new trial. However, the state of Texas eventually decided not to retry the case. The film, made more powerful because it dramatizes a true story, meticulously documents evidence to suggest that Adams had been framed. Its depiction of why the key witnesses had reason to lie helped to free Adams and provides a useful counter to the popular conception that eyewitness testimony is the most reliable testimony in criminal cases.

By Timothy L. Hall

primary source of wrongful conviction. Anecdotal accounts of such wrongful convictions have been cited by many observers. In 1996 the National Institute of Justice collected cases of people convicted of a crime who had later been conclusively exonerated by DNA evidence. Seventy-five percent of the hundred clearly wrongful convictions studied were based upon mistaken eyewitness identification, which offers systematic proof of the fallibility of eyewitness testimony.

The 1992 Innocence Project (hereafter 'Project') is an attempt to exonerate ' the wrongly convicted through DNA testing' and to bring about reforms in the criminal justice system to prevent further injustice. The Project identifies eyewitness misidentification as the greatest contributor to wrongful convictions which is proven by DNA testing. More than Seventy per cent of the decisions have been overturned, the report says, based on DNA testing.

Encouraged by recommendations from the National Institute of Justice, efforts were begun during the late 1990's to improve the gathering of eyewitness evidence by many police departments. These included the use of open-ended, nonsuggestive interview questions; better constructed lineups, with foils all generally similar to description of the offender; and presenting suspects to the witness in succession, thus avoiding the forced-choice implications of the common simultaneously presented lineup. Police officials were cautioned against reinforcing witness responses and of the importance of remaining noncommittal. Subsequently, in October 2014, the National Academy of Sciences, in a report, identified reforms (promoted by the Project) especially in the area of police practices, which include blind administrators (officer administering line-up is also unaware of who the suspect is thereby preventing statements, gestures or cues influencing the witness); close resemblance of the line-up to the eyewitness's description of the perpetrator; with clear instruction to the person viewing the line-up that the perpetrator may or may not be in the line-up (thereby reducing the pressure on the person to pick a perpetrator); recording the identification procedures whenever possible, etc.

The American system of justice must necessarily rely upon the reports of eyewitnesses. This is not always a problem. In some crimes the offender is well known to the victim. Often major features of a crime are confirmed by concurring witnesses. Yet identification by those who experience a fleeting contact with a criminal-stranger or testimony by those whose memories have been contaminated with distorting suggestions must be viewed with caution. A mandate of forensic science is that of distinguishing valid from flawed eyewitness accounts and establishing procedures for collecting such accounts that ensure their reliability.

Thomas E. DeWolfe
Updated by Tania Sebastian

Further Reading

Doyle, James M., Learning from error in American Criminal Justice, The Journal of Criminal Law & Criminology 100 (2010), 109-148.

'Identifying the Culprit: Assessing Eyewitness Identification', by the Committee on Scientific Approaches to Understanding and Maximizing the Validity and Reliability of Eyewitness Identification in Law Enforcement and the Courts Committee on Science, Technology, and Law Policy and Global Affairs Committee on Law and Justice Division of Behavioral and Social Sciences and Education (The National Academies Press, 2014, Washington D.C.), available at: http://www.innocenceproject.org/wp-content/uploads/2016/02/NAS-Report-ID.pdf

Lang, Angela, "The Role of Memory and Eye Witness Testimony" (2010). Senior Honors Projects I, Paper 181, available at: http://digitalcommons.uri.edu/srhonorsprog/181

Loftus, Elizabeth F. *Eyewitness Testimony.* 2d ed. Cambridge, Mass.: Harvard University Press, 1996. A psychologist discusses research upon conditions influencing the reliability of eyewitness testimony.

Loftus, Elizabeth F. (1979). Eyewitness testimony. Cambridge, MA: Harvard University Press.

Wells, G. L., and Elizabeth F. Loftus. "Eyewitness for People and Events." In *Handbook of Psychology*, edited by A. M. Goldstein and I. B. Weiner. New York: John Wiley Sons, 2003. Outlines factors that affect event memory and result in mistaken identification.

Wells, G. L., and Elizabeth A. Olson. "Eyewitness Testimony." *Annual Review of Psychology* 54 (2003): 277-295. This review discusses cases of convicts cleared by DNA evidence.

Wells, G. L., et al. "From the Lab to the Police Station: A Successful Application of Eyewitness Research." *American Psychologist* 55 (2000): 581-598. Account of the national guidelines for collecting and using eyewitness testimony.

Wrightsman, L. S., E. Greene, M. T. Nietzel, and W. H. Fortune. *Psychology and the Legal System.* Belmont, Calif.: Wadsworth, 2002. Chapter 7 of this textbook reviews the work on conditions that influence the reliability of eyewitness testimony.

Garrett, Brandon L. & Neufeld, Peter J., Invalid Forensic Science Testimony and Wrongful Convictions Virginia Law Review 95(1), (Mar., 2009), pp. 1-97.

See also Circumstantial evidence; Criminal prosecution; Cross-examination; DNA testing; Evidence, rules of; Expert witnesses; False convictions; Forensic psychology; National Institute of Justice; Perjury; Police lineups; Testimony; Trials; Witnesses.

False convictions

Definition: Occasions in which innocent persons are convicted of crimes that they have not committed

Criminal justice issue: Appeals; Convictions; Defendants; Verdicts

Significance: In addition to being grossly unfair to defendants who are erroneously convicted, false convictions damage public confidence in the criminal justice system. Moreover, public safety becomes an issue when convictions of the wrong persons allow guilty criminals to remain at large.

The criminal justice system is designed to protect society by identifying and bringing to justice individuals who have violated the law. Determining guilt or innocence requires the services and expertise of police officials, prosecutors, defense attorneys, judges, and jurors. The system, therefore, contains numerous decision points involving human judgment and, because fallible human beings are involved in the process, errors can sometimes occur which produce a false conviction. False convictions have long been a concern of responsible members of the criminal justice community. In the eighteenth century, British theorist and philosopher Jeremy Bentham, whose ideas influenced the US Constitution and the American criminal justice system, called false convictions "mis-seated punishment." Modern research concerning the causes and frequency of false convictions did not begin until the early twentieth century, when Yale law professor Edwin Borchard published case studies of sixty-five false convictions that occurred in the United States between 1812 and 1930. Borchard's pioneering work was followed, from the 1950s through the early 1980s, by a small number of other publications identifying additional cases.

During the mid-1980s the topic of false convictions began receiving increased attention from both researchers and the popular media—primarily as a result of the unprecedented availability of DNA testing. Because each person's DNA is unique, it has become possible for some prisoners to have old evidence that was used to convict them—evidence such as specimens of blood, hair, tissue, semen, or other body fluids—reexamined in order to determine if the results of earlier, less accurate tests were misleading or faulty. Between 1989—when the first DNA exoneration occurred—and 2004, at least 145 falsely convicted individuals were cleared using DNA testing. Additionally, several hundred other cases of false conviction have come to light using other investigative techniques. Many of these cases have received widespread newspaper and television coverage. According to data from the Innocence Project, an organization formed in 1992 that is dedicated to exonerating people who have been wrongfully convicted through the use of DNA testing, 341 convicted individuals have been exonerated through DNA testing as of 2016. Some of the reasons cited for these false convictions include eyewitness misidentification, false confessions, and unvalidated forensic science. The Innocence Project's data shows that of these cases, 78 percent involved eyewitness misidentification, 28 percent involved false confessions, and 46 percent involved misapplication of forensic science. Due to the concerted effort of organizations such as the Innocence Project, as of early 2016, almost 150 true suspects and perpetrators had been identified.

Amidst the increasing concern over the possible number of innocent people losing several years of their lives in prison, the University of Michigan Law School published the National Registry of Exonerations in 2012, tracking exonerations of the wrongfully convicted beginning in 1989. According to their data, as of 2016, more than 1,700 people had been exonerated of the crimes of which they were convicted. Along with DNA, the factors behind the exonerations included victim recantations, misconduct by authorities, and fabricated crimes. The most exonerations occurred in Illinois, Texas, New York, and California.

Repercussions of False Convictions

False convictions in the criminal justice process carry high personal and social prices. First, they compromise public safety. When a falsely accused person is convicted of a crime, that individual is punished in place of the one who actually committed the offense. Therefore, for virtually every person falsely convicted of a crime, there is a corresponding guilty person who has not been brought to justice and who may be continuing to commit crimes in the community.

False convictions also undermine the public's confidence in the judicial system. Every year, stories are published in the media concerning individuals who have languished in prison for years and are later found to have been falsely convicted. Stories of this nature can shake citizens' faith in the ability of the criminal justice system to separate the innocent from the guilty and to do justice. False convictions can, therefore, damage the symbolic status of the criminal justice process—a process that symbolizes the United States' moral stance against crime and the desire to achieve justice. A loss of confidence in the criminal justice system can have serious and widespread negative consequences. For example, if jurors become skeptical of police testimony or prosecutorial judgment, they are more likely to acquit a guilty individual. A loss of confidence in the criminal justice system can also lead to vigilante-style justice.

Additionally, when an innocent person is falsely convicted, several separate injustices occur. Primarily, the falsely convicted persons unjustly suffer. They are often subjected to the horrors of prison life, are denied freedom (often for several years), and possibly face execution. Death-penalty opponents are quick to point out that individuals falsely convicted of capital crimes may be executed before they can be exonerated. The average time between sentencing and exoneration in false-conviction cases is slightly more than ten years. By contrast, the average time between sentencing and execution of death penalties is also approximately ten years.

The families of the falsely convicted also unjustly suffer when there are separations of husbands from wives, parents from children, and brothers from sisters, as well as possibly substantial losses in income and public shame. Moreover, family members typically exhaust all their available resources when attempting to correct their relatives' false convictions. Other participants in the criminal justice process may also suffer. Often jury members, witnesses, police officers, prosecutors, defense attorneys, and judges are distressed when they discover their actions have contributed to sending innocent persons to prison, or worse, to death row.

Dysfunctions in the Criminal Justice System

False convictions allow researchers opportunities to analyze system dysfunctions. Once victims of false conviction are identified, details of their cases can be examined from the moments when they enter the system until their convictions, in order to determine where the system has failed. For example, analysis of a false conviction case may reveal flawed procedures used by police in the handling of eyewitnesses. Evidence of police or prosecutorial overzealousness or corruption may be exposed. Errors by defense attorneys or forensic experts might be discovered. Knowledge of this kind can be used to improve the criminal justice process through implementation of better procedures and increased training, accountability, and funding. Ultimately, this information should lead to improvements in the criminal justice process that will reduce false convictions and advance the system of justice.

False Convictions and Prison Populations

Estimates of the frequency of false convictions have ranged from as low as 0.5 percent to as high as 20 percent of all criminal convictions. More than two million convicts were incarcerated in U.S. jails and prisons in 2005. Given that number, a false-conviction rate of only 1 percent would mean that more than 20,000 people were incarcerated in 2005 for crimes they did not commit. A 5 percent error rate would mean that false convictions account for 100,000 prisoners, and a rate of 20 percent would mean that more than 400,000 people in jails and prisons did not belong there.

How frequently false convictions occur is unknown. The hidden nature of so many aspects of false convictions creates numerous challenges to researchers attempting to determine the true extent of the problem. In the past, criminal justice professionals tended to believe that false convictions only rarely occurred. Edwin Borchard's 1932 book *Convicting the Innocent* was written in response to a local district attorney who had commented, "Innocent men are never convicted.... It's a physical impossibility." Even as late as the mid-1980's, some members of the criminal justice system were stating that false convictions never occurred. However, such notions have now been largely dispelled because hundreds of individuals have been proved to be victims of false convictions since 1989.

Many researchers believe that the cases revealed so far represent only the "tip of the iceberg." Cases that have been discovered are sometimes the result of modern DNA testing, which is only available in a small percentage of criminal cases in which evidence such as hair, tissue, or body fluids is present. Also, the great majority of false convictions exposed since 1989 have involved only two types of cases: rape—in which DNA testing has unique detection power—and death-penalty cases—in which intense appellate court review is most likely to occur. It is probable that many false convictions involving other types of offenses such as theft, assault, or drug crimes would be uncovered if similar appellate efforts were expended or if powerful tools similar to DNA testing could be used. Of the cases included in the National Registry of Exonerations, only 12 percent were for crimes such as robbery and drug or white-collar crimes; however, many of the exonerations did not involve the use of DNA.

Why False Convictions Occur

Research has isolated many factors associated with false convictions. These factors generally fall into the categories of unintentional error or misconduct. Every major study of false convictions has concluded that unintentional eyewitness error is the primary factor associated with false convictions. Crime witnesses or victims are notoriously unable to provide precise accounts of what they see. Mistaken identification is particularly harmful to innocent defendants because judges and jurors tend to believe the veracity of eyewitnesses' claims over those of accused defendants.

Another type of unintentional error associated with false convictions is the presentation of evidence by prosecution "expert" witnesses that is later found to be misleading or erroneous. Unintentional errors by criminal justice officials often occur because of heavy caseloads. Judges, in order to move cases and relieve heavy dockets, encourage plea bargaining instead of full fact-finding trials. Police and prosecutors, without the time and financial resources necessary to properly process cases, can take part in rushes to judgment that ultimately result in false convictions.

Poorly trained or underprepared defense attorneys also contribute to the incidence of false conviction. Competent counsel can uncover police practices responsible for misidentifications, coerced confessions, or false confessions, and faulty forensic science. Because falsely convicted individuals are usually indigent, even competent attorneys may not have the necessary financial resources or time to investigate and defend their clients' claims of innocence properly. Young offenders and individuals with diminished mental capacity are especially vulnerable to system pressures.

Some of the more unsettling findings in cases of false convictions are incidents of intentional misconduct by police, prosecutors, defense attorneys, and judges. All members of the criminal justice profession are subject to biases, prejudices, and personal ambitions that may affect their judgment and decision making. Police, in order to bolster their cases, have been found to suppress exculpatory evidence or to make unduly suggestive comments to witnesses during pretrial identification procedures.

In some cases, police officers have been found to have planted evidence on innocent people in order to gain convictions. For example, between 1999 and 2000, the Rampart scandal in Los Angeles involved police officers who planted evidence or otherwise framed nearly one hundred suspects. In 2003, a dishonest undercover police officer from Tulia, Texas, was found to have framed thirty-nine innocent people during a drug-operation investigation.

False convictions involving prosecutorial misconduct most often entail the suppression of exculpatory evidence and knowingly using false testimony. When prosecutors have weak cases, they may also elicit testimony from so-called jailhouse snitches, who are willing to testify they overheard other inmates confess to crimes in return for reduced sentences. Several cases of false conviction have occurred because of the use of these snitches.

Although errors can be categorized as unintentional or intentional, the practice of listing cases by a single type of error can be misleading and can present an oversimplification of the dynamics of false conviction. In most cases of false conviction, multiple factors are simultaneously at work.

Robert J. Ramsey

Further Reading
Christianson, Scott. *Innocent: Inside Wrongful Conviction Cases.* New York: New York UP, 2004. Print.
Connors, E., T. Lundregan, N. Miller, and T. McEwen. *Convicted by Juries, Exonerated by Science: Case Studies in the Use of DNA Evidence to Establish Innocence After Trial.* Alexandria: Natl. Inst. of Justice, 1996. Print.
"DNA Exonerations in the United States." *Innocence Project.* Innocence Project, 2016. Web. 27 May 2016.
Gross, S., et al. *Exonerations in the United States: 1989-2003.* New York: Open Soc. Inst., 2004. Print.
Huff, C. R., A. Rattner, and E. Sagarin. *Convicted but Innocent: Wrongful Conviction and Public Policy.* Thousand Oaks: Sage, 1996. Print.
Radelet, Michael L., Hugo A. Bedau, and Constance E. Putnam. *In Spite of Innocence: Erroneous Convictions in Capital Cases.* Boston: Northeastern UP, 1992. Print.
"Researchers: More Than 2,000 False Convictions in Past 23 Years." *NBC News.* NBCNews.com, 21 May 2012. Web. 27 May 2016.
Scheck, Barry, Peter Neufeld, and Jim Dwyer. *Actual Innocence: Five Days to Execution, and Other Dispatches from the Wrongly Convicted.* New York: Random House, 2000. Print.

See also Appellate process; Confessions; Convictions; DNA testing; Double jeopardy; Expert witnesses; Eyewitness testimony; *Habeas corpus*; Justice; Miscarriage of justice; Pardons; Plea bargaining; Police corruption; Police lineups.

Faretta v. California

The Case: U.S. Supreme Court ruling on self-representation
Date: Decided on June 30, 1975
Criminal justice issue: Attorneys; constitutional protections; defendants

Significance: In this case, the Supreme Court ruled that the Sixth Amendment guarantees criminal defendants the right to conduct their own defense.

Charged with grand theft, Anthony Faretta was appointed a public defender at his arraignment. Worried that the public defender's heavy caseload would prevent him from giving his case adequate attention, Faretta asked to represent himself. He had previously represented himself in a case, but his trial judge in this case was hesitant to grant his request. Nevertheless, after cautioning Faretta of the ramifications of waiving counsel, the judge accepted his request. Before the trial began, the judge reviewed Faretta's ability to represent himself by questioning him on jury selection and on the hearsay rule. Not satisfied with Faretta's responses, the judge revoked his earlier decision and appointed a public defender for Faretta.

Faretta was tried and found guilty. Afterward, he appealed his conviction on the basis that he had been denied the right to conduct his own defense. An appellate court upheld the lower court's decision, noting that Faretta had no constitutional right to represent himself, and the Supreme Court of California refused to review the case. Faretta then appealed his case to the U.S. Supreme Court.

The Court decided in Faretta's favor, ruling that the Sixth Amendment's phrase "assistance of counsel" means that defendants are primarily responsible for their own defense. The Court added that counsel must be available to provide aid to receptive defendants. In essence, therefore, the Sixth Amendment confers a right to self-representation. The Court also noted that when defendants "knowingly and intelligently" give up right to counsel after being apprised of the dangers of self-representation, their choices should be noted in the court records. Therefore, in forcing Faretta to accept a state-appointed public defender against his will, the California court deprived him of his constitutional right to conduct his own defense.

The right to counsel is guaranteed in the Sixth Amendment to the U.S. Constitution. Criminal defendants are always reminded of this right when the Miranda warning is read to them. A corollary to this right to counsel, however, is that counsel must be effective. To be certain that lay persons unfamiliar with the intricacies of the law do not jeopardize their cases, even when they are innocent, defendants are encouraged to use the knowledge and skills of professional counsel. Nevertheless, defendants may waive the assistance of counsel and represent themselves in court.

Judges have the responsibility to determine if defendants are capable of acting as their attorneys. They consider several matters in making this determination: Can the defendants communicate effectively in English? Have they enough basic legal knowledge to conduct their defenses without unnecessary interruptions, delays, or the possibility of mistrials or appeals? Defendants who choose to defend themselves cannot afterward complain that they lacked effective counsel.

Victoria M. Time

Further Reading
Acker, J. R., and D. C. Brody. *Criminal Procedure: A Contemporary Perspective.* 2d ed. Sudbury, Mass.: Jones and Bartlett, 2004.
Roberson, C. *Criminal Procedure Today: Issues and Cases.* 2d ed. Upper Saddle River, N.J.: Prentice-Hall, 2003.
Stuckey, G. B., C. Roberson, and H. Wallace. *Procedures in the Justice System.* 7th ed. Upper Saddle River, N.J.: Prentice-Hall, 2004.
Zalman, M. *Criminal Procedure: Constitution and Society.* 3d ed. Upper Saddle River, N.J.: Prentice-Hall, 2002.

See also Counsel, right to; Defendant self-representation; Supreme Court, U.S.

Fines

Definition: Monetary payments required of defendants that provide compensation to either the government or the victim
Criminal justice issue: Punishment; restorative justice; sentencing; white-collar crime
Significance: Fines are popular sanctions that have been used as alternatives to probation and prison. They are also imposed on defendants when restitution is to be made to the victims of the crimes. Fines are not as popular in the United States as in European countries but are commonly used in the United States as punishments for traffic violations and white-collar crimes.

Monetary punishments have a long history in criminal justice, dating back to before ancient Rome. Through succeeding centuries, their use decreased as prisons were used more frequently to punish criminals, and as the belief in the effectiveness of deterrence-based policies. While deterrence policies focus on decreasing the likelihood that convicted criminals will repeat their crimes, fines fulfill the goals of greater efficiency and restitution.

Indeed, fines are currently becoming more popular again in the United States, through the expansion of restitution programs and increasingly critical concern about the budgets of criminal justice correctional programs.

Fines provide a number of cost-effective advantages for criminal justice, while also providing alternatives to overburdened correctional programs, such as incarceration and probation. The financial cost of prison and probation programs have been a source of controversy, and some claim that they can increase the criminal tendencies of nonviolent criminals. By contrast, fines can provide a sense of justice whereby victims and governments are repaid for the offenders' crimes, while sheltering nonviolent offenders themselves from more hardened criminals in the correctional system.

Fines are now most commonly used in the United States for minor offenses and for white-collar crime. This contrasts with their use in Europe, where fines are the preferred method of punishment for most offenses, particularly property crimes. The distinction between Europe and the United States may in part be due to the greater retributive desires of the American populace. Fines are viewed by many in the United States as too lenient to be assessed as punishments for most crimes, and ineffective as deterrents. The use of fines for punishment also generates much controversy because of the disproportionate punitive impact that they have on the rich and the poor.

Brion Sever

Further Reading
Burns, Ronald, and Michael Lynch. "Another Fine Mess...The Preliminary Examination of the Use of Fines by the National Highway Traffic Safety Administration." *Criminal Justice Review* 27 (2002): 1-25.
Raine, John, Eileen Dunstan, and Alan Makie. "Financial Penalties as a Sentence of the Court: Lessons of Policy and Practice from Research Magistrates Courts of England and Wales." *Criminal Justice* 3 (2003): 181-197.
Waldfogel, Joel. "Are Fines and Prison Terms Used Efficiently? Evidence on Federal Fraud Offenders." *Journal of Law and Economics* 38 (1995): 107-139.
Waring, Elin. "Incorporating Co-offending in Sentencing Models: An Analysis of Fines Imposed on Antitrust Offenders." *Journal of Quantitative Criminology* 14 (1996): 283-305.

See also Animal abuse; Color of law; Contempt of court; Drunk driving; Environmental crimes; Jaywalking; Misdemeanors; Punitive damages; Regulatory crime; Sentencing; Traffic fines; Traffic law; Trespass.

Ford v. Wainwright

The Case: U.S. Supreme Court ruling on capital punishment
Date: Decided on June 26, 1986
Criminal justice issue: Capital punishment; defendants; mental disorders
Significance: This case forced the criminal justice system to examine controversies surrounding mental illness and the death penalty, in particular what types of mental conditions should spare condemned prisoners from execution.

On July 19, 1974, Alvin Bernard Ford was convicted of first-degree murder after shooting a Fort Lauderdale police officer in a robbery attempt. Ford was sentenced to death by electric chair in the Florida court system. During his trial and sentencing, Ford appeared to be mentally competent. After his first year of prison, Ford received only one disciplinary report for his behavior. In 1982, his mental condition gradually began to decline, and he started having delusions. For example, Ford thought that his family was being held hostage at the prison and that the Ku Klux Klan had made him a target of conspiracy. Ford's communication skills deteriorated; his writing and speaking became incoherent.

Florida law stipulated that if the governor is informed that a death-row inmate may be insane, a commission of psychiatrists must be appointed to examine the person. The examiners must determine whether the person understands the consequences of the death penalty and why it is being imposed. After a thirty-minute interview, two of the three psychiatrists diagnosed Ford as psychotic, yet all three determined that Ford was competent enough to be executed. Relevant testimony of two psychiatrists who had worked with Ford over time, however, was not included in the fact-finding process. They concluded that Ford was severely psychotic and not competent to be executed. No opportunity was given to other knowledgeable experts to dispute the findings of the state-appointed commission. Based on the commission's results, the governor found Ford to be competent and issued a death warrant for his execution.

Florida's Eleventh Circuit Court of Appeals stayed the execution to hear the issues. The court decided against Ford. The U.S. Supreme Court agreed to hear Ford's appeal. In a 5-4 decision, the Supreme Court overturned the decision of the Florida court and ordered that the case be remanded to federal district court for a full hearing. Justice Thurgood Marshall wrote the majority opinion of the Supreme Court. He concluded that the Eighth Amendment prohibits the states from imposing the death penalty on prisoners who are insane. The court found that Florida's process of evaluating condemned prisoners did not provide adequately for deciding whether Ford was competent to be executed.

Before the federal district court could determine Ford's competency, Alvin Ford died in prison. His death left issues unresolved, such as how competency is defined, what should be done in cases where the inmate wavers between stages of competency and incompetence, whether medication should be used to restore an inmate's mental health before execution, and whether mentally retarded inmates are competent for execution.

Michelle R. Royle

Further Reading
Conley, R., R. Luckasson, and G. N. Bouthilet. *The Criminal Justice System and Mental Retardation: Defendants and Victims*. Baltimore: Brookes, 1992.
Fabrega, H. "Culture and Formulation of Homicide: Two Case Studies." *Psychiatry* 67 (2004): 178-196.
Lewis, Dorothy Otnow. *Guilty by Reason of Insanity: A Psychiatrist Explores the Minds of Killers*. New York: Ivy Books, 1999.
Monahan, J. *Mental Illness and Violent Crime*. Washington, D.C.: U.S. Department of Justice, 1996.
Whitlock, Francis Antony. *Criminal Responsibility and Mental Illness*. London: Butterworths, 1963.

See also Capital punishment; Cruel and unusual punishment; Insanity defense; Supreme Court, U.S.

Furman v. Georgia

The Case: U.S. Supreme Court ruling on capital punishment
Date: Decided on June 29, 1972
Criminal justice issue: Capital punishment; civil rights and liberties; constitutional protections
Significance: Ruling that existing laws for imposing capital punishment were unconstitutional because of their random and unpredictable application, the Court appeared to imply that any capital punishment laws might be found unconstitutional.

William Furman, Lucious Jackson, and Elmer Branch were convicted and sentenced to death in the states of Georgia and Texas. After the three defendants were unsuccessful in their appeals to the supreme courts of the two states, their attorneys appealed to the U.S. Supreme Court, which granted review and consolidated the cases into one decision.

The majority of the Court voted 5 to 4 to strike down Georgia's and Texas's laws for imposing the death penalty, and the effect was to nullify all death-penalty statutes in the United States. With the justices sharply divided, the majority announced the ruling in a short, unsigned *per curiam* opinion, followed by 231 pages of individual opinions by the nine justices. The majority agreed that existing laws allowed judges and juries so much discretion on whether to impose the death sentence that the result was arbitrary, irrational, and contrary to due process of law. Two members of the majority argued in concurring opinions that capital punishment was always unconstitutional, one concurring opinion emphasized the equal protection clause of the Fourteenth Amendment, and two other concurring opinions addressed only the arbitrary, unpredictable application of the penalty.

Justice William Brennan's concurrence presented a vigorous argument for the idea that capital punishment always was "cruel and unusual punishment." Like others of the majority, he quoted statements (called *dicta*) in *Trop v. Dulles* (1958) that the Eighth Amendment draws its meaning "from the evolving standards of decency that mark the progress of a maturing society" and that the amendment prohibited "inhuman treatment." From this perspective Brennan severely criticized capital punishment for four reasons: that it violated human dignity, that it was applied arbitrarily, that its declining use showed that it was increasingly unacceptable to contemporary society, and that it was excessive since it was not more effective than a less severe punishment.

In contrast, Justice William Rehnquist and the other dissenters emphasized that capital punishment was envisioned by the Framers of the Constitution. They argued that it was undemocratic for judicial authority to strike down legislative enactments without being able to point to explicit statements in the Constitution.

Since *Furman* ruled that all existing laws providing for capital punishment were unconstitutional, the decision escalated controversy about capital punishment. Although the decision left the constitutionality of capital punishment unclear, thirty-five states soon enacted new legislation that took the concerns of *Furman* into account. Portions of these laws would later be declared unconstitutional, but in *Gregg v. Georgia* (1976) the majority of the Court would decide that capital punishment is constitutional so long as there are proper procedures and regulations.

Thomas Tandy Lewis

Further Reading

Bohm, Robert M. *Deathquest: An Introduction to the Theory and Practice of Capital Punishment in the United States.* Cincinnati: Anderson Publishing, 2003.

Carter, Linda E., and Ellen Krietzberg. *Understanding Capital Punishment Law.* Newark, N.J.: LexisNexis, 2004.

Latzer, Barry, ed. *Death Penalty Cases: Leading Supreme Court Cases on Capital Punishment.* 2d ed. Burlington, Mass.: Butterworth Heinemann, 2002.

Sarat, Austin. *When the State Kills: Capital Punishment and the American Condition.* Princeton, N.J.: Princeton University Press, 2001.

See also Bill of Rights, U.S.; Capital punishment; *Coker v. Georgia*; Cruel and unusual punishment; *Gregg v. Georgia*; *Tison v. Arizona*; *Witherspoon v. Illinois*; Supreme Court, U.S.

Gag orders

Definition: Declarations by trial judges forbidding everyone involved in trial proceedings from discussing the cases with the media

Criminal justice issue: Judges; legal terms and principles; media; trial procedures

Significance: Gag orders help courts to conduct their business without having information relating to cases be improperly released to the public. Judges implement the orders to protect the actors in the cases from being overwhelmed by the media and to protect the cases themselves from being tainted by false or exaggerated information that finds its way into the news.

Courts and judges impose gag orders during trials to limit the information presented to the public about court proceedings. Such orders are most commonly used in high-profile cases to limit information access by the media to actual court proceedings, case evidence, and testimony. Gag orders also restrict the access of jury members to information about their trials when they are not sequestered.

Gag orders are imposed not only on attorneys and their staffs but also on witnesses and potential witnesses, law-enforcement officers, and any other persons who participate in court proceedings. Orders are imposed to make sure there are no leaks of unauthorized material to the press or public. If only attorneys were under the orders, they might speak with staff members who, in turn, could release information if they were not also covered by the orders. Any person who violates a gag order can be held in contempt of court and punished as a result.

An example of a high-profile case in which a gag order was imposed was the California trial of Scott Peterson for the murder of his wife and her unborn child that concluded with Peterson's conviction in December, 2004. That trial was subjected to saturation media coverage, and the presiding judge in the case imposed a gag order throughout the full duration of Peterson's trial. The order was imposed during the preliminary stages of the trial to protect ongoing investigations and to protect witnesses and others presenting testimony.

Jenephyr James

Further Reading

Chermak, Steven M. *Victims in the News: Crime and the American News Media.* Boulder, Colo.: Westview Press, 1995.

Chiasson, Lloyd, ed. *The Press on Trial: Crimes and Trials as Media Events.* Westport, Conn.: Greenwood Press, 1997.

Surette, Ray. *Media, Crime, and Criminal Justice.* 2d ed. Pacific Grove, Calif.: Brooks/Cole Publishing, 1998.

See also Contempt of court; Judges; Print media; Television news; Trial publicity.

Gideon v. Wainwright

The Case: U.S. Supreme Court ruling on right to counsel
Date: Decided on March 18, 1963
Criminal justice issue: Attorneys; defendants
Significance: The Supreme Court ruled that states must provide legal counsel to poor defendants in criminal trials because the right to counsel guaranteed by the Sixth Amendment applies without reservation to the states.

Prior to this case, considerable confusion existed as to whether the Sixth Amendment's "right to counsel" provision applied to the states as well as to the federal government. In 1932, in the famous "Scottsboro" case of *Powell v. Alabama*, the Supreme Court had stressed the vulnerability of the accused and concluded that their conviction transgressed the fair trial provisions of the Sixth Amendment because they had not benefited from legal representation. That case, however, teemed with qualifying circumstances. The accused were a half dozen young, transient black defendants with little education and, in some instances, with diminished intelligence, who were tried without effective counsel and sentenced to death for raping two white women. Nevertheless, it was believed that the Supreme Court had, in *Powell*, made the right-to-counsel provision of the Sixth Amendment applicable to the states.

This conclusion prevailed for a decade before the Supreme Court explicitly corrected that misunderstanding in *Betts v. Brady* (1942). Stressing the exceptional circumstances involved in the Scottsboro cases, a majority concluded in *Betts* that the right to a fair trial does not require that the criminally accused be represented by an attorney under ordinary circumstances in state proceedings, even in capital cases. Following the *Betts* decision, it was generally supposed that the accused could adequately represent themselves, especially if they had previously witnessed the judicial system at work. Remarkable circumstances such as those of the *Powell* case were an exception to the rule.

Gideon v. Wainwright challenged this assumption. Clarence Gideon fit the *Betts* test. He had been on the wrong side of the bar more than once, and he had actively represented himself in his trial. In accepting the case on appeal, the Supreme Court committed itself to determining whether the concept of a fair trial requires counsel as a general proposition. No other basis existed for deciding the case.

From the outset it appeared that *Gideon* would be a landmark case. Abe Fortas, one of Washington, D.C.'s most celebrated lawyers and later a Supreme Court justice, represented Gideon on a *pro bono* basis. In Fortas's view, Gideon had repeatedly made errors in defending himself that most first-year law students would have avoided. The Supreme Court agreed, overturning *Betts* on the basis of the complex and often confusing nature of judicial proceedings to the ordinary citizen. "The right of one charged with crime to counsel may not be deemed fundamental and essential to fair trials in some countries," Justice Hugo L. Black summarized for the majority, "but it is in ours." Shortly thereafter, the right to counsel was extended to pretrial accusatory proceedings and custodial arrests (*Escobedo v. Illinois*, 1964; *Miranda v. Arizona*, 1966). Meanwhile, in his retrial, with a qualified attorney representing him, Gideon was acquitted of the crime for which he had been previously convicted.

Joseph R. Rudolph, Jr.

Further Reading

Lewis, Anthony. *Gideon's Trumpet.* New York: Vintage Books, 1989.

Reiman, Jeffrey. *The Rich Get Richer and the Poor Get Prison: Ideology, Crime and Criminal Justice.* Boston: Allyn & Bacon, 2004.

Smith, Christopher E. *Courts and the Poor.* Chicago: Nelson-Hall, 1991.

Taylor, John B. *Right to Counsel and Privilege Against Self-Incrimination: Rights and Liberties Under the Law.* Santa Barbara, Calif.: ABC-Clio, 2004.

Tomkovicz, James J. *The Right to the Assistance of Counsel: A Reference Guide to the United States Constitution.* Westport, Conn.: Greenwood Press, 2002.

See also *Argersinger v. Hamlin*; Bill of Rights, U.S.; *Certiorari*; Counsel, right to; Defendant self-representation; Due process of law; Equal protection under the law; *Habeas corpus*; Incorporation doctrine; Public defenders; Supreme Court, U.S.

Grand juries

Definition: Legal bodies formally charged with determining if there is sufficient evidence in criminal investigations to proceed to trials

Criminal justice issue: Investigation; Procedures; Prosecution

Significance: Arrest and arraignment; prosecution; trial procedures

In US criminal proceedings, grand juries, unlike trial juries, do not determine the guilt or innocence of the accused. Rather, they assess whether or not the government has enough evidence to advance to a criminal trial (grand juries do not operate in civil proceedings). In this sense, the grand jury is intended, in the words of the Supreme Court, to "serve as a buffer or referee between the government and the people who are charged with crimes."

The grand jury was imported to America as part of English law and was originally meant to protect the colonies against capricious actions of royalist courts. Grand juries are explicitly recognized in the Fifth Amendment to the US Constitution, which specifies that "no person shall be held to answer for a capital, or otherwise infamous crime, unless on a presentment or indictment of a Grand Jury," although it also lists a limited number of exceptions for those engaged in military or militia service.

Operation and Composition

Grand jury proceedings, which occur as part of the criminal process at both state and federal levels, usually begin when a "bill of indictment," or a written accusation of a crime, is submitted to the jury by a prosecutor. The grand jury then examines the government's case, conducting hearings in which witnesses are called and evidence is presented. Again, in contrast to trial proceedings, these hearings are conducted in secret, the public is excluded from attendance, and the accused has no right to present evidence, although the jury may grant this right. Grand juries operate without the direct supervision of a judge—who still exercises some oversight outside the jury chamber—and proceedings are usually dominated by the prosecution, in part because defense attorneys are generally excluded from participation. Although grand juries are normally formed to assess evidence presented by prosecutors, at times they are constituted as independent investigative bodies, the basic function of which is to determine whether there is enough evidence of a crime to proceed to trial.

Federal grand juries have twenty-three members, while state grand juries vary in size from five to twenty-three members. If a legally specified number of jurors from this group believes that the evidence is sufficient to continue prosecution, the grand jury issues an indictment, also known as a "true bill," to the court with jurisdiction over the case. If a true bill is not returned, the case is dismissed and a no bill or ignoramus" is rendered. At the federal level, twelve jurors are needed to return an indictment or ignoramus; at the state level, the number varies depending on the juries' overall size. In any event, unanimity is not required. By some estimates, grand juries issue indictments 95 percent of the time.

Grand jury members are usually selected at random from voting rolls, although the process varies somewhat at the state level. Grand jurors generally serve for three to eighteen months, although the terms of service can run shorter or longer. Thus, a single grand jury typically reviews a large number of cases.

Powers of the Grand Jury

Witnesses who appear before grand juries possess few procedural rights. Prosecutors are not required to consider or present evidence that might demonstrate the innocence of the accused. In *Williams v. United States* (1992), the US Supreme Court ruled that federal prosecutors need not present evidence favorable to the defense in seeking indictments. Moreover, although the accused may know the names of those testifying before the grand jury, they have no right to confront and cross-examine them. Some evidence inadmissible before trial juries is acceptable in the context of a grand jury inquiry, including hearsay. Those appearing before a grand jury have no right to representation by counsel, although they may request to consult with an attorney outside the grand jury chamber. Some states permit attorneys to be brought into the jury room.

The courts have consistently upheld the broad powers and prerogatives of the grand jury, including the secrecy

Early Federal Grand Jury. (Public domain, via Wikimedia Commons)

of its proceedings and its power to compel witnesses to appear, testify, and provide evidence. However, in *Kastigar v. United States* (1972), the U.S. Supreme Court found that grand juries' power to subpoena witnesses and compel testimony must be balanced against constitutional protections against self-incrimination found in the Fifth Amendment. The Court ruled that compelled testimony and any information or evidence directly derived therefrom cannot be used in subsequent criminal proceedings against the testifying individual—who might still be prosecuted through evidence obtained independently from the grand jury. The Court has consistently avoided insisting that the grand jury is constitutionally required at the state level, making the grand jury provisions of the Fifth Amendment one of the few portions of the Bill of Rights that have not been applied to the states. In *Hurtado v. California* (1884), the Court held that the grand jury protections of the Fifth Amendment need not be extended to the states.

Informations and Presentments

While numerous states authorize the grand jury system, many others use an alternate process known as an "information" to determine whether the prosecution's case should proceed to trial. In an information, a prosecutor provides a written accusation of a crime to the court with the initial authority to hear the case. Usually the prosecution's accusation is initially inspected by a magistrate to ensure its propriety.

On occasion, grand juries go beyond simply determining the sufficiency of the evidence before them by offering "presentments." Although not quite indictments,

Early Federal Grand Jury. (Public domain, via Wikimedia Commons)

presentments draw attention to alleged illegal or corrupt activities. In 1974, for example, a grand jury presentment identified President Richard M. Nixon as an "unindicted coconspirator" for his role in the Watergate scandal.

Grand juries are used in most federal felony prosecutions, although the information is employed in noncapital criminal cases at the district court level and in some civil cases. The state use of grand juries varies widely, with some states employing them optionally and others relegating them to certain classes of investigations, such as in the event of corruption charges against public officials. Grand juries are no longer employed in England; their importance in the US legal system is unique.

The grand jury has been the object of frequent criticism, both from those who find it a cumbersome element of the legal system and from those who consider it a menace to criminal rights and civil liberties in general. The former critics often point to the "information" as a preferable, more efficient procedure for advancing the course of a criminal investigation. Those who object that grand juries have great potential for abuse argue that prosecutors' unbridled authority within the grand jury chamber allows them to intimidate witnesses and cajole jurors, so that the indictment becomes more of a foregone conclusion than an actual check against improper investigations. Defenders of the existing grand jury insist that it serves a critical function in ensuring that the charges against a suspect stem from well-considered evidence rather than from malice, haste, or expedience.

Bruce G. Peabody

Further Reading

Abraham, Henry J. *The Judicial Process: An Introductory Analysis of the Courts of the United States, England, and France.* 7th ed. New York: Oxford UP, 1998. Print.

Clark, Leroy D. *The Grand Jury: The Use and Abuse of Political Power.* New York: Quadrangle, 1975. Print.

del Carmen, Rolando V. *Criminal Procedure: Law and Practice.* 9th ed. Belmont: Wadsworth, 2014. Print.

Diamond, Paul S. *Federal Grand Jury Practice and Procedure.* 5th ed. Huntington: Juris, 2012. Print.

Frankel, Marvin E., and Gary P. Naftalis. *The Grand Jury: An Institution on Trial.* New York: Hill, 1977. Print.

Thomas, Suja A. *The Missing American Jury: Restoring the Fundamental Constitutional Role of the Criminal, Civil, and Grand Juries.* New York: Cambridge UP, 2016. Print.

Younger, Richard D. *The People's Panel: The Grand Jury in the United States, 1634–1941.* Providence: Brown UP, 1963. Print.

See also Criminal procedure; Criminal prosecution; *Hurtado v. California*; Indictment; Information; Jury system; Organized crime; Preliminary hearings; Public prosecutors; Testimony; Trials.

Gregg v. Georgia

The Case: U.S. Supreme Court ruling on capital punishment

Date: Decided on July 2, 1976

Criminal justice issue: Capital punishment; constitutional protections; punishment

Significance: The Court ruled that the death penalty itself was not a cruel and unusual punishment but that procedural safeguards were required to prevent its use in an arbitrary and unpredictable manner.

At the trial stage of bifurcated proceedings, a jury found Troy Gregg guilty of the murder of two men while engaged in armed robbery. In the penalty stage of proceedings, the judge instructed the jury to consider both mitigating and aggravating circumstances and not to impose the death penalty unless it found aggravating circumstances to exist beyond a reasonable doubt. Based on these instructions, the jury returned a verdict of death. The Georgia Supreme Court, which was required by law to review the record, upheld the sentence as not excessive or disproportionate to penalties in similar cases. Gregg and his lawyer then petitioned the U.S. Supreme Court for review.

A few years earlier, in *Furman v. Georgia* (1972), the Supreme Court had ruled that all existing laws allowing capital punishment were in violation of the Eighth Amendment because they failed to prevent arbitrary and unpredictable application. Many observers thought that it would be impossible to devise new laws that would satisfy the concerns expressed in the *Furman* decision, but between 1972 and 1976, thirty-five states, including

Georgia, had passed new statutes authorizing the death penalty. With this background, observers were keenly interested in whether the Court would strike down Georgia's new legislation.

In *Gregg*, the Court voted 7 to 2 to uphold the statutory system under which Troy Gregg had been sentenced. The major idea in Justice Potter Stewart's majority opinion was that capital punishment is not unconstitutional per se. Stewart referred to the historical acceptance of capital punishment in American history and to the fact that the majority of state legislatures had recently indicated that they did not consider the punishment to be cruel and unusual. The death penalty, moreover, appeared to be a "significant deterrent" for some people, and the notion of retribution, while not the dominant goal in criminal law, was not forbidden or inconsistent with the recognition of human dignity. Stewart found that Georgia's laws prevented death from being imposed in an arbitrary or capricious manner, and he specifically endorsed three elements: first, the bifurcated proceedings; second, the judge's instructions to consider the defendant's character and the nature of the circumstances; and third, mandatory review by Georgia's high court to determine whether the death sentence was disproportionate.

Two liberal dissenters on the Court, Justices William Brennan and Thurgood Marshall, argued that capital punishment was always excessive, was not a significant deterrent, and was inconsistent with the concept of human dignity.

The *Gregg* decision indicated that in the foreseeable future the Supreme Court would allow capital punishment, but that its application would be slow, expensive, and rare because of the Court's insistence on procedural safeguards to prevent arbitrary or disproportionate sentencing. *Gregg* appeared to reflect the complex views of a public that was increasingly concerned about the growth of violent crime. By 1991 some twenty-five hundred persons were under sentence of death in the United States, but during that year there were only fourteen executions.

Thomas Tandy Lewis

Further Reading

Bohm, Robert M. *Deathquest: An Introduction to the Theory and Practice of Capital Punishment in the United States.* Cincinnati: Anderson Publishing, 2003.

Carter, Linda E., and Ellen Krietzberg. *Understanding Capital Punishment Law.* Newark, N.J.: LexisNexis, 2004.

Latzer, Barry, ed. *Death Penalty Cases: Leading Supreme Court Cases on Capital Punishment.* 2d ed. Burlington, Mass.: Butterworth Heinemann, 2002.

Sarat, Austin. *When the State Kills: Capital Punishment and the American Condition.* Princeton, N.J.: Princeton University Press, 2001.

See also Bill of Rights, U.S.; Capital punishment; *Coker v. Georgia*; Cruel and unusual punishment; *Furman v. Georgia*; Supreme Court, U.S.; *Tison v. Arizona*; *Witherspoon v. Illinois*

Habeas corpus

Definition: Court order, or writ, to bring a person being detained before a court or judge to determine whether the person's imprisonment is lawful

Criminal justice issue: Appeals; Arrest and arraignment; Habeas corpus; Jurisdiction; Legal terms and priniciples

Significance: Habeas corpus has long been part of the common law to protect people from unlawful imprisonment; the judicial branch of government has authority over the executive police power in this regard. When prisoners' appeals are exhausted, the writ of *habeas corpus* provides an avenue through which they can request reviews of their convictions.

Petitions for writs of *habeas corpus*, also known as the Great Writ, are among the most commonly used proceedings to test the constitutionality of detentions and imprisonments. Habeas corpus is a Latin phrase that translates as "that you have the body." Prisoners or detainees who apply for the writ are usually known as petitioners, and the named respondents are the persons who have legal custody of them. Petitions may be brought either under state law or, if certain conditions have been met, under federal law. Although persons who are being detained pending trials or other proceedings can also petition for the writs, by far the largest category of petitioners includes those who have already been convicted of crimes.

Procedures

The procedures used to petition for state writs of *habeas corpus* vary from state to state and are governed by state statutes and court rules. In the federal system, petitions for writs of *habeas corpus* by state prisoners and detainees cannot be filed until all available remedies under state law have been exhausted. This exhaustion rule is based upon the concept of comity, which requires the courts of one jurisdiction to avoid interfering in the affairs of other jurisdictions unless absolutely necessary.

The exhaustion requirement gives the states the opportunity to address constitutional issues raised by their own prisoners and detainees, perhaps avoiding the need for the federal courts to become involved. Federal writs of *habeas corpus* are further limited by the requirement that federal petitions be filed within one year after convictions, or other actions, become final. This limit was imposed by the Antiterrorism and Effective Death Penalty Act of 1996. Finally, in order to prevent abuse of the writ, there are stringent requirements on the filing of second or successive writs addressing the same issues.

Federal writs of *habeas corpus* are used by detainees and prisoners who claim that their continued detention or imprisonment violates the US Constitution. Errors of state law do not support habeas relief, unless those errors also violate a federal constitutional provision. Detainees usually complain that they are being held without probable cause in violation of the Fourth Amendment, or that they have not been provided with speedy trials, as guaranteed by the Sixth Amendment.

Petitions of convicted prisoners often raise numerous points attacking their state convictions on federal constitutional grounds. However, *habeas corpus* does not constitute an appeal and is governed by different standards from those that govern essentially the same grounds in direct appeals. For example, a state court error-even an error that violates the federal Constitution-will not support relief unless the state court has also acted unreasonably. In other words, the state court must not only be wrong but must also have been unreasonable in reaching its incorrect decision. The federal courts must also presume that a state court's factual findings are correct, unless a prisoner can prove that the findings are incorrect by clear and convincing evidence.

Grounds for Habeas Corpus

The grounds urged by prisoners in federal habeas petitions fall into two general categories. The first contains errors relating to conduct of trials that do not relate to particular constitutional rights. Such trial errors support habeas relief only when they are so grossly prejudicial that they fatally infect the trials and deny the fundamental fairness that is the essence of due process. Federal courts approach such grounds with considerable self-restraint, and it is usually only the most egregious of errors that entitle state prisoners to federal habeas relief.

The second category contains grounds based upon violations of particular constitutional rights, such as the right to effective counsel or the right against self-incrimination. When state prisoners can prove violations of such

John Rosselli (right) checks over a writ of habeas corpus with his lawyer, Frank Desimone, after Rosselli surrendered to the US Marshall. (Public domain, via Wikimedia Commons)

fundamental rights, it is more likely that relief will be granted.

Petitions for *habeas corpus* can also be used by prisoners to attack the execution of their sentences rather than the convictions themselves. In other words, prisoners can use writs to complain that their sentence has not been computed correctly or that their earned sentence credits have been lost. However, just as with petitions attacking convictions, petitions attacking execution of sentences must allege violation of the federal Constitution. Such petitions are usually based upon the due process clause of the Fourteenth Amendment. When petitions are granted, the prisoners are not set free unless corrections of the errors result in enough sentence credits to entitle them to immediate release.

Most petitions for *habeas corpus* in noncapital cases are filed by prisoners *pro se*, that is, without legal representation. Prisons ordinarily provide preprinted forms to be used by prisoners who wish to file petitions for *habeas corpus*. They also provide law libraries for them to do legal research. When a court determines that a hearing should be conducted on a prisoner's petition, counsel is usually appointed to assist the prisoner. However, most petitions are resolved without the need for hearings.

Habeas Corpus and Guantánamo Bay

Since 2008, the issue of the right to the writ of *habeas corpus* for the prisoners held at the US detention facility at Guantánamo Bay, Cuba, has remained controversial.

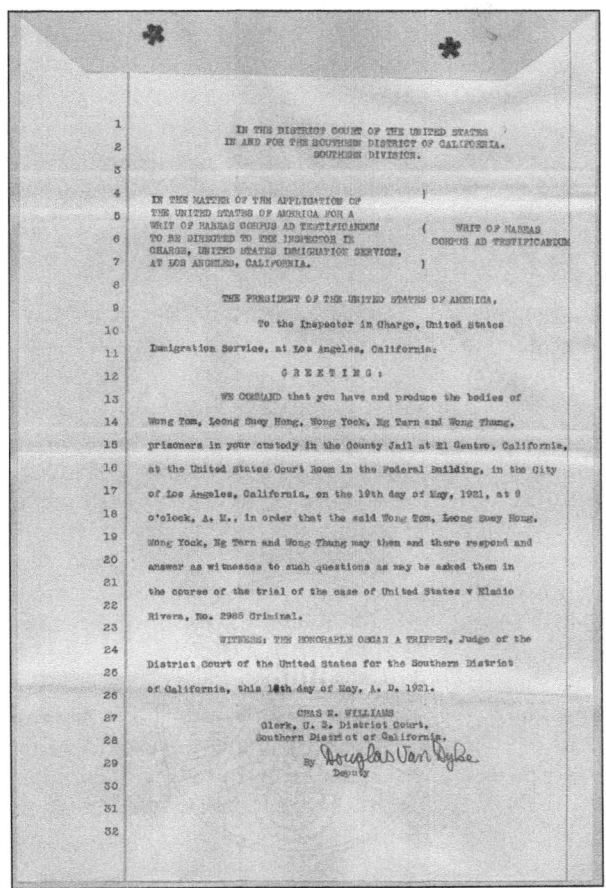

Writ of Habeas Corpus Ad Testificandum. (Public domain, via Wikimedia Commons)

That year, in the case of *Boumediene v. Bush*, the Supreme Court ruled in a 5-4 majority that the inmates at Guantánamo Bay had the right to *habeas corpus* to challenge the legality of their military detention, and that the previous Military Commissions Act of 2006 was unconstitutional. However, as of 2015, it had been noted by the media that since 2010, the Supreme Court had refused the majority of *habeas corpus* petitions submitted by individuals being held at the Cuban detention camp under US jurisdiction.

Sharon K. O'Roke

Further Reading

Barnes, Patricia G. *CQ's Desk Reference on American Criminal Justice: Over Five Hundred Answers to Frequently Asked Questions from Law Enforcement to Corrections.* Chicago: U of Chicago P, 2000. Print.

Hanson, Roger A. *Federal Habeas Corpus Review: Challenging State Court Criminal Convictions.* Washington, DC: US Dept. of Justice, Bureau of Justice Statistics, 1995. Print.

Lewis, Anthony. *Gideon's Trumpet.* New York: Vintage, 1989. Print.

Sacks, Mike. "Supreme Court Declines Guantanamo Bay Cases: It's Been 4 Years of Silence." *Huffington Post.* HuffingtonPost.com, 11 June 2012. Web. 4 Feb. 2015.

Schmalleger, Frank. *Criminal Justice Today: An Introductory Text for the Twenty-first Century.* 8th ed. Upper Saddle River: Pearson, 2005. Print.

See also Antiterrorism and Effective Death Penalty Act; Appellate process; Bill of Rights, U.S.; Certiorari; Cruel and unusual punishment; Defendant self-representation; Effective counsel; False convictions; *Gideon v. Wainwright*; Judicial review; Magna Carta; Mandamus; Martial law; Procedural justice.

Harmelin v. Michigan

The Case: U.S. Supreme Court ruling on mandatory sentences

Date: Decided on June 27, 1991

Criminal justice issue: Punishment; substance abuse

Significance: Upholding a Michigan drug possession law that carried a mandatory term of life imprisonment, the Supreme Court rejected the plaintiff's argument that the sentence was "cruel and unusual punishment" and therefore in violation of the Eighth Amendment.

Under Michigan law, the petitioner, Ronald Allen Harmelin, was convicted of possessing 672 grams of cocaine and sentenced to mandatory life imprisonment because the amount was in excess of the 650-gram threshold specified in the law for imposing the mandatory sentence. The Michigan State Court of Appeals upheld the sentence, rejecting Harmelin's claim that the sentence violated the protection against "cruel and unusual punishment" guaranteed by the Constitution. Harmelin argued that the sentence violated that restriction because it was "disproportionate" to his crime and, further, that because it was mandatory it provided for no "mitigating circumstances" that would allow a judge any latitude in sentencing.

Harmelin's appeal to the U.S. Supreme Court was denied and his sentence upheld. Justice Antonin Scalia delivered the Court's principal opinion. It concluded that because there is no proportionality provision in the Eighth Amendment, a sentence cannot be deemed cruel or unusual on the basis that it is disproportionate to the crime involved. Furthermore, it argued that Harmelin's claim that his mandatory sentence deprived him of his right to a consideration of mitigating circumstances had no precedent in constitutional law. It observed that mandatory penalties, though they could be harsh or extreme, were common enough in the history of the United States and had never been construed as cruel and unusual in the constitutional sense of that phrase. While granting that Harmelin's argument had support in the so-termed individualized capital-sentencing doctrine of the Court's death-penalty legal theory, the majority dismissed Harmelin's claim because of the qualitative difference between execution and all other forms of punishment.

Justice Anthony Kennedy, joined by Justices Sandra Day O'Connor and David Souter, although concurring with the judgment against Harmelin, claimed that the Eighth Amendment's cruel and unusual punishment provision does encompass "a narrow proportionality principle that applies to noncapital sentences." Citing various precedents, these justices argued that the Court, though not clearly or consistently, had previously determined the constitutionality of noncapital punishments based on that principle, although said precedents had taken under review only the length of a punishment's term, not its type.

Having again broached the issue of proportionality, the Supreme Court was likely to face more challenges to mandatory sentencing. From state to state, in statutes imposing mandatory sentences, there is no uniform-sentencing code governing types of punishment or their length. Although in *Harmelin* the Court argued that state legislatures must retain the prerogative of establishing their own penal codes, where there is a wide discrepancy between mandatory penalties imposed for the same crime by one state and another, plaintiffs may seek relief from enforcement of the more severe penalty.

John W. Fiero

Further Reading

Gaines, Larry K., and Peter B. Kraska, eds. *Drugs, Crime, and Justice*. Prospect Heights, Ill.: Waveland Press, 2003.

Tonry, Michael. *Reconsidering Indeterminate and Structured Sentencing*. Washington, D.C.: U.S. Department of Justice, Office of Justice Programs, National Institute of Justice, 1999.

_____. *Sentencing Matters*. New York: Oxford University Press, 1996.

United States Sentencing Commission. *Federal Sentencing Guidelines Manual 2003*. St. Paul, Minn.: West Group, 2004.

See also Cruel and unusual punishment; Drugs and law enforcement; Mandatory sentencing; Punishment; *Rummel v. Estelle*; Supreme Court, U.S.

Harmless error

Definition: Legal mistake made during the course of a defendant's progress through the justice system that is not considered to be damaging to the defendant's case

Criminal justice issue: Appeals; convictions; legal terms and principles; prosecution

Significance: The principle of harmless error holds that mistakes made by prosecutors should not be the basis of reversing trial results on appeal, if those mistakes do not significantly alter court proceedings or outcomes or substantially violate the constitutional rights of the parties.

If a legal mistake, or error, is made during a trial, the results of the trial often may be reversed on appeal. For example, a conviction may be overturned by an appellate court for such a prosecutorial error as admitting illegally seized evidence into trial. However, if the error is a minor mistake that can be proven beyond a reasonable doubt not to influence the outcome of the trial or create prejudice against the defendant, the error may be considered "harmless," and the trial result will be allowed stand. The principle of harmless error prevents appellate courts from overturning judicial decisions for unimportant courtroom mistakes.

During the early twentieth century, convictions were sometimes reversed for errors as trivial as omitting the word "the" from "peace and dignity of the state" at the end of an indictment. Recognizing the need for "harmless error," the U.S. Congress began including it in legislation in 1911. In 1948, harmless error was added to procedural law.

Jennifer C. Gibbs

Further Reading

Garner, Bryan A., ed. *Black's Law Dictionary*. 8th ed. St. Paul, Minn.: Thomson/West, 2004.

"Harmless Constitutional Error: A Reappraisal." *Harvard Law Review* 83, no. 4 (February, 1970).

See also Appellate process; *Arizona v. Fulminante*; Attorney ethics; Case law; Criminal procedure; Criminal prosecution; Exclusionary rule; Judicial review; Reversible error; Search and seizure.

Hearings

Definition: Formal meetings used for inquiries, examinations, and determinations of issues arising within legal actions

Criminal justice issue: Investigation; trial procedures

Significance: Hearings often play important roles in deciding procedural and substantive issues before legal actions go to trial.

Hearings are formal or quasi-formal proceedings used by courts, legislatures, administrative agencies, and government departments to address specific issues. Judicial hearings normally focus an individual issues, or groups of issues, arising from larger cases. Hearings may be used as procedural tools to guarantee that due process rights are being protected. Examples of common hearings held in criminal cases include arraignments, which are used to enter initial pleas, review bail, and protect due process rights; preliminary hearings, in which probable cause in felony cases is examined; and motion hearings, in which procedural and substantive legal issues are considered.

As a rule, hearings before a court require the attendance of all parties to the cases. In most hearings, every party has a right to be heard regarding the issues at hand. An *ex parte* hearing is one in which only one party to a case is present. Such hearings are generally reserved to matters of an emergency nature, when notice and opportunity to be heard cannot reasonably be given to all parties.

Some hearings, such as preliminary hearings, may also require the attendance and testimony of witnesses and the presentation of evidence. Other hearings focus on legal questions only and typically provide the parties or their attorneys opportunities to address the courts on specific issues. In the most formal hearings, court reporters or other court officers preserve records of the matters discussed. In less formal hearings, no recording is done and the only record is the order entered by the judge following the hearing.

In criminal matters the most common hearings are preliminary hearings, in which questions of probable cause are examined by courts. Other hearing types include hearings on motions, evidence, and arraignment. Hearings *in camera* are held in the privacy of judges' chambers or anterooms, outside the normal confines of courtrooms.

Hearings are also used by legislative bodies to make inquiries into factual or legal issues of interest to the legislature. Such hearings are commonly conducted by committees or subcommittees of the entire legislature. In many instances, the legislative bodies or committees may possess the power of subpoena to compel witnesses to appear and testify. Such power affords legislative bodies the authority to investigate, normally a government action reserved to the executive branch, and to make inquiries into matters affecting legislation.

Government administrative agencies also use hearings as quasi-judicial exercises of their power. Such agencies are generally afforded this power through the legislation that creates them, and the purposes of such hearings are to take enforcement, corrective, or investigative action into matters arising under the agencies' authority. A common example can be found in many cases arising from charges of driving under the influence. The criminal charges are handled by the courts, but the question of how such crimes affect the offenders' driving privileges is normally handled through the administrative procedures of state driver's license bureaus.

Carl J. Franklin

Further Reading
Acker, J. R., and D. C. Brody. *Criminal Procedure: A Contemporary Perspective.* 2d ed. Sudbury, Mass.: Jones and Bartlett, 2004.
LaFave, Wayne R., Jerold H. Israel, and Nancy J. King. *Criminal Procedure.* 4th ed. St. Paul, Minn.: Thomson/West, 2004.

See also Arraignment; Criminal procedure; Inquests; Parole; Preliminary hearings; Testimony; Witnesses.

Hung juries

Definition: Juries that are unable to reach innocent or guilty verdicts by the required voting margin
Criminal justice issue: Juries; Trial procedures; Verdicts
Significance: The controversy over the phenomenon of hung juries has been the catalyst for empirical research and jury reform.

The occurrence of hung juries within the criminal justice system has long been a controversial and intriguing phenomenon. Hung juries have remained an issue of concern over time because of their potential negative consequences, which include the emotional impact on the victims and families and the costs of retrying cases. There are many explanations as to why jury members fail to convict or acquit a defendant. A hung jury may be the result of individual, group, or evidentiary factors. Many critics of the jury system propose that hung juries result from failures within the group interaction during deliberation. Hung juries have been attributed to jurors' poor intelligence, personality eccentricities, corruption, difficulty with evidence comprehension, and outright refusal to follow the law (such as jury nullification). In addition, ambiguous or inadequate evidence presentation by the attorneys may also result in a jury deadlocking.

Understanding the actual factors contributing to hung juries is challenging. For example, many jurisdictions do not maintain systematic records of jury trials that hang because they occur so infrequently. More specifically, jury deliberations have long been viewed as a "black box" demanding absolute confidentiality. As a result, early research on juries, and more specifically on hung juries, was scarce before the mid-1970s. Groundbreaking and early empirical research was conducted on the American jury by Harry Kalven, Jr. and Hans Zeisel. Their study briefly addressed the issue of hung juries and found that hung juries occurred at a rate of 5.5 percent, or roughly one in twenty.

The catalyst for empirical research on the jury system and hung juries was the U.S. Supreme Court decision in *Apodaca v. Oregon* (1972). In *Apodaca*, the Supreme Court decided unanimous verdicts were not constitutionally mandated in noncapital cases and that a majority vote by jurors could convict or acquit a defendant. The Court's reasoning was that allowing majority-rule verdicts would increase the efficiency of the court process and decrease the cost of a jury trial, with little or no negative consequences on the quality of jury deliberations.

Subsequent research confirmed that the rate of hung juries and the length of jury deliberations decreased when majority-rule verdicts were used. However, empirical research also revealed that nonunanimous verdicts decreased the quality of deliberation and decreased juror satisfaction with the deliberation process. For example, once a majority verdict was met, the minority or dissenting opinions no longer needed to be considered.

Erin J. Farley

Further Reading
Abramson, Jeffery. *We, the Jury: The Jury System and the Ideal of Democracy*. Cambridge: Harvard UP, 1994. Print.
Hannaford-Agor, Paula L., Valerie P. Hans, Nicole L. Mott, and G. Thomas Munsterman. *Are Hung Juries a Problem?* Williamsburg: National Center for State Courts, 2002. Print.
Kalven, Harry, and Hans Zeisel. *The American Jury*. Boston: Little, Brown, 1966. Print.

See also Dismissals; Jury nullification; Jury sequestration; Jury system; Trials.

Immunity from prosecution

Definition: Legally binding promise not to prosecute a potential defendant, typically offered in exchange for testimony

Criminal justice issue: Defendants; immunity; trial procedures

Significance: Offering immunity from prosecution permits the government to compel testimony that might otherwise be blocked by the Fifth Amendment right against self-incrimination.

A successful prosecution sometimes depends upon testimony by an accomplice of the accused. This is particularly true for crimes that lack witnesses external to the criminal enterprise, such as a specific victim or a third-party observer. These crimes include conspiracy, bribery, white-collar crimes such as securities fraud, or organized crimes involving the distribution of forbidden goods or services such as drugs or prostitution. Although testimony can ordinarily be compelled, that of an accomplice, who is also guilty of criminal activity, is shielded by the self-incrimination clause of the Fifth Amendment to the U.S. Constitution.

To circumvent this impediment, prosecutors offer a binding promise of nonprosecution in exchange for the testimony. Because prosecution is now foreclosed, witnesses' interests in not being turned into the tool of their own legal undoing are adequately satisfied. Even if witnesses deem the bargain a bad one, they may not refuse the immunity, and testimony may now be required before any compulsory forum, including grand juries, trials, or legislative investigations.

"Transactional immunity" offers complete protection from prosecution on any matter related to the testimony given. The more limited "use immunity" bans future prosecution based upon the witness's testimony or on leads developed as a result of the testimony but does not bar prosecution based upon evidence acquired wholly independently of the witness's testimony. The latter, as an equivalent for the right against self-incrimination, was upheld by the U.S. Supreme Court in 1972, in *Kastigar v. United States*.

John C. Hughes

Further Reading
Amar, Akhil Reed. *The Constitution and Criminal Procedure*. New Haven, Conn.: Yale University Press, 1997.
Taylor, John B. *Right to Counsel and Privilege Against Self-Incrimination*. Santa Barbara, Calif.: ABC-Clio, 2004.

See also Amnesty; Conspiracy; Criminal liability; Diplomatic immunity; Police civil liability; Self-incrimination, privilege against; Witness protection programs.

Impeachment of judges

Definition: Procedure for removing from office judges who engage in serious misconduct

Criminal justice issue: Government misconduct; judges

Significance: Impeachment of federal officials is uncommon. Most impeachment proceedings against federal officials have been against judges, but even these are relatively rare.

The closing years of the twentieth century witnessed the impeachment of three federal judges: Harry Claiborne, Alcee Hastings, and Walter Nixon. Frequently, but not inevitably, judicial impeachment follows a criminal conviction for some offense. Judge Claiborne was impeached during the 1980's after being convicted of tax fraud, and Judge Nixon was impeached after his conviction for perjury. Judge Hastings, on the other hand, was acquitted of criminal charges but was subsequently impeached by the Senate.

One might imagine that impeachment proceedings would be unnecessary in cases in which judges have been convicted of criminal violations. In fact, judges so convicted frequently resign and thus escape the further indignity of impeachment. However, such resignations are not inevitable and certainly not always quickly accomplished. Federal judge Robert Collins was imprisoned in 1991 but continued to draw his annual salary until his resignation in August, 1993. Harry Claiborne, unwilling to consider resignation, drew his judicial salary for two years while he served a prison term in the 1980's, until Congress finally impeached him.

Attempts to impeach judges have not been reserved simply for the rank and file of the judiciary. Even judicial luminaries, such as Supreme Court justices, have sometimes had to endure the stern gaze of a Congress willing to consider their impeachment. In 1805, for example, Justice Samuel Chase faced impeachment proceedings against him but ultimately prevailed, causing Thomas Jefferson to grouse that the prospect of impeachment was "not even a scarecrow." In the twentieth century, Justice William O. Douglas had to fend off impeachment charges led by then-House minority leader Gerald R. Ford. Douglas was ultimately vindicated when the House Judiciary committee refused to recommend impeachment articles to the House.

Timothy L. Hall

Further Reading
Black, Charles Lund, Jr. *Impeachment: A Handbook*. New Haven: Yale University Press, 1998.
Kuo, M. E., ed. *Impeachment: An Overview of Constitutional Procedures and Practices*. New York: Nova Science Publishers, 2003.
Trial of Samuel Chase, an Associate Justice of the Supreme Court of the United States, Impeached by the House of Representatives for High Crimes and Misdemeanors Before the Senate of the United States. Reprint. 2 vols. New York: Da Capo Press, 1970.

See also Judges; Political corruption; Supreme Court, U.S.

Newspaper illustration of Chief Justice Salmon Chase (right) being sworn in before testifying at his own impeachment trial. (Library of Congress)

In forma pauperis

Definition: Latin phrase, meaning "as a poor pauper," that is applied to legal matters involving poor persons

Criminal justice issue: Defendants; legal terms and principles

Significance: The legal principle of *in forma pauperis* allows poor defendants to file motions or complaints in courts without cost. The purpose of this provision is to make courts accessible to all citizens, regardless of their means.

When a person seeking help from a court cannot afford to pay the standard fees, the costs are covered by the state or federal government. In such cases, the normal costs are waived by the court, which might also provide an indigent person assistance of an attorney. *In forma pauperis* petitions are available at both the state and federal levels. *In forma pauperis* filings are generally considered to be confidential. When trial courts accept them, the applicants' eligibility for relief continues through any appellate proceedings that follow the initial court actions.

Eligibility for *in forma pauperis* help is based on income, and the standards may vary widely. However, in most states, persons receiving public assistance or using food stamps are generally eligible to file *in forma pauperis*. The principle also applies to state and federal prisoners who are without resources.

The best-known *in forma pauperis* criminal case was the U.S. Supreme Court's *Gideon v. Wainwright* ruling in 1963. The case originated when Clarence Gideon was tried for burglary. He asked for an attorney at his trial but was denied and was eventually convicted. While in prison, he filed an appeal with the U.S. Supreme Court, arguing that he had been denied his Sixth Amendment right to an attorney. The Court accepted his *in forma pauperis* petition and heard the matter. In a 9-0 vote, the justices agreed with Gideon and reversed his conviction. The Court stated that the issue Gideon's case raised was of such broad significance that it made its ruling retroactive—something virtually unheard of.

Lawrence C. Trostle

Further Reading
Galloway, Russell W. *Justice for All? The Rich and Poor in Supreme Court History, 1790-1990*. 2d ed. Charleston, N.C.: Carolina Academic Press, 1991.
Lewis, Anthony. *Gideon's Trumpet*. New York: Vintage Books, 1989.
Reiman, Jeffrey. *The Rich Get Richer and the Poor Get Prison: Ideology, Class, and Criminal Justice*. 7th ed. Boston: Allyn & Bacon, 2004.

See also *Argersinger v. Hamlin*; *Certiorari*; Counsel, right to; Equal protection under the law; *Gideon v. Wainwright*; *Miranda v. Arizona*; Public defenders.

Indeterminate sentencing

Definition: System of awarding prison sentences whose terms are defined by minimum and maximum lengths
Criminal justice issue: Punishment; Sentencing

Significance: Federal and most state courts no longer use the once-universal system of awarding prison terms of indeterminate length, a change that has reduced the role of discretion in all parts of the criminal justice system.

As recently as the mid-1970s, the judicial systems of every US state, the District of Columbia, and the federal government had indeterminate sentencing systems. Under those systems, legislature set statutory maximums on authorized prison sentences. When awarding sentences, judges could choose between prison, probation, and fines and could set maximum prison terms. Corrections officials could determine good time and early releases, and parole boards could set release dates. Virtually all those decisions were free from appellate review. By 2004, most states and the federal government had switched to a system of structured sentencing.

Indeterminate sentencing takes its name from the fact that at the time convicted offenders are sentenced, they do not know exactly how long they will be in prison or under supervision. Under such a system, the sentences that judges award to offenders are defined by ranges of years, usually divided into "low" and "upper" ranges. In most systems, offenders are required to serve at least 100 percent of their low range and not more than 100 percent of their upper range.

The goal of indeterminate sentencing was to allow sentencing decisions to be based on the individual characteristics of the cases and offenders. At every stage of the sentencing and corrections process, officials had the authority to tailor punishments and treatments to the needs of individual offenders. By the mid-1970s, indeterminate sentencing systems were beginning to erode. Civil and prisoner rights activists claimed that the broad discretion afforded by indeterminate sentencing systems produced arbitrary and unpredictable decisions that were often racially biased. Opponents of indeterminate sentencing also claimed that standardless discretion denied offenders constitutional due process of law.

Critics have also claimed that indeterminate sentencing removed links between the seriousness of crimes and the sentences that were awarded. They argued that offenders should receive specific punishments for specific crimes so that nothing depreciates the seriousness of the crimes. Another criticism is that indeterminate sentencing allows judges and other officials involved in sentencing decisions to negate public perceptions and views of punishments.

There are many arguments in support of indeterminate sentencing as well. One argument is exactly the reverse of the argument that the indeterminate process insulates the public from the punishment process. Proponents of indeterminate sentencing argue that leaving punishment decisions to criminal justice experts, such as judges, rather than to legislatures is more likely to result in rehabilitation of the offenders.

Proponents would also argue that indeterminate sentencing does a better job of taking into account rehabilitation and public safety goals than do determinate sentencing systems. At the heart of indeterminate sentencing is the idea that humans are malleable and redeemable and that if they are given the opportunity to better themselves in exchange for earlier release dates, they will reform. Indeterminate sentencing allows judges and correctional officials, professionals who routinely work with offenders, to determine the risk factors and recommend release dates and plans. By giving professionals who know the individual offenders the opportunity to determine their release date, public safety concerns are given top priority.

Jennifer R. Albright

Further Reading

Branham, Lynn S. *The Law and Policy of Sentencing and Corrections in a Nutshell*. 9th ed. St. Paul: West, 2013. Print.

Tonry, Michael. *Reconsidering Indeterminate and Structured Sentencing*. Washington: Dept. of Justice, Office of Justice Programs, Natl. Inst. of Justice, 1999. Sentencing & Corrections: Issues for the 21st Century. *National Criminal Justice Reference Service*. Web. 26 May 2016.

Tonry, Michael, and Richard S. Frase, eds. *Sentencing and Sanctions in Western Countries*. New York: Oxford UP, 2001. Print.

Ulmer, Jeffery T. *Social Worlds of Sentencing: Court Communities under Sentencing Guidelines*. Albany: State U of New York P, 1997. Print.

See also Blended sentences; Concurrent sentences; Good time; Just deserts; Mandatory sentencing; Presentence investigations; Rehabilitation; Sentencing; Sentencing guidelines, U.S.; Medical model of offender treatment; Parole boards.

Indictment

Definition: Formal criminal charges issued by grand juries

Criminal justice issue: Pleas; prosecution; trial procedures

Significance: American federal law and the laws of many states provide that no one may be held for trial for a crime without being indicted by a grand jury.

In some states, a defendant may be bound over for trial by a judge after a preliminary hearing without being indicted by a grand jury. The purpose of indictments is to prevent arbitrary arrest. Before arrests are made (except in a few cases of hot pursuit), impartial grand juries must secretly consider the evidence and decide whether an arrest would be justified. The indictment requirement grew out of the tendency of English officials, including the English Parliament itself, to simply arrest persons they did not like.

An indictment by a grand jury does not mean that a person is guilty. It means only that the grand jury finds compelling evidence of two things: that a crime has been committed and that there is good reason to believe that the defendant in question might have committed the crime. A regular trial before a jury or a judge, a plea of guilty, or a decision to dismiss the case must follow before the action is complete. Indictments may be sealed and opened at a later date, such as when an arrest is made.

Indictments by grand juries are not required by the U.S. Constitution in state criminal justice systems, although many states use them. The U.S. Supreme Court so ruled in the 1884 case of *Hurtado v. California*. In that case, the Court said that whatever procedure is used must afford the defendant as much protection as was provided under the old common law of England. In English common law, informations rather than indictments were used. Informations are accusations by a public official that an individual has committed a crime. The common law is no longer used as justification, but "settled usage" is, and information is "settled usage." In 1937, Justice Benjamin Cardozo wrote that the Bill of Rights injunction to use indictments at the federal level was not extended to the states by the Fourteenth Amendment as many sections of the Bill of Rights were, because the Fourteenth Amendment extended only those portions of the Bill of Rights that "are of the very essence of a scheme of ordered liberty," such as freedom of speech. Cardozo wrote that the right to indictment by a grand jury is not of that nature.

Therefore, states may and often do use informations rather than indictments to bring persons to court, and in many states it is customary for a judge at a preliminary hearing, rather than for a grand jury, to determine whether a crime has been committed and whether the defendant ought to be summoned to a trial for that crime.

Dwight Jensen

Further Reading
Abraham, Henry J. *The Judicial Process*. 6th ed. New York: Oxford University Press, 1993.
Del Carmen, Rolando V. *Criminal Procedure: Law and Practice*. 6th ed. Belmont, Calif.: Thomson/Wadsworth, 2004.
Frankel, Marvin E., and Gary P. Naftalis. *The Grand Jury: An Institution on Trial*. New York: Hill & Wang, 1977.
Garcia, Alfredo. *The Fifth Amendment: A Comprehensive Approach*. Westport, Conn.: Greenwood Press, 2002.
Neubauer, David W. *America's Courts and the Criminal Justice System*. 8th ed. Belmont, Calif.: Wadsworth/Thomson Learning, 2005.

See also Bill of particulars; Criminal prosecution; Defendants; Grand juries; *Hurtado v. California*; Information; Judges; Jury system; Misdemeanors; Public prosecutors; Speedy trial right; Trials.

Inquests

Definition: Formal government inquiries into legal matters, particularly homicides
Criminal justice issue: Homicide; investigation; medical and health issues
Significance: Inquests are used as judicial inquiries or official examinations to gather evidence before trials begin.

The purpose of a legal inquest is to obtain information to determine whether a crime has been committed or not. Inquests are solely investigatory and are most commonly used in murder cases. During the inquests, judges oversee all judicial procedures related to the cases in question before actual trial dates are set. In state courts, assistant district attorneys represent the government and present all evidence having any legal bearing on the cases.

All forms of evidence gathered during inquests help determine whether criminal charges should be filed. The evidence gathered is then presented to the courts under sworn testimony. This includes any physical evidence, such as firearms or other weapons that might be involved with the alleged crimes. At this time, witness testimony is also presented to the courts under oath. Results of any autopsies completed by county coroners are also presented, as well as results of any ballistic testing and any other medical tests relevant to the cases.

Inquest hearings themselves are closed to both the public and the media. Only persons having personal interests in the outcomes of the cases may attend the initial hearings. These people may include legal representation of any suspects under investigation. After an inquest is completed, the presiding judge forwards all the evidence submitted to the relevant court, which is likely to be a superior court. At that time, evidence gathered through the inquest is accessible only to attorneys general, district attorneys, and defendant counsel.

After reviewing all information on a case, a district attorney or an attorney general decides whether charges should be filed. If no charges are found and it is determined that there will be no criminal trial, the information and evidence gathered by the inquest are opened to the public. After an open finding is reported to the public, an inquest can be reopened if new evidence is presented to the coroner.

The most common types of inquest are medical examinations into the causes of suspicious deaths. County coroners normally perform these duties. The requirements for qualified coroners are vast and vary from jurisdiction to jurisdiction. However, most jurisdictions require their coroners to have legal training. Other examples of inquests include inquiries into environmental disasters and cases of severe corruption resulting in possible impeachment or incarceration.

Emily I. Troshynski

Further Reading
Blanche, Tony, and Brad Schreiber. *Death in Paradise: An Illustrated History of the Los Angeles County Department of Coroner*. New York: Four Walls Eight Windows, 2001.
Schneir, Walter, and Miriam Schneir. *Invitation to an Inquest*. New York: Pantheon, 1983.

See also Autopsies; Coroners; Grand juries; Preliminary hearings; Trial publicity; Trials; Verdicts.

Jessica's Law/Jessica Lunsford Act (2005)

Definition: The Jessica Lunsford Act of 2005, also known as Jessica's Law, was named after a nine-year-old girl who was abducted and murdered by a convicted sex offender (John Evander Couey) in Florida. The law mandates a minimum sentence of twenty-five years in prison and lifetime electronic monitoring for adults who have been convicted for certain sex crimes against children less than twelve years old.

Criminal justice issue: Criminal justice issues: Sex offenses; sentencing; punishment; victims

Significance: After Florida passed the Jessica Lunsford Act in 2005, many states adopted their own version of the law, which was designed to prevent the recidivism of convicted sex offenders by increasing the penalty, monitoring offenders via an electronic device, and/or restricting their residency.

The Jessica Lunsford Act, which was signed by Florida Governor Jeb Bush in 2005, was named after a nine-year-old girl who was abducted and murdered by a convicted sex offender in Florida. In responding to the fact that Jessica's killer had a lenient sentence for his previous sex crime, the act aims to protect young children from sexual offenders by revising sexual predator criteria and sentencing, and enforcing stricter scrutiny for sex offenders under supervision. The main components of the Act are a mandatory minimum sentence of twenty-five years in prison and lifetime electronic monitoring (LEM) for adult offenders who have been convicted of lewd, unchaste, or licentious acts against a victim less than twelve years old. Furthermore, the sexual battery or the rape of a child less than twelve years old is punishable by life imprisonment with no chance of parole.

Other states quickly followed Florida and have enacted similar reform acts, which have been referred to as "Jessica's Law." Currently, more than forty states have some form of a Jessica's Law. For example, in California, with the overwhelming support of the voters, Proposition 83, also known as Jessica's Law, was approved in 2006 to increase the legal penalties for sex offenses, require LEM for felony registered sex offenders, and prohibit registered sex offenders from residing within 2,000 feet of any school or park. Similarly, Ohio Senate Bill 260, which is the Ohio version of Jessica's Law, imposed a mandatory prison sentence of fifteen to twenty-five years for gross sexual imposition with a minor and intensified monitoring of sex offenders after their release. Most recently, New Jersey, which was among the few states that did not have a Jessica's Law, finally enacted a law in 2014 that increased penalties for those convicted of aggravated sexual assault of a child under thirteen years old. A federal version of the Jessica Lunsford Act was proposed to Congress in 2005 but was not enacted.

Unintended Consequences

The proponents of Jessica's Law argue that increasing the penalties and strengthening the supervision for those who commit sexual offenses would prevent offenders from committing other crimes and protect children whom they might victimize. Furthermore, the citizens would feel more secure and safe by knowing that those offenders are free from where children regularly gather such as parks and schools.

However, the deterrence effects of Jessica's Law are not well-supported by research-based evidence. A 2004 study of resident restrictions of sexual offenders in Colorado found that residential restrictions of supervised sex offenders did not deter the sex offender from reoffending. Similarly, a study conducted by the Minnesota Department of Corrections in 2003 that tracked the most serious sex offenders who were released in Minnesota between 1997 and 1999, found that none of those who were rearrested for committing new sex offenses resided in close proximity to schools or parks at the time of their arrests.

Some research suggests that residency restrictions actually led to serious unintended collateral consequences for offenders. According to a task force report in 2010 by the California Department of Corrections, many offenders are now homeless due to residency restrictions, and such an unstable living arrangement makes them more prone to recidivate. Also, a report in Minnesota showed that residency restrictions forced them to move to rural remote areas where they are likely to become increasingly isolated with few employment opportunities, a lack of social support, and limited availability of medical treatment, counseling, and other rehabilitative social services.

After numerous legal challenges to the constitutionality of part of the law, California decided to alter the blanket residency restrictions and impose the residence restriction only on pedophiles and others whose sex crimes involved children. The Iowa legislators revised the law after determining the housing restriction was unenforceable. Nonetheless, Jessica's Law has enjoyed enormous support from the public in its goal to protect young children from horrific sexual predators given the continuing memory of Jessica Lunsford.

Yoshiko Takahashi

Further Reading
Dierenfeldt, R., and J. Carson."Examining the Influence of Jessica's Law on Reported Forcible Rape: A Time-Series Analysis." *Criminal Justice Policy Review*. 2014. doi:10.1177/0887403414563139.

Griffin, T., and J. Wooldredge. "Judges' Reactions to Ohio's "Jessica's Llaw." *Crime & Delinquency* 59, no. 6 (2013): 861-85.

Hautala, L. "State High Court Strikes at Jessica's Law in San Diego," 128, no. 41 (2015): 3.

Hamilton, A., and A. Moines. "Banning the Bad Guys: Nobody Wants a Pedophile Living Next Door: But Will New Residency Restrictions for Sex Offenders Really Make Kids Safer?" *Time* 166, no. 10 (2005): 72.

Minnesota Department of Corrections. *Level Three Sex Offenders Residential Placement Issues 2003 Report to the Legislature*. https://ccoso.org/sites/default/files/MNresidencerestrictions.pdf.

Zucker, B. "Jessica's Law Residency Restrictions in California: The Current State of the law." *Golden Gate University Law Review* 44, no. 2 (2014): 101.

See also Victims of Crime Act, Victimology, Crime victimization: primary and secondary, and Victims of Trafficking Act (2014).

Judges

Definition: Appointed and elected public officials who are charged with authoritatively and impartially resolving disputes presented in courts of law

Criminal justice issue: Jurisdictions; Judges; Professional standards; Verdicts

Significance: Judges play a critical role in the criminal justice system, both as authoritative managers of courtroom proceedings and often as the impartial arbiters of facts, guilt, and sentences. Judges are therefore expected to possess a number of valuable qualities that equip them to meet the high standards and demanding tasks of their office.

The United States tends to employ what is known as an adversary system in courtrooms, which means that the parties in legal disputes are expected to present their cases in their own best interests. In such settings, judges are not expected to assist either side to make its case or even to seek out evidence and facts. Instead, it is expected that such evidence will be made available by the parties either through deliberately presenting pertinent facts or through cross-examination. The judge's role thus becomes one of enforcing the rules and ensuring that a fair trial takes place. Some describe this role as akin to that of a referee enforcing the rules of a game. However, the judge's role typically goes beyond the tasks implied by this analogy.

The complexities of US law, coupled with the sometimes tense emotions and deliberate deceptions in the courtroom, can conspire to make the judge's task of ensuring a fair trial extremely difficult. The judge can be expected to exercise an almost superhuman combination of wisdom, compassion, logic, circumspection, integrity, and objectivity. While they may fall short of this ideal, judges typically are better trained and more disciplined than the general population. Almost all federal and state judges have law degrees and extensive courtroom experience, often as attorneys. Standards for municipal judges are usually less demanding. However, the respect accorded to the profession overall is valuable to judges in maintaining authority in the courtroom.

Deciding Verdicts and Imposing Sentences

In addition to managing courtroom proceedings, judges frequently must pass judgment at the conclusion of a trial. This function is sometimes served partly or wholly by juries. Judges can be called upon to determine guilt or innocence, to pass sentences in criminal trials, and to ascertain damages in civil trials.

In determining guilt or assigning blame, judges often must choose between two well-presented and plausible arguments. Sometimes, however, they are faced with two problematic and poorly presented arguments. Either way, they are frequently forced to make a definitive decision based on conflicting and incomplete information. In doing this, they must draw on a thorough knowledge of the law and a keen understanding of human nature while being familiar with the facts of a case.

Once guilt is determined, sentencing remains a difficult and complex task faced by judges. Most crimes can warrant a range of penalties, depending on the particular circumstances. Judges are expected to weigh such matters as the violence or damage caused by the crime, personal information about the defendant (such as age, criminal record, and evident contrition), and the conclusiveness of the conviction. This last point is especially relevant when a jury, rather than the judge, decides the matter of guilt.

Judges are usually constrained in their sentencing decisions by statutes that limit the types and lengths of sentences. In some cases their sentencing discretion is broad. In others the range of permissible sentences is quite narrow. For example, judges are often bound by guidelines on mandatory sentencing for certain crimes. Many of these guidelines were enacted in the 1970s and 1980s by legislative bodies that were frustrated by the wide divergence of sentences for essentially the same crimes handed down by different judges. Some judges lost their jobs because of their alleged unwillingness to mete out suitably harsh penalties. During the 1980s, for example, several California supreme court justices lost their reelection bids in the wake of public anger that they repeatedly overturned death-penalty convictions. During the late 1990s the federal government and many state governments passed

American judge talking to a lawyer. (By maveric2003, via Wikimedia Commons)

"three-strikes" laws, which required that persons convicted of three felonies be sentenced to life imprisonment. Thus, judges are subjected to legal and political constraints in their sentencing duties that can limit judicial independence.

Judicial Independence

Of all the qualities judges must have, impartiality is perhaps the most important. If a judge possesses personal interests linked to the outcome of a trial or if a judge is subject to political pressure, then the entire criminal justice system can be undermined. Different jurisdictions promote judicial independence in a variety of ways: by establishing lifetime (or at least long-term) judicial appointments, by requiring that judges recuse themselves from cases in which they have a personal interest, by paying them generous salaries to reduce their susceptibility to bribes, or by prohibiting them from practicing law while in office.

Federal judges in the United States are appointed by the president of the United States and confirmed by the US Senate. Similarly, judges in many state systems are appointed by the governor and confirmed by the state legislature, although in many other states judges are elected or periodically reaffirmed through a popular vote. In a small number of states judges are nominated by a special nominating commission appointed by a state officer, serve for a fixed "probationary" period, and are then subjected to a popular confirmation vote to earn a full term. In each system of judicial appointment, there is some effort to balance the competing needs of independence and accountability.

The legitimacy of the judiciary relies not only on judicial objectivity and independence but also on the public perception of these qualities. Governments therefore make deliberate efforts to symbolically illustrate judicial independence: courts and judicial chambers are usually separated from executive and legislative buildings; judges wear somber, ecclesiastical-looking black robes; judicial elections are studiously nonpartisan; and courtrooms are frequently adorned with images of scales, swords, and other symbols of justice.

As either a supplement or alternative to the principle of impartiality, the notion of judicial balance is sometimes put forward as an important factor in ensuring justice. That is, multimember courts (such as supreme courts and many appeals courts) are sometimes composed of judges with a range of ideological backgrounds. The idea is that both "liberal" and "conservative" views should be represented on the bench. During the late twentieth century more controversial efforts were undertaken to ensure that the judges of a given jurisdiction reflect the ethnic, racial, and gender diversity of the populations they serve. These and other efforts to achieve balance among judges challenge the notion of justice as an absolute quality to be sought in each judge's actions and decisions.

Steve D. Boilard

Further Reading
Coffin, Frank M. *On Appeal: Courts, Lawyering, and Judging.* New York: Norton, 1994. Print.
Gunther, Gerhard. *Learned Hand: The Man and the Judge.* New York: Knopf, 1994. Print.
Kelly, Zachary A. *Judges and Lawyers.* Vero Beach: Rourke, 1999. Print.
McIntosh, Wayne V., and Cynthia L. Cates. *Judicial Entrepreneurship: The Role of the Judge in the Marketplace of Ideas.* Westport: Greenwood, 1997. Print.
O'Brien, David M., ed. *Judges on Judging: Views from the Bench.* 2nd ed. Washington, DC: CQ, 2004. Print.
Philips, Susan U. *Ideology in the Language of Judges: How Judges Practice Law, Politics, and Courtroom Control.* New York: Oxford UP, 1998. Print.
Vile, John R., ed. *Great American Judges: An Encyclopedia.* 2 vols. Santa Barbara: ABC, 2003. Print.

See also *Amicus curiae* briefs; Appellate process; Case law; Change of venue; Clerks of the court; Contempt of court; Gag orders; Impeachment of judges; Judicial system, U.S.; Objections; Opinions; Plea bargaining; Sentencing; Sentencing guidelines, U.S.; Summonses; Three-strikes laws; Trials; *Voir dire.*

Judicial review

Definition: Power of the courts to examine laws to determine their constitutionality and to declare null and void laws failing to meet that standard

Criminal justice issue: Appeals; constitutional protections; courts

Significance: The power of judicial review is a significant and controversial power of the U.S. federal and state judicial system. Although the power to create laws belongs to the legislative branch of government (and to the executive branch through the power of executive order), the courts, given their power of judicial review, have the final say in declaring what is the law.

The broad power of judicial review was not explicitly assigned to the judicial branch of government by the Constitutional Convention of 1787. Rather, its creation can be traced to the judicial branch itself—in particular, to the 1803 decision in *Marbury v. Madison* by the U.S. Supreme Court led by Chief Justice John Marshall. This decision opened the way for the judicial branch, in interpreting the law, to become at least as powerful as the legislative and executive branches.

Controversy over the principle of judicial review does not, however, stem from questions about its historical legitimacy but rather from the processes by which justices acquire their positions in the courts. While many judges at the state level are elected to their positions, the justices of the U.S. Supreme Court are appointed to their positions for life. This causes many to worry that the power of judicial review, at least at the federal level, is undemocratic in its very nature, granting such power to the judicial branch that it threatens the balance of power among the three branches of government.

The concern that the principle of judicial review unduly extends the power of the courts and "politicizes" the power of the judiciary is shared by both conservatives and liberals alike. Liberals worry that in the hands of a conservative Supreme Court the power of judicial review could be used to overturn progressive social legislation, such as affirmative action laws. Around the turn of the twentieth century new laws creating more favorable working conditions for laborers were deemed invalid in the case of *Lochner v. New York* (1905) and other decisions. Conservatives worry that in the hands of a liberal Supreme Court the power of judicial review could be used by justices to promote social change. As an example of so-called judicial activism they point to *Roe v. Wade* (1973), which, on the basis of an implicit constitutional right to privacy, overturned a statute making abortions illegal in the state of Texas. Controversy over the power of judicial review aside, the existence of this power exerts an influence over lawmakers that many would claim is beneficial, as the knowledge that laws are subject to judicial review can lead to greater care and conscientiousness on the part of lawmakers in crafting legislation.

Diane P. Michelfelder

Further Reading

Baum, Lawrence. *The Supreme Court*. 8th ed. Washington, D.C.: CQ Press, 2003.

Greenberg, Ellen. *The Supreme Court Explained*. New York: W. W. Norton, 1997.

Lewis, Thomas T., and Richard L. Wilson, eds. *Encyclopedia of the U.S. Supreme Court*. 3 vols. Pasadena, Calif.: Salem Press, 2001.

McGuire, Kevin. *Understanding the U.S. Supreme Court*. New York: McGraw-Hill, 2002.

Neubauer, David W. *America's Courts and the Criminal Justice System*. 8th ed. Belmont, Calif.: Wadsworth/Thomson Learning, 2005.

See also Appellate process; Case law; *Certiorari*; Constitution, U.S.; Court types; Due process of law; *Habeas corpus*; Harmless error; Jurisdiction of courts; *Stare decisis*; Supreme Court, U.S.

Judicial system, U.S.

Definition: One of the three co-equal branches of American state and federal governments that provides forums for applying laws and resolving civil and criminal cases

Criminal justice issue: Courts; Federal Law; Law codes

Significance: The American court system embodies the adversary system of justice, in which it is the role of all parties in cases to take the lead in investigating the facts, presenting evidence, and formulating legal arguments to demonstrate why they, and not their adversaries, should prevail, within the settings of neutral forums.

The U.S. judicial system is actually made up of fifty-two distinct and separate judicial systems: the federal court system and fifty-one autonomous systems for each of the U.S. states and the federal District of Columbia. Moreover, the military forces and U.S. territories also have their own separate systems. However, the federal and state court systems share the same basic structures and follow similar procedures in their proceedings. Also, both types of court systems contain trial and appellate courts, though the individual courts may function somewhat differently.

Trial and Appellate Courts

Trial courts are courts of the first instance; they hear evidence, determine the facts, and make initial decisions in cases. In addition, trial court proceedings are conducted by judges who sit alone, without other judges, and decide the applicable legal principles and make initial rulings as to issues of procedure and admission of evidence. When cases are being tried by juries, the presiding judges' roles are usually limited to those functions, and the trial juries have responsibility for deciding the facts and reaching verdicts.

In bench trials, which have no juries, the judges alone make findings on the facts and pronounce verdicts. Although trial courts are situated at the base of the judicial system, the fact-finding roles of these courts often have greater importance than the courts' ultimate decisions because determinations as to the facts cannot be re-argued when cases are appealed.

On the level above trial courts are appellate courts, which hear and decide appeals of decisions made below by the trial courts. Depending on the courts and their jurisdictions, the losing parties' ability to bring appeals may be automatic or may be solely at the discretion of the appellate courts. The main function of appellate courts is to review decisions of the trial courts below them and to resolve questions of law, regardless of whether the original cases were decided by judges or juries.

The facts of cases that are found by the trial courts are accepted as "given" on appeal, and panels of judges instead hear arguments about whether the trial courts have made errors in applying the law. For example, a losing party at trial may argue on appeal that the factual evidence does not support an ultimate judgment of liability in a civil case, that a judge was mistaken in admitting certain witness testimony into evidence in a criminal case, or that a judge or jury misinterpreted the law. These examples demonstrate that the main benefit of appellate review is to create opportunities to have second looks at disputed aspects of cases in order to correct errors that may have affected their outcomes.

Procedures in trial and appellate courts differ significantly. In trial courts, in which evidence of facts is admitted, the trial judges preside over processes in which attorneys representing opposing sides call witnesses to testify and answer questions. The judges resolve issues as to the admissibility of the evidence, ensure that both sides in cases have fair opportunities to argue their sides, and then instruct the juries on the laws that should guide their decisions when they consider the evidence and endeavor to reach verdicts.

Proceedings in appellate courts are less complex. No testimony is accepted. Rather, panels of appellate judges allot each attorney certain amounts of time to argue the legal issues orally on behalf of their clients and to answer questions posed by the judges. Additionally, the attorneys submit written arguments or "briefs" to elaborate their arguments further. Afterward, the appellate judges consider the cases and decided either to affirm (agree with) or reverse (disagree with) the trial court decisions, based on applicable laws. On occasion, appellate courts reverse and remand cases back to the trial courts for reconsideration of specified aspects of the cases.

State Courts

Judges in state courts are usually elected or appointed. At the base of state court systems are courts that possess special or limited authority. For example, suits involving small amounts of money or highly particular legal matters may be resolved in small-claims courts or traffic courts or before magistrates or justices of the peace. Some states require that small claims be submitted first to arbitration before panels of lawyers. In most of these courts, the litigating parties represent themselves, without professional counsel, and the proceedings are less formal than in trial courts. Losing parties in these proceedings usually have the right to bring their cases before trial courts for new hearings.

State court systems are geographically divided into subdivisions or judicial districts. Most state trial courts have general authority to hear wide ranges of civil and criminal cases. Some trial courts may be large enough to be subdivided into sections based on the types of cases they hear, such as civil, criminal, and domestic-relations divisions.

Whether general or specific, a court's authority to hear a particular type of case is referred to as its subject-matter jurisdiction. Trial courts have authority to decide criminal prosecutions against defendants who commit crimes within their states. In addition, trial courts in civil cases must have jurisdiction over either the persons or the property involved in disputes. For example, when a dispute is about title to, or rights in, property located within the state, the court has *in rem* jurisdiction to decide the case.

By contrast, personal jurisdiction is based on the locations, residences, or activities of the parties within the state. Even defendants who do not reside with a state may

The U.S. judicial system comprises thousands of courts under federal, state, and territorial jurisdictions, but all the courts are ultimately answerable to the Supreme Court of the United States (above), whose seat is in Washington, D.C. (Library of Congress)

be subject to the jurisdiction of its courts if they have been doing business in the state or have established other significant connections to the state. Cases that are filed in trial courts, or that are brought to trial courts from small-claims courts or magistrates, are decided in the manner described earlier. Once final decisions are reached in the trial courts, the losing parties may appeal.

Most state court systems have intermediate appellate courts, in which losing parties have a guaranteed right to bring appeals, and supreme court, in which the ability to bring appeals rests at the discretion of the courts' judges. A few states have no intermediate appeals courts. In such states, appeals from trial courts go directly to their supreme courts. Unless a case involves only state-law issues, the U.S. Supreme Court sometimes agrees to hear appeals from decisions of state supreme courts, particularly when aspects of federal law are at issue or when a party's U.S. constitutional rights are involved. For example, defendants who are found guilty of crimes in state courts but who believe that their federal constitutional right to due process was violated by police during their arrests may petition the U.S. Supreme Court to review their cases.

Federal Courts

Judges in the federal system are appointed by the U.S. president and confirmed by the U.S. Senate. In the federal court system, lawsuits begin in district courts, which are the federal equivalents of state trial courts. Every state has at least one federal district court within its boundaries that operates separately, but alongside the state's trial courts. As in state trial courts, proceedings in federal district courts are presided over by judges who decide questions of applicable law. Determinations of facts may be made by either jurors or judges. As in state trial courts, federal district courts must have jurisdiction over the subject matter of the cases they try.

Federal district courts have jurisdiction over defendants charged with federal crimes. The courts have authority to hear civil cases as matters of either diversity jurisdiction or federal question jurisdiction. Diversity jurisdiction exists when the opposing parties in a case are citizens of different states, or when at least one party is a citizen of a foreign nation, and when the amounts in dispute exceed $75,000. Federal question jurisdiction exists when the claims arise under issues pertaining to the U.S. Constitution or federal statutes or treaties of the United

States. There is no required amount in controversy for federal question jurisdiction.

There are also a few more specialized types of federal courts. Bankruptcy courts hear petitions under the federal bankruptcy law. The Court of International Trade hears cases involving customs and import or export of goods. The Court of Federal Claims decides cases brought against the U.S. government.

As in many state court systems, losing parties in federal district courts have an automatic right to appeal. Thus, defendants who have been convicted of crimes in federal district courts may file appeals as a matter of right in order to challenge their convictions. The U.S. courts of appeal operate as all appellate courts do, typically with panels of three judges reviewing cases for errors of law and accepting the facts as decided in the district courts.

The United States is divided into thirteen circuits, each with its own court of appeals. Eleven circuits cover several states and hear appeals from criminal and civil cases decided by federal district courts sitting within those states. The District of Columbia has its own circuit court of appeals, and a federal circuit court of appeals exists to hear specific appeals involving patents, claims against the federal government, and customs and international trade matters.

U.S. Supreme Court

The U.S. Supreme Court is the highest court for both federal and state court systems. Except in rare circumstances, the Supreme Court functions as an appellate court, hearing appeals from the federal courts of appeal and state supreme courts. The Court comprises eight associate justices and a chief justice, whose official title is "chief justice of the United States." All the Supreme Court justices are appointed by the president and confirmed by the Senate.

In almost all cases, the Supreme Court has discretion as to whether to hear specific appeals and agrees to hear only a small fraction of the cases submitted for its consideration. The Court usually defers to state supreme courts on matters of state law or in interpreting a state's constitution. Most appeals heard by the Supreme Court involve significant questions of federal law or constitutional rights or issues of national importance that are subjects of disagreement among various circuit courts of appeal.

Kurt M. Saunders

Further Reading

Corley, Pamela C., Artemus Ward, and Wendy L. Martinek. *American Judicial Process: Myth and Reality in Law and Courts*. New York: Routledge, 2016. Print.

Abraham, Henry J. *The Judicial Process*. New York: Oxford UP, 1998. Print.

Hall, Timothy L., ed. *The U.S. Legal System*. 2 vols. Pasadena: Salem Press, 2004. Print.

Janosik, Robert J., ed. *Encyclopedia of the American Judicial System: Studies of the Principal Institutions and Processes of Law*. New York: Scribner's, 1987. Print.

Kelly, Zachary A. *Judges and Lawyers*. Vero Beach: Rourke, 1999. Print.

Meador, Daniel J. *American Courts*. St. Paul: West, 1991. Print.

Meador, Daniel J., and Jordana S. Bernstein. *Appellate Courts in the United States*. St. Paul: West, 1994. Print.

Pacelle, Richard L. *The Supreme Court in a Separation of Powers System: The Nation's Balance Wheel*. New York: Routledge, 2015. Print.

Smith, Christopher E. *Courts and Trials: A Reference Handbook*. Santa Barbara: ABC-Clio, 2003. Print.

See also Appellate process; Court types; Criminal justice in U.S. history; Criminal justice system; Criminal procedure; Discretion; Judges; Judicial review; Jurisdiction of courts; Jury system; Justice; Opinions; *Stare decisis*; Supreme Court, U.S.; Trials.

Jurisdiction of courts

Definition: Authority of different types of courts to hear and decide cases

Criminal justice issue: Courts; Jurisdictions

Significance: Jurisdiction is a complicated but important issue. In criminal matters, a court is without authority to decide a criminal case unless it has both the jurisdiction to decide the particular kind of criminal case and jurisdiction over the defendant.

One of the most important issues facing a court in any case is whether it has jurisdiction over the case. In its broadest sense, "jurisdiction" is the authority of any branch of the justice system to interpret or apply the law. For example, the jurisdictions of federal law-enforcement agencies are explicitly defined by law. Within the court system, however, jurisdiction refers to the authority of courts to hear and decide cases. A court cannot decide a case unless it exercises authority that is appropriate to its own jurisdiction.

Both federal and state courts face limitations in the kinds of cases they can decide. The US Constitution, state constitutions, and federal and state laws grant and limit the jurisdiction of courts. A court must have both subject-matter jurisdiction and personal jurisdiction to make legally valid decisions.

Subject-Matter Jurisdiction

Subject-matter jurisdiction refers to the kinds of cases that a specific type of court is authorized to hear. In criminal cases, subject-matter jurisdiction refers to whether particular courts can hear and decide criminal cases, and if so, what kinds of criminal cases the courts can decide. Most criminal matters fall under the subject-matter jurisdiction of state courts because the US Constitution explicitly provides that the states have the duty of protecting the general welfare of the people. This duty includes deciding what acts should be criminal and what punishments should be awarded for committing specific crimes. A state's criminal laws, known as a penal or criminal code, and its criminal procedure laws define the subject-matter jurisdiction for that state's courts.

The US Constitution and laws enacted by the US Congress provide the subject-matter jurisdiction of federal courts. In criminal matters, federal courts have subject-matter jurisdiction over cases concerning violations of federal criminal laws. In addition, federal courts can review convictions from state courts when defendants raise constitutional issues. In some instances, state and federal courts have concurrent jurisdiction over the same actions. Concurrent jurisdiction refers to the authority of different courts to decide the same case that occurs within the same territory, and over the same subject matter. For example, state criminal laws define robbery as a crime. Therefore, a state court would have subject-matter jurisdiction over a defendant charged with robbing a bank in its state. However, robbery of a bank that is federally insured is also a violation of federal law. Consequently, a federal court would have subject-matter jurisdiction over the same defendant under applicable federal law.

Courts also differ in terms of whether their subject-matter jurisdiction is limited or general. Limited-jurisdiction courts can decide only specific matters, while general-jurisdiction courts are not so limited. Each state has courts of general jurisdiction that can hear both civil and criminal matters. However, states also have lower-level courts that can decide specific kinds of cases.

Limited Jurisdiction Courts

While there is enormous variation among state court systems, some examples will illustrate the idea of limited jurisdiction. Many state laws provide that family courts have jurisdiction over matters such as child abuse, domestic violence, child custody, and child support. States often give surrogate courts the authority to adjudicate matters concerning wills, trusts, and estates. In criminal matters, town and justice courts frequently have jurisdiction over misdemeanors, while higher-level courts have jurisdiction over felonies. Thus, a court of limited criminal jurisdiction does not have the authority to hear and decide a murder case.

In the federal court system, the issue of subject-matter jurisdiction is more complex. Federal courts are courts of limited subject-matter jurisdiction that are divided into three separate areas: diversity jurisdiction (suits between citizens of different states), ancillary jurisdiction (matters not ordinarily under federal jurisdiction that are associated with federal offenses), and federal-question jurisdiction. Federal criminal cases usually do not involve either diversity jurisdiction or ancillary jurisdiction. However, federal-question jurisdiction can involve criminal matters. Federal courts can hear two types of matters that fall under federal-question jurisdiction: violations of federal law and issues arising under the US Constitution. Federal-question jurisdiction explains why federal courts can decide cases concerning violations of federal criminal law as well as cases from state courts in which defendants raise constitutional issues.

Finally, subject-matter jurisdiction concerns the ideas of original and appellate jurisdiction. A court has original jurisdiction when it can hold trials and rule on matters directly, while appellate jurisdiction refers to courts that rule on matters previously decided by other courts. All states specify the courts that have original jurisdiction and appellate jurisdiction. In federal courts, US district courts exercise original jurisdiction, while courts of appeals and the US Supreme Court exercise appellate jurisdiction. However, there are certain cases in which the Supreme Court can exercise original jurisdiction. These kinds of cases do not involve criminal matters.

Personal Jurisdiction

Also called *in personam* jurisdiction, personal jurisdiction refers to the authority that courts have over persons who are subjects of cases. Personal jurisdiction is sometimes confused with venue, a term for the location of a trial or proceeding. Personal jurisdiction concerns the question of whether a court has the authority to make a determination concerning a particular defendant.

For a court to exercise personal jurisdiction over a defendant, the defendant must have some contact with the state that is to hear the case. In civil matters, the issue of personal jurisdiction is often a complicated question, especially when a defendant lives out of state. In criminal proceedings, a defendant's contact with a state merges with the idea of territoriality. Therefore, personal jurisdiction exists over persons who commit offenses that affect the interests of that state. In federal criminal matters, personal jurisdiction exists over persons who commit offenses within the territory of the particular federal judicial district.

Patricia E. Erickson

Further Reading

Barkan, Steven E., and George J. Bryjak. *Fundamentals of Criminal Justice: A Sociological View.* 2nd ed. Sudbury: Jones, 2011. Print.
Latzer, Barry. *State Constitutions and Criminal Justice.* Westport: Greenwood, 1991. Print.
Meyer, Jon'a F., and Diana R. Grant. *The Courts in Our Criminal Justice System.* Upper Saddle River: Prentice, 2003. Print.
Miller, William S. *A Primer on American Courts.* New York: Pearson, 2005. Print.
Neubauer, David W., and Henry F. Fradella. *America's Courts and the Criminal Justice System.* 11th ed. Belmont: Wadsworth, 2014. Print.
Stolzenberg, Lisa, and Stewart J. D'Alessio. *Criminal Courts for the 21st Century.* 3rd ed. Miami: Dept. of Criminal Justice, Florida Intl. U, 2010. Print.

See also Appellate process; Change of venue; Court types; Criminal procedure; Criminal prosecution; Judicial review; Judicial system, U.S.; Multiple jurisdiction offenses; Precedent; Supreme Court, U.S.; Trials; World Court.

Jury nullification

Definition: Power of juries to change, alter, or modify the law or facts in cases they are considering in trials
Criminal justice issue: Juries; Principles; Trial procedures
Significance: Jury nullification presupposes a jury's inherent power to either disregard a judge's instructions on the law, or, in addition, disregard some or all of the evidence presented in litigation. Although it is difficult to establish just how much jury nullification takes place, many experts on jury behavior believe it is on the rise.

It is argued that the jury, as the community's conscience, must be allowed to operate as a brake on the misapplication of the law in particular circumstances. Criminal cases, in particular, offer a fertile field for the application of the nullification principle. For example, verdicts in so-called "mercy killing" trials, trials involving politically charged issues, and trials of battered women charged with spousal killing often exhibit jury nullification at work. Likewise, many Americans have taken the position that the O. J. Simpson acquittal by a predominantly African American jury in 1995 was a clear example of jury nullification premised on race.

John Adams was in favor of jury nullification. (Public domain, via Wikimedia Commons)

There is an on-going debate in American criminal justice about whether or not jury nullification, if carried too far, will lead to a lawless society. On the other hand, if no discretion were allowed a jury to nullify what it believed to be an oppressive rule of law, the outcome might be technically legal but morally outrageous. All the nation's Founding Fathers were in favor of the trial jury's discretionary power to nullify. John Adams, Alexander Hamilton, and Thomas Jefferson were robustly in favor of granting to the trial jury the power to determine both the law and the facts, unburdened by either a judge's instructions or the rules of evidence.

In both theory and practice it is assumed that at the end of judicial proceedings the judge instructs the jury on the rules of law to be applied to the case at hand. Using these instructions, the jury applies the law to the facts they find during their deliberations. However, since no two cases are alike and since every case is infected, to a greater or lesser extent, with both legal and factual ambi-

Thomas Jefferson was in favor of jury nullification. (Public domain, via Wikimedia Commons)

guity, the jury is often left to view the law and the facts through its own peculiar prism. It is at this point that the cry of jury nullification is often heard by the losing side.

Most American trial and appellate judges are not in favor of instructing the jury on its power to disregard the law or the facts in a particular case. Judges arguably fear a total disregard for both legal principles and relevant facts if juries are simply left to their own devices. Thus, while a jury still holds a sort of veto power over the rigidity and inaptness of certain legal principles, trial judges and their appellate counterparts are generally content to remain silent on a jury's power to nullify.

John C. Watkins, Jr.

Further Reading
Abramson, Jeffery. *We, the Jury: The Jury System and the Ideal of Democracy.* Cambridge, Mass.: Harvard University Press, 1994.
Conrad, Clay S. *Jury Nullification: The Evolution of a Doctrine.* Durham, N.C.: Carolina Academic Press, 1998.
Ferguson, Andrew G. *Why Jury Duty Matters: A Citizen's Guide to Constitutional Action.* New York: NYU Press, 2012. *eBook Collection (EBSCOhost).* Web. 26 May 2016.
Freedman, Monroe H.1. "Jury Nullification: What It Is, and How to Do It Ethically." *Hofstra Law Review* 42.4 (2014): 1125-1138. *Legal Source.* Web. 26 May 2016.
Jonakait, Randolph N. *The American Jury System.* New Haven, Conn.: Yale University Press, 2003.

See also Hung juries; Jury sequestration; Jury system; Miscarriage of justice; Trials; Verdicts.

Jury sequestration

Definition: Isolation of jurors from the public during trials
Criminal justice issue: Juries; media; trial procedures; verdicts
Significance: Impartiality is essential to jurors, and sequestration prevents them from being improperly influenced by news reports, family members, friends, or other sources of information.

A paramount concern for judges during jury trials is ensuring that jurors' decisions are based on properly presented evidence. In controversial cases there are fears that jurors' exposure to news reports or opinionated acquaintances will improperly affect jury deliberations and the verdict. In such cases judges may order the jury to be sequestered in order to shield jurors from improper sources of information. Because jurors must live together in a hotel away from their friends and family, jury sequestration imposes significant costs on the personal lives of jurors. Sequestration also generates significant expenses for the court, which must pay for the jurors' food and lodging throughout the course of the trial.

Sequestration may occur in cases involving highly publicized crimes or well-known defendants. Sequestration may be particularly appropriate when the news media informs the public about information and evidence that is not admissible in court. For example, if the police found a bloody weapon in the defendant's home but that weapon could not be presented at trial because it was found during an illegal search, the judge may sequester the jury to prevent the jurors from reading about the weapon in the newspapers.

Because of the cost and inconvenience of jury sequestration, judges rarely order it. Judges must often make a decision about sequestration at the beginning of a trial. If sequestration is possible, judges may ask potential jurors during jury selection if sequestration would create special hardships that would make it exceptionally unfair or difficult for them to serve. For example, the mother of a young child may be excused from jury duty if the judge agrees that sequestration would pose an exceptional hardship for the mother and child.

When jurors are sequestered, bailiffs must monitor their contact with the outside world. In some situations, bailiffs cut out and destroy all newspaper articles about the trial before the newspapers are given to the jurors. Bailiffs also monitor television programs watched by jurors to make sure that they do not watch news stories about the trial. Judges also instruct jurors on the importance of their responsibilities and warn them to avoid all news reports and conversations about the trial. If the bailiffs or other jurors inform the judge that a specific juror has read prohibited newspaper articles, talked about the case with outsiders, or otherwise undertaken forbidden behavior, the judge may dismiss the juror from the case and seat an alternate. In major cases, alternate jurors are sequestered along with the regular jurors and hear the same evidence presented in court, even if they are not ultimately permitted to participate in deliberating the verdict.

Christopher E. Smith

Further Reading

Abramson, Jeffery. *We, the Jury: The Jury System and the Ideal of Democracy*. Cambridge, Mass.: Harvard University Press, 1994.

Jonakait, Randolph N. *The American Jury System*. New Haven, Conn.: Yale University Press, 2003.

Schwartz, Victor E., et al. *Safeguarding the Right to a Representative Jury: The Need for Improved Jury Service Laws*. Washington, D.C.: National Legal Center for the Public Interest, 2003.

Stanley, Jacqueline. *Jurors' Rights*. Naperville, Ill.: Sourcebooks, 1998.

See also Bailiffs; Hung juries; Jury nullification; Jury system; Trial publicity; Trials.

Jury system

Definition: System in which groups of citizens who are representative of their communities hear testimony and assess evidence in court cases to determine the truth or falsehood of such testimony and evidence

Criminal justice issue: Courts; Juries; Trial procedures; Verdicts

Significance: A right guaranteed by the U.S. Constitution, trial by jury is a central component of Anglo-American justice and is especially important in criminal trials. The jury system affords those accused of crimes to receive a hearing by a cross section of ordinary citizens in whose hands the determination of guilt or innocence rests.

During the late twentieth century, four of every five jury trials in the world was conducted in the United States. Despite the inadequacies to which legal scholars, criminologists, and legislators have repeatedly pointed in the jury system, the system is more securely entrenched in the American justice system than in any other system in the world. Moreover, despite modifications that various state governments have made in it, one can safely predict that the jury system will remain intact in the United States for many years to come.

The jury system is a fundamental part of the American justice system largely because the authors of the Declaration of Independence listed as one of their major complaints against the British crown government that it was "depriving us, in many Cases, of the Benefits of Trial by Jury." Given this background, the nation's founders made provision for the jury system when they drew up the U.S. Constitution.

Constitutional Mandates

Article III of the U.S. Constitution promises those accused of any federal crimes—except for impeachment—the right to trial by jury. The Fifth Amendment specifies that no citizen shall be answerable for the commission of any capital or "otherwise infamous crime, unless on a presentment or indictment of a Grand Jury," thereby placing the judgment of testimony and evidence in the hands of a representative body of the citizenry.

The Sixth Amendment guarantees a speedy public trial "by an impartial jury of the State and district wherein the crime shall have been committed." The word "impartial" is particularly important in this amendment and has been the basis for empaneling disinterested jurors to hear both criminal and civil cases. The Seventh Amendment states that "in suits of common law, where the value in controversy shall exceed twenty dollars, the right of trial by jury shall be preserved, and no fact tried by a jury, shall be otherwise reexamined in any Court of the United States, than according to the rules of the common law." This amendment, which firmly establishes the right to trial by jury, also establishes the all-important guarantee against double jeopardy.

The Fourteenth Amendment guarantees the right of a jury trial to any defendant accused of a crime, federal or state, that carries a penalty of more than six months' imprisonment. The protection of this amendment, which has been tested in the courts, is not extended to those accused of minor offenses.

Given constitutional guarantees that resulted from zealous reactions to widespread dissatisfaction with

The one man power in our jury system. (Public domain, via Wikimedia Commons)

Great Britain's governance of the colonies, the American judicial system could not easily be moved to abandon the jury system. For all the faults jurists have found with the system, it is so fundamentally a part of American justice that it is inconceivable to envision the American justice system without it.

Grand Juries

Grand juries are bodies that usually consist of between sixteen and twenty-three jurors. They are subdivided into two types of juries, those that charge defendants and those that investigate. The first of these examines evidence brought forth against suspects to determine whether it is sufficient to warrant formal charges that will lead to court trials by other, smaller juries. If the evidence suggests that there is probable cause for trials, indictments are issued that set in motion the machinery for jury trials.

Investigatory grand juries examine evidence against public officials suspected or accused of criminal misconduct in office. They also investigate alleged criminal activity in other segments of society, such as organized crime. They, too, can issue indictments if the testimony and evidence suggest probable cause.

Hearings held by grand juries are closed to the public. The rights of those suspected of violations are protected meticulously, and all suspects enjoy the presumption of innocence. Indictments are not declarations of guilt; they merely indicate the need for further investigation.

Petit Juries

The type of jury with which most Americans are familiar is the petit, or petty, jury, so designated because of its comparatively small size. In the United States, petit juries generally contain twelve jurors and some alternates. However, in some states juries may range in size from six to ten members.

In criminal cases, petit juries decide whether defendants are guilty or innocent of the crimes of which they have been accused. In civil cases, juries establish liability and determine the damages awarded to successful complainants. The courtrooms in which cases are tried by petit juries are generally open to the public. However, judges may limit the numbers of observers and are empowered, under certain circumstances, to clear their courtrooms of spectators when they believe that their presence is disrupting proceedings. All defendants in criminal cases that petit juries hear are deemed innocent until their guilt is proved to the jury beyond a reasonable doubt. Presumption of innocence is the keystone of the American justice system. If a reasonable doubt exists about any defendant's guilt, a verdict of acquittal must be returned.

Coroners' Juries

In most jurisdictions, coroners' juries are composed of six members. It is their purpose to hold investigations, termed inquests, into causes of death in cases in which doubt exists. They are frequently called upon, for example, to determine whether deaths are the result of murder or suicide. They work closely with forensic pathologists, who perform autopsies that provide the juries with the information they need to make reasonable judgments.

The Making of Juries

Stringent rules govern how juries are constituted. To begin with, pools of jurors must be representative of the general population of the United States. Moreover, no

U.S. citizen may be excluded from a pool of jurors on such arbitrary grounds as race, gender, or class. Furthermore, jurors drawn from the jury pool to judge specific cases must also be representative of the community wherein the indictment has been issued.

In the distant past, juror pools were drawn only from members of communities who owned property. However, that method of selection was successfully challenged by those who contended that it imposed a class distinction upon jury selection. Eventually, jury pools came to be drawn from voting rolls. Before ratification of the Nineteenth Amendment guaranteed women the right to vote in all states in 1920, however, women were excluded from the voting rolls in most states. Until the Voting Rights Act of 1965, voting rolls in many southern states held the names of few black voters, making it impossible to impanel truly representative juries in those states.

Toward the end of the twentieth century, other methods began to be employed to develop pools of jurors. The most common of these draws pools from lists of licensed drivers as well as registered voters. This method broadened substantially the composition of jury pools and constituted a major advance toward making juries more representative of the general population than they had previously been.

In deciding who will serve on juries slated to hear specific cases, in a process known as *voir dire*, attorneys for both defense and prosecution question potential jurors drawn from the pool. The selection of appropriate juries is essential to the successful defense or prosecution of any case. Effective attorneys select juries with great care and deliberation, sometimes employing consultants specially trained in jury selection to guide them toward the best choices. When attorney questioning uncovers obvious biases that might cloud jurors' objectivity or give reason to suspect that potential jurors have already reached conclusions about the cases to be tried, attorneys on either side may reject them as jurors. Such dismissals are called objections for cause. Attorneys are permitted an unlimited number of such objections.

Attorneys are also allowed limited numbers of peremptory challenges. These challenges do not require them to offer any explanations or justifications to the courts. For example, an attorney may legitimately issue a peremptory challenge to exclude a retiree dependent upon investment income in a trial of a stockbroker accused of fraudulent dealings with elderly clients. Likewise, an attorney might exclude the president of a local temperance organization from serving on a jury in a drunk driving case.

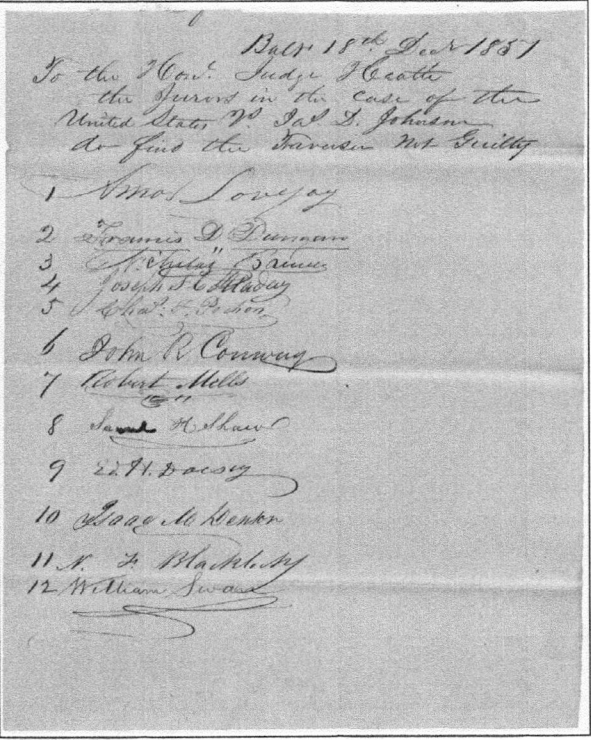

A verdict is part of the jury system. (Public domain, via Wikimedia Commons)

However, peremptory challenges that are clearly made on the basis of race or gender may lead to mistrials.

Jury Verdicts

In most jurisdictions, decisions to find defendants guilty in criminal cases must be unanimous. If even a single juror votes against conviction and cannot be persuaded in subsequent jury balloting to change the vote, a deadlock is declared in the trial and a hung jury is said to exist. There are no official limits on how many ballots juries may take during their deliberations.

When jury deliberations result in hung juries, defendants in the cases are still presumed innocent. However, the accusations against them remain intact. Prosecutors may later elect to reopen their cases and hold new trials. However, in many instances the press of other cases makes prosecutors reluctant to do so. Prosecutors may also come under administrative pressures to consider costs to the government over the pursuit of justice. Some jurisdictions have sought to overcome the problem of hung juries by allowing specified majority votes of guilty—often ten out of twelve—to produce convictions. In Scotland, it has long taken only a simple majority vote to convict.

The secrecy of what goes on in jury rooms generally remains sacrosanct after trials. Although jurors may be individually polled after their foreperson announces their verdict, they are under no obligation to explain their votes to anyone at any time.

Roots of the Jury System

The American jury system is a product of a millennium of English and American history. It originated in medieval England and grew out of the development of codified laws and statutes that came to be accepted by society to replace or at least supplement many of the controls that earlier resided in the family, whose eldest male member usually served a judicial function. The rules that governed such a system were often capricious, whereas law as society conceives it is meant to be uniform, and justice as society conceives it is ideally blind.

When the Norman ruler William the Conqueror invaded England in 1066, right (which was often determined by combat) did not always triumph over might. Persons who accused others of crimes besmirched the integrity of the other persons, who then might feel honor-bound to engage in combat with their accusers to avenge the insults. In such situations, might was right. The stronger combatants won, regardless of whose case was more valid in their disputes.

In many societies, trial by ordeal was a popular form of determining guilt or innocence until three or four centuries ago. Accused persons who could walk over glowing embers without blistering their feet or carry several pounds of hot coals in their hands without injury were considered innocent of all charges against them. Innocence, needless to say, was seldom the outcome in such primitive judicial procedures.

Before the year 1000, England's King Ethelred I, recognizing that the English system of justice was deficient, appointed twelve of his most trusted followers to investigate illegal activities and make formal accusations against suspects, much as grand juries do in modern society. After their evidence was heard, guilty votes by at least eight of the twelve resulted in convictions. It is probably this early English model of twelve-man juries that eventually led to twelve members being the standard for modern petit juries in the United States.

In the Anglo-Saxon era, with society centered in small villages or feudal keeps, people knew one another well. As early as 850, England's King Alfred divided every community in his domain into units of ten families that were mutually responsible for one another's behavior. Each ten groups of such families, or "tithings," constituted a judicial unit called a "hundred." County courts run by sheriffs met twice a year to hear cases brought by the "hundredors," as they were called. Cases were heard by twelve members of the hundredors who were selected because of their personal knowledge of each case being tried.

Among the early British, reputation carried great weight and honor was valued above all else. If people well respected in the community were accused of crimes by others, they either owned up to the accusations and made amends or, upon their honor, vowed innocence. Such vows were readily accepted from people who were known to be honest. However, strangers who vowed innocence were often subjected to ordeals to prove their claims.

When groups of people made accusations, the accused were expected to find eleven thanes who would swear to their honesty and honor. If they could not persuade that many to testify, they were usually subjected to physical ordeals and, predictably, adjudged guilty. These earliest juries of thanes selected by the accused were quite opposite to the impartial juries that are fundamental to modern jury systems. They were selected because they had already made up their minds and were predisposed in favor of the defendants. Under modern judicial systems, when prospective jurors are found to have any bias for or against defendants, they are precluded from serving. Studies of judicial decisions in England between 1550 and 1750 reveal that during those two centuries, juries consistently voted to acquit people they knew and voted to convict people they did not know.

Objections to the Jury System

The jury system has been tried and abandoned in many countries. Generally it has been observed that whenever a nation attempts to impose such a jury system upon its established judicial system, the attempt soon fails. In such situations, modifications in the system are usually so great as to make it almost unrecognizable as a jury system. For example, in France, Germany, and Denmark, experiments with juries were eventually replaced by trial systems that involve judges and lay assessors who help to weigh evidence.

Outside the United States, the jury system seems most firmly entrenched in Great Britain, where it was originally established and refined quite early. In Australia, New Zealand, and Canada, jury systems are strong because they were established as the original system in those countries—all of which inherited the British legal system.

A major objection to trial by jury is that many jurors lack the intelligence, backgrounds, or stamina to assess effectively evidence given within a legal context. This objection has been heard increasingly as law cases have placed increasing demands on jurors, expecting them to understand highly technical evidence, such as the results of polygraph tests, DNA (deoxyribonucleic acid) testing, and other modern laboratory procedures that are now applied to gathering and evaluating evidence.

Another type of complaint about the jury system is the proven fact that some jurors can be bribed by parties to the cases being tried. This problem can be largely eliminated by sequestering juries, which is sometimes done in highly publicized trials. In such trials, juries are sometimes cut off from communication with the outside world for periods lasting several months. In cases that involve organized crime, jurors may have ample cause to fear for their physical welfare and safety during and after trials. On the other hand, jurors assigned to high-profile cases are occasionally eager to serve because they have ulterior motives, such as plans to profit from their experience after the trials by writing books or taking to the television talk-show circuit.

Sometimes, potentially competent jurors are excused because of the disruptions to their lives that long sequestration might cause them. Occasionally, members of sequestered juries finish their service and find that they have lost their jobs or that their marriages or other personal relationships are foundering.

Criticism has also been directed toward juries in civil cases that award unrealistically high settlements to complainants whose cases succeed. Appellate courts have often reduced or eliminated some of the most unrealistic settlements, but appealing a verdict is a cumbersome process that is costly to the complainants, the defendants, and the government.

R. Baird Shuman

Further Reading
Abramson, Jeffrey. *We, the Jury: The Jury System and the Ideal of Democracy.* Cambridge, Mass.: Harvard UP, 2000.
Guinther, John, and Bettyruth Walter. *The Jury in America.* New York: Facts On File, 1988.
Holland, Barbara. "Do You Swear that You Will Well and Truly Try . . . ?" *Smithsonian* 25 (March 1995).
Lesser, Maximus A., and William S. Hein. *The Historical Development of the Jury System.* Buffalo: W. S. Hein, 1992.
Schwartz, Victor E., et al. *Safeguarding the Right to a Representative Jury: The Need for Improved Jury Service Laws.* Washington, DC: National Legal Center for the Public Interest, 2003.

See also *Batson v. Kentucky*; Burden of proof; Criminal procedure; Grand juries; Hung juries; Judicial system, U.S.; Jury nullification; Jury sequestration; Verdicts; *Voir dire*; *Witherspoon v. Illinois*.

Just deserts

Definition: The concept that punishments for crimes should match the severity of the crimes themselves
Criminal justice issue: Legal terms and principles; Prevention; Punishment; Sentencing
Significance: The concept of just deserts, related to the retributive philosophy of criminal justice, has gained in popularity as the crime problem in the United States has grown.

Just deserts, from an archaic form of the word "desert" meaning "what is deserved," refers to a punishment or consequence that is seen as fitting in regard to the crime or misbehavior. In many contexts the misspelling "just desserts" is accepted and even more common. The concept is part of the retributivist justice model that has deep roots in many world cultures. In addition to being a common phrase in public use it has been incorporated to varying degrees in different criminal justice systems.

Receiving just deserts: punishing a wife beater in Peking, China. (Library of Congress)

In a 1976 report entitled *Doing Justice* criminologist Andrew von Hirsch and other members of the Committee for the Study of Incarceration called for a turning away from the then-prevailing philosophy of rehabilitation of offenders and moving toward a sentencing model that emphasizes giving criminals what they "deserve" for the particular crimes they have committed. Under the rehabilitative model, indeterminate sentencing and wide discretion on the part of sentencers are viewed as desirable. The so-called just deserts model, by contrast, shifts the focus in sentencing to the seriousness of the offender's crime. Proponents of this approach generally favor reducing sentencing disparities and using guidelines that prescribe standardized sentences. The general aim is to give the same punishment to all individuals who commit the same crime.

The just deserts model draws some inspiration from the classical retributivist theory of punishment, which builds on concepts beginning with the well-known ancient concept of "an eye for an eye" and including theories such as that of the eighteenth-century German philosopher Immanuel Kant. According to Kant, judicial punishment "must in all cases be imposed on [the criminal] only on the ground that he has committed a crime." It is a matter of opinion and the subject of much debate as to what the appropriate punishment is for any given crime, however. Among the factors usually considered are the seriousness of the crime, the criminal's previous record, and the amount of harm done to the criminal's victim.

Mario F. Morelli

Further Reading
Cooper, Alison. *A Punishment to Fit the Crime?* North Mankato, Minn.: Sea to Sea Publications, 2005.
Davis, Michael. *To Make the Punishment Fit the Crime: Essays in the Theory of Criminal Justice.* Boulder, Colo.: Westview Press, 1992.
Friedman, Lawrence M. *Crime and Punishment in American History.* Portland, Oreg.: Basic Books, 1994.
Garland, David. *Punishment and Modern Society.* Chicago: University of Chicago Press, 1990.
Gerber, Monica M., and Jonathan Jackson. "Retribution as Revenge and Retribution as Just Deserts." *Social Justice Research* 26.1 (2013): 61–80. Print.
Gervasi, Alexa. "Is There Justice in 'Just Deserts?'" *American Criminal Law Review.* American Criminal Law Review, 8 May 2015. Web. 26 May. 2016.

See also Community-based corrections; Criminal justice system; Deterrence; Discretion; Incapacitation; Mandatory sentencing; Probation, adult; Punishment; Recidivism; Rehabilitation; Sentencing; Sentencing guidelines, U.S.; United States Sentencing Commission; Victimology; Schools of criminology.

Mandamus

Definition: A writ of *mandamus* is a court order requiring a lower court or government agency to carry out its lawfully mandated duties and functions

Criminal justice issue: Courts; federal law; legal terms and principles

Significance: Used only in unusual emergencies, writs of *mandamus* are most commonly issued by superior courts to correct abuses of power by lower courts.

The federal Judiciary Act of 1789 established the federal court system and gave the federal courts the power to issue writs of *mandamus*. These writs require that legally mandated acts be carried out by government or its agents. For example, Arkansas has one of the most liberal freedom of information acts of the fifty states. That Arkansas law requires that virtually all documents of government be open to public viewing during the normal operating hours of a public agency. The law requires that all criminal case files possessed by the police, excepting cases still under investigation, be made available to public viewing during the normal operating hours of the police agencies. If a police department were to refuse public access to those closed criminal case files, a citizen could petition a court to issue a writ of *mandamus* ordering the police department to open those files during normal operating hours.

Lawrence M. Salinger

Further Reading
Meyer, J. F., and D. R. Grant. *The Courts in Our Criminal Justice System.* Upper Saddle River, N.J.: Prentice-Hall, 2003.
Neubauer, D. W. *America's Courts and the Criminal Justice System.* 7th ed. Belmont, Calif.: Wadsworth, 2002.
Wood, Horace G. *A Treatise on the Legal Remedies of Mandamus and Prohibition: Habeas Corpus, Certiorari, and Quo Warranto.* 3d ed. Revised and enlarged by Charles F. Bridge. Littleton, Colo.: Fred B. Rothman, 1997.

See also *Certiorari*; *Habeas corpus*; Subpoena power; Summonses.

Mandatory sentencing

Definition: Laws requiring judges to impose predetermined penalties for certain specified crimes or third felony convictions

Criminal justice issue: Judges; Prisons; Punishment; Sentencing

Significance: The adoption of mandatory sentencing guidelines during the 1980s and 1990s limited judicial discretion in sentencing offenders and contributed to sharp increases in prison populations.

Mandatory sentences for certain offenses have existed since the foundation of the United States. In the early days of the republic, specific sentences were imposed for certain crimes, including gossiping and murder. Early mandatory sentences reflected the forms of punishment used at the time and ranged from dunking stools for gossipers to hanging for convicted murderers.

Special habitual-offender laws that could impose life imprisonment for third felony convictions became common during the twentieth century. However, broader uses of mandatory minimum sentences did not develop until mid-century, when increasing public concern about drug abuse led to the creation of new sentences for drug offenses. For example, in 1952, the US Congress passed the Boggs Act, which specified minimum sentences for federal narcotics offenses, with no possibility of parole or probation after first convictions. Many states then passed legislation modeled on the Boggs Act that specified mandatory minimum sentences for violations of their own drug laws.

During the 1960s, mandatory sentences were heavily criticized for eliminating judicial discretion, treating first-time offenders as harshly as violent criminals and for the failure of the sentences to reduce drug violations. Such criticisms helped prompt Congress to pass the Comprehensive Drug Abuse Prevention and Control Act of 1970, which repealed most of the federal mandatory minimums for drug offenses. However, the 1970s saw a push for more uniform federal sentencing policies and the elimination of indeterminate sentencing in favor of determinate sentences, without the possibility of parole. At the same time, some states were enacting mandatory minimum sentences for drug offenses on their own.

In 1973, New York passed a series of laws that required mandatory fifteen-year prison sentences for possession or sales of small quantities of narcotics. Michigan passed a similar law in 1978. Michigan's law was dubbed the "650 lifer law" because it required mandatory life imprisonment for the possession, sale, or conspiracy to sell or possess 650 grams of cocaine or heroin. By 1983, forty states had similar mandatory sentencing laws.

Sentencing Reform in the 1980s

The bulk of sentencing reform took place in the 1980s, due in large part to the Reagan administration's war on drugs. In 1984, Congress passed the Comprehensive Crime Control Act and the Sentencing Reform Act, which transformed the federal system of indeterminate sentencing to a system of determinate sentencing. Parole was eliminated and the United States Sentencing Commission was established to develop federal sentencing guidelines for judges. The Crime Control Act successfully limited judicial discretion on sentences for drug crimes, while adding new mandatory sentences for other crimes. The new requirements included adding five years to drug-offense sentences for using or carrying guns during drug crimes or crimes of violence. The law also mandated fifteen-year sentences for simple possession of firearms by persons with three previous convictions for burglary or robbery.

The Anti-Drug Abuse Act of 1988 established most of the drug-related mandatory minimums, including five- and ten-year sentences tied to quantities of illegal drugs. Further adding to the mandatory minimum sentences, the Omnibus Crime Control Act of 1988 mandated minimum sentences of five years for simple possession of crack cocaine; however, simple possession of other drugs remained a misdemeanor. The mandatory minimum for crack cocaine versus powder cocaine, often referred to as the 100:1 ratio, required five-year sentences for possession of 500 grams of powder cocaine or 5 grams of crack cocaine. The act made crack cocaine the only drug to carry a federally mandated sentence for simple possession. Another significant provision of the 1988 law was an increase in penalties for drug conspiracy, which could be applied equally to both major dealers and low-level participants in drug deals.

"Get Tough on Crime" Era

The punitive sentencing reforms adopted during the 1990s reflected the so-called "get tough on crime" attitudes of the public and the administration at the time. During that decade, additional federal mandatory sentencing laws were enacted, including some that did not apply to drugs. Many states also legislated mandatory sentences for felons possessing firearms or using firearms in the commission of crimes.

Washington (1993) and California (1994) both enacted mandatory life sentences for offenders receiving third felony convictions. Similar laws mandating sentences for habitual offenders were on the books in most states but were not widely used. However, they became an important issue in the 1990s after some highly publicized crimes, including the murder of a young girl in California by a repeat offender. California's new law, dubbed " three strikes and you're out," set mandatory twenty-five-year to life sentences for offenders convicted of third felonies. California's law became controversial because it applied to any third felony conviction. As a consequence, some highly publicized cases arose when nonviolent offenders were sentenced to exceptionally long prison terms for crimes as minor as shoplifting.

Mandatory sentencing laws were also heavily criticized for giving disproportionate punishment to nonviolent drug offenders by sentencing them to long prison terms. Appeals were made to Congress for relief, and in 1994 Congress enacted a so-called "safety valve" exception to the mandatory minimum sentences. The safety valve applied to nonviolent, low-level, and first-time drug offenders, but its eligibility criteria were so narrow that nonviolent drug offenders continued to be sentenced to long prison terms under the mandatory laws. The only way most defendants could avoid mandatory minimum sentences was to provide law enforcement with "substantial assistance" by disclosing information on other drug dealers or testifying against them in court.

Proponents of mandatory sentencing laws argue that these laws provide desirable sentencing uniformity. Critics argue that mandatory sentencing laws have placed unnecessary financial strains on the criminal justice system while failing to reduce the numbers of drug violations. Appeals have been made to Congress to address the large disparity in sentences awarded to crack cocaine and powder cocaine users. Congress has responded by introducing bills that would increase sentences for powder cocaine offenses while retaining the mandatory five-year minimum for simple possession of crack cocaine. Meanwhile, additional mandatory sentencing laws continue to be proposed in Congress.

In 2005, the US Supreme Court held in *United States v. Booker* that the US Sentencing Guidelines, which allowed judges to enhance sentences based on facts not reviewed by a jury, were a violation of the Sixth Amendment right to trial by jury. In 2013, in a similar case, *Alleyne v. United States*, the Supreme Court held that if any element of a crime increases the mandatory minimum punishment, it must be disclosed to the jury and found to be true beyond a reasonable doubt. In responsem the US Justice Department announced that it would refine its policy regarding mandatory minimums for certain nonviolent, low-level drug offenders, reserving severe mandatory minimum penalties for serious, high-level, or violent drug traffickers.

Tammy L. Castle

Further Reading

Allen, Harry E., Edward J. Latessa, and Bruce S. Ponder. *Corrections in America: An Introduction*. 14th ed. Upper Saddle River: Pearson Education, 2015. Print.

Clark, J., J. Austin, and D. A. Henry. *Three Strikes and You're Out: A Review of State Legislation*. Washington, DC: National Institute of Justice, Government Printing Office, 1997. Print.

Demleitner, Nora V., Douglas A. Berman, Marc L. Miller, and Ronald F. Wright. *Sentencing Law and Policy: Cases, Statutes, and Guidelines*. New York: Aspen, 2003. Print.

Krantz, Sheldon, and Lynn Branham. *The Law of Sentencing, Corrections, and Prisoners' Rights*. St. Paul: West, 1997. Print.

Stith, Kate, and Jose A. Cabranes. *Fear of Judging: Sentencing Guidelines in the Federal Courts*. Chicago: U of Chicago P, 1998. Print.

Tonry, Michael. *Reconsidering Indeterminate and Structured Sentencing*. Washington, DC: US Department of Justice, Office of Justice Programs, National Institute of Justice, 1999. Print.

Tonry, Michael. *Sentencing Matters*. New York: Oxford UP, 1996. Print.

"US: Repeal Mandatory Federal Drug Sentences." *Human Rights Watch*. Human Rights Watch, 2 Feb. 2016. Web. 31 May 2016.

Zimring, Franklin E., G. Hawkins, and S. Kamin. *Punishment and Democracy: Three Strikes and You're Out in California*. Oxford: Oxford UP, 2001. Print.

See also Comprehensive Crime Control Act; Comprehensive Drug Abuse Prevention and Control Act; Concurrent sentences; Discretion; Drug courts; Felonies; *Harmelin v. Michigan*; Incapacitation; Indeterminate sentencing; Just deserts; Prison overcrowding; Recidivism; *Rummel v. Estelle*; Sentencing; Sentencing guidelines, U.S.; United States Sentencing Commission.

Massiah v. United States

The Case: U.S. Supreme Court ruling on the right to counsel

Date: Decided on May 18, 1964

Criminal justice issue: Attorneys; confessions; defendants; interrogation

Significance: This case expanded the exclusionary rule to disallow the prosecution from using any evidence that the police have deliberately elicited from an indicted defendant when not in the presence of a lawyer.

A federal grand jury indicted Winston Massiah and a codefendant on charges of illegally trafficking in cocaine. Massiah retained a lawyer and was released on bail. Unknown to Massiah, his codefendant agreed to cooperate with federal officers in exchange for a reduced sentence. In a private conversation with the codefendant, Massiah made incriminating statements that were overheard by an agent operating a transmitter.

At the subsequent trial, the judge allowed the agent to testify about Massiah's statements, which were tantamount to a confession. Based on this evidence, the jury quickly decided that Massiah was guilty. In appealing the conviction, defense lawyers pointed to the precedent of *Spano v. New York* (1959), in which the Supreme Court had held that the prosecution may not make use of a confession that police officers obtained by intimidating a defendant who had already been indicted. In getting Massiah to confess, however, the police had used only trickery, not threats or other forms of coercion.

The Supreme Court, by a 6-3 vote, overturned Massiah's conviction. Writing for the majority, Justice Potter Stewart held that once adversarial proceedings have been initiated, any statements deliberately elicited by government agents outside the presence of a defense lawyer must be excluded from a criminal trial, except if the defendant had explicitly waived his Sixth Amendment right to counsel. The justices in the majority made a linkage between this right and the Fifth Amendment privilege against self-incrimination, which they interpreted to mean that confessions not given voluntarily and intentionally are inadmissible as evidence. In this case, therefore, it was irrelevant that the police had not forcefully compelled Messiah to made incriminating statements to his colleague.

The *Massiah* holding applied only to statements obtained by law-enforcement officers after a person has been formally charged with a crime. Later that year, in *Escobedo v. Illinois*, the Court recognized that a suspect yet to be indicted has a right to counsel when in custody for the purpose of interrogation. The famous case of *Miranda v. Arizona* (1966) obligated the police to inform suspects of this right before interrogation. The Court further expanded the prohibition against using trickery to elicit information from detained suspects outside the presence of counsel in *Brewer v. Williams* (1977). In *Henry v. United States* (1980), the Court suppressed a conversation in which an incarcerated defendant made incriminating statements to a cellmate cooperating with the police, even though the cellmate had simply listened and had not encouraged the defendant to discuss the crime.

Thomas Tandy Lewis

Further Reading
Taylor, John B. *Right to Counsel and Privilege Against Self-Incrimination: Rights and Liberties Under the Law.* Santa Barbara, Calif.: ABC-Clio, 2004.
Whitebread, Charles, and Christopher Slobogin. *Criminal Procedures: An Analysis of Cases and Concepts.* 4th ed. New York: Foundation Press, 2000.

See also Confessions; Counsel, right to; Electronic surveillance; *Escobedo v. Illinois*; Exclusionary rule; Police ethics; Supreme Court, U.S.

McCleskey v. Kemp

The Case: U.S. Supreme Court ruling on capital punishment
Date: Decided on April 22, 1987
Criminal justice issue: Capital punishment; civil rights and liberties
Significance: This Supreme Court ruling rejected a death-row inmate's claim that Georgia's system of sentencing people to death was unconstitutional because it discriminated on the basis of race.

In 1978, Warren McCleskey, a black man, was convicted of killing a white police officer during an armed robbery of a store in Atlanta, Georgia. McCleskey's jury—which consisted of eleven whites and one black—sentenced him to die in Georgia's electric chair. McCleskey sought a writ of *habeas corpus*, arguing, among other things, that the Georgia capital sentencing process was administered in a racially discriminatory manner and violated the U.S. Constitution. According to McCleskey, the jury's decision to execute him violated the Eighth Amendment because racial bias rendered the decision arbitrary and capricious. Also, the equal protection clause of the Fourteenth Amendment was violated because McCleskey, a black man, was treated differently than white defendants in the same position.

To support his claim of racial discrimination, McCleskey offered as evidence a careful statistical study performed by Professor David B. Baldus and his colleagues at the University of Iowa (the Baldus study). The Baldus study showed that race played a dual role in deciding whether convicted murderers in Georgia would be sentenced to death. First, the race of the murder victim played a large role in whether a defendant would be sentenced to die. According to the study, defendants charged with killing whites received the death penalty in 11 percent of the cases. Defendants charged with killing African Americans received the death penalty in only 1 percent of the cases. After taking account of thirty-nine variables that could have explained the disparities on nonracial grounds, the Baldus study concluded that, in Georgia, defendants charged with killing white victims were 4.3 times as likely to receive a death sentence as defendants charged with killing African Americans.

Second, the race of the defendant played an important role during capital sentencing. According to the Baldus study, black defendants were 1.1 times as likely to receive a death sentence as other defendants. Thus, the study showed that black defendants such as McCleskey who had killed white victims had the greatest likelihood of receiving the death penalty.

By a 5-4 vote, the Supreme Court ruled against McCleskey. The Supreme Court accepted the validity of the Baldus study but held that McCleskey failed to prove "that decision makers in his case acted with discriminatory purpose." In other words, McCleskey failed to show that his constitutional rights were violated because he did not prove that anyone involved in his particular case intentionally discriminated against him based on his race. Justice Lewis Powell's opinion for the majority expressed special concern that if the Court accepted McCleskey's argument—that racial bias impermissibly tainted capital sentencing proceedings—all criminal sentences would be subject to attack based on allegations of racial discrimination. The *McCleskey* decision is a landmark ruling in the modern era of capital punishment.

Warren McCleskey died in Georgia's electric chair on September 25, 1991. That same year Justice Powell, whose 5-4 majority opinion sealed Warren McCleskey's fate, told a biographer that he would change his vote in that case (thus sparing McCleskey's life) if he could. Also, although executions had resumed in the United States in 1977, 1991 marked the first time in the modern era of American capital punishment that a white defendant (Donald "Pee Wee" Gaskins) was actually executed for killing a black person.

Randall Coyne

Further Reading
Bohm, Robert M. *Deathquest: An Introduction to the Theory and Practice of Capital Punishment in the United States.* Cincinnati: Anderson Publishing, 2003.
Carter, Linda E., and Ellen Krietzberg. *Understanding Capital Punishment Law.* Newark, N.J.: LexisNexis, 2004.
Latzer, Barry, ed. *Death Penalty Cases: Leading Supreme Court Cases on Capital Punishment.* 2d ed. Burlington, Mass.: Butterworth Heinemann, 2002.
Sarat, Austin. *When the State Kills: Capital Punishment and the American Condition.* Princeton, N.J.: Princeton University Press, 2001.

See also Capital punishment; Equal protection under the law; Supreme Court, U.S.

Minnick v. Mississippi

The Case: U.S. Supreme Court ruling on the right to counsel
Date: Decided on December 3, 1990
Criminal justice issue: Arrest and arraignment; confessions; defendants; interrogation
Significance: This Supreme Court decision found that a reinitiated interrogation of a murder suspect who had been advised of his Miranda rights and received counsel still violated the suspect's Fifth Amendment rights because it was conducted without counsel being present.

Robert S. Minnick, the petitioner, sought reversal of his conviction for murder in the circuit court of Lowndes County, Mississippi, on the grounds that his constitutional rights against self-incrimination had been violated when his confession was taken during an interrogation conducted without counsel present. Minnick, a fugitive from prison, had been arrested and held in a California jail, where two federal agents, after reading the Miranda warnings to him, began an interrogation on a Friday. He requested that they return on the following Monday, when he would have counsel present. The agents complied, breaking off their questioning. An appointed attorney then advised Minnick to speak to no one about the charges against him. After an interview with the agents on Monday, Minnick was questioned by a deputy sheriff from Mississippi. The deputy advised Minnick of his Miranda rights, and the accused, who refused to sign a waiver of those rights, confessed to the murder for which he was subsequently tried and sentenced to death.

At Minnick's murder trial in Mississippi, he filed a motion to suppress the confession, but his request was denied. The conviction was then upheld by the Supreme Court of Mississippi, which ruled that Minnick's right to counsel, as set forth in the Fifth Amendment, had been granted in accordance with the guidelines established in *Edwards v. Arizona* (1981), which stipulates that a defendant who requests counsel during questioning cannot be subjected to further interrogation until the counsel is "made available" to the defendant. According to the Mississippi Supreme Court, that condition had been met when Minnick consulted with his appointed attorney.

The U.S. Supreme Court, on *certiorari*, reversed and remanded in a 6-2 decision. In the majority opinion, written by Justice Anthony Kennedy, the justices ruled that in a custodial interrogation, once counsel is provided, questioning cannot be resumed without counsel being present. It stipulated that the *Edwards v. Arizona* ruling regarding protection against self-incrimination is not met, nor is that protection terminated or suspended, by the mere provision of counsel outside the interrogation process. The majority found that Minnick's confession to the Mississippi deputy sheriff should have been inadmissible at his murder trial. In a dissenting opinion, Justice Antonin Scalia argued the contrary, holding that the *Edwards v. Arizona* rule excluding self-incrimination without counsel was not applicable after Minnick's first interview with his appointed attorney.

The Court's relatively narrow interpretation of what constitutes right to counsel leaves a legacy of stringent procedural requirements on law-enforcement agencies, which must comply with a suspect's right to have counsel present during custodial interrogations that had been broken off and later resumed. From the point of view of such agencies, its practical effect is to inhibit an expeditious interrogation of suspects.

John W. Fiero

Further Reading

Dressler, Joshua. *Understanding Criminal Procedure*. 3d ed. New York: LexisNexis, 2002.

Taylor, John B. *Right to Counsel and Privilege Against Self-Incrimination: Rights and Liberties Under the Law*. Santa Barbara, Calif.: ABC-Clio, 2004.

Tomkovicz, James J. *The Right to the Assistance of Counsel: A Reference Guide to the United States Constitution*. Westport, Conn.: Greenwood Press, 2002.

See also Confessions; Counsel, right to; Self-incrimination, privilege against; Supreme Court, U.S.

Miscarriage of justice

Definition: Legal act, verdict, or punishment that is clearly unfair or unjust

Criminal justice issue: Government misconduct; Trial procedures; Verdicts

Significance: Whether a criminal justice outcome should be considered a miscarriage of justice is often difficult to determine and can be a source of controversy between groups with opposing viewpoints. Attention placed on an actual or perceived miscarriage of justice can result in political debate and sometimes government policy changes.

Miscarriages of justice fall into two basic groups: unfair acquittals of the guilty and unfair convictions of the inno-

Protesters who believed that the acquittal of George Zimmerman was a miscarriage of justice. (By Brian Stansberry, via Wikimedia Commons)

cent. Acquittals of defendants whom many people believe are guilty—such as former football star O. J. Simpson—often generate as much or more attention in the media as punishments of the guilty. Although acquittals of offenders who are perceived to be guilty can cause considerable heartache to the victims of crime and their families and can increase public skepticism about criminal justice, most people would consider false convictions of innocent defendants to be the more serious of the two types of miscarriages of justice.

Miscarriages of justice occur not only in trial outcomes but also at other steps of the criminal justice system. For example, the wrongful arrest of an innocent person is as much a miscarriage of justice as a police officer's conscious decision not to arrest a guilty offender who has harmed another person.

Brion Sever

Further Reading

Dwyer, Jim, Peter Neufeld, and Barry Scheck. *Actual Innocence: Five Days to Execution and Other Dispatches from the Wrongly Convicted*. Garden City: Doubleday, 2000. Print

Gershman, Bennett. "Themes of Injustice: Wrongful Convictions, Racial Prejudice, and Lawyer Incompetence." In *Criminal Courts for the Twenty-first Century*, edited by Lisa Stolzenberg and Stewart D'Alessio. Upper Saddle River: Prentice-Hall, 1998. Print.

Westervelt, Saundra, and John Humphrey. *Wrongly Convicted: Perspectives on Failed Justice*. New Brunswick: Rutgers UP, 2001. Print.

See also Appellate process; Cruel and unusual punishment; Exclusionary rule; False convictions; Harmless error; Jury nullification; Pardons; Perjury; Police corruption; Presumption of innocence; Scottsboro cases.

Night courts

Definition: Courts holding their sessions during evening hours

Criminal justice issue: Courts; jurisdictions

Significance: Court proceedings conducted at times other than those considered normal working hours are becoming an increasingly common part of the modern criminal justice system.

Almost entirely criminal courts, night courts have become a necessity as a result of several federal court rulings. Due process requirements, mandated by state and federal courts, and state statutes require that individuals arrested or detained by the police must be brought before a magistrate and given formal notice of charges against them within twenty-four to forty-eight hours in an effort to minimize the time a presumably innocent individual spends in jail.

Jurisdictions unable to handle staggering caseloads during regular working hours have been forced to operate courts twenty-four hours a day, seven days a week as a result. The Criminal Court of New York City, for example, the largest and busiest court in the United States, handled approximately 40 percent of its 1997 arraignments during the night and early morning hours. Many other court systems, especially those in densely populated areas, have been forced to establish similar courts or risk being forced to release criminals who might be denied their due process rights.

Donald C. Simmons, Jr.

Further Reading

Meyer, J. F., and D. R. Grant. *The Courts in Our Criminal Justice System.* Upper Saddle River, N.J.: Prentice-Hall, 2003.

Neubauer, D. W. *America's Courts and the Criminal Justice System.* 7th ed. Belmont, Calif.: Wadsworth, 2002.

Warner, Ralph. *Everybody's Guide to Small Claims Court, National Edition.* Berkeley, Calif.: Nolo Press, 2004.

See also Court types; Criminal law; Judges; Misdemeanors; Traffic courts; Traffic fines; Traffic law.

Nolle prosequi

Definition: Announcement made into a court record that a plaintiff or prosecutor will not proceed forward with a lawsuit or indictment

Criminal justice issue: Legal terms and principles; prosecution; trial procedures

Significance: In criminal law, prosecutors enter *nolle prosequi* motions to terminate their cases early; however, such motions are rare and usually require the approval of judges.

From a Latin phrase meaning "we shall no longer prosecute," *nolle prosequi* is a type of defendant disposition occurring after the filing of a case, but before judgment, in court. Such a filing means that the plaintiff in a civil case, or prosecutor in a criminal case, wishes to drop prosecution of all or part of a suit or indictment.

In civil cases, a *nolle prosequi* is considered an agreement by the plaintiff to not proceed, either against some of the defendants, or to part of the suit. It may be entered for one of several counts, or for one of several defendants. In criminal cases, *nolle prosequi* is an entry made on records by prosecutors stating that they will no longer pursue prosecution. Common reasons for *nolle prosequi* include insufficient evidence, reluctance of witnesses to testify, and police errors. Such motions are extremely rare, however, and prosecutors who wish to file them generally need the permission of judges to do so.

The awarding of a *nolle prosequi* is not a bar to future action for the same cause, as it does not prevent the charge from being brought up at a later date. Conversely, in some jurisdictions, a *nolle prosequi* of a charge enables the defendant later to file a petition requesting expungement of police records and court records relating to the charge.

Pati K. Hendrickson

Further Reading

Champion, Dean John. *The American Dictionary of Criminal Justice.* 2d ed. Los Angeles: Roxbury Publishing, 2001.

Territo, Leonard, James B. Halsted, and Max L. Bromley. *Crime and Justice in America: A Human Perspective.* 6th ed. Upper Saddle River, N.J.: Pearson Prentice-Hall, 2004.

See also Acquittal; Criminal procedure; Discretion; District attorneys; Public prosecutors; Trials.

Nolo contendere

Definition: Plea that refuses to contest charges brought against a defendant

Criminal justice issue: Defendants; legal terms and principles; pleas; trial procedures

Significance: *Nolo contendere* pleas are most commonly made when civil cases against defendants are possible. Although this form of plea has been criticized for lacking logical and theoretical purpose, some authorities argue that the passage of time has shown *nolo contendere* to perform a useful and practical function in the court process.

Defendants in criminal court are provided the option to plead guilty, not guilty, and, sometimes, *nolo contendere*. Latin for "no contest," the term *nolo contendere* indicates that defendants are not contesting the charges against them. Instead, the defendants are essentially accepting penalties without admitting guilt. Defendants who plead no contest are thus subject to the same penalties they would receive if they instead simply pleaded guilty to the charges. *Nolo contendere* pleas are also similar to guilty pleas in that they must be made voluntarily and without force or threats. However, *nolo contendere* pleas differ from guilty pleas in not acknowledging wrongdoing. For that reason, they cannot be used against defendants in later civil proceedings resulting from the same offenses.

While the right to plead guilty or not guilty is a fundamental right in the American justice system, defendants do not have an unqualified right to plead *nolo contendere*. *Nolo contendere* pleas are allowed in federal courts and in the majority of states but are mainly used for misdemeanor offenses. In cases that qualify for *nolo contendere* pleas, defendants usually have to acquire permission from either the prosecution, the court, or both.

Brion Sever

Further Reading
ABA Standards for Criminal Justice: Pleas of Guilty. Chicago: American Bar Association, 1999.
Burnett, C. "*Nolo Contendere*: Efficient or Effective Administration of Justice?" *Criminal Law Bulletin* 23 (1987): 117-134.

See also Arraignment; Convictions; Criminal procedure; Plea bargaining; Pleas; Self-incrimination, privilege against.

Objections

Definition: Expression of disagreement with a statement or procedure during a trial by an attorney involved in a case
Criminal justice issue: Attorneys; courts; trial procedures
Significance: The ability to object during trials gives attorneys a means to alert judges that they believe statements or procedures should not be permitted.

During the trial process, attorneys can verbally object to the admission of evidence into the proceedings. That evidence may include oral testimony, physical evidence, or the types of questions being asked by opposing attorneys. If the latter, attorneys may raise their objections after questions are asked but before they are answered. They may object on the grounds that the questions are irrelevant, immaterial, prejudicial, or call for witnesses to speak on subjects about which they have no direct knowledge.

Once an objection is made, the judge rules on it. The judge may decide to sustain the objection or overrule it. A judge who sustains an objection is stating that the objection itself has merit. In such a case, the offending attorney may be instructed to rephrase a question or discontinue a behavior, such as being rude or harsh to a witness. A judge who decides that an objection lacks merit will overrule it and allow the other attorney to continue as before. Occasionally, there are instances in which a judge does not make an immediate ruling on an objection. In some instances, the judge may require the attorneys to argue the legal point outside the presence of the jury, in what is known as a side-bar conference.

Jenifer A. Lee

Further Reading
Neubauer, David W. *America's Courts and the Criminal Justice System*. 8th ed. Belmont, Calif.: Wadsworth/Thomson Learning, 2005.
Rabe, Gary A., and Dean John Champion. *Criminal Courts: Structure, Process, and Issues*. Upper Saddle River, N.J.: Prentice-Hall, 2002.

See also Judges; Subpoena power; Testimony; Trials; Witnesses.

Obstruction of justice

Definition: Efforts to interfere with the operations of court or their officials
Criminal justice issue: Courts; trial procedures
Significance: Obstructing justice may deny a party the right to due process or justice.

Obstruction of justice is an attempt to impede justice by any means. It may include physical disruption of trial courts in session; attempts to interfere with judges, court officials, or jurors; and attempts to bribe or create doubt regarding the integrity of those involved in court proceedings. Concealing or falsifying evidence obstructs justice, as does resisting a court-appointed process server.

Because police are officers of the court, intentional interference with their duties may be considered an obstruction of justice. In federal practice, obstruction extends to agencies, departments, and committees conducting their work. A witness concealing evidence from an investigation by a congressional committee is as guilty of obstruction as a person concealing evidence in a trial court.

Elizabeth Algren Shaw

Further Reading
Del Carmen, Rolando V. *Criminal Procedure: Law and Practice*. 6th ed. Belmont, Calif.: Thomson/Wadsworth, 2004.
Garner, Bryan A., ed. *Black's Law Dictionary*. 8th ed. St. Paul, Minn.: Thomson/West, 2004.
Wood, J. D., and Linda Picard, eds. *Dictionary of Law*. Springfield, Mass.: Merriam-Webster, 1996.

See also Contempt of court; Corporate scandals; Evidence, rules of; Perjury; Subpoena power.

Opinions

Definition: Written explanations by judges of the reasons for their rulings
Criminal justice issue: Appeals; judges; trial procedures
Significance: The judicial system generally expects judges who decide cases to explain their decisions in written opinions. The collected opinions of relatively important courts—state appellate courts and federal courts—form the bases for subsequent judicial decisions. Later courts strive to adhere to the results of previously published opinions in keeping with the judicial principle of *stare decisis*, which means, "let the decision stand."

To facilitate the legal system's reliance on previous opinions to guide subsequent ones, legal publishers have traditionally collected judicial opinions into bound volumes referred to generically as "reporters." Reporters may collect all the opinions of a specific court, such as the *United States Reports*, which includes the opinions of the U.S. Supreme Court. Other reporters contain the opinions of courts in a particular geographic region, such as the *Pacific Reporter*, which includes opinions from the courts of California and other western states. Computerized databases and Internet sites now make most, if not all, reported opinions available to those without access to bound volumes of reporters.

In the U.S. system appellate judges write most opinions. Appellate courts generally have three or more members, a majority of whom determine the outcome in particular cases. One member of this majority then typically writes the opinion explaining the result, or holding, of the case. This opinion is called the majority opinion. Sometimes a judge who agrees with the majority's result in a case may nevertheless not agree with the reasoning offered by the majority opinion or may wish to explain the decision in some fashion other than that adopted by the majority. This judge may write what is referred to as a concurring opinion. A judge who disagrees not only with the reasoning of a case but with the result reached by the majority might write a dissenting opinion to express this disagreement. Finally, in a few cases judges may agree about a decision and publish a *per curiam* opinion, which bears the name of no particular author. Courts publish *per curiam* opinions most frequently to express decisions in minor or noncontroversial cases.

Timothy L. Hall

Further Reading
Amar, Akhil Reed. *The Constitution and Criminal Procedure: First Principles*. New Haven, Conn.: Yale University Press, 1997.
Lewis, Thomas T., and Richard L. Wilson, eds. *Encyclopedia of the U.S. Supreme Court*. 3 vols. Pasadena, Calif.: Salem Press, 2001.
Rehnquist, William. *The Supreme Court*. New York: Alfred A. Knopf, 2001.

See also Appellate process; Case law; Court types; Precedent; Supreme Court, U.S.

Palko v. Connecticut

The Case: U.S. Supreme Court ruling on double jeopardy
Date: Decided on December 6, 1937
Criminal justice issue: Constitutional protections; defendants
Significance: In this case, while refusing to apply the Fifth Amendment right against double jeopardy to the states, the Supreme Court established an influential test for determining which fundamental rights contained within the Bill of Rights are incorporated into the Fourteenth Amendment's due process clause.

On the night of September 29, 1935, Bridgeport, Connecticut, police officers Wilfred Walker and Thomas J. Kearney were shot and killed. Frank Palko was charged with first-degree murder, a charge which carried a death sentence. On January 24, 1936, a trial jury found Palko guilty of only second-degree murder because the killings were not sufficiently premeditated. Palko received a sentence of life imprisonment. On July 30, 1936, the Supreme Court of Errors of Connecticut ordered a new trial by finding that the trial judge gave improper instructions to the jury. On October 15, 1936, a second jury found Palko guilty of first-degree murder, and he was sentenced to death. Palko's case came to the U.S. Supreme Court with the claim that the second trial violated his Fifth Amendment right to not "be subject for the same offense to be twice put in jeopardy of life or limb." At the time, however, the Supreme Court had applied the Fifth Amendment right against double jeopardy only to criminal cases in federal, rather than state, courts.

For most of American history, the provisions of the Bill of Rights protected individuals only against actions by the federal government. The ratification of the Fourteenth Amendment in 1868 applied constitutional rights to protection against the states, but those rights were vaguely worded protections involving "due process" and "equal protection." People repeatedly brought cases to the Supreme Court asserting that the provisions of the Bill of Rights should apply against state as well as federal government officials. Beginning in 1925, the Supreme Court gradually incorporated a few rights—speech, press, and religion—into the Fourteenth Amendment's due process clause and thereby made those rights applicable to the states.

Unfortunately for Palko, the Court was unwilling to incorporate the Fifth Amendment's protection against double jeopardy in 1937. Thus Palko's conviction was affirmed, and he was subsequently executed for the murders. Justice Benjamin Cardozo's majority opinion, however, established a test for determining which rights to incorporate by declaring that only rights which are "fundamental" and "essential" to liberty are contained in the right to due process in the Fourteenth Amendment. In analyzing Palko's case, Cardozo decided that many criminal justice rights contained in the Bill of Rights, such as trial by jury and protection against double jeopardy and self-incrimination, are not fundamental and essential because it is possible to have fair trials without them.

The importance of *Palko v. Connecticut* is that Cardozo's test established an influential standard for determining which provisions of the Bill of Rights apply against the states. Although justices in later decades disagreed with Cardozo's specific conclusions and subsequently incorporated double jeopardy and other rights for criminal defendants, most justices continued to use Cardozo's basic approach of evaluating whether each specific right was fundamental and essential to liberty.

Christopher E. Smith

Further Reading
Garcia, Alfredo. *The Fifth Amendment: A Comprehensive Approach*. Westport, Conn.: Greenwood Press, 2002.
Holmes, Burnham. *The Fifth Amendment*. Englewood Cliffs, N.J.: Silver Burdett Press, 1991.
Rudstein, David S. *Double Jeopardy: A Reference Guide to the United States Constitution*. Westport, Conn.: Praeger, 2004.

See also Bill of Rights, U.S.; Double jeopardy; Due process of law; Incorporation doctrine; Supreme Court, U.S.

Pardons

Definition: Legal release from the punishment for a crime
Criminal justice issue: Government misconduct; Pardons and parole; Political issues
Significance: The power of government to pardon criminals is an essential part of the checks and balances of the American constitutional system, as it allows executive branches to check the fairness of rulings from the judicial branches.

Modern government's power to pardon has its origin in ancient Hebrew law. It also existed within European churches and monarchies that had the power of clemency during medieval times. Centuries later, in England, the pardon power was recognized as the "royal prerogative of mercy." In the United States, pardons are viewed as a way for the executive branches of state and federal government to check the judiciary.

Many scholars view the pardon power as antidemocratic because it permits one person to subvert the rulings of the criminal justice system. However, the Framers of the US Constitution supported the idea of a pardon power because it allowed executive leaders to use well-timed pardons during times of crisis to quell rebellion among dissatisfied segments of the population.

The chief executive officers at the national and the state levels may issue pardons in particular cases. In each of the fifty states, a board of pardons makes recommendations—often in consultation with the state boards of parole—on persons who should be given pardons. Three main goals are served through the use of the pardon power: remedying injustice, removing the disgrace of conviction, and mitigating the punishment stage of the criminal justice system. It is rare for pardons to be issued for injustices, but many convicted persons are released from prison after they are found to have been wrongfully convicted. Pardons are more commonly employed in cases in which young offenders seek to expunge their criminal records in order to pursue careers that are not open to convicted felons. Pardons allow all former convicts to find employment more easily and generally remove the disgrace of criminal records.

Presidential Pardons

The US Constitution provides US presidents with the power to pardon individuals for offenses against the United States, except in cases of impeachment. President pardons generally receive little attention, but they have been exercised frequently throughout history. In *Ex parte Garland* (1866), the US Supreme Court ruled that Congress cannot limit the president's pardon power through legislation. Hence, the power to pardon at the federal level is potentially unlimited. Moreover, presidents can issue pardons at any time during judicial proceedings and for any offense. In fact, offenses do not even have to be specified, and a person need not be convicted of a crime to be issued a pardon.

By contrast, a large majority of states have placed limitations on their governors' power to pardon. For example, many states have imposed postconviction requirements upon governors, requiring that a person must first be convicted of a crime to be eligible for a pardon.

The Pardon of Richard M. Nixon

The most controversial pardon in American history was issued on September 8, 1974, when President Gerald R. Ford pardoned former president Richard M. Nixon one month after succeeding Nixon as president. At that moment, Nixon had not even been charged with any crime; however, he was under investigation for his involvement in a burglary at the Democratic headquarters at the Watergate hotel in Washington, DC. Nevertheless, Ford's proclamation pardoned Nixon for all offenses against the United States that he may have committed during his presidency.

Many Americans believed that Ford's pardon of Nixon was motivated by partisan interests and contradicted the assumption of the Framers of the Constitution that presidents would not break the law. In fact, some speculated

President Ford announces his decision to pardon former President Richard Nixon. (Public domain, via Wikimedia Commons)

that Ford promised to pardon Nixon even before Nixon named him vice president on Spiro Agnew's resignation, thus putting him in line for the presidency. Nevertheless, in *Murphy v. Ford* (1975), a federal district court judge upheld the constitutionality of Ford's pardon of Nixon. Citing *Ex parte Garland* as precedent, the judge reaffirmed that the president's power to pardon is not subject to any limitations.

Bush's Pardons of Iran-Contra Figures

In December 1992, President George Bush pardoned six key figures in the Iran-Contra scandal, which involved members of President Ronald Reagan's administration illegally selling weapons to Iran during the 1980s in exchange for funds to support the Contras who were fighting against Nicaragua's Sandinista government. Congress had specifically addressed the issue of the Contras by passing legislation to keep the US government out of the Nicaraguan civil war. In December 1992, Reagan's former vice president, George Bush, was himself a lame-duck president, after losing his bid for reelection in November. Bush pardoned former defense secretary Caspar Weinberger, three Central Intelligence Agency officials, and two former advisers to Reagan. By pardoning these people, Bush halted the criminal justice process and prevented more information from surfacing about the scandal. His action was troubling because many people speculated that Bush was acting in his own self-interest, as criminal trials might have produced information about his own involvement in the scandal during his time as vice president.

The pardon power is a significant grant of authority bestowed upon US presidents. The pardons issued by Ford and Bush demonstrate that the power might be used for political purposes and, more important, might pose risks to democratic government. The pardon power has the potential of being used by governors and presidents to conceal criminal and other government misconduct. Therefore, some politicians, such as former senator Walter Mondale of Minnesota, have proposed constitutional amendments to place a postconviction limitation on the president's power to pardon individuals for federal crimes. Until such an amendment is ratified, however, the US Supreme Court's interpretation of the pardon power prohibits restrictions upon presidents.

Scott P. Johnson

Further Reading

Chabot, Steve. *Presidential Pardon Power: Hearing Before the Committee on the Judiciary, US House of Representatives*. Collingdale: Diane, 2003. Print.
Genovese, Michael. *The Power of the American Presidency, 1789-2000*. New York: Oxford UP, 2000. Print.
Johnson, Scott P., and Christopher E. Smith. "White House Scandals and the Presidential Pardon Power: Persistent Risks and Prospects for Reform." *New England Law Review* (1999). Print.
Macgill, Hugh C. "The Nixon Pardon: Limits on the Benign Prerogative." *Connecticut Law Review* (1974). Print.
Mollenhoff, Clark R. *The Man Who Pardoned Nixon*. New York: St. Martin's, 1976. Print.

See also Amnesty; Clemency; Constitution, U.S.; Criminal justice system; False convictions; Good time; Miscarriage of justice; Parole; Parole officers; Political corruption; Probation, adult; Parole Commission, U.S..

People v. George Zimmerman (2013)

Definition: The *People v. Zimmerman* (2013) was a case involving the criminal prosecution of George Zimmerman under the charge of second-degree murder for the shooting and killing of seventeen-year-old Trayvon Martin.
Criminal justice issue: Criminal justice issues: Courts; defendants; homicide; hate crime; verdicts
Significance: This case brought to light and reignited discussion of civil liberties—specifically the issue of racial profiling—and the "stand your ground" doctrine in the United States.

On a Sunday evening in February of 2012, Trayvon Martin, a seventeen-year-old Black American boy was walking down the sidewalk on the way to his father's home in Sanford, Florida. Trayvon had just made a trip to the local 7-Eleven to buy a snack for himself and his brother. At

Protesters calling for justice after the acquittal of George Zimmerman. (By Brian Stansberry, via Wikimedia Commons)

the same time, George Zimmerman, a neighborhood watch leader, was driving down the street when he spotted Martin. Upon seeing Martin, Zimmerman thought there was something suspicious about him. To date, it is unknown exactly what made Zimmerman suspicious about Martin. Sources have speculated that the suspicion could have arisen due to Martin's race and attire (i.e., Martin wore a hooded sweatshirt).

Due to his suspicions, Zimmerman called the police. The dispatch officer informed him that an officer was on the way and that he should take no further action until the officer arrived. However, Martin took off running soon after. Zimmerman felt compelled to follow Martin, thereby disobeying the dispatch officer's earlier warning to stand down. There are conflicting accounts of what happened in the four minutes between this moment and the arrival of the police. Specifically, whether Martin or Zimmerman was the primary aggressor in the altercation that ensued, whether Martin saw Zimmerman's gun and reached for it, and whether Zimmerman should have had more injuries if Martin had beaten him as badly as he had claimed.

According to Zimmerman, Martin was allegedly the primary aggressor and knocked him to the ground, repeatedly punched him, and pounded his head against the pavement several times. To escape the attack, Zimmerman claimed he had no option other than to shoot Martin in self-defense. However, Zimmerman did not testify to this at trial.

Since Martin did not survive the altercation, the only existing account of the alleged events was relayed by a friend, Rachel Jeantel, whom Martin was conversing with on the phone leading up to the altercation. According to the witness, Martin had reported that a man was watching and following him. Jeantel testified that she warned Martin to walk away from the man because he might be a rapist. She later reported hearing the beginning stages of the altercation between the pair. According to her testimony, Jeantel believed that Zimmerman attacked Martin and allegedly heard screams from Martin pleading with Zimmerman to "get off." The defense may have effectively damaged the witness's credibility by eliciting testimony from her that she had lied about her age and reasoning for failing to attend Martin's wake.

Regardless of the account, the ending remains the same: Trayvon Martin was shot and killed by George Zimmerman. The next critical question became whether this was an act of self-defense, as Zimmerman claimed, or of second-degree murder or manslaughter. The decision in this matter was one for the court to decide. Put before the court, a jury deliberated for sixteen hours over two days before returning a not guilty verdict for all charges, thereby acquitting George Zimmerman of the killing of Trayvon Martin.

The case brought two key issues to light, sparking conversations and protests about: (1) racial profiling and (2) Stand Your Ground laws. In regards to racial profiling, the argument was put forth that Zimmerman had used Martin's race as the sole factor in concluding that Martin was engaging in the suspicious behavior that led him to call dispatch, follow Martin, and eventually enter into a physical altercation. While using race or ethnicity to stop, search, arrest, or investigate an individual is illegal for law enforcement agents, George Zimmerman was a civilian neighborhood watch captain, not a law enforcement agent. Even though racial profiling was heavily debated among members of the public, the judge in the case forbade the discussion and presentation of evidence during trial that Zimmerman had racially profiled Martin.

The Stand Your Ground laws in the state of Florida are considered to be some of the most extreme in the United States. These laws allow individuals who believe they or someone else is in danger of being seriously harmed to use deadly force against the perpetrator. Such laws allow individuals, even if they can safely avoid the conflict and flee from danger, to stand their ground and meet "force with force." In this case, Zimmerman waived his right to the Stand Your Grand pretrial immunity hearing afforded to him. A ruling in favor of Zimmerman in the pretrial immunity hearing would have meant that no criminal or civil trial against him could proceed. Instead, Zimmerman decided to have his attorneys try the case as a self-defense case.

Since being acquitted of all charges related to Martin's death, Zimmerman has had several run-ins with the law including speeding violations, domestic violence charges, an alleged road-rage incident, and faced possible charges for aggravated assault with a weapon. On February 24, 2016, the Justice Department closed its investigation into the death of Trayvon Martin. The Justice Department concluded that the standard of proof for prosecuting the incident as a federal hate crime had not met.

Andrea Arndorfer

Further Reading
Correll, J., B. Park, C. M. Judd, and B. Wittenbrink. "The Police Officer's Dilemma: Using Ethnicity to Disambiguate Potentially Threatening Individuals." *Journal of Personality and Social Psychology*. 83 (2002): 1314-29. doi:10.1037//0022-3514.83.6.1314.
Jones, D. M. "He's a Black Male...Something Is Wrong with Him!" The Role of Race in the Stand Your Ground Debate." *University of Miami Law Review* 68 (2014): 1025-50.
Jones Thomas A., and S. M. Blackmon. "The Influence of the Trayvon Martin Shooting on Racial Socialization Practices of African American Parents." *Journal of Black Psychology* 41 (2015): 75-89. doi:10.1177/0095798414563610.
Lawson, T. F. "A Fresh Cut in an Old Wound—A Critical Analysis of the Trayvon Martin Killing: The Public Outcry, the Prosecutors' Discretion, and the Stand Your Ground Law." *University of Florida Journal of Law and Public Policy* 23 (2012): 271-312.
Rice Lave, T. "Shoot to Kill: A Critical Look at Stand Your Ground Laws." *University of Miami Law Review* 67 (2013): 827-60.
Reitzel, J., and A. R. Piquero. "Does It Exist? Studying Citizens' Attitudes of Racial Profiling." *Police Quarterly* 9 (2006): 161-83. doi:10.1177/1098611104264743.
Sommers, S. R., and S. A. Marotta. "Racial Disparities in Legal Outcomes: On Policing, Charging Decisions, and Criminal Trial Proceedings." *Policy Insights from the Behavioral and Brain Sciences*. 1, (2014): 103-11.: doi:10.1177/2372732214548431.

See also Racial profiling; Use of force; Preventive patrol; Self-defense; Right to bear arms; Reasonable force; Law enforcement; Citizen's arrests.

Plea bargaining

Definition: Negotiations between prosecuting and defense attorneys designed to reduce criminal charges against defendants in return for guilty pleas
Criminal justice issue: Convictions; Defendants; Pleas; Trial procedures
Significance: Plea bargaining is a frequent practice, with many criminal cases being resolved out of court when

both sides reach an agreement. Both sides in cases see advantages for themselves by striking successful bargains. Defendants seek reduced sentences and perhaps less damning criminal records; prosecutors seek to reduce the costs and time consumed by trials while assuring convictions.

Plea bargains might be initiated by either side in criminal cases. One study indicates that one reason for plea bargaining is to save the cost, time, and reputation of the defense attorney. That person must deal with the same judge, prosecutor, and police officers in other cases and does not want to get a bad reputation. Furthermore, the defense attorney must make a living and does not want to get bogged down in difficult cases for little money. However, the plea bargain might be initiated by a more self-sacrificing defense attorney or by the state.

The plea bargain typically involves reducing the seriousness of charges against a defendant. Instead of battery, for example, the charge might be changed to assault or to disturbing the peace. Instead of murder, the accusation might be changed to manslaughter. Another type of plea bargain involves dropping some charges against the defendant and keeping others. For example, encouraging the prosecution to drop a charge of selling cocaine and retain a charge of possessing marijuana might be the goal of plea bargaining. Still another objective of plea bargaining involves a defendant's pleading guilty to a charge with the understanding that the sentence will be lighter instead of heavier.

The judge is officially not in on the bargain, and whether the judge has been consulted is a matter that only the judge and the attorney know. Some judges refuse to be consulted, and all or almost all conduct themselves as if they had not been consulted. It is typical, for example, for judges to tell defendants in court that they cannot, and have not been asked to, reduce the defendants' sentences in return for pleas of guilty. The defendants must act on faith and on the advice of their defense attorneys. An attorney who finds that the prosecution (and the judge, if consulted) will not abide by the bargain is unlikely to bargain again, and that can be harmful to the offending attorney.

Some defendants plead guilty to charges even though they consider themselves to be innocent in order to be spared the expenses of trials or the ordeals of long sentences. It is difficult to say how often that happens, because many defendants contend after sentencing that they are innocent. Plea bargaining is frequently condemned by the public and by politicians, but unless the time, help, and budget of the prosecutor is unlimited, it is likely to continue.

Dwight Jensen

Further Reading
Fisher, George. *Plea Bargaining's Triumph: A History of Plea Bargaining in America*. Stanford: Stanford UP, 2003. Print.
"How Courts Work: Steps in a Trial: Plea Bargaining." *American Bar Association*. ABA, n.d. Web. 31 May 2016.
Rakoff, Jed S. "Why Innocent People Plead Guilty." *New York Review of Books*. NYREV, 20 Nov. 2014. Web. 31 May 2016.
Rosett, Arthur I. *Justice by Consent: Plea Bargains in the American Courthouse*. New York: Lippincott Williams & Wilkins, 1976. Print.
Vogel, Mary E. *Coercion to Compromise: Social Conflict and the Emergence of Plea Bargaining, 1830-1920*. Rev. ed. New York: Oxford UP, 2005. Print.

See also Arraignment; *Brady v. United States*; Convictions; Criminal prosecution; Defendants; Discretion; District attorneys; *Nolo contendere*; Pleas; Public prosecutors; *Rummel v. Estelle*; *Santobello v. New York*; Sentencing; Trials; Unabomber.

Pleas

Definition: Formal statements of guilt or otherwise by defendants in response to formal charges or indictments
Criminal justice issue: Arrest and arraignment; defendants; pleas; verdicts
Significance: Pleas are crucial components in the arraignment phase of the criminal process.

During the arraignment the judge presents the criminal charges, advises defendants of the right to court-appointed counsel, schedules hearings, determines the trial date, and resolves issues with regard to bail. At the arraignment defendants respond with a plea of not guilty, guilty, or *nolo contendere*. The defendants' choice of pleas is critical, as the disposition of the case rests on the plea.

Not Guilty and Guilty Pleas

The first option, and the one most often selected, is not guilty. The not guilty plea allows defendants time to consider the strength of their cases and to determine the chances of a favorable outcome in court. Therefore, the plea does not necessarily mean that defendants are innocent; it means that they wish to have their cases heard in court and want a judge or jury to determine whether there is enough evidence to return a guilty verdict. If defendants do not enter a plea, the court automatically enters a not guilty plea based on the precept that one is innocent until proven guilty. Persons who plead not guilty have a right to have a judge or jury trial. At trial the decision makers listen to the evidence. In order for a judge or jury to return a guilty verdict in a criminal proceeding, the prosecutor must demonstrate guilt beyond a reasonable doubt.

Defendants may also choose to plead guilty. The implications of this decision are serious. Defendants waive their right to a trial and to prepare a defense, the right against self-incrimination, the right to confront witnesses, and the right to appeal the decision. Thus, when defendants relinquish such fundamental rights, the judge must question them to determine whether they understand the implications of the guilty plea. The judge must determine whether the plea is voluntarily made or whether threats or promises were made to force a guilty plea. The judge also must ensure that defendants understand the charges against them and the corresponding sentences or fines.

Last, the judge must ascertain the factual basis of the plea to make sure that there is proof that defendants have actually engaged in the conduct with which they are charged. If defendants choose this plea and the judge has determined that they understand the ramifications of pleading guilty, the court may immediately convict as if a judge or jury returned a guilty verdict in a trial. Defendants may be sentenced at the arraignment or the judge may order a presentencing report and schedule a sentencing hearing.

Nolo Contendere

The last plea option allows defendants to plead *nolo contendere*, which means no contest, or "I do not wish to contend." Typically, defendants use this plea in order to avoid an admission of wrongdoing in the event of a subsequent civil suit regarding the same matter. If defendants are sued for monetary damages, a guilty verdict would provide evidence of wrongdoing, whereas a plea of *nolo contendere* would not. When defendants plead *nolo contendere*, a conviction is handed down, just as a guilty plea is adjudicated. The defendants relinquish their rights just as persons who plead guilty and are subject to the same sentences or fines as persons who plead guilty and are convicted. The judge must take the same precautions to ensure that defendants are aware of the relinquishment of rights involved in the plea of *nolo contendere* and that the decision is voluntary.

Ann Burnett

Further Reading
ABA *Standards for Criminal Justice: Pleas of Guilty*. Chicago: American Bar Association, 1999.
Bergman, Paul, and Sara J. Berman-Barrett. *The Criminal Law Handbook*. Berkeley, Calif.: Nolo Press, 1997.
Farnsworth, E. Allan. *An Introduction to the Legal System of the United States*. 3d ed. New York: Oceana, 1996.

See also Arraignment; Convictions; Criminal prosecution; Defendants; Insanity defense; *Nolo contendere*; Plea bargaining; Presumption of innocence; Reasonable doubt; Trials.

Powell v. Alabama

The Case: U.S. Supreme Court ruling on effective counsel
Date: Decided on November 7, 1932
Criminal justice issue: Capital punishment; defendants; juries
Significance: The Court ruled that the concept of due process requires states to provide effective counsel in capital cases when indigent defendants are unable to represent themselves.

In 1931, Ozie Powell and eight other black youths whose ages ranged from twelve to nineteen, known as the "Scottsboro boys," were tried and convicted before an all-white jury in Scottsboro, Alabama, charged with having raped two white women while traveling on a freight train. Although the Alabama constitution required the appointment of counsel for indigent defendants accused of capital crimes, no lawyer was definitely appointed to represent the defendants until the day of their trial. An atmosphere of racial hostility influenced the proceedings, and after a trial lasting one day, seven of the youths were sentenced to death, while the two youngest were transferred to the juvenile authorities. The trial attracted considerable attention, so that procommunist lawyers of the International Labor Defense volunteered to represent the young men on appeal. After the majority of the Alabama Supreme Court affirmed the convictions, the U.S. Supreme Court granted review.

The Court voted 7 to 2 to reverse the conviction and to remand the case to Alabama for a new trial. Writing for the majority, Justice George Sutherland did not speak of the Sixth Amendment, which had not yet been made applicable to the states, but rather asked whether the defendants had been denied the right of counsel, contrary to the due process clause of the Fourteenth Amendment. Sutherland noted that from the time of arraignment to the time of the trial, the defendants had not had "the aid of counsel in any real sense." The right to be heard implied the right to be heard with the assistance of counsel, for even most educated and intelligent persons would not have the training or experience to represent themselves in a criminal trial. Sutherland was impressed with "the ignorance and illiteracy of the defendants" and with the "circumstances of public hostility." In this particular case, therefore, the failure of the trial court to make "an effective appointment of counsel" was a denial of due process within the meaning of the Fourteenth Amendment.

The "Scottsboro boys case" represented transitional steps in three important directions. First, the decision came very close to incorporating the right to counsel into the meaning of the Fourteenth Amendment, so that this portion of the Sixth Amendment would apply to the states. Second, it recognized that at least in capital cases, the state must provide counsel for indigents unable to defend themselves. Third, it included the provocative suggestion that the state had the obligation to provide "effective" assistance of counsel. These three issues would become increasingly important in subsequent cases.

Thomas Tandy Lewis

Further Reading
Carter, Dan T. *Scottsboro: A Tragedy of the American South.* Rev. ed. Baton Rouge: Louisiana State University Press, 1979.
Goodman, James E. *Stories of Scottsboro.* New York: Pantheon Books, 1994.
Horne, Gerald. *"Powell v. Alabama": The Scottsboro Boys and American Justice.* New York: Franklin Watts, 1997.
National Association for the Advancement of Colored People. *Guide to the Papers of the NAACP, Part 6: The Scottsboro Case, 1931-1950.* Frederick, Md.: University Publications of America, 1986.

See also *Argersinger v. Hamlin*; Counsel, right to; Due process of law; Equal protection under the law; Incorporation doctrine; Scottsboro cases; Supreme Court, U.S.

Precedent

Definition: Court rulings that guide later court interpretations of the law
Criminal justice issue: Courts; Judges; Law codes
Significance: When judges see factual similarities between current cases and earlier cases, they look for rules of law on which the earlier cases were based and apply them to their present cases.

Judges use precedent in cases. (Public domain, via Wikimedia Commons)

Much law is written in terms that do not lend themselves to a single, unequivocal interpretation. For example, the First Amendment to the US Constitution states that "Congress shall make no law . . . abridging the freedom of speech." However, because the authors of the Bill of Rights did not anticipate the invention of radio and television, contemporary judges must decide whether electronic communications broadcasts over the airwaves are a form of "speech."

When judges confront such ambiguous situations for the first time, they apply the written Constitution according to what they consider just principles. In doing so they effectively fill in the blank spaces in the document. In that sense they are actually making constitutional law. Because judges are bound to follow established law when they make decisions, all judges in similar cases in the future must follow the precedent established in the earlier case.

Law made by legislatures—called "statutory law"—is often characterized by the same ambiguity. When the US Congress passed the Sherman Anti-Trust Act of 1890, the Supreme Court had to decide whether the law's prohibition of "every contract, combination . . . or conspiracy in restraint of trade or commerce" made union-organized strikes illegal. In *Loewe v. Lawlor*

(1908) the Court said that a union strike was such an illegal restraint of trade. This decision prompted Congress to amend the antitrust law six years later to exempt union activity from its coverage.

US legislators do not write laws to cover every conceivable circumstance. If judges find that there simply is no applicable statute, they must make a decision in the case on the basis of their understanding of justice. Such judge-made law is called common law and is found in judges' written decisions. Once a judge has made a common-law decision, the decision carries the force of law, and other judges must apply the principle in deciding future cases.

A precedent is binding only in the jurisdiction in which it has been decided. Thus, if a Maine court decides that an optometrist's failure to test for glaucoma constitutes negligence, that decision does not bind a Mississippi judge. When it comes to federal constitutional and statutory law, the US Supreme Court's interpretations govern the entire country.

It is possible to overturn a precedent. Common law can be overruled by a statute. A court's interpretation of a statute may be overruled by a subsequent statute. A court may overrule itself but rarely does so. A precedent may or may not be a good law, but as former US Supreme Court Justice Harlan Fiske Stone said, "It is often more important that a rule of law be settled than that it be settled right."

William H. Coogan

Further Reading

Amar, Akhil Reed. *The Constitution and Criminal Procedure: First Principles*. New Haven: Yale UP, 1997. Print.

Burge, Mark Edwin. "Without Precedent: Legal Analysis in the Age of Non-Judicial Dispute Resolution." *Cardozo Journal of Conflict Resolution* 15.1 (2013): 143-91. Print.

Hitt, Matthew P. "Measuring Precedent in a Judicial Hierarchy." *Law & Society Review* 50.1 (2016): 57-81. Print.

Meyer, J. F., and D. R. Grant. *The Courts in Our Criminal Justice System*. Upper Saddle River: Prentice, 2003. Print.

Neubauer, D. W. *America's Courts and the Criminal Justice System*. 7th ed. Belmont: Wadsworth, 2002. Print.

See also Annotated codes; Case law; Common law; Constitution, U.S.; Jurisdiction of courts; Opinions; *Stare decisis*; Statutes.

Preliminary hearings

Definition: Proceedings held to determine whether a crime has been committed and whether the accused should be tried

Criminal justice issue: Arrest and arraignment; Trial procedures

Significance: In this phase of the judicial process, the prosecutor attempts to present enough evidence to demonstrate the accused's probable guilt. The judge must then decide whether to proceed toward trial.

In the US judicial process, if the prosecution believes that it has collected enough evidence to prove that the accused has committed a felony, the next step is either a grand jury or a preliminary hearing. If a state offers both options, the prosecutor may choose which one to pursue. At a preliminary hearing, the prosecutor must prove to a judge that there is sufficient evidence, known as probable cause, that a crime has occurred and that the accused has committed that crime. (In grand jury proceedings, the prosecution presents the evidence to the jury rather than the judge.) A preliminary hearing is scheduled after the prosecutor has filed a criminal complaint. The preliminary hearing is sometimes known as a preliminary examination or an evidentiary hearing.

A preliminary hearing must take place within a specified amount of time, usually within a few days after charges are filed and an arraignment is held. Defendants can waive the preliminary hearing and are sometimes advised to do so by their counsel.

During the preliminary hearing, the prosecutor presents only the amount of evidence necessary to demonstrate probable guilt. If the presiding judge determines that there is probable cause, the case will proceed to the next phase. In some states, this next phase may still be a grand jury hearing, and in others it may be the trial. If the presiding judge determines that there is insufficient evidence to indict the accused, the charges are dropped. The prosecution may next choose to take the evidence to the grand jury.

Kimberley M. Holloway

Further Reading

Bergman, Paul. "Preliminary Hearings." *Criminal Law: A Desk Reference*. 3rd ed. Berkeley: Nolo, 2016. Print.

Glannon, Joseph W. *Civil Procedure*. 7th ed. Frederick: Wolters, 2013. Print.

See also Arraignment; Criminal procedure; District attorneys; Due process of law; Grand juries; Hearings; Indictment; Information; Inquests; Presumption of innocence; Testimony.

Presentence investigations

Definition: Reports drafted by probation officer or court officials detailing significant information that may be considered by the sentencing judge when sentencing a criminal defendant

Criminal justice issue: Investigation; probation and pretrial release; sentencing

Significance: Presentence investigation reports are essential to ensure that all relevant circumstances of both the offense and the offender are taken into account in formulating just sentences.

Before defendants are sentenced for crimes in most criminal courts, judicial officers—most frequently probation officers—are asked to complete presentence investigations. These written reports offer information about the defendants and their crimes that may assist the court in determining appropriate sentences. Factors such as the defendants' criminal histories, their educational and employment backgrounds, and their medical and psychological histories all may be appropriate for inclusion in a presentence investigation. These reports are not intended as exhaustive life histories; it is important that reports be succinct and not burden courts with extraneous information.

In addition to the reports, statements of the defendants, which may show either mitigating circumstances in the commission of the offenses or remorse on the part of the defendants, may play a role. The rights of victims are also addressed to some extent by the inclusion of statements assessing the impact of the crimes on the victims and the possibilities of restitution.

Numerous options are available for sentencing, and specific recommendations are frequently made by the judicial officers. For example, probation may be granted if offenders demonstrate amenabililty to supervision and the capacity of living crime-free lives and have not broken laws that mandate incarceration or other punishments. Alternatively, fines may be imposed. If incarceration occurs, presentence investigations may influence the classification of the correctional settings for the defendants. Options such as community release may be affected by the defendants' histories in particular settings. Also, some individuals may have had previous experiences in certain programs that had either positive or negative effects on their behavior.

Although offender characteristics play a role in the sentencing process, some offenses do not offer substantial flexibility in the actual sentences conveyed. Mandatory sentencing statutes and presumptive sentencing guidelines sometimes control or at least constrain the sentence imposed, sometimes even taking precedence over mitigating circumstances or offender characteristics.

John C. Kilburn, Jr.
Updated by Charles E. MacLean

Further Reading

The Presentence Investigation. Washington, D.C.: Division of Probation, Administrative Office of U.S. Courts, 1984.

Stith, Kate, and Jose A. Cabranes. *Fear of Judging: Sentencing Guidelines in the Federal Courts.* Chicago: University of Chicago Press, 1998.

Tonry, Michael. *Reconsidering Indeterminate and Structured Sentencing.* Washington, D.C.: U.S. Department of Justice, Office of Justice Programs, National Institute of Justice, 1999.

See also Convictions; Discretion; Judges; Pleas; Punishment; Sentencing; Verdicts; Victim and Witness Protection Act; Technology's transformative effect; Victim impact statements.

Prosecutorial abuse

Definition: Misuse or abuse of authority by governmental officials charged with investigating and prosecuting crime

Criminal justice issue: Government misconduct; immunity; professional standards; prosecution; trial procedures

Significance: When prosecutors abuse their authority, they undermine the integrity of the criminal justice process, jeopardize criminal defendant's rights, and risk wrongful convictions.

Prosecutorial abuse occurs when a prosecutor violates the legal and ethical duties of the office of the prosecutor. A prosecutor is a government official charged with investigating and prosecuting crime in a just and ethical manner. Prosecutors must abide by certain legal and ethical standards as they execute their governmental duties. Failure to follow those laws and standards constitutes prosecutorial abuse. Examples of abuse of the powers associated with the office include biased decisions about whom to prosecute, evidence suppression, fabrication of evidence, jury tampering, grand jury violations, or efforts to obtain wrongful convictions. Some forms of prosecutorial abuse are crimes and render the prosecutor subject to legal action, but in many cases prosecutors enjoy immunity for actions they take in their official capacities. The research community generally agrees that the number and frequency of prosecutorial abuses are underreported, with dangerous consequences for the criminal justice system. Analysts speculate that abuses go unreported for several reasons. Prosecutors enjoy a great deal of professional discretion; the ethical rules for their behavior are vague and inconsistent; and they are not subject to any meaningful mechanisms of external oversight. Moreover, the remedies for prosecutorial misconduct are few in number, relatively toothless, and poorly enforced. The majority of states provide statutory guidance, particularly with respect to prosecutors' evidentiary disclosure requirements. But those laws do not expressly or consistently address prosecutors' behaviors. The laws and regulations governing prosecutorial conduct largely derive from case law, from state and federal ethics rules, and from national professional organizations, which collectively create inconsistent and unpredictable standards. .

Prosecutorial abuse can take a number of forms during both the investigatory and trial stages. During investigations, prosecutorial abuses occur when prosecutors destroy evidence, hide evidence, or do not disclose that they have potentially exculpatory evidence. The Supreme Court established in *Brady v. Maryland* that failure to disclose exculpatory evidence violates the Fifth and Fourteenth Amendments Due Process Clauses. The affirmative duty to disclose such evidence was affirmed in *Kyles v. Whitley*. Threats against witnesses, rescission of immunity agreements to elicit testimony, and failing to disclose immunity agreements to defendants also constitute abuses of power. Making false statements to the grand jury and violating grand jury confidentiality are both actionable abuses, as was the case in the 2016 conviction of disbarred Pennsylvania Attorney General Kathleen Kane for leaking grand jury evidence to the media. Finally, prosecutors may breach their duties if, like the disbarred district attorney in the Duke lacrosse case, they make improper or misleading pretrial statements to media about defendants, victims, or evidence.

There are countless examples of prosecutorial abuses during trial. A 2016 California study identifies comprehensively catalogs improper prosecutorial behaviors during trial: (1) improper comments during opening statements and closing arguments; (2) misstatements of law; (3) eliciting misleading, inaccurate, or perjured testimony; (4) *Brady* violations; (5) criticisms of defendant exercising the right to remain silent at trial or declining to call witnesses (Griffin); (6) ad hominin attacks on opposing counsel or defendants' expert witnesses; (7) editorializing about or "vouching" for witness credibility; (8) improper appeals to jurors' passions or prejudices; (9) improper commentary on defendants' lack of remorse; (10) use of unduly prejudicial victim impact statements; (11) improper comments on defendants' alleged potential for future dangerousness; (12) misleading statements or comments on the merits of the case during voir dire; and (13) using peremptory challenges improperly to exclude jurors based on race or gender in violation of *Batson v. Kentucky*.

For decades following the *Brady* decision, courts consistently maintained that prosecutors could be held liable and potentially punished criminally if they actively interfered in defendants' abilities to receive a fair trial. Then in 2011, the Supreme Court appeared to limit this long line of case law when it announced in *Connick v. Thompson* that prosecutors could not be held liable for Brady violations committed by their subordinate attorneys. Specifically, the Supreme Court announced that the district attorney's failure to train his subordinate attorneys on how to comply with Brady was not an actionable violation of his professional duties. Many subsequent cases confirmed this limitation on prosecutorial abuse. But then, in an unrelated case, Texas passed the Michael Morton Act in 2013 to promote transparency in criminal investigations and the discovery process. Morton, who was wrongfully convicted of murdering his wife, served twenty-five years before deoxyribonucleic acid (DNA) evidence cleared him. He was released and provided with compensation and services under applicable state law. Ken Anderson, the prosecutor, confessed to withholding exculpatory evidence that suggested another man had committed the murder, and he failed to disclose exculpatory testimony from a witness. Anderson served a ten-day jail term, paid fines, and was disbarred. Morton's story inspired national dialogue about prosecutorial accountability. The Morton Act is Texas state law, and not all states have similar statutes. *Brady* remains good law, but states have interpreted its parameters differently depending upon their understandings of *Connick* and subsequent cases.

If prosecutors engage in criminal misconduct, they can be prosecuted under relevant state law. Many civil cases for breaches of their duties arise under 42 U.S. Code, Section 1983, which allows for plaintiffs to pierce prosecutors' immunity and seek legal damages. Potential remedies include dismissal of charges, suppression of tainted evidence, mistrial, acquittal, and monetary compensation. Defendants also may pursue civil lawsuits for damages and injunctive relief for such misconduct.

Anne S. Douds, JD, PhD

Further Reading

Brady v. Maryland, 373 U.S. 83 (1963).

Caldwell, H. M. "Everybody Talks about Prosecutorial Conduct but Nobody Does Anything About It: A 25-Year Survey of Prosecutorial Misconduct and a Viable Solution."*University of Illinois Review* (forthcoming 2016).

Browning, J. G. "Prosecutorial Misconduct in the Digital Age."*Albany Law Review* 77 (2013): 881.

Coleman, J. P., and J. Lockey. "Brady Epidemic Misdiagnosis: Claims of Prosecutorial Misconduct and the Sanctions to Deter It."*University of San Francisco Law Review* 50 (2016): 199

Imbler v. Pachtman, 424 U.S. 409 (1976).

Joy, P. A. "The Relationship between Prosecutorial Misconduct and Wrongful Convictions: Shaping Remedies for a Broken System."*Wisconsin Law Review* ___ (2006): 399.

Lawless, J. F. "Prosecutorial Misconduct: Law, Procedure, Forms." LexisNexis. 2015.

See also Attorney ethics; Convictions; Criminal prosecution; Discovery; District attorneys; False convictions; Nolle prosequi; Trials.

Public defenders

Definition: Government attorneys assigned to represent criminal defendants who cannot afford to hire private attorneys

Criminal justice issue: Attorneys; Defendants; Professional standards

Significance: By representing criminal defendants who cannot afford to pay for their own attorneys, public defenders play an important role in ensuring that the right of all defendants to counsel is satisfied.

Persons charged with a crime in the United States are entitled to have a lawyer represent them. Those who cannot afford to hire their own lawyer are entitled to representation by a lawyer appointed by the court and paid for by the government. In most US cities and many states, this representation is provided by a lawyer or group of lawyers called public defenders. These attorneys are employed by the government specifically to represent those who cannot afford to hire their own counsel.

The Constitutional Right to Counsel

Before 1963 most persons charged with a crime who could not afford to hire a lawyer to represent them simply represented themselves. Even in very serious cases, poor, and sometimes poorly educated, people had to present their own cases to juries and judges. There was no nationally recognized right to have a lawyer appointed to represent indigent defendants. The US Supreme Court held in 1942 that criminal defendants were entitled to the appointment of a lawyer at government expense only when special circumstances required a lawyer to make a defendant's trial fair. The Court held that the constitutional guarantee of "due process" required only that defendants have fair trials and that in most cases trials could be fair even if the defendant did not have a lawyer.

The Supreme Court recognized two exceptions to this "special circumstances" rule, but these exceptions had limited applicability. First, persons charged with crimes against federal law in federal rather than state courts were entitled under the Sixth Amendment to the US Constitution to have a lawyer appointed to represent them. The assistance of counsel clause of the amendment provides that "in all criminal prosecutions, the accused shall . . . have the assistance of counsel for his defense." Second, persons charged in federal or state courts with capital crimes, for which they could receive the death penalty, were entitled to the appointment of a lawyer. Because the vast majority of criminal charges did not carry a possible death sentence as punishment and most criminal offenses were (and still are) prosecuted in state rather than in federal courts, most people charged with most crimes were represented by a lawyer only if they had the money to hire one. Even persons charged with very serious crimes that could result in long prison terms were routinely tried without counsel.

These rules changed dramatically in 1963, when the US Supreme Court decided in the case of *Gideon v. Wainwright* that having a lawyer represent an accused person was essential to ensuring that every criminal trial was fair. The source of this right was the Sixth Amendment's guarantee of the assistance of counsel. For the first time, the Court ruled that the Sixth Amendment's guarantee of the assistance of counsel was fully applicable to the states and required that all indigent persons charged with felonies in state courts, not just in federal courts, had to be provided with a lawyer at government expense.

The Creation of the Public Defender

The Supreme Court's *Gideon v. Wainwright* decision resulted in the creation of public defender offices and programs throughout the nation. Some jurisdictions established public defenders to handle most criminal cases against indigent persons, while others relied on the appointment of private lawyers to handle these cases. In 1972 the Supreme Court expanded the right to an appointed lawyer to include those persons charged with misdemeanors as well as felonies. It later limited this right to those misdemeanor cases in which persons are actually

Public defender's office. (By Michael Rivera, via Wikimedia Commons)

sentenced to imprisonment, excluding cases in which punishment is limited to fines.

The right to have an appointed lawyer can begin at any critical stage of a case, even before it comes to trial, such as at an initial or preliminary hearing. This right can begin as soon as a person is arrested, when a person is questioned by police and given the Miranda warnings—that is, the notification of the arrested person of their the rights to speak with a lawyer, to have a lawyer appointed if they cannot afford to hire one, and to remain silent in order to avoid self-incrimination. Often the lawyer appointed is a public defender. Poor persons charged with a crime have a right to the services of a lawyer free of charge during trial, sentencing, and one appeal. The right does not provide for representation for further appeals or for representation in civil cases.

Modern Public Defenders

Although the Supreme Court has held that the US Constitution requires that indigent persons charged with crimes be provided a lawyer at government expense, it has not specified how this must be done. Jurisdictions in the United States use three basic methods to provide such representation: public defenders, assigned counsels, and contract attorneys. Public defenders are lawyers who exclusively represent indigent criminal defendants. They may be organized into offices by city, county, or state, and they are usually employees of one of these units of government. Federal courts have a federal defender system, which provides representation to indigent persons charged with federal crimes. Assigned counsels are private lawyers who makes themselves available for appointment by the court on a case-by-case basis. They may or may not specialize in criminal defense, and they may or may not be screened or specially trained to handle criminal cases. They are paid a fee, which is usually fixed but can vary according to the time they spend on a case or on the type of case they are handling. Contract attorneys are members of organizations, such as law firms or bar associations, that contract with cities, counties, or states to handle a certain number of appointed cases for a set period of time.

Most modern American criminal justice systems and virtually all urban ones rely on some combination of these options to provide representation to a large proportion of criminal defendants. A US Department of Justice study found that in 1996 about 82 percent of defendants charged with felonies in the nation's seventy-five largest counties were represented by court-appointed counsel. The estimated cost of these services to both state and local governments was more than $2.3 billion in 2007, which was approximately 3.5 times what these services cost in inflation-adjusted constant dollars in 1979. This rise in expenditures for the representation of poor defendants corresponds to the dramatic increase in incarceration rates in the United States during the 1980s and has led to concerns that increased caseloads and reduced funding may cause poor persons charged with crimes to have less fair trials than wealthy criminal defendants.

Problems of Public Defense

Although public defenders receive their salaries from the government, they are legally and ethically obligated to represent their clients, the accused persons, against the government. This has sometimes made the public, and even some clients, resentful or mistrustful of public defenders. Early studies of the system of public defenders during the late 1960s suggested that public defenders sometimes saw themselves as part of a team, which included the prosecutor and the judge, whose goal was to convince clients to plead guilty. Another strand of critical thinking challenged this critique, noting that effective public defenders could often obtain favorable plea bargains for their clients even if they did so through what appeared to be a less aggressive or less adversarial approach. Whatever their views of themselves, public defenders have become essential components of the criminal justice system in most densely populated US jurisdictions.

During the 1980s and 1990s, many American jurisdictions experienced dramatic increases in the demand for public defender services. Between 1982 and 1986, for example, the US Justice Department found that the caseloads of public defenders in the United States increased by 40 percent. This increase was caused in large part by increased prosecution of drug offenses, often characterized as the "war on drugs." In some jurisdictions, public defenders were each appointed to handle hundreds of cases a year, which raised questions about their effectiveness as defense lawyers and the quality of representation their clients received.

Some public defenders responded by going to court and refusing to accept additional cases without being provided with additional resources. All lawyers have an ethical obligation to represent clients competently, and some public defenders contended that no one could competently represent hundreds of different clients a year, with each case involving different facts and legal issues. Some courts responded to this demand for the services of public defenders by appointing private lawyers to represent indigent defendants *pro bono*, without compensation, as part of their obligation to serve the public. Because many of these lawyers had little experience practicing criminal law, this practice raised serious concerns about the quality of the representation they provided.

Standards for Criminal Justice

In an effort to establish uniform standards of practice for criminal defense lawyers, including public defenders, the American Bar Association (ABA), the nation's largest bar association, promulgated *Standards for Criminal Justice*. First published in 1968 and for the third time in 1992, the *Standards* set forth guidelines for effective and ethical conduct by both prosecutors and defense lawyers, as well as benchmarks for effective provision of defense services. They seek to provide to all eligible persons "quality" legal representation, as opposed to just competent counsel. They also stipulate that no public defender or appointed counsel should accept workloads that interfere with providing high-quality representation and that government must provide adequate funding for these services. Although these standards are only recommendations and have no legal weight, they have been influential in defining the role and operation of modern public defender offices.

David M. Siegel

Further Reading

American Bar Association. *ABA Standards for Criminal Justice: Providing Defense Services*. 3rd ed. Washington: Author, 1992. Print.

Harlow, Caroline Wolf. *Defense Counsel in Criminal Cases*. Washington: Office of Justice Programs, Dept. of Justice, 2009. *Bureau of Justice Statistics*. Web. 30 May 2016.

Kunen, James S. *"How Can You Defend Those People?": The Making of a Criminal Lawyer*. New York: Random, 1983. Print.

Langton, Lynn, and Donald J. Farole Jr. *Public Defender Offices, 2007-Statistical Tables*. Washington: Office of Justice Programs, Dept. of Justice, 2009. *Bureau of Justice Statistics*. Web. 30 May 2016.

Lewis, Anthony. *Gideon's Trumpet*. 1964. New York: Vintage, 1989. Print.

McIntyre, Lisa J. *The Public Defender: The Practice of Law in the Shadows of Repute*. Chicago: U of Chicago P, 1987. Print.

Wice, Paul B. *Public Defenders and the American Justice System*. Westport: Praeger, 2005. Print.

Wormser, Richard. *Defending the Accused: Stories from the Courtroom*. New York: Watts, 2001. Print.

See also *Argersinger v. Hamlin*; Attorney ethics; Counsel, right to; Criminal justice system; Criminal procedure; Defendants; Defense attorneys; Effective counsel; Equal protection under the law; *Escobedo v. Illinois*; *Gideon v. Wainwright*; Privileged communications; Public prosecutors.

Public prosecutors

Definition: Attorneys serving as the public officials responsible for overseeing the prosecution of criminal cases by setting charges, conducting plea negotiations, and presenting evidence in court on behalf of the government

Criminal justice issue: Attorneys; Political issues; Professional standards; Prosecution

Significance: The prosecutor is one of the most powerful actors in the justice system because of the office's broad discretionary powers to determine which cases will be pursued and which defendants will be permitted to plead guilty to lesser charges.

The prosecutor is the public official who acts as the attorney representing the government and the public in pursuing criminal convictions. The prosecutor possesses broad powers to determine which defendants to prosecute, what charges to pursue, and which cases to terminate through plea bargains. The prosecutor must oppose the defense attorney during trials and present sufficient and appropriate evidence to persuade a judge or jury to render a verdict of guilty.

The Prosecutorial System

The concept of the American prosecutor was drawn from English legal tradition, in which a representative of the king sought to persuade jurors that a particular individual should be charged and convicted of a crime. In the United States, prosecutorial responsibilities are divided among the various levels of government. Federal prosecutors are known as US attorneys. They are appointed to office by the president and are each responsible for prosecuting federal crimes in one of the ninety-four federal district courts throughout the United States. Within each courthouse, they are assisted with their tasks by teams of assistant prosecutors. Their work is often coordinated by the attorney general of the United States and the US Department of Justice.

Prosecutor. (Public domain, via Wikimedia Commons)

At the state level, each state has an elected attorney general who, in most states, possesses the power to initiate prosecutions for violations of state laws. In three states—Alaska, Delaware, and Rhode Island—the attorney general oversees all local prosecutors. In most states, however, the focus of prosecutorial power is the local prosecutor. These local prosecutors are sometimes known as district attorneys, or states' attorneys. In all states except Connecticut and New Jersey, local prosecutors are elected officials who have primary responsibility for investigating and prosecuting violations of state criminal laws within their counties. In Connecticut and New Jersey, local prosecutors are appointed and supervised by state officials. By contrast, local prosecutors in other states are accountable to the voters within their counties. They are usually visible political figures who seek to please and impress the voters with their efforts to combat crime.

Many attorneys use the office of county prosecutor as a stepping-stone to higher offices as judges, state legislators, or members of Congress. The prosecutor's office serves this purpose especially well because of its high visibility in the local community and because the prosecutor can show tangible success in battling crime—an issue of widespread concern to voters. Moreover, prosecutors do not have to become involved in controversial issues that divide the community such as welfare spending or education. They can devote their time to publicizing their success in the battle against crime, which enjoys unified public support.

Because of the visibility and power of the local prosecutor's office, political parties frequently devote significant energy and resources to battling each other during election campaigns for the prosecutor's office. As a result, political leaders often select prosecutorial candidates based on their ability to raise campaign funds and their attractiveness to the voters rather than on their prior experience as attorneys. Attorneys who have never handled criminal cases before in their lives sometimes win elections as prosecutors. If their offices are anywhere but in rural areas, however, they usually have experienced assistant prosecutors who handle the steady flow of cases and teach them about criminal law. In small towns and rural counties, the local prosecutor may not have many assistant prosecutors, if any.

Because of prosecutors' involvement in politics, political considerations sometimes affect their decisions. They may use their offices to provide jobs (as assistant prosecutors and investigators) for loyal members of their political party. They may prosecute vigorously any questionable activity by political opponents while turning a blind eye to wrongdoing by influential citizens or by their political supporters. Because no official supervises or commands the local prosecutors in most states, it is up to the local voters to ensure that prosecutors perform according to professional standards. Voters are the only ones who possess the power to remove most prosecutors from office.

Prosecutor Decision Making

Prosecutors possess broad powers. They can use their discretion to determine which defendants are charged, what charges are pursued, which plea bargains to approve, and what strategies to employ during trials. Prosecutors even possess the power to drop charges against defendants without providing any reasons. This power to drop charges cannot be stopped or reversed by any other official, not even a judge or the governor. The primary pressure that keeps prosecutors from having unchecked power is the risk that the public will be unhappy with their decisions and vote them out of office in future elections.

Prosecutors are responsible for many key decisions in the criminal process. They must evaluate the evidence brought to them by the police in order to determine which charges, if any, to file against each defendant. Prosecutors make recommendations about whether defendants should be released on bail. Studies show that judges are usually very deferential to prosecutors' recommendations about whether bail is to be granted, the bail amount, and the conditions of release. Prosecutors also control the process for the grand jury by presenting evidence against the suspects that they have chosen without any defense attorneys in the courtroom to argue against the issuance of indictments. In states that do not use grand juries, prosecutors initiate charges against a defendant by filing an information describing the charges to be pursued based on the evidence thus far available. Prosecutors handle plea negotiations on behalf of the government and recommend sentences when defendants plead guilty. Prosecutors also develop trial strategies and determine how evidence will be presented to the jury for those few cases that are not terminated through plea bargains.

Prosecutors' decision making is influenced by their need to please several constituencies. Because prosecutors' jobs depend on public support, prosecutors typically try to develop good relations with the news media. They want news reports to show them as making tough, intelligent decisions in identifying and prosecuting criminal suspects. Prosecutors must also have good relationships with the police, because they must rely on the police to do a good job in making arrests and gathering appropriate evidence. Prosecutors do not want to displease police officers by dropping charges or agreeing to light sentences during plea bargaining, because the police then may be less enthusiastic and cooperative in investigating subsequent cases. Prosecutors also rely on good relationships with the local county commission, city council, or state legislature that provides the annual budget for the prosecutor's office. If the prosecutors cannot please these elected officials, then they may receive inadequate resources in the following year's budget. Although prosecutors have broad discretionary power, their relationships with political constituencies influence their decisions and actions.

Prosecutors' decisions are also influenced by their need to process a steady flow of cases with their office's limited resources. For most prosecutors, this situation helps to encourage their participation in plea bargaining. Most offices do not have the time, money, or personnel to bring every case to trial. Moreover, prosecutors gain definite convictions when they can negotiate a guilty plea. If cases go to trial, there is always a risk that unpredictable juries might not render guilty verdicts. Through plea bargaining, prosecutors gain quick convictions with a minimal expenditure of resources.

Plea Bargaining

Prosecutors usually hold the upper hand in plea bargaining because they can initially charge defendants with multiple offenses, even if they are not sure that they can prove all the charges. This gives the prosecutor the ability to apply pressure to the defendant by scaring the defendant with the prospect of multiple convictions and punishments if a guilty plea is not forthcoming. The US Supreme Court has decided that prosecutors can threaten defendants with additional charges during plea negotiations. Although the judge officially controls sentencing, most judges will routinely approve whatever sentence the prosecutor recommends as part of a plea agreement. Because more than 90 percent of cases terminate through plea bargains, the prosecutor effectively influences the sentences imposed on offenders in most cases.

The plea-bargaining process in many courthouses becomes streamlined through cooperative relationships that develop among prosecutors, public defenders, and judges. Frequently, the same assistant prosecutor, public defender, and judge are in the same courtroom day after day discussing plea bargains in one case after another. Before long, they come to understand one another's assessments of the seriousness of specific kinds of crimes and of the appropriate severity of punishment for each crime. Once they develop common understandings about the sentences to be imposed for specific offenses or repeat offenders, they can quickly develop consistent plea agreements in each new case that arrives before them.

Prosecutors and the Adversary System

Because the American justice process employs an adversary system that pits prosecutors against defense attorneys, many critics fear that prosecutors are encouraged to seek convictions at all costs rather than examine each case carefully to determine whether someone arrested by the police is, in fact, guilty. In an adversary system, attorneys can become too focused on simply defeating the opponent rather than ensuring that justice is accomplished through the conviction of guilty defendants. There is a risk that attorneys, including prosecutors, will attempt to hide information from their opponents, even when that evidence might cast doubt on the guilt of a defendant and thereby increase the probability that an innocent person receives unjustified punishment.

In other countries (in Germany, for example), prosecutors are appointed government officials who are under the supervision of a national office. They have secure positions, and their decisions are less susceptible to political pressures. They are obligated to reveal any evidence that questions the defendant's guilt, and their ultimate objective as professionals is to see that correct decisions are made. By contrast, as elected officials in an adversary system, American prosecutors are under pressure from the community to solve crimes. They may be blamed by the public and subsequently lose office if highly publicized crimes remain unsolved. This pressure may create incentives for prosecutors to pursue cases aggressively against defendants, even in instances in which the available evidence may be less than compelling. If prosecutors are unethical, their lack of the job security possessed by government-employee prosecutors in other countries may lead them to manufacture evidence against selected individuals simply to avoid public blame for unsolved crimes. Such problems are not widespread, but they have occurred with sufficient frequency over American history to raise questions about whether elected prosecutors in an adversarial system can make sufficiently objective decisions to avoid misuse of prosecutors' broad powers.

Christopher E. Smith

Further Reading

Cole, George F., and Christopher Smith. *American System of Criminal Justice*. 10th ed. Thomson, 2004. Print.
Heilbroner, David. *Rough Justice: Days and Nights of a Young D.A.* New York: Pantheon, 1990. Print.
Jacoby, Joan E. *The American Prosecutor: A Search for Identity.* Lexington: Lexington, 1980. Print.
McDonald, William F., ed. *The Prosecutor*. Beverly Hills: Sage, 1979. Print.
Stewart, James B. *The Prosecutors*. New York: Simon, 1987. Print.

See also Attorney General, U.S.; Attorneys general, state; Criminal justice system; Defense attorneys; Grand juries; Indictment; *Miranda v. Arizona*; Plea bargaining; Public defenders.

Punishment

Definition: Intentional infliction of harm by government on individuals for offenses against law
Criminal justice issue: Capital punishment; Sentencing
Significance: Because punishment of criminal offenders usually involves inflicting harm on them in ways that would be considered unacceptable or immoral in other circumstances, competing theories attempt to justify or abolish the practice.

Punishment in the modern United States is a massive and costly enterprise. In 2014, approximately 2.2 million people were serving time in prison or jail, a 500 percent increase over the previous forty years. The Sentencing Project reports that changes in sentencing laws have driven up the US incarceration rate, not changes in crime rates. In 2013, state governments in the United States spent $51.9 billion on corrections. Moreover, that figure does not include money spent on providing police protection and the court system.

The United States leads the world in incarceration rates, with 698 individuals per 100,000 incarcerated in 2015. Rwanda has the world's second-highest incarceration rate, with 492 individuals serving time per 100,000, followed by Russia (446) and Brazil (301). Residents of the United States are 8.9 times more likely to be incarcerated than residents of Germany—the most prosperous country in Europe—which has an incarceration rate of 78 per 100,000. Despite the fact that US incarceration rates are so disproportionately high compared to the rates of other countries, the United States experiences far more violent crime per capita than other high-income democracies. In 2015, the reported homicide rate was approximately 5 per 100,000 population forin the United States; in Western and Central European countries, the murder rates are often below 1 per 100,000.

Meanwhile, the United States invests more in punishing offenders than any other nation—both in financial outlays and in the loss of freedom for millions of incarcerated convicts—but even this price has not made for a safer society. All these disparities between crime and punishment rates raise fundamental questions about punishment: What justifies it? What are its objectives? How can those objectives be achieved? Finally, how important are those objectives compared to others, such as the preservation of civil liberties?

Philosophical Bases for Punishment

Until the eighteenth century, punishments for criminal offenses in Western societies typically consisted of sporadic public displays of spectacular corporal violence. Some of these punishments would now be considered forms of torture. A particularly gruesome example was known as "drawing and quartering": Ropes attached to each of a convicted criminal's limbs were tied to four draft animals, which pulled them in four different directions, eventually tearing the convict into four parts, hence, the "quartering." Severe punishments such as that served several objectives. They demonstrated the authority of the state, exacted revenge on criminal offenders, and issued warning to all those who might be considering committing similar offenses.

Punishment did not become a subject of serious systematic study until the mid-eighteenth century, when Cesare Beccaria published *On Crimes and Punishments* (1764). Beccaria argued that deterring offenders was the only legitimate function of punishment and it was best accomplished by standardizing penalties, publicizing them so that everyone understood and had notice of the harm they could suffer, and enforcing sanctions regularly and fairly. Beccaria further claimed that excessive punishments were inhumane and unnecessary to deter.

The late eighteenth-early nineteenth century English philosopher and reformer Jeremy Bentham developed Beccaria's insights into a comprehensive theory of law governed by the central premise of what has come to be known as utilitarianism. He argued that legislation should promote the greatest good, or utility, and the least suffering for the greatest number of people. According to his utilitarian philosophy, punishment should be forward-looking because its only legitimate purpose is preventing future crimes. From this perspective, three possible justifications for punishment arise: deterrence, incapacitation, and rehabilitation.

Deterrence functions as a disincentive to committing a crime. For example, it may be in the interest of students to steal books from libraries because they prefer having them exclusively to themselves and prefer not to have to return them. If no penalty exists for stealing books, the students have little reason not to steal them, other than their moral convictions. However, utilitarians believe it is foolish to rely on people's moral beliefs to prevent them from doing things that benefit themselves but decrease overall happiness for others. For utilitarians, threats of punishment shift the balance of incentives. If the book-stealing students risk paying burdensome fines or facing jail time, they are much less likely to steal books to avoid the minor inconvenience of having to return them. Criminal sanctions therefore alter incentive structures so that it becomes in each individual's best interest to obey the law. Breaking the law thus becomes unworthy of the risk.

To maintain this risk/reward deterrent ratio, the public must understand the laws and their sanctions, believe there is an adequate degree of likelihood that they will be apprehended and subjected to punishment, and agree that the punishment is not so extreme that its application would produce suffering that outweighs the happiness or utility it is intended to promote. For this latter reason, punishments designed to deter must not be too harsh—what in American constitutional language would be considered cruel and unusual—and must not violate rights of offenders by denying them due process of law or equal protection under the law. The punishments must be proportionate to the crimes that are committed, so that perpetrators of more serious crimes receive more severe punishments. Finally, they must only be as severe as is required to accomplish the penological objective and therefore not be excessive. This argument presumes that a substantial portion of potential offenders engage in rational cost-benefit analyses to determine whether criminal activity is worth the risk of punishment, and some critics doubt whether potential criminals engage in such deliberations.

The Rationale for Incapacitation

Utilitarianism also regards incapacitation as a legitimate strategy for reducing crime. Incapacitation renders convicts incapable of committing further crimes against the general public, either by incarcerating the convicts or physically debilitating them. These ends may be achieved by such means as capital punishment for murderers and chemical or surgical castration for sex offenders. The belief that individuals who commit crimes will continue to commit them unless incapacitated underlies this theory, which is the basis of recidivist statutes, such as "three-strikes" laws, that impose more severe punishments for repeat offenders.

The value of incapacitation is undermined if serving time actually increases the likelihood of the convicts committing more crimes upon their release. That might happen, for example, if their experiences of living among other convicts in prison conditions them to think of themselves as career criminals. Released convicts might also turn back to crime if they find that their opportunities for success in noncriminal life are worse after their release than they were before they entered the criminal justice system, such as higher rates of unemployment due to having a criminal record.

To some degree, warehousing convicts in prisons does prevent them from committing offenses against society. However, it is widely acknowledged that crime rates within prisons are higher than crime rates outside them. A consistent utilitarian cannot discount the pain caused by offenses committed inside prisons; however, most advocates of incapacitating criminals pay little attention to the consequences of segregating the most troubled populations in such arrangements. Moreover, in the light of the fact that African American men are nearly six times more likely than white men to be incarcerated, this concentration of violence raises troubling questions about fairness and discrimination.

The Goal of Rehabilitation

Rehabilitation is another legitimate means of preventing crime for utilitarians. It seeks to reform offenders so they no longer commit crimes, and under this theory, sentences may seem more like treatments than punishment. Rehabilitation can take many forms, including substance abuse therapy, vocational training, and education. Instead of conceiving of prison as a depository for offenders, rehabilitative theory seeks to use sentences as occasions to remove offenders who had strayed from law-abiding life from whatever social forces had corrupted them.

Early prisons practicing the rehabilitative model, such as those at Auburn and Sing Sing, New York, and Pittsburgh, Pennsylvania, during the 1820s, therefore isolated inmates from one another to prevent them from tempting one another to deviate from their paths toward the straight and narrow. Left to hard work, their conscience, and the Bible, reformers believed that the inmates' good natures would return. Rehabilitative ideals are committed to a belief that humans are good, equal, and redeemable and deserve the opportunity to correct their lives and restore their full citizenship. According to this position, governments are responsible for helping their citizens along this path.

In addition to rehabilitating individual offenders, utilitarianism also attempts to prevent crime by addressing the social causes of crime and "rehabilitate" the broader culture as well as individuals. If drug abuse, poverty, unemployment, or racial discrimination cause crime, utilitarians would seek to uproot criminal behavior by eliminating the cultural forces that generate millions of criminals rather than simply incarcerating all of these criminals once they commit offenses. In this sense, utilitarian rehabilitation attempts to diagnose and cure the social diseases that cause crime rather than simply treating individuals once they have symptoms of criminal behavior.

Critics of the rehabilitative model question its effectiveness, doubting whether even the most thorough therapeutic treatment can reform incorrigible criminals. Others find rehabilitative objectives vague and difficult to measure, leaving too much of sentencing indeterminate and subjective. Further, some fear that rehabilitation blurs the line between treatment and punishment and thus results in extended criminal detention of those needing only therapy. Many individuals with mental illness, for example, have difficulty ever leaving the criminal justice system.

Retributivist Theories

The most trenchant criticism of rehabilitation is leveled by those who disagree with the entire utilitarian view of punishment and find that "coddling" prisoners with psychological treatment and education in this way suffers from a fundamental confusion: Criminals simply deserve to suffer punishment. By this view, it is morally imperative to punish murderers, for example, regardless of whether doing so might reduce crime rates.

The word "retribution," from a Latin word for paying back, traces its Western origins to the biblical *lex talionis* or "eye for an eye." Unlike the forward-looking orientation of utilitarianism, retributivism seeks to address the wrongs of the past by forcing offenders to pay their debts to victims and society. In other words, the retributivist believes that punishment should balance the scales of justice by causing offenders to suffer pain commensurate with that of their victims. In this sense, retribution exacts revenge in proportion to the moral desert of the offenders.

Immanuel Kant's late-eighteenth-century ethical writings provide the philosophical underpinnings for modern retributivism. The human ability to reason, Kant claimed, enables each person to think freely and understand universal moral truths. By determining what is right from one's own reasoning, rather than from the authority of another, employing one's will to rise above the corrupting influences of culture and desire, and performing the good, one becomes self-governing and free. This understanding of humanity, wherein people use their reason to realize and live by objective ethical truth, provides the foundation for the Enlightenment's secular conception of human dignity. Because humans have dignity, Kant argued, they must always be treated as ends in themselves, rather than as mere means. He named this requirement that people not use others exclusively as tools the "practical imperative."

Utilitarian justifications of punishment violate the practical imperative because they use offenders merely to reduce crime rates. To preserve offenders' dignity, the justice system must hold them responsible for their crimes and treat them as if they were capable of freely making moral choices. Although this may seem odd, from a Kantian perspective offenders have a right to be punished. Otherwise they are but children or animals. In all utilitarian forms of punishment, offenders are denied dignity in this respect: rehabilitation seeks to cure them of their disease, deterrence treats them as rats that need shocks to keep them from eating cheese, and incapacitation simply denies them any ability to make moral choices. Anthony Burgess's novel *A Clockwork Orange* (1962), which was made into a 1971 film by Stanley Kubrick, dramatically explores these tensions between freedom and crime prevention.

Retributivists also claim that because preventing crime is the sole objective of utilitarian punishment, utilitarians would permit grievous injustices such as framing innocent people if such sacrifices furthered that goal. Although commentators repeat this criticism in most discussions about justifications of punishment, it does not appear to raise serious problems. Utilitarianism originated as a legal theory that demanded several institutional conditions for the public pursuit of utility, including security of person and property, legality, legislative supremacy, democratic accountability, publicity, and transparency. These utilitarian political procedures would preclude framing an innocent person.

Critics of retributivism find that its refusal to consider the objective of reducing future crime contradicts the most basic practical justification for punishment. Parents punish children, for example, to foster their development into moral citizens, rather than to balance metaphysical scales of justice. Society would surely find it reprehensible if parents were to assault a child physically and explain that they have administered corporal punishment as a vendetta because the child "deserves to suffer." Retributivism thus appears to offend the intuitive maxim that "two wrongs do not make a right."

To many, the retributive demand for "just deserts" provides a thinly veiled excuse for a lust for vengeance similar to the righteous indignation accompanying violence committed in the name of religion. As the Indian nationalist leader Mohandas K. Gandhi warned in his pacifist philosophy, "an eye for an eye" makes the whole world blind." In addition, retributive theories claim that punishment must be proportionate with the offense, yet they offer no convincing explanation for how to go about matching offenses with crimes other than the bare assertion of *lex talionis*.

Sentencing decisions also raise problems of incommensurability. In what sense, for example, is any prison term proportionate with a drug offense? Even if society executes a murderer, the murderer's death is not in any meaningful way equivalent to the death of a particular victim. Death, suffering, and loss endure regardless of the pain that is inflicted on an offender.

Hybrid Theories

Debates between utilitarian and retributive theories of punishment have led some to adopt hybrid theories. The most common such theory calls for a consequentialism constrained by deontological boundaries. Attempts to synthesize the best of both theories, however, fail to resolve their incompatible foundations.

The "restorative justice" movement has recently been offered as a progressive alternative to retribution, as it emphasizes repairing the damaged relationships between offenders and victims through reconciliation programs rather than punishment. Still others advance the increasingly popular "restitution" theory of punishment. Following the principles advanced by the law and economics movement, it argues that offenders should pay their debts to society and their victims financially rather than through conventional penalties such as prison sentences. Some take the radical position that attempts to justify punishment will fail because such state-sanctioned violence is ultimately unjustifiable. The fact that punishment may make human affairs more orderly does not necessarily mean that it necessarily has ethical foundations, and if it does not, it should be abolished. In its place, abolitionists would understand crime as conflicts requiring resolution rather than the infliction of more pain. Abolitionists share many ideological commitments with pacifists and are subjected to similar criticisms, including the charge that abolishing punishments would fail to protect victims from aggressors.

Social scientists have become increasingly skeptical of the ability to deter or rehabilitate with punishment. This has led to a rebirth in the popularity of retributive arguments, which were thought to be barbaric only a few generations ago. This rise of retributivism, coupled with the brute efficacy of incarceration, has created a culture in which offenders are thought to deserve long sentences. The US Sentencing Guidelines formalized these trends, requiring longer sentences and removing much of the discretion previously granted to judges to tailor individual sentences. Add to this situation lengthy mandatory sentences for drug offenders—who already constitute 40 percent of US federal prison populations and 15.7 percent of US state prison populations—and the staggering incarceration rates continue to grow.

Nick Smith

Further Reading

Beccaria, Cesare. *On Crimes and Punishments*. Indianapolis: Bobbs-Merrill, 1963. Print.
Bentham, Jeremy. *Introduction to the Principles of Morals and Legislation*. New York: Hafner, 1961. Print.
Bianchi, J., and P. Pettit, eds. *Abolitionism: Towards a Non-Repressive Approach to Crime*. Amsterdam: Free UP, 1986. Print.
Binder, Guyora, and Nick Smith. "Framed: Utilitarianism and Punishment of the Innocent." *Rutgers Law Journal* 32 (2000): 115. Print.
Clear, Todd R., Michael D. Reisig, and George F. Cole. *American Corrections*. 11th ed. Boston: Cengage, 2016. Print.
Duff, R. A. *Trials and Punishments*. Cambridge: Cambridge UP, 1986. Print.
Duff, R. A., and David Garland, eds. *A Reader on Punishment*. Oxford,: Oxford UP, 1994. Print.
Fact Sheet: Trends in U.S. Corrections. Washington, DC: Sentencing Project, Dec. 2015. PDF file.
Foucault, Michel. *Discipline and Punish: The Birth of the Prison*. Trans. Alan Sheridan. New York: Vintage, 1995. Print.
Garland, David. *Punishment and Modern Society: A Study in Social Theory*. Oxford: Oxford UP, 1993. Print.
Hatch, Virginia Leigh, and Anthony Walsh. *Capital Punishment: Theory and Practice of the Ultimate Penalty*. Oxford: Oxford UP, 2015. Print.
Honderich, T. *Punishment: The Supposed Justifications*. Harmondsworth: Penguin, 1984. Print.
Kant, Immanuel. *Foundations of the Metaphysics of Morals*. Trans. Lewis White Beck. Indianapolis: Bobbs-Merrill, 1959. Print.
Kaplan, John, Robert Weisberg, and Guyora Binder, eds. *Criminal Law: Cases and Materials*. 6th ed. New York: Aspen, 2008. Print.
Primoratz, Igor. *Justify Legal Punishment*. Atlantic Highlands: Humanities, 1989. Print.

See also Capital punishment; Community-based corrections; Corporal punishment; Cruel and unusual punishment; Deterrence; Incapacitation; Just deserts; Punitive damages; Rehabilitation; Restorative justice; Sentencing; Sentencing guidelines, U.S.; Medical model of offender treatment; Pennsylvania system of corrections; Scandinavia's prison experience.

Restitution

Definition: Punishment requiring convicted offenders to pay their victims or society for the costs incurred as a result of their crimes
Criminal justice issue: Convictions; Punishment; Sentencing
Significance: The use of restitution is increasing and in many states is now a mandatory sanction that courts are required, by law, to impose on offenders.

Until the late decades of the twentieth century, few formal restitution programs existed in the United States. Now, all US states have restitution programs and every state gives its courts the right to order restitution to be paid by offenders. Within the United States, restitution is used as a form of punishment both in the adult criminal justice system and juvenile justice system systems. In both cases, restitution is often part of offenders' terms of probation. Restitution is also sometimes used as an alternative form of punishment, in place of incarceration. One type of restitution program requires offenders to pay monetary damages directly to victims. Monetary restitution may be ordered to cover such things as medical expenses, lost wages, counseling costs, loss of property, and funeral expenses resulting from the offenders' crimes. Instead of repaying the victims themselves with money, victim service restitution requires offenders to perform services for the victims of their crimes. Another type of restitution, community service, usually requires offenders to pay society back by engaging in community-service projects. Instead of being sentenced into the prison or jail system, offenders may be required to perform services in nursing homes, parks, hospitals, libraries, schools, animal shelters, or other public institutions. Judges may impose whatever number of service hours they regard as commensurate with the crimes committed. All these forms of restitution may be ordered for crimes against property, such as vandalism, or violent crimes against persons, such as assault.

As both a sole punishment and a condition of one's probation, restitution provides several advantages over other forms of punishment. Restitution programs save the taxpayers millions of dollars, as offenders are not placed in secure facilities, such as prisons, jails, or halfway houses. Secondly, these programs provide offenders with fresh chances to become productive citizens without suffering the negative effects of incarceration. Most important, restitution programs provide victims and communities with both tangible benefits and feelings of vindication for the harm they suffer.

Research has found that restitution programs for both juveniles and adults have higher success rates than other alternative forms of punishment. However, those who have completed restitution programs may not necessarily stay away from future contact with law-enforcement officials. Thus, while the majority of offenders complete their court-ordered restitution programs, the recidivism effects of these programs remain in doubt.

Karen F. Lahm

Further Reading

Allen, Harry E., Clifford E. Simonsen, and Edward J. Latessa. *Corrections in America: An Introduction*. 10th ed. Upper Saddle River, N.J.: Pearson Education, 2004.

"Restitution." *National Center for Victims of Crime*. Natl. Center for Victims of Crime, 2004. Web. 1 June 2016.

"Returning Money to Victims." *Offices of the United States Attorneys*. US Dept. of Justice, 8 July 2015. Web. 1 June 2016.

Senna, Joseph, and Larry J. Siegel. *Essentials of Criminal Justice*. 3d ed. Belmont, Calif.: Wadsworth, 2001.

Siegel, Larry J. *Juvenile Delinquency: The Core*. Belmont, Calif.: Wadsworth, 2002.

See also Blended sentences; Community service; Execution of judgment; Fines; Juvenile courts; Juvenile justice system; Probation, adult; Probation, juvenile; Rehabilitation; Restorative justice; Sentencing; Victim-offender mediation; Victimology; Australia's "Reintegrative Shaming" approach; Peacemaking criminology.

Restorative justice

Definition: Philosophy of justice that focuses on repairing harm caused by offenses

Criminal justice issue: Crime prevention; restorative justice; victims

Significance: Restorative justice is a modern holistic approach to justice that aims to treat both offenders and their victims, while involving the community in restitution and punishment.

A philosophical approach that is currently being used in both the adult and juvenile justice systems in the United States, restorative justice focuses on repairing the harm caused by offenses. It involves the victims of the crimes, the communities that are affected, and the offenders in the justice process. The U.S. Department of Justice has identified six components of restorative justice that must be considered in its application to any given case: the nature of the crime, the victims, the offenders, the local community, the overriding goal of justice, and the role of the criminal or juvenile justice system.

The nature of the crime, the impact on the victim and the attitude of the offender, are key factors in the success of restorative justice, and not all crimes are suitable for its application. For example, particularly violent crimes that traumatize their victims and crimes involving uncooperative offenders are generally unsuitable for restorative justice techniques.

The primary goal of restorative justice—and the one that gives it its name—is to repair damage and relationships that are harmed by crimes. This goal contrasts with the goal of retributive justice, which is to assign blame and administer punishments. Also unlike traditional retributive justice, in which victims have little involvement in the corrections process, restorative justice offers victims active roles in offender rehabilitation. For example, the victims may play a part in recommending restitution and participate in offender-victim mediation and conflict resolution, victim-offender circles, offender mentor programs, and in the supervising of community service.

Techniques

One of the most widely used techniques in restorative justice is victim-offender mediation, which brings victims and offenders together, along with trained mediators, to seek resolutions to the crimes. VOM is typically implemented after the offenders are charged, but it can also be used after the offenders complete their sentencing. During VOM, victim may share with the offenders the impact of the latters' crimes, including personal, social, and community elements. VOM is often used with burglary and other property crimes, in juvenile justice matters, and in other family court matters.

Offenders play a critical role in the success of restorative justice techniques. They must be willing to admit that they have caused harm to their victims and their communities and must be committed to repairing that harm. In addition to working with their victims, offenders must be able to identify their own needs in successful rehabilitation.

Community leaders and other community members are also involved in the restorative justice process. Their role is to work with both offenders and victims in restitution agreements. They offer resources for successful completion of the restorative programs, involve themselves in implementing restitution agreements, identify needs, and work toward crime prevention.

One example of community-led restorative justice initiatives is sentencing circles, which have been used by Native Americans for many years. The focus of circles is on the victims, their concerns, and the concerns of the community. Sentencing circles traditionally incorporate elements of both shaming and healing. The shaming works when the offenders are among their neighbors, friends, and community leaders.

A final key to the success of restorative justice is the role played by the formal criminal justice or juvenile justice system. In addition to ensuring that the restorative justice process is embraced by all the various parts of the justice system, there must be some kind of accountability within the process. As a whole, the justice system and its administrators need to know whether restorative justice measures are an effective response to criminal behavior. Research on the effectiveness of restorative justice has not yet been widely established in the United States. However, in countries in which it began earlier, such as Canada, four outcomes of restorative justice have been studied: victim satisfaction, offender satisfaction, restitution compliance, and lower recidivism rates.

Research conducted in Canada on more than thirty restorative justice programs has found that the programs have higher victim and offender satisfaction than traditional retributive justice responses, that they are better at achieving restitution compliance from offenders, and that they appear to reduce recidivism rates. It should be noted, however, that restorative justice programs are, by their very nature, likely to be more successful because they involve only positively motivated offenders and victims.

A restorative justice program that has received national attention and served as a model for other programs is the offender-victim circles held at the maximum security facility in Green Bay, Wisconsin. The circle lasts for three days and offenders convicted of serious offenses, such as murder, rape, and aggravated assault, meet with their victims in a secure environment under the supervision of psychologists and counselors. Offenders report that meeting their victims face to face and confronting the horror of their own crimes leaves a lasting impression on them.

Obstacles

There are some barriers to overcome in implementing restorative justice programs. Some critics argue that restorative justice approaches do not address the issue of deterrence, particularly deterrence of serious crime. Others maintain that victims' rights may not be addressed equally or appropriately. Overcoming cultural barriers is also important when establishing restorative justice programs. Failure to account for cultural differences can lead to miscommunication and misunderstanding. In a brief on cross-cultural issues in restorative justice, the Department of Justice advises that differences in communication styles, such as physical proximity, body movements, paralanguage (vocal cues such as hesitations and changing timbre of voice), and density of language, should be understood by all parties involved in the restorative justice process.

Gaining the support of community members and ensuring the program meets state and federal guidelines will help ensure the success of restorative justice programs.

Monica L. P. Robbers

Further Reading

Johnstone, Gerry. *Restorative Justice: Ideas, Values, Debates*. Portland, Oreg.: Willan, 2002. Broad discussion of arguments for and against restorative justice programs.

Karp, David R., and Todd R. Clear. *What Is Community Justice? Case Studies of Restorative Justice and Community Supervision*. Thousand Oaks, Calif.: Sage Publications, 2002. Sociological study of actual restorative justice programs in action with detailed descriptions.

Rawls, John. *Justice as Fairness: A Restatement*. Edited by Erin Kelly. Cambridge, Mass.: Belknap Press, 2001. Collection of essays assembled by the distinguished American ethicist John Rawls that consider a wide variety of questions about the nature of justice.

Zehr, Howard, and Barb Toews, eds. *Critical Issues in Restorative Justice*. Chicago: Criminal Justice Press, 2004. This book provides an introduction to restorative justice and explores programs that have been implemented around the world. Both successes and failures are discussed.

See also Community service; Community-based corrections; Juvenile Justice and Delinquency Prevention, Office of; Juvenile justice system; Prison and jail systems; Punishment; Rehabilitation; Restitution; Victim assistance programs; Victim-offender mediation.

Restraining orders

Definition: Court orders in the nature of injunctions, usually temporary, that forbid parties from doing specified acts

Criminal justice issue: Crime prevention; domestic violence; victims

Significance: This remedy preserves a plaintiff's rights to avoid irreparable injury, pending final determination of the parties' rights; a variant of the restraining order helps protect victims of domestic violence.

In the usual course of a civil legal proceeding, the court makes no order affecting either party's substantive rights until the final judgment. In some situations, however, a plaintiff's rights may be irreparably damaged if the defendant continues taking some action. In such a case, the plaintiff may apply to the court for a temporary restraining order (also known as a "temporary injunction").

In order to be granted this extraordinary relief, the party seeking the order must show that immediate and irreparable harm is likely to result from a continuation of the status quo, or that the defendant is acting in a manner that will make any final judgment on the merits ineffectual. The burden is on the plaintiff to show entitlement to the order, and the court is likely to balance the relative inconveniences to the plaintiff and the defendant in determining whether the order should be issued. The temporary restraining order is effective only until a final judgment is issued. If the plaintiff is ultimately successful in the adjudication, the court may replace the temporary restraining order with a permanent injunction.

One special type of restraining order is the domestic violence restraining order. All fifty states have statutes authorizing a court to issue a restraining order against the alleged perpetrator of domestic violence, upon application by the intimate partner or former partner of the alleged perpetrator. Although the law varies among jurisdictions, this type of restraining order typically orders the respondent to refrain from further violence, harassment, or intimidation of the petitioner. It typically orders the respondent to vacate the home and to avoid contact with the petitioner at work, church, and school. The order also usually establishes custody and visitation for minor children, if necessary, and may order child or spousal support.

The typical procedure for obtaining a domestic violence restraining order is for the petitioner to make application for the court in an *ex parte* hearing—a hearing before the court in which only the petitioner is present, not the respondent. If the court finds that the statutory requirements are met, it issues a restraining order, which is then served upon the respondent. The respondent has a period of time (usually twenty-one days) in which to contest the order at a hearing. The restraining order typically is in effect for one year, unless vacated earlier by the court. Violation of the restraining order is punishable by civil or criminal penalties, and the violation itself (such as an assault) is also a separately punishable crime.

Gwendolyn Griffith

Further Reading

Haugaard, J. J., and L. G. Seri. "Stalking and Other Forms of Intrusive Contact Among Adolescents and Young Adults from the Perspective of the Person Initiating the Intrusive Contact." *Criminal Justice and Behavior* 31, no. 1 (2004): 37-54.

Meyer, J. F., and D. R. Grant. *The Courts in Our Criminal Justice System*. Upper Saddle River, N.J.: Prentice-Hall, 2003.

Neubauer, D. W. *America's Courts and the Criminal Justice System*. 7th ed. Belmont, Calif.: Wadsworth, 2002.

See also Cease-and-desist orders; Domestic violence; Stalking; Trespass; Victim assistance programs.

Reversible error

Definition: Error made during a trial that warrants a reversal of a guilty verdict

Criminal justice issue: Appeals; convictions; trial procedures; verdicts

Significance: Trial court verdicts can be reversed when appellate courts determine that defendants' cases have been seriously harmed by mistakes made during their trials.

> **Examples of Reversible Errors**
> - incompetent counsel
> - judicial bias
> - jury bias
> - trial testimony based on coerced confessions
> - failure of judge to recognize statutory requirements
> - incomplete jury instructions

One of the primary functions of federal and state appellate courts is to review and correct errors committed during trials. Errors can occur at any stage of the trial. Appellate courts may also review the competence and impartiality of the actors involved in the trials, including defense attorneys, judges, witnesses, and jury members.

Under English common law almost all findings of trial errors resulted in reversals, Now, however, American courts classify errors into two principal types: harmless and reversible. A harmless error is one considered to be a simple mistake made during the course of a trial that does not affect the decision of the judge or jury. By contrast, a reversible error is a mistake committed during a trial that is considered so serious that it warrants a reversal of the verdict, either because it negatively affects the outcome of the trial or because it abridges the defendant's fundamental constitutional rights.

Errors of a constitutional nature are regarded as more serious than nonconstitutional errors. Appellate courts have held that constitutional errors warrant reversals when there is a possibility they have contributed to decisions of the judges or juries. Nonconstitutional errors can be grounds for reversal only when appellate courts determine that they have significantly influenced verdicts.

Margaret E. Leigey

Further Reading
Traynor, Roger J. *The Riddle of Harmless Error*. Columbus: Ohio State University Press, 1970.
Whitebread, Charles H., and Christopher Slobogin. *Criminal Procedure: An Analysis of Cases and Concepts*. New York: Foundation Press, 2000.

See also Appellate process; Court types; *Habeas corpus*; Harmless error; Trials.

Robinson v. California

The Case: U.S. Supreme Court ruling on cruel and unusual punishment

Date: Decided on June 25, 1962
Criminal justice issue: Punishment; substance abuse
Significance: This case, which held that it was cruel and unusual punishment to incarcerate drug addicts simply because of their addictions, was for some critics emblematic of the Warren court's "softness" on crime.

Robinson, the plaintiff in this case, was originally convicted under a California statute making it a crime to be a drug addict and was sentenced to ninety days in jail. The statute did not require the state to prove that the accused had either bought or purchased drugs or that he possessed them—the mere status of being a drug addict was enough to convict a defendant. Robinson appealed, and the Supreme Court overturned the conviction on grounds that incarceration for ninety days for what amounts to an illness constitutes cruel and unusual punishment.

Because of such rulings as *Mapp v. Ohio* (1961), which extended guarantees against unreasonable search and seizure to state defendants, the Court overseen by Chief Justice Earl Warren was criticized for "coddling" criminals. *Robinson* was doubly controversial because it is based on the assumption that drug addiction is an illness over which the addict has no control. Indeed, six years later the Court declined to follow its own precedent in *Powell v. Texas* (1968), in which it upheld the criminal conviction of a chronic alcoholic, declaring that the state of knowledge regarding alcoholism was inadequate to permit the enunciation of a new constitutional principle.

The *Robinson* decision is important for making the cruel and unusual punishment clause of the Eighth Amendment applicable at the state as well as the federal level. The case was a continuation of the "due process revolution," championed initially by Justice Hugo Black, that reached its high-water mark during Earl Warren's tenure as chief justice. By means of the due process clause of the Fourteenth Amendment, the guarantees of the Bill of Rights limiting federal action were "incorporated" into the Fourteenth Amendment, thus becoming applicable to state governments. The Fourteenth Amendment, passed in the wake of the Civil War, makes all persons born in the United States citizens whose privileges and immunities cannot be restricted and whose rights of due process and equal protection cannot be denied.

Some framers of the Fourteenth Amendment indicated that the privileges and immunities extended therein included the guarantees of the Bill of Rights, but this point was left ambiguous. In *Palko v. Connecticut* (1937), the Court explicitly addressed the issue for the first time, stating that some of the rights embodied in the first ten amendments to the Constitution were so fundamental that the Fourteenth Amendment obligated states to observe them. Then, writing in dissent in *Adamson v. California* (1947), Justice Black argued that the Fourteenth Amendment obligated states to honor all aspects of the Bill of Rights. The Court has never quite adopted this view, but by the time Earl Warren's leadership ended in 1969, most of the Bill of Rights had been applied to the states.

Lisa Paddock

Further Reading
Berkson, Larry. *The Concept of Cruel and Unusual Punishment.* Lexington, Mass.: Lexington Books, 1975.
Gaines, Larry K., and Peter B. Kraska, eds. *Drugs, Crime, and Justice.* Prospect Heights, Ill.: Waveland Press, 2003.
Liska, Ken. *Drugs and the Human Body, with Implications for Society.* 7th ed. Saddle River, N.J.: Prentice-Hall, 2004.
Orcutt, James D., and David R. Rudy, eds. *Drugs, Alcohol, and Social Problems.* Lanham, Md.: Rowman & Littlefield, 2003.

See also Cruel and unusual punishment; Drugs and law enforcement; Due process of law; *Rummel v. Estelle*; Supreme Court, U.S.

Rummel v. Estelle

The Case: U.S. Supreme Court ruling on mandatory sentences
Date: Decided on March 18, 1980
Criminal justice issue: Fraud; punishment; sentencing
Significance: In this case, the Supreme Court found no cruel and unusual punishment in a state's mandatory life-imprisonment statute as applied to a man convicted of three fraudulent offenses involving only $229.11.

In 1973, William Rummel was convicted under the Texas recidivist statute, which required a mandatory life sentence after three felony convictions, even for nonviolent offenses. In 1964 Rummel had been convicted of his first felony, the fraudulent use of a credit card to obtain goods worth $80.00. Four years later he had been found guilty of passing a forged check for $28.36. Finally, in 1973 he was charged with a third felony of receiving $120.75 by false pretenses. Rummel might have avoided the life sentence if he had yielded to the state's pressure to accept a plea bargain without a jury trial, but he insisted on a trial. Rummel sought relief in federal court, with the argument that his life sentence was "cruel and unusual" because it was grossly excessive and disproportionate to the penalties for more serious crimes. The district court and court of appeals rejected the argument, and Rummel appealed to the U.S. Supreme Court.

The Court voted 5 to 4 to affirm the constitutionality of Rummel's punishment. Writing for the majority, Justice William H. Rehnquist maintained that the doctrine that the Eighth Amendment prohibited sentences disproportionate to the severity of the crime was relevant only in death-penalty cases, because this penalty was unique in its total irrevocability. Rehnquist found that the Texas statute had two legitimate goals: to deter repeat offenders and to isolate recidivists from society as long as necessary after they had demonstrated their incapacity to obey the law. The states generally had the authority to determine the length of isolation deemed necessary for such recidivists. Rehnquist also made much of the fact that the Texas statute allowed the possibility of parole.

In an important dissent, Justice Lewis F. Powell, Jr., argued that the doctrine of disproportionality also applied to penalties in noncapital cases. He pointed to precedents that could be interpreted as prohibiting grossly excessive penalties, especially *Weems v. United States* (1910) and *Robinson v. California* (1962). Powell observed that in Texas, even those convicted of murder or aggravated kidnapping were not subject to mandatory life sentences. In addition, he maintained that the possibility of parole should not be considered in assessing whether the penalty was grossly disproportionate.

The *Rummel* decision would prove to be limited and uncertain in its application as a precedent. In 1983, when the Court encountered a life sentence without any chance of parole based on a recidivist statute in *Solem v. Helm*, Justice Powell would write the majority opinion while Rehnquist would write a dissent. While *Solem* did not directly overturn *Rummel*, the *Solem* majority did endorse the idea that a prison sentence might be unconstitutional if it was disproportionate to punishments for other crimes. Yet in upholding a life sentence for the possession of 650 grams of cocaine in *Harmelin v. Michigan* (1991), the Court would indicate its continued reluctance to apply the doctrine of disproportionality in noncapital cases.

Thomas Tandy Lewis

Further Reading
Demleitner, Nora V., Douglas A. Berman, Marc L. Miller, and Ronald F. Wright. *Sentencing Law and Policy: Cases, Statutes, and Guidelines.* New York: Aspen Publishers, 2003.
Tonry, Michael. *Sentencing and Sanctions in Western Countries.* New York: Oxford University Press, 2001.
_____. *Sentencing Matters.* New York: Oxford University Press, 1996.

United States Sentencing Commission. *Federal Sentencing Guidelines Manual 2003.* St. Paul, Minn.: West Publishing, 2004.

See also *Brady v. United States*; Cruel and unusual punishment; Mandatory sentencing; Plea bargaining; Supreme Court, U.S.

Santobello v. New York

The Case: US Supreme Court ruling on plea bargaining
Date: Decided on December 20, 1971
Significance: In this case, which granted the petitioner the right to either a resentencing or a new trial, the Supreme Court confirmed the binding nature of plea-bargaining agreements made by prosecutors with defendants in criminal proceedings.

In 1969, in New York, Rudolph Santobello was arraigned on two criminal counts of violating state antigambling statutes. At first, Santobello entered a plea of not guilty, but later, after negotiations with his prosecutors, he changed his plea to guilty to a lesser-included charge, which carried a maximum penalty of one year in prison. Between the entering of the new guilty plea and the sentencing, there was a delay of several months, and in the interim Santobello obtained a new defense attorney, who immediately attempted to have the guilty plea removed and certain evidence suppressed. Both motions were denied.

At Santobello's sentencing, a new prosecutor recommended the maximum penalty of one year in prison. The defense quickly objected, using the argument that the petitioner's plea-bargaining agreement had stipulated that the prosecution would make no recommendation regarding sentencing. The judge, rejecting the relevancy of what prosecutors claimed they would do, sentenced Santobello to the full one-year term on the grounds that he was a seasoned and habitual offender. Subsequently, the Appellate Division of the Supreme Court of the State of New York unanimously upheld the conviction.

The US Supreme Court found that the prosecution had breached the plea-bargaining agreement and remanded the case to the state court to determine whether the circumstances required only resentencing before a different judge or whether the petitioner should be allowed to withdraw his guilty plea and be granted a new trial on the two counts as originally charged. The fact that the breach in the plea-bargaining agreement was inadvertent was deemed irrelevant, as was the sentencing judge's claim that he was not influenced by the prosecutor's recommendation. Chief Justice Warren E. Burger, in the court's ruling, argued that the plea-bargaining procedure in criminal justice "must be attended by safeguards to ensure the defendant what is reasonably due in the circumstances." Therefore, any agreement made in the plea-bargaining process, because it is part of the inducement used to encourage a plea of guilty, constitutes "a promise that must be fulfilled."

In its decision in *Santobello*, the Supreme Court both confirmed its formal recognition of plea bargaining, first granted in *Brady v. United States* (1970), and established its binding nature. Although in later decisions it would review and somewhat modify its position, as, for example, in *Mabry v. Johnson* (1984), it established an extremely important principle: that prosecutors and courts could not unilaterally renege on promises made in plea-bargaining agreements. The *Santobello* decision had the effect of encouraging wider use of the plea-bargaining process, an important aid in expediting justice.

John W. Fiero

Justice Thurgood Marshall gave the dissent in the case. (Public domain, via Wikimedia Commons)

Further Reading
Fisher, George. *Plea Bargaining's Triumph: A History of Plea Bargaining in America.* Stanford, Calif.: Stanford University Press, 2003.

Rosett, Arthur I. *Justice by Consent: Plea Bargains in the American Courthouse.* Philadelphia: Lippincott, 1976.
"Santobello v. New York." *FindLaw.* FindLaw, 2016. Web. 27 May, 2016.
"Santobello v. New York." *Oyez.* Chicago-Kent College of Law at Illinois Tech, n.d. Web. 27 May, 2016.
Vogel, Mary E. *Coercion to Compromise: Social Conflict and the Emergence of Plea Bargaining, 1830-1920.* Rev. ed. New York: Oxford University Press, 2005.

See also *Brady v. United States;* Criminal justice system; Criminal procedure; District attorneys; Plea bargaining; Supreme Court, U.S.

Scottsboro cases

The Event: Celebrated cases arising from the arrest, on false charges of rape, of nine young African American men who were subsequently convicted by all-white juries and subjected to years of incarceration
Date: March 25, 1931-July, 1937
   Place: Alabama
Criminal justice issue: Appeals; civil rights and liberties; juries
Significance: The Scottsboro cases showed the racist nature of justice in the American South and led to the U.S. Supreme Court's establishment of new rules concerning lawyers and juries.

On March 25, 1931, Alabama authorities arrested nine young black men, Olen Montgomery, Clarence Norris, Haywood Patterson, Ozie Powell, Willie Roberson, Charlie Weems, Eugene Williams, Andrew Wright, and Leroy Wright, and charged them with raping two white women, Ruby Bates and Victoria Price. The alleged rape took place on top of a boxcar on a freight train moving rapidly through Jackson County in northeastern Alabama. The "Scottsboro boys," as the nine African Americans were called, denied having seen the girls on the train, but within five days an all-white grand jury indicted them for rape, and a week later, April 6, the first defendants were brought to trial before an all-white jury.

The Initial Trials

After two days of testimony, largely from Price and Bates, the jury found Clarence Norris and Charlie Weems guilty of rape and sentenced them to death. The court-appointed defense attorney, who appeared to be quite drunk during the proceedings, did not bother to cross-examine witnesses and asked few questions of anyone. The next day, another all-white jury convicted Haywood Patterson on the basis of the same testimony and sentenced him to death. He had the same inept lawyer as did the first two defendants.

On April 8 and 9, four more of the accused, including fifteen-year-old Eugene Williams, sat in the Scottsboro courthouse and heard similar evidence and the same verdict: death by the electric chair. The final trial took place on the afternoon of April 9 but ended in a mistrial for the thirteen-year-old Leroy Wright. Several members of the jury rejected the prosecution's demand for a life sentence for the youngest of the accused, wanting Leroy to die instead. After the mistrial he was released and not retried. In short, in three days of legal proceedings, eight of the nine defendants were sentenced to death after quick trials before all-white juries and with inadequate legal representation.

The Appeals

The convictions made newspaper headlines across the country and caught the attention of the National Association for the Advancement of Colored People (NAACP). The group quickly sent a team of lawyers to Alabama to appeal the verdicts in state and federal courts. The American Communist Party also dispatched a prominent lawyer, Samuel Leibowitz, to Scottsboro (it hoped to use the case to build its membership in the African American community). The NAACP and the Communist Party fought for months over who would have chief responsibility for the appeals. Finally, Leibowitz took full charge of the case. The Alabama Supreme Court denied the appeals of all the convicted men except Eugene Williams. The court ordered his release because he was a juvenile at the time of his conviction. The appeal to the federal courts had much greater success, however, and in November, 1932, the U.S. Supreme Court ordered new trials for all seven of the "boys" now sitting on death row. The Court ruled in this case, *Powell v. Alabama* (1932), that none of the defendants had been provided with an adequate lawyer, so they had been denied their right to due process under the Fourteenth Amendment.

Second Series of Trials

During a second series of trials in March, 1933, in Decatur, Alabama, a safer distance from the scene of the alleged crime, but also before all-white juries, Haywood Patterson and Clarence Norris were found guilty again and sentenced to death. This happened even though one of the supposed victims, Ruby Bates, reversed her earlier testimony and denied that any rape had taken place. The trial judge, however, in an unusual move, set aside the

Defendant Haywood Patterson during the 1933 trial. (National Archives)

conviction of Patterson and ordered a third trial for him. At that new trial in December, the jury heard from Price one more time but not from Bates, who by this time was attending Communist Party rallies in the North calling for the immediate release of the Scottsboro boys. The third all-white jury convicted Patterson a third time and ordered his execution. A few days later, at Norris's second trial, he also was sentenced to the electric chair. Testimony from a farmer who claimed to have witnessed the event from his hayloft about a quarter of a mile away from the fast-moving train helped make the state's case.

In the new round of appeals the Alabama supreme court upheld the new convictions, and the prisoners remained on death row. They continued to be abused by vicious guards and wardens. In 1935 the U.S. Supreme Court stepped in once more and reversed the convictions of Norris and Patterson. The Court held in *Norris v. Alabama* (1935) that neither defendant had received a fair trial because of a "long-continued, unvarying and wholesale exclusion of Negroes from jury service" on the part of the state of Alabama. A short time later, the first black man in the state's history was placed on the Jackson County grand jury, and the defendants were quickly reindicted.

In January, 1936, Haywood Patterson stood trial for a fourth time. The same witnesses presented the same testimony, but this time the jury recommended a seventy-five-year sentence rather than electrocution, and Patterson was returned to the state prison. The Alabama Supreme Court upheld this conviction, and the U.S. Supreme Court this time found no reason for reversal. In July, 1937, Clarence Norris was tried for a third time, convicted, and sentenced to death. Andy Wright and Charlie Weems got ninety-nine years and seventy-five years respectively. In a major surprise, the state dropped all charges against Eugene Williams, Olen Montgomery, Willie Roberson, and Roy Wright. After six years on death row, they were released.

Aftermath

A year later, Alabama governor Bibb Graves reduced Norris's death sentence to life imprisonment but denied pardons to the remaining Scottsboro defendants despite promises he had previously made to lawyers for the NAACP. Not until 1943 did a new governor release Charlie Weems, followed the next year by Norris and Andrew Wright. Both men immediately violated their paroles by leaving the state. Norris was hunted down and returned to prison in 1944. Two years later he got a second parole; Ozie Powell was also released. Andy Wright was returned by Georgia authorities and sent back to prison. In 1948, Haywood Patterson escaped from Kilby State Prison and headed to Detroit. The FBI tracked him down as a parole violator, but Michigan governor G. Mennen Williams refused to extradite him to Alabama. Patterson died four years later after spending more than seventeen years in prison for a crime he never committed. The last surviving "Scottsboro boy," Clarence Norris, received a pardon from Alabama governor George Wallace in October, 1976. Norris died in quiet obscurity in 1989.

The Scottsboro cases demonstrated the great biases and inequalities in American law, especially for African Americans in the South. Nine defendants suffered greatly because of biased juries, inadequate lawyers, and the disregard for the basic constitutional rights of black Americans. Still, the U.S. Supreme Court made two key decisions in the cases that helped affirm these basic rights in the future. *Powell v. Alabama* and *Norris v. Alabama* established the right to effective council in death-penalty cases and the guarantee of an unbiased jury.

Leslie V. Tischauser

Further Reading
Carter, Dan T. *Scottsboro: A Tragedy of the American South*. Rev. ed. Baton Rouge: Louisiana State University Press, 1979.
Goodman, James E. *Stories of Scottsboro*. New York: Pantheon Books, 1994.
Horne, Gerald. *"Powell v. Alabama": The Scottsboro Boys and American Justice*. New York: Franklin Watts, 1997.
Miller, Loren. *The Petitioners: The Story of the Supreme Court of the United States and the Negro*. New York: Pantheon Books, 1966.
National Association for the Advancement of Colored People. *Guide to the Papers of the NAACP, Part 6: The Scottsboro Case, 1931-1950*. Frederick, Md.: University Publications of America, 1986.
Record, Wilson. *Race and Radicalism: The NAACP and the Communist Party in Conflict*. Ithaca, N.Y.: Cornell University Press, 1964.

See also Appellate process; Counsel, right to; Equal protection under the law; *Gideon v. Wainwright*; Jim Crow laws; Miscarriage of justice; *Powell v. Alabama*.

Self-incrimination, privilege against

Definition: Privilege found in the Fifth Amendment to the U.S. Constitution that protects persons from being compelled to be witnesses against themselves in state or federal criminal proceedings

Criminal justice issue: Confessions; defendants; immunity; interrogation
Significance: The privilege against self-incrimination is an important procedural safeguard against the awesome power of the government in the accusatorial system of criminal justice, designed to protect the individual.

Basic concerns and questions concerning self-incrimination and its interlink between voluntariness and free have puzzled philosophers for centuries and represent one of history's Gordian knots.

The privilege against self-incrimination originated in England in the twelfth century, when English subjects were summoned to appear before the ecclesiastical courts, the courts of High Commission, and the infamous Star Chamber to take oaths *ex officio*. Without being informed whether they were being accused of any crime, suspects were obliged to swear that they would answer truthfully any and all questions put to them.

To object, subjects invoked the ancient maxim *nemo tenetur* ("no man is bound to accuse himself"), insisting that they could not be required to accuse themselves of crimes before formal judicial proceedings, and the courts relented. Parliament prohibited administration of oaths *ex officio* and, by the eighteenth century, English courts had extended to defendants and witnesses in criminal trials the right to refuse to testify against themselves. Because the accused was disqualified from testifying at the trial, the privilege became the chief protection against forced confessions.

The Fifth Amendment

The privilege was carried over to the American colonies. The fact that twelve of the twenty-three rights in the Bill of Rights (the first ten constitutional amendments, ratified in 1791) deal with criminal procedures is some indication of the importance of balancing individual rights against the government's power to prosecute crime. The Fifth Amendment reads, in part: "No person . . . shall be compelled in any Criminal Case to be a witness against himself." The Fifth Amendment acted as a limitation only on the federal government for a time. Beginning in the 1930's, the Supreme Court relied on the Fourteenth Amendment to reverse state criminal convictions based on confessions that it determined were involuntary under a "totality of the circumstances" evaluation (*Brown v. Mississippi*, 1936). Then, in *Malloy v. Hogan* (1964), the Court decided that the right against self-incrimination itself was so fundamental that it should be applied in state criminal prosecutions, under the so-called incorporation doctrine.

The values underlying the privilege against self-incrimination form the core of the American criminal justice system, which is based on an accusatorial rather than an inquisitorial system of criminal justice. The privilege obliges the government to meet its burden of proving guilt beyond a reasonable doubt without forcing the accused to join the prosecution. The Supreme Court has recognized the premium this system places on individual dignity, even the dignity of those accused of serious crime. The privilege obliges the government to play by the rules: Police and prosecutors may not rely on physical abuse, inhumane techniques, or deceit and trickery. A criminal defendant need not testify at all. The prosecutor may not comment on the failure to testify, and the jury may not take the defendant's silence as any indication of guilt.

The privilege is not without limits. It applies in civil or administrative proceedings only if an answer might tend to be incriminating in a later criminal proceeding. It can be claimed only by individuals and not by corporations, and thus business records usually may be seized. It protects only evidence elicited from the defendant, not incriminating statements of a third party. It is limited to testimonial evidence; a defendant may be obliged to furnish real evidence such as fingerprints or a blood sample. Even a person with a valid claim of privilege may be compelled to testify if the government grants immunity and promises not to use the testimony in any later criminal prosecution.

Interrogations

The Supreme Court first took a Sixth Amendment/right to counsel approach to custodial interrogations and held that accused persons had the right to be informed by their lawyer of their privilege against self-incrimination, once an investigation had focused on them (Escobedo v. Illinois, 1964). Then in 1966, the Court decided the landmark case Miranda v. Arizona, and held that without a waiver, the assistance of counsel during interrogation is necessary to vindicate the right against self-incrimination.

The police must deliver the well-known Miranda warning to the suspect: He has a right to remain silent; anything he says may be used against him in court; he has a right to a lawyer's assistance before and during interrogation; a lawyer will be appointed if he cannot afford one. If the suspect requests a lawyer or invokes the right to remain silent, then the interrogation is supposed to stop.

Unless the suspect is expressly and fully afforded this warning and knowingly and voluntarily waives these rights, any confession or statement is not admissible in evidence at trial.

This decision touched off a heated public argument over the advisability of requiring this warning, which was part of a larger debate over the appropriateness of the U.S. Supreme Court elaborating rights for those accused of crime. In numerous subsequent decisions, the Supreme Court has refined the Miranda holding and its exceptions in an apparent effort to accommodate legitimate interests in law enforcement. The central requirement of a formal warning has remained intact.

Further questions are raised as to the use of 'truth serum' as a method of interrogation by the police. Use of this unconventional technique, known as narco-analysis has been in question, especially in conflict with the Fifth Amendment. The US Supreme Court's interpretation of the Fifth Amendment as against self-incrimination extends to mean that there is no prohibition for the use of unconventional methods (by court orders), all that is prohibited is the admissibility of narco-analysis as evidence. The evidence, could, however, be used to lead an investigation in a non-criminal case.

The question at the heart of self-incrimination and narco-analysis is whether injecting truth serum can be unconstitutional when the suspect has refused to comply with the legal obligation to answer questions truthfully and under oath. The answer is reflected in the fact that law enforcement authorities, given leeway would expand on the forms of torture that are acceptable, which would then be dangerous for an individual's freedom.

Thomas E. Baker
Updated by Tania Sebastian

Further Reading

Berger, Mark. *Taking the Fifth: The Supreme Court and the Privilege Against Self-Incrimination*. Lexington, Mass.: Lexington Books, 1980. Useful summary of U.S. Supreme Court rulings on self-incrimination issues.

Garcia, Alfredo. *The Fifth Amendment: A Comprehensive Approach*. Westport, Conn.: Greenwood Press, 2002. Part of the publisher's Contributions in Legal Studies series, this book examines the interconnections among the Fifth Amendment's three clauses relating to criminal justice: the privilege against self-incrimination, the right to a grand jury indictment, and protection against double jeopardy.

Levy, Leonard W. *Origins of the Fifth Amendment*. New York: Oxford University Press, 1968. Though old, still one of the best available histories of the Fifth Amendment, which provides the constitutional basis of the protection against self-incrimination.

Meltzer, Milton. *The Right to Remain Silent.* New York: Harcourt Brace Jovanovich, 1972. Very readable book on the privilege against self-incrimination written for younger readers.

Taylor, John B. *Right to Counsel and Privilege Against Self-Incrimination: Rights and Liberties Under the Law.* Santa Barbara, Calif.: ABC—Clio, 2004. Comprehensive and up-to-date text on the privilege against self-incrimination in the post-September 11, 2001, environment.

Hinman, Lawrence M. *Contemporary Moral Issues: Diversity and Consensus* (4th edition, Routledge USA, 2016)

Amar, Akhil Reed and Lerner, Renee Lettow, "Fifth Amendment First Principles: The Self-Incrimination Clause" (1995). *Faculty Scholarship Series.* Paper 993. Available at: http://digitalcommons.law.yale.edu/fss_papers/993

Godsey, Mark A. *Rethinking the Involuntary Confession Rule: Toward a Workable Test for Identifying Compelled Self-Incrimination,* 93 Cal. L. Rev. 465 (2005). Available at: http://scholarship.law.berkeley.edu/californialawreview/vol93/iss2/2

Dershowitz, Alan M. "Is there a Torturous Road to Justice," *Los Angeles Times,* Nov 8, 2001, available at: http://articles.latimes.com/2001/nov/08/local/me-1494

See also Bill of Rights, U.S.; *Brady v. United States*; Constitution, U.S.; Counsel, right to; Criminal justice system; Criminal procedure; Defendants; Due process of law; Immunity from prosecution; *Minnick v. Mississippi*; Miranda rights; *Miranda v. Arizona*; *Nolo contendere*; Supreme Court, U.S.

Sentencing

Definition: Handing down to convicted defendants of specified penalties, such as incarceration or probation

Criminal justice issue: Convictions; Probation and pretrial

Significance: Sentences are not simply punishments; they may include nonpunitive responses such as psychological treatment.

Historically, when people committed acts of violence, the focus was on making matters whole again, often through restitution to the victims or the victims' families. With the rise in state power and the inability of the peasantry to pay monetary compensation, society increasingly resorted to corporal forms of punishment such as branding, whipping, and execution. It was not until the nineteenth century that prison was accepted as a reformed method of corporal punishment.

Types of Sentences

There are currently four basic types of sentences: fines, whereby governments collect money from convicted offenders; community sentences, whereby the convicted follow behavioral rules, such as restitution or treatment programs; incarceration in jails, prisons, and community treatment facilities; and capital punishment, whereby the convicted are executed. Each year, the United States Sentencing Commission issues or amends its *Guidelines Manual* for sentencing. This manual contains rules and precedents set in previous cases to aid a judge in determining the appropriate sentence.

The specific blend of these sentencing forms may depend on which of five sentencing goals are held most important. Those who believe in deterrence hope that punishment will prevent offenders or potential criminals from committing additional crimes. Those who seek long prison terms hope that they can select and incapacitate future criminals. Those who focus on punishment for its own sake seek retribution for past acts. Those who focus on rehabilitation hope to teach offenders not to commit future bad acts. Those who focus on restitution hope that offenders' future behavior will be altered through their efforts to compensate victims and that victims will regain some sense of wholeness. In addition to these sentencing goals, many argue that sentencing laws and decisions are highly responsive to political pressures and that organizational considerations such as courtroom efficiency and the capacity of the correctional system have a major impact on such decisions.

Prison sentences are either indeterminate or determinate. Indeterminate sentences give offenders both a minimum and a maximum sentence, say from five to fifteen years, whereby the corrections department is given the discretion to release inmates based on appropriate behavior. Determinate sentences set a single period of incarceration, although judges may be given the discretion to pass sentences from a wide range of possibilities. This discretion has increasingly been restricted by laws on mandatory sentencing, such as Massachusetts's requirement of a one-year sentence for illegal firearms possession. Similarly, recent sentencing-guideline statutes allow judges to vary sentences only slightly, often by only a few months, in the case of multiple-year sentences. Studies have shown that between indeterminate and determinate sentencing systems, there is little overall difference in the time inmates actually serve. In the 2015 federal fiscal year, 8,602 convicted offenders were subject to serve mandatory minimum sentences.

Recent attempts at innovation involve community sentences, such as shock incarceration boot camps, high-tech solutions such as electronic monitoring, and efforts to include offenders in "restoring" victims to their previctimized state.

Sentencing Process

The three branches of government—the legislative, judicial, and administrative—have different levels of responsibility for setting criminal sentences. A legislature takes increasing responsibility if it establishes mandatory sentences or strict sentencing guidelines. Often a judge, the prosecutor, and occasionally a jury make choices within a broad range of options set by the legislature, giving them the primary power in sentencing. Correctional officials may have significant responsibility if the sentences are indeterminate, for they largely decide when an inmate will be released from prison.

The vast majority of defendants plead guilty before trial as a result of a plea bargain with the prosecutor. Such agreements usually include sentence recommendations. Most judges either accept such agreements or must give mandatory or highly restricted sentences. Thus, many argue that prosecutors are now the most powerful sentencing agents in the criminal justice system.

Actual sentences are handed down at sentencing hearings, which, for the majority of defendants, take place either the same day or the day after they are convicted. For the majority of defendants, the only information the judge has in sentencing are attorney recommendations and the prior conviction record of the defendant. Some jurisdictions require a presentence report, especially for serious crimes. A probation agent or court official gives the information to the judge for consideration after investigating the crime, its victims, and the defendant.

Legal Rights in Sentencing

Compared to the guilt phase of the criminal process, the US Supreme Court has recognized very few defendants' rights during the sentencing phase of a criminal proceeding. Defendants have the right, under the Sixth Amendment to the Constitution, to have an attorney assist them at the sentencing hearing, but only if an actual jail or prison term is imposed. Defendants do not have the right of allocution—that is, the right to address the court on their own behalf. They also have no right to a presentence report nor do they have the right to see or comment on a presentence report or to call witnesses on their own behalf unless they face the death penalty. Defendants also have no right to cross-examine witnesses or to ask that judges give reasons for their decisions.

Sentencing decisions can easily be biased by unfair information, but the U.S. Supreme Court has said that the quantity of information is very important, saying that a judge may consider almost any information, including alleged prior criminal acts for which the defendant has not been convicted. Some lower courts have even said that judges may consider charges for which defendants have been found not guilty. Also, if judges believe that defendants lied when testifying, they can use this belief to punish defendants at sentencing. If defendants refuse to provide information about another person's criminal activity, they can also be additionally punished at sentencing. Evidence that may not be admitted in criminal trials because it was illegally seized may be admitted during sentencing hearings. Evidence showing the impact of the crime on victims or victims' families is allowed, as are victims' personal characteristics. Only victims' or family members' opinions about how a defendant should be sentenced are not allowed.

While the US Supreme Court has recognized very limited rights for defendants, some state legislatures and

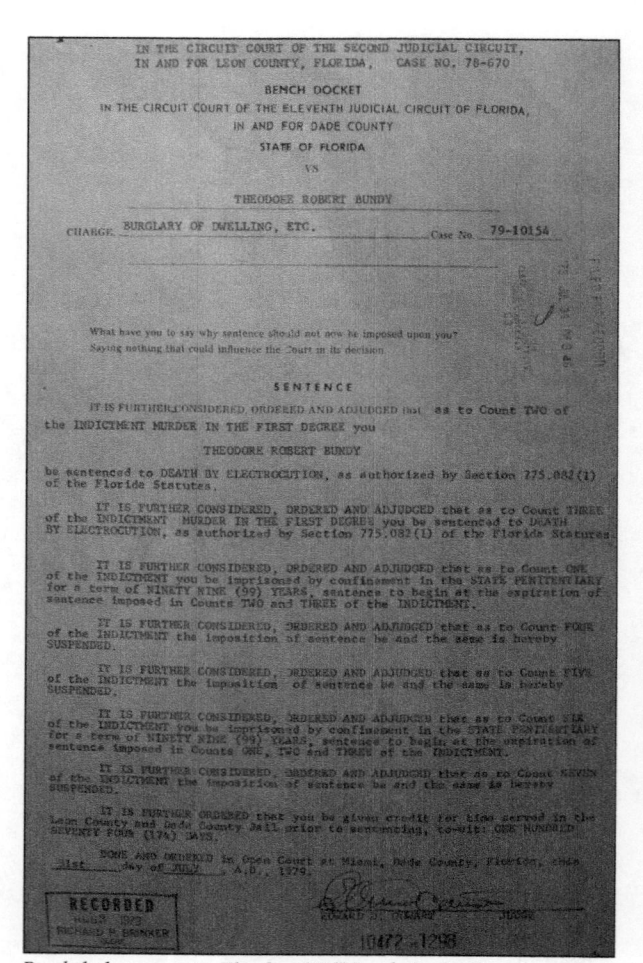

Bench docket sentencing Theodore "Ted" Bundy for the crimes he was convicted of in the Chi Omega murders of Jan. 15, 1978. (By dbking, via Wikimedia Commons)

courts have recognized that defendants have additional rights during sentencing, and some judges, using their discretion, may also provide defendants with such additional benefits.

Peter Gregware

Further Reading

Allen, Harry E., Clifford E. Simonsen, and Edward J. Latessa. *Corrections in America: An Introduction*. 10th ed. Upper Saddle River, N.J.: Pearson Education, 2004. Introductory discussion of the history of corrections, sentencing, incarceration, alternatives to confinement, types of offenders under correctional supervision, and reintegration.

Byrne, James, Arthur Lurigio, and Joan Petersilia, eds. *Smart Sentencing: The Emergence of Intermediate Sanctions*. Newbury Park, Calif.: Sage Publications, 1992. Collection of a broad range of views on issues and controversies surrounding such community sanctions as electronic monitoring and boot camps.

Demleitner, Nora V., Douglas A. Berman, Marc L. Miller, and Ronald F. Wright. *Sentencing Law and Policy: Cases, Statutes, and Guidelines*. New York: Aspen Publishers, 2003. Comprehensive text on all aspects of sentencing, with numerous case studies and texts of relevant laws and the actual federal guidelines.

Krantz, Sheldon, and Lynn Branham. *The Law of Sentencing, Corrections, and Prisoners' Rights*. St. Paul, Minn.: West Publishing, 1997. Excellent legal text that includes most of the important legal decisions related to sentencing and offers examples of state sentencing systems.

Stith, Kate, and Jose A. Cabranes. *Fear of Judging: Sentencing Guidelines in the Federal Courts*. Chicago: University of Chicago Press, 1998. Critical evaluation of the impact of federal sentencing guidelines on court decisions.

Tonry, Michael. *Reconsidering Indeterminate and Structured Sentencing*. Washington, D.C.: U.S. Department of Justice, Office of Justice Programs, National Institute of Justice, 1999. Federal government report on impact of sentencing guidelines on the entire U.S. justice system.

_____. *Sentencing Matters*. New York: Oxford University Press, 1996. Excellent history of sentencing with an analysis of contemporary reforms, such as sentencing guidelines, intermediate sanctions, and mandatory penalties.

United States Sentencing Commission. "Federal Sentencing Guidelines Manual 2015." *United States Sentencing Commission*. Office of Public Affairs, .1 Nov. 2015. Web. 1 June 2016.

Zimring, Franklin, and Gordan Hawkins. *Incapacitation: Penal Confinement and the Restraint of Crime*. New York: Oxford University Press, 1995. Examination of the relationship between theories of incapacitation and its actual impact.

See also Bifurcated trials; Community-based corrections; Community service; Concurrent sentences; Discretion; Indeterminate sentencing; Just deserts; Mandatory sentencing; Plea bargaining; Rehabilitation; Sentencing guidelines, U.S.; Suspended sentences; Three-strikes laws; United States Sentencing Commission; Restitution; Victim impact statements; Australia's Reintegrative Shaming Approach.

Sentencing guidelines, U.S.

Definition: Parameters established by Congress and state legislatures that courts must follow to determine the maximum and minimum sentences allowed for any criminal offense

Criminal justice issue: Punishment; sentencing

Significance: In the "get-tough-on-crime" era, many people feel that criminals should be spending more time behind bars. Sentencing guidelines seek to ensure lengthy prison sentences for offenders.

In the criminal courts of the United States, the judge decides what punishment the convicted offender will receive in the sentencing phase of a trial. The U.S. court system was set up so that judges could carefully weigh all the factors in each case and determine the most appropriate punishment for each offender. Traditionally, a judge might decide in one case that the offender would benefit from doing community service work or attending some type of treatment program. In another case, the judge might decide that the crime was so heinous that the offender needed to spend a lengthy sentence in prison. The judge had the discretionary power to decide each sentence on a case-by-case basis.

By the 1970's, many observers felt that criminals were punished too lightly for their crimes, and some said that criminals should spend more time behind bars. In addition, critics felt that judges had too much discretionary power and that sentences were being arbitrarily meted out. For example, an African American man who was convicted of a first-time burglary offense may have gotten the same sentence as a white man with three prior convictions. As for the most extreme sentence, death, African Americans were being handed this sentence much more often than whites who had committed similar crimes.

In an attempt to address both concerns, sentencing guidelines were proposed. Eventually, most states and the federal government adopted some type of sentencing guidelines. These vary by jurisdiction. Regardless of the specific content of the guidelines, they all serve the same function: to take complete discretion in sentencing away from the judge and to establish specific parameters within which a person can be sentenced. As a result, each offender within the same jurisdiction who is convicted of the same kind of crime will receive a similar sentence, regardless of age, race, sex, or any other factor.

Although these parameters have satisfied some critics, many judges are not happy with sentencing guidelines because they restrict judges' discretionary powers. These judges feel their role is to hand out a sentence after having considered the person's crime, criminal history, remorse, and other factors. Under sentencing guidelines, judges may be forced to hand down sentences they feel are either too severe or too light. In extreme cases, judges have resigned in order to avoid handing out a sentence with which they did not agree.

Neil Quisenberry

Further Reading
Tonry, Michael. *Reconsidering Indeterminate and Structured Sentencing.* Washington, D.C.: U.S. Department of Justice, Office of Justice Programs, National Institute of Justice, 1999.
Tonry, Michael, and Richard Fraser. *Sentencing and Sanctions in Western Countries.* New York: Oxford University Press, 2001.
Ulmer, Jeffery T. *Social Worlds of Sentencing: Court Communities Under Sentencing Guidelines.* Albany: State University of New York Press, 1997.
United States Sentencing Commission. *Federal Sentencing Guidelines Manual 2003.* St. Paul, Minn.: West Publishing, 2004.

See also Community service; Discretion; Indeterminate sentencing; Judges; Just deserts; Mandatory sentencing; Punishment; Sentencing; United States Sentencing Commission.

Solem v. Helm

The Case: U.S. Supreme Court ruling on cruel and unusual punishment
Date: Decided on June 28, 1983
Criminal justice issue: Constitutional protections; punishment
Significance: In this case, the Supreme Court interpreted the Eighth Amendment's prohibition on cruel and unusual punishments to limit the ability of states to impose life sentences for multiple convictions on nonviolent felony charges.

In 1979, Jerry Helm was convicted of issuing a "no account" check for one hundred dollars. This was his seventh felony conviction in South Dakota. In 1964, 1966, and 1969, he had been convicted of third-degree burglary. He had been convicted of obtaining money under false pretenses in 1972, and in 1973 he was convicted of grand larceny. Moreover, his third drunk-driving conviction in 1975 counted as a felony offense. All the offenses were nonviolent, none involved personal, physical victimization of another person, and alcohol was a contributing factor in each case.

Although the maximum penalty for writing a "no account" check in South Dakota was normally five years in prison and a five-thousand-dollar fine, Helm was sentenced to life imprisonment without possibility of parole because defendants convicted of four felonies under South Dakota law may be given the maximum penalty for class 1 felonies—even if they have never actually committed a class 1 felony. The purpose of the state's tough sentencing law was to put habitual offenders away forever so that they could not commit additional offenses.

On appeal, the South Dakota Supreme Court rejected Helm's claim that the sentence of life without parole for a nonviolent offense constituted cruel and unusual punishment in violation of the Eighth Amendment. The U.S. Court of Appeals disagreed and invalidated Helm's sentence. When the U.S. Supreme Court reviewed the case, a narrow five-member majority agreed with Helm's argument.

In a prior decision (*Rummel v. Estelle*, 1980), the U.S. Supreme Court had permitted Texas to impose a life sentence on a man who, over the course of a decade, was convicted of three separate theft offenses in which he stole less than $250. The Supreme Court regarded the *Helm* case as different because South Dakota, unlike Texas, did not permit people with life sentences to become eligible for parole. Thus the realistic impact of Helm's sentence was much harsher than that of life sentences imposed in other states where prisoners typically earn an eventual parole release if they exhibit good behavior. The Court decided that Helm's punishment was disproportionate to his crimes because sentences of life without parole are typically reserved for people convicted of first-degree murder, kidnapping, or treason—not for people who commit nonviolent offenses involving modest amounts of money.

The importance of *Solem v. Helm* is that the Supreme Court placed limitations on the ability of the states to impose severe sentences on people convicted of multiple nonviolent felonies. The case also reinforced the Court's view that the Eighth Amendment contains an implicit requirement that sentences cannot be disproportionate to the crimes committed.

Christopher E. Smith

Further Reading
Berkson, Larry. *The Concept of Cruel and Unusual Punishment.* Lexington, Mass.: Lexington Books, 1975.

Demleitner, Nora V., Douglas A. Berman, Marc L. Miller, and Ronald F. Wright. *Sentencing Law and Policy: Cases, Statutes, and Guidelines*. New York: Aspen Publishers, 2003.
Tonry, Michael. *Sentencing and Sanctions in Western Countries*. New York: Oxford University Press, 2001.
United States Sentencing Commission. *Federal Sentencing Guidelines Manual 2003*. St. Paul, Minn.: West Publishing, 2004.

See also Bill of Rights, U.S.; Cruel and unusual punishment; *Rummel v. Estelle*; Sentencing; Supreme Court, U.S.

Speedy trial right

Definition: Constitutional right of defendants to have their cases tried without unreasonable delays
Criminal justice issue: Constitutional protections; probation and pretrial release; trial procedures
Significance: The constitutional guarantee that accused persons have the right to a speedy trial is one of the fundamental features of U.S. constitutional law.

The Sixth Amendment to the U.S. Constitution provides that in all criminal prosecutions the accused shall enjoy the right to a speedy trial. Applying the due process clause of the Fourteenth Amendment, the U.S. Supreme Court ruled in *Klopfer v. North Carolina* (1967) that this right applies to state trials as well. Chief Justice Earl Warren wrote that "the right to a speedy trial is as fundamental as any of the rights secured by the Sixth Amendment," and like the right to counsel, he reasoned, it should also be applied to the states.

Not only do trial delays create an enormous backlog of cases that clog the judicial system, but they also make it difficult for the accused to present an adequate defense. Even if the accused person is free on bail, employment may be disrupted, reputations harmed, and financial resources depleted.

Delay is a common defense tactic, because there are many instances in which delay favors the accused. Most often it puts pressure on the prosecution to make concessions. To avoid a lengthy trial a prosecutor may offer to reduce the charges against a defendant in return for a guilty plea. There is also the danger that a person on bail awaiting trial may commit other crimes or forfeit bail.

The term "speedy trial" is vague at best, and over the years the U.S. Supreme Court has attempted to clarify its meaning. In *Barker v. Wingo* (1972) the Court stated that the factors to be considered in determining whether a delay is justified are, generally, the length of the delay, the reason for the delay, the defendant's claim to the right to a speedy trial, and prejudice toward the defendant. In *Barker* a delay of five and a half years caused by sixteen state-requested continuances was allowed because of the need to convict a codefendant before proceeding against the accused and because of the illness of the chief investigating officer. When Willie Barker was eventually brought to trial, he was convicted and given a life sentence. The Court held that since the defendant did not ask for a speedy trial and did not assert that his right had been violated until three years after his arrest, he had not been deprived of his due process right to a speedy trial.

Most states have statutes that fix the period of time during which an accused must be brought to trial. In addition, to ensure that a person's trial in a federal court not be unduly delayed or that a suspect not be held in custody indefinitely, the U.S. Congress passed the Speedy Trial Act of 1974. According to this act, which was supposed to go into effect by 1979, federal cases had to be brought to trial within one hundred days of a person's arrest. If cases were not tried within this period, federal prosecutors faced the possibility that their charges against defendants would be dismissed. Despite the planned five-year delay in the implementation of the Speedy Trial Act, the federal courts were backlogged with cases to such an extent that Congress was forced to postpone its implementation indefinitely.

Raymond Frey

Further Reading
Campbell, Andrea. *Rights of the Accused*. Philadelphia: Chelsea House, 2001.
Garcia, Alfredo. *The Sixth Amendment in Modern American Jurisprudence*. Westport, Conn.: Greenwood Press, 1992.
Lewis, Thomas T., ed. *The Bill of Rights*. 2 vols. Pasadena, Calif.: Salem Press, 2002.
Smith, Christopher E. *Courts and Trials: A Reference Handbook*. Santa Barbara, Calif.: ABC-Clio, 2003.

See also Bail system; *Barker v. Wingo*; Bill of Rights, U.S.; Citations; Criminal prosecution; Defendants; Indictment; Plea bargaining; Trials.

Standards of proof

Definition: Rules determining how much and what sort of evidence is enough to win cases in courts of law
Criminal justice issue: Evidence and forensics; professional standards; trial procedures

Significance: Without well-established and uniformly applied standards of proof, no one would be assured of a fair trial.

There are three separate standards of proof, two for "civil" (noncriminal) cases and another for criminal cases. In most civil cases, the standard is generally said to require proving a case "by a preponderance of the evidence." This means convincing the court that one side's position is more likely true than the other side's position. In these cases, the same standard applies to both sides.

In some civil cases, such as those involving fraud, the party bringing the lawsuit is required to prove a case by providing "clear and convincing evidence." Under this standard, the court must be persuaded that the accusation or claim is highly probable, not merely more likely true than not true.

These civil standards are basically "judge-made"; that is, they were developed as part of the English common law, and those traditions have been followed by American courts. The distinction between the two types of civil cases has its origin in ancient English law, where there were two court systems, one of law and one of "equity." Cases heard in law courts were decided under the "preponderance" standard, while those heard in courts of equity were decided under the "clear and convincing" standard.

Although most modern American court systems have only courts of law, the ancient distinction still remains. Sometimes the standard to be applied is included in the law the court is asked to enforce; where the statute does not say, however, the courts resort to the common-law tradition and to their understanding of the legislature's purposes in passing the law.

In a criminal case, the party bringing the case is the government, which is usually far more powerful and with much less to lose than the other side. A much higher standard of proof is applied to the government: Before it can win, it must prove its position "beyond a reasonable doubt." That means the accused person cannot be found guilty unless the court is convinced that the government has definitely proved every necessary part of its case. This standard has long been followed in both England and the United States, and it has been expressly required in American criminal cases since 1970, when the U.S. Supreme Court formally adopted that language in *In re Winship* (1970).

Douglas E. Baker

Further Reading
ABA *Standards for Criminal Justice: The Prosecution Function.* 3d. ed. Washington, D.C.: American Bar Association, 1992.
Reid, Sue Titus. *Criminal Justice.* 6th ed. Cincinnati: Atomic Dog Publishing, 2001.
Samaha, J. *Criminal Law.* 8th ed. Belmont, Calif.: Thomson/Wadsworth, 2004.

See also Burden of proof; Criminal procedure; Evidence, rules of; Presumption of innocence; Reasonable doubt; Sobriety testing.

Stanford v. Kentucky

The Case: U.S. Supreme Court ruling on cruel and unusual punishment
Date: Decided on June 26, 1989
Criminal justice issue: Capital punishment; juvenile justice
Significance: In this case, the Supreme Court held that the Eighth Amendment's prohibition against cruel and unusual punishment did not prevent the execution of individuals who were juveniles at the time they committed the crimes for which they were executed.

The Supreme Court's decision addressed two cases, one involving a seventeen-year-old male convicted of first-degree murder for having robbed a gas station and then raped, sodomized, and shot to death a station attendant, and the other involving a sixteen-year-old sentenced to death for having robbed a convenience store, stabbed the attendant, and left her to die. Both criminal defendants had been tried as adults.

The Supreme Court held that the Eighth Amendment's "cruel and unusual punishment" clause did not bar states from executing individuals who were sixteen and seventeen years of age at the time they committed the applicable crimes. The Court noted that such executions were not the kinds of punishment considered cruel and unusual at the time the Bill of Rights was adopted. Furthermore, the Court concluded that the executions at issue in the case were not contrary to "evolving standards of decency that mark the progress of a maturing society." Justice Sandra Day O'Connor concurred in this holding but wrote separately to emphasize her belief that the Court had a constitutional obligation to assure in each case that a particular defendant's blameworthiness was proportional to the sentence imposed. Justice Antonin Scalia, who wrote the majority opinion and the opinion of four justices on this point, argued that the Court had never invalidated a punishment solely because of an asserted disproportion between the punishment and the defendant's blameworthiness.

Justices William J. Brennan, Thurgood Marshall, Harry A. Blackmun, and John Paul Stevens dissented. These justices stated that the "cruel and unusual punishment" clause of the Eighth Amendment bars the execution of any person for a crime committed while the person was under age eighteen. Justice Brennan, writing for the dissenters, asserted that such executions violated contemporary standards of decency. He pointed out that the laws of a majority of states would not have permitted the executions at issue in this case and that in the vast majority of cases involving juvenile offenders, juries did not impose the death penalty. The justice concluded by arguing that the imposition of the death penalty for juvenile crimes served the interests of neither retribution nor deterrence. Capital punishment in these cases did not serve the interests of retribution since, according to Justice Brennan, the penalty was disproportionate to the defendants' blameworthiness. The punishment did not advance the interests of deterrence since juveniles were not likely to make the kind of cost-benefit analysis that would dissuade them from committing a crime for fear of receiving the death penalty.

Timothy L. Hall

Further Reading

Bedau, Hugo Adam, and Paul Cassell. *Debating the Death Penalty: Should America Have Capital Punishment? The Experts on Both Sides Make Their Best Case.* Oxford, England: Oxford University Press, 2003.

Berkson, Larry. *The Concept of Cruel and Unusual Punishment.* Lexington, Mass.: Lexington Books, 1975.

Bohm, Robert M. *Deathquest: An Introduction to the Theory and Practice of Capital Punishment in the United States.* Cincinnati: Anderson Publishing, 2003.

Cox, Steven M., John J. Conrad, and Jennifer M. Allen. *Juvenile Justice: A Guide to Theory and Practice.* 5th ed. New York: McGraw Hill, 2003.

See also Bill of Rights, U.S.; Capital punishment; Constitution, U.S.; Cruel and unusual punishment; Juvenile justice system; Punishment; Supreme Court, U.S.

Stare decisis

Definition: Deciding of cases on the basis of judicial precedent in similar cases

Criminal justice issue: Appeals; Law codes; Legal terms and principles; Trial procedures

Significance: This principle gives continuity and predictability to the entire body of common-law decisions.

Stare decisis comes from a Latin term meaning "to stand by things that have been settled." Under this principle of law, judicial decisions that have been made in cases similar to the one under consideration are accepted as authoritative. *Stare decisis* involves, in addition to how judges in the past decided similar cases, what the basic judicial principles followed were. (It is accepted that specific circumstances will vary.) Often more than one case will be cited to illustrate the stability and continuity of the principles judged to apply in the current case. The principle applies only to the actual decision and not to the arguments substantiating that decision. Thus, a later case could be decided similarly to an earlier one but for different reasons.

Many arguments on questions of the law have already been settled in earlier cases. When the same point is again in controversy in a trial court, the earlier precedent is judged to be binding on the later court decision. This principle provides a degree of certitude as to what the law actually says about similar issues. It gives a consistency to court decisions that might not be possible if earlier decisions were not consulted. Appellate courts similarly follow the principle of *stare decisis*, but they are not under the same obligation as is a trial court. If two principles of the law come into conflict, or if the court seeks to remedy a continued and obvious injustice, appellate courts can deviate from judicial precedent and break new ground.

Precedents can be overruled and, in fact, have been many times. Courts often look at the presumed results of a decision. Occasionally such a prediction will prompt the judge to alter a decision. The judicial philosophy of a particular judge or justice can also influence a court decision. Judicial activists are more likely to overturn a precedent than are judges who believe it is their duty to defer to legislative intent. In the absence of clear legislation, that philosophy tends to follow decisions of earlier courts.

In *Helvering v. Hallock* (1940), Supreme Court Justice Felix Frankfurter called *stare decisis* "a principle of policy and not a mechanical formula," especially when adhering to the principle would involve "collision with a prior doctrine more embracing in its scope, intrinsically sounder, and verified by experience." It is not unusual for the US Supreme Court to overrule its own decisions. The New Deal era Court, for example, did that several times. The most celebrated Court reversal was *Brown v. Board of Ed-*

The United States Reports would be used for stare decisis. *(Public Domain, via Wikimedia Commons)*

ucation in 1954, which overruled the "separate-but-equal" segregation doctrine of *Plessy v. Ferguson* (1896).

Overruling judicial precedent is a serious responsibility because it not only changes what has been accepted as law but also implies that the judge or judges making the earlier rules were either mistaken or philosophically wrong. A court must show respect for the knowledge and intelligence of previous judges. Even when an earlier decision can be shown to be legally or constitutionally flawed, stability is a consideration. If changing a decision would disrupt society excessively or create political chaos, judges are reluctant to break with the continuity of precedent.

Closely related to *stare decisis* is the principle of *res judicata* ("a matter settled by judgment"). This means that once a matter is judicially settled by the courts, continued suits on the same matter will not be permitted. Once decided, a decision is laid to rest.

William H. Burnside

Further Reading

Garner, Bryan A., ed. *Black's Law Dictionary*. 8th ed. St. Paul, Minn.: Thomson/West, 2004.

Holmes, Oliver Wendell, Jr. *The Common Law*. Boston: Little, Brown, 1909.

Pekelis, Alexander H. *Law and Social Action*. New York: Da Capo Press, 1970.

Schwartz, Bernard. *The Law in America: A History*. New York: McGraw-Hill, 1974.

See also Annotated codes; Appellate process; Case law; Common law; Evidence, rules of; Judicial review; Judicial system, U.S.; Opinions; *Payne v. Tennessee*.

Subpoena power

Definition: Power of courts to require persons to appear in court to testify or to produce documents that are relevant to cases

Criminal justice issue: Courts; judges; trial procedures; witnesses

Significance: The word "subpoena" comes from a Latin word that literally means "under penalty"-which is the essence of the legal authority behinds a subpoena.

Whereas a summons merely indicates that legal action is being taken against the person receiving it, that person would not be breaking the law by not appearing in court. However, a subpoenaed witness is ordered to appear to give testimony at a specified time and place and is subject to penalty if the order is disobeyed. An individual receiving a subpoena to appear as a witness may be ordered to testify in court, before an administrative or other body, or to a court reporter. The Sixth Amendment to the U.S. Constitution guarantees that criminal defendants have the right to have witnesses subpoenaed in their favor, and it is typically wise to do so in order to guarantee that the witnesses will appear at the legal proceedings.

Subpoenas are issued for a variety of reasons by a variety of legal authorities, including a lawyer for the parties involved in a suit, a grand jury for witnesses to a crime, a prosecutor, a court clerk, a coroner, legislative committees, and administrative agencies. There are two basic types of subpoenas. The type referred to simply as a subpoena requires that an individual testify as a witness. The other type, a *subpoena duces tecum*, requires that witnesses must bring with them any documents or papers in their possession that may be relevant to the case under investigation. Before formal charges have been filed in a case, investigatory subpoenas may be issued requiring witnesses to appear at a hearing and to bring with them any pertinent documents or papers. Likewise, after formal charges are filed in a case, subpoenas can again be issued requiring witnesses to appear at a hearing or in court to give depositions or produce relevant documents or papers.

A valid subpoena must be issued by an officer authorized by the court, and it must typically be delivered personally within the proper time and to the proper place. It is very important that a person who has been subpoenaed appear at the specified time and place stated in the subpoena. An individual failing to do so can be held in contempt of court, fined, or imprisoned and may also be liable for damages sustained by the aggrieved party. For legitimate reasons, such as illness or a family death, a subpoenaed individual may postpone the appearance date.

It is wise for individuals to consult a lawyer if they object to a subpoena. A lawyer may raise objections to a subpoena prior to the appearance date by making a motion to quash the subpoena or by filing a formal objection in writing. In either case, a hearing will be held to consider the lawyer's request, and a decision will be rendered as to whether or not the subpoena will be enforced.

Alvin K. Benson

Further Reading
Meyer, J. F., and D. R. Grant. *The Courts in Our Criminal Justice System.* Upper Saddle River, N.J.: Prentice-Hall, 2003.
Neubauer, D. W. *America's Courts and the Criminal Justice System.* 7th ed. Belmont, Calif.: Wadsworth, 2002.
Rabe, Gary A., and Dean John Champion. *Criminal Courts: Structure, Process and Issues.* Upper Saddle River, N.J.: Prentice-Hall, 2002.

See also Discovery; Expert witnesses; Hearings; *Mandamus*; Obstruction of justice; Summonses; Testimony; Witnesses.

Summonses

Definition: Judicial instruments used to initiate legal proceedings or to call for the appearance of persons before courts or other bodies
Criminal justice issue: Courts; pleas; trial procedures
Significance: Important instruments in criminal justice, summonses expedite proceedings by using the full weight of the courts and other government bodies to order defendants, witnesses, and other persons to make appearances.

In a civil action summonses are formal notices issued by clerks of the court that notify defendants of actions against them. A summons normally gives notice of the nature of the lawsuit and demands that the defendant appear to answer the allegations. Failure to answer, either through further pleadings or by not appearing in person, generally subjects the defendant to a default judgment.

Other forms of summonses include jury summonses, which command citizens to appear before the court to serve as jurors. A jury summons carries the authority of the court, and a failure to appear in response to it may subject the person to severe civil or criminal penalties. A summons may also be used in lieu of a subpoena to order a witness to appear to give testimony.

In criminal matters summonses are also used to command the appearance of defendants before the court. Whereas a warrant generally requires the arrest of the named person, a summons simply commands the person's appearance before the court. This technique is used frequently when dealing with misdemeanors or violations. For example, the owner of a tavern may receive a summons to appear before a magistrate to answer for violations of liquor laws or health codes. Likewise, motorists typically receive summonses when they are issued citations for moving violations. The tickets issued by police officers are forms of summonses that command the motorists to appear before courts or otherwise answer the allegations.

Summonses may also be issued by officials charged with enforcing various legal codes of municipalities, counties, and states. They might include a summons directing a food vendor to appear before health inspectors for serving food without a license or for operating a restaurant that fails to meet health code regulations. This type of summons, much like a traffic ticket, usually serves two purposes in the sense that it is both the actual complaint and the summons to appear.

Carl J. Franklin

Further Reading
Del Carmen, Rolando V. *Criminal Procedure: Law and Practice.* 6th ed. Belmont, Calif.: Thomson/Wadsworth, 2004.
Samaha, Joel. *Criminal Procedure.* 3d ed. St. Paul, Minn.: West Publishing, 1996.

See also Citations; Judges; Subpoena power.

Supreme Court, U.S., and criminal rights

Identification: Highest court in the US justice system
Criminal justice issue: Appeals; Civil rights and liberties; Constitutional protections; Courts
Significance: As the highest court of appeal in the United States, the Supreme Court has played an important role in shaping the American criminal justice process, especially in regard to the interpretation of the rights of criminal suspects.

The legal basis for the creation of the US Supreme Court can be found in Article III of the US Constitution, which was ratified in 1789. The Constitution does not spell out the Court's specific responsibilities and powers, but the

Court has come to play a central role in the American political system in interpreting the constitutional bases of laws and exercising the power of final judicial review over all appeals that reach it from state and lower federal courts.

The Court's power of judicial review empowers it to declare governmental acts unconstitutional. Judicial review is controversial because it appears undemocratic when a president signs a law approved by a majority of the people's representatives in Congress, only to have a majority of the Court's nine justices-none of whom is elected by the people-declare the law unconstitutional. The principle of judicial review was established in 1803, in the landmark case of *Marbury v. Madison*, in which the Supreme Court ruled that the power was implied within the judiciary's duty to interpret the law.

Early History

During the late eighteenth century and the nineteenth century, the Supreme Court played a significant role in defining the structure and institutions of the American political system. The Court issued rulings that defined the powers of the national government and its relationship with the states and also interpreted the powers of the executive and legislative branches of government. During that period, however, the court performed only a minor role in matters related to civil liberties, including the rights of criminal defendants. After the US Congress passed the Judiciary Act of 1925, the court began expanding its role in the political system by interpreting the scope of the freedoms listed in the Bill of Rights and the due process clause of the Fourteenth Amendment.

Also known as the Judges' Bill, the Judiciary Act of 1925 established the Supreme Court's discretionary jurisdiction, which has given the court more flexibility in case selection. The modern court selects cases for review without interference from Congress, although Article III of the US Constitution gives Congress the power to define the process of how cases are appealed to it. The power of Congress to define the appellate jurisdiction of the Supreme Court is one of the checks within the system of checks and balances established by the Framers of the Constitution. However, commercialization, urbanization, and industrialization made laws so complex that Congress decided that the court was better able to select cases for itself.

The Judiciary Act also established the writ of *certiorari* petition, which has since become the most common way for cases to be accepted for review by the Supreme Court. Parties appealing decisions to the court must file writs of *certiorari* requesting that relevant lower court records be delivered to the Supreme Court. Four of the nine justices on the court must vote in favor of a writ of *certiorari* petition for a case to be granted review.

Throughout the twentieth century, the Supreme Court incorporated nearly all the protections of the Bill of Rights to make them apply to state governments through the due process clause of the Fourteenth Amendment. Before the Bill of Rights protections were extended to the states, their protections were guaranteed in federal courts, but not necessarily in state or local courts. However, the Fourteenth Amendment, which was ratified immediately after the Civil War to protect newly freed slaves, asserted that states could not deny due process to all their citizens. The Court used the Fourteenth Amendment's due process clause as a vehicle to require the individual states to respect most of the freedoms and protections enumerated in the Bill of Rights.

The Court and Rights of Criminal Defendants

The incorporation of the Bill of Rights upon states was especially significant for persons accused of crimes because about 90 percent of criminal cases are tried in state and local courts. Before the Bill of Rights protections were incorporated, it was common for criminal defendants to be treated roughly by law-enforcement officials during searches and seizures and interrogations and by prosecutors and judges in trials in ways that are now no longer permitted. Criminal suspects were frequently denied due process of law in states whose constitutions and local practices ran contrary to the rights of criminals defined in the federal Bill of Rights.

The Warren Court

With the appointment of Earl Warren as chief justice of the United States by President Dwight D. Eisenhower in 1953, the Supreme Court began an era of liberal interpretations of criminal defendants' rights. Warren expanded the meaning of criminal defendants' rights by nationalizing most of the liberties during the 1960s and by establishing a code of conduct for police officers in dealing with criminal suspects. Landmark decisions by the Warren court revolutionized the criminal justice system by providing more protection for criminal defendants. For example, the court's decision in *Gideon v. Wainwright* in 1963 required states to provide attorneys for defendants accused of felonies who could not afford their own representation. The court's 1966 decision in *Miranda v. Arizona* required police officers to inform suspects of their right to remain silent and their right to counsel.

The Supreme Court Building of the United States from the dome of the capitol building. (By Farragutful, via Wikimedia Commons)

The Warren court did not rule directly on the constitutionality of the death penalty. However, in *Trop v. Dulles* (1958), it established that punishments had to meet evolving standards of decency or risk violating the Eighth Amendment's cruel and unusual punishment clause.

The Warren court also nationalized a controversial principle known as the exclusionary rule in its landmark *Mapp v. Ohio* decision in 1961. The exclusionary rule bars illegally obtained evidence from being used in court against criminal defendants. The rule is controversial because guilty defendants might be set free if crucial evidence is excluded from trials. The rule applies to illegal police searches and coercive interrogations conducted by police officers without the presence of attorneys to advise suspects. Hence, the exclusionary rule relates to provisions in the Fourth, Fifth, and Sixth Amendments.

While political liberals applauded the Warren court's rulings, conservatives were offended by them and viewed the Supreme Court as "soft on crime." It was common during Warren's era to see billboards calling for Warren's impeachment, especially in conservative states such as Texas and Indiana.

Conservative Counterrevolution

In reaction to the Warren court's liberal decisions, Richard M. Nixon campaigned for the presidency in 1968 on a "law and order" platform. A Republican, Nixon promised the voters that he would appoint conservative justices to the Court who would favor law-enforcement officers, or what he called the "peace forces." After Nixon was elected, he had the unusual fortune of appointing four justices to the court during his first term. His appointments included Chief Justice Warren Burger, who served on the court from 1969 until 1986.

Republican Presidents Ronald W. Reagan and George Bush followed Nixon's lead by appointing six justices to the court during the 1980s and early 1990s, including Chief Justice William H. Rehnquist in 1986. Meanwhile, no Democratic president appointed a justice between 1968 and 1993. The increased conservatism the Republican appointments gave to the court significantly altered the court's rulings in a variety of areas, including criminal justice.

During the 1980s and 1990s, the Supreme Court handed down rulings that created exceptions to allow illegally obtained evidence to be used in criminal trials. For example, the court allowed police officers to conduct searches with invalid warrants when they acted in "good faith." The court also created a "public safety" exception to allow police to coerce suspects into providing information about locations of dangerous weapons in public places. This exception allowed police to avoid the problems associated with issuing Miranda warnings during emergency situations in which speedy police action was crucial. The Supreme Court also created the "inevitable discovery" exception to admit illegally obtained evidence into court under the presumption that if such evidence had not been obtained illegally, it would have been found eventually.

Exceptions such as these are examples of how Warren court decisions have been interpreted in a more conservative manner by the Burger and Rehnquist courts. However, while legal scholars agree that a conservative counterrevolution has, in fact, occurred since Warren retired in 1969, many of his court's landmark decisions, such as *Gideon*, *Miranda*, and *Mapp*, have not been overturned. However, these decisions have been interpreted to provide more support for law-enforcement officials, prosecutors, and judges in their battle against criminal defendants.

The post-Warren court has also made conservative rulings in matters of sentencing and punishment. In *Gregg v. Georgia* (1976), for example, the court ruled that the death penalty did not violate the Eighth Amendment's cruel and unusual punishment clause. The Rehnquist court has also made it easier to apply the death penalty by issuing decisions that limit the number of federal appeals for death row inmates, to allow states to execute defendants under the age of eighteen, and to allow relatives of murder victims to issue emotional statements to juries during the sentencing phases of death penalty trials. Although more than one-half of death row inmates are of African American and Hispanic heritage, the court ruled in *McClesky v. Kemp* (1987) that the death penalty was not being implemented in a racially discriminatory manner. Clearly, the rights of criminal suspects had been limited by the decisions of the Burger and Rehnquist courts, while a movement favoring a strict enforcement of the laws had been expanded.

President George W. Bush nominated John Glover Roberts to take over as chief justice upon the death of Rehnquist in 2005. As of 2016, under Roberts's reign, the court had handed down several important decisions involving controversial topics such as the environment, abortion, health care, campaign finance, and same-sex marriage. As for criminal rights, the court passed rulings that limited police searches during arrests, protected the privacy of information stored on cell phones in terms of evidence, and prohibited the placement of global positioning system (GPS) devices on the vehicles of suspects.

Scott P. Johnson

Further Reading

Baum, Lawrence. *The Supreme Court*. 8th ed. Washington, DC: CQ, 2004. Print.
Campbell, Andrea. *Rights of the Accused*. Philadelphia: Chelsea, 2001. Print.
Cole, George F., and Christopher E. Smith. *The American System of Criminal Justice*. 10th ed. Belmont: Wadsworth, 2004. Print.
Epstein, Lee, and Thomas G. Walker. *Constitutional Law for a Changing America: Rights, Liberties, and Justice*. 5th ed. Washington, DC: CQ, 2003. Print.
Greenberg, Ellen. *The Supreme Court Explained*. New York: Norton, 1997. Print.
Hall, Kermit. *The Rights of the Accused: The Justices and Criminal Justice*. New York: Garland, 2001. Print.
Lewis, Thomas T., ed. *The Bill of Rights*. 2 vols. Pasadena: Salem, 2002. Print.
Lewis, Thomas T., and Richard L. Wilson, eds. *Encyclopedia of the US Supreme Court*. 3 vols. Pasadena: Salem, 2001. Print.
O'Brien, David M. *Constitutional Law and Politics*. 6th ed. New York: Norton, 2005. Print.
Wolf, Richard. "Chief Justice John Roberts' Supreme Court at 10, Defying Labels." *USA Today*. USA Today, 29 Sept. 2015. Web. 30 May 2016.

See also Bill of Rights, U.S.; Capital punishment; Constitution, U.S.; Counsel, right to; Court types; Due process of law; Incorporation doctrine; Judicial review; Judicial system, U.S.; Jurisdiction of courts.

Suspended sentences

Definition: Postponements of the execution of sentences handed down by courts
Criminal justice issue: Convictions; Pardons and parole
Significance: The power to suspend sentences allows courts discretion in awarding actual punishments while satisfying statutory requirements for justice.

Depending upon federal and state sentencing guidelines, suspended sentences may be rendered in a number of ways. Courts may suspend pronouncement of sentences on convicted defendants. They may impose sentences at the time of conviction and then suspend the actual implementation of those sentences; or, they may impose sentences, incarcerate the convicted defendants and later suspend the remainder of their sentences. When courts impose suspended sentences by delaying their renderings of the sentences, they review the cases at designated future dates and later render sentences that are appropriate for their later judgments. For example, a court may suspend sentence on payment of court costs. If the convicted individual pays the costs as ordered, the court will render the sentence as costs of court with no incarceration. If the convicted individual fails to pay costs as ordered, the court may at a later date impose a sentence that includes incarceration. Many states allow the sentences of first-time offenders-especially for less serious crimes-to be postponed in this manner. Such suspensions help make space in overcrowded prisons for repeat offenders and those who perpetrate more serious crimes.

Courts may pronounce sentences and then suspend incarcerating the defendants, subject to additional requirements. For example, a court may hand down a suspended sentence of eighteen months, court costs, and admission of the convicted defendant to a drug-treatment facility. A court might also hand down a suspended sentence of three months, court costs, and performance of one hundred hours of community service. In both examples, the sentences rendered may be consistent with sentencing guidelines for the crimes committed, while giving the convicted defendant some choice in the matter of being incarcerated at the time of sentencing. Most states use some form of suspended sentencing whenever possible, not only to relieve overcrowding in prisons, but also to render sentences more likely to reduce recidivism, or repeat offenses.

The form of suspended sentence that is most common falls under the guidelines of parole. After convicted defendants serve some portion of the sentences, they petition to have their incarceration terminated or postponed. Granting of parole does not nullify the original sentence, as persons who violate their parole terms may be required to serve out their full sentences.

Suspended sentences are not considered final judgments. Suspended sentences render the case proceedings inactive within the courts subject to re-activation upon violation of conditions imposed with the suspension.

Taylor Shaw

Further Reading

Hoffman, Peter B. *History of the Federal Parole System*. Chevy Chase, Md.: U.S. Department of Justice, 2003.

Tonry, Michael. *Sentencing Matters*. New York: Oxford University Press, 1996.

_____, ed. *The Future of Imprisonment*. New York: Oxford University Press, 2004.

See also Appellate process; Blended sentences; Execution of judgment; Parole; Probation, adult; Sentencing.

Testimony

Definition: Evidence provided by witnesses in trials that is given under oath, either orally or in the form of affidavits or depositions

Criminal justice issue: Evidence and forensics; trial procedures; witnesses

Significance: Testimony is critical in criminal trials because it provides support for arguments and positions advocated by either side in a legal proceeding.

Although testimony can loosely be defined as evidence, it is distinguishable from evidence derived from writings or other sources. For evidence to be testimony, a witness must present it under oath to a judge or tribunal, in person or through a sworn deposition.

Testimony is a component in three aspects of the legal process: grand jury hearings, preliminary hearings, and trials. A grand jury consists of a body of citizens who determine if there is probable cause to believe that a crime has been committed. In order to make that determination, they hear testimony from witnesses presented by the state, or prosecution. If they determine that probable cause exists, they return an indictment against the defendant. In a preliminary hearing, a judge hears testimony from prosecution witnesses and makes a decision as to whether or not an individual should be held for trial. In a criminal or civil trial, witnesses are questioned through direct and cross-examination, and a judge or jury listens to the testimony in order to reach a verdict. In all three instances, witnesses take oaths in which they swear or affirm to tell the truth.

Testimony in a grand jury is usually secret and is not used in later trials. However, testimony in a preliminary hearing is preserved for later use, either by a court reporter or a tape recorder. The testimony provided in a preliminary hearing might be used in a trial to refresh a witness's memory or to demonstrate inconsistencies in the testimony. The testimony in a preliminary hearing may also be used at trial if a witness dies or becomes unavailable to testify.

The prosecution in a criminal case and the plaintiff in a civil case present their testimony first because they have the burden of proof. Testimony is provided in brief question and answer format; witnesses usually do not tell their stories in a continuous narrative. In direct examination, the attorneys question the witnesses who support their side of a case. Typically, the questions are open-ended in order for the witnesses to elaborate on their testimony, thus presenting a strong case. In cross-examination, the attorneys question the witnesses on the opposing side. The attorney may attempt to obtain testimony by using closed-ended or leading questions so that the witness does not have a chance to elaborate on answers. During closing arguments, attorneys make convincing arguments and provide reasons for the jurors or judge to return a verdict in their favor. They draw on the testimony of witnesses to help support their arguments.

Ann Burnett
Updated by Christine Wilson

Further Reading
Loftus, Elizabeth F. *Eyewitness Testimony.* 2d ed. Cambridge, Mass.: Harvard University Press, 1996.
Weiss, K. "Confessions and Expert Testimony." *Journal of the American Academy of Psychiatry and Law* 31 (2003): 451-458.
Wrightsman, L. S., E. Greene, M. T. Nietzel, and W. H. Fortune. *Psychology and the Legal System.* Belmont, Calif.: Wadsworth, 2002.

See also Court reporters; Cross-examination; Discovery; Evidence, rules of; Expert witnesses; Eyewitness testimony; Grand juries; Hearsay; Perjury; Preliminary hearings; Subpoena power; Witnesses.

Three-strikes laws

Definition: Laws mandating lengthy prison sentences for third felony convictions
Criminal justice issue: Judges; Punishment; Sentencing
Significance: Three-strikes laws are largely symbolic in most of the United States, but in California they helped to swell the prison population and escalated the critical problems of prison overcrowding and fiscal crisis.

As the politically motivated get-tough-on-crime campaigns against crime and drugs escalated during the 1980s, US government policymakers moved to adapt the baseball concept of "three strikes and you're out" to sentencing of repeat offenders, and multiple states and the federal government rushed to create politically popular, draconian mandatory minimum sentencing laws.

The goal behind these laws was to punish serious and violent repeat offenders with prison sentences as long as from twenty-five years to life, while reducing victimization and improving community safety through the casting out and incapacitating of the worst criminals. Despite the initial popularity of the concept of three-strikes laws, they have been little used in most states. However, one state, California, pursued the concept with such vigor that it became an integral part of the state's corrections and fiscal landscape, leading to a massive prison population.

The United States

In 1993, voters in the state of Washington responded to a particularly heinous violent sexual crime by a recidivist parolee by approving an initiative that mandated life in prison without the possibility of parole for persons convicted of committing serious offenses such as murder, rape, and robbery a third time. Within two years, more than twenty-five other states and the federal government approved their own variations of three-strikes laws. While there was some variation in the crimes covered by these new laws, the principles of "three strikes" and long mandatory sentences adopted in Washington State were followed in virtually all the new laws.

Over the next decade, state legislatures and court systems showed appropriate restraint by sentencing only a few thousand criminals under three-strikes laws throughout the entire nation. For example, between 1993 and 2004, the state of Washington sentenced fewer than two hundred criminals under its three-strikes laws. Generally, the original intent of the law was upheld, as most of the criminals sentenced under these laws were violent robbers, sex offenders, murderers, and individuals convicted of serious assaults.

California

Meanwhile, by 1994, both the legislature and voters of California had adopted three-strikes laws. California's laws included a unique feature: the provision of a second-strike enhancement that doubled sentences, as well as the ability of prosecutors to file third-strike charges on nonviolent and nonserious felony offenses, many of which would ordinarily have been treated as misdemeanors. For example, shoplifting offenses could be prosecuted as petty theft if the offenders had prior convictions.

California's approach was controversial and raised important issues relating to the Eighth Amendment and its cruel and unusual punishment clause and the principle of proportionality. In the 2003 landmark companion cases of *Lockyer v. Andrade* and *Ewing v. California*, the US Supreme Court

voted 5 to 4 in favor of allowing California to set the sentencing laws approved by its voters.

The most striking result of California's three-strikes law was a large increase in the state's prison population. Of the 160,000 inmates incarcerated in California in early 2004, about 25 percent were second and third strikers. The large number of prisoners placed unprecedented strains on the state's budget. The average cost of housing an inmate in California was $31,000 per year in 2004. As prisoners age beyond fifty, their increasing health problems raise the average cost of housing to between $60,000 and $75,000 per year. A study of California's three-strikes law estimated that during its first decade, the law cost taxpayers more than $8 billion in increased corrections costs. Moreover, more than 50 percent of that extra expenditure went to incarcerating nonviolent third strikers.

The 1990s found California, like the rest of the nation, experiencing significant crime reductions. Experts believe that reductions in crime were more likely to be due to the robust economy of that period, the increased availability of jobs, the maturation of community policing, and other criminal justice and corrections systems improvements rather than to the advent of three-strikes laws. Support for this observation can be found in the fact that the national reduction in crime occurred fairly evenly throughout the nation, including the one-half of the states that had no three-strikes laws.

In November 2004, Californians voted on an initiative that would have eased the state's three-strikes law by allowing judges to impose milder prison sentences on nonviolent offenders. That measure failed to pass. In 2012, California voters approved Proposition 36, which significantly amended the states' three-strikes law: the requirement for sentencing a defendant as a third-strike offender were changed to twenty-five years to life by requiring the new felony be a serious or violent felony and the addition of a mean by which defendants currently serving a third-strike sentence could petition the court for a reduction of their term.

Kevin Meehan

Further Reading

"Bill Clinton Regrets 'Three Strikes' Bill." *BBC News*. BBC, 16 July 2015. Web. 31 May 2016.

Clark, John Austin, James Henry, and D. Alan Henry. *"Three Strikes and You're Out": A Review of State Legislation*. Washington, DC: National Institute of Justice, 1997. Print.

Couzens, J. Richard, and Tricia A. Bigelow. "The Amendment of the Three Strikes Sentencing Law." *California Courts*. Judicial Council of California, May 2016. Web. 31 May 2016.

Ehlers, Scott, Vincent Schiraldi, and Jason Ziedenberg. *Still Striking Out: Ten Years of California's Three Strikes*. Washington, DC: Justice Policy Institute, 2004. Print.

LaCourse, R. David, Jr. *Three Strikes in Review*. Seattle: Washington Policy Center, 1997. Print.

Taibbi, Matt. "Cruel and Unusual Punishment: The Shame of Three Strikes Laws." *Rolling Stone*. Rolling Stone, 27 Mar. 2013. Web. 31 May 2016.

Tonry, Michael. *Sentencing Matters*. New York: Oxford UP, 1996. Print.

Zimring, Franklin E., G. Hawkins, and S. Kamin. *Punishment and Democracy: Three Strikes and You're Out in California*. New York: Oxford UP, 2001. Print.

See also Criminal records; Cruel and unusual punishment; Discretion; Incapacitation; Judges; Mandatory sentencing; Prison overcrowding; Recidivism; Sentencing; Supreme Court, U.S.; Violent Crime Control and Law Enforcement Act; Punishment.

Tison v. Arizona

The Case: U.S. Supreme Court ruling on capital punishment

Date: Decided on April 21, 1987

Criminal justice issue: Capital punishment; sentencing

Significance: In this case, the Supreme Court created a flexible standard for applying the death penalty to felony-murder accomplices who demonstrate reckless disregard for human life even though they do not directly participate in killing a victim.

On July 30, 1978, brothers Donny, age twenty-one, Ricky, age twenty, and Raymond Tison, age nineteen, smuggled guns into the Arizona State Prison and helped in the escape of their father, Gary, who was a convicted murderer, and another convicted murderer. The group changed cars and made their escape on a desert highway. When they had a flat tire, they flagged down a passing car containing young parents, a baby, and a teenage cousin and held the family at gunpoint. Gary Tison ordered his sons to load their possessions into the young family's car. As the brothers loaded the car and pushed their own disabled car into the desert, their father and the other prison escapee brutally murdered the entire family, including the baby, with shotgun blasts at close range.

The escaping group traveled for several more days before encountering a police roadblock. During the ensuing shoot-out, Donny was killed, Gary escaped into the desert but soon died from exposure, and Ricky, Raymond, and the other convict were captured.

As accomplices to the killing of the young family, Ricky and Raymond Tison were charged with felony murder. When they were sentenced to death, they appealed their sentences based on a Supreme Court decision (*Enmund v. Florida*, 1982) which had declared that felony-murder accomplices cannot be sentenced to death if they do not directly participate in the actual killing. After the Arizona Supreme Court upheld the sentences, the Tisons took their case to the U.S. Supreme Court.

In a 5-4 decision, the U.S. Supreme Court created a flexible standard for imposing the death penalty. The Court declared that felony-murder accomplices could receive the death penalty if they demonstrated "reckless disregard for human life," even if they did not directly participate in the killing. The justices used this new standard to uphold the capital sentences imposed on the Tisons because they viewed the brothers' active involvement in supplying weapons to convicted murderers and kidnapping the young family as a demonstration of "reckless disregard."

In *Tison v. Arizona* the Supreme Court gave state prosecutors greater flexibility to seek the death penalty against accomplices who participate in crimes that result in homicides. This new flexibility came at the price of greater inconsistency in the application of capital punishment. Under the prior rule, it was relatively clear which offenders were eligible for the death penalty, based on their direct participation in a killing. By contrast, under the *Tison* rule, jurors and judges applying the vague "reckless indifference" standard have broad opportunities to impose capital punishment based on their negative feelings toward the accomplice or their revulsion at the crime without precise consideration of the defendant's actual participation.

Christopher E. Smith

Further Reading

Banner, Stuart. *The Death Penalty: An American History*. Cambridge, Mass.: Harvard University Press, 2002.

Bedau, Hugo Adam, and Paul Cassell. *Debating the Death Penalty: Should America Have Capital Punishment? The Experts on Both Sides Make Their Best Case*. Oxford, England: Oxford University Press, 2003.

Bohm, Robert M. *Deathquest: An Introduction to the Theory and Practice of Capital Punishment in the United States*. Cincinnati: Anderson Publishing, 2003.

Latzer, Barry, ed. *Death Penalty Cases: Leading U.S. Supreme Court Cases on Capital Punishment*. 2d ed. Boston: Butterworth-Heinemann, 2002.

See also Accomplices and accessories; Capital punishment; Cruel and unusual punishment; Felonies; Murder and homicide; Supreme Court, U.S.

Traffic courts

Definition: Courts that deal with infractions of traffic laws that are considered less serious than misdemeanors and felonies

Criminal justice issue: Courts; traffic law

Significance: Traffic courts alleviate crowding in the justice system, for if traffic violations led to full criminal trials, the system would be overwhelmed with juries, lawyers, and convictions. Costs would be enormous, and many persons would be upset with the police and justice system for the vigorous enforcement of what are perceived to be insignificant crimes.

Traffic courts were established to handle routine traffic violations, such as speed law violations, driver and vehicle safety code infractions, parking tickets, and offenses against other rules of the road. Traffic crimes did not fit well into traditional state criminal court systems.

There are more than 150 million licensed drivers in the United States and a total of more than 25 million automobile accidents every year, more than 50,000 of which involve fatalities. The costs of these accidents reach more than $30 billion a year. The purpose of traffic law enforcement and traffic courts is to reduce the number of accidents and deaths. One result is that more than 20,000 traffic citations are filed every day in the United States.

Routine traffic violations are handled differently from more serious offenses such as driving under the influence of alcohol or drugs (DUI). For crimes such as speeding or running through a traffic sign, there is no need to prove criminal intent, as is true with other types of crimes. Simply committing the act is proof of guilt. Traffic courts were established specifically to handle proceedings involving what are legally called "traffic infractions." Most U.S. states have three types of criminal acts: misdemeanors, felonies, and infractions. Infractions are dealt with by civil rather than criminal procedures. The right to an attorney or trial by jury may not apply in cases involving infractions. Convictions do not result in prison or probation, and fines are often held to $50 or less. More serious traffic crimes, such as driving under the influence, are handled in more traditional court proceedings, in which defendants have the right to an attorney and a trial by jury.

Creating Order on the Highways

Highways can be very dangerous. Traffic laws have done a good job in creating order out of potential chaos. Drivers generally respect speed laws, traffic signs, and traffic lights, even when no police cars are visible. The success of the system is illustrated by the fact that the long-term trend has shown a decrease in traffic fatalities. The National Safety Council reports that there is only one serious traffic accident for every 60,000 miles driven, and Americans drive more than 2 trillion miles a year. The effect of traffic law enforcement by police and courts is demonstrated by the success of state laws requiring motorcyclists to wear helmets. Prior to passage of laws requiring helmets, only 50 percent of cyclists wore helmets, but after vigorous enforcement by the police and judges, that number grew to almost 100 percent, and the number of deaths in motorcycle accidents dropped dramatically. In the three states that refused to pass such laws, the number of fatalities remained at a very high level.

The strict enforcement of laws and efficient procedures in traffic courts have, according to many studies, led to fewer accidents and better driving habits. Studies of speed law enforcement have shown that it is not so much the severity of the penalty as the likelihood of being caught and convicted that reduces violations. On the other hand, studies have not indicated that there is any real benefit to sending traffic law violators to traffic school.

Leslie V. Tischauser

Further Reading

Haas, Carol. *Your Driving and the Law: A Crash Course in Traffic Tickets and Court, Auto Accidents and Insurance, and Vehicle-Related Lawsuits.* Bountiful, Utah: Horizon, 1991.

Hand, B., A. Sherman, and M. Cavanagh. *Traffic Investigation and Control.* New York: Macmillan, 1980.

U.S. Department of Transportation. *Traffic Safety and Crime: Keeping Pace.* Washington, D.C.: National Highway Traffic Safety Administration, 1996.

See also Citations; Drunk driving; Hit-and-run accidents; Misdemeanors; Traffic fines; Traffic law.

Traffic fines

Definition: Monetary penalties imposed for traffic violations

Criminal justice issue: Punishment; traffic law

Significance: Traffic fines are a serious issue because safety on the roadways is a substantial problem; however, public opinion views traffic offenses as noncriminal acts, even when serious injuries result, and traffic fines appear not to deter chronic offenders from repeating their offenses.

Traffic fines are imposed by states as sanctions to deter bad driving of motor vehicles. However, studies have shown that traffic fines are not effective in deterring chronic traffic offenders, particularly drunk drivers. Improving road safety is difficult when many in the general public do not view most traffic offenses as serious issues.

Amounts of traffic fines are usually tied directly to the types of driving violations, with more serious violations receiving higher fines. Police officers may make arrests and issue citations, summonses, tickets, and other documents for violations of traffic laws. Depending on the seriousness of violations, motorists may be required to appear in court or simply to pay fines for their violations.

Fines are usually nominal amounts designed to be high enough to impress upon drivers the seriousness of their violations, without being so high that drivers may be unable to pay them and consequently face imprisonment. New technologies such as traffic cameras are now increasingly used to detect traffic violations, such as running stoplights; citations are simply mailed to the registered owners of the offending vehicles; and fines are paid without the need for appearances in court.

Police agencies have long recognized that enforcing traffic laws uniformly is more important than having uniformity in the traffic laws themselves. Traffic fines may vary from jurisdiction to jurisdiction, but the general public expects fairness. Drivers get upset when they perceive that they are being ticketed and fined while other drivers who are doing the same things, or worse, are not. Police officers are thus expected to be consistent in their awarding of tickets.

Police officers who take money directly from drivers instead of issuing them tickets are practicing a form of corruption. In years past, small towns in isolated regions occasionally ran "speed-trap" operations in which police and court officials worked in tandem to collect excessive fines from motorists passing through their communities.

David R. Forde

Further Reading

Boyle, John M. *National Survey of Speeding and Other Unsafe Driving Actions*. Washington, D.C.: U.S. Dept. of Transportation, National Highway Traffic Safety Administration, 1998.

Carroll, Alex. *Beat the Cops: The Guide to Fighting Your Traffic Ticket and Winning*. Santa Barbara, Calif.: Ace, 1995.

Haas, Carol. *Your Driving and the Law: A Crash Course in Traffic Tickets and Court, Auto Accidents and Insurance, and Vehicle-Related Lawsuits*. Bountiful, Utah: Horizon, 1991.

Matheson, Tim. *Traffic Tickets, Fines, and Other Annoying Things*. Secaucus, N.J.: Citadel Press, 1984.

See also Citations; Misdemeanors; Night courts; Traffic courts; Traffic law.

Trial publicity

Definition: Information about trial disseminated through print or broadcast media

Criminal justice issue: Media; trial procedures

Significance: Issues regarding trial publicity emerge from two opposing principles: the right of the accused to a fair trial and the constitutional imperative that court proceedings be public. The two concerns conflict when trial publicity threatens to impermissibly affect the outcome of a trial.

Traditionally, tacit professional limitations were imposed on attorneys, restricting the information they could reveal to the news media. By the late twentieth century the potential for instantaneous, in-depth trial coverage by electronic media made trial publicity a broader social issue involving the whole judicial system, the public's right to know, and the professional conduct of journalists. The result is freer movement of information to the public and less accountability for any one party or institution.

The principle of publicity was key to the development of modern democracies in Europe and America. It was through the publicizing of the private affairs of kings and other ruling authorities that a public sphere of discourse developed. Consequently, most modern constitutions call for conducting the affairs of state in public. The Sixth Amendment to the U.S. Constitution provides that "the accused shall enjoy the right to a speedy and public trial." This ensures that justice will be carried out under the watchful eye of other private citizens.

A Musical Lampoon of the News Media

The Academy-Award winning film *Chicago* (2002), based on a musical by Bob Fosse and Fred Ebb, depicts the legal travails of a nightclub singer (Catherine Zeta-Jones) and a chorus girl (Renée Zellweger) during the 1920's. Both women are arrested for murder and are represented by the same media-hound lawyer (Richard Gere). The lawyer's efforts for each client wax and wane as the publicity their cases generate go up and down. By this measure, his efforts for the chorus girl increase as public interest in the nightclub singer wanes. Eventually, both women—though acquitted of their crimes—are relegated to the dustbin of media attention, and the lawyer moves on with new clients.

Chicago may be an accurate reflection of the public's fickle interest in headline cases in the past, but its theme is not equally relevant in modern American society. In the early twenty-first century, media coverage of sensational legal cases typically morphs into book deals and made-for-television films. In the current media environment, sensational criminal cases—such as those involving O. J. Simpson, Robert Blake, Kobe Bryant, and Michael Jackson—can occupy the public's attention for long periods of time.

By Timothy L. Hall

In the eighteenth and nineteenth centuries the right to a public trial meant that private citizens and print journalists could attend court proceedings. In the twentieth century access was sometimes extended to radio and television broadcasters as well. However, the U.S. Supreme Court has been reluctant to grant to broadcast journalists the access given to citizens and print journalists. The Supreme Court takes the position that broadcast technology could adversely affect court proceedings by affecting the behavior of those in the courtroom, including the judge, attorneys, parties, and witnesses.

In some cases the individual's right to privacy takes precedence over the public's right to know. In certain states an attorney can move to close the courtroom. If the attorney shows good cause the judge may remove spectators from the courtroom for part or all of the proceedings. This is most often done in cases involving juveniles, adoptions, or rape. Judges may also clear the courtroom if witnesses must provide embarrassing evidence, usually in cases involving sexual assault. As often as not, criminal defendants successfully object to these attempts to close the courtroom; after all, the right to a public trial is the defendant's right, not the judge's right.

Typically, trial publicity is limited to coverage of a crime, the police investigation, and regular reports on courtroom testimony. In the majority of trials, publicity is not a problem. If a judge believes that trial publicity may bias the proceedings, a gag order can be issued restricting what parties in the trial may say to journalists. A judge may also sequester a jury by cutting off jurors' access to news broadcasts and newspapers and by restricting them to their hotel rooms and court facilities. However, it is rare for gag orders to be enforced or for a jury to be sequestered.

If excessive local publicity makes it impossible to impanel a jury of impartial jurors that have not been exposed to the publicity, a judge may also call for a change of venue by moving the trial to an area in which the pool of potential jurors has been less exposed to news coverage of the case in question. Although changes of venue are suboptimal in that the citizens in the jurisdiction where the crime occurred will not sit in judgment of the accused, changes of venue are essential in high-publicity cases to ensure that the accused's constitutional right to a fair trial by impartial jurors is scrupulously honored.

Thomas J. Roach
Updated by Charles E. MacLean

Further Reading
Chermak, Steven M. *Victims in the News: Crime and the American News Media*. Boulder, Colo.: Westview Press, 1995.
Chiasson, Lloyd, ed. *The Press on Trial: Crimes and Trials as Media Events*. Westport, Conn.: Greenwood Press, 1997.
Clehane, Dianem, and Nancy Grace. *Objection! How High-Priced Defense Attorneys, Celebrity Defendants, and a 24/7 Media Have Hijacked Our Criminal Justice System*. New York: Hyperion, 2005.
Surette, Ray. *Media, Crime, and Criminal Justice*. 2d ed. Pacific Grove, Calif.: Brooks/Cole, 1998.

See also Attorney ethics; Change of venue; Constitution, U.S.; Gag orders; Inquests; Jury sequestration; Jury system; Print media; Television news; *Voir dire*.

Trials

Definition: Formal processes of adjudication, from arraignment through verdicts
Criminal justice issue: Courts; defendants; judges; trial procedures
Significance: Judicial trials represent a high point in criminal justice processing and symbolize justice. When they are conducted fairly, they reinforce public confidence in the criminal justice system, raise public awareness that crime does not pay, and demonstrate the principle that under constitutional government, the innocent are vindicated.

Judicial trials take two forms: bench trials and jury trials. Bench trials are nonjury trials in which judges act as the sole arbiters. Jury trials are judicial processes in which groups of selected impartial average citizens are sworn to reach verdicts by considering relevant facts to find the truth. The history of jury trials is deeply rooted in English history, going back at least as far as King John's signing in 1215 of the Magna Carta, which granted the right to trial by jury of peers to English noblemen.

In the United States, jury trials are a right guaranteed by the U.S. Constitution, which provided that trials of all crimes were to be by juries selected in the states in which the crimes were allegedly committed. That right was further affirmed in 1791 by the ratification of the Bill of Rights, whose Sixth Amendment, which gives accused persons the right to speedy and public trials by impartial juries in all criminal prosecutions.

Fundamental to court trials is the fact that the United States practices an adversarial system of justice, which is based on the premise that every dispute has two sides to it. Trials offer the opposing sides-prosecution and defense—the opportunity to present their evidence and arguments before judges or impartial juries.

Typical court trial processes consist of a series of major steps, beginning with opening statements and ending with the verdict. The underlying purpose of all trials is to find the truth-guilty verdicts when charges against defendants are proven, and acquittals when the charges are not proven beyond a reasonable doubt. Where not guilty verdicts are rendered, the accused are immediately discharged. When guilty verdicts are rendered, sentencing and appeals may follow.

Types of Trials
The two basic types of court trials in the United States are criminal and civil. Criminal trials are proceedings designed to enforce or protect public rights. Penalties in criminal trials range from simple fines to death, depending on the charges and the circumstances in which the crimes are committed.

Civil trials, on the other hand, are proceedings designed to permit individuals, organizations, and institutions to seek monetary redress, to protect private rights, and prevent private wrongs. Penalties in civil trials are almost always monetary awards.

> ## Hollywood Goes to Court
>
> Film depictions of trials are often unrealistic, but it is unusual for films to stray as far from legal reality as *Suspect* (1987) and *...And Justice for All* (1979). In director Peter Yates's *Suspect*, singer Cher stars as a public defender assigned to represent a homeless deaf man (Liam Neeson) accused of murder. During the ensuing trial, one of the jurors (Dennis Quaid) secretly offers advice to the public defender, then helps her actively investigate the case and develop a romantic relationship with her. Although suspenseful, *Suspect* receives low marks for accuracy in the depiction of a criminal case. Contact between lawyers and jurors is specifically prohibited, and it is inconceivable that a defense counsel would pursue a relationship with a juror in the midst of a trial. The film also makes other kinds of errors. For example, the prosecutor at trial, with little evidence to prove the guilt of the homeless defendant, offers evidence of the defendant's previous criminal behavior. Similar evidence is commonly spotlighted in movie trials but is not generally admissible in real-life trials. In the main, rules of evidence prevent prosecutors from trying to show that because defendants have done something wrong in the past that they have probably done something wrong more recently.
>
> In director Norman Jewison's *...And Justice for All* Al Pacino plays a lawyer who is representing a judge (John Forsythe) accused of rape. After the lawyer discovers that his client is actually guilty, he announces this fact during his opening statements at his client's trial. This action, completely unbelievable, would certainly lead to the lawyer's disbarment. In fact, almost nothing about the film's treatment of legal issues is realistic. For example, the judge-defendant elects to be tried by another judge, not by a jury. In real life, no criminal defense lawyer would allow his client to be tried by a judge—especially one known as a law-and-order judge, as is the film's judge. The film also misrepresents plea bargains, which are agreements between prosecutors and defense attorneys, not between defense attorneys and judges, as the film seems to suggest. Finally, lawyers are not allowed to have private conversations with judges about pending cases; such *ex parte* communications are strictly forbidden.
>
> *By Timothy L. Hall*

Stages in Judicial Trials

The first step in any jury court trial is jury selection. It begins with the summoning of eligible citizens—whose names are taken from the master jury lists—who are then questioned in a process known as *voir dire* to determine their eligibility to serve as jurors. The master jury list is usually compiled from voter registration lists, driver's license lists, or city telephone directories. By employing unlimited challenges for cause and limited peremptory challenges, counsel for the prosecution and the defense whittle down the numbers of potential jurors to the required size, which is usually twelve jurors and several alternates.

The second step is presentation of brief opening statements by prosecutors and defense attorneys that outline what each side intends to prove in evidence. The primary purpose of opening statements is to acquaint judges and jurors with the essentials of the cases and to prepare them for the arguments that are to come. These statements are often limited to the scope of what the prosecutors and defense attorneys intend to cover in evidence. The prosecution usually presents its opening statement first.

Prosecution Strategies and Procedures

The next step in court trial is the fuller presentation of the plaintiff or prosecution's case. In judicial trials, the plaintiff or prosecution is typically the first to present its case to the judge or jury. It is an opportunity to call and lead witnesses in evidence, as well as to present other evidence that will bolster the case. Prosecution witnesses present their evidence through direct examination as led by the prosecutors. They may include victims, eyewitnesses, police officers, and expert witnesses such as forensic scientists and medical specialists.

Four basic types of evidence may be presented at trial: real evidence, testimonial evidence, direct evidence, and circumstantial evidence. Real evidence includes physical objects of almost any kind, such as weapons, documents, and other tangibles, that are related to the case. Testimonial evidence consists of statements of any sort by competent witnesses. Direct evidence consists of eyewitness testimony by third parties who have observed incidents relating to the cases. Circumstantial evidence is indirect evidence, that is, indirect proofs of material facts relating to cases without direct observation of the action.

After prosecutors directly examine witnesses, the defense attorneys are given the opportunity to cross-examine the same witnesses. In cross-examinations, the defense attorneys ask questions to clarify the defendants' roles in the cases. The defense also uses cross-examination to point out inconsistencies in witnesses' testimony that damage their cases and, if possible, raise doubts in the minds of the juries about the credibility of the witnesses and their testimony.

In like manner, the defense may also challenge the reliability and relatedness of other types of evidence presented by the prosecution. However, the judges ultimately rule on the admissibility or nonadmissibility of contested evidence. Prosecutors may reexamine their own witnesses after defense cross-examinations are completed to provide answers to new information and points raised during cross-examination.

Defense Tactics and Procedures

Immediately following the presentation of the prosecution's case, the defense may request the court to dismiss the case on grounds of failure of the prosecution to prove its case. If the motion is sustained, the judge will direct the jury to acquit the defendant and then dismiss the case. If motion is denied, then the defense presents its own case.

Defense attorneys present their cases in the same manner as the prosecution by calling their own witnesses. The defense usually involves direct examination of defense witnesses and presentation of other types of evidence. As the defense finishes examining witnesses, the prosecution can cross-examine them. The prosecution tries to establish inconsistencies in the defense witnesses' testimony, just as the defense has earlier tried to discredit the prosecution witnesses.

It should be noted that because defendants are deemed innocent until proven guilty, the defense may elect not to present any witnesses or evidence at all. The prosecution carries the burden of proof—the legal standard requiring it to prove the accused guilty beyond any reasonable doubt.

Rebuttal and Surrebuttal

At the conclusion of the defense case, the prosecution may present rebuttal witnesses or evidence. Rebuttal evidence is evidence that tends to refute the opponents' evidence or undermine their alibis. It may also take the form of discrediting the credibility of defense witnesses based on misrepresentations of facts or proof of incentives to lie, especially for witnesses who have criminal conviction records of their own.

Sometimes rebuttals may involve bringing in new evidence that was not introduced during the prosecutors' case. The defense may choose to exercise a surrebuttal by examining rebuttal witnesses, and may in turn introduce other evidence or witnesses. Surrebuttal is evidence directed toward countering rebuttal evidence, or strengthening the defense evidence. Rebuttal/surrebuttal exchanges may continue indefinitely, until both parties exhaust all witnesses and new evidence. When that happens, the defense may again submit a motion for directed verdict. If the motion is denied, both the prosecution and defense present their closing arguments.

From Closing Arguments to Jury Deliberation

Closing arguments are summary statements delivered by the prosecution and the defense following the presentation of all evidence. Defense attorneys usually present their arguments first, followed by the prosecutors, who wrap up the cases. The goal of each closing statement is to attack the credibility of the opponent's evidence and witnesses. Closing statements must be based on facts, supported by evidence, and aimed at convincing judges or juries as to why they must rule in favor of their arguments. Factual summaries may be either short or prolonged.

After the closing arguments, the judges inform jurors of the general legal principles and standards they are to observe as they deliberate to reach their verdicts. Judges typically remind jurors that the accused are be deemed innocent until they are proven guilty and that convictions must be based on proof beyond a reasonable doubt. The judges also advise jurors on any special aspects of the crimes in question that may be relevant to their deliberations.

Because jurors are mostly average citizens, the instructions they receive are designed to educate them on the legal rules, principles, and standards applicable to the particular cases, as well as general principles. The instructions are also designed to clear away any misconceptions that may constitute grounds for appeal. Sometimes, judges invite the prosecutors and defense attorneys to participate in drawing up their jury instructions.

After jurors hear the judges' instructions, they retire into seclusion to discuss the cases and reach verdicts. Deliberation processes may involve exhaustive discussions and analyses of all evidence presented at trial. When in doubt about specific points, the jurors may call for clarification from the judges on aspects of their instructions or for portions of the case transcripts.

During their deliberations, jurors are cut off from all outside influences until they reach their verdicts. Deliberations may last only a few hours or drag on for several days. When jurors cannot reach verdicts in one day, they are instructed by the judges not to discuss the cases with anyone until they return the next day to continue their deliberations. In highly politicized or celebrated cases, jurors may be sequestered in jury or hotel rooms and not allowed to leave until after they reach verdicts. Sequestration is the keeping together of juries and separating them from the general public throughout trials or deliberation processes to protect them from outside influences that may affect their decisions unfairly.

Verdicts

Verdicts represent the jurors' final decisions after detailed analyses of all evidence presented in cases. Typical jury verdicts are either guilty or not guilty. Jury decisions must be unanimous in all criminal cases, and guilty verdicts must meet the standard of proof beyond all reasonable doubt, that is, a clear and convincing belief that any reasonable person would accept that the defendant is guilty as charged.

When jurors fail to reach agreement after deliberating, the trials are said to end in hung juries. In some jurisdictions, a hung jury constitutes grounds for a judge to declare a mistrial and dismiss the jury. Mistrials mean the termination of trials before verdicts are reached due to intervening circumstances that make it impossible to secure fair trials or for the trials to continue. When hung juries or mistrials are declared, charges are dismissed and the defendants are released. However, prosecutors reserve the right to file for new trials of the defendants on the same charges without breaching the defendants' constitutional right against double jeopardy.

When juries inform the judges that they have reached verdicts, they are invited back into the courtrooms to announce their verdicts. Trial verdicts of not guilty bring cases to an end, and the defendants are freed of all pending bonds. On the other hand, when jury forepersons announce guilty verdicts, the jurors are usually polled individually to voice their decisions in open court. After guilty verdicts are finalized, judges order presentencing investigations and set dates for sentencing the convicted defendants.

Postverdict Motions and Sentencing

After guilty verdicts are announced, defense attorneys can file two types of postconviction motions in the hope of giving their clients second opportunities at freedom. The first type of motion is a motion in arrest of judgment. This type of motion asks the court to set aside and reverse the jury verdict on grounds that errors were made by the jury in the trial that require the case to be dismissed and the defendant acquitted. The second type is a motion for a new trial. This unusual request is based on assertions that serious errors have been made at trial by either the trial judge or the prosecutor. Sometimes the motions are based on newly discovered evidence that justifies setting aside a guilty verdict and granting a new trial. However, such motions are rarely granted by presiding judges.

Sentences are penalties imposed by courts on persons found guilty of criminal wrongdoing. It is the responsibility of the presiding judges to impose criminal sentences. Penalties are often tied to recommendations made by probation officers in presentence investigation (PSI) reports. Types of judicial penalty include monetary fines, probation, imprisonment, restitution, intermediate sanctions, commitment to hospitals or other treatment agencies, and death. Judicial sanctions may combine two or three of these punishments.

Appeals

Appeals mark the end of the road in court trial processes. Losing sides in trials may file for judicial reviews from appellate courts when the trial court judges refuse their post-trial motions for relief from the verdicts. Possible reasons for appeals include refusals of trial judges to admit relevant or exculpatory evidence during trial, inclusion of irrelevant or damaging evidence at trial, and improper jury instruction—especially when the losing attorneys' objections to such measures are ignored by the trial judges.

The first major step in the appeals process involves the filing of formal notice of appeal document in the appellate court. The next phase is to apply for a transcript proceeding from the trial court. On fixed dates, both the prosecution and the defense present their cases to the appeals courts under a regulated schedule. Appellate court decisions may include upholding the rulings of the lower court or reversing the trial court decisions and discharging the cases. Appellate courts may also reverse and remand cases for fresh trials.

Emmanuel C. Onyeozili
Updated by Christine Wilson

Further Reading

Baum, Lawrence. *American Courts: Process and Policy*. 5th ed. Boston: Houghton Mifflin, 2001. Standard textbook covering all aspect of U.S. courts, from their organization and structure to the procedures they employ.

Bodenhamer, David J. *Fair Trial: Rights of the Accused in American History*. New York: Oxford University Press, 1997. Succinct history of changing constitutional rulings that have steadily ensured greater fairness in criminal procedures.

Carp, Robert A., and Ronald Stidham. *Judicial Process in America*. 5th ed. Washington, D.C.: CQ Press, 2001. Congressional Quarterly, 1996. General survey of trial procedures in the larger context of criminal justice processes.

Epstein, Lee, and Thomas G. Walker. *Constitutional Law for a Changing America: Rights, Liberties, and Justice*. 5th ed. Washington, D.C.: CQ Press, 2004. Up-to-date study of constitutional law with considerable attention to the role of the Supreme Court.

Mauet, Thomas A. *Trial Techniques*. 6th ed. New York: Aspen Publishers, 2002. Textbook explaining trial procedures and the tactics and strategies that prosecution and defense attorneys can employ.

Neubauer, David W. *America's Courts and the Criminal Justice System*. 8th ed. Belmont, Calif.: Wadsworth/Thomson Learning, 2005. Comprehensive analysis of the dynamics of criminal justice in action as seen in the relationship of judge, prosecutor, and defense attorney.

Siegel, Larry J. *Criminology*. 8th ed. Belmont, Calif.: Wadsworth/Thomson Learning, 2004. Gives a thorough overview of the discipline of criminology and the entire criminal justice process, legal concepts, and justice perspectives, featuring high-profile cases, events, and relevant materials in a comprehensive, balanced, and objective fashion.

Wellman, Francis L. *The Art of Cross-Examination*. 4th ed. New York: Macmillan, 1936. Reprint. New York: Simon and Schuster, 1998. Reprint of a classic work on the crucial trial attorney skill of cross-examination.

See also Acquittal; Bifurcated trials; Burden of proof; Court types; Criminal prosecution; Discovery; Dismissals; District attorneys; Evidence, rules of; Hung juries; Judges; Judicial system, U.S.; Jurisdiction of courts; Reasonable doubt; Speedy trial right; Verdicts; Witnesses.

United States Sentencing Commission

Identification: Independent federal judicial agency responsible for developing federal sentencing guidelines and acting as a research resource for the executive and legislative branches of the federal government
Date: Established in 1984
Criminal justice issue: Federal law; judges; sentencing
Significance: The commission is responsible for determining federal sentencing guidelines, thereby removing discretion from federal judges.

The United States Sentencing Commission was established by the Sentencing Reform Act of 1984 as an independent federal agency located within the judicial branch of the government. The commission was tasked with setting the lower and upper bounds of permissible punishments for federal offenses.

The commission's duties also include collecting and analyzing federal sentencing data and determining its effect on the federal criminal justice system. The commission uses this data to recommend federal sentencing changes to Congress. It also reviews various crime and sentencing research and refines the federal guidelines based on the findings of this research. The commission also monitors the outcomes and cases from the Court of Appeals and congressional action. In addition, the commission trains thousands of criminal justice professionals in the proper use of the federal sentencing guidelines and publishes numerous reports every year (all of which are posted on its Web site).

The makeup of the commission is mandated by federal statute. Seven voting members are appointed by the president and confirmed by the Senate for six-year terms. Also included are two nonvoting members. One additional voting member is appointed by the commission's chairperson. No more than three of the commissioners may be federal judges, and no more than four may belong to the same political party. In addition, the U.S. attorney general and the chairperson of the U.S. Parole Commission are ex officio members of the commission.

The commission was established in an effort to combat disparity in federal sentencing. Prior to the Sentencing Reform Act of 1984, federal judges were not required to use the same sentencing standards. Judges could impose sentences ranging from probation to the statutory maximum for any given offense. The Sentencing Reform Act was passed in an attempt to achieve greater fairness and certainty of punishment in the federal courts.

Since its inception, the sentencing commission has been a point of contention between the federal judiciary and the legislative branch of government. In April, 2003, the Protect Act was passed, although it focused on child welfare, it also included provisions requiring the commission to issue new limits to federal judges' discretion in sentencing above or below the sentencing guidelines. The federal judiciary voted in the fall of 2003 to support legislation counter to the sentencing provisions in the Protect Act in an effort to restore more judicial discretion. This placed the commission in the middle of a political battle between the federal judiciary and some members of Congress.

The Justice Department and Republican members of Congress tended to support the new rules, stating that they were needed in order to keep sentencing in the federal courts uniform and to keep maverick judges in line. The protests from the judiciary were not just from a few disgruntled liberal judges. Chief Justice William Rehnquist has also protested the changes, stating that they go too far in eliminating judicial discretion and flexibility. Statistics from the sentencing commission show that federal judges depart from the guidelines about 18 percent of the time, usually at the request of prosecutors, as a reward for cooperative defendants.

However, this discussion was rendered moot in 2005 when the Supreme Court ruled, in *United States v. Booker*, that all sentencing standards issued by the commission are only advisory, not mandatory. Congress could pass legislation mandating minimum and maximum sentences for various crimes, while the commission, as part of the judicial branch, could not legislate sentences; rather it could only offer guidelines to be consulted by judges. While this ruling technically overturned the reason for the creation of the commission, the commission continues to exist and influence federal sentences, although, as might be expected, initial studies of the post Booker period have indicated a greater disparity of sentences among individuals sentenced for the same crime.

The commission continually refines its guidelines, but a major change occurred in 2015. The commission substantially lowered the sentencing guidelines for certain types of drug convictions, and stated that they should be applied retroactively to those previously sentenced for these crimes. The Justice Department began processing possible changes for individuals whose cases could be affected by the new guidelines. The new guidelines included a provision that no prisoners could be released prior to November, 2016. Initial estimates are that over 40,000 individuals could be affected by this change.

Jennifer R. Albright
Updated by Donald A. Watt

Further Reading

Stith, Kate, and Jose A. Cabranes. *Fear of Judging: Sentencing Guidelines in the Federal Courts.* Chicago: University of Chicago Press, 1998.

United States Congress Committee on the Judiciary Subcommittee on Criminal Justice Oversight. *Oversight of the United States Sentencing Commission: Are the Guidelines Being Followed? Hearing Before the Subcommittee on Criminal Justice Oversight of the Committee on the Judiciary, United States Senate, One Hundred Sixth Congress, Second Session, October 13, 2000.* Washington, D.C.: U.S. Government Printing Office, 2001.

Von Hirsh, Andrew, Michael Tonry, and Kay Knapp. *Sentencing Commission and Its Guidelines.* Boston: Northeastern University Press, 1987.

United States Sentencing Commission. "Chapter One—Introduction, Authority, and General Application Principles." *Federal Sentencing Guidelines Manual 2015-2016.* Washington: United States Sentencing Commission: Guidelines Archive, 2015. Web. 28 September 2016.

See also Comprehensive Crime Control Act; Discretion; Just deserts; Mandatory sentencing; Sentencing; Sentencing guidelines, U.S.; Parole Commission, U.S.; Sentencing; Sentencing guidelines, U.S.

Verdicts

Definition: Formal decisions or findings made by juries or judges upon matters of fact submitted to them for deliberation and determination

Criminal justice issue: Trial procedures; verdicts

Significance: Verdicts in criminal justice cases can differ from those in civil cases, as defendants who are issued verdicts of acquittal cannot be tried again.

In legal cases the court interprets the applicable law associated with a given case and explains the law to the jury. Based on the presented evidence the jury must determine the facts in the case and make a proper application of the law relating to those facts to arrive at a verdict. In general, the jury's verdict must be unanimous, but many states have modified the condition of unanimity, particularly in civil cases, so that verdicts can be rendered by designated majorities of the juries.

Verdicts may be either general or specific. A general verdict is that in which the jury pronounces "guilty" or "not guilty" and thus decides whether the plaintiff or the defendant wins the case. A general verdict is the verdict most often rendered in criminal cases. Moreover, in criminal cases the verdict must generally be unanimous and must be returned by the jury to the judge in open court. This verdict is based on every material fact submitted for the consideration of the jury. The court may also submit to the jury appropriate forms for a general verdict and, in some cases, a list of written questions concerning one or more of the relevant issues to the case that must be answered in the process of determining the verdict.

When the jury is asked by the court to answer specific questions of fact but leaves any decisions based on the law to the court, it is called a special verdict. The court often requires that the jury return a special verdict in the form of a special written finding upon each issue of fact, and the court determines if the defendant is guilty or not based on those answers. Civil cases may be decided by either a general or a special verdict.

When the verdict is presented in court, the defendant and all the jury members must be present. In most jurisdictions, both the plaintiffs and the defendants have the right to have the jury polled. When they are polled, the jury members are asked if the stated verdict is the one that they favored. A verdict will not stand if the required number of jurors does not answer this question in the affirmative.

When the evidence conclusively dictates a clear verdict in favor of one of the litigants, the judge has the authority in many states to direct the jury to render a verdict in favor of either the plaintiff or the defendant. If it is evident to the court that a verdict is against the weight of the evidence, the court may order a new trial. However, in criminal cases, a verdict of acquittal is conclusive upon the prosecution (the state) so that the defendant will not be subjected to double jeopardy. However, in the event that the jury cannot reach a verdict, the defendant may be tried again.

Alvin K. Benson

Further Reading

Kavlen, Harry, and Hans Zeisel. *The American Jury*. Boston: Little, Brown, 1966.

Litan, Robert E., ed. *Verdict: Assessing the Civil Jury System*. Washington, D.C.: Brookings Institution, 1993.

See also Acquittal; Convictions; Defendants; Dismissals; Double jeopardy; Hung juries; Jury system; Punitive damages; Reasonable doubt; Reversible error; Testimony; Trials.

Voir dire

Definition: Preliminary process in selection of persons to serve on juries

Criminal justice issue: Juries; Legal terms and principles; Trial procedures

Significance: The process of empaneling jurors can be one of the most important and most difficult tasks during a trial.

A French legal phrase, *voir dire* means "to speak the truth." It is the process by which prospective jurors are questioned to determine whether they hold any biases or prejudices that might interfere with their role as objective jurors. The circumstances of cases or high-profile status of persons involved in cases make it difficult at times for jury selection to remain bias-free. *Voir dire* allows defense attorneys and prosecutors to eliminate jurors whom they believed are biased or who may be unlikely to accept their sides' versions of events. This is done using two types of challenges—challenges for cause and peremptory challenges. Challenges for cause can be made by either set of attorneys and are unlimited in number. However, judges make the final decisions about excusing specific prospective jurors. Challenges for cause are rarely made and are rarely granted.

Peremptory challenges are made by either side and are limited in number. However, judges are not involved in these decisions to exclude jurors. Peremptory challenges are strategically used and require no explanation to the judges. In the past, such challenges were used systematically to remove jurors on the basis of their race or gender—a practice that is now legally prohibited.

As with other aspects of the trial process, *voir dire* exists to protect the integrity of the criminal justice system. It is meant to allow citizens to participate in the trial process while allowing that process to be as unbiased and impartial as possible.

Jenifer A. Lee

Further Reading

Abadinsky, H. *Law and Justice: An Introduction to the American Legal System*. Upper Saddle River, N.J.: Prentice-Hall, 2003.

Browning, John G. "Should Voir Dire Become Voir Google? Ethical Implications of Researching Jurors on Social Media." *SMU Science & Technology Law Review* 17 (2014): n. pag. Web. 26 May 2016.

Costanzo, Mark, and Daniel Krauss. *Forensic and Legal Psychology: Psychological Science Applied to Law*. New York: Worth, 2012. Print.

Frederick, Jeffrey T. *Mastering Voir Dire and Jury Selection*. 2nd ed. Chicago: Amer. Bar Assn., 2005. Print.

Johnson, Vida. "Presumed Fair? Voir Dire on the Fundamentals of Our Criminal Justice System." *Seton Hall Law Review* 45.2 (2015): 545-580. *Index to Legal Periodicals & Books Full Text (H.W. Wilson)*. Web. 26 May 2016.

Rabe, Gary A., and Dean John Champion. *Criminal Courts: Structure, Process, and Issues*. Upper Saddle River, N.J.: Prentice-Hall, 2002.

See also Death qualification; Defendants; Defense attorneys; District attorneys; Judges; Jury system; Print media; Trial publicity; Trials.

Witherspoon v. Illinois

The Case: U.S. Supreme Court ruling on juries in capital punishment cases

Date: Decided on June 3, 1968

Criminal justice issue: Capital punishment; juries

Significance: In this groundbreaking decision, the Supreme Court decided that prospective jurors with reservations about the death penalty could not be excluded from service in criminal proceedings.

The Sixth Amendment to the U.S. Constitution guarantees accused citizens the right to trial by an impartial jury of peers. This deceptively simple guarantee has come under fire in cases too numerous to mention. During the 1960's, many noteworthy cases advanced to the Supreme Court regarding the composition and unanimity of the jury in criminal cases. In 1968, the *Witherspoon* case compounded the jury-selection question with the issue of capital punishment.

Using an Illinois statute, the prosecution at William Witherspoon's murder trial in Cook County, Illinois, eliminated almost half of the potential jurors by challenging those who had reservations about their ability to impose a death sentence. This exclusion occurred without any determination of the level of reservation; that is, the potential jurors were excluded for any degree of uncertainty about imposition of a death sentence. The defendant, Witherspoon, appealed his case on the grounds that such a broad exclusion of jurors prevented him from being tried by an impartial jury as guaranteed in the Sixth Amendment. Witherspoon claimed that a jury absent of those opposed or at least uncertain about capital punishment would under no circumstances be impartial or representative of the community.

The Supreme Court agreed in a majority opinion written by Justice Potter Stewart. Witherspoon's death sentence was voided by the Court; however, his conviction was not overturned. The Court agreed with the defendant that a jury devoid of objectors to capital punishment was sure to be "woefully short" of the impartiality guaranteed by the Sixth Amendment and extended to the states under the Fourteenth Amendment. In the majority opinion, the Court stated that those prospective jurors who expressed a total disinclination toward ever imposing the death penalty could be excluded; however, persons who merely had reservations in the matter could not be excluded for their reservations alone.

The Court went on to state that juries must attempt to mirror the feelings of the community. In any given community there will be a certain number of people who are unsure of their feelings about capital punishment. This point of view should not be avoided in jury selection, the Court ruled, as inclusion of such undecided jurors will ensure neutrality on the sentencing issue and will allow the jury more adequately to reflect the conscience of the community.

While ruling that a jury totally committed to the imposition of the death penalty cannot be selected deliberately, as this would deprive a defendant of life without due process, the Court did not issue a constitutional rule that would have required the reversal of every jury selected under the Illinois statute. The Court did not state that a jury composed of persons in favor of capital punishment would be predisposed to convict, only that such a jury would be predisposed in the sentencing element of a trial.

The *Witherspoon* decision was an early test of the Supreme Court's position on capital punishment as well as on jury composition and selection. The Court indicated its willingness to uphold criminal convictions while examining the sentencing procedures being used in the states. At no point in its opinion did the Court express disfavor for the death penalty; rather, the opinion targeted only the constitutional implications of the jury-selection process. In other words, the *Witherspoon* decision indicated that within constitutional bounds, communities would be left to choose whether or not to impose the death penalty.

Donna Addkison Simmons

Further Reading
Bohm, Robert M. *Deathquest: An Introduction to the Theory and Practice of Capital Punishment in the United States*. Cincinnati: Anderson Publishing, 2003.
Carter, Linda E., and Ellen Krietzberg. *Understanding Capital Punishment Law*. Newark, N.J.: LexisNexis, 2004.
Latzer, Barry, ed. *Death Penalty Cases: Leading Supreme Court Cases on Capital Punishment*. 2d ed. Burlington, Mass.: Butterworth Heinemann, 2002.
Sarat, Austin. *When the State Kills: Capital Punishment and the American Condition*. Princeton, N.J.: Princeton University Press, 2001.

See also Capital punishment; Criminal law; Criminal procedure; Death qualification; Jury system; Supreme Court, U.S.

Witness protection programs

Definition: Government programs designed to ensure the safety of key witnesses during and after court proceedings
Criminal justice issue: Crime prevention; trial procedures; witnesses
Significance: Witness protection programs provide security for witnesses whose testimony is critical in important court proceedings.

Some U.S. states have developed state-managed witness protection programs. The most frequently used program is the federal Witness Protection Program. Since the program's inception, under Title V of the Racketeer Influenced and Corrupt Organizations (RICO) Act of 1970, as a tool to combat organized crime, more than five thousand witnesses have been part of the Witness Protection

Program. Beyond providing for the safety of witnesses, the program also provides for the health, relocation, psychological welfare, and social adjustment of witnesses. Federal protection through the Witness Protection Program has been extended to provide protection for any witnesses and their families who are recommended to the attorney general by a state U.S. attorney's office. After the program was evaluated by the Witness Security Review Committee in 1977, the Witness Security Reform Act, part of the Comprehensive Crime Control Act of 1984, was adopted to correct a number of deficiencies that existed in the original 1970 act.

A victim's compensation fund was established through an adjustment made to the Witness Protection Program by the Reform Act. This fund compensates persons or beneficiaries for death or physical injury that may occur during relocation. However, injuries that occur to witnesses cannot be used as a cause of action against the United States. Also, for those witnesses who are sentenced to and remain in prison, placement in one of the five protected witness units in special areas of federal penitentiaries is necessary. Located throughout the country, these units are operated by the Federal Bureau of Prisons.

Guidelines and Procedures

Before accepting witnesses in the Witness Protection Program, the attorney general considers the danger in which a community will be placed if a witness is relocated there. The safety of the town or region must be considered, because many of the witnesses in the program are criminals who, in exchange for revealing information, are provided with protection and a reduction in fines or prison time. However, the significance of witnesses' testimony may outweigh the danger in which the witnesses place the community. Witnesses and those close to them must have their criminal histories reviewed and pass a psychological examination.

The attorney general, with aid from the U.S. marshals, assists witnesses accepted into the program in a variety of ways. Witnesses may be provided with new identities, including new names and social security cards. Those involved in the program may then use the new information to obtain other pieces of identification, such as driver's licenses. Consequently, witnesses' birth identities cease to exist in the public domain, and the records of witnesses' birth identities are turned over to the marshals service.

Once the decision to relocate a witness is made, local law-enforcement officials are notified that there is a protected witness in their territory. A relocation inspector is provided to witnesses to help them adjust to their new locations and identities. The inspector advises the witnesses about improved living strategies, such as answering people's questions about the past. The witnesses are also provided with housing. For some, this may be a temporary safe house; for others, it may be a new permanent location. The transportation of previously owned household furniture and personal property to the witnesses' new locations may also be provided. However, the type of personal property relocated with the witnesses is regulated, because certain personal items could connect the witnesses to their previous identities.

The witnesses are provided with a stipend to meet basic living expenses. The amount and duration of the stipend are regulated by the attorney general. Once witnesses are able to support themselves, monetary aid ceases. They are also assisted with obtaining employment. Although employment aid from the government entails paying for job training, government aid does not include providing false job résumés or references. Beyond these specific guidelines, witnesses generally are assisted in other ways that are necessary to achieve independence. The decision to reveal or not to reveal witnesses' identities or locations is made by the attorney general after weighing the danger to the witnesses, to the public, to the success of the program, and to the forthcoming trial. However, the attorney general must reveal any requested information if ordered to do so by the court.

Witness Agreement

Once approved for the program, witnesses must sign a memorandum of understanding with the attorney general. The memorandum of understanding includes the agreement to testify and to provide information related to the proceedings to appropriate law-enforcement officials. To provide for the safety of the community, protected witnesses must agree not to commit any crimes and to take necessary steps to avoid detection. The witnesses must comply with legal obligations and civil judgments and must cooperate with reasonable requests of government employees who are involved in the protection process. Witnesses are allowed to designate persons to serve as their agents, who make sworn statements regarding the witnesses' legal obligations, such as child custody and any outstanding debts. Witnesses are also advised to resolve the issue of child custody before entering the program, ensuring that their children's best interests are considered in making a decision. Protected witnesses must inform witness protection officials of probation and parole responsibilities, of other activities, and of their current addresses.

Memorandums of understanding are entered into with all participants in the protection program who are over eighteen years of age. Before completing the evaluation that determines whether witnesses qualify for the program, the attorney general may decide to provide protection to witnesses immediately. Immediate protection is necessary in situations in which the lack of immediate protection would harm the investigation. The attorney general also has the power to terminate the protection of the witnesses if the memorandum of understanding is breached or the witnesses provide false information. The decision to terminate protection is not open to judicial review.

Kim Kochanek

Further Reading
Earley, Pete, and Gerald Shur. *WITSEC: Inside the Federal Witness Protection Program.* New York: Bantam Books, 2002. Inside view of the federal Witness Protection Program, based on Shur's twenty-five-year career as an attorney in the Department of Justice.
Fyfe, Nicholas R. *Protecting Intimidated Witnesses.* Aldershot Burlington, Vt.: Ashgate, 2001. Detailed study of a witness protection program in Great Britain, with emphasis on Scotland.
Hill, Henry, with Gus Russo. *Gangsters and Goodfellas: The Mob, Witness Protection, and Life on the Run.* New York: M. Evans, 2004. Firsthand account of a former criminal living under the Witness Protection Program by the man whose criminal life was dramatized in the film *Goodfellas* (1990).
Sabbag, Robert. "The Invisible Family." *New York Times Magazine* (February 11, 1996). Offers a personal understanding of the witness protection program and general information.

See also Immunity from prosecution; Marshals Service, U.S.; Organized crime; Testimony; Witnesses.

Witnesses

Definition: Persons whose testimony under oath or affirmation is received as evidence in courts of law or in depositions
Criminal justice issue: Evidence and forensics; trial procedures; witnesses
Significance: Under the common law, witnesses should speak only what they know firsthand and testify only as to facts. That is, they cannot offer opinions, make inferences, or draw conclusions.

The rule requiring firsthand personal knowledge has been preserved by the Federal Rules of Evidence (FRE). Because the meaning of the key terms "fact" and "opinion" is often unclear, the FRE have also liberalized the admissibility of lay opinions. Lay opinions are now allowed whenever they would be helpful, provided that they are rationally based on the witness's perceptions. The latter requirement simply means that the witness must have firsthand (personal) knowledge of the matter at issue. Thus, witnesses are allowed to say that a person was (or appeared to be) angry, kidding, dying, strong, sober, or drunk. Speed may be estimated, even sometimes in such terms as fast or slow. Other examples include "It was a sturdy fence" and "The apple was rotten."

The requirement of firsthand knowledge should not be confused with the hearsay rule. If a witness states "Jack shot Mary" but knows this only from others, the witness violates the firsthand personal knowledge rule. If the same witness in the same circumstances testifies that "Joe told me Jack shot Mary," the firsthand rule is not violated, but the hearsay rule may be violated. Hearsay rules govern the admissibility of a declarant's out-of-court statements. Accordingly, hearsay may be recounted in court pursuant to an exception or exemption; in such instances, the lack of firsthand knowledge would affect the weight rather than the admissibility of the witness's testimony.

Incompetency or Disqualification of Witnesses

Competent witnesses are those who testify to what they have seen, heard, or otherwise observed. Trial courts recognize two kinds of witness incompetencies that result in automatic disqualification: lack of personal knowledge and failure to take the oath or affirmation regarding telling the truth.

In the past, witnesses have been ruled incompetent because they have personal interests in cases, past criminal convictions, drug or alcohol intoxication or addiction, marital relationships with involved parties, or mental incapacity. Moreover, persons who are too young may be disqualified as witnesses. Such matters are mainly deemed factors to consider for whatever they are worth in the realms of relevance and credibility.

Persons who are to be offered as witnesses are often subjected to a special series of questions (often outside the presence of the jury) to ascertain foundational facts. This series of questions is to determine whether prospective witnesses understand the duty to tell the truth, can distinguish fact from fantasy, and have the ability to communicate meaningfully with the jury. Children over six years old are rarely found to be incompetent. Although state laws may differ, the FRE generally treat children, at least in principle, no differently from other witnesses.

> ### Attorneys as Witnesses
>
> *Inherit the Wind*, a 1960 film directed by Stanley Kramer, is a fictional re-creation of the famous Scopes "monkey" trial of 1925, when a high school biology teacher was charged with violating a Tennessee state law prohibiting the teaching of evolution in classrooms. The film's climactic moment occurs when the counsel for defense (Spencer Tracy), a lawyer modeled on Clarence Darrow, cross-examines the prosecutor (Fredric March), who is modeled on the historical William Jennings Bryan. Such an occurrence is highly unusual in trials, but the film scene is based on an actual courtroom confrontation between Darrow and Bryan. Lawyers are not generally permitted to serve as both advocates and necessary witnesses in cases, except in matters of what would considered noncontroversial issues—such as the fees they are entitled to be paid for their work in cases.
>
> *Timothy L. Hall*

These rules allow for the exclusion of child witnesses only for compelling reasons, which must be something other than mere age.

Witness Preparation and Sequestration

There are almost no formal limits on bona fide efforts to prepare a prospective witness for taking the witness stand. Thus, in preparing to testify, a witness may review documents, recordings, notes, and other pieces of documentation. The witness may also be rehearsed by attorneys but not prompted to tell an untruth.

In most jurisdictions there is a process called "sequestration," whereby witnesses may be prevented from listening to other testimony in the case. Questions have arisen as to whether this bars trial witnesses from reading transcripts, attending depositions, listening to oral reports of what transpired at hearings, or watching televised portions of trials. The Oklahoma bombing trials of the late 1990's raised the question as to whether families of the deceased victims were permitted to view the trial if they planned to give victim-impact statements at the death-penalty sentencing phase. The trial judge, upheld by the court of appeals, concluded that they could not. The U.S. Congress then legislated, specifically with retroactive effect, that such witnesses in such cases could view the trials.

Additionally, the FRE exempts from sequestration witnesses who are parties, the designated representatives of organizations that are parties, or essential persons, such as experts needed at counsel's table to assist the attorneys. This rule also requires the judge to enter a sequestration order upon an attorney's request or upon the judge's own motion. The judge's order serves to clarify the scope of witness sequestration in a particular case.

Procedure for Examining Witnesses

The basic pattern of trials after jury selection and the opening statements of counsel is that plaintiffs present their cases through witnesses, documents, and other evidence. Then the defendants present their cases, which may consist of both denying facts asserted in the plaintiffs' cases and establishing affirmative defenses.

A witness presented at either phase will normally be examined directly by the attorney presenting the witness, by the attorney from the opposing side during cross-examination, by the proponent to redirect examination and repair the damage caused during cross-examination, and finally by the opposing attorney in a second cross-examination to repair the damage of the proponent. In the absence of an exercise of the judge's discretion, repair is the only acceptable purpose of the last two sequences. Furthermore, repair may be severely limited or disallowed completely by the judge when the contribution of additional examination would be minimal. Further redirects and recrosses are always possible if necessary.

The order of presentation of witnesses in both civil and criminal trials is basically the same. The most significant difference is that the U.S. Constitution's Fifth Amendment privilege against self-incrimination prohibits the prosecution from calling criminal defendants to the stand as witnesses. In civil trials the plaintiff's lawyers often call defendants before other witnesses.

On direct examination attorneys usually must ask for and get yes-no or short answers. However, many jurisdictions give the judge discretion to permit extended narratives to the extent that they help develop the witness's testimony. Leading questions, those that suggest the answer, are generally improper on direct examination, with exceptions for forgetful, older, young, hostile, or adverse witnesses. In the case of forgetful, older, or young witnesses, leading questions serve a valid function in refreshing their memory or directing their attention. When lawyers call hostile or adverse witnesses to the stand, the danger that the witness will consciously or unconsciously acquiesce to the examiner's version of the truth is minimal, and leading questions are thus allowed. When witnesses are hostile to the examiner, the need for forcing them to answer the lawyer's questions is greater than the danger that leading questions present.

Witnesses in The Caine Mutiny Court-Martial

One of the most famous trials in American fiction occurs in Herman Wouk's 1951 novel *The Caine Mutiny*, a story made even more famous by the 1954 film adaptation starring Humphrey Bogart. The novel's trial is a court-martial proceeding against Lieutenant Steve Maryk, the executive officer of the USS *Caine*, a Navy minesweeper, and it realistically portrays both the inconsistencies in testimony of witnesses to the same events and the difficulty of punishing perjurers.

Early in *The Caine Mutiny*, Maryk is harassed by fellow lieutenant Thomas Keefer's constant complaints about the irrational behavior of their captain, Lieutenant Commander Philip Francis Queeg. Finally, when the ship's safety is threatened in a typhoon, Maryk concludes that Captain Queeg is mentally unbalanced and relieves him of command—a momentous action for any naval officer to undertake. Afterward, Maryk is court-martialed for "conduct to the prejudice of good order and discipline." However, his attorney, Lieutenant Barney Greenwald, wins his acquittal. Although Keefer has been the lead instigator of Queeg's removal from command, at trial he betrays Maryk by denying that Queeg is unbalanced. However, under intense cross-examination by Greenwald, Queeg himself begins acting erratically on the witness stand, becoming the defense's most persuasive witness.

The trial in *The Caine Mutiny* is realistic in that events that seem to be of clear import at one time are found by the time of trial to be subject to differing interpretations. For a time, at least, before he is rattled by Greenwald's cross-examination, Queeg is able to present himself in a different light from that in which his ship's crew has seen him while at sea. Also realistic is Keefer's willingness to perjure himself and his ability to get away with this conduct. Although witnesses appear in court under oath, it is ordinarily difficult to marshal evidence sufficient to convict a lying witness of perjury.

Timothy L. Hall

In common-law jurisdictions there are restrictions not only on leading questions but also on those deemed argumentative, misleading, compound, or otherwise multifaceted. The FRE treat these matters by reposing power in the judge to supervise witness examinations. Specifically, the FRE exhort the judge to take reasonable measures to promote effectiveness and efficiency in ascertaining the truth and to protect witnesses from harassment or undue embarrassment.

There are two views as to the permissible scope of cross-examinations. The restrictive rule confines the cross-examiner to matters within the scope of direct examination. The wide-open rule allows any material issue in the case to be explored. The federal rules adopt the restrictive rule but allow the judge to make exceptions. Convenience of witnesses and trial efficiency often dictate that the judge exercise discretion regarding the proper scope of a witness's cross-examination.

Witnesses' Character and Credibility

By introducing personal testimony about a witness's character, it is possible to judge whether the witness has testified accurately, lied, or made a mistake; whether a person did or did not commit rape; whether a person was or was not careful; or whether a person turned a corner in an automobile in a particular way. However, such character-type propensity evidence is sometimes prejudicial, misleading, too time-consuming, or unfair. Accordingly, there is a general ban on the use of character-type propensity evidence unless it fits special rules for special exceptions. The exceptions are many.

It must be shown that reputation or character witnesses are familiar with the reputation of the person about whom they are testifying. Thus, in the case of reputation testimony, courts normally require that the witness and the subject have lived or done business in reasonable proximity to each other for a substantial period in the fairly recent past. Also, the reputation reported must be the subject's reputation in the relevant community and relatively current.

A prerequisite for the admissibility of personal opinions about another's propensities is that the person providing personal opinions had some substantial recent contact or relationship with the other person that would furnish a reasonable basis for a current opinion. Weaknesses in these foundational elements affect the weight rather than the admissibility of character-type propensity evidence. Rules of impeachment govern the efforts to test the opposing witnesses' credibility.

Everyone's Duty to Testify

Two kinds of witnesses may appear at a trial or deposition: ordinary lay witnesses or expert witnesses. A properly subpoenaed witness who fails to show up at the time and date specified is subject to arrest. Except for the reimbursement of costs of coming to court, ordinary witnesses may not be paid to testify. Because of the truth-seeking function of the court, parties and other witnesses can be compelled to give testimony, even if it is damaging to themselves or others. Accordingly, a person normally cannot prevent another person from disclosing confidences, secrets, or other matters. However, privileges are a narrow exception to these general rules. The privileges for confidential communications in the attorney-client, physician-patient, psychotherapist-patient, and husband-wife contexts are examples of such exceptions. Privileges operate to exclude relevant evidence in the name of some other social objective. Most true privileges are designed to promote certain kinds of relationships and particularly to promote confidential communications within these socially desirable relationships.

W. Dene Eddings Andrews

Further Reading

Bergman, Paul. *Transcript Exercises for Learning Evidence*. St. Paul, Minn.: West Publishing, 1992. Practical workbook containing various questions, answers, and judicial rulings from a variety of civil and criminal cases. This book is helpful for understanding the legal propriety of common objections.

_____. *Trial Advocacy in a Nutshell*. 3d ed. St. Paul, Minn.: West Publishing, 1995. This book and the book Bergman coauthored with Berman-Barnett, listed below, are easy-to-read, helpful, and inexpensive paperbacks. They review the fundamentals of direct examinations and cross-examinations and offer numerous examples.

Bergman, Paul, and Sara J. Berman-Barnett. *Represent Yourself in Court: How to Prepare and Try a Winning Case*. 2d ed. Berkeley, Calif.: Nolo Press, 1998.

Graham, Kenneth. *Casenotes Law Outlines: Evidence*. Santa Monica, Calif.: Casenotes, 1996. Offers discussions of the evidence rules on which common objections are based.

Loftus, Elizabeth F. *Eyewitness Testimony*. 2d ed. Cambridge, Mass.: Harvard University Press, 1996. Discussion by a psychologist of research on conditions influencing the reliability of eyewitness testimony.

Rothstein, Paul F., Myrna Raeder, and David Crump. *Evidence: State and Federal Rules in a Nutshell*. 3d ed. St. Paul, Minn.: West Publishing, 1997.

Technical Working Group for Eyewitness Evidence. *Eyewitness Evidence: A Guide for Law Enforcement*. Washington, D.C.: U.S. Department of Justice, Office of Justice Programs, National Institute of Justice, 1999. Practical guide for law-enforcement professionals in evaluating testimonies of witnesses.

See also Cross-examination; Depositions; Diplomatic immunity; Discovery; Expert witnesses; Objections; Perjury; Privileged communications; Subpoena power; Testimony; Trials; Witness protection programs.

World Court

Identification: International Court of Justice
Date: Held first session in April, 1946
Place: The Hague, the Netherlands
Criminal justice issue: Criminal justice issue: International Law
Significance: Legal systems have historically been established solely within sovereign nations. The International Court of Justice—or World Court, as it is better known—handles cases among nations and international disputes that are beyond the scope of any one nation's justice system.

Although the International Court of Justice (ICJ) was created as part of the United Nations after World War II, it was neither the first attempt to establish a mechanism to arbitrate disputes among countries nor the first World Court. However, it is the first court to become truly global in membership and recognition. The weakness of the court is that it cannot coerce participation by its sovereign member countries, nor can it enforce judgments. Even with these weaknesses, however, the court is seen by most to play a positive role within the international community.

Forerunners to the World Court include the Permanent Court of Arbitration, which was established in 1899 to assist in cases of international arbitration and other related matters. The first international body with independently appointed justices who heard cases brought before it was the Permanent Court of International Justice (PCIJ). Operating from 1922 to 1946, this court was created in conjunction with the League of Nations but was not formally part of the League.

Post-World War II plans for the United Nations included the International Court of Justice. The new World Court was understood to be a successor to the PCIJ with broader powers. In contrast to its predecessor body, the new World Court was created as an integral part of the United Nations. In 2005, it recognized the right of 191 sovereign nations to bring cases before it.

The court comprises fifteen justices who serve nine-year terms. One-third of them are elected every three years, and no two justices may be from the same country. The justices are elected by the U.N. General Assembly and Security Council, which vote separately on nominations. The function of the court is to settle disputes between independent countries (contentious cases) and to give opinions on international matters, as requested by agencies within the United Nations (advisory opinions).

The court hears contentious cases between two nations only when the governments of both nations agree to accept the court's jurisdiction over their dispute. From its inception through mid-2004, the court delivered seventy-nine contentious-case rulings and twenty-five advisory opinions. The court's activities were not spread evenly over those years, as its activities reflected changing global political moods. For example, between July, 1962, and August, 1971—at the height of Cold War tensions—only one new case was brought before the court and only one advisory opinion was sought. Between 1990 and 2004—after the Cold War ended—more than forty-five contentious cases (many interrelated) were brought before the court; however, the court did not rule in all these cases.

As the world's nations were becoming more comfortable with the idea of international tribunals, a new international court came into existence in 1998: the International Criminal Court. Completely independent of the World Court, this new court deals exclusively with matters of international crimes.

Donald A. Watt

Further Reading

Broomhall, Bruce. *International Justice and the Criminal Court: Between Sovereignty and the Rule of Law.* New York: Oxford University Press, 2003.

Cassese, Antonio. *International Criminal Law.* New York: Oxford University Press, 2003.

Kolba, Boris. *International Courts.* Milwaukee: World Almanac Library, 2004.

Meyer, Howard N. *The World Court in Action: Judging Among the Nations.* Lanham, Md.: Rowman & Littlefield, 2002.

See also Diplomatic immunity; International law; Jurisdiction of courts; War crimes.